THE LETTERS OF EMILY DICKINSON

THE LETTERS OF

Emily Dickinson

Edited by

THOMAS H. JOHNSON

Associate Editor

THEODORA WARD

THE BELKNAP PRESS
of HARVARD UNIVERSITY PRESS
Cambridge, Massachusetts, and London, England

Designed by Burton J Jones, Jr.

Printed in the U.S.A.

CONTENTS

ILLUSTRATIONS

Following page 154

The house on Pleasant Street occupied by the Dickinsons, 1840–1855. [*Houghton Library*.]

The Dickinson homestead on Main Street, showing Emily's conservatory. [*Houghton Library*.]

Daguerreotype of Austin Dickinson, early 1850's. [*Houghton Library*.]

Daguerreotype of Susan Gilbert, about 1855. [*Houghton Library*.]

Daguerreotype of Lavinia Norcross Dickinson, early 1850's. [*Houghton Library*.]

Daguerreotype of Martha Gilbert, about 1855. [*Houghton Library*.]

John L. Graves, as a student at Amherst College. [*Houghton Library*.]

Elizabeth Chapin Holland, about 1878. [*Houghton Library*.]

Following page 534

Thomas Wentworth Higginson, about 1870. [*Harvard University Archives*.]

Helen Hunt Jackson. [*Harvard University Archives*.]

The Reverend Jonathan L. Jenkins. [*Houghton Library*.]

Samuel Bowles, about 1875. [*Houghton Library*.]

Samuel Bowles with friends in California, 1865. [*Houghton Library*.]

Following page 582

Facsimiles of letters showing Emily Dickinson's handwriting:

1842. Letter 1. Ink. One large sheet, addressed on fold: *Wm – Austin Dickinson*/Easthampton/Mass. Last three lines on verso; shown entire, reduced about one half. [*Houghton Library*.]

ix

1861. Letter 232. Ink. One page, torn on fold. Shown entire, reduced about one quarter. [*Houghton Library.*]

1869. Letter 330. Ink. Six pages, first page shown, slightly enlarged. [*Boston Public Library.*]

1881. Letter 711. Pencil. Two pages, both shown, reduced about one half. [*Houghton Library.*]

ACKNOWLEDGMENTS

With the publication of these letters, the task of editing the poetry and prose of Emily Dickinson, undertaken in the spring of 1950, is brought to its conclusion. The introductions and notes which follow herein extend the narrative begun in the 1955 edition of the poems, and, together with the interpretive biography issued likewise in 1955, set forth the story of Emily Dickinson's life and writing as fully as I know how to tell it.

I take pleasure in recording again the acknowledgments which I made in *The Poems of Emily Dickinson*. The work of preparing the poems and letters constantly overlapped, and the generosity of those who have assisted the first undertaking extends equally to this. My initial debt, most gladly owned, is to Mr. Gilbert H. Montague, whose gift to Harvard College Library provided funds for the purchase of the Dickinson manuscripts and other family papers from the late Alfred Leete Hampson, the heir to the literary estate. Mrs. Alfred Leete Hampson has always stood ready to extend help upon request and her assistance, effectively and quietly given, has been important.

I wish to thank those who have served in an advisory capacity: Mr. Frederick B. Adams, Jr., Mr. Edward C. Aswell, Mr. Julian P. Boyd, and Mr. Robert E. Spiller.

I take pleasure in expressing gratitude to the following persons who willingly gave me access to Dickinson letters which they owned: Dr. J. Dellinger Barney, Mr. Clifton Waller Barrett, Dr. Mary Bennett, Mrs. Graham B. Blaine, Mr. Francis Bowles, Mrs. John Nicholas Brown, Mr. Orton L. Clark, Mr. H. B. Collamore, Mrs. T. Franklin Currier, Mrs. Morgan B. Cushing, Mr. Frank Davidson, Miss Elizabeth S. Dickerman, Mr. Clarence Dickinson, Miss Marion E. Dodd, Miss Julia S. L. Dwight, Mrs. Edward T. Esty, Mrs. Howard B. Field, Mrs. Leon Godchaux, Mrs. William L. Hallowell, Mr. Francis Russell Hart, Mr. Seth P. Holcombe, Mr. Josiah G. Holland, Mr. Richard Hooker, Mr. Parkman Howe, Miss Helen Jackson, Sister Mary James,

Miss Marcelle Lane, Mrs. Vivian Y. Laramore, Mr. Josiah K. Lilly, Mr. Samuel Loveman, Mr. Thomas O. Mabbott, Mr. Julian E. Mack, Mrs. William T. Mather, Miss Edith L. Pinnick, Mrs. Frederick J. Pohl, Mrs. Fairfield Porter, Mrs. Doheny H. Sessions, Mrs. H. T. Sheldon, Mrs. Susan H. Skillings, Mrs. Grant Squires, Mrs. Elizabeth S. Walcott, and Mrs. Alison H. Yaeger. The kindnesses of Mr. Robert P. Esty I recall with special pleasure.

It was Mabel Loomis Todd whose pioneer work in editing many of the Dickinson letters in 1894 saved much which otherwise would have been lost. I am grateful for the researches of her daughter Millicent Todd Bingham, who has devotedly carried on her mother's work and has herself contributed much to our knowledge of the poet. The present edition would not have been possible if the collection of manuscripts recently transferred by her to Amherst College had not been made available, as well as the transcripts made by Mrs. Todd, when preparing her edition, of letters which the owners subsequently destroyed or lost.

The following institutions gave willing access to their Dickinson holdings: American Antiquarian Society; Amherst College; Boston Public Library; Colby College Library; Goodell Library, University of Massachusetts; Harvard College Library; Huntington Memorial Library, Oneonta, New York; Jones Library, Amherst; The Pierpont Morgan Library; Mount Holyoke College Library; New York Public Library; Princeton University Library; The Rosenbach Foundation; Smith College Library; and Yale University Library. I wish also to thank Williston Academy for supplying the record of Austin Dickinson's enrollment, and the Baker Library of Dartmouth College for access to the Bartlett papers.

I am grateful to those who have shared their reminiscences: the late Margaret (Mrs. Orton L.) Clark, Dr. Kendall Emerson, Miss Louise B. Graves, Mrs. William T. Mather, and Mrs. Stuart Reynolds.

Mrs. Raymond W. Jones placed family diaries and memorabilia at my disposal. Mr. Russell S. Smith's unpublished study of Emily Dickinson's use of the Bible was a constant help. Mr. William H. McCarthy has assisted the enterprise from the beginning, and his innumerable kindnesses have been unfailing. The aid given to these labors by Mr. Jay Leyda, who himself is preparing a documentary record of the life of Emily Dickinson, has been so extensive that it virtually constitutes him a research associate.

The grant of a fellowship by the John Simon Guggenheim Foundation gave assurance that the work of editing the poems and letters of one of America's major writers would be completed.

In conclusion I take special pleasure in recognizing the interest bestowed upon this undertaking, in behalf of myself and Mrs. Ward, by Mr. William A. Jackson and the staff of the Houghton Library, where most of the work has been done. It has become an association at a personal level.

THOMAS H. JOHNSON

Jaffrey, New Hampshire
August 1957

INTRODUCTION

James Russell Lowell, himself a letter writer of distinction, most admired in that literary form the letters of Gray, Cowper, Walpole, and Lamb. "I hold that a letter which is not mainly about the writer of it lacks the prime flavor. The wine must smack a little of the cask," he said to his friend Charles Eliot Norton.[1] "Letters, so it seems to me,/ Our careless quintessence should be," he wrote. By "careless" Lowell obviously does not mean *slack* or *heedless*, or even *unpremeditated*. He has in mind what writers in the early nineteenth century meant by *genial* when they used the word in the sense of innate; and such precisely is the wine that smacks of the cask. Lowell would certainly have added Keats to his list had enough letters of Keats been published at the time for Lowell to savor them. Perhaps he would have added Emily Dickinson.

The noteworthy characteristic of the Dickinson letters, like that of the poems, is acute sensitivity. Indeed, early in the 1860's, when Emily Dickinson seems to have first gained assurance of her destiny as a poet, the letters both in style and rhythm begin to take on qualities that are so nearly the quality of her poems as on occasion to leave the reader in doubt where the letter leaves off and the poem begins. Such intensity of feeling was a handicap that she bore as one who lives with a disability, and her friends must have increased the burden by often making her aware that they felt sympathy for a pathetic situation. It left her, as those who observed her knew, though they never so phrased it, emotionally naked. In all decency, she did not dare to appear in the drawing room when guests were present. "In all the circumference of Expression," she wrote in 1884, "those guileless words of Adam and Eve never were surpassed, 'I was afraid and hid Myself.'" But the disability need not be pitied, for she knew that though she could expect no deliverance from it, she could devise compensations, and her ability to do so vests her informal correspondence

[1] *New Letters* . . . , ed. Howe, New York (1932) IV, 278.

with a charm which time does not alloy. "How frugal is the Chariot/ That bears a Human soul!" The husbandry of those whose sensibilities threaten disaster must be austere. As she herself expressed the thought in 1863, renunciation is a piercing virtue.

Letter writing became a part of Emily Dickinson's life while she was still a child. Her need of contact with those she loved led her to set whole mornings or afternoons aside to pen with intimate sprightliness missives of considerable length. Such being true of her own capabilities, she expected in return, during her adolescent years, letters of equal sociability and endurance, and repeatedly bullies or cajoles those whose replies do not measure to her expectation or are delayed longer than she feels may be a reasonable period — perhaps a day or two. She was only eleven when she wrote the earliest surviving letter, in which she expresses herself with ease and charming felicity. But it is in the letter she wrote to Abiah Root in August 1845 that one sees the culmination of her development as a child. Now fourteen, she is natural, eager, interested in people, in her studies, the world about her, and in the development of her own new dimensions as a person. This realization she unconsciously discloses by saying: "I never enjoyed myself more than I have this summer."

Yet in the same year, and but a few weeks later, her next letter to Abiah reveals how her enthusiasm for school was regarded by her parents as a sign of overstimulation, for which a term of housekeeping instruction would be a salutary remedy. "Mother thinks me not able to confine myself to school this term. She had rather I would exercise. . ." The parents had good reason to watch for signs of excitability. They had found it necessary to send her away from home for a month in the previous year after Emily had been permitted to witness for a few moments, at her own insistence, the approaching death of young Sophia Holland, a girl of her own age, and the story of that experience as Emily recounted it to Abiah in March 1846 goes far to explain the nature of the child. Emily Dickinson's quest for the unknowable began at a very early age.

The fascination of genius is in its paradox. Emily Dickinson was still a child, and on occasion of course acted childishly, but she was equipped even now with a substantial vocabulary, and had no difficulty in filling what she rightly described as a "mammoth sheet" with her thoughts and feelings. Such are discernibly the lines of force which made her the woman and poet she became. She commented to Abiah in March 1847, in a context that looks back, and also forward to the Seminary she expects to enter in the fall: "I am always in love with my teachers." The expression has that quality of candor and accurate self-evaluation which gives stature to Emily Dickinson as a person and a poet. Throughout her life she turned for leadership to a "master." After 1862 Higginson stood in that relation to her, as all her letters to him make emphatically clear. It was her feeling, certainly in part, about Dr. Wadsworth, and perhaps about others now undiscoverable. But the need for a tutor or guide, who might conduct her in the manner Dante was led through the visions of a divine comedy, is the logical extension of all sentient being, and one especially needful to poets, who seek to translate mankind to greener pastures through the symbol of language. Emily Dickinson's quest for a guide she expressed with admirable forthrightness to Higginson in August 1862. Without reticence and with clear self-appraisal she said: "I had no Monarch in my life, and cannot rule myself, and when I try to organize – my little Force explodes – and leaves me bare and charred –"

The sensitivity was present from the beginning, but the poet was as yet unborn. Her susceptibility to atmosphere invigorates the letters written in the late 1840's by pointing up the contrast of those written from home and those she wrote upon arrival at South Hadley. Before she entered the Seminary she was still writing whimsically and dwelling upon recollection of past associations which she hopes a demand visit from Abiah Root or Jane Humphrey will recapture. But the simple, factual accounts she wrote of her life at Mount Holyoke tell the inevitable story of youthful maturity. The disciplines of a good institutional experience are timeless.

Homesickness increased as the year at Mount Holyoke advanced, and the strain within was one that both parents recognized, for her father decided not to send her back for a second year, or acceded to her wish to stay home. It was typical of the Dickinson family not to accept any separation, even when it was for the good of the absent member. Such a trait shows itself in the fact that when Austin went to law school he was on the end of a tether. Home affairs, the annual and cherished Cattle Show for instance, took precedence over his occupations elsewhere. He could be sent for at any time. With the independence characteristic of the Dickinsons, who paid little heed to other people's rules, Austin was late in arriving at Cambridge for his law school classes; though he was graduated with his class, he did not bother to be present to receive his diploma, choosing instead to accompany his mother, evidently at her request, to a reunion at Monson Academy. "I think we miss each other more every day that we grow older," Emily wrote her brother on 8 April 1853, "for we're all unlike most everyone, and are therefore more dependent on each other for delight." During the same month she commented to him on some visiting cousins: "The Newmans seem very pleasant, but they are not *like us*. What makes a few of us so different from others? It's a question I often ask myself." It is a question to which she had unconsciously supplied the answer likewise during the same month: "I wish we were children now. I wish we were *always* children, how to grow up I dont know." These were the years when she was signing her letters "Emilie." To grow up meant to leave the clan. The tie with the Norcross cousins, even in later years, gave an outlet to that side of her nature which persisted in the game of "little girlhood." "Did you know there had been a fire here," she wrote them on July fourth, 1879, "and that but for a whim of the wind Austin and Vinnie and Emily would have all been homeless? . . . Vinnie came soft as a moccasin, 'Don't be afraid, Emily, it is only the fourth of July.' I did not tell that I saw it, for I thought if she felt it best to deceive, it must be that it was."

The sense of being closely knit reveals itself also in the Dickinson habit of lampooning neighbors. Though the quotations are Emily's words, the spirit is that of the clan. " 'Mrs Skeeter' [perhaps Mrs. Luke Sweetser] is very feeble," she wrote Austin in March 1852, " 'cant bear Allopathic treatment, cant have Homeopathic' — dont want Hydropathic — Oh what a pickle she is in — should'nt think she would deign to *live* — it is so decidedly vulgar!" As she grew older, she became more expert as a satirist. "Libbie goes to Sunderland, Wednesday," she informed the Norcross cousins in October 1863, speaking of the redoubtable aunt Elizabeth, "for a minute or two; leaves here at 6 1/2 — what a fitting hour — and will breakfast the night before; such a smart atmosphere! The trees stand right up straight when they hear her boots, and will bear crockery wares instead of fruit, I fear. She hasn't starched the geraniums yet, but will have ample time, unless she leaves before April." On occasion the witticisms became sardonic, and, as her sister's are reported to have been, they are somewhat grim. In a letter written to the Norcrosses in the same month she remarks: "No one has called so far, but one old lady to look at a house. I directed her to the cemetery to spare expense of moving."

There came a time in Emily Dickinson's life, very near her thirtieth year, when she deliberately chose never willingly to leave her home again. The decision reflects itself clearly in the letters written after 1860. Before then they are enthusiastic, sometimes ardently sentimental, and usually long. Such is especially true of the letters written in the early fifties. She easily took fright about her friendships which, because of their importance to her, seemed hazardous. Her informality has charm during these years, but the protestations of affection and the repeated concern for Austin's health as well as for her own compel the reader to traverse arid stretches. The fantastic letters in the early part of 1850 lead to the speculation that this might have been the period when she commenced in earnest to write poetry. Benjamin Newton had left Amherst, but was not married. He had sent her Emerson's poems and she was writing to him. It was in 1858 that she began to assemble her poems into the small, thread-tied manuscript "volumes" or packets, and early in 1862 she felt enough assurance in her destiny to initiate her correspondence with T. W. Higginson.

During these latter years she underwent a profound emotional change, which the letters vividly reflect. Letters now became more important to her than they ever do to most people, since they were the sole means of escape from a self-elected incarceration. They enabled her to control the time and the plane of her relationships. The degree and nature of any intimacy was hers to choose. Henceforth the letters are composed with deliberation, each with the chosen recipient in mind, and it becomes clear that a letter written to Higginson, for instance, could never have been intended for Bowles or anyone else. The letters are briefer because the thought is tersely ordered. Many, if not most of them, were now written first in rough draft and then recopied. Such is especially true of those she wrote in later years, often with cordial intimacy, to correspondents like Mrs. Todd or Professor Chickering whom she never met. And after she came to accept Higginson's verdict in 1862 that her poetry was not for publication, they served as a conveyance for her poems. They literally became her "letter to the world."

Since Emily Dickinson's full maturity as a dedicated artist occurred during the span of the Civil War, the most convulsive era of the nation's history, one of course turns to the letters of 1861–1865, and the years that follow, for her interpretation of events. But the fact is that she did not live in history and held no view of it, past or current. Walt Whitman projected himself into the world about him so intensely that not only the war but the nation itself is continuously the substance of his thought in prose and verse. The reverse was true for Dickinson, to whom the war was an annoyance, a reality only when it was mirrored to her in casualty lists. Such evidently was true in some degree for all the Dickinsons, since Austin, when drafted, exercised his privilege of paying the five-hundred-dollar fee to arrange for a substitute. Emily wrote Mrs. Bowles in the summer of 1861: "I shall have no winter this year – on account of the soldiers – Since I cannot weave Blankets, or Boots – I thought it best to omit the season." Only once again does she make any general allusion to this mighty conflict, the repercussions of which are clearly audible even after the lapse of a century. "A Soldier called – ," she wrote Bowles just a year later, "a Morning ago, and asked for a Nosegay, to take to Battle. I suppose he thought we kept an Aquarium."

The attitude of mind that could prompt such shallow facetiousness can be understood in the light of her personal intent in living. Years later, on the eve of the first election of President Cleveland, she made clear to Mrs. Holland the nature and extent of her concern with social history. "Before I write to you again, we shall have had a new Czar. Is the Sister a Patriot? 'George Washington was the Father of his Country' – 'George Who?' That sums all Politics to me." The rejection of society as such thus shows itself to have been total, not only physically but psychically. It was her kind of economy, a frugality she sought in order to make the most of her world; to focus, to come to grips with those universals which increasingly concerned her.

When Emily Dickinson made use of current news in her letters, and she often did so, she employed it as part of the metaphor of her speech. In thanking Theodore Holland for a sketch he sent her in the summer of 1884, she acknowledged it with the comment: "I approve the Paint – a study of the Soudan, I take it, but the Scripture assures us our Hearts are all Dongola." She has in mind that the fate of General Gordon, whose headquarters were at Dongola in the Soudan, was in the balance, and that no man can foretell his fate. She similarly employed quotations from scripture or from Shakespeare, not as embellishment but as pointed commentary on tense situations. Taken by themselves, the words from *Coriolanus* which constitute one note to Sue in 1876 seem quite meaningless: "Doth forget that ever he heard the name of Death." But if Sue put the words in context, as she was expected to do, they constitute a tender note of apology for one whose quick tongue sometimes betrayed her stalwart heart, an apology perhaps in this case for her sister Lavinia.

It is possible in the letters to discover something about the books and authors that gave the chiefest pleasure, and something too about the way poetry is written, but on the whole the comments are desultory, often cryptic, or enthusiastic. She told Higginson in her second letter to him that among poets she admired Keats and the Brownings, among prose writers Ruskin and Sir Thomas Browne. This does not go far, and omits Shakespeare, her truest master. She singles out the book of Revelation in the Bible, yet it is but one of many books from that great repository which was her constant source of inspiration, allusion, and quotation. Whitman, an innovator of the first order himself, she told Higginson that she had read nothing of, and the statement may have remained true throughout her life. In the early years, Emerson, the Brontës, and Dickens were favorites; later she avidly awaited the appearance of a new novel by George Eliot, but she evinced no marked interest in her other contemporaries. The striking originality, and on occasion profundity, of her own verse never reveals itself in the few critical assessments scattered through her letters.

It is for a quite different reason that the letters attain stature. They are the expression of her unique personality, and of a mind which could phrase the thought, "There is always one thing to be grateful for, – that one is one's self and not somebody else." Though she never wrote about herself after adolescence, the letters nevertheless are always self-portraits, written by one who has observed herself frankly and with no self-pity or regrets. Such indeed remains true whether the letter is penned to a child or an adult, to an intimate or a casual acquaintance. They validate another statement that, like the above, she made to Higginson, one which expresses the deliberateness with which she chose her way of living. When he asked her whether, not even seeing visitors, she felt sorry not to have something to do, she answered: "I never thought of conceiving that I could ever have the slightest approach to such a want in all future time." She paused and added: "I feel that I have not expressed myself strongly enough."

NOTES ON THE PRESENT TEXT

With the exception of letters presumably destroyed, all those which at the present time Emily Dickinson is known to have written are here assembled. The method of arrangement used in *The Poems of Emily Dickinson* (1955), the companion edition to this volume of *Letters*, has been followed here. As far as possible the letters are placed chronologically, each is numbered and is directly followed by data concerning manuscript location and publication history. The explanatory notes for each letter briefly identify persons and events mentioned. (Recipients of letters and persons frequently named are more fully identified in the biographical sketches in Appendix 1.) The source of literary allusions and quotations is given wherever it is known.

Since Emily Dickinson rarely dated her letters after 1850, except by an occasional "Wednesday" or "Saturday," the dates that she gave are moved to the notes unless the day named is part of the significance of the communication (for example, letter no. 777). Frequently internal evidence sets the date precisely. Often the date can be limited to a given week or month. But sometimes an assigned date must derive solely from the evidence of handwriting, and such letters are therefore spoken of as having been written "about" a probable year. A detailed study of the "Characteristics of the Handwriting," written by Mrs. Ward, is set forth in the introduction to *Poems* (1955), xlix–lix, illustrated by twenty facsimile reproductions of the handwriting as it revealed itself over the years. In instances where an autograph is missing, the text derives from the earliest published source, unless the note specifies otherwise.

One feels virtually certain that more Dickinson letters will eventually come to light, though painstaking search over a period of several years has not turned them up. Even so, there is little reason to expect that the number of undiscovered letters is large. Many letters are known to be irrecoverable, and among them some that would be especially interesting. Such are the early letters written to Benjamin F. Newton, to George H. Gould, and to William H. Dickinson, letters which Mrs. Todd could not trace when she was preparing her edition of *Letters of Emily Dickinson*, published in 1894.[2] There were the letters to the Reverend Charles Wadsworth, almost certainly destroyed, and to others, whose names may not be known at present. Some now lost Mrs. Todd secured, at least from transcripts, during the 1890's. The Norcross cousins, for instance, never showed Mrs. Todd the large number they had received over the years, but supplied copies of such extracts as they thought appropriate; all were destroyed at the time of Louise Norcross's death in 1919. The present text of all such letters derives either from *Letters of Emily Dickinson* (ed. 1931) or from the Norcross transcripts themselves.[3]

The question of whether to publish letters written to Emily Dickinson never rose, because only a handful of such letters survived. After Emily's death, Lavinia Dickinson destroyed almost all of them. A few written by Helen Hunt Jackson, by the editor Thomas Niles, and by Thomas Wentworth Higginson were saved, or escaped destruction. Because all were written by persons important to American letters in the nineteenth century, and clarify points in several Dickinson letters, they are here included.

In round figures, some 1150 letters and prose fragments are included, and the texts of three-quarters of the number derives from Dickinson autographs. The remainder perforce reproduces the text of transcripts or of an earlier publication. About one hundred letters are published for the first time, including almost all of the letters to Jane Humphrey, and to Mrs. J. Howard Sweetser. This figure does not include those which derive from transcripts made by the recipient, such as those written to Catherine Scott Anthon and to Susan Dickinson. Actually the new material is much more extensive than a

[2] See *Ancestors' Brocades: The Literary Debut of Emily Dickinson*, by Millicent Todd Bingham, New York, 1945, pages 254 and 263. Mabel Loomis Todd fortuitously set herself the task of collecting the letters within the decade following the death of Emily Dickinson. Many that survive today might well have been destroyed had she less systematically undertaken her labors. The story is told in detail by her daughter in *Ancestors' Brocades*, especially in the chapters "Collecting the Letters" (188–209), and "Emily's Correspondents" (247–266).

[3] The spelling of Louise's nickname is here given as *Loo* (not *Lou*), since that is the spelling Emily Dickinson always used.

tabulation would show, for a very large number of letters were subject to extensive deletion when they were previously published.[4]

All autograph letters are presented in their verbatim form.

It is to be expected that autographs privately owned will change hands. Ownership is here ascribed as it was last known.

Names of recipients are given and indexed as Emily Dickinson knew them when she was writing to them. Abiah Root and Jane Humphrey, for instance, were married after the correspondence with them had come to an end. All letters were written in Amherst except those for which the headings specify a different location.

SYMBOLS USED TO IDENTIFY MANUSCRIPTS

At the present time Dickinson autograph letters are located in about fourteen institutions. Some two score individuals are known to possess one autograph or more. Individuals are named in the list of acknowledgments and identified by last name in the notes of the

[4] The present editing of the letters to Abiah Root requires a special note. During the early 1890's Abiah Root Strong loaned almost all the letters that she had received from Emily Dickinson to Mrs. Todd, who made complete transcripts and then returned them to Mrs. Strong. When Mrs. Todd published *Letters* (1894), she omitted large portions from the letters to Abiah Root, in part at the request of the recipient, in part because some sections dwelt at length on schoolgirl news.

Evidently Mrs. Todd made printer's copy by clipping out portions from the transcripts she had made, supplying the printer with the remainder. When she prepared the second edition (1931), she restored some of the omitted portions. Among her papers in the Bingham collection (AC) is an envelope filled with the portions still unused.

This edition reproduces the 1931 edition of the text of those letters to Abiah Root for which no autograph is known. It does not incorporate the text of the remaining clippings into the body of the letters, because the position cannot be exactly determined, and because the association of a clipping with a given letter is at best conjecture. Most of her omissions Mrs. Todd noted with dots, but not all, and not always at the right place. They therefore are placed separately, and at the end of letters no. 5, 6, 8, 9, 12, 14, 39, 69, and 91. Of the two remaining letters to Abiah Root for which no autographs are known, no. 15 appears to be complete as published in 1931, and no. 23 may be complete with the additional paragraph which now follows it.

Since Mrs. Strong could not recall the names of many of her schoolmates, when she discussed the letters with Mrs. Todd (see AB 188–189, 206–209), it is impossible to be sure of identification now. For instance, Sarah Gray, Sarah Taylor, and Sarah S. T. may all have been the same Sarah — namely, Sarah Tracy. Blank spaces indicate words which Mrs. Todd could not decipher, and therefore left blank.

text. Institutions likewise are named in full in the list and briefly identified in the notes. Certain symbols are used throughout.

AAS — The American Antiquarian Society, Worcester, Massachusetts.

AC — Amherst College Library. All autograph letters, and transcripts of autograph letters, at Amherst College are in the Millicent Todd Bingham Collection, except letters to the following persons, presented by other donors: Mrs. James S. Cooper, Mr. Kendall Emerson, Mrs. Richard H. Mather, Mrs. William Henry Prince, and Mrs. Edward Tuckerman.

BPL Higg — The Thomas Wentworth Higginson papers in the Galatea Collection, Boston Public Library.

HCL — Harvard College Library. HCL ARS (letters to Abiah Root Strong); HCL B (manuscripts which had special association for Martha Dickinson Bianchi); HCL E (letters to Henry Vaughan Emmons); HCL G (letters to John L. Graves); HCL H (letters to Dr. and Mrs. Josiah Gilbert Holland); HCL JH (letters to Jane Humphrey); HCL L (letters formerly in the possession of Lavinia Norcross Dickinson or Susan Gilbert Dickinson or their heirs)

NYPL — New York Public Library.

YUL — Yale University Library.

SYMBOLS USED TO IDENTIFY PUBLICATION

AB *Ancestors' Brocades: The Literary Début of Emily Dickinson.* By Millicent Todd Bingham. New York: Harper, 1945.

AM *The Atlantic Monthly* (1875 – current).

FF *Emily Dickinson Face to Face: Unpublished Letters with Notes and Reminiscences.* By Martha Dickinson Bianchi. Boston: Houghton Mifflin, 1932.

FN *Emily Dickinson: Friend and Neighbor.* By MacGregor Jenkins. Boston: Little, Brown, 1930.

Home *Emily Dickinson's Home: Letters of Edward Dickinson and His Family, with documentation and comment.* Edited by Millicent Todd Bingham. New York: Harper, 1955.

L (1894) *Letters of Emily Dickinson.* Edited by Mabel Loomis Todd. 2 vols. Boston: Roberts Brothers, 1894.

L (1931) *Letters of Emily Dickinson.* New and enlarged edition. Edited by Mabel Loomis Todd. New York: Harper, 1931.

LH *Emily Dickinson's Letters to Dr. and Mrs. Josiah Gilbert Holland.* Edited by Theodora Van Wagenen Ward. Cambridge: Harvard, 1951.

LL *The Life and Letters of Emily Dickinson.* By Martha Dickinson Bianchi. Boston: Houghton Mifflin, 1924.

NEQ *The New England Quarterly* (1927 – current).

Poems (1955) *The Poems of Emily Dickinson, Including variant readings critically compared with all known manuscripts.* Edited by Thomas H. Johnson. 3 vols. Cambridge: Harvard, 1955.

Revelation *Emily Dickinson: A Revelation.* Edited by Millicent Todd Bingham. New York: Harper, 1954.

I

LETTERS

1–14

[1842–1846]

". . . the Hens
lay finely . . ."

Emily Dickinson's twelfth year brought the first interruption to the close companionship in her home, when Austin was sent away to school for a single term. His father's first letter to him said: "I sent you there to improve," and one infers that family and neighbor associations were becoming distractions not good for his studies.

The record of enrollments at Amherst Academy in the forties gives a bewildering impression of casualness in the matter of school attendance, and may reflect a similar condition elsewhere. Emily herself was in and out of school, for reasons of health, several times during her adolescent years. Some of her friends were girls sent to Amherst from other towns, to live with relatives or board in the homes of schoolmates while in residence for a term or two. Only one among the group of five who were her special friends during these years was Amherst bred.

The letters of this earliest surviving group were written to her brother and to two school friends. Her mind was developing rapidly, but she was still in the immediate world of childhood when she wrote the three letters of 1842 with which the series begins.

To *Austin Dickinson*   *18 April 1842*

My dear Brother

As Father was going to Northampton and thought of coming over
to see you I thought I would improve the opportunity and write you
a few lines – We miss you very much indeed you cannot think how
odd it seems without you there was always such a Hurrah wherever
you was I miss My bedfellow very much for it is rare that I can get
any now for Aunt Elisabeth is afraid to sleep alone and Vinnie has to
sleep with her but I have the privilege of looking under the bed every
night which I improve as you may suppose the Hens get along nicely
the chickens grow very fast I am afraid they will be so large that you
cannot perceive them with the naked Eye when you get home the
yellow hen is coming off with a brood of chickens we found a hens
nest with four Eggs in it I took out three and brought them in the next
day I went to see if there had been any laid and there had not been
any laid and the one that was there had gone so I suppose a skonk had
been there or else a hen In the shape of a skonk and I dont know
which – the Hens lay finely William gets two a day at his house we
5 or 6 a day here there Is one Creeper that lays on the ground the
nests are so high that they cannot reach them from the ground I Expect we shall have to make some ladders for them to get up on William
found the hen and Rooster after you went away that you could not
find we received your letter Friday morning and very glad we were
to get it you must write oftener to us the temperance dinner went off
very well the other day all the Folks Except Lavinia and I there were
over a Hundred there the students thought the dinner too cheap the
tickets were a half a dollar a piece and so they are going to have a
supper tomorrow Evening which I suppose will be very genteel Mr
Jones has found in looking at his policy that his insurance is 8 thousand dollars instead of 6 which makes him feel a great deal better than
he did at first Mr Wilson and his wife took tea here the other night
they are going to move wednesday – they have made out to get one of

the Mt Pleasant Buildings to its place of distination which is a matter of great rejoicing to the public it was really was Enough to make
ones Eyes ache and I am glad it has got out of sight and hearing too –
there are going to be great fixing up I expect in those buildings we
are all very well and hope you are the same – we have very pleasant
weather now Mr Whipple has come and we expect Miss Humphrey
tomorrow – Aunt Montague – has been saying you would cry before
the week was out Cousin Zebina had a fit the other day and bit his
tongue into – as you say it is a rainy day and I can think of – Nothing
more to say – I shall Expect an answer to my letter soon Charles Richardson has got back and is in Mr Pitkins store Sabra is not running
after him at all she had not seen him when I last saw her which was
Saturday I suppose she would send her *respects to you* if *she knew
I was going to write* to you – I *must now close* – all send a great deal
of love to you and hope you are getting along well and – Enjoy your
self –

Your affectionate Sister Emily –

MANUSCRIPT: HCL (L 53). Ink. Unpublished. Addressed on the fold:
Wm Austin Dickinson/Easthampton/Mass. On the date line she wrote
"Amherst," and her aunt Elizabeth Dickinson added: "Mass. April 18th
1842."
  A few days before his thirteenth birthday, Austin was sent to Williston
Seminary, newly opened as an endowed institution at Easthampton, to
attend the spring term. His father wrote to him a few days after his enroll-
ment, and followed his letter with a visit, carrying Emily's letter with him.
Sabra was the daughter of A. P. Howe, landlord of the Amherst House.

2

To Austin Dickinson   *1 May 1842*

My dear Brother
  As it was Sunday Afternoon and all the folks gone to meeting Except – mother and myself I thought I would improve the opportunity
and write you a few lines – we are all very well – but very lonely without you – I am glad you took the Latin lexicon – if it can be of any
use to [you] because I have had good luck in borrowing one – your
Clothes came – safe by Mr Pr[?]er and we were very glad to hear that

you were well and in good spirits – the hens get along nicely – we brought in 9 Eggs yesterday – We generally get about 7 a day Mrs – Washburn was very much pleased with the Eggs mother sent her – the other day Francis brought your Rooster home and the other 2 went to fighting him while I was gone to School – mother happened to look out of the window and she saw him laying on the ground – he was most dead – but she and Aunt Elisabeth went right out and took him up and put him in a Coop and he is nearly well now – while he is shut up the other Roosters – will come around and insult him in Every possible way by Crowing right in his Ears – and then they will jump up on the Coop and Crow there as if they – wanted to show that he was Completely in their power and they could treat him as they chose – Aunt Elisabeth said she wished their throats would split and then they could insult him no longer – I had an opportunity to write to Jane Humphrey which I improved and wrote her a short note as I had not time to write a long one the Man who was going to carry them having but a short time to stay in Amherst – I can think of nothing more to say but that we shall all be glad when you come home again – a great deal of love from all to you if you could I wish you – would send Sabra a paper she would be so pleased with it – I want you to answer this letter as soon as you can – Our garden is not made yet – our trees are all very full of blossoms now and – they look Very handsome – your Clothes that you sent home are all in good order – for you to put on – John Wheelock has been very sick and still continues to be so – though he is not as bad now as he was I do not think – Pa says he saw Mr Armsby here to Meeting to day – I like Miss Humphrey very much as a teacher – I recite to her in all My Studies Except Latin – the Horse is not very well and is staying at Mr Frinks to be taken care of till he is better I can think of nothing more to say now –

Your affectionate Sister Emily
ps – we expect Grandpa Norcross and Uncle William up here this week – Sabra Howe has had a handsome present of a gold ring from Charles Richardson She dont seem to care much about him but he hangs on to her – and will not let go his hold – in hopes I suppose she will come back to him which she does not seem inclined to do I will put in her respects because I know she would send them if she knew I was agoing to write –

My dear Austin.

I have yielded to Emily's solicitations to write you a few words. I am not in the habit of writing to gentlemen more than *once* if I do not receive an answer, however I will not *censure* you, for not writing me – I know you are busy as examination is so near – hope to see you next week Wednesday – I do not know of any news to tell you – except that three of your hens strayed away to Major Kellogg's – and were brought home by Henry Howe to-day, – after an absence of several days. Eggs are very abundant – 11 were brought in to-day. The lattice-work & grape-arbor have been painted to-day – Mr Howe is having his house painted – Col Smith's house is just finished – this street is fast improving – come home as soon as you can for we are lonesome. Accept much love from your

affectionate aunt,
Elizabeth

excuse all haste for it is late –

MANUSCRIPT: HCL (L 54). Ink. Unpublished. Dated: Amherst May 1 1842. Addressed on the fold: Wm Austin Dickinson/Easthampton/Mass.

"Aunt Elizabeth," then a girl of nineteen living in her older brother's home, added a note on the same sheet on Monday, while the letter was still waiting for a bearer. Her note is dated: Amherst, Mass. May 2nd 1842.

3

To Jane Humphrey   *12 May 1842*

My dear Jane

I have been looking for a letter from you this long time but not receiving any I plucked up all the remaining courage that I had left and determined to make one more effort to write you a few lines – I want to see you very much for I have got a great deal to tell you about school matters – and besides you are one of my dear friends. Sabra has had a beautiful ring given to her by Charles you know who as well as I do – the Examination at Easthampton is today – and Austin is coming home tonight. Father is sick with the Rheumatism and can not go but Mother has gone with somebody else – it is very unpleasant today – it showers most all the time – your sister is very well indeed – I believe she has gone to South hadley this afternoon – I miss you more and more every day, in my study in play at home indeed every where I miss my beloved Jane – I wish you would write to me – I should think more of it than of a mine of gold – when you write me I wish you would write me a great long letter and tell me all the news that you know of – all your friends send a great deal of love to you Austin and William Washburn send their respects to you – this Afternoon is Wednesday and so of course there was Speaking and Composition – there was one young man who read a Composition the Subject was think twice before you speak – he was describing the reasons why any one should do so – one was – if a young gentleman – offered a young lady his arm and he had a dog who had no tail and he boarded at the tavern think twice before you speak. Another is if a young gentleman knows a young lady who he thinks nature has formed to perfection let him remember that roses conceal thorns he is the sillyest creature that ever lived I think. I told him that I thought he had better think twice before he spoke – what good times we used to have jumping into bed when you slept with me. I do wish you would come to Amherst and make me a great long visit – how do you get along in Latin. I am in the class that you used to be in in Latin – besides Latin I study History and Botany I like the school very much indeed – your Sister sends a great deal of love to all your folks and to every one she knows there – My Plants grow beautifully – you know that elegant old Rooster that Austin thought so much of – the others fight him and killed him – answer this letter as soon as you can – I can think of nothing more to say now yours affectionately

Emily

MANUSCRIPT: Rosenbach 1170/17 (1). Ink. Dated: Amherst May 12 1842. Addressed on the fold: Miss Jane Humphrey/Southwick/Mass. Postmarked: Amherst Ms May 12. Written in pencil, in a different hand, is the draft of the beginning of a letter – possibly Jane's reply: "My very dear Friend/I Know you are thinking of m[e] (if thinking of me at all) as a very neg[ligent] . . ."

PUBLICATION: George Frisbie Whicher, *This Was a Poet* (1938) 43–44, in part.

Jane Humphrey had lived with the Dickinsons while she briefly attended Amherst Academy. Sabra Howe, William Washburn, and Charles Richardson were school friends. Jane's sister Helen Humphrey, was one of ED's teachers, and another sister, Mary, was a student at the Academy.

4

To Austin Dickinson   *autumn 1844*

Dear brother Austin

As Mr Baker was going directly to where you are I thought I would write a line to inform you that if it is pleasant day after tomorrow we are all coming over to see you, but you must not think too much of our coming as it may rain and spoil all òur plans. however if it is not pleasant so that we do not come over father says that you may come home on Saturday, and if we do not come he will make some arrangement for you to come and write you about it.

I attend singing school. Mr Woodman has a very fine one Sunday evenings and has quite a large school. I presume you will want to go when you return home. We had a very severe frost here last night and the ground was frozen — hard. We all had our noses nipped a little. the Ladys Society meets at our house tomorrow and I expect we shall have a very pleasant meeting. If you was at home it would be perfectly sure. We wish much to hear from you, and if you have time I wish you would write a line and send by Mr Baker. Mother wishes if your stockings are any of them thin, that you should do them up in a little bundle & send them by Mr Baker. Accept much love from us all.

Your affectionate sister E

If we dont come Wednesday we may Thursday if not father will write you.

MANUSCRIPT: AC. Pencil. Dated: Monday. A.M. Addressed on the fold: William A. Dickinson, per Mr Baker.

PUBLICATION: *Home* 66–67.

Austin was a student in the Classical Department of Williston Seminary for the term ending 10 August 1842, and for the year 1844–1845. This letter was probably written in the autumn of 1844, when the early appearance of frozen ground would draw comment. Mrs. Bingham's speculation seems reasonable: "'Mr. Baker,' the bearer of the note, may have been the

prosperous farmer Alfred Baker, or his brother Osmyn, a well-known lawyer who moved his office from Amherst to Northampton in 1844" (*Home*
66).

5

To Abiah Root   23 *February 1845*

Dear Abiah,

After receiving the smitings of conscience for a long time, I have
at length succeeded in stifling the voice of that faithful monitor by
a promise of a long letter to you; so leave everything and sit down
prepared for a long siege in the shape of a bundle of nonsense from
friend E.

. . . I keep your lock of hair as precious as gold and a great deal
more so. I often look at it when I go to my little lot of treasures, and
wish the owner of that glossy lock were here. Old Time wags on
pretty much as usual at Amherst, and I know of nothing that has
occurred to break the silence; however, the reduction of the postage
has excited my risibles somewhat. Only think! We can send a letter
before long for five little coppers only, filled with the thoughts and
advice of dear friends. But I will not get into a philosophizing strain
just yet. There is time enough for that upon another page of this mammoth sheet. . . . Your *beau idéal* D. I have not seen lately. I presume
he was changed into a star some night while gazing at them, and
placed in the constellation Orion between Bellatrix and Betelgeux.
I doubt not if he was here he would wish to be kindly remembered to
you. What delightful weather we have had for a week! It seems more
like smiling May crowned with flowers than cold, arctic February
wading through snowdrifts. I have heard some sweet little birds sing,
but I fear we shall have more cold weather and their little bills will
be frozen up before their songs are finished. My plants look beautifully. Old King Frost has not had the pleasure of snatching any of
them in his cold embrace as yet, and I hope will not. Our little pussy
has made out to live. I believe you know what a fatality attends our
little kitties, all of them, having had six die one right after the other.
Do you love your little niece J. as well as ever? Your soliloquy on the
year that is past and gone was not unheeded by me. Would that we
might spend the year which is now fleeting so swiftly by to better
advantage than the one which we have not the power to recall! Now

I know you will laugh, and say I wonder what makes Emily so sentimental. But I don't care if you do, for I sha'n't hear you. What are
you doing this winter? I am about everything. I am now working a
pair of slippers to adorn my father's feet. I wish you would come and
help me finish them. . . . Although it is late in the day, I am going
to wish you a happy New Year, — not but what I think your New Year
will pass just as happily without it, but to make a little return for
your kind wish, which so far in a good many respects has been granted,
probably because you wished that it might be so. I am trying to think
of some news to inform you of and while I write the fire burns which
is a very natural inference as it is a chilly, uncomfortable day. I go
to singing-school Sabbath evenings to improve my voice. . . . Don't
you envy me? . . .

I do wish you would come, 'Biah, and make me a long visit. If
you will, I will entertain you to the best of my abilities, which you
know are neither few nor small. Why can't you persuade your father
and mother to let you come here to school next term, and keep me
company, as I am going? Miss ——, I presume you can guess who I
mean, is going to finish her education next summer. The finishing
stroke is to be put on at [Norton]. She will then have learned all that
we poor foot-travellers are toiling up the hill of knowledge to acquire.
Wonderful thought! Her horse has carried her along so swiftly that
she has nearly gained the summit, and we are plodding along on foot
after her. Well said and sufficient this. We'll finish an education sometime, won't we? You may then be Plato, and I will be Socrates, provided you won't be wiser than I am. Lavinia just now interrupted my
flow of thought by saying give my love to A. I presume you will be
glad to have some one break off this epistle. All the girls send much
love to you. And please accept a large share for yourself.

From your beloved
Emily E. Dickinson.

I received your note by Sabra for which you have my hearty thanks.
I intended to write you by Sabra, but as usual she went off in a hurry
and I had no time, and I thought as all the other girls wrote you, my
letter if I wrote one, would seem no smarter than any body else, and
you know how I hate to be common. There, haven't I made a fine lot
of excuses for not writing you. I also received your paper last week

Friday. How exceedingly witty it was. The one about the little boy who was fearful of [ ] out before he went to [ ] was so sharp I was afraid of cutting off some of my fingers. Don't think of the Bookmark dear A [ ]

I presume by this time you are thirsting for some news from friends S. G., A. W., H. M. and S. P. They are all well and happy for aught I know. Sarah [Tracy?] alias Virgil is as consistent and calm and lovely as ever. Abby goes to school and is storing her mind with knowledge as the bee sips the nectar from the flowers. Hatty is making fun as usual, and Sabra [ ]. Sarah S. groweth up like the green [ ] the [ ]. Mr. [ ]

Sabra Howe has gone to Baltimore to stay several months or a year. Anna Taylor is [ ] on the single [ ]. Jane Gridley struts as badly as ever.

Have you heard anything from S[ ] Newton. I had a paper from her a few days ago. She was well and sent much love to all her friends. I suppose you consider yourself one and as such will take some of this article to yourself. Dont you wish Jane Kim[ ] would come back. I cant bear to think she is so far away. I have sent her a letter and a catalogue since she went away, and I dont know whether she ever received them or not as I [ ] of her friends have heard from her except to know that she reached there in safety and was very well. *I go to singing-school Sabbath evenings to improve my voice as a matter of [ ], & have the pleasure of a glimpse at nearly all the [ ] and [ ] in the town. I have seen nothing of Jane Brigham since last term. I presume she is at her old lodgings in Prescott. Mary Snell has a little sister which they think of calling Ellena (?) Is n't it a beautiful name?
* I hope this letter wont be broken open. *If it is folks will wonder who has got so much nonsense to tell, wont they?
Do write soon and a huge letter too may it be, much more so than mine. I hope the little dove will bear the letter safely. [*drawing of a hand*] Dont laugh at that clumsy hand. Give my love to all inquiring friends. I have so many in S[pringfield] I fear you will be troubled to give them all the particulars respecting my health. You know I always mean what I say.

[11]

* Please send me a copy of that Romance you was writing at Amherst. *I am in a fever to read it. *I expect it will be against my Whig feelings.

MANUSCRIPT: missing. See note 3 in "Notes on the Present Text." All of the letter above the signature has been published. All the rest is unpublished except the sentences marked by asterisks; these have been published in whole or in part in *Letters* (1931). The letter concludes with brief messages written as postscripts by other friends at ED's invitation, and signed: "Harriette Merrill," "Sarah S. T.," "Anna N. Tyler," and "Not Emily."

The section in the second paragraph above the signature, beginning "Although it is late," concludes with the statement that the day is chilly and uncomfortable. Earlier in the same paragraph, and separated by dots to indicate omitted material, is the sentence "It seems more like smiling May . . . than cold, arctic February." Both sections were first added in the 1931 edition, and the latter section may belong in another letter, or certainly in a different part of this one if the letter, begun one day, was finished on another.

PUBLICATION: *L* (1894) 2–4, in small part; *LL* 109–110, in small part; *L* (1931) 1–4, all that precedes the signature. It is dated (presumably by ED): Amherst, Feb. 23, 1845.

Attending the same school continuously seems not to have been expected, and by the time ED was fourteen she had made another friend who had come to Amherst and had gone again. After Abiah Root's terms at the Academy were over, ED saw her only when she came to Amherst to visit her cousins the Palmers. The friendship lasted for ten years, but no letter exchange is known to have taken place after Abiah's marriage in 1854 (see letter no. 166).

6

To Abiah Root   7 *May 1845*

Dear Abiah,

It seems almost an age since I have seen you, and it is indeed an age for friends to be separated. I was delighted to receive a paper from you, and I also was much pleased with the news it contained, especially that you are taking lessons on the "piny," as you always call it. But remember not to get on ahead of me. Father intends to have a piano very soon. How happy I shall be when I have one of my own! Old Father Time has wrought many changes here since your last short visit. Miss S. T. and Miss N. M. have both taken the marriage vows upon themselves. Dr. Hitchcock has moved into his new house, and Mr. Tyler across the way from our house has moved into President Hitchcock's old house. Mr. C. is going to move into Mr. T.'s former house, but the worst thing old Time has done here is he has walked so fast as to overtake Harriet Merrill and carry her to Hartford on last week Saturday. I was so vexed with him for it that I ran after him and made out to get near enough to him to put some salt on his tail, when he fled and left me to run home alone. . . . Viny went to Boston this morning with father, to be gone a fortnight, and I am left alone in all my glory. I suppose she has got there before this time, and is probably staring with mouth and eyes wide open at the wonders of the city. I have been to walk to-night, and got some very choice wild flowers. I wish you had some of them. Viny and I both go to school this term. We have a very fine school. There are 63 scholars. I have four studies. They are Mental Philosophy, Geology, Latin, and Botany. How large they sound, don't they? I don't believe you have such big studies. . . . My plants look finely now. I am going to send you a little geranium leaf in this letter, which you must press for me. Have you made you an herbarium yet? I hope you will if you have not, it would be such a treasure to you; 'most all the girls are making one. If you do, perhaps I can make some additions to it from flowers growing around here. How do you enjoy your school this term? Are the teachers as pleasant as our old schoolteachers? I expect you have a great many prim, starched up young ladies there, who, I doubt not, are perfect models of propriety and good behavior. If they are, don't let your free spirit be chained by them. I don't know as there [are] any in school of this stamp. But there 'most always are a few, whom the teachers look up to and regard as their satellites. I am growing handsome very fast indeed! I expect I shall be the belle of Amherst when I reach my 17th year. I don't doubt that I shall have perfect crowds of admirers at that age. Then how I shall delight to make them await my bidding, and with what delight shall I witness their suspense while I make my final decision. But away with my nonsense. I have written one composition this term, and I need not assure you it was exceedingly edifying to myself as well as everybody else. Don't you want to see it? I really wish you

[13]

could have a chance. We are obliged to write compositions once in a fortnight, and select a piece to read from some interesting book the week that we don't write compositions.

We really have some most charming young women in school this term. I sha'n't call them anything but women, for women they are in every sense of the word. I must, however, describe one, and while I describe her I wish Imagination, who is ever present with you, to make a little picture of this self-same young lady in your mind, and by her aid see if you cannot conceive how she looks. Well, to begin. . . . Then just imagine her as she is, and a huge string of gold beads encircling her neck, and don't she present a lively picture; and then she is so bustling, she is always whizzing about, and whenever I come in contact with her I really think I am in a hornet's nest. I can't help thinking every time I see this singular piece of humanity of Shakespeare's description of a tempest in a teapot. But I must not laugh at her, for I verily believe she has a good heart, and that is the principal thing now-a-days. Don't you hope I shall become wiser in the company of such virtuosos? It would certainly be desirable. Have you noticed how beautifully the trees look now? They seem to be completely covered with fragrant blossoms. . . . I had so many things to do for Viny, as she was going away, that very much against my wishes I deferred writing you until now, but forgive and forget, dear A., and I will promise to do better in future. Do write me soon, and let it be a long, long letter; and when you can't get time to write, send a paper, so as to let me know you think of me still, though we are separated by hill and stream. All the girls send much love to you. Don't forget to let me receive a letter from you soon. I can say no more now as my paper is all filled up.

Your affectionate friend,
Emily E. Dickinson.

Abby Wood & I sit together, and have real nice times. There is just room enough at our table for you and Hatty Merrill. How I wish you were both here this moment. I had a newspaper as large as life from Miss Adams our dear teacher. She sent me a beautiful little bunch of pressed flowers which I value very much as they were from her. How happy we all were together that term we went to Miss Adams. I wish it might be so again, but I never expect it. I have had two letters from S since her mother died. She is keeping house now. She says they have a good girl & get along very well, though she misses her mother very much. I pity her very much she must be so lonely without her mother. I dont know of any news in particular to tell you, except that Emeline Kellogg is preparing to go away to school. Jane Gridley, Miss Gridley I should have said, has gone to Norton to school. Martha Gilbert still lives and moves and has her being pretty much as ever.

Sarah and Abby both send their best love to you, also Sabra. Sarah wishes you to write to her soon without waiting to hear from her first, and Abby wishes the same. You must excuse me, Biah, for not writing this letter in order to have reached you on last Wednesday, but . . .

MANUSCRIPT: missing. See note 3 in "Notes on the Present Text." All of the letter above the signature has been previously published.

PUBLICATION: L (1894) 5–8; LL 110–113; L (1931) 4–6; dated (presumably by ED): Amherst, May 7, 1845.

When ED was visiting her uncle William Dickinson in Worcester, in 1844, her father wrote her on 4 June: "Tell Uncle Wm. that I want a Piano when he can buy good ones, at a fair price." (HCL). It was nearly a year later that the intent was realized (see letter no. 7). In recommending to Abiah that she make an herbarium, ED does not say whether she had started her own. She was studying botany at the time, and perhaps this letter marks the beginning of her collection of pressed plants, still extant (HCL), which she assembled with meticulous care. The allusion here to Shakespeare is the first of many which appear in her letters. One conjectures that it might be to the situation described by Puck in *A Midsummer-Night's Dream* (III, ii) which he sums up by the words: "Lord, what fools these mortals be!"

7

To Abiah Root   *3 August 1845*

Dear Abiah

I have now sit down to write you a long, long, letter. My writing apparatus is upon a stand before me, and all things are ready. I have no flowers before me as you had to inspire you. But then you know I can imagine myself inspired by them and perhaps that will do as well. You cannot imagine how delighted I was to receive your letter.

It was so full — & everything in it was interesting to me because it came from you. I presume you did not doubt my gratitude for it, on account of my delaying so long to answer it for you know I have had no leisure for anything. When I tell you that our term has been 16 weeks long & that I have had 4 studys & taken Music lessons you can imagine a little how my time has been taken up lately. I will try to be more punctual in such matters for the future. How are you now. I am very sorry to hear that you are unable to remain in your school on account of your health, it must be such a disappointment to you. But I presume you are enjoying yourself much to be at home again. You asked me in your last letter if Old Father Time wagged on in Amherst pretty much as ever. For my part I see no particular change in his movements unless it be that he goes on a swifter pace than formerly, and that he wields his sickle more stern than ever. How do you like taking music lessons. I presume you are delighted with it. I am taking lessons this term, of Aunt Selby who is spending the summer with us. I never enjoyed myself more than I have this summer. For we have had such a delightful school and such pleasant tea[c]hers, and besides I have had a piano of my own. Our Examination is to come off next week on Monday. I wish you could be here at that time. Why cant you come. If you will — You can come and practice on my piano as much as you wish to. I am already gasping in view of our examination, and although I am determined not to dread it I know it is so foolish. Yet in spite of my heroic resolutions, I cannot avoid a few misgivings when I think of those tall, stern, trustees, and when I known that I shall lose my character if I dont recite as precise as the laws of the Medes and Persians. But what matter will that be a hundred years hence. I will distress you no longer with my fears, for you know well enough what they are without my entering into any explanations. Are you practising now you are at home — I hope you are, for if you are not you would be likely to forget what you have learnt. I want very much to hear you play. I have the same Instruction book that you have, Bertini, and I am getting along in it very well. Aunt Selby says she shant let me have many tunes now for she wants I should get over in the book a good ways first. Oh Abiah. If Sarah [Tracy?], Hatty, and yourself were only here this summer what times we should have. I wish if we cant be together all the time that we could meet once in a while at least. I wish you would all come to our house and then Abby come too and such times as we should have would be a caution. I want to see you all so much, that it seems as if I could not wait. Have you heard anything from Miss Adams Our dear teacher – I have not – I sent her a paper about 3 weeks ago – but I have received no answer, and therefore I do not know where she is now. How much I would give to see her once more – but I am afraid I never shall. She is so far away – You asked me in your letter to tell you all the news worth telling and though there is not much yet I will endeavor to think of everything that will be news to you. In the first place, Mrs Jones and Mrs S Mack have both of them a little *daughter*. Very promising *Children* I understand. I dont doubt if they live they will be ornaments to society. I think they are both to be considered as Embryos of future usefullness Mrs. Washburn. Mack has now two grand daughters. Isnt she to be envied. Sabra Howe and J Gridley have both returned home. I do not see as they have altered much. They have both been attending school, and have now come to honor us poor Country folks with their presence a little while. Dont you think we ought to feel highly honored by such condescension. Jane will not return to Norton again. But Sabra will go back to Baltimore in the course of a few weeks probably to spend some time – Emeline Kellogg is expected home from school in a short time. Martha Gilbert looks and appears just as she ever did. Your Protege, Nancy Cutler is well and attending school, and Abby and I are plodding over our books pretty much as ever. Have you heard from – Hatty or Sarah – lately. I have received one paper from Sarah and a note from Hatty since I last wrote you. They were both well and happy. I do not understand your hints in regard to Abby taking so much interest in Deacon Macks family. Now Sarah is absent, I take it William is the member of the family whom you allude to. But I did not know as Abby had any partiality for him. That William is a smart boy. However as you did not mean to insinuate I will make no more comments on him, except to add that I think he will make a devoted *husband*. Dont you. I am sorry that you are laying up Hattys sins against her. I think you had better heap coals of fire upon her head by writing to her constantly until you get an answer. I have some patience with these – School Marms. They have so many trials. I hope you will decide to blot out her iniquities against her. I dont know about this Mr Eastcott giving you concert tickets. I think for my part it looks

[17]

rather suspicious. He is a young man I suppose. These Music teachers are always such high souled beings that I think they would exactly suit your fancy. My Garden looks beautifully now. I wish you could see it. I would send you a boquet if I could get a good opportunity. My House plants look very finely now. You wished me to give you some account of Sabra Palmer. She is attending school this term & studying Latin & Algebra. She is very well and happy and sends much love to you. All the girls send much love to you, and wish you to write to them. I have been working a beautiful book mark to give to one of our school girls. Perhaps you have seen it. It is an arrow with a beautiful wreath around it. Have you been working any lately. I get but very little time to work now days, there are so many other things to be done. Have you altered any since I have seen you. Isnt it a funny question for one friend to ask another. I havnt altered any, I dont think except that I have my hair done up and that makes me look different. I can imagine just how you look now. I wonder what you are doing this moment. I have got an idea that you are knitting edging. Are you. Wont you tell me when you answer my letter whether I guessed right or not. Have you got any Forget me not in your garden this summer. I am going to send you as a present in my letter next time. I am pressing some for all the girls and it is not dry yet. You gave me a compliment in your letter in regard to my being a faithful Correspondent. I must say I think I deserve it. I have been learning several beautiful pieces lately. The Grave of Bonaparte is one. Lancers Quick Step—Wood up, and Maiden Weep no more, which is a sweet little song. I wish much to see you and hear you play – I hope you will come to A. before long – Why cant you pass Commencement here. I do wish you would. Do write me often – and tell me all the news, and I will be sure to answer your letters in better season than this one. I have looked my letter over and find I have written nothing worth reading. However you must excuse it on the plea that I have written in great haste – Dont look at the writing and dont let any one see the letter. I want you should keep the seal and whenever you look at it you can think that I am looking at you at the same time.

Accept much love
from you aff friend Emily E D.
Give my love to all inquiring friends – Am I not safe enough in saying

this – Abby in particular sends love to you and wishes you to write her.

MANUSCRIPT: HCL (ARS 1). Ink. Addressed on the fold: Miss Abiah P. Root/Feeding Hills/Mass. Postmarked: Amherst Ms Aug 4. Dated: Sabbath eve.

PUBLICATION: L (1894) 8–12, many omissions; LL 113–115, further omissions; L (1931) 6–10, several omissions.

The Dickinsons' piano arrived shortly after ED last wrote to Abiah, and here she is able to report progress in her playing. Her music is in a large, bound volume (HCL), but the only piece therein that is mentioned here is "The Grave of Bonaparte," a song, with music by L. Heath, Boston, Oliver Ditson, 1843. No reliable account of her playing has been preserved, though Mrs. Bianchi recorded (FF 157) her mother's memory of ED's improvisations. Most of the compositions in her early collection are popular marches, waltzes, and quicksteps. The expression "heap coals of fire," though originating in the Bible (Proverbs 25.22 and Romans 12.20), had become so well known that its use here as a figure of speech would not necessarily mean that ED felt it to be a scripture allusion.

8

To Abiah Root   *25 September 1845*

Dearest Abiah,

As I just glanced at the clock and saw how smoothly the little hands glide over the surface, I could scarcely believe that those self-same little hands had eloped with so many precious moments since I received your affectionate letter, and it was still harder for me to believe that I, who am always boasting of being so faithful a correspondent, should have been guilty of negligence in so long delaying to answer it. . . . I am very glad to hear that you are better than you have been, and I hope in future disease will not be as neighborly as he has been heretofore to either of us. I long to see you, dear Abiah, and speak with you face to face; but so long as a bodily interview is denied us, we must make letters answer, though it is hard for friends to be separated. I really believe you would have been frightened to have heard me scold when Sabra informed me that you had decided not to visit Amherst this fall. But as I could find no one upon whom to vent my spleen for your decision, I thought it best to be calm, and therefore have at length resigned myself to my cruel fate, though with not a very good grace. I think you do well to inquire whether anything has been heard from H. I really don't know what has become of her, unless procrastination has carried her off. I think that must be the case. I think you have given quite a novel description of the wedding. Are you quite sure Mr. F., the minister, told them to stand up and he would tie them in a great bow-knot? But I beg pardon for speaking so lightly of so solemn a ceremony. You asked me in your letter if I did not think you partial in your admiration of Miss Helen H[umphrey], ditto Mrs. P[almer]. I answer, Not in the least. She was universally beloved in Amherst. She made us quite a visit in June, and we regretted more than ever that she was going where we could not see her as often as we had been accustomed. She seemed very happy in her prospects, and seemed to think distance nothing in comparison to a home with the one of her choice. I hope she will be happy, and of course she will. I wished much to see her once more, but was denied the privilege. Abby Wood, our particular friend, and the only particular friend among the girls, is well and sends much love to you. . . . You asked me if I was attending school now. I am not. Mother thinks me not able to confine myself to school this term. She had rather I would exercise, and I can assure you I get plenty of that article by staying at home. I am going to learn to make bread to-morrow. So you may imagine me with my sleeves rolled up, mixing flour, milk, salaratus, etc., with a deal of grace. I advise you if you don't know how to make the staff of life to learn with dispatch. I think I could keep house very comfortably if I knew how to cook. But as long as I don't, my knowledge of housekeeping is about of as much use as faith without works, which you know we are told is dead. Excuse my quoting from the Scripture, dear Abiah, for it was so handy in this case I couldn't get along very well without it. Since I wrote you last, the summer is past and gone, and autumn with the sere and yellow leaf is already upon us. I never knew the time to pass so swiftly, it seems to me, as the past summer. I really think some one must have oiled his chariot wheels, for I don't recollect of hearing him pass, and I am sure I should if something had not prevented his chariot wheels from creaking as usual. But I will not expatiate upon him any longer, for I know it is wicked to trifle with so reverend a personage, and I fear he will make me a call in person to inquire as to the remarks which I have made concerning him. Therefore I will let him alone for the present. . . . How are you getting on with your music? Well, I hope and trust. I am taking lessons and am getting along very well, and now I have a piano, I am very happy. I feel much honored at having even a doll named for me. I believe I shall have to give it a silver cup, as that is the custom among old ladies when a child is named for them. . . . Have you any flowers now? I have had a beautiful flower-garden this summer; but they are nearly gone now. It is very cold to-night, and I mean to pick the prettiest ones before I go to bed, and cheat Jack Frost of so many of *the treasures* he calculates to rob to-night. Won't it be a capital idea to put him at defiance, for once at least, if no more? I would love to send you a bouquet if I had an opportunity, and you could press it and write under it, The last flowers of summer. Wouldn't it be poetical, and you know that is what young ladies aim to be now-a-days. . . . I expect I have altered a good deal since I have seen you, dear Abiah. I have grown tall a good deal, and wear my golden tresses done up in a net-cap. Modesty, you know, forbids me to mention whether my personal appearance has altered. I leave that for others to judge. But my [*word omitted*] has not changed, nor will it in time to come. I shall always remain the same old sixpence. . . . I can say no more now, as it is after ten, and everybody has gone to bed but me. Don't forget your affectionate friend,

Emily E. D.

I was very unwell at the time I received your letter & unable to busy myself about anything. Consequently I was down-spirited and I give you all the credit of restoring me to health. At any rate, you may have your share. It really seemed to give me new life to receive your letter, for when I am rather low-spirited nothing seems to cheer me so much as a letter from a friend. At every word I read I seemed to feel new strength & have now regained my usual health and spirits.

Abby Wood and myself have each received a paper & note from her [Harriet Merrill] since she left. Mrs. Merrill has received 1 paper from her and that is all. I have written her two letters, sent her two papers & a package containing a very handsome book mark since I have received anything from her. [ ] really cant help thinking she has forgotten the many happy hours we spent together, and though I try to banish the idea from my mind, for it is painful to me, I am afraid she has forgotten us, but I hope not.

[21]

I think she [Helen Humphrey] must be missed much in Southwick, & her mother and sisters must be very lonely without her. Did you visit the friend whom you spoke of in your letter, the following week, & how did you find her. I hope better. I thought of you as perfectly happy all that week. You know you gave me permission in your letter to imagine you in a state of felicity.

*Abby Wood our particular friend, and the only particular friend among the girls, is well and sends much love to you. She is going to write you soon. She keeps me company at home this term, her aunt thinks it not best for her to attend school so steadily as she has done, and so we are both laid by for a while. Abby had a letter from Sarah [Tracy?] two or three weeks since. She was well and happy and sent much love to all her friends. I think if there is one in the world, who deserves to be happy, that one is Sarah. She is a noble girl, and I love her much. I shall write her soon, and tell her what has been going on here since she left. I received a letter from S Norton a few days ago who now lives in Worcester, formerly lived in Amherst. She lost her mother last spring & I have had two letters from her since. She seems to feel very lonely, now her mother is dead, and thinks were she only alive it would be all she would ask. I pity her much, for she loved her mother devotedly and she feels her loss very keenly. [ ] I had nearly forgotten to mention that Sabra Howe has been spending most of her time in Baltimore, with an uncle and aunt for the last year. She came home 3 or 4 weeks ago to make a visit, & is going to return week after next for a year if nothing happens to prevent. I should think her mother would wish her at home, some of the time with her. But she seems to think it best for Sabra to acquire her education away from home.

. . . much love to you, and wants much to hear from you.

Do write me soon, for as I cannot see you, I must hear from you often, very often. I suppose you will return to Springfield to school before long. I really wish I was going too. But as our dear teacher Miss Adams used to say, if wishes were horses, then beggars might ride. So I will wish no longer, but be content to stay where I am placed. Sabra, Viny, Abby and all the Girls send much love to you.

MANUSCRIPT: missing. See note 3 in "Notes on the Present Text." All of the letter above the signature has been published; all below it is unpublished except the sentence marked by an asterisk, which is in *Letters* (1931).

PUBLICATION: L (1894) 12–15; LL 115–118; L (1931) 10–12, dated (presumably by ED): Thursday, Sept. 26 [*sic*], 1845.

The marriage referred to is that of Helen Humphrey to Albert Palmer. Sabra Palmer was a member of the same family; it was they whom Abiah visited when she came to Amherst.

This is the earliest known letter in which ED paraphrases lines from the Bible and from Shakespeare, the two sources to which she returns again and again throughout her life for quotation or allusion. Here the paraphrase is self-consciously introduced. The scripture source for the first is James 2. 17: ". . . faith, if it hath not works, is dead. . ." The second is from *Macbeth* V, iii, 22–23: "My way of life/Is fall'n into the sere, the yellow leaf."

9

To Abiah Root   *12 January 1846*

Abiah, my dear,

Since I received your precious letter another year has commenced its course, and the old year has gone never to return. How sad it makes one feel to sit down quietly and think of the flight of the old year, and the unceremonious obtrusion of the new year upon our notice! How many things we have omitted to do which might have cheered a human heart, or whispered hope in the ear of the sorrowful, and how many things have we done over which the dark mantle of regret will ever fall! How many good resolutions did I make at the commencement of the year now flown, merely to break them and to feel more than ever convinced of the weakness of my own resolutions! The New Year's day was unusually gloomy to me, I know not why, and perhaps for that reason a host of unpleasant reflections forced themselves upon me which I found not easy to throw off. But I will no longer sentimentalize upon the past, for I cannot recall it. I will, after inquiring for the health of my dear Abiah, relapse into a more lively strain. I can hardly have patience to write, for I have not seen you for so long that I have worlds of things to tell you, and my pen is not swift enough to answer my purpose at all. However, I will try to make it communicate as much information as possible and wait to

[23]

see your own dear self once more before I relate all my thoughts which have come and gone since I last saw you. I suppose from your letter that you are enjoying yourself finely this winter at Miss Campbell's school. I would give a great deal if I was there with you. I don't go to school this winter except to a recitation in German. Mr. C[oleman] has a very large class, and father thought I might never have another opportunity to study it. It takes about an hour and a half to recite. Then I take music lessons and practise two hours in a day, and besides these two I have a large stand of plants to cultivate. This is the principal round of my occupation this winter. . . . I have just seen a funeral procession go by of a negro baby, so if my ideas are rather dark you need not marvel. . . . Old Santa Claus was very polite to me the last Christmas. I hung up my stocking on the bedpost as usual. I had a perfume bag and a bottle of otto of rose to go with it, a sheet of music, a china mug with *Forget me not* upon it, from S. S., — who, by the way, is as handsome, entertaining, and as fine a piano player as in former times, — a toilet cushion, a watch case, a fortune-teller, and an amaranthine stock of pin-cushions and needlebooks, which in ingenuity and art would rival the works of Scripture Dorcas. I found abundance of candy in my stocking, which I do not think has had the anticipated effect upon my disposition, in case it was to sweeten it, also two hearts at the bottom of all, which I thought looked rather ominous; but I will not enter into any more details, for they take up more room than I can spare.

Haven't we had delightful weather for a week or two? It seems as if Old Winter had forgotten himself. Don't you believe he is absent-minded? It has been bad weather for colds, however. I have had a severe cold for a few days, and can sympathize with you, though I have been delivered from a stiff neck. I think you must belong to the tribe of Israel, for you know in the Bible the prophet calls them a stiff-necked generation. I have lately come to the conclusion that I am Eve, alias Mrs. Adam. You know there is no account of her death in the Bible, and why am not I Eve? If you find any statements which you think likely to prove the truth of the case, I wish you would send them to me without delay.

Have you heard a word from Harriet Merrill or Sarah [Tracy?] I consider them lost sheep. I send them a paper every week on Monday, but I never get one in return. I am almost a mind to take a hand-car and go around to hunt them up. I can't think that they have forgotten us, and I know of no reason unless they are sick why they should delay so long to show any signs of remembrance. Do write me soon a very long letter, and tell me all about your school and yourself too.

Your affectionate friend,
Emily E. Dickinson.

Abby stays at home & I must stay to keep her company you know [ ] Since I last wrote you there have[been] a number of changes in Amherst. In the first place Mr. David Parsons has taken a wife to be the solace of his old age. She is a very superior lady. She has been a widow this number of years. Mr. P. found her in Hartford. She has a daughter about 20 years old, who is going to set up a dress maker's shop here. I am glad he has got a good wife to take care of his children. A. Taylor has gone to Bradford to school for a year. Mr. and Mrs. Carter have moved to Boston and their little charge, Lily Baker, has gone to Ashfield to live. Mr. Baker has gone to Northampton to live. Mr. Holland has been to the west, & brought home a niece just Sophia's age whom he has adopted as his daughter in Sophia's place. She resembles Sophia very much & Mr. Holland seems happier than he has for this long while before[.] Jane Houghton has gone to the south this winter to remain until her sister comes home. Martha Gilbert has gone to Pittsfield to school. Dr. Gridley has gone representative to Boston, this winter.

Viny wishes not to be forgotten in her share of love.

Now if you dont answer this letter soon I shall — I shall do something dreadful. So if you wish to save me the commission of some terrible deed you must write me very soon. Are you not coming to Amherst this winter. I wish father would let me go down to Springfield to see you, and then we could talk over old times. I suppose you are getting along finely in music. I had forgotten to ask after your adorable Mr. Eastcott.

There are a number of additions to the society of girls my age this winter. Mrs. S. Mack has a cousin staying with her, a very pretty girl. Emily Fowler has a cousin with her, Kate Hand by name, a very fine scholar. Then there is a Mrs. Sawtelle spending the winter here whose husband is at Washington, who has a daughter Henrietta who attends school. But I would give more to have Harriet, Sarah and yourself back than all the new comers. How is your friend Elizabeth Smith this winter. I hope better, though this season is bad for persons who are consumptive.

You cannot think how delighted I was to receive your letter. I had almost feared you had forgotten me. I carried it up to Abby's the same day that I received it.

Abby sends a great deal of love to you and says she shall write you very soon. Nancy Cutler too sends a great deal of love to you and wants much to hear from you. Why do you not ride over to A. this beautiful sleighing. I should be delighted to see you.

Sabra is well and sends much love to you, or would if she knew I was writing.

MANUSCRIPT: missing. See note 3 in "Notes on the Present Text." All of the letter above the signature has been published; all below it is unpublished.

PUBLICATION: *L* (1894) 16–18; *LL* 118–119, in small part; *L* (1931) 13–15, dated (presumably by ED): Amherst, Jan. 12, 1846.

Abiah Root was now attending Miss Campbell's School in Springfield, while Sarah Tracy and Harriet Merrill were at a school for girls in Pittsfield. (*Letters*, ed. 1931, expanded the initials S. T., used in *Letters*, ed. 1894, to Sarah Taylor). An obituary notice in the *Hampshire and Franklin Express* reads: "In this town, Jan. 9 [1846], an infant child of Mr. Charles Wilson, aged 7 months. (Colored)." The Reverend Dr. David Parsons was for many years pastor of the First Church. On Osmyn Baker, see the note for letter no. 4. On the death of Seneca Holland's daughter Sophia, see ED's full account in letter no. 11.

Dorcas, in Acts 9.36–43, is described as "full of good works." The Israelites are referred to as a "stiffnecked people" in Deuteronomy 9.6.

10

To Abiah Root   31 *January 1846*

Dear Abiah.

I fear you have thought me very long in answering your affectionate letter and especially considering the circumstances under which you wrote. But I am sure if you could have looked in upon me Dear A. since I received your letter you would heartily forgive me for my long delay.

I was delighted to receive an answer to my own so soon. Under any other circumstances I should have answered your letter sooner. But I feared lest in the unsettled state of your mind in regard to which choice you should make, I might say something which might turn your attention from so all important a subject. I shed many tears over your letter — the last part of it. I hoped and still I feared for you. I have had the same feelings myself Dear A. I was almost persuaded to be a christian. I thought I never again could be thoughtless and worldly — and I can say that I never enjoyed such perfect peace and happiness as the short time in which I felt I had found my savior. But I soon forgot my morning prayer or else it was irksome to me. One by one my old habits returned and I cared less for religion than ever. I have longed to hear from you — to know what decision you have made. I hope you are a christian for I feel that it is impossible for any one to be happy without a treasure in heaven. I feel that I shall never be happy without I love Christ.

When I am most happy there is a sting in every enjoyment. I find no rose without a thorn. There is an aching void in my heart which I am convinced the world never can fill. I am far from being thoughtless upon the subject of religion. I continually hear Christ saying to me Daughter give me thine heart. Probably you have made your decision long before this time. Perhaps you have exchanged the fleeting pleasures of time for a crown of immortality. Perhaps the shining company above have tuned their golden harps to the song of one more redeemed sinner. I hope at sometime the heavenly gates will be opened to receive me and The angels will consent to call me sister. I am continually putting off becoming a christian. Evil voices lisp in my ear — There is yet time enough. I feel that every day I live I sin more and more in closing my heart to the offers of mercy which are presented to me freely — Last winter there was a revival here. The meetings were thronged by people old and young. It seemed as if those who sneered loudest at serious things were soonest brought to see their power, and to make Christ their portion. It was really wonderful to see how near heaven came to sinful mortals. Many who felt there was nothing in religion determined to go once & see if there was anything in it, and they were melted at once.

Perhaps you will not beleive it Dear A. but I attended none of the meetings last winter. I felt that I was so easily excited that I might again be deceived and I dared not trust myself. Many conversed with me seriously and affectionately and I was almost inclined to yeild to the claims of He who is greater than I. How ungrateful I am to live along day by day upon Christs bounty and still be in a state of emnity to him & his cause.

Does not Eternity appear dreadful to you. I often get thinking of it and it seems so dark to me that I almost wish there was no Eternity. To think that we must forever live and never cease to be. It seems as if Death which all so dread because it launches us upon an unknown world would be a releif to so endless a state of existense. I dont know why it is but it does not seem to me that I shall ever cease to live on earth – I cannot imagine with the farthest stretch of my imagination my own death scene – It does not seem to me that I shall ever close my eyes in death. I cannot realize that the grave will be my last home — that friends will .weep over my coffin and that my name will be mentioned, as one who has ceased to be among the haunts of the living, and it will be wondered where my disembodied spirit has flown. I cannot realize that the friends I have seen pass from my sight in the prime of their days like dew before the sun will not again walk the streets and act their parts in the great drama of life, nor can I realize that when I again meet them it will be in another & a far different world from this. I hope we shall all be acquitted at the bar of God, and shall receive the welcome, Well done Good & faithful Servants., Enter Ye into the Joy of your Lord. I wonder if we shall know each other in heaven, and whether we shall be a chosen band as we are here. I am inclined to beleive that we shall — and that our love will be purer in heaven than on earth. I feel that life is short and time fleeting — and that I ought now to make my peace with my maker – I hope the golden opportunity is not far hence when my heart will willingly yield itself to Christ, and that my sins will be all blotted out of the book of remembrance. Perhaps before the close of the year now swiftly upon the wing, some one of our number will be summoned to the Judgment Seat above, and I hope we may not be separated when the final decision is made, for how sad would it be for one of our number to go to the dark realms of wo, where is the never dying worm and the fire which no water can quench, and how happy if we may be one un-broken company in heaven. *I carried your letter to Abby* and she perused it with the same feelings as myself, and we wished together that you might choose that better part which shall not be taken from you. Abby sends much love to you and many wishes for your happiness both temporal and eternal. She hopes to hear from you soon, very soon, and Abby and I shall be in a state of suspense until we hear from you & know what choice you have made or whether you have ceased to think of serious things. Do write me very soon and tell me all about yourself & your feelings, and do forgive me for so long neglecting to answer your letter. Although I am not a christian still I feel deeply the importance of attending to the subject before it is too late.

Your aff friend,
Emily E. D. –

I am delighted to think you are coming here to school next summer, and what delightful times we shall have to be together again as in the days that are past.

We have had a Donation Party here since I received your last letter. Mr & Mrs Colton had some very valuable presents from their friends. I went with Abby Maria, in the evening and had a very pleasant time. The next day the children all met & A & myself, went to help take care of them –

Sabra is well and sends much love to you. She says that she has owed you a letter this long while and shall write you soon as she has time. S. goes to school and finds little time for anything except her studys. Your Uncles family are all well. Please excuse those blots on the first page of my letter, as they [are] Austins work, and accidental. Also excuse the writing for I have written in great haste. I have 4 other letters to answer now. But I have written you first –

I can hardly wait for spring to come, for I so long to see you. It seems to me I shall be almost perfectly happy to see you again.

Have you heard anything yet from Harriet and Sarah. I have not, and I hardly know what to think of it. Miss H. Merrill says she has not heard from Harriet but once since she went away.

I shall write them both soon. Viny sends her love to you and says she shall be very glad to see you back again as shall all the rest of us. Dont fail to answer this letter soon.

Yours,
Emily E. Dickinson –

Manuscript: HCL (ARS 2). Ink. Unpublished. Addressed on the fold: Miss Abiah P. Root/Care of Miss Mary Campbell,/Springfield,/ Mass. Postmarked: Amherst Ms Feb 2. ED's date line: Saturday eve. 1846.

ED's confession of a religious struggle was prompted by Abiah's confidences about her own uncertainties. The more spontaneous side of religious life at Amherst is shown in the celebration in honor of the Reverend Aaron Colton. While it was customary to eke out the minister's salary with gifts of food and firewood, this donation party expressed appreciation for an able young pastor whom the people loved. The scripture allusions and biblical phrases throughout this and the following letter are such as would be heard almost weekly from the pulpit, and indeed daily in the course of revival meetings.

11

To Abiah Root   *28 March 1846*

Dearest Abiah

It is Sabbath Eve. All is still around me & I feel in a mood to answer your affectionate letter. I am alone before my little writing desk, & wishing I could write news to you as joyful as your letter to me contained. I am alone with God, & my mind is filled with many solemn thoughts which crowd themselves upon me with an irresistible force. I think of Dear Sarah & yourself as the only two out of our circle of five who have found a Saviour. I shed many a tear & gave many a serious thought to your letter & wished that I had found the peace which has been given to you. I had a melancholy pleasure in comparing your present feelings with what mine once were, but are no more. I think of the perfect happiness I experienced while I felt I was an heir of heaven as of a delightful dream, out of which the Evil one bid me wake & again return to the world & its pleasures. Would that I had not listened to his winning words! The few short moments in which I loved my Saviour I would not now exchange for a thousand worlds like this. It was then my greatest pleasure to commune alone with the great God & to feel that he would listen to my prayers. I determined to devote my whole life to his service & desired that all might taste of the stream of living water from which I cooled my thirst. But the world allured me & in an unguarded moment I listened to her syren voice. From that moment I seemed to

[30]

lose my interest in heavenly things by degrees. Prayer in which I had taken such delight became a task & the small circle who met for prayer missed me from their number. Friends reasoned with me & told me of the danger I was in of grieving away the Holy spirit of God. I felt my danger & was alarmed in view of it, but I had rambled too far to return & ever since my heart has been growing harder & more distant from the truth & now I have bitterly to lament my folly — & also my own indifferent state at the present time.

I feel that I am sailing upon the brink of an awful precipice, from which I cannot escape & over which I fear my tiny boat will soon glide if I do not receive help from above. There is now a revival in College & many hearts have given way to the claims of God. What if it should extend to the village church & your friends A. & E. feel its influence. Would that it might be so.

Although I feel sad that one should be taken and the others left, yet it is with joy that Abby & I peruse your letter & read your decision in favor of Christ & though we are not in the fold yet I hope when the great sheperd at the last day separates the sheep from the goats we may hear his voice & be with the lambs upon the right hand of God. I know that I ought now to give myself away to God & spend the springtime of life in his service for it seems to me a mockery to spend life's summer & autumn in the service of Mammon & when the world no longer charms us, "When our eyes are dull of seeing & our ears of hearing, when the silver cord is loosed & the golden bowl broken" to yield our hearts, because we are afraid to do otherwise & give to God the miserable recompense of a sick bed for all his kindness to us. Surely it is a fearful thing to live & a very fearful thing to die & give up our account to the supreme ruler for all our sinful deeds & thoughts upon this probationary term of existence. I feel when I seriously reflect upon such things as Dr Young when he exclaimed, O! what a miracle to man is man —

Yesterday as I sat by the north window the funeral train entered the open gate of the church yard, following the remains of Judge Dickinson's wife to her long home. His wife has borne a long sickness of two or three years without a murmur. She relyed wholly upon the arm of God & he did not forsake her. She is now with the reedeemed in heaven & with the savior she has so long loved according to all human probability. I sincerely sympathise with you Dear A. in the loss of your friend E. Smith. Although I had never seen her, yet I loved her from your account of her & because she was your friend. I was in hopes I might at sometime meet her but God has ordained otherwise & I shall never see her except as a spirit above. I do not recollect ever hearing you speak of her religious views but I hope her treasure was in heaven. What a blow to the fond hopes of her parents & friends must her early death be. I have never lost but one friend near my age & with whom my thoughts & her own were the same. It was before you came to Amherst. My friend was Sophia Holland. She was too lovely for earth & she was transplanted from earth to heaven. I visited her often in sickness & watched over her bed. But at length Reason fled and the physician forbid any but the nurse to go into her room. Then it seemed to me I should die too if I could not be permitted to watch over her or even to look at her face. At length the doctor said she must die & allowed me to look at her a moment through the open door. I took off my shoes and stole softly to the sick room.

There she lay mild & beautiful as in health & her pale features lit up with an unearthly – smile. I looked as long as friends would permit & when they told me I must look no longer I let them lead me away. I shed no tear, for my heart was too full to weep, but after she was laid in her coffin & I felt I could not call her back again I gave way to a fixed melancholy.

I told no one the cause of my grief, though it was gnawing at my very heart strings. I was not well & I went to Boston & stayed a month & my health improved so that my spirits were better. I trust she is now in heaven & though I shall never forget her, yet I shall meet her in heaven. I know what your feelings must have been at her death, & rejoice that you have consolation from on high to bear it with submission.

Your aff.

Emily E Dickinson.

Please not let S. or any one see this letter. It is only for you. I carried your letter to Abby, & we read it together. I shall show it to no one else, of course, as I never show any of the letters of the 'five' to any one but Abby as she is one of them.

You ask me to excuse the freedom of your letter Dear A. I think all things should be free with friends, & therefore there is nothing to excuse. Do write me a long letter soon, & be sure & come home with

Sabra, for I cannot wait any longer to see you. I really envy Sabra the pleasure of seeing you so soon & should not allow her to have any of you, did she not promise me faithfully to bring you home with her. Sabra says you have a new Piano & I rejoice with you that you have one. Viny says, give my love to Biah — as she always calls you & all the girls send much love to you. Now as a last warning, Dear A. Dont forget to come home with Sabra for it would so bitterly dissappoint us if you should not come.

MANUSCRIPT: HCL (ARS 3). Ink. Unpublished. Dated: Amherst. March. 28. 1846. Addressed on the fold: Miss Abiah P. Root/Feeding Hills./Mass./Per. Sabra. [Palmer].

ED's awakening to the reality of death came when Sophia Holland, daughter of Seneca Holland of Amherst, died on 29 April 1844. She was so deeply affected that her parents sent her to visit Mrs. Dickinson's sister Lavinia (Mrs. Loring Norcross) in Boston. (Emily's first visit to this loved aunt had occurred before Mrs. Norcross's marriage, and shortly after the birth of Emily's sister Lavinia, when both mother and baby were ill. At two and a half Emily was described in a letter by her aunt as "A very good child"; and the writer noted: "She has learned to play on the piano — she calls it the *moosic*.") On her way home from Boston she stopped at Worcester to visit her uncle William Dickinson. She later recalled that the day after her return to Amherst she first met Abiah. (See letter no. 91.) The circle of five girls to whom she refers include, beside herself, Abiah Root, Abby Wood, Harriet Merrill, and Sarah Tracy.

The scripture reference in the third paragraph combines Matthew 13.15 with Ecclesiastes 12.6: "For this people's heart is waxed gross, and their ears are dull of hearing, and their eyes they have closed. . ." "Or ever the silver cord be loosed, or the golden bowl be broken. . ." The paragraph concludes by quoting line 84 (Night I) of Young's *Night Thoughts*.

12

To Abiah Root   26 June 1846

My dear Abiah,

Though it is a long time since I received your affectionate epistle, yet when I give you my reasons for my long delay, I know you will freely forgive and forget all past offences.

It seems to me that time has never flown so swiftly with me as it has the last spring. I have been busy every minute, and not only so, but hurried all the time. So you may imagine that I have not had a spare moment, much though my heart has longed for it, to commune with an absent friend. . . . I presume you will be wondering by this time what I am doing to be in so much haste as I have declared myself to be. Well, I will tell you. I am fitting to go to South Hadley Seminary, and expect if my health is good to enter that institution a year from next fall. Are you not astonished to hear such news? You cannot imagine how much I am anticipating in entering there. It has been in my thought by day, and my dreams by night, ever since I heard of South Hadley Seminary. I fear I am anticipating too much, and that some freak of fortune may overturn all my airy schemes for future happiness. But it is my nature always to anticipate more than I realize. . . . Have you not heard that Miss Adams — dear Miss Adams — is here this term? Oh, you cannot imagine how natural it seems to see her happy face in school once more. But it needs Harriet, Sarah, and your own dear self to complete the ancient picture. I hope we shall get you all back before Miss Adams goes away again. Have you yet heard a word from that prodigal, — Harriet? . . .

Your affectionate friend,

Emily E. D.

I send you a memento in the form of a pressed flower, which you must keep.

A converted Jew has been lecturing here for the last week. His lectures were free, and they were on the present condition of the Jews. Dr. Scudder, a returned missionary, is here now, and he is lecturing also. Have you seen a beautiful piece of poetry which has been going through the papers lately? *Are we almost there?* is the title of it. . . . I have two hours to practise daily now I am in school. I have been learning a beautiful thing, which I long to have you hear. . . .

You cannot imagine how cruelly you disappointed Abby & I in not coming to visit us the last spring. We charged Sabra when she visited you at Feeding Hills, not to return without you & we could hardly speak peaceably to her when she returned alone. I anticipated more than I can express in seeing you & it seemed as if I could not wait to press you to my arms. Why did you not come, dear A. Sabra did not give any reason for your staying away, only that you could not come, which did not at all satisfy A & myself. We had been planning a great many pleasure excursions — & a great deal of enjoyment against your arrival. Abby was to have you at her house part of the time, I the other part, & Sabra was to have you – how much? Not at all! !

Was not that a contrivance? But now you are out of our reach, & we have no hope of you at present.

Was not your going to Norwich very sudden, & how long do you intend to stay there? Mrs Palmer told me you was not well at all when you left, & I am very anxious to hear a word from you as soon as possible.

& I begin to think she [Harriet Merrill] has entirely forgotten us. I cannot bear to think she has forgotten the many happy hours we used to pass together in each other's society. I hear from Sarah once in a long while.

Mrs.! Deacon! Washburn! Mack! wrote to Sarah telling her that Miss Adams was here & inviting her to spend the summer here. But she wrote that they intended to have a family meeting this summer & her father wished her to remain with them this summer.

You know Sarah is an obedient daughter! & she preferred to gratify her father rather than to spend the summer with her friends in Amherst. Do write me soon, dear A. & a long letter may it be.

MANUSCRIPT: missing. See note 3 in "Notes on the Present Text." All of the letter above the signature, and the first two paragraphs below it, have been published; the rest is unpublished.

PUBLICATION: L (1894) 18–20; LL 119–120; L (1931) 15–16, dated (presumably by ED): Friday Eve, 1846.

Matthew Berk, the "converted Jew," lectured at Amherst on June 18, 21, and 22. The poem "Are we almost there" had appeared in newspapers as early as 1833. Written by Florence Vane, it was published as a song by Oliver Ditson in 1845, with music by the author. On the sheet, the story of its origin is told thus: "A young lady had visited the South for her health, but finding she hourly grew worse, her friends hurried her home. On the journey she was very much exhausted and continually inquired 'Are we almost there?' A friend, who accompanied her, wrote the song after her death."

Deacon David Mack, as his third wife, married Harriet Parsons Washburn in 1844. She was the widow of the Reverend Royal W. Washburn, pastor of the First Church until his death in 1833.

To *Abiah Root*   *Boston, 8 September 1846*

My dear friend Abiah.

   It is a long – long time since I received your welcome letter & it
becomes me to sue for forgiveness, which I am sure your affectionate
heart will not refuse to grant. But many & unforeseen circumstances
have caused my long delay. My health was very poor all the latter part
of spring & continued so through the summer. As you may have heard,
Dear Miss Adams is teaching in Amherst & I was very anxious to attend the Academy last term on that account & did go for 11 weeks,
at the close of which I was so unwell as to be obliged to leave school.
It cost me many a severe struggle to leave my studies & to be considered
an invalid, but my health demanded a release from all care & I made
the sacrifice. I had a severe cough for several weeks attended with a
difficulty in my throat & general debility. I left school & did nothing
for some time excepting to ride & roam in the fields. I have now entirely got rid of my cough & all other bad feelings & am quite well &
strong. My health affected my spirits & I was quite down spirited for
some time, but have with renewed health regained my usual flow of
spirits. Father & Mother thought a journey would be of service to
me & accordingly, I left for Boston week before last. I had a delightful
ride in the cars & am now quietly settled down, if there can be such a
state in the city. I am visiting in my aunt's family & am happy. Happy!
Did I say? No not happy, but contented. I have been here a fortnight
to day & in that time I have both seen & heard a great many wonderful
things. Perhaps you might like to know how I have spent the time
here. I have been to Mount Auburn, to the Chinese Museum, to
Bunker hill. I have attended 2 concerts, & 1 Horticultural exhibition.
I have been upon the top of the State house & almost everywhere that
you can imagine. Have you ever been to Mount Auburn? If not you
can form but slight conception – of the "City of the dead." It seems
as if Nature had formed the spot with a distinct idea in view of its
being a resting place for her children, where wearied & dissappointed
they might stretch themselves beneath the spreading cypress & close
their eyes "calmly as to a nights repose or flowers at set of sun."

The Chinese Museum is a great curiosity. There are an endless variety of Wax figures made to resemble the Chinese & dressed in their costume. Also articles of chinese manufacture of an innumerable variety deck the rooms. Two of the Chinese go with this exhibition. One of them is a Professor of music in China & the other is teacher of a writing school at home. They were both wealthy & not obliged to labor but they were also Opium Eaters & fearing to continue the practice lest it destroyed their lives yet unable to break the "rigid chain of habit" in their own land They left their family's & came to this country. They have now entirely overcome the practice. There is something peculiarly interesting to me in their self *denial*. The Musician played upon two of his instruments & accompanied them with his voice. It needed great command over my risible faculty to enable me to keep sober as this amateur was performing, yet he was so very polite to give us some of his native music that we could not do otherwise than to express ourselves highly edified with his performances. The Writing Master is constantly occupied in writing the names of visitors who request it upon cards in the Chinese language – for which he charges 12½ cts. apiece. He never fails to give his card besides to the person[s] who wish it. I obtained one of his cards for Viny & myself & I consider them very precious. Are you still in Norwich & attending to music. I am not now taking lessons but I expect to when I return home.

Does it seem as though September had come? How swiftly summer has fled & what report has it borne to heaven of misspent time & wasted hours? Eternity only will answer. The ceaseless flight of the seasons is to me a very solemn thought, & yet Why do we not strive to make a better improvement of them?

With how much emphasis the poet has said, "We take no note of Time, but from its loss. T'were wise in man to give it then a tongue. Pay no moment but in just purchase of it's worth & what it's worth, ask death beds. They can tell. Part with it as with life reluctantly." Then we have higher authority than that of man for the improvement of our time. For God has said. "Work while the day lasts for the night is coming in the which no man can work." Let us strive together to part with time more reluctantly, to watch the pinions of the fleeting moment until they are dim in the distance & the new coming moment claims our attention. I am not unconcerned Dear A. upon the all important subject, to which you have so frequently & so affectionately called my attention in your letters. But I feel that I have not yet made my peace with God. I am still a s[tran]ger – to the delightful emotions which fill your heart. I have perfect confidence in God & his promises & yet I know not why, I feel that the world holds a predominant place in my affections. I do not feel that I could give up all for Christ, were I called to die. Pray for me Dear A. that I may yet enter into the kingdom, that there may be room left for me in the shining courts above. Why do you not come to Amherst? I long to see you once more, to clasp you in my arms & to tell you of many things which have transpired since we parted. Do come & make me a long – long, visit this autumn. Will you not? There have been many changes in Amherst since you was there. Many who were then in their bloom have gone to their last account & "the mourners go about the streets." Abby was in Athol when I left home on a visit to her mother & brothers. She is very well & as lovely as ever. She will write you soon. Abby & I talk much of the happy hours we used to spend together with yourself, Sarah & Hatty Merrill. Oh! what would I give could we all meet again. Do write me soon Dear A & let it be a long – long letter. Dont forget – !!!!!

> Your aff. friend
> Emily E. D.

Sabra Palmer was well the last time I saw her & she talked of going to Feeding Hills. She may be there now for ought I know. Do you not think it has been unusually hot the past summer. I have really suffered from the heat the last week. I think it remarkable that we should have such weather in September. There were over 100 deaths in Boston last week, a great many of them owing to the heat. Mr Taylor, Our old Teacher, was in Amherst at Commencement time. Oh! I do love Mr. Taylor. It seemed so like old times to meet Miss Adams & Mr Taylor again. I could hardly refrain from singing Auld Lang Syne. It seemed so very apropos. Have you forgotten the memorable ride we all took with Mr Taylor, "Long, Long, ago."

I hear from Sarah Tracy quite often, but as to Hatty I will not ask you if you ever hear from her for it would oblige you to leave room in your next letter, to say. No, not a word. Sarah writes in very good spirits & I think she is very happy. I am so glad to think Sarah has so good a home & kind friends for she is every way worthy of them. How glad I should be to find you in A. when I return home. Dont you recollect it was the day I returned from Boston before that I first met you & introduced myself so unceremoniously?

Have you any flowers in Norwich? My garden looked finely when I left home. It is in Viny's care during my absence. Austin entered college last Commencement. Only think!!!!!! I have a brother who has the honor to be a Freshman – Will you not promise me that you will come to Commencement when he graduates? Do! Please! Viny told me if I wrote you while I was gone to give her best love to you. I have altered very much since you was here. I am now very tall & wear long dresses near[l]y. Do you beleive we shall know each other when we meet. Dont forget to write soon.

E.

MANUSCRIPT: HCL (ARS 4). Ink. Dated: Boston. Sep. 8. 1846. Addressed on the fold: Miss Abiah P. Root/Care of D. B. Tucker Esq/Norwich/Connecticut [readdressed and forwarded to: Feeding Hills/Springfield/Mass]. Postmarked: Boston Sep 10 5 cts [and] Norwich Ct. Sep 14.

PUBLISHED: L (1894) 20–23, in part; LL 120, in small part; L (1931), 16–19, in part.

The strain evident in the preceding short letter is explained by this account of ED's eager preparation for entering Mount Holyoke. Again she was sent to visit her aunt, Mrs. Loring Norcross. The quotation from Young's *Night Thoughts* must have been from memory:

> We take no note of time
> But from its loss: to give it then a tongue
> Is wise in man.
>
> *Night* I, lines 54–56

> . . . . . pay
> No moment, but in purchase of its worth;
> And what its worth, ask death-beds; they can tell.
> Part with it as with life, reluctant . . .
>
> *Night* II, lines 49–52

ED affixed a small paper seal or wafer, bearing the printed legend "Till we meet," to the addressed surface of the letter. The scripture quotation in the eighth sentence above her signature is from Ecclesiastes 12.5.

14

To Abiah Root   *late autumn 1846*

My dear Abiah,

When I last wrote you I was in Boston, where I spent a delightful visit of four weeks. I returned home about the middle of September in very good health and spirits, for which it seems to me I cannot be sufficiently grateful to the Giver of all mercies. I expected to go into the Academy upon my return home, but as I stayed longer than I expected to, and as the school had already commenced, I made up my mind to remain at home during the fall term and pursue my studies the winter term, which commences a week after Thanksgiving. I kept my good resolution for once in my life, and have been sewing, practising upon the piano, and assisting mother in household affairs. I am anticipating the commencement of the next term with a great deal of pleasure, for I have been an exile from school two terms on account of my health, and you know what it is to "love school." Miss Adams is with us now, and will remain through the winter, and we have an excellent Principal in the person of Mr. Leonard Humphrey, who was the last valedictorian. We now have a fine school. I thank you a thousand times for your long and affectionate letter. . . . I found a quantity of sewing waiting with open arms to embrace me, or rather for me to embrace it, and I could hardly give myself up to "Nature's sweet restorer," for the ghosts of out-of-order garments crying for vengeance upon my defenceless head. However, I am happy to inform you, my dear friend, that I have nearly finished my sewing for winter, and will answer all the letters which you shall deem worthy to send so naughty a girl as myself, at short notice. . . .
    Write soon.

                              Your affectionate

                                        Emily E. D.

    Are you never coming to Amherst? You say in your last letter that you are coming in the spring, but your friends Abby & myself after discussing the matter at large have decided that if you have a spark of affection left in your heart for us you must come before. Why can you not come at Thanksgiving time, or at least after snow comes. Do come as soon as you can possibly & be sure that when you do come be it early or late you will find two warm friends ready to welcome you, by the names of Abby & Emily. Write soon, your aff.

Emily E. D.

I have much to tell you of when I see you, & let that be speedy. Abby sends bushels of love to you, & also a note which I enclose. Have you yet heard from Dear Harriet? I have not. Miss Merrill has written to Harriet & Frances inviting them to spend Thanksgiving. I need not tell you how much I wish to see her & learn the cause of her long silence. How I wish we could all meet at Thanksgiving time. How much we should have to say of the times that are gone. Write very soon.

MANUSCRIPT: missing. See note 3 in "Notes on the Present Text." All of the letter above the first signature has been published; all below it is unpublished.

PUBLICATION: L (1894) 24–25; LL 120–121; L (1931) 20–21, dated (presumably by ED): Sabbath Eve, 1846.

Elizabeth Adams, recently made preceptress of Amherst Academy, remained only until March 1847 (see letter no. 15). Leonard Humphrey, just out of college, was principal for this one year only.

It is probable that the first paragraph of the unpublished section is a concluding section preceding "Write soon. Your affectionate Emily E. D.," and that the remainder is a postscript.

II

LETTERS

15–26

[1847–1848]

"I am really
at Mt Holyoke . . ."

When Emily Dickinson wrote to Abiah Root in 1846 of her happiness in the prospect of going to Mount Holyoke, she did so with the eagerness of a girl whose growth demands wider opportunities. The Seminary proved to be all that she expected, and she had no difficulties adjusting to her studies or to her newfound friends. In spite of a bronchial ailment which enforced a long absence, she completed the courses for the year satisfactorily. But, as the weeks advanced, her spirit grew less settled. The religious atmosphere of all such institutions at that time was heavily charged, and Emily was oppressed by it. Her tie to her home was strengthened rather than loosened by her absence. She returned happily to Amherst in August 1848, her formal education at an end, leaving her only record of the year in the letters she wrote to Austin and to Abiah Root while she was at South Hadley.

15

To Abiah Root   *14 March 1847*

Ever dear Abiah.

I was delighted to receive your affectionate letter & to know that
I was not quite forgotten & should have answered it speedily had I
been able. The influenza has been very prevalent & severe here this
winter & at the time your letter reached me, I was quite sick with it,
so that I could scarcely sit up or do anything at all. My cold was very
severe in my head at first, but after I had partly recovered from that,
my cold settled upon my lungs & I had a hard cough for 3 or 4 weeks.
I am happy to say that I am pretty well now & yours is the first letter
which I have answered since I was sick. Surely you will forgive me
this once!! I suppose that your term at Miss C[ampbell]'s school is
near its close, if it has not already closed. Our term in the academy has
closed. We have spent our vacation of a fortnight, & school has commenced again since you wrote me. I go this term & am studying Algebra, Euclid, Ecc[lesiastical] History & reviewing Arithmetic again, to
be upon the safe side of things next autumn. We have a delightful
school this term under the instruction of our former principals, & Miss
R. Woodbridge – daughter of Rev. Dr. W. of Hadley, for preceptress.
We all love her very much. Perhaps a slight description of her might
be interesting to my dear A. – She is tall & rather slender, but finely
proportioned, has a most witching pair of blue eyes – rich brown hair –
delicate complexion – cheeks which vie with the opening rose bud –
teeth like pearls – dimples which come & go like the ripples in yonder
little merry brook – & then she is so affectionate & lovely. Forgive my
glowing description, for you know I am always in love with my
teachers. Yet, much as we love her, it seems lonely & strange without
"Our dear Miss Adams." I suppose you know that she has left Amherst,
not again to return as a teacher. It is indeed true, that she is to be married. Are you not astonished? Nothing was known, but that she was to
return to the school, until a few days before she left for Syracuse,
where she has gone to make her "wedding gear." She is to be married

the first of next April, to a very respectable lawyer in Conway, Mass. She seemed to be very happy in anticipation of her future prospects, & I hope she will realize all her fond hopes. I cannot bear to think that she will never more wield the sceptre, & sit upon the throne in our venerable schoolhouse, & yet I am glad she is going to have a home of her own & a kind companion to take life's journey with her. I am delighted that she is to live so near us, for we can ride up & see her often. You cannot imagine how much I enjoyed your description of your Christmas fete at Miss Campbell's. How magnificent the "Christmas tree" must have been, & what a grand time you must have had, so many of you!!! Oh!!! I had a great many presents, Christmas, & New Year's holidays – both – but we had no such celebration of the former which you describe.

Do you ever hear from Dear Sarah & Harriet. I have heard nothing from either of them this age. I sent Hatty a paper the other day & hope it may remind her of old & I fear, forgotten friends. However time will decide. Mrs. Merrill has not heard a word since last fall & does not know why. She thinks Hatty is so busy that she cant get time to write any of us. But if so busy why does she not send us a paper or speak of us when she writes her grandmother? There is a mystery about her silence to me. I hope she is happy & – but I will say no more of her till I see you "face to face" & we can "commune as a man communeth with his friend" one with another. I have one little note that Hatty wrote me soon after she went home, which I value as my own self. It is a precious communication & I will show it to you when you come. You see how much I am anticipating your visit to Amherst & you must not again dissapoint my fond expectations. Sabra told me the other day that her father was going to Michigan in May to bring on the widow and orphan child of your lamented "Cousin Albert" & that she had written you not to come until that time on account of their being alone at that time. Abby & I are talking constantly of your intended visit here & I expect we shall quarrel all the time when you really do come about who shall have the most of you. However I do not think we shall conduct quite as warlike as that! You must not think of staying less than a fortnight when you come for so long have we known each other only by symbols traced upon paper, that our words will be many & our intercourse full of affection for those of our number who are distant from us & of joy at our meeting.

Do write me soon — a long letter & tell me how soon you are coming & how long we can keep you when you come.

Your aff.

Emily E. Dickinson

Abby desires to be particularly remembered to you & Viny also sends much love to "Biah." When Miss Adams went away she wished me to tell you when I saw or wrote you that she had been trying to answer your letter this long while & should as soon as she got time. I think that Abby – you & I had better write her a congratulatory letter after she arrives at her new home, telling her of our joy at her union with so worthy a man & giving her sundry bits of advice on the importance of her station & her household cares. What do you think of this idea? If it is your pleasure you will please to signify it by the usual sign in your next letter. Let me hear from you very soon & I will answer speedily.

Manuscript: missing. The text is reproduced from a photostat (AC), formerly in the possession of Mrs. Todd. The letter is dated: Sabbath eve, 1847. A notation on the photostat, in Mrs. Todd's writing, records the address on the envelope: Miss Abiah P. Root/care of Miss Mary Campbell/Springfield/Mass. The address was canceled and the letter forwarded to Feeding Hills. The postmark is given as March 15, 1847.

Publication: L (1894) 25–26, in part; L (1931) 21–24, entire, together with a facsimile of the last page.

The spring term at Amherst Academy in 1847 began on March 5. The new preceptress, Rebecca M. Woodbridge, daughter of the Hadley minister, was a girl of twenty. The widow brought home from the West was Helen Humphrey Palmer, Jane Humphrey's sister, who had been one of ED's teachers five years before. The other friends here mentioned are probably Sabra Palmer, Harriet Merrill, Sarah Tracy, and Abby Wood.

16

To Austin Dickinson   *South Hadley, 21 October 1847*

My dear Brother. Austin.

I have not really a moment of time in which to write you & am taking time from "silent study hours," but I am determined not to break my promise again & I generally carry my resolutions into effect. I watched you until you were out of sight Saturday evening & then went to my room & looked over my treasures & surely no miser ever counted his heaps of gold, with more satisfaction than I gazed upon the presents from home.

The cake, gingerbread, pie, & peaches are all devoured, but the – apples – chestnuts & grapes still remain & will I hope for some time. You may laugh if you want to, in view of the little time in which so many of the good things have dissappeared but you must recollect that there are *two* instead of *one* to be fed & we have keen appetites over here. I cant tell you now how much good your visit did me. My cough is almost gone & my spirits have wonderfully lightened since then. I had a great mind to be homesick after you went home, but I concluded not to, & therefore gave up all homesick feelings. Was not that a wise determination? How have you all been at home since last week? I suppose nothing of serious importance has occurred, or I should have heard of it, before this time. I received a long letter from Mary. Warner, last evening & if you see her, please give my love to her & tell her I will answer it the first moment, I have to spare from school. By the way, there has been a Menagerie, here this week. Miss. Lyon. provided, "Daddy Hawks" as a *beau,* for all the Seminary girls, who wished to see the *bears* & monkeys, & your sister not caring to go, was obliged to decline the gallantry of said gentleman, which I fear I may never have another opportunity to avail myself of. The whole company stopped in front of the Seminary & played for about a quarter of an hour, for the purpose of getting custom in the afternoon I opine. Almost all the girls went & I enjoyed the solitude finely.

I want to know when you are coming to see me again, for I wish to see you as much as I did before. I went to see Miss Fiske. in her room yesterday & she read me, her letter from Sam & a right merry letter it was too. It sounded like him for all the world. I love Miss. Fiske. very much & think I shall love all the teachers, when I become better acquainted with them & find out their ways, which I can assure you are almost "past finding out." I had almost forgotten to tell you of a dream which I dreamed, last night & I would like to have you turn Daniel & interpret it to me, or if you dont care about going through all the perils which he did I will allow you to interpret it without, provided you will try to tell no lies about it. Well, I dreamed a dream & Lo!!! Father had failed & mother said that "our rye field which she & I planted, was mortgaged to Seth Nims." I hope it is not true but do write soon & tell me for you know "I should expire with mortification" to have our rye field mortgaged, to say nothing of it's falling into the merciless hands of a loco!!! Wont you please to tell me when you answer my letter who the candidate for President is? I have been trying to find out ever since I came here & have not yet succeeded. I dont know anything more about affairs in the world, than if I was in a trance, & you must imagine with all your "Sophomoric discernment," that it is but little & very faint. Has the Mexican war terminated yet & how? Are we beat? Do you know of any nation about to besiege South Hadley? If so, do inform me of it, for I would be glad of a chance to escape, if we are to be stormed. I suppose Miss Lyon. would furnish us all with daggers & order us to fight for our lives, in case such perils should befall us.

Tell mother, that she was very thoughtful to inquire in regard to the welfare of my shoes. Emily has a shoe brush & plenty of blacking, & I brush my shoes to my heart's content. Thank Viny 10,000. times for the beautiful ribbon & tell her to write me soon. Tell father I thank him for his letter & will try to follow its precepts. Do excuse the writing for I am in furious haste & cant write another word.

Your aff. Emily

Give much love to Father, mother, Viny, Abby, Mary, Deacon Haskell's family & all the good folks at home, whom I care anything about. I shall write Abby & Mary very soon. Do write me a long letter soon & answer all my questions, that is if you can read them. Come & see me as often as you can & bring a good load every time.

Miss Fiske. told me if I was writing to Amherst to send her love. Not specifying to whom, you may deal it out, as your good sense & discretion prompt.

Be a good boy & mind me.

MANUSCRIPT: AC. Ink. Dated: Thursday noon. Addressed on the fold: Austin Dickinson, Esq./Amherst./Mass. Postmarked: South Hadley Mass. Oct 22.

PUBLICATION: L (1894) 65–67, in part; L (1931) 63–65, in part; Home 68–70, entire.

For Mary Lyon (1797–1849), founder and principal of the Seminary, this was the last full year of teaching. Her associate principal was Mary C. Whitman. Of the nine other teachers, only one is here mentioned, Rebecca W. Fiske, a recent Seminary graduate whose brother Sam was at the time a junior at Amherst College. Mary Warner and Abby Wood were Amherst friends with whom ED had grown up. The Emily who is mentioned as having the shoebrush was ED's cousin from Monson, Emily Lavinia Norcross, a senior and her roommate. ED had now been at the Seminary for three weeks.

The term "loco-foco," originally applied to any antimonopolistic wing of New York City Democrats (1835), was now used by the Whigs to describe any Democrat, and Democrats in the judgment of the Dickinsons were persons who would bear watching. Seth Nims, a Democrat, was the Amherst postmaster during the presidencies of Polk (1845–1849), Pierce, and Buchanan (1853–1861). The same tone about Nims is evident in letter no. 130, and in one from Lavinia to her brother in 1853 (*Home* 318): "Mr Nims is making awful blunders in the post office. I hope he'll be requested to retire."

ED's comment on the politics of the times, here focused on the Mexican war, should be compared with one written in similar vein near the end of her life (letter no. 950).

17

To Austin Dickinson   *South Hadley, 2 November 1847*

My dear Brother. Austin.

I have this moment finished my recitation in History & have a few minutes, which I shall occupy in answering your short, but welcome letter. You probably heard that I was alive & well, yesterday, unless, Mr. E. Dickinson was robbed of a note, whose contents were to that effect. But as robbers are not very plenty now a days, I will have no forebodings on that score, for the present. How [are] you! do you get along without me now & does "it seem any more like a funeral," than it did before your visit to your *humble servant* in this place? Answer me!! I want much to see you all at home & expect to 3. weeks from tomorrow, if nothing unusual, like a famine or pestilence, occurs to prevent my going home. I am anticipating much in seeing you on this week Saturday & you had better not dissappoint me!! for if you do, I will harness the "furies" & pursue you with a "whip of scorpions," which is even worse you will find, than the "long oat" which you may remember. Have you heard from Sarah Pynchen. lately & have you found out "those particular reasons" which prevent her corresponding with me, much to her sorrow & my inexpressible regret, for having few letters to write, now I am away from home, it would be a pleasant method of employing my liesure time & keep my mind from vain & foolish thoughts in the leisure time before mentioned. How long is Mary. Warner. to be absent from home? I received a long letter from her a few days since & sent her a letter directed to Medford, today. I hear often from Abby. & think she has not forgotten me, though absent. She is now my debtor to the amount of one long letter & I wish you would inform her, if you have an opportunity, that I am anxiously waiting to receive it. I received a letter last eve, of an amusing nature & signed by the writer as "John Klima." I read it, but as I found the postage was 10. cts. I concluded it was not intended for me & sent it back to the office. The postmark, was so faint that I could not decipher it & I have not a little curiosity respecting it. If you can give me any clue to the mystery, I will be obliged to you, in due proportion to the amount of information which you are able to give me. How do the plants look now & are they as flourishing as before I went away? I wish much to see them. Some of the girls here, have plants, but it is a cold place & I am very glad that I did not bring any, as I thought of doing. A young lady by the name of Beach, left here for home this morning. She could not get through her examinations & was very wild beside. Miss Lyon. said she should write her father, if she did not change her course & as she did not, her father came for her last night. He was an interesting man & seemed to feel very badly that his daughter should be obliged to leave, on account of bad conduct. Perhaps you saw an account some time since, of a carriage, being presented to Henr⁻ Clay. by a Mr. Beach. It was the self same. Why dont Sarah Thompson's brother come over to see her, if he has one spark of affection for her? Please tell him, she is very anxious to see him & will not receive him if he dont come soon. You must tell mother that I was delighted to see her handwriting once more, but that she need not put herself out to write me, for I know just how much she has to do & on that account do not expect to see letters from her very often. Please tell Viny, that if she has any time from the cares of her household to write a line to me, that I would receive it with all due deference to her age & majesty & honors. I suppose "Cook" occupies most of her time & will therefore excuse her long delay for the past, but not for the future. Cousin Emily. had a letter from Grandmother., last night and she mentioned in her letter, that Mrs Coleman & Eliza were daily expected in Monson & would probably spend some time at Aunt Flynt's. It seems impossible to me that Mrs. Frink. is dead. How is Jacob. Holt. now? I have not heard a word from him since you were here & feel quite anxious to know how he is. Give much love to him & tell him I will write him as soon as I can find a spare moment for it. Are Thompson. & Newton. going away before I come home? Give much love to Father, Mother, Viny & Abby, also thank Abby for her note & tell her I consider it only a type of what is forthcoming. Do write a long letter to

Your aff Sister.

Emily.

Tell Father, I am obliged to him much, for his offers of *"picauni-ary"* assistance, but do not need any. We are furnished with an account-book, here & obliged to put down every mill, which we spend & what we spend it for & show it to Miss. Whitman every Saturday, so you perceive your sister is learning to keep accounts in addition to the other branches of her education. I am getting along nicely in my studies & am happy – quite for me. Wont you ask father for Aunt Elisabeth's address & give it to me when you write me for I wish to write her & dont know to whose care to send it.

South-Hadley — Seminary.
Novr 2d.   —   1847 —
Bill of. Fare.

Roast. Veal.
Potatoes.
Squash.
Gravy.
Wheat & Brown-Bread.
Butter.
Pepper & Salt.

Dessert.
Apple-Dumpling.
Sauce.

Water.

Is'nt that a dinner fit to set before a King.

Emily. E. Dickinson.

MANUSCRIPT: AC. Ink. Dated: Tuesday noon. Addressed on the fold: Austin Dickinson, Esq./Amherst./Mass. Postmark illegible. ED transcribed the "Bill of Fare" onto a separate sheet.

PUBLICATION: L (1894) 68–69, in part; L (1931) 65–67, in part; *Home* 71–73, entire.

Austin was now a sophomore at Amherst College. Jacob Holt was an Amherst boy who had attended the Academy with both ED and Abiah Root five years before. She pasted into the back of her Bible a poem by Dr. Holt, clipped from the *Hampshire and Franklin Express* of 6 June 1848, together with an obituary notice from a Boston paper. His demise was therefore one which she wished to recall, though it never had the import clearly evident after the death of Benjamin Newton (see the note to letter no. 153). She solicitously mentions Holt twice again in letters to Austin (nos. 19 and 22), but when she wrote Abiah Root a few days after Holt's death on 12 May 1848 (letter no. 23), she was not moved enough to record the fact, even though she was in Amherst during the weeks of his final illness. The scripture quotation is a reference to 1 Kings 12.11: ". . . my father hath chastised you with whips, but I will chastise you with scorpions." (See also letter no. 57.)

18

To Abiah Root   *South Hadley, 6 November 1847*

My dear Abiah.

I am really at Mt Holyoke Seminary & this is to be my home for a long year. Your affectionate letter was joyfully received & I wish that this might make you as happy as your's did me. It has been nearly six weeks since I left home & that is a longer time, than I was ever away from home before now. I was very homesick for a few days & it seemed to me I could not live here. But I am now contented & quite happy, if I can be happy when absent from my dear home & friends. You may laugh at the idea, that I cannot be happy when away from home, but you must remember that I have a very dear home & that this is my first trial in the way of absence for any length of time in my life. As you desire it, I will give you a full account of myself since I first left the paternal roof. I came to S. Hadley six weeks ago next Thursday. I was much fatigued with the ride & had a severe cold besides, which prevented me from commencing my examinations until the next day, when I began.

I finished them in three days & found them about what I had anticipated, though the old scholars say they are more strict than they ever have been before. As you can easily imagine, I was much delighted to finish without failures & I came to the conclusion then, that I should not be at all homesick, but the reaction left me as homesick a girl as it is not usual to see. I am now quite contented & am very much occupied now in reviewing the Junior studies, as I wish to enter the middle class. The school is very large & though quite a number have left, on account of finding the examinations more difficult than they anticipated, yet there are nearly 300. now. Perhaps you know that Miss. Lyon is raising her standard of scholarship a good deal, on account of the number of applicants this year & on account of that she makes the examinations more severe than usual.

You cannot imagine how trying they are, because if we cannot go through them all in a specified time, we are sent home. I cannot be too thankful that I got through as soon as I did, & I am sure that I never would endure the suspense which I endured during those three days again for all the treasures of the world.

I room with my Cousin Emily, who is a Senior. She is an excellent room-mate & does all in her power to make me happy. You can imagine how pleasant a good room-mate is, for you have been away to school so much. Everything is pleasant & happy here & I think I could be no happier at any other school away from home. Things seem much more like home than I anticipated & the teachers are all very kind & affectionate to us. They call on us frequently & urge us to return their calls & when we do, we always receive a cordial welcome from them.

I will tell you my order of time for the day, as you were so kind as to give me your's. At 6. oclock, we all rise. We breakfast at 7. Our study hours begin at 8. At 9. we all meet in Seminary Hall, for devotions. At 10¼. I recite a review of Ancient History, in connection with which we read Goldsmith & Grimshaw. At .11. I recite a lesson in "Pope's Essay on Man" which is merely transposition. At .12. I practice Calisthenics & at 12¼ read until dinner, which is at 12½ & after dinner, from 1½ until 2 I sing in Seminary Hall. From 2¾ until 3¾. I practise upon the Piano. At 3¾ I go to Sections, where we give in all our accounts for the day, including, Absence — Tardiness — Communications — Breaking Silent Study hours — Receiving Company in our rooms & ten thousand other things, which I will not take time or place to mention. At 4½. we go into Seminary Hall, & receive advice from Miss. Lyon in the form of a lecture. We have Supper at 6. & silent-study hours from then until the retiring bell, which rings at 8¾, but the tardy bell does not ring until 9¾, so that we dont often obey the first warning to retire.

Unless we have a good & reasonable excuse for failure upon any of the items, that I mentioned above, they are recorded & a *black mark* stands against our names: As you can easily imagine, we do not like very well to get "exceptions" as they are called scientifically here. My domestic work is not difficult & consists in carrying the Knives from the 1st tier of tables at morning & noon & at night washing & wiping the same quantity of Knives. I am quite well & hope to be able to spend the year here, free from sickness. You have probably heard many reports of the food here & if so I can tell you, that I have yet seen nothing corresponding to my ideas on that point from what I have heard. Everything is wholesome & abundant & much nicer than I should imagine could be provided for almost 300. girls. We have also a great variety upon out tables & frequent changes. One thing is certain & that is, that Miss. Lyon & all the teachers, seem to consult our comfort & happiness in everything they do & you know that is pleasant. When I left home, I did not think I should find a companion or a dear friend in all the multitude. I expected to find rough & uncultivated manners, & to be sure, I have found some of that stamp, but on the whole, there is an ease & grace a desire to make one another happy, which delights & at the same time, surprises me very much. I find no Abby. or Abiah. or Mary, but I love many of the girls. Austin came to see me when I had been here about two weeks & brought Viny & Abby. I need not tell you how delighted I was to see them all, nor how happy it made me to hear them say that "they were *so lonely.*" It is a sweet feeling to know that you are missed & that your memory is precious at home. This week, on Wednesday, I was at my window, when I happened to look towards the hotel & saw Father & Mother, walking over here as dignified as you please. I need not tell you that I danced & clapped my hands, & flew to meet them for you can imagine how I felt. I will only ask you do you love your parents? They wanted to surprise me & for that reason did not let me know they were coming. I could not bear to have them go, but go they must & so I submitted in sadness. Only to think Abiah, that in 2½ weeks I shall be at my *own dear home* again. You will probably go home at Thanksgiving time & we can rejoice with each other.

You dont [know] how I laughed at your description of your introduction to Daniel Webster & I read that part of your letter to Cousin. Emily. You must feel quite proud of the acquaintance & will not I hope be vain in consequence. However you dont know Govr Briggs & I do, so you are no better off than I. I hear frequently from Abby & it is a great pleasure to receive her letters. Last eve, I had a long & very precious letter from her & she spoke of see^g a letter from you. You probably have heard of the death of *O. Coleman.* How melancholy!! Eliza. had written me a long letter giving me an account of her death, which is beautiful & affecting & which you shall see when we *meet again.*

Abiah, you must write me often & I shall write you as often as I have time. But you know I have many letters to write now I am away from home. Cousin. Emily says "Give my love to Abiah."

From your aff

Emily E. D—

MANUSCRIPT: Mount Holyoke College. Ink. Dated: Mt Holyoke. Seminary. Novr 6. 1847.

PUBLICATION: L (1894) 27–31, in part; LL 124–127, in part: *Mt. Holyoke Alumnae Quarterly* IX (1926), 153–155, entire; L (1931) 24–28, in part.

Edward Dickinson was a member of the executive council (1846–1847) of Governor George N. Briggs; both Briggs and his wife had been overnight guests in the Dickinson home. Olivia Coleman, the older sister of ED's friend Eliza, died at Princeton, New Jersey, on September 28, two days before ED had left Amherst for South Hadley. Her father Lyman Coleman, currently teaching at the College of New Jersey (Princeton), had been principal of Amherst Academy (1844–1846) when ED was a student there.

19

To Austin Dickinson   *South Hadley, 11 December 1847*

My dear Brother. Austin.

I heard today that Mr. Colton. from Amherst was to preach here tomorrow & am writing a word, hoping to send by him to you. You probably thought me very sisterly, grateful &c. not to answer your kind letter by Mary. Snell, but I had no time to write by her & since then I have been occupied every moment & could find no time to write you. I was not very well when Mary. was here, but think that I am better now.

I finished my examination in Euclid last eve & without a failure at any time. You can easily imagine how glad I am to get through with 4. books, for you have finished the whole *forever*. I am looking forward to next Wednesday very impatiently — as I expect you and Mary. Warner, then. Surely you will not disappoint me. How are you all at home & what are you doing this vacation? You are reading Arabian Nights, according to Viny's statement. I hope you have derived much benefit from their perusal & presume your powers of imagining will vastly increase thereby. But I must give you a word of advice too. Cultivate your other powers in proportion as you allow Imagination to captivate you! Am not I a very wise *young lady*? I had almost forgotten to tell you what my studies are now. "Better *late* than *never*." They are, Chemistry, Physiology & quarter course in Algebra. I have completed four studies already & am getting along well. Did you think that it was my birthday — yesterday? I dont believe I am *17*. Is. Jacob. Holt any better than when you wrote last & is there any hope of him? Give much love to all home friends & tell them I will write a long letter soon. Knowing you to be fond of gimcracks I wish you would accept the enclosed Box of Wafers. Hope you will use them on all extra important occasions, such as writing notes for example &, but I will not specify. My best love to father, mother, Viny, Abby & Mary.

From your aff. Sister

Emily.

MANUSCRIPT: AC. Ink. Dated: Saturday. *P.M.* Envelope addressed: Austin. W. Dickinson./Amherst./Mass./*Per Mr Colton.*

PUBLICATION: L (1894) 70, in part; L (1931) 68, in part; *Home* 74, entire.

The Reverend Mr. Aaron Colton had been pastor of the First Church since 1840. Mary Snell, about the age of ED, was a daughter of Ebenezer S. Snell, professor of mathematics at Amherst College. The wafers which ED enclosed were probably similar to those mentioned in letter no. 13.

20

To Abiah Root   *South Hadley, 17 January 1848*

My dear Abiah.

Your welcome epistle found me upon the eve of going home & it is needless to say very happy. We all went home on Wednesday before Thanksgiving & a stormy day it was, but the storm must not be in our way, so we tried to make the best of it & look as cheerful as we could. Many of the girls went very early in the morning in order to reach home the same day & when we all sat down to the breakfast table, it seemed lonely enough to see so many places vacant. After breakfast, as we were not required to keep all the family rules, a number of us met together at one of the windows in the Hall to watch for our friends, whom we were constantly expecting. No morning of my life ever passed so slowly to me & it really seemed to me they never were coming, so impatiently did I wait their arrival. At last almost tired out I spied a carriage in the distance & surely Austin was in it. You who have been away so much, can easily imagine my delight & will not laugh, when I tell you how I dashed down stairs & almost frightened my dignified – brother out of his senses. All was ready in a moment or less than a moment & Cousin Emily & myself, not forgetting the driver, were far on our way towards home. The rain fell in torrents & the wind howled around the sides of the mountain over our heads & the brooks below filled by the rain rushed along their pebbly beds almost frightfully, yet nothing daunted, we rode swiftly along & soon the Colleges & the spire of our venerable Meeting House, rose to my delighted vision. Never did Amherst look more lovely to me & gratitude rose in my heart to God, for granting me such a safe return to my *own* DEAR HOME. Soon the carriage stopped in front of our own house & all were at the door to welcome the returned one, from Mother with tears in her eyes down to Pussy who tried to look as gracious as was becoming her dignity. Oh! Abiah, it was the first meeting as it had been the first separation & it was a joyful one to all of us. The storm did not at all subside that night, but in the morning I was waked by the glorious sun himself – staring full in my face. We went to church in the morning & listened to an excellent sermon from our own minister, Mr. Colton. At noon we returned & had a nice dinner, which, you well know cannot be dispensed with on Thanksgiving day. We had several calls in the afternoon and had four invitations out for the evening. Of course, we could not accept them all, much to my sorrow, but decided to make two visits.

At about 7. oclock, Father, Mother, Austin, Viny, Cousin Emily & myself to bring up the rear, went down to Profʳ Warner's, where we spent an hour delightfully, with a few friends & then bidding them good eve, we young folks, went down to Mrs. S. Mack's accompanied by *Sister Mary*.

There was quite a company of young people assembled, when we arrived and after we had played many Games, we had in familiar terms a "Candy Scrape." We enjoyed the evening much & returned not until the clock pealed out "Remember 10 oclock my dear, remember 10, oclock." After our return, Father wishing to hear the Piano, I like an obedient daughter, played & sang a few tunes, much to his apparent gratification. We then retired & the next day & the next were as happily spent as the eventful Thanksgiving day itself. You will probably think me foolish thus to give you an inventory of my time while at home, but I did enjoy so much in those short four days, that I wanted you to know and enjoy it too. Monday came so soon & with it came a carriage to our door & amidst tears falling thick & fast away I went again. Slowly & sadly dragged a few of the days after my return to the Seminary and I was very homesick, but "after a storm there comes a calm" and so it was in my case. My sorrows were soon lost in study & I again felt happy, if happiness there can be away from "home, sweet home."

Our term closes, this week on Thursday & Friday, I hope to see home and friends once more. I have studied hard this term & aside from my delight at going home, there is a sweetness in approaching rest to me. This term is the longest in the year & I would not wish to live it over again, I can assure you. I love this Seminary & all the teachers are bound strongly to my heart by ties of affection. There are many sweet girls here & dearly do I love some new faces, but I have not yet found the place of a *few* dear ones filled, nor would I wish it to be here. I am now studying "Silliman's Chemistry" & Cutler's Physiology, in both of which I am much interested. We finish Physiology before this term closes & are to be examined in it at the Spring Examinations, about five weeks after the commencement of the next term. I already

[59]

begin to dread that time for an examination in Mt. Hol. Sem. is rather more public than in our old academy & a failure would be more disgraceful there, I opine, but I hope to use my father's own words "that I shall not disgrace myself."

What are you studying now? You did not mention that item in your last letters to me & consequently I am quite in the dark as regards your progress in those affairs. All I can say is, that I hope you will not leave *poor me* far behind. Mr Humphrey. brought Mary. Warner. over to see me the other day & we had a delightful time, you well know. Cousin Emily sends much love & wishes you to write her a note, when you answer my letter & may it be speedily.

Your aff. *Sister.*

Emily E. Dickinson

Our Section have commenced reading Compositions & we read once in a month, during which time we *write two.*

You remember that you wished a remembrance to Jane. Humphrey when you last wrote me & I did [give] the message to her. She sends much love to you & wishes much to see you. In my last letter from home, Viny said that Mrs. A. Palmer. returned to Southwick a fortnight since. Do you not think her very lovely in her garb of mourning? Mary is a sweet child & bids fair to be as interesting as her mother. Helen. seems perfectly bound up in her child and I trust she will be a great comfort to her in her solitary & lonely hours. It seems a very long time since our last meeting and I long to see you once more. There is a great deal of religious interest here and many are flocking to the ark of safety. I have not yet given up to the claims of Christ, but trust I am not entirely thoughtless on so important & serious a subject.

Do you not think we have had some delightful weather for winter & does it not remind you of spring?

MANUSCRIPT: HCL (ARS 5). Ink. Dated: Mt. Hol. Fem. Sem. Jan. 17, 1848. Addressed on the fold: Miss. Abiah P. Root./Care of. Miss. Mary. Campbell./Springfield./Mass. Postmarked: South Hadley Mass. Jan. 19.

PUBLICATION: L (1894) 31–35, in part; LL 128–129, in part; L (1931) 29–32, in part.

No Christmas recess customarily was granted at this time in New England schools and colleges, for the season was still associated in the orthodox Congregational mind with other Christian orthodoxies which were strongly disapproved. At Mount Holyoke a two-week holiday was scheduled between the terms, and ED was to go home again on the twenty-first of the month. Helen H. Palmer was last mentioned in a letter to Abiah written in the previous spring (no. 15).

21

To Austin Dickinson   *South Hadley, 15 February 1848*

My dear Austin.

Miss Fiske. has been to my room & left word that she is going to Amherst, tonight & I can send home by her if I wish. It seemed desolate enough here for a *few days* after my return as Emily. had not come & I was all alone, but I have now got settled down in the *old track* and feel quite at home. I am pretty well & have got rested from my *dissipation*. You have probably recovered from the effects of my visit by this time & can retire in season. Miss. Mann. came in to see me soon after father went home and spoke of enjoying her visit at our house very much.

Emily Norcross. came yesterday about 5. o clock & glad was I to see her I can assure you. She left all Monson folks, well. You probably know that Mary Hills. went home yesterday & dont know when she will return. When is Harriet. Parsons coming back, or has she decided to remain at home?

Please give much love to all at home & to Mary & Abby. Also remember me to your room mate if you please to do so. I do hope you will come & see me as often as you can, for I want much to see you already; it is [such] good sleighing, that you need make no great sacrifice to ride over here I am sure. You must not expect to hear from me often, for I have but little time to write, but you must write me as often as possible.

Your aff.
Emily.

MANUSCRIPT: AC. Pencil. Dated: Tuesday noon. Envelope addressed in ink: Austin W. Dickinson./Amherst./Mass./Per Miss Fiske.

PUBLICATION: *Home* 76–77.

The new term at Mount Holyoke began on February 4. Margaret Mann was one of the Seminary teachers. Mary Hills and Harriet Parsons were Amherst friends attending the Seminary.

22

To Austin Dickinson   *South Hadley, 17 February 1848*

My dear Austin.

You will perhaps imagine from my date, that I am quite at leisure & can do what I please even in the forenoon, but one of our teachers, who is engaged, received a visit from her intended, quite unexpectedly yesterday afternoon & she has gone to her home to show him I opine & will be absent until Saturday. As I happen to recite to her in one of my studies, her absence gives me a little time in which to write. Your *welcome* letter found me all engrossed in the history of Sulphuric Acid!!!!! I deliberated for a few moments after it's reception on the propriety of carrying it to Miss. Whitman, your friend. The result of my deliberation was a conclusion to open it with moderation, peruse it's contents with sobriety becoming my station, & if after a close investigation of it's contents I found nothing which savored of rebellion or an unsubdued will, I would lay it away in my folio & forget I had ever received it. Are you not gratified that I am so rapidly gaining correct ideas of female propriety & sedate deportment? After the proposed examination, finding it concealed no dangerous sentiments I with great gravity deposited it with my other letters & the impression that I once had such a letter is entirely obliterated by the waves of time. I have been quite lonely since I came back, but cheered by the thought that I am not to return another year I take comfort & still hope on. My visit at home was happy, very happy to me & had the idea of in so short a time returning, been constantly in my dreams, by night & day I could not have been happier. "There is no rose without a thorn" to me. Home was always dear to me & dearer still the friends around it, but never did it seem so dear as now. All, all are kind to me but their tones fall strangely on my ear & their countenances meet. mine not like home faces, I can assure you, most sincerely. Then when tempted to feel sad, I think of the blazing fire, & the cheerful meal & the chair empty now I am gone. I can hear the cheerful voices & the merry laugh

& a desolate feeling comes home to my heart, to think I am alone. But my good angel only waits to see the tears coming & then whispers, only this year!! Only 22. weeks more & home again you will be to stay. To you, all busy & excited, I suppose the time flies faster, but to me slowly, very slowly so that I can see his chariot wheels when they roll along & himself is often visible. But I will no longer imagine, for your brain is full of Arabian Nights fancies & it will not do to pour fuel on your already *kindled imagination.* You cant think how dissappointed I was to know that Viny was not coming until next week, for I had made all my plans to welcome her on Friday of this week instead of next. But it will be better the longer it is in coming I suppose. All the girls are waiting with impatience to see her & to about a dozen I have given her dimensions. Tell her she must look her prettiest or they will be dissappointed for I have given a glowing account of her.

I suppose you have written a few & received a quantity of Valentines this week. Every night I have looked & yet in vain for one of Cupid's messengers. Many of the girls have received very beautiful ones & I have not quite done hoping for one. Surely *my friend* THOMAS, has not lost all his former affection for me. I entreat you to tell him I am pining for a Valentine. I am sure I shall not very soon forget last Valentine week nor any the sooner, the fun I had at that time. Probably, Mary, Abby & Viny have received scores of them from the infatuated wights in the neighborhood while your *highly accomplished & gifted elder sister* is entirely overlooked. Monday afternoon, *Mistress* Lyon arose in the hall & forbade our sending "any of those foolish notes called Valentines." But those who were here last year, knowing her opinions, were sufficiently cunning to write & give them into the care of Dickinson, during the vacation, so that about 150. were despatched on Valentine morn, before orders should be put down to the contrary effect. Hearing of this act, Miss Whitman by & with the advice & consent of the other teachers, with frowning brow, sallied over to the Post office, to ascertain if possible, the number of Valentines and worse still, the names of the offenders. Nothing has yet been heard as to the amount of her information, but as Dickinson is a good hand to help the girls & no one has yet received sentence, we begin to think her mission unsuccessful. I have not written one nor do I now intend to. Your injunction to pile on the wood has not been unheeded for we have been obliged to obey it to keep from freezing up. I have had a severe cold for a few days, but think it is better now. We cannot have much more cold weather I am sure, for spring is near. Have you decided who to bring when you come? As to my opinion on that point, I confess I am in a strait betwixt two, Mary & Abby. Your better judgment will I am certain decide in the right and I will therefore leave it entirely in your hands.

Do you intend to give Miss. Whitman a ride? You had better resign that honor to your room-mate when he comes over again I judge. I had a note from E. Coleman, a few days since, but she said not a word of any of the family. You can probably imagine the drift of her remarks, without further information. I cannot say half that I want to for want of space.

Your affectionate Sister.

Emily.

How is Jacob. Holt now? I wish much to hear from him as not one word have I heard since I left home about him. Does your Rooster yet persist in his foolish habit of crowing under his window? I hope he has long ere this repented him of his folly. Professor. Smith. preached here last Sabbath & such sermons I never heard in my life. We were all charmed with him & dreaded to have him close. I understand the people of S. Hadley have given Mr. Belden of East-street a call to settle here. If he accepts, I hope it *will*, WILL not be until my year is out. Will you ask Viny. to get my History & Topic book, of Harriet. Parsons & bring them with her, for reviews commence very soon & I shall need them. Also will she bring a little Sweet Flag & that Comb, which I did my hair up with when I came home from Boston? Write me as long a letter as this is very soon.

Give my best love to Father, Mother, Viny, Mary, Abby, Dea. Haskell's family & all who inquire for me.

Please not to show this letter for it is strictly confidential & I should feel badly to have you show it.

MANUSCRIPT: AC. Ink. Dated: Thursday morn. Addressed on the fold: Austin. W. Dickinson./Amherst./Mass. Postmark illegible. The letter is sealed with a diamond-shaped wafer on which is printed "Believe me," followed by the first bar of the well-known musical rendering of "Believe me, if all these endearing young charms."

PUBLICATION: L (1894) 70–73, in part; LL 130–132, in part; L (1931) 69–71, in part; *Home* 78–80, entire.

As the year advanced, ED's homesickness increased. The strain must have been apparent to her family, for her father had already decided not to send her to Mount Holyoke for a second year.

The custom of exchanging valentines was not limited at this time to one day, but extended through the entire "Valentine week." The Reverend Henry B. Smith was a member of the Amherst College faculty; the Reverend Pomeroy Belden was pastor of the East Parish church in Amherst. ED's friend Thomas has not been identified.

23

To Abiah Root   *South Hadley, 16 May 1848*

My dear Abiah,

You must forgive me, indeed you must, that I have so long delayed to write you, and I doubt not you will when I give you all my reasons for so doing. You know it is customary for the first page to be occupied with apologies, and I must not depart from the beaten track for one of my own imagining. . . . I had not been very well all winter, but had not written home about it, lest the folks should take me home. During the week following examinations, a friend from Amherst came over and spent a week with me, and when that friend returned home, father and mother were duly notified of the state of my health. Have you so treacherous a friend?

Now knowing that I was to be reported at home, you can imagine my amazement and consternation when Saturday of the same week Austin arrived in full sail, with orders from head-quarters to bring me home at all events. At first I had recourse to words, and a desperate battle with those weapons was waged for a few moments, between my *Sophomore* brother and myself. Finding words of no avail, I next resorted to tears. But woman's tears are of little avail, and I am sure mine flowed in vain. As you can imagine, Austin was victorious, and poor, defeated I was led off in triumph. You must not imbibe the idea from what I have said that I do not love home — far from it. But I could not bear to leave teachers and companions before the close of the term and go home to be dosed and receive the physician daily, and take warm drinks and be condoled with on the state of health in general by all the old ladies in town.

Haven't I given a ludicrous account of going home sick from a boarding-school? Father is quite a hand to give medicine, especially if it is not desirable to the patient, and I was dosed for about a month after my return home, without any mercy, till at last out of mere pity my cough went away, and I had quite a season of peace. Thus I remained at home until the close of the term, comforting my parents by my presence, and instilling many a lesson of wisdom into the budding intellect of my only sister. I had almost forgotten to tell you that I went on with my studies at home, and kept up with my class. Last Thursday our vacation closed, and on Friday morn, midst the weeping of friends, crowing of roosters, and singing of birds, I again took my departure from home. Five days have now passed since we returned to Holyoke, and they have passed very slowly. Thoughts of home and friends "come crowding thick and fast, like lightnings from the mountain cloud," and it seems very desolate.

Father has decided not to send me to Holyoke another year, so this is my *last term*. Can it be possible that I have been here almost a year? It startles me when I really think of the advantages I have had, and I fear I have not improved them as I ought. But many an hour has fled with its report to heaven, and what has been the tale of me? . . . How glad I am that spring has come, and how it calms my mind when wearied with study to walk out in the green fields and beside the pleasant streams in which South Hadley is rich! There are not many wild flowers near, for the girls have driven them to a distance, and we are obliged to walk quite a distance to find them, but they repay us by their sweet smiles and fragrance.

The older I grow, the more do I love spring and spring flowers. Is it so with you? While at home there were several pleasure parties of which I was a member, and in our rambles we found many and beautiful children of spring, which I will mention and see if you have found them, — the trailing arbutus, adder's tongue, yellow violets, liverleaf, blood-root, and many other smaller flowers.

What are you reading now? I have little time to read when I am here, but while at home I had a feast in the reading line, I can assure you. Two or three of them I will mention: *Evangeline, The Princess, The Maiden Aunt, The Epicurean,* and *The Twins and Heart* by

Tupper, complete the list. Am I not a pedant for telling you what I have been reading? Have you forgotten your visit at Amherst last summer, and what delightful times we had? I have not, and I hope you will come and make another and a longer, when I get home from Holyoke. Father wishes to have me at home a year, and then he will probably send me away again, where I know not. . . .

Ever your own affectionate
Emilie E. Dickinson.

P. S. My studies for this series are Astronomy and Rhetoric, which take me through to the Senior studies. What are you studying now, if you are in school, and do you attend to music? I practise only one hour a day this term.

MANUSCRIPT: missing.

PUBLICATION: L (1894) 36–39; LL 133–136; L (1931) 32–35, dated (presumably by ED): Mt. Holyoke Female Seminary. May 16, 1848.

Longfellow's *Evangeline* and Tennyson's *The Princess* were both reviewed in the *Hampshire and Franklin Express,* 30 March 1848. *The Maiden Aunt* is a novel by Marcella Bute Smedley; *The Epicurean,* a prose romance by Thomas Moore; and *The Twins* and *The Heart* are two novels (bound together) by Martin Tupper.

[The paragraph that follows was published by itself in L (1931) 28, among the letters to Abiah Root. It is probably part of this letter, omitted at the point indicated by dots in the fourth paragraph.]

I tremble when I think how soon the weeks and days of this term will all have been spent, and my fate will be sealed, perhaps. I have neglected the *one thing needful* when all were obtaining it, and I may never, never again pass through such a season as was granted us last winter. Abiah, you may be surprised to hear me speak as I do, knowing that I express no interest in the all-important subject, but I am not happy, and I regret that last term, when that golden opportunity was mine, that I did not give up and become a Christian. It is not now too late, so my friends tell me, so my offended conscience whispers, but it is hard for me to give up the world. I had quite a long talk with Abby while at home and I doubt not she will soon cast her burden on Christ. She is sober, and keenly sensitive on the subject, and she says she only desires to be good. How I wish I could say that

[67]

with sincerity, but I fear I never can. But I will no longer impose my own feelings even upon my friend. Keep them sacred, for I never lisped them to any save yourself and Abby.

24

To Austin Dickinson   *South Hadley, 29 May 1848*

My dear **Austin**.

I received a letter from home on Saturday, by Mr. Gilbert Smith and father wrote in it that he intended to send for Cousin Emily. & myself on Saturday of this week to spend the Sabbath at home. I went to Miss. Whitman, after receiving the letter & asked her if we could go if you decided to come for us. She seemed stunned by my request & could not find utterance to an answer for some time. At length, she said "did you not know it was contrary to the rules of the Seminary to ask to be absent on the Sabbath"? I told her I did not. She then took a Catalogue, from her table & showed me the law in full at the last part of it.

She closed by saying that we could not go & I returned to my room, without farther ado. So you see I shall be deprived of the pleasure of a visit home & you that of seeing me, if I may have the presumption to call it a *pleasure*!! The Teachers are not willing to let the girls go home this term as it is the last one & as I have only nine weeks more to spend here, we had better be contented to obey the commands. We shall only be the more glad to see one another after a longer absence, that will be all.

I was highly edified with your *imaginative* note to me & think your flights of fancy indeed wonderful at your age!! When are you coming to see me, or dont you intend to come at all? Viny told us, you were coming this week & it would be very pleasant to us to receive a visit from *your highness* if you can be absent from home long enough for such a purpose:

Is there anything new at home & wont you write me a long letter telling me all news? Mary. Warner. has not yet answered the note which I sent her at the commencement of the term. I cant write longer.

Your aff.

Emilie.

Manuscript: AC. Ink. Dated: Monday morn. Addressed on the fold: Austin. W. Dickinson./Amherst./Mass.
Publication: L (1894) 74–75, in part; LL 132–133, in part; L (1931) 71–72, in part; Home 81–82, entire.

The Seminary rule for that year which ED refers to reads thus: "The young ladies do not make or receive calls on the Sabbath. Neither should they spend a single Sabbath from the Seminary in term time. . . . The place of weekly labors is the most favorable spot for the scenes of the Sabbath."

25

To Austin Dickinson   *South Hadley, 25 June 1848*

My dear Austin.

I was very glad to see your friend, Bowdoin, for so long a time had passed since I last heard from home, that I began to consider myself entirely deserted.

Your note & father's letter, were both acceptable, only they were quite too brief, not lengthy enough, to suit me. I am much delighted with the idea of going home, but dont expect to realize it until fairly there, within sight & sound of you all. I wonder if you know, that today is the seventh Sabbath, since I left home. Quite a long time since I have seen you all and the many good people in Amherst. Bowdoin, tells me of no news, excepting the following. Cherries are fast getting ripe & the new generation attended the Senior Levee, a short time since, both of which facts, were received by me, with proper resignation. Surely, things must have changed in quiet, peace loving Amherst.

Jane Humphrey. wishes me to tell you that she would be happy to accept your invitation, but as Misses. Lyon & Whitman. are not willing & tell her it will lower her classification if she goes, she feels obliged to decline. I believe, Miss. Fiske. has given up the idea of going also. Father wrote that you were expecting Uncle Joel. [Norcross] at our house, yesterday and you are probably having grand times among yourselves. Louisa. Dickinson & Antoinette. Baker., went home on Friday last & expect to return tomorrow morning. She could not have had permission, had it not been that her friends from New. York. were there and desired to see her. Bowdoin. had quite an adventure about seeing me, which he will tell you. Yesterday afternoon I had a call from a sister of Tutor [Lewis] Greene's, who has been teaching school in Brooklyn & is quite intimate in Aunt Kate's family. She said Aunt. Catharine. was coming to Amherst, next week. I received a long letter from Cousin Zebina [Montague], about a fortnight since & answered it last week. I want much to see you all & think Monday & Tuesday will be rather dull days to me. I do wish they might seem as long to you. One thing in your note made me feel badly, & you can guess what it was. Give my best love to Father, Mother, Viny & Uncle Joel, if he is indeed at our house. Tell Viny, the letter she sent me last, was not received & I guess it was lost on the way. I hope a similar fate will not befall any others, I should otherwise obtain. I have an action against John. Spencer, which you shall hear of at my coming. Emily & I shall be all ready at precisely 5. o,clock.

Your aff. Sister.

Emilie.

My love to Abby & Mary. What an honor, Viny had in attending the Levee. I hope she bears that & others similar, in becoming humility. Cousin Emily. can hardly eat or sleep, so perfectly happy is she with the idea of going home with me to the great Festival. She sends her love to all the household.

MANUSCRIPT: AC. Ink. Dated: Sabbath noon. Addressed on the fold: Austin. W. Dickinson./Amherst./Mass.

PUBLICATION: *Home* 83–84.

The term at Mount Holyoke was not to end until August 3, but ED had a short visit at home when she and her cousin, among others, were allowed to go to Amherst for the opening of the new "Cabinet," a small museum at Amherst College. The ceremony coincided with the Junior Exhibition on June 29.

26

To Abiah Root   *29 October 1848*

My own dear Abiah,

For so I will still call you, though while I do it, even now I tremble at my strange audacity, and almost wish I had been a little more humble not quite so presuming.

Six long months have tried hard to make us strangers, but I love you better than ever notwithstanding the link which bound us in that golden chain is sadly dimmed, I feel more reluctant to lose you from that bright circle, whom I've called *my friends* I mailed a long letter to you the 1st of March, & patiently have I waited a reply, but none has yet cheered me.

Slowly, very slowly, I came to the conclusion that you had forgotten me, & I tried hard to forget you, but your image still haunts me, and tantalizes me with fond recollections. At our Holyoke Anniversary, I caught one glimpse of your face, & fondly anticipated an interview with you, & a reason for your silence, but when I thought to find you search was vain, for "the bird had flown." Sometimes, I think it was a fancy, think I did not *really* see my old friend, but her spirit, then your well known voice tells me it was no spirit, but yourself, living, that stood within that crowded hall & spoke to me – Why did you not come back that day, and tell me what had sealed your lips toward me? Did my letter never reach you, or did you coolly decide to love me, & write to me no more? If you love me, & never received my letter – then may you think yourself wronged, and that rightly, but if you dont want to be my friend any longer, say so, & I'll try *once* more to blot you from my memory. Tell me very soon, for suspense is intolerable. I need not tell you, this is from,

Emilie.

MANUSCRIPT: HCL (ARS 6). Ink. Unpublished. Dated: Amherst. October 29th – 1848.

The "Anniversary" at which ED caught a glimpse of Abiah was the Seminary commencement excercises, held on August 3. She was mistaken about the time that had passed since her last letter, which was written in mid-May.

III

LETTERS

27–39

[1849–1850]

"Amherst is alive
      with fun this winter . . ."

The years 1849–1850 were a time of expansion for Emily Dickinson. Her health was better, and new books and interests absorbed her. After her return from Mount Holyoke, she made new friends in the town and the college, and it was at this time that she enjoyed the happy companionship of Ben Newton. She afterward felt that the friendship was one of the experiences which had most enlarged her mind. None of her letters to him have survived.

In 1850, Austin was a senior at Amherst College, and some of his classmates, as well as the young tutors at the college, came frequently to the house. Lavinia was away at school, not at Mount Holyoke, but at Wheaton Seminary in Ipswich, where Mary Lyon had taught before she founded her own institution.

Among the girls at Amherst whom Emily saw most often was Susan Gilbert, who had returned in the autumn of 1848, after completing her schooling at Utica, New York. Another was Emily Fowler, whom she had not known well as a child because of a difference in age. One of the amusements of the winter season was the sending of valentines, and it is with a letter of the valentine season that this group begins.

27

To William Cowper Dickinson   *14 February 1849*

Cousin William,

Tis strange that a promise lives, and brightens, when the day that fashioned it, has mouldered, & stranger still, a promise looking to the day of Valentines for it's fulfillment.

Mine has been a very pleasant monitor, a friend, and kind companion, not a stern tyrant, like your own, *compelling* you to do what you would not have done, without compulsion.

Last Wednesday eve, I thought you had forgotten all about your promise, else you looked upon it as one foolish, & unworthy of fulfillment, now, I know your memory was faithful, but I sadly fear, your inclination, quarrelled with *it's* admonitions.

A little condescending, & sarcastic, your Valentine to me, I thought; a little like an Eagle, stooping to salute a Wren, & I concluded once, I dared not answer it, for it seemed to me not quite becoming — in a bird so lowly as myself — to claim admittance to an Eyrie, & conversation with it's King.

But I have changed my mind — & you are not too busy, I'll chat a while with you.

I'm a "Fenestrellan captive," if this world *be* "Fenestrella," and within my dungeon yard, up from the silent pavement stones, has come a plant, so frail, & yet so beautiful, I tremble lest it die. Tis the first living thing that has beguiled my solitude, & I take strange delight in it's society. It's a mysterious plant, & sometimes I fancy that it whispers pleasant things to me — of freedom — and the future. Cans't guess it's name? T'is "Picciola"; & to *you* Cousin William, I'm indebted for my wondrous, new, companion.

I know not how to thank you, for your kindness. Gratitude is poor as poverty itself — & the "10,000 thanks" so often cited, seem like faintest shadows, when I try to stamp them here, that I may send their impress to you. "Picciola's" first flower — I will keep for you. Had not

it's gentle voice, & friendly words – assured me of a "kind remembrance" – I think I should not have presumed thus much.

The last week has been a merry one in Amherst, & notes have flown
around like, snowflakes. Ancient gentlemen, & spinsters, forgetting
time, & multitude of years, have doffed their wrinkles – in exchange
for smiles – even this aged world of our's, has thrown away it's staff –
and spectacles, & *now* declares it will be young again.

Valentine's sun is setting now however, & before tomorrow eve, old
things will take their place again. Another year, a long one, & a stranger
to us all – must live, & die, before it's laughing beams will fall on us
again, & of "that shadowy band in the silent land" may be the present
writers of these merry missives.

But I am moralizing, forgetful of you, sisterless — and for *that* reason prone to mournful reverie – perhaps. Are you happy, now that she
is gone? I know you must be lonely since her leave, and when I think
of you nowdays, t'is of a "melancholy gentleman, standing on the banks
of river Death – sighing & beckoning Charon to convey him over."

Have I guessed right, or are you merry as a "Fine old English
Gentleman – all of the Olden time"?

I'll write to Martha soon, for tis *as* desolate to be without her letters;
more desolate than you can think. I wont forget some little pencil marks
I found in reading "Picciola," for they seem to me like silent sentinels,
guarding the towers of some city, in itself — too beautiful to be unguarded; I've read those passages with hightened interest on their
account.

Long life to Mr Hammond, & a thousand Valentines for every
year of it.

Pardon my lengthiness — if it be not unpardonable.

Sincerely, your cousin,
Emily E. Dickinson.

MANUSCRIPT: Dickinson. Ink. Dated: Valentine morn. Unpublished.
William Cowper Dickinson, valedictorian of the class of 1848, was a
friend but not a close relative of ED. He returned as tutor in 1851, but
this letter clearly was written before that time. Charles Hammond was
principal of Monson Academy where Dickinson was teaching.
Picciola is the title of a romantic tale of Napoleonic times by X. B.
Saintine (Joseph Xavier Boniface), published in 1839. In the following

decade it went through many European and American editions, the latest of which was a profusely illustrated one with decorated binding, published at Philadelphia in 1849. The story concerns a political prisoner in the stronghold of Fenestrella, whose observation of a plant growing between the stones of his prison courtyard transforms his philosophy and changes his fortunes. The Italian jailer's exclamation, "Povera picciola!" (poor little thing), provides the name which the prisoner gives the unknown flower.

28

To Elbridge G. Bowdoin   *about December 1849*

Mr Bowdoin.

   If all these leaves were altars, and on every one a prayer that Currer Bell might be saved — and you were God — would you answer it?

MANUSCRIPT: AC. Ink.
PUBLICATION: L (1894) 137; LL 136; L (1931) 136.
   The date given by Mrs. Todd, December 1849, is confirmed by the handwriting. A penciled note on the third page of the folded sheet, in Bowdoin's hand, reads: "On returning Jane Eyre. The leaves mentioned were box Leaves, sent to me in a little bouquet." ED cannot be alluding to an illness of Charlotte Brontë (who died in 1855), for the book had been published only the year before, and the identity of the writer was still unknown. Her plea simply expresses her hope that Currer Bell will live long and write many more books.

29

To Joel Warren Norcross   *11 January 1850*

Dearest of all dear Uncles.

   Sleep carried me away, and a dream passed along, a dream all queer, and curious — it was a dream of warning — I ought not to hide it from whom it concerns — God forbid that you trifle with vision so strange — the Spirit of love entreat you — the Spirit of warning guide — and the all helping hold — and prevent you from falling! And I dreamed — and beheld a company whom no man may number — all men in their youth — all strong and stout-hearted — nor feeling their burdens for strength – nor waxing faint – nor weary. Some tended their flocks – and some sailed on the sea – and yet others kept gay stores, and deceived the foolish who came to buy. They made life one summer day – they danced to the sound of the lute – they sang old snatches of song – and they quaffed the rosy wine – One promised to love his friend and one vowed to defraud no poor – and *one* man told a lie to his niece – they all did sinfully – and their lives were not yet taken. Soon a change came – the young men were old – the flocks had no sheperd – the boat sailed alone – and the dancing had ceased – and the wine-cup was empty – and the summer day grew cold – Oh fearful the faces then! The Merchant tore his hair – and the Sheperd gnashed his teeth – and the Sailor hid himself – and prayed to die. Some kindled the scorching fire – some opened the earthquake's mouth – the winds strode on to the sea – and serpents hissed fearfully. Oh I was very much scared and I called to see who they were – this torment waited for – I listened – and up from the pit *you* spoke! You could'nt get out you said – no help could reach so far – you had brought it upon yourself – I left you alone to die – but they told me the whole of the crime – you had broken a promise on earth – and now t'was too late to redeem it. Do you wonder at my alarm – do you blame me for running to tell you? It was'nt *all* a dream – but I know it will be fulfilled unless you stop sinning now – it is not too late to do right. Do you take any hints I wonder – can you guess the meaning of things – not yet aroused to the truth. You villain without a rival – unparraleled doer of crimes – scoundrel unheard of before – disturber of public peace – "creation's blot and blank" – state's prison filler – *magnum bonum* promise maker – harum scarum promise breaker – Oh what can I call you more? Mrs Caudle would call you "a gentleman" – that is altogether too good. Mrs Partington "a very fine fellow" – neither does this apply – I call upon all nature to lay hold of you – let fire burn – and water drown – and light put out – and tempests tear – and hungry wolves eat up – and lightning strike – and thunder stun – let friends desert – and enemies draw nigh and gibbets *shake* but never *hang* the house you walk about in! My benison not touch – my malison pursue the body that hold your spirit! Any other afflictions which now slip my mind shall be looked up and forwarded to you immediately. How will you bear them all – will they depress – and make life hang too heavily? Would that they might thus do – but I look for no such results – you will bear them like a Salamander. Old fashioned Daniel could'nt take things more coolly. Does sarcasm affect you – or the sneers of the world? "Burn flame – simmer heat – swelter toad – I have cursed thee – and thou art accursed."

Dont remember a letter I was to receive when you got back to Boston – how long and how broad – how high – or deep it should be – how many cars it should sink – or how many stages tip over – or the shaking of earth when it rested – Hav'nt the faintest recollection of the hearts to be lighter – the eyes to grow brighter and the life made longer with joy it should give – a most unfortunate mem'ry – the owner deserves our pity! Had you a pallid hand – or a blind eye – we would talk about coming to terms – but you have sent my father a letter – so there remains no more but to fight. War Sir – "my voice is for war!" Would you like to try a duel – or is that too quiet to suit you – at any rate I shall kill you – and you may dispose of your affairs with that end in view. You can take Chloroform if you like – and I will put you beyond the reach of pain in a twinkling. The last duel I fought did'nt take but five minutes in all – the "wrapping the drapery of his couch about him – and lying down to pleasant dreams" included. Lynch laws provide admirably now for wifes – and orphan children – so duels seem differently from what they formerly did to me. Uncle Loring – and Aunt Lavinia *will* miss you some to be sure – but trials *will* come in the best of families – and I think they are usually for the best – they give us new ideas – and *those* are not to be laughed at. How have you been bodily, and mentally since you were up to see us? How do you sleep o *nights* – and is your appetite waning? These are infallible symptoms, and I only thought I'd inquire – no harm done I hope. Harm is one of those things that I always mean to keep clear of – but somehow my intentions and me dont chime as they ought – and people will get hit with stones that I throw at my neighbor's dogs – not only *hit* – *that* is the least of the whole – but they insist upon blaming *me* instead of the *stones* – and tell me their heads ache – why it is the greatest piece of folly on record. It would do to go with a story I read – one man pointed a loaded gun at a man – and it shot him so that he died – and the people threw the owner of the gun into prison – and afterwards hung him for *murder*. Only another victim to the misunderstanding of society – such things should not be permitted – it certainly is as much as one's neck is worth to live in so stupid a world –

and it makes one grow weary. Life is'nt what it purports to be. Now when I walk into your room and pluck your heart out that you die – I kill you – hang me if you like – but if I stab you while sleeping the dagger's to blame – it's no business of mine – you have no more right to accuse me of injuring you than anything else I can think of. That we understand capital punishment, and one another too I verily believe – and sincerely hope – for it's so trying to be read out of the wrong book when the right one is out of sight.

Your friends in town are comfortable – or *were* at the last accounts – tho' I hav'nt been into the Kelloggs' for several days now. Still I have seen neither Doctor, or Sexton around, and will take the fearful responsibility of assuring you that they live, and are well. You will perceive that the whole stands for a part in this place – it being one of those exceedingly *aspeny* cases that the bungling had better let alone. Have you found *Susannah* yet? "Roses will fade – time flies on – Lady of beauty," – the whole hymn is too familiar to you now for me to repeat it. Amherst is alive with fun this winter – might you be here to see! Sleigh rides are as plenty as people – which conveys to my mind the idea of very plentiful plenty. How it may seem to you I don't calculate at all – but presume you can see the likeness if you get the right light upon it. Parties cant find fun enough – because all the best ones are engaged to attend balls a week beforehand – beaus can be had for the taking – maids smile like the mornings in June – Oh a very great town is this! Chorus – a "still greater one is this." "Now for the jovial bowl," etc. You are fond of singing – I think – and by close, and assiduous practise may learn these two before I see you again. Exertion never harmed anybody – it wont begin now.

Are you all well – how are the children – please give the love of all our household to all the members of your's. Dont leave Cousin Albert out in my part! Vinnie has been to see you – she wrote what splendid times she had. We are very lonely without her – hope to linger along till she comes home. Will you write me before you go hence? Any communications will be received gratefully.

Emilie – I believe.

My kind regards to the gentlemen – White – and Leavitt. Heaven's choicest blessings attend them – and evil pass by without turning either to the right hand – or the left. Very particular indeed about the left hand – as they would be a little most likely to be there. "God bless you" to Wm Haskell – and civilized messages to all the rest of my friends.

Austin did'nt get to Boston somehow or other. He spent all but the fag end of vacation reading Hume's History – and it nearly used him up.

Had a long and very interesting letter from Emily [Norcross] a few days since. She seems contented – almost happy – says she will be glad to see us all, tho.

MANUSCRIPT: AC. Ink. Dated: Amherst New Year 11th/50.
PUBLICATION: L (1931) 57–61.

White and Leavitt were the business partners of Norcross. The character of Mrs. Caudle, a voluble scold, was created by Douglas William Jerrold for *Punch*, and *Mrs. Caudle's Curtain Lectures* was published in 1846. Mrs. Partington, a village Malaprop, was a character created by Benjamin P. Shillaber for a Boston newspaper in 1847. The first quotation in the second paragraph recalls *Paradise Lost*, II, 51: "My sentence is for open war"; the second quotation in the same paragraph, the conclusion of Bryant's *Thanatopsis*: "Like one who wraps the drapery of his couch/ About him, and lies down to pleasant dreams."

30

To Jane Humphrey   23 *January 1850*

Dear Jane.

I have written you a great many letters since you left me – not the kind of letters that go in post-offices – and ride in mail-bags – but queer – little silent ones – very full of affection – and full of confidence – but wanting in proof to you – therefore not valid – somehow you will not answer them – and you *would* paper, and ink letters – I will try one of those – tho' not half so precious as the other kind. I have written *those* at night – when the rest of the world were at sleep – when only God came between us – and no one else might hear. No need of shutting the door – nor of whispering timidly – nor of fearing the ear of listeners – for night held them fast in his arms that they could not interfere – and his arms are brawny and strong. Sometimes I did'nt know but you were awake – and I hoped you wrote with that spirit pen – and on sheets from out the sky. *Did* you ever – and were we together in any

[81]

of those nights? I *do* love – and remember you Jane – and have tried to convince you of it ocularly – but it is not easy to try just as we *are* at home – Vinnie away – and my two hands but *two* – not four, or five as they ought to be – and so *many* wants – and me so *very* handy – and my time of so *little* account – and my writing so *very* needless – and really I came to the conclusion that I should be a villain unparralleled if I took but an inch of time for so unholy a purpose as writing a friendly letter – for what need had *I* of sympathy – or very much less of affection – or less than they all – of friends – mind the house – and the food – *sweep* if the spirits were low – nothing like exercise to strengthen – and invigorate – and help away such foolishnesses – work makes one strong, and cheerful – and as for society what neighborhood so full as my own? The halt – the lame – and the blind – the old – the infirm – the bed-ridden – and superannuated – the ugly, and disagreeable – the perfectly hateful to me – all *these* to see – and be seen by – an opportunity rare for cultivating meekness – and patience – and submission – and for turning my back to this very sinful, and wicked world. Somehow or other I incline to other things – and Satan covers them up with flowers, and I reach out to pick them. The path of duty looks very ugly indeed – and the place where *I* want to go more amiable – a great deal – it is so much easier to do wrong than right – so much pleasanter to be evil than good, I dont wonder that good angels weep – and bad ones sing songs. It is a great while since I've seen you Jane – and really I miss you sincerely – the days would go swifter were you in the end – and the sight of your hood would lift me up certainly – I *do* wish that you could be here. The year went away so fast we had'nt time to think – had I known it would carry you with it I certainly would have thought. Only another *too late* to put with the rest – one more to reproach – and to look sadly out of large – dark eyes – and there will be more – and more if we live to help make them. It seemed so pleasant to have you – to know that I might see you – that I sank into a kind of stupor – and did'nt know – or care – or think that I could not see you always – and while I slept you faded all away – and was gone when I waked up. "Why where am I – how came I here – who put me in – who'll take me out – where's my servant – where are my friends – you hav'nt got any." The immortal Pickwick himself could'nt have been more amazed when he found himself soul – body and – spirit incarcerated in the pound than was I myself when they said *she* had gone – gone! Gone *how* – or *where* – or *why* – who saw her go – help – hold – bind – and keep her – put her into States-prison – into the House of Correction – bring out the long lashed whip – and put her feet in the stocks – and give her a number of stripes and make her repent her going! They say you are teaching in Warren – are happy – then I know you are good – for none *but* the good are happy – you are out of the way of temptation – and out of the way of the tempter – I did'nt mean to make you wicked – but I was – and am – and shall be – and I was with you so much that I could'nt help contaminate. Are you ever lonely in Warren – are you lonely without me – very lonely the last to be sure – but I want to know.

Vinnie you know is away – and that I'm very lonely is too plain for me to tell you – I am *alone* – *all* alone. She wrote that she'd heard from you – and had written you herself – did she say she was home-sick? She knew that her letters to me would be *family* affairs – and she cant tell me anything at all – she dont dare to – and I'd rather she would'nt either. When I knew Vinnie must go I clung to you as the dearer than ever friend – but when the grave opened – and swallowed you both – I murmured – and thought I had a right to – I hav'nt changed my mind yet – either. I love to be surly – and muggy – and cross – then I remember you – and feel that I do a kind of justice to you – and myself – which eases my conscience wonderfully. Oh ugly time – and space – and boarding-school contemptible that tries to keep us apart – laugh now if you will – but you shall howl hereafter! Eight weeks with their bony fingers still poking me away – how I *hate* them – and would love to do them harm! Is it wicked to talk so Jane – what *can* I say that isn't? Out of a wicked heart cometh wicked words – let us sweep it out – and brush away the cob-webs – and garnish it – and make ready for the Master! There is a good deal going on just now – the two last weeks of vacation were full to the brim of fun. Austin was reading Hume's History until then – and his getting it through was the signal for general uproar. Campaign opened by a sleigh ride on a very magnificent plan to which my dear Jane would have been joyfully added – had she been in town – a party of ten from here met a party of the same number from Greenfield – at South-Deer-field the evening next New Year's – and had a frolic, comprising char-ades – walking around *indefinitely* – music – conversation – and supper – set in most modern style; got home at two o'clock – and felt no worse for it the next morning – which we all thought was very remarkable. Tableaux at the President's followed next in the train – a Sliding party close upon it's heels – and several cozy sociables brought up the rear. To say nothing of a party *universale* at the house of Sydney Adams – and one *confidentiale* at Tempe Linnell's. How we miss *our friend* at all of these things! I would gladly exchange them all for one evening's talk with the friends I love – but it may not be. If every prayer was answered, there would be nothing left to pray for – we *must* "suffer – and be strong." Shall we be strong – wont suffering make weaker this human – it makes stronger not *us* – but what God gave, and what he will take – mourn our bodies ever so loudly. We do not know that he is God – and *will* try to be still – tho' we really had rather complain. The Sewing Society has commenced again – and held its first meeting last week – now all the poor will be helped – the cold warmed – the warm cooled – the hungry fed – the thirsty attended to – the ragged clothed – and this suffering – tumbled down world will be helped to it's feet again – which will be quite pleasant to all. I dont attend – notwithstanding my high approbation – which must puzzle the public exceedingly. I am already set down as one of those brands almost consumed – and my hardheartedness gets me many prayers. Spencer is slowly improving – said he heard from you a little while ago – and seemed much gratified. Abby Haskell too is much better – I verily believe they will live in spite of the "angel of death." Tolman I do not see – guess he is pining away – and cant say I blame him in view of the facts in the case. I shant tell you what ails him – for it is a *private* matter – and you ought not to know! How could you be so cruel Jane – it will certainly be the death of him – and t'will be laid at *your* door if it *is*. Write me soon darling!

Very sincerly yrs –
Emily E. Dickinson.

Have you ever seen Carpenter in Warren? Has he recovered yet – I saw him at the Levee – and remembered him – and I want to know about him. Abby Wood is in Athol. Her only brother is very low – and probably cannot recover. I pity the child with my whole heart – she is too young to suffer so. I had a letter – and Ralph Emerson's Poems – a beautiful copy – from Newton the other day. I should love to read you them both – they are very pleasant to me. I can write him in about three weeks – and I *shall*. Did you know that Payson had gone to Ohio to live? I was so sorry to have him go – but everyone is going – we shall all go – and not return again before long. Kavanagh says "there will be mourning – mourning – mourning at the judgment seat of Christ" – I wonder if that is true? I had a letter from Lyman a little while since – you may read it sometime.

Two cousins of mine from South-Hadley are staying their vacation with us. I can hardly tell whether I am enjoying their visit, or not – but I rather think I am, as I dont certainly know – now do you ever tell of this – and I will certainly put you into a sleep which you cant wake up from! Abiah Root has been in Amherst – stayed only a week – but long enough for me to know her anew as a splendid girl. She is a treasure surely. She has written me since she went home – and we are going to correspond again. I have written to *Belvidere* – and young "D. D." will feel some things I think – at any rate I intended he should – and wrote accordingly. It would have done your own heart good. All send you much love.

MANUSCRIPT: Rosenbach 1170/ 17 (2). Ink. Dated: Amherst. January 23^d/50.

PUBLICATION: G. F. Whicher, *This Was a Poet* . . . , New York (1938) 89, three sentences only.

Jane Humphrey, recently preceptress at Amherst Academy (1848–1849), was now teaching at Warren. Lavinia was attending Wheaton Female Seminary at Ipswich. The cousins who had been visiting were Mary Ann and Sarah J. Dickinson of Romeo, Michigan, who attended Mount Holyoke for a year. Abby Wood's home was in Athol, but she was now living with her uncle and aunt, the Luke Sweetsers, near neighbors of the Dickinsons. John Laurens Spencer (AC 1848) was now the principal of Amherst Academy. Harvey Sessions Carpenter (AC 1853) was a freshman from Warren. Albert Tolman (AC 1845) was a tutor in the college. "Belvidere" (James Parker Kimball, AC 1849) had given ED a copy of Holmes's poems (HCL), inscribed: Miss Emily E. Dickinson/ From J. P. K./"Philopena"/Amherst Jan. 18th 1849. Meanwhile evidently the friendship had cooled.

Ben Newton probably gave ED the copy of Emerson's *Poems* (1847) shortly before leaving Amherst to continue the study of law at Worcester, his native town. He was still unmarried. The cryptic sentence "I can write him in about three weeks – and I *shall*" presumably was clear to Jane Humphrey. This is probably ED's first letter to Jane after Jane's departure from Amherst, and therefore what knowledge the girls shared had derived from conversations. The tone of the remark suggests that ED had acceded to some parental interdiction placed upon a headlong correspondence. That ED felt a deep friendship for Newton is certain. That she was in love with him is most unlikely (see letter no. 153).

ED's expression in the second paragraph, "Out of a wicked heart cometh wicked words," is a paraphrase of Luke 6.45.

31

To Abiah Root   *29 January 1850*

Very dear Abiah.

The folks have all gone away – they thought that they left me alone, and contrived things to amuse me should they stay long, and *I* be lonely. Lonely indeed – they did'nt look, and they could'nt have seen if they had, who should bear me company. *Three* here instead of *one* — would'nt it scare them? A curious trio, part earthly and part spiritual two of us – the other all heaven, and no earth. *God* is sitting here, looking into my very soul to see if I think right tho'ts. Yet I am not afraid, for I try to be right and good, and he knows every one of my struggles. He looks very gloriously, and everything bright seems dull beside him, and I dont dare to look directly at him for fear I shall die. Then *you* are here – dressed in that quiet black gown and cap – that funny little cap I used to laugh at you about, and you dont appear to be thinking about anything in particular, not in one of your *breaking dish* moods I take it, you seem aware that I'm writing you, and are amused I should think at any such friendly manifestation when you are already present. *Success* however even in making a fool of one's-self is'nt to be despised, so I shall persist in writing, and you may in laughing at me, if you are fully aware of the value of time as regards your immortal spirit. I cant say that I advise you to laugh, but if you are punished, and I warned you, that can be no business of mine. So I fold up my arms, and leave you to fate – may it deal very kindly with you! The trinity winds up with me, as you may have surmised, and I certainly would'nt be at the fag end but for civility to you. This selfsacrificing spirit will be the ruin of me! I am occupied principally with a cold just now, and the dear creature *will* have so much attention that my time slips away amazingly. It has heard *so* much of New

[86]

Englanders, of their kind attentions to strangers, that it's come all the way from the Alps to determine the truth of the tale – it says the half was'nt told it, and I begin to be afraid it was'nt. Only think, came all the way from that distant Switzerland to find what was the truth! Neither husband – protector – nor friend accompanied it, and so utter a state of loneliness gives friends if nothing else. You are dying of curiosity, let me arrange that pillow to make your exit easier! I stayed at home all Saturday afternoon, and treated some disagreable people who insisted upon calling here as tolerably as I could – when evening shades began to fall, I turned upon my heel, and walked. Attracted by the gaiety visible in the street I still kept walking till a little creature pounced upon a thin shawl I wore, and commenced riding – I stopped, and begged the creature to alight, as I was fatigued already, and quite unable to assist others. It would'nt get down, and commenced talking to itself – "cant be New England – must have made some mistake, disappointed in my reception, dont agree with accounts, Oh what a world of deception, and fraud – Marm, will [you] tell me the name of this country – it's Asia Minor, is'nt it. I intended to stop in New England." By this time I was so completely exhausted that I made no farther effort to rid me of my load, and travelled home at a moderate jog, paying no attention whatever to it, got into the house, threw off both bonnet, and shawl, and out flew my tormentor, and putting both arms around my neck began to kiss me immoderately, and express so much love, it completely bewildered me. Since then it has slept in my bed, eaten from my plate, lived with me everywhere, and will tag me through life for all I know. I think I'll wake first, and get out of bed, and leave it, but early, or late, it is dressed before me, and sits on the side of the bed looking right in my face with such a comical expression it almost makes me laugh in spite of myself. I cant call it interesting, but it certainly *is* curious – has two peculiarities which would quite win your heart, a huge pocket-handkerchief, and a very red nose. The first seems so very *abundant*, it gives you the idea of independence, and prosperity in business. The last brings up the "jovial bowl, my boys," and such an association's worth the having. If it *ever* gets tired of *me*, I will forward it to *you* – you would love it for *my* sake, if not for it's own, it will tell you some queer stories about me – how I sneezed so loud one night that the family thought the last trump was sounding, and climbed into the currant-bushes to get out of the way – how the rest of the people arrayed in long night-gowns folded their arms, and were waiting – but this is a wicked story, it can tell some *better* ones. Now my dear friend, let me tell you that these last thoughts are fictions – vain imaginations to lead astray foolish young women. They are flowers of speech, they both *make*, and *tell* deliberate falsehoods, avoid them as the snake, and turn aside as from the *Bottle* snake, and I dont *think* you will be harmed. Honestly tho', a snake bite is a serious matter, and there cant be too much said, or done about it. The big serpent bites the deepest, and we get so accustomed to it's bites that we dont mind about them. "Verily I say unto you fear *him.*" Wont you read some work upon snakes – I have a real anxiety for you! *I* love those little green ones that slide around by your shoes in the grass – and make it rustle with their elbows – they are rather my favorites on the whole, but I would'nt influence *you* for the world! There is an air of misanthropy about the striped snake that will commend itself at once to your taste, there is no monotony about it – but we will more of this again. Something besides severe colds, and serpents, and we will try to find *that* something. It cant be a garden, can it, or a strawberry bed, which rather belongs to a garden – nor it cant be a school-house, nor an Attorney at Law. Oh dear I dont know *what* it is! Love for the absent dont *sound* like it, but try it, and see how it goes.

I miss you very much indeed, think of you at night when the world's nodding, "nidnid nodding["] – think of you in the daytime when the cares of the world, and it's toils, and it's continual vexations choke up the love for friends in some of our hearts; remember your warnings sometimes – try to do as you told me sometimes – and sometimes conclude it's no use to try; then my heart says it *is*, and new trial is followed by disappointment again. I wondered when you had gone why we did'nt talk more – it was'nt for want of a subject, it never *could be* for *that*. Too many perhaps, such a crowd of people that nobody heard the speaker, and all went away discontented. You astounded me in the outset – perplexed me in the continuance – and wound up in a grand snarl – I shall be all my pilgrimage unravelling. Rather a dismal prospect certainly – but "it's always the darkest the hour before day," and this early sunset promises an earlier rise – a sun in splendor – and glory, flying out of it's purple nest. Would'nt you love to see God's bird, when it first tries it's wings? If you were here I would tell you something – *several* somethings which have happed since you went away, but time, and space, as usual, oppose themselves, and I put my treasures away till "we *two* meet again." The hope that I shall continue in love towards you – and *vica versa* will sustain me till then. If you are thinking soon to go away, and to show your face no more, just inform me – will you – I would have the "long lingering look" which you cast behind – It would be an invaluable addition to my treasures, and "keep your memory green." "Lord keep all our memories green," and help on our affection, and tie "the link that doth us bind" in a tight bow-knot that will keep it from separation, and stop us from growing old – if *that* is impossible – make old age pleasant to us – put it's arms around us kindly, and when we go home – let that home be called *Heaven*!

Your very sincere, and *wicked* friend,

Emily E Dickinson.

Abby has not come home yet – and I hav'nt written her. She must be very sad, and need all comfort from us. She will be left *alone* – wont she?

Had a letter from Vinnie after you left – it expressed great regret at not seeing you – both on her part and Jane's. They come home in seven weeks.

I hav'nt thanked you for your letter yet, but not for want of gratitude. I will do so *now* most sincerely, most heartily – gladly – and gratefully. You will write me another soon – that I may have *four right* feelings again! They dont come for the asking. I have been introducing you to me in this letter so far – we will traffick in "joys" – and "sorrows" some other day. Colds make one very carnal and the spirit is always afraid of them. You will excuse all *mistakes* in view of ignorance – all *sin* in view of "the fall," all *want* of *friendly affection* in the sight of the verse "the deepest stream the stillest runs," and other general deficiencies, on the ground of universal incapacity! Here is surely room for Charity, and heavenly visiter would'nt have come but for these faults. "No loss without a gain." I called to see your cousins an evening since – they were well, and evidently delighted to see one another – and us. Lucy spoke in high praise of visiting, of visiting Abiah more especially, and of visiting Abiah's mother, more especially still. When your letter came I had two western cousins – now at S-Hadley Sem^y staying their vacation with me. They took an unbounded delight in a sentence I read them – and to pay for it, send you their love. Write me a letter!

MANUSCRIPT: HCL (ARS 7). Ink. Dated: Amherst. January 29. 1850. PUBLICATION: L (1894) 39–45, in part; LL 137–140, in part; L (1931) 35–40, in part, with conclusion misplaced.

Following ED's letter to Abiah of 29 October 1848 (no. 26), there had been a break in their correspondence. With this letter ED carries out the purpose she mentioned to Jane Humphrey a few days earlier, and renews it. The paraphrase "we *two* meet again" recalls the opening line of *Macbeth*: "When shall we three meet again?" The "long lingering look" echoes the last line of stanza 22 in Gray's *Elegy in a Country Churchyard*: "Nor cast one longing ling'ring look behind." "Lord, keep my memory green" is the last line in the Christmas book, published in 1848, by Dickens: *The Haunted Man and the Ghost's Bargain*.

32

To Emily Fowler (Ford) early 1850?

I wanted to write, and just tell you that *me*, and *my spirit* were fighting this morning. It is'nt known generally, and you must'nt tell anybody.

I dreamed about you last night, and waked up putting my shawl, and hood on to go and see you, but this wicked snow-storm looked in at my window, and told me I could'nt. I hope God will forgive me, but I am very unwilling to have it storm – he is merciful to the sinning, is'nt he?

I cannot wait to be with you – Oh ugly time, and space, and uglier snow-storm than all! Were you happy in Northampton? I was very lonely without you, and wanted to write you a letter *many* times, but Kate was there too, and I was afraid you would both laugh. I should be stronger if I could see you oftener – I am very puny alone.

You make me so happy, and glad, life seems worth living for, no matter for all the trials. When I see you I shall tell you more, for I know you are busy this morning.

That is'nt an *empty* blank where I began – it is so full of affection that you cant see any – that's all. Will you love, and remember, *me* when you have time from worthier ones? God keep you till I have seen you again!

Very earnestly yrs –

Emily.

MANUSCRIPT: NYPL. Ink. Addressed on the fold: Miss Emily E Fowler./Austin. Unpublished.

This note, in the handwriting of 1850, may have been written about the same time as the two foregoing. The "Kate" referred to was probably Catharine Hitchcock (1826–1895), daughter of Edward Hitchcock, President of Amherst College.

33

To William Cowper Dickinson   *about February 1850*

> "Life is but a strife –
> T'is a bubble –
> T'is a dream –
> And man is but a little *boat*
> Which paddles down the stream"

MANUSCRIPT: Dickinson. Ink. Addressed: Mr William C Dickinson / Amherst – / Mass –. Unpublished. The date is conjectured from the handwriting.

Although the spirit of this verse seems removed from that of the usual valentine, it seems to have been sent as such. It is illustrated with small cuts clipped from old books and papers, one cutting taken from the *New England Primer*. After line one: a man, a woman, and a boy in a doorway, beating off dogs with a broom and sticks; after line two: two boys and a girl blowing bubbles; after line three: (1) a sleeping king (from the *Primer*), and (2) a small sailboat.

34

To George H. Gould?   *February 1850*

Magnum bonum, "harum scarum," zounds et zounds, et war alarum, man reformam, life perfectum, mundum changum, all things flarum?

[91]

Sir, I desire an interview; meet me at sunrise, or sunset, or the new moon — the place is immaterial. In gold, or in purple, or sackcloth — I look not upon the *raiment*. With sword, or with pen, or with plough — the weapons are less than the *wielder*. In coach, or in wagon, or walking, the *equipage* far from the *man*. With soul, or spirit, or body, they are all alike to me. With host or alone, in sunshine or storm, in heaven or earth, *some* how or *no* how — I propose, sir, to see you.

And not to *see* merely, but a chat, sir, or a tete-a-tete, a confab, a mingling of opposite minds is what I propose to have. I feel sir that we shall agree. We will be David and Jonathan, or Damon and Pythias, or what is better than either, the United States of America. We will talk over what we have learned in our geographies, and listened to from the pulpit, the press and the Sabbath School.

This is strong language sir, but none the less true. So hurrah for North Carolina, since we are on this point.

Our friendship sir, shall endure till sun and moon shall wane no more, till stars shall set, and victims rise to grace the final sacrifice. We'll be instant, in season, out of season, minister, take care of, cherish, sooth, watch, wait, doubt, refrain, reform, elevate, instruct. All choice spirits however distant are ours, ours theirs; there is a thrill of sympathy — a circulation of mutuality — cognationem inter nos! I am Judith the heroine of the Apocrypha, and you the orator of Ephesus.

That's what they call a metaphor in our country. Don't be afraid of it, sir, it won't bite. If it was my *Carlo* now! The Dog is the noblest work of Art, sir. I may safely say the noblest — his mistress's rights he doth defend — although it bring him to his end — although to death it doth him send!

But the world is sleeping in ignorance and error, sir, and we must be crowing cocks, and singing larks, and a rising sun to awake her; or else we'll pull society up to the roots, and plant it in a different place. We'll build Alms-houses, and transcendental State prisons, and scaffolds — we will blow out the sun, and the moon, and encourage invention. Alpha shall kiss Omega — we will ride up the hill of glory — Hallelujah, all hail!

Yours, truly,

C.

MANUSCRIPT: missing.
PUBLICATION: *The Indicator* (Amherst College), II, 7, February 1850.

This valentine letter, dated "Valentine Eve," is typical of the nonsense ED could evoke for such occasions. Some of the expressions, such as "magnum bonum, harum scarum" she also used in her letter (no. 29) to Joel Norcross. *The Indicator* was published by a group of students among whom was George H. Gould, Austin's good friend. The preparation of the "Editor's Corner," in which the letter appears, was for this issue in the hands of Henry Shipley. It was preceded by a comment in which the editor says: "I wish I knew who the author is. I think she must have some spell, by which she quickens the imagination, and causes the high blood 'run frolic through the veins.'" On Carlo, see letters no. 194 and 314.

35

To Jane Humphrey   *3 April 1850*

Jane, *dear* Jane.

The voice of *love* I heeded, tho' *seeming* not to; the voice of affliction is louder, more earnest, and needs it's friends, and they know this need, and put on their wings of affection, and fly towards the lone one, and sing, sing sad music, but there's something sustaining in it. Your *first* words found me far out in the world, crowding, and hurrying, and busying, the last ones have found me there, but I have struggled with some success, and am free to be with you a little. Trouble is with you, and trial, and your spirit is sorely cumbered, and I can hardly dare to talk, *earthly* things seem faded, and fallen; could I speak with a right of Heaven, and the Savior, and "rest for the weary" I know I could bring strength to you, and could lift you above this cumbering; but I can tell you how dearly I love you, if *this* will make you happier. I have been much with you since you first wrote me, *always* with you, but *more* since *then,* for the last few days you have been *very* near, very dear *indeed,* and I have wished, and prayed to *see* you, and to *hear* you, and to feel your warm heart beating near me, what music in such quiet ticking! You mourn Jennie, how does it *seem* to mourn, you *watch,* and the lamp is waning, where is your spirit resting, have you any dear friend to be near you, and to tell you of peace? It would be very precious to *me* to do so, to be a strong arm you might lean on when you looked all around, and could find none, this is none of it permitted now, and I think, and strive, and attempt, but come no nearer the end.

[93]

Can I console so far off, wont the comfort waste in conveying, and be *not*, when my letter gets there? How long had your father been sick, and why hav'nt you told me before, we have *certainly* loved one another! How very much you have suffered, and I hav'nt known anything about it, but supposed you away in Warren, teaching, and thinking of home, and *sometimes* of us, and a place we wish *was* your home. I have dreamed of you, and talked of you, and wished for you, and have almost thought I should see you, it has seemed that some way would help me, and a providence would bring you, and yet you have not come, and I am so very tired of waiting. Some one said you would come in vacation, and I looked towards it very eagerly, made my treasures ready against it, and prepared my mind, and heart to welcome you in so kindly, and disappointment put a great cloud in my sky, and it's so high I cannot reach it, and it's doing a deal of harm. How lonely this world is growing, something so desolate creeps over the spirit and we dont know it's name, and it wont go away, either Heaven is seeming greater, or Earth a great deal more small, or God is more "Our Father," and we feel our need increased. Christ is calling everyone here, all my companions have answered, even my darling Vinnie believes she loves, and trusts him, and I am standing alone in rebellion, and growing very careless. Abby, Mary, Jane, and farthest of all my Vinnie have been seeking, and they all believe they have found; I cant tell you *what* they have found, but *they* think it is something precious. I wonder if it *is?* How strange is this sanctification, that works such a marvellous change, that sows in such corruption, and rises in golden glory, that brings Christ down, and shews him, and lets him select his friends! In the day time it seems like Sundays, and I wait for the bell to ring, and at evening a great deal stranger, the "still small voice" grows earnest and rings, and returns, and lingers, and the faces of good men shine, and bright halos come around them; and the eyes of the disobedient look down, and become ashamed. It *certainly* comes from God — and I think to receive it is blessed — not that I know it from *me*, but from those on whom *change* has passed. They seem so very tranquil, and their voices are kind, and gentle, and the tears fill their eyes so often, I really think I envy them. You know all about John Sanford, and Thurston, and all the rest, and I cant say more about it. You must pray when the rest are sleeping, that the hand may be held to me, and I may be led away.

[94]

How long does it seem since you left me, has the time been fleet, or lagging – been filled with hope, and the future, or waste, and a weary wilderness – and no one who knew the road? I would whisper to you in the evening of many, and curious things – and by the lamps eternal read your thoughts and response in your face, and find what you thought about me, and what I have done, and am doing; I know you would be surprised, whether in pleasure, or disappointment it does'nt become me to say – I have dared to do strange things – bold things, and have asked no advice from any – I have heeded beautiful tempters, yet do not think I am wrong. Oh I have needed my trusty Jane – my friend encourager, and sincere counciller, my rock, and strong assister! I could make you tremble for me, and be very much afraid, and wonder how things would end – Oh Jennie, it would relieve me to tell you all, to sit down at your feet, and look in your eyes, and confess what *you only* shall know, an experience bitter, and sweet, but the sweet did so beguile me – and life has had an aim, and the world has been too precious for your poor – and striving sister! The winter was all one dream, and the spring has not yet waked me, I would *always* sleep, and dream, and it never should turn to morning, so long as night is so blessed. What do you weave from all these threads, for I know you hav'nt been idle the while I've been speaking to you, bring it nearer the window, and I will see, it's all wrong unless it has one gold thread in it, a long, big shining fibre which hides the others – and which will fade away into Heaven while you hold it, and from there come back to me. I hope belief is not wicked, and assurance, and perfect trust – and a kind of a twilight feeling before the moon is seen – I hope human nature has truth in it – Oh I pray it may not deceive – confide – cherish, have a great faith in – do you dream from all this what I mean? Nobody *thinks* of the joy, nobody *guesses* it, to all appearance old things are engrossing, and new ones are not revealed, but there *now* is nothing old, things are budding, and springing, and singing, and you rather think you are in a green grove, and it's branches that go, and come. I shall see you *sometime* darling, and that sometime *may* not be distant, try to grow fast, and live really, and endure, and wait in patience – and reward *cannot* be distant. Be strong Jennie in remembrance, dont let "bygones *be* bygones" – love what you are taken from, and cherish us tho, so dim. Dont put us in narrow graves – we shall *certainly rise* if you do, and scare you most prodi-

[95]

giously, and carry you off perhaps! "This is the end of earth."

Very affectionately your friend

Emily E Dickinson.

Vinnie and Jane send much love, and want to know whether you received two long letters from them a great while ago.

Abby says she is waiting patiently. She is well, and sends you much love; Mother, and Austin unite in the same.

Mrs Brewster has lost a sister, her beautiful sister Celia who went away on a mission; she is deeply, and greatly afflicted, and hardly knows how to submit – she cherished that sister, and loved her, and she cannot resign her so soon. Her remains will be brought to Blandford as soon as the 1st of May, and as she is preserved in spirit, they hope she will still be natural, and they can part with her then more willingly.

Mr Spencer is very comfortable – I have faith that the spring will revive him, and give him some newness of life, and strength. No news from our "Theologian" Jennie, he must have "made way with himself" – I really dont care if he *has*. I am hushed as the night when I write *her*, and of *him* I hear not *a tiding*. I only prayed for *pride* – I have received yet more; indifference, and he may go "where he listeth," and never a bit care I. Something else has helped me forget *that,* a something surer, and higher, and I sometimes laugh in my sleeve. Dont betray me Jennie – but love, and remember, and write me, and I shall one day meet you.

MANUSCRIPT: HCL (JH 1). Ink. Dated: Amherst. April 3d. 1850. Unpublished.

Jane Humphrey had been compelled to resign her teaching position at Warren and return home because of the serious illness of her father, who died on the day this letter was written (see letter no. 36). Mrs. Brewster was the wife of John Milton Brewster, who practiced medicine at Amherst from 1843 until 1853. She herself died in the following year. Her sister, Celia Wright, a girl of nineteen, married John C. Strong in 1846, and accompanied him on his mission among the Choctaw Indians (1847–1849). Benjamin E. Thurston (AC 1852) later went West into business. "Our theologian" was James P. Kimball, whom ED finds it difficult to warm toward (see letter no. 30); and the person referred to as "her" was probably his sister Maria. The Jane mentioned in the sentence following the signature was Vinnie's friend Jane Hitchcock.

36

To Abiah Root   *7 and 17 May 1850*

Dear Remembered.

The circumstances under which I write you this morning are at once glorious, afflicting, and beneficial — glorious in *ends,* afflicting in *means,* and *beneficial* I *trust* in *both.* Twin loaves of bread have just been born into the world under my auspices — fine children – the image of their *mother* — and *here* my dear friend is the *glory.*

On the lounge asleep, lies my sick mother, suffering intensely from Acute Neuralgia — except at a moment like this, when kind sleep draws near, and beguiles her, *here* is the *affliction.*

I need not draw the *beneficial* inference — the good I myself derive, the winning the spirit of patience the genial house-keeping influence stealing over my mind, and soul, you know all these things I would say, and will seem to suppose they are *written,* when indeed they are only *thought.* On Sunday my mother was taken, had been perfectly well before, and could remember no possible imprudence which should have induced the disease, everything has been done, and tho' we think her gradually throwing it off, she still has much suffering. I have always neglected the culinary arts, but attend to them now from necessity, and from a desire to make everything pleasant for father, and Austin. Sickness makes desolation, and "the day is dark, and dreary," but health will come back I hope, and light hearts, and smiling faces. We are sick hardly ever at home, and dont know what to do when it comes, wrinkle our little brows, and stamp our little feet, and our tiny souls get angry, and command it to go away. Mrs *Brown* will be glad to see it, old-ladies *expect* to die, as for *us,* the young, and active, with all longings "for the strife," *we* to "perish by the road-side, weary with the march of life" no – no my dear "Father Mortality," get out of our way if you please, we will call if we ever want you, Good-morning Sir, ah Good-morning! When I am not at work in the kitchen, I sit by the side of mother, provide for her little wants – and try to cheer, and encourage her. I ought to be glad, and grateful that I *can* do anything now, but I do feel so very lonely, and so anxious to have her cured. I

[97]

hav'nt repined but *once*, and you shall know all the why. While I washed the dishes at noon in that little "sink-room" of our's, I heard a well-known rap, and a friend I love *so* dearly came and asked me to ride in the woods, the sweet-still woods, and I wanted to exceedingly – I told him I could not go, and he said he was disappointed – he wanted me very much – then the tears came into my eyes, tho' I tried to choke them back, and he said I *could*, and *should* go, and it seemed to me unjust. Oh I struggled with great temptation, and it cost me much of denial, but I think in the end I conquered, not a glorious victory Abiah, where you hear the rolling drum, but a kind of a helpless victory, where triumph would come of itself, faintest music, weary soldiers, nor a waving flag, nor a long-loud shout. I had read of Christ's temptations, and how they were like our own, only he did'nt sin; I wondered if *one* was like mine, and whether it made him angry – I couldnt make up my mind; do you think he ever did?

I went cheerfully round my work, humming a little air till mother had gone to sleep, then cried with all my might, seemed to think I was much abused, that this wicked world was unworthy such devoted, and terrible sufferings, and came to my various senses in great dudgeon at life, and time, and love for affliction, and anguish.

What shall we do my darling, when trial grows more, and more, when the dim, lone light expires, and it's dark, so very dark, and we wander, and know not where, and cannot get out of the forest – whose is the hand to help us, and to lead, and forever guide us, they talk of a "Jesus of Nazareth," will you tell me if it be he?

I presume you have heard from Abby, and know what she now believes – she makes a sweet, girl christian, religion makes her face quite different, calmer, but full of radiance, holy, yet very joyful. She talks of herself quite freely, seems to love Lord Christ most dearly, and to wonder, and be bewildered, at the life she has always led. It all looks black, and distant, and God, and Heaven are near, she is certainly very much changed.

She has told you about things here, how the "still small voice" is calling, and how the people are listening, and believing, and truly obeying — how the place is very solemn, and sacred, and the bad ones slink away, and are sorrowful — not at their wicked lives — but at this strange time, great change. I am one of the lingering *bad* ones, and so do *I* slink away, and pause, and ponder, and ponder, and pause, and do work without knowing why—not surely for *this* brief world, and more sure it is not for Heaven—and I ask what this message *means* that they ask for so very eagerly, *you* know of this depth, and fulness, will you *try* to tell me about it?

It's *Friday* my dear Abiah, and that in another week, yet my mission is unfulfilled—and you so sadly neglected, and dont know the reason why. Where do you think I've strayed, and from what new errand returned? I have come from "*to* and *fro,* and walking up, and down" the same place that Satan hailed from, when God asked him where he'd been, but not to illustrate further I tell you I have been dreaming, dreaming a *golden* dream, with eyes all the while wide open, and I guess it's almost morning, and besides I have been at work, providing the "food that perisheth," scaring the timorous dust, and being obedient, and kind. *I* call it kind obedience in the books the Shadows write in, it may have another name. I am yet the Queen of the court, if regalia be dust, and dirt, have three loyal subjects, whom I'd rather releive from service. Mother is still an invalid tho' a partially restored one—Father and Austin still clamor for food, and I, like a martyr am feeding them. Would'nt you love to see me in these bonds of great despair, looking around my kitchen, and praying for kind deliverance, and declaring by "Omar's beard" I never was in such plight. *My* kitchen I think I called it, God forbid that it was, or shall be my own—God keep me from what they call *households,* except that bright one of "faith"!

Dont be afraid of my imprecations, they never did anyone harm, and they make me feel so cool, and and [*sic*] so very much more comfortable!

Where are you now Abiah, where are your thoughts, and aspirings, where are your young affections, not with the *boots,* and *whiskers;* any with *me* ungrateful, *any* tho' drooping, dying? I presume you are loving your mother, and loving the stranger, and wanderer, visiting the poor, and afflicted, and reaping whole fields of blessings. Save me a *little* sheaf—only a very little one! Remember, and care for me sometimes, and scatter a fragrant flower in this wilderness life of mine by writing me, and by not forgetting, and by lingering longer in prayer, that the Father may bless one more!

Your aff friend,

Emily.

It's a great while since I've seen your cousins, they were all very well when I did. When will you come again – Speedily, will you?

Vinnie is still at school, and I sit by my lonely window, and give bright tears to her memory. Tears are my angels now.

Do you hear from our dear Jennie Humphrey, do you know' who's staying now? I feel impatiently, *very* it's so long since I've heard about her. When her father was sick she wrote me, and as soon as I could I replied; I afterwards saw his death, the day that my letter reached her. She must be bereaved indeed, and I wish I could go, and console her. She has the "Great Spirit" tho', and perhaps she does'nt need me. Do you know how she bears her trial. She is a very dear friend to me, and all of these things I think of.

What a beautiful mourner is her sister, looking so crushed, and heart-broken, yet never complaining, or murmuring, and waiting herself so patiently! She reminds me of suffering Christ, bowed down with her weight of agony, yet smiling at terrible will. "Where the weary are at rest" these mourners all make me think of — in the sweet still grave. When shall it call us?

MANUSCRIPT: HCL (ARS 8). Ink. Dated: Amherst. May 7th/50.

PUBLICATION: L (1894) 46–50, in part; LL 141–145, in part; L (1931) 40–43, in part, with part misplaced on pages 28–29.

Lavinia was still in school at Ipswich. The religious revival was of such proportions that on June 8 the *Springfield Republican* could report that it was still in progress. Edward Dickinson made confession of his faith and joined the church on 11 August. In the third paragraph ED quotes from Longfellow's "The Rainy Day," a poem to which she alludes no fewer than six times during these early years (see letters no. 54, 69, 74, 88, 98). In the eighth paragraph the quotation is from Longfellow's "Footsteps of Angels."

37

To Austin Dickinson   *27 October 1850*

Suppose "Topknot" should come down, and speak to his brothers, and sisters, or bind up the broken hearts of divers deserted friends, suppose he should doff his crown, and lay down his lofty sceptre, and once more a patient child receive reproof, and correction, salute the insulted rod, and bow to the common Lord!

An affection of nin[e]teen years for the most ungrateful of brothers jogs now and then at my elbow, and calls for paper and pen. Permit me to tie your shoe, to run like a dog behind you. I can bark, see here! Bow wow! Now if that is'nt fine I don't know! Permit me to be a stick, to show how I will not beat you, a stone, how I will not fling, musquito, I will not sting. Permit me to be a fowl, which Bettie shall dress for dinner, a bantam, a fine, fat hen. I will crow in my *grave* if you will, Chanticleer being still, tho' sleeping. Herein I "deign to condescend to stoop so low," what a high hill between me, and thee, a *hill*, upon my word, it is a *mountain*, I dare not climb. Let's call it "Alp," or "*Ande*," or yet the "Ascension Mount." I have it! — you shall be "Jove" a sitting on great "Olympus," a whittling the lightnings out, and hurling at your relations. Oh, "Jupiter"! fie! for shame! *Kings* sometimes have fathers and mothers. Father and I are going to have a Cattle Show Wednesday. School masters and Monkeys half price. I guess you had better "come down." They've appointed *you* joint committee on the "Beast with the seven horns.["] If time, and ability fail you, they'll omit the remaining horn. There's an old hand they call "Revelation." I dare say he will give you a lift! Bowdoin is pretty well, except now and on ailing, he *may* hold on a good while yet, you know that life is *unsartin*!

To the Boy of brass buttons, clasped hands, and fervent expression, send greetings.

That Miss Field may abstain from *meadow*, nor ever be found of *Groves*, is the prayer of your anxious friend.

"Serve God, and fear the King"! Exit *Sue*!!!

MANUSCRIPT: AC. Ink. Dated: Sunday evening. Envelope addressed: Austin Dickinson./Sunderland./Mass. Postmarked: Amherst MS. Oct. 28.

PUBLISHED: *Home* 109–110.

Austin was graduated from Amherst College in August 1850, and in September went to teach at Sunderland, a few miles north of Amherst. He had already become interested in Susan Gilbert, whose "exit" ED predicts. His letters to Sue from Sunderland are extant (HCL).

38

To Susan Gilbert (Dickinson)   *about December 1850*

Were it not for the *weather* Susie — my little, unwelcome face would come peering in today – I should steal a kiss from the sister —

the darling Rover returned – Thank the wintry wind my dear one, that spares such daring intrusion! *Dear* Susie – *happy* Susie – I rejoice in all *your* joy – sustained by that dear sister you will never again be lonely. Dont forget all the little friends who have tried so hard to *be* sisters, when indeed you *were* alone!

You do not hear the wind blow on this inclement day, when the *world* is shrugging it's shoulders; your little "Columbarium is lined with warmth and softness," there is no "silence" there — so you differ from bonnie "Alice." I *miss one* angel face in the little world of sisters – dear Mary – *sainted* Mary – Remember lonely one – tho, *she* comes not to us, *we* shall return to her! My love to *both* your sisters — and I want so much to see Matty.

Very aff yours,

Emily

MANUSCRIPT: HCL (B 131). Ink. Dated: Thursday noon.
PUBLICATION: *FF* 186–187.

Susan Gilbert's sister Mary, married for less than a year to Samuel J. Learned, died on 14 July 1850. The other unmarried sister, Martha, who had been in Michigan, joined Sue in December at the home of the eldest sister Harriet (Mrs. William Cutler), in Amherst. The "Alice" here alluded to is Alice Archer in Longfellow's *Kavanagh*, whose room is described as "that columbarium lined with warmth, and softness, and silence."

39

To Abiah Root *late 1850*

I write Abiah to-night, because it is cool and quiet, and I can forget the toil and care of the feverish day, and then I am *selfish* too, because I am feeling lonely; some of my friends are gone, and some of my friends are sleeping – sleeping the churchyard sleep — the hour of evening is sad — it was once my study hour — my master has gone to rest, and the open leaf of the book, and the scholar at school *alone*, make the tears come, and I cannot brush them away; I would not if I could, for they are the only tribute I can pay the departed Humphrey.

You have stood by the grave before; I have walked there sweet summer evenings and read the names on the stones, and wondered who would come and give me the same memorial; but I never have

[102]

laid my friends there, and forgot that they too must die; this is my first affliction, and indeed 'tis hard to bear it. To those bereaved so often that home is no more here, and whose communion with friends is had only in prayers, there must be much to hope for, but when the unreconciled spirit has nothing left but God, that spirit is lone indeed. I don't think there will be any sunshine, or any singing-birds in the spring that's coming. I shall look for an early grave then, when the grass is growing green; I shall love to call the bird there if it has gentle music, and the meekest-eyed wild flowers, and the low, plaintive insect. How *precious* the grave, Abiah, when aught that we love is laid there, and affection would fain go too, if that the lost were lonely! I will try not to say any more — my rebellious thoughts are many, and the friend I love and trust in has much *now* to forgive. I wish I were somebody else — I would pray the prayer of the "Pharisee," but I am a poor little "Publican." "Son of David," look down on me!

'Twas a great while ago when you wrote me, I remember the leaves were falling — and *now* there are falling snows; who maketh the two to differ — are not leaves the brethren of snows?

Then it *can't* be a great while since then, though I verily thought it *was*; we are not so young as we once were, and time seems to be growing long. I dream of being a grandame, and banding my silver hairs, and I seem to be quite submissive to the thought of growing old; no doubt you ride rocking-horses in your present as in young sleeps — quite a pretty contrast indeed, of me braiding my own gray hairs, and my friend at play with her childhood, a pair of decayed old ladies! Where *are* you, my *antique* friend, or my very dear and young one — just as you please to please — it *may* seem quite a presumption that I address you at all, knowing not if you habit here, or if my "bird has flown" in which world her wing is folded. When I think of the friends I love, and the little while we may dwell here, and then "we go away," I have a yearning feeling, a desire eager and anxious lest any be stolen away, so that I cannot behold them. I would have you here, all here, where I can *see* you, and *hear* you, and where I can say "Oh, no," if the "Son of Man" ever "cometh"!

It is not enough, now and then, at long and uncertain intervals to hear you're alive and well. I do not care for the body, I love the timid soul, the blushing, shrinking soul; it hides, for it is afraid, and the bold obtrusive body — Pray, marm, did you call *me*? We are very small, Abiah — I think we grow still smaller — this tiny, insect life the portal to another; it seems strange — strange indeed. I'm afraid we are all unworthy, yet we shall "enter in."

I can think of no other way than for you, my dear girl, to come here — we are growing away from each other, and talk even now like strangers. To forget the "meum and teum," *dearest* friends must meet sometimes, and then comes the "bond of the spirit" which, if I am correct, is "unity."

. . . You are growing wiser than I am, and nipping in the bud fancies which I let blossom — perchance to bear no fruit, or if plucked, I may find it bitter. The shore is safer, Abiah, but I love to buffet the sea — I can count the bitter wrecks here in these pleasant waters, and hear the murmuring winds, but oh, I love the danger! You are learning control and firmness. Christ Jesus will love you more. I'm afraid he don't love me *any*! . . . Write when you *will*, my friend, and forget all amiss herein, for as these few imperfect words to the full communion of spirits, so this small giddy life to the *better*, the life eternal, and that *we* may live this life, and be filled with this true communion, I shall not cease to pray.

E.

Abby has been to see you, and you had the happiest time. *I* know how you talked, and wa[l]ked, and I saw the weary eyelids, drooping, fainting, falling. Oh you are both asleep, and your hand is fast in Abby's. I stand by the fond young bedside, and think of "Babes in the Wood" – large babes – the ones we hear of were *small* ones – I seem to myself a robin covering you with leaves – the Babies we *were are* buried, and their shadows are plodding on. Abby is better now – she has just made another visit – a kind of friendly tour among her kith and kin. She seems better in mind and body – by which I mean stronger physically, and more cheerful in mind. I wonder that Abby's head-aches do not depress her more – she endures and bears like a martyr.

I see but little of Abby; she cannot come to see me, and I walk so far not often, and perhaps it's all right and best. Our lots fall in different places; mayhap we might disagree. We take different views of life, our thoughts would not dwell together as they used to when we were young — how long ago that seems! She is more of a woman than I am, for I love so to be a child – Abby is holier than me – she does more good in her lifetime than ever I shall in mine – she goes among the poor, she shuts the eye of the dying – she will be had in memorial when I am gone and forgotten. Do not think we are aught than friends — though the "silver cord *be* loosed" the "golden bowl" is *not* broken. I have talked thus freely of Abby because we three were friends, because I trust we three *are* friends, and shall meet in bliss together, because the golden links, though dimmed, are no less golden, and I love to hold them up, and see them gleam in the sunshine; you and I, too, are more alike than Abby and I are sometimes, and the name of each is dear and is cherished by the other.

Won't you say what you think of Abby – I mean of her heart and mind – when you write me. I think it is a license which friend may take with friend, without at all detracting from aught we like or love. And tell me of *some one else* – what *she* is thinking and doing, and whether she still remembers the loves of "long ago," and sighs as she remembers, lest there be no more as true – "sad times, sweet times, two bairns at school, but a' one heart" – *three* bairns, and the tale had been truer.

MANUSCRIPT: missing. See note 3 in "Notes on the Present Text." All of the letter above the signature has been published. The final two paragraphs below the signature (which directly follow the paragraph which precedes them) were published in *Letters* (1931) 49–50, and by mistake separated from the rest of the letter. The first paragraph below the signature is unpublished.

PUBLICATION: L (1894) 50–53; L (1931) 44–46, dated (presumably by ED): Tuseday Evening. It is said to have been postmarked 2 January. The letter seems to have been written on 31 December 1850.

Leonard Humphrey died, 13 November 1850, at his home in North Weymouth. Abby Wood had been greatly affected during the religious revival of the previous summer, and joined the church in August.

IV

LETTERS

40–176

[1851–1854]

"... *we do not have much poetry,*
father having made up his mind
that its pretty much all real life."

The close relationship between Emily Dickinson and her brother Austin is clearly shown, both in the great number of letters she wrote to him when he was away, and in the fact that he preserved so many of them. In the course of these years, while Austin was teaching in Boston and later attending Harvard Law School, the daily intimacy of home life was constantly kept before him in her frequent letters.

It was at this time, also, that Austin's courtship of Susan Gilbert was taking shape, culminating in their publicly acknowledged engagement by the end of 1853. Emily's intimacy with Sue grew with Sue's closer tie to Austin. Fond as she still was of the girls with whom she had been intimate in earlier years, Emily's feeling for Sue took precedence over other friendships, and her letters during Sue's absences were as much a part of her daily life as were those to Austin.

The letters to these two close companions dominate the correspondence of the period, but her feeling for others was not excluded. She enjoyed exchanges of books and thoughts with Henry Vaughan Emmons during his undergraduate years. And her cousin, John L. Graves, who introduced Emmons to her, she counted as a friend of her own.

40

To Emily Fowler (Ford)   *about 1851*

I'm so afraid you'll forget me dear Emily – through these cold winter days, when I cannot come to see you, that I cannot forbear writing the least little bit of a note – to put you in mind of me; perhaps it will make you laugh – it may be foolish in me but I love you so well sometimes – not that I do not *always* – but more dearly sometimes – and with such a desire to see you that I find myself addressing you almost ere I'm aware. When I am as old as you and have had so many friends, perhaps they wont seem so precious, and then I shant write any more little "billet doux" like these, but you will forgive me *now*, because I cant find many so dear to me as you – then I know I cant have you always – some day a "brave dragoon" will be stealing you away and I will have farther to go to discover you *at all* – so I shall recollect all these sweet opportunities and feel so sorry if I did'nt improve them. I wish I had something new, or very happy, to tell you, which would fill that lofty kitchen with sunshine all day long, but there *is* nothing new – neither indeed there *can* be – for things have got so old; but something happy there *is* if the remembrance of friends is always sweet and joyful. Solve this little problem, dear Emily, if you possibly can: You have "so many" friends – *you* know how *very* many – then if all of them love you *half* so well as me, say – how much will it make?

I fancy I catch you *ciphering* on the funniest little slate, with the airiest little pencil – I will not interrupt you –

Dear Emilie –

Goodbye!

MANUSCRIPT: NYPL. Ink. Dated: Thursday morning. Addressed on the fold: Miss Emily E Fowler/by Vinnie.

PUBLICATION: L (1894) 136–137, in part; L (1931) 136, in part.

The date is conjectured from the handwriting. This is the second known letter (see no. 32) written to Emily Fowler, who was one of ED's earliest friends. ED wrote several more over the years, an especially large number in 1853, the year of Emily Fowler's marriage. But the quality of disembodiment, uncharacteristic of most letters, is peculiarly evident in those to Emily Fowler, who was more than four years older than ED.

41

To Elbridge G. Bowdoin   *February 1851*

I weave for the Lamp of *Evening* — but fairer colors than *mine* are twined while stars are shining.

I know of a shuttle swift — I know of a fairy gift — mat for the "Lamp of *Life*" — the little Bachelor's wife!

MANUSCRIPT: AC. Ink. Dated: 1851. Addressed: Mr. Bowdoin./ Present.
PUBLICATION: L (1931) 138.
This valentine seems to have accompanied a lamp mat made by ED.

42

To Austin Dickinson   *8 June 1851*

It might not come amiss dear Austin to have a tiding or two concerning our state and feelings, particularly when we remember that "Jamie is gone awa."

Our state is pretty comfortable, and our feelings are *somewhat solemn* which we account for satisfactorily by calling to mind the fact that it is the "Sabbath Day." Whether a certain passenger in a certain yesterday's stage has any sombre effect on our once merry household, or the reverse "I dinna choose to tell," but be the case as it may, we are rather a crestfallen company to make the *best* of us, and what with the sighing wind, the sobbing rain, and the whining of nature *generally*, we can hardly contain ourselves, and I only hope and trust that your this evening's lot is cast in far more cheery places than the ones you leave behind.

We are enjoying this evening what is called a "northeast storm" — a little north of east, in case you are pretty definite. Father thinks "it's amazin raw," and I'm half disposed to think that he's in the right about it, tho' I keep pretty dark, and dont *say* much about it! Vinnie is at the instrument, humming a pensive air concerning a young lady who thought she was "almost there." Vinnie seems much grieved, and I really suppose *I* ought to betake myself to weeping; I'm pretty sure that I *shall* if she dont abate her singing.

Father's just got home from meeting and Mr Boltwood's, found the last quite comfortable, and the first not quite so well.

Mother is warming her feet, which she assures me confidently are "just as cold as ice.["] I tell her I fear there is danger of icification, or ossification — I dont know certainly which! Father is reading the Bible — I take it for *consolation*, judging from outward things. He and mother take great delight in dwelling upon your character, and reviewing your many virtues, and Father's prayers for you at our morning devotions are enough to break one's heart — it is really very touching; surely "our blessings brighten" the farther off they fly! Mother wipes her eyes with the end of her linen apron, and consoles herself by thinking of several future places "where congregations ne'er break up," and Austins have no end! This being a favorite sentiment with you, I trust it will find a response in all patriotic bosoms. There has not been much stirring since when you went away — I should venture to say *prudently* that matters had come to a stand — unless something new "turns up" I cannot see anything to prevent a *quiet season*. Father takes care of the doors, and mother of the windows, and Vinnie and I are secure against all outward attacks. If we can get our *hearts "under"* I dont have much to fear — I've got all but *three* feelings down, if I can only keep them!

Tutor Howland was here *as usual*, during the afternoon — after tea I went to see Sue — had a nice little visit with her — then went to see Emily Fowler, and arrived home at 9 — found Father is great agitation at my protracted stay — and mother and Vinnie in tears, for fear that he would kill me.

Sue and Martha expressed their sorrow that you had gone away, and are going to write a postscript in the next letter I send.

Emily F[owler] talked of you with her usual deal of praise. The girls all send their love. Mother wants me to say that if you like *Aunt L's Bonnet*, and can find one for *her just like it*, that "Barkis is very willin." Vinnie sends her love, and says she is "pretty comfortable." I shall think of you tomorrow with four and twenty Irish boys — all in a row! I miss you very much. I put on my bonnet tonight, opened the gate very desperately, and for a little while, the suspense was terrible — I think I was held in check by some invisible agent, for I returned to the house without having done any harm!

If I had'nt been afraid that you would "poke fun" at my feelings, I had written a *sincere* letter, but since the "world is hollow, and Dollie is stuffed with sawdust," I really do not think we had better expose our feelings. Write soon to *me*, they all send love to you and all the folks — love to Lizzie if there. Vinnie has commenced snoring.

Your dear Sister

Emily.

MANUSCRIPT: AC. Ink. Dated: Sunday evening.

PUBLICATION: L (1894) 75–76, in part; LL 149–151, in part; L (1931) 72–74, in part; Home 128–129, entire.

Austin left home on Saturday, 7 June 1851, to begin a year's engagement as teacher in the boys' section of the Endicott School in the North End of Boston, settled largely by Irish immigrants who had fled the potato famine of 1847. His uncle Loring Norcross was a member of the school committee. At first he lived with the Norcrosses, but shortly moved to a boarding house (see letter no. 43), though his mailing address continued to be through the Norcrosses.

The quotation "where congregations ne'er break up" is from the familiar hymn "Jerusalem! My happy home!" The William Burkitt version (1693) first introduced the word "congregations" at the end of the second stanza: "Where congregations ne'er break up,/And Sabbaths have no end."

43

To Austin Dickinson   *15 June 1851*

From what you say Dear Austin I am forced to conclude that you never received *my letter* which was mailed for Boston *Monday*, but *two days* after you left — I dont know where it went to, Father wrote on the outside, and to care of Uncle Loring, and waiting from day to day and receiving no reply, I naturally grew rather crusty and resolved to reserve my mss for youths more worthy of them; this will account for the fact that you heard nothing by Bowdoin. In neither of your letters, for which I heartily thank you, have you made any mention of my departed letter — Bowdoin *thinks* you told him you had not heard from home, and quite surprised at it, and grieved to have you think you were forgotten *so* quick, I will try the post again, if I cant be more successful. I'm glad you are so well pleased, I am glad you are *not* delighted, I would not that *foreign* places should wear the smile of home. We are quite alarmed for the *boys*, hope you wont *kill*, or *pack away* any of em, so near Dr. Webster's bones t'ant strange you have had temptations! You would not take it amiss if I should say we *laughed some* when each of your letters came — your respected parents were *overwhelmed* with glee, and as for the *young ladies* they gave a smile or so by way of recognizing your *descriptive* merits. Father remarks quite briefly that he "thinks they have found their master," mother bites her lips, and fears you "will be *rash* with them" and Vinnie and I say masses for poor Irish boys souls. So far as *I* am concerned I should like to have you kill some — there are so many now, there is no room for the Americans, and I cant think of a death that would be more after my mind than *scientific destruction, scholastic dissolution*, there's something lofty in it, it smacks of *going up*! Wont you please to state the *name* of the boy that turned the faintest, as I like to get such *facts* to set down in my *journal*, also anything else that's *startling* which you may chance to know — I dont think deaths or murders can ever come amiss in a young woman's journal — the country's *still* just now, and the severities alluded to will have a salutary influence in waking the people up — speaking of *getting up*, how early are *metropolitans* expected to wake up, *especially* young men — *more* especially *schoolmasters*? I miss "my department" mornings — I lay it quite to heart that I've no one to wake up. Your room looks lonely enough — I do not love to go in there — whenever I pass thro' I find I 'gin to whistle, as we read that little boys are wont to do in the graveyard. I am going to set out *Crickets* as soon as I find time that they by their shrill singing shall help disperse the gloom — will they grow if I *transplant* them?

You importune me for *news*, I am very sorry to say "Vanity of vanities" there's no such thing as news — it is almost time for the cholera, and *then* things will take a start!

We have had a man to take tea, a Mr Marsh by name — he went to school with Father.

I think him a "man of cares" tho' I know nothing concerning him —

[113]

another important item, so far as I can judge — I think he's for "law and order." Susie and Martha come often. Sue was here on Friday, for all afternoon yesterday — I gave the *manslaughter* extract to the infinite fun of Martha! They miss you very much — they send their "united loves." Vinnie rode with Howland yesterday, and Emily Fowler and [William Cowper] Dickinson also, at the same time — had a fine ride. The Reading club seems lonely — perhaps it weeps for you.

Dwight Cowan does very well — the Horse is quite "uncommon." Hunt is shingling the barn. We are going to have some new hens — a few.

I reserve the close for bad news — we cant come to hear Jennie — we are coming, but cant now. There are several reasons why — the first we are not near ready — Miss Leonard is coming this week — Grandmother is coming to see us — if we go now we cant *stay* any — we cannot come now and again — it would be all haste and confusion — we should have to hurry home, and we do not think it best. We shall come before long, when we are all prepared — "two monuments of the past" would make quite a stir in Boston! You must'nt be disappointed, nor blame the folks at all — they would be perfectly willing if we tho't best ourselves. Give our love to our friends, thank them *much* for their kindness; we *will* come and see them and you tho' now it is not convenient. All of the folks send love.

Your aff
Emily.

Mother says if there's anything more you want, if you will only write us Mrs Kimberly will make it — also if you have any things which you would like to send home Henry Kellogg is there, and you can send by him. Write as often as possible. Take care of yourself —

Special love to Emily, and the little cousins.

MANUSCRIPT: AC. Ink. Dated: Sunday Evening. Envelope addressed: Wm Austin Dickinson./Care of Loring Norcross Esq./Boston./Mass. Postmarked: Amherst Ms. Jun 16.

PUBLICATION: L (1894) 80, in part; LL 154, in part; L (1931) 77–78, in part; Home 130–139, entire, with facsimile reproduction.

Austin wrote twice in the first week of his absence, and urged his sisters to come to Boston to hear Jenny Lind. ED cites the coming of the dressmaker as one reason for refusal. "Dr. Webster's bones" alludes to the notorious murder in a Harvard laboratory of Dr. George Parkman by his colleague Dr. John W. Webster in 1849. Webster was hanged, and buried in Mount Auburn Cemetery, which ED had visited in 1846.

44

To Austin Dickinson   *22 June 1851*

I rec'd your letter Austin, permit me to thank you for it, and to request some more as soon as it's convenient—permit me to accord with your discreet opinion concerning Swedish Jennie, and to commend the heart brave eno' to express it—combating the opinion of two civilized worlds, and New York into the bargain, must need considerable daring—indeed it had never occurred to me that amidst the Hallelujahs one tongue would dare to be dumb—and much less I assure you that this dissenting one should be my romantic Brother! For I had looked for delight and a very high style of rapture in such a youth as you—Father perused the letter and verily for joy the poor man could hardly contain himself—he read and read again, and each time seemed to relish the story more than at first. Fearing the consequences on a mind so formed as his, I seized the exciting sheet, and bore it away to my folio to amuse nations to come.

"If it had only come" in the language of your Father, "a single day before," in the twinkling of an eye "it had been transferred to the *Paper*" to tell this foolish world that one man living in it dares to say what he *thinks*—nor heeds if some dog bark. So soon as he was calm he began to proclaim your opinion—the effect cannot be described—encomium followed encomium—applause deafened applause —the whole town reeled and staggered as *it* were a drunken man— rocks rent—graves opened—and the seeds which had'nt come up were heard to set up growing—the sun went down in clouds—the moon rose in glory—Alpha Delta, All Hail!

We have all been rather *piqued* at Jennie's singing so well, and this first calumnious whisper pleases us so well. We rejoice that we did not come—our visit is yet before us.

The *Bonnet* came safely Saturday, and is pronounced by *us all* to be *very beautiful*—mother is very much pleased with it, says it is "just

[115]

to her mind," you could'nt have suited us better *possibly* if you'd tried.

Mother wants me to thank you for all your pains and trouble, and says you "are very kind to do so much for your mother."

You hav'nt told us yet as you promised about your home — what kind of people they are — whether you find them pleasant — whether those timid gentlemen have yet "found tongue to say" — do you find the life and living any more annoying than you at first expected — do you light upon any friends to help the time away — have you whipped any more bad boys — all these are solemn questions, pray give them proper heed!

Two weeks of your time are gone, I cant help wondering sometimes if you would love to see us, and come to this still home — I cant help wanting to see you now and then at times and my interviews with you at the *Barn* are frought with a saddened interest. I suppose I am a fool — you always said I was one, and yet I have some feelings that seem sensible to me, and I have desires to see you now that you are gone which are really quite intelligent. Dont take too much encouragement, but really I have the hope of becoming before you come quite an *accountable being!*

Why not an "eleventh hour" in the life of the *mind* as well as such an one in the life of the *soul* — greyhaired sinners are saved — simple maids may be *wise*, who knoweth?

The yard round the house has been mowed and presents quite a fine appearance — Dwight continues to do very well, Baalis Sanford was here last week; has gone to Bridgwater now, and will be here again sometime this week.

Our Reading Club still is, and becomes now very pleasant — *Stebbins* comes in to read now, and *Spencer* — t'would not be so if *you* were here — the *last* time *Charles* came in when we had finished reading, and we broke up with a *dance* — make your own reflections at the story I just told you — the Tutors come after us, and walk home with us — we *enjoy that!* A *Senior Levee* was held at Prof and Mrs Haven's on Tuesday of last week — quite an oldfashioned time — Vinnie and dodging *Chapin* was the only fun they had there — Vinnie played pretty well! There's another at the President's this next Friday evening — "Clarum et venerabile" Seniors! Emily Fowler inquires for you — also M. and Susie — Give my love to my friends, and write me as soon as you can — the folks all send their love. *B F N. is married.*

MANUSCRIPT: AC. Ink. Dated: Sunday evening.
PUBLICATION: L (1894) 77–78, in part; LL 151–152, in part; L (1931) 74–75, in part; Home 143–145, entire.
Professor Haven came to Amherst in 1850. The president, at this time, was Edward Hitchcock. B. F. Newton, married on June 4, was already stricken with pulmonary tuberculosis, and died within two years; his wife was twelve years older than he. Austin was a member of Alpha Delta Phi fraternity.

45

To Austin Dickinson   *29 June 1851*

At my old stand again Dear Austin, and happy as a queen to know that while I speak those whom I love are listening, and I am happier still if I shall make *them* happy.

I have just finished reading your letter which was brought in since church. *Mr* Pierce was not out today, the wife of this same man took upon her *his* duties, and brought the letter *herself* since we came in from church. I like it grandly – very – because it is so long, and also it's *so* funny – we have all been laughing till the old house rung again at your delineations of men, women, and things. I feel quite like retiring, in presence of one so grand, and casting my small lot among small birds, and fishes – you say you dont comprehend me, you want a simpler style. *Gratitude* indeed for all my fine philosophy! I strove to be exalted thinking I might reach *you* and while I pant and struggle and climb the nearest cloud, you walk out very leisurely in your slippers from Empyrean, and without the *slightest* notice request me to get down! As *simple* as you please, the *simplest* sort of simple – I'll be a little ninny – a little pussy catty, a little Red Riding Hood, I'll wear a Bee in my Bonnet, and a Rose bud in my hair, and what remains to do you shall be told hereafter.

Your letters are richest treats, send them always just such warm days – they are worth a score of fans, and many refrigerators – the only "diffikilty" they are so very *queer*, and *laughing* such hot weather is *anything* but *amusing*. A little more of earnest, and a little less of jest until we are out of August, and then you may joke as freely as the Father of Rogues himself, and we will banish care, and daily die a laughing! It is *very* hot here now, I dont believe it's any hotter in

Boston than t'is here — we cant lie down to sleep lest we wake up in burning. I verily *baked* in bed the last time I retired, but now adopt a method of keeping up all night which having never *tried* I think will turn out nicely! I hope you're very careful in working, eating and drinking when the heat is so great — there are temptations there which at home you are free from — beware the juicy fruits, and the cooling ades, and cordials, and do not eat *ice-cream*, it is so very *dangerous* — the folks think much about you, and are so afraid you'll get sick by being rash or imprudent — for our sakes Austin wont you try to be careful? I know *my* sake a'nt much, but Vinnie's is considerab[l]e — it weighs a good many pounds — when *skin and bones* may plead, I will become a *persuasion*, but you have *other* friends who are much more substantial. I know of *sisters twain* – Oh Youth, come back again, they sing — you ask me of the "postscript" — it's coming — the writers are well, and come often to see Vinnie and me — they do not have any *rides* except Martha went with Barton on horseback the other morning. Root has quite left the field — our little neighbor Jones we are happy to say is faithful. We talk of you together, and intersperse remarks with snatches from your letters.

You ask about the carriage, it is to be done this week, when you get home we'll ride, perhaps we will "take a tour."

Mother feels quite anxious to know about your *clothes*, washing, ironing, &c. Vinnie suggests in connection that she may sometimes occur to mind when you would like collars washed — I told her I would'nt tell you — I hav'nt however decided whether I will or not. I often put on five knives, and four and another tumbler forgetting for the moment that "we are not all here," it occurs to me however, and I remove the extra and brush a tear away in memory of my brother.

We miss you now and always — when God bestows but *three* and one of those is witholden the *others* are left alone. *Moody Cook* took tea here Saturday — he came to see "his pony" and it being suppertime Father asked him to stay — he took *your* seat at the table which led to some remarks concerning yourself, and your absence, which your ear may hear. "Somehow he and Austin always *were* good friends — *he* was none of your *mean* boys — doing *small mean* things, and there was something in him which always made *folks mind* — when Austin was at home Austin was *in town*" tho' this I comprehend not the nescessity of *stating* it seeming quite instinctive, and not needful to prove. Father told him about your early youth, your love for trade and driving – instanced *Hens* and *Bees* as nearest illustrations. By the way – I forgive you that *fraud* of 25 cts and hope Almighty Jove will be very merciful! Father thinks Moody Cook put spirit in the cider when he was here in the spring and thinks *you* understand it, and that yourself and Moody are in some way joking him – he has thought so much about it that he said he should write, and ask you – we young ones laugh in our sleeves, and think he is rather crazy. Father is as uneasy when you are gone away as if you catch a trout, and put him in Sahara – when you *first* went away he came home very frequently – walked gravely towards the barn, and returned looking very stately – then strode away down street as if the foe was coming – *now* he is more resigned – contents himself by fancying that "we shall *hear* today," and then when we *do not* hear, he wags his head profound, and thinks without a doubt there will be news "tomorrow." "Once one is two" once one *will be* two ah I have it here! I wish you could have some cherries – if there was any way we would send you a basket of them – they are very large and delicious, and are just ripening now – little Austin Grout comes every day to pick them, and mother takes great comfort in calling him by name, from vague association with her departed boy. Austin, to tell the *truth*, it is very still and lonely. I do wish you were here despite the darkened Laddy – they are bad enough in darkness, I really dont feel willing that they should come to light thro' such a daring medium – Emeline and Sarah took a trip sometime since, and have not yet returned – from all that I can learn I conclude that "I tell Eliza" is his consoling now – in other language Austin – she has become "Miss Mills."

Root has been here twice – B Harrington once, and others in due proportion – W. Dickinson is going to write you – Bowdoin is "around." The railroad is a "workin" – my love to all my friends. I am on my way down stairs to put the teakettle boiling – writing and taking tea cannot sympathize – if you forget me now your right hand *shall* it's cunning.

Emilie.

MANUSCRIPT: AC. Ink. Dated: Sunday afternoon. Envelope addressed: Wm Austin Dickinson./Care of Loring Norcross Esq./Boston./Mass. Postmarked: Amherst Ms Jun 30.

PUBLICATION: L (1894) 85–87, in part; L (1931) 84–86, in part; *Home* 146–148, entire.
The references to persons in this letter are so obscure as to make identification unwarrantable. An enclosed note from Lavinia suggests that Emeline Kellogg, who lived next door, and Henry Nash, whom she later married, may have been the ones principally concerned.

46

To Austin Dickinson   *6 July 1851*

I have just come in from Church very hot, and faded, having witnessed a couple of Baptisms, three admissions to church, a Supper of the Lord, and some other minor transactions time fails me to record. Knowing Rev A. M. Colton so thoroughly as you do, having received much benefit from his past ministrations, and bearing the relation of "Lamb" unto his fold, you will delight to know that he is well, and preaching, that he has preached *today* strange as it may — must seem, that just from his benediction I hurry away to you. No doubt you can call to mind his eloquent addresses, his earnest look and gesture, his calls of *now today* — no doubt you can call to mind the impetus of spirit received from this same gentleman and his enlivening preaching — therefore if you should fancy I'd looked upon the *wine* from walk or conversation a little fierce or fiery, bear all these things in mind!

Our church grows interesting, Zion lifts her head — I overhear remarks signifying Jerusalem, I do not feel at liberty to say any more today! I wanted to write you *Friday*, the night of Jennie Lind, but reaching home past midnight, and *my room* sometime after, encountering several perils starting, and on the way, among which a *kicking horse*, an inexperienced driver, a number of Jove's thunderbolts, and a very terrible rain, are worthy to have record. All of us went — just four — add an absent individual and that will make full five – the concert commenced at eight, but knowing the world was *hollow* we thought we'd start at six, and come up with everybody that meant to come up with us — we had proceeded some steps when one of the beasts showed symptoms, and just by the *blacksmith's shop* exercises commenced, consisting of kicking and plunging on the part of the horse, and whips and moral suasion from the *gentleman* who drove — the horse refused to proceed, and your respected family with much chagrin dismounted, advanced to the hotel, and for a season halted — another horse procured, we were politely invited to take our seats, and proceed, which we refused to do till the animal was warranted — about half thro' our journey thunder was said to be heard, and a suspicious *cloud* came travelling up the sky — what words express our horror when rain began to fall — in drops — sheets — cataracts — what *fancy conceive* of drippings and of drenchings which we met on the way — how the stage and its mourning captives drew up at Warner's hotel — how all of us alighted, and were conducted in, how the rain did not abate, how we walked in silence to the old Edwards Church and took our seats in the same, how Jennie came out like a child and sang and sang again, how boquets fell in showers, and the roof was rent with applause — how it thundered outside, and inside with the thunder of God and of men — judge ye which was the loudest — how we all loved Jennie Lind, but not accustomed oft to her manner of singing did'nt fancy *that* so well as we did *her* — no doubt it was very fine — but take some notes from her "Echo" — the Bird sounds from the "Bird Song" and some of her curious trills, and I'd rather have a Yankee.

Herself, and not her music, was what we seemed to love – she has an air of *exile* in her mild blue eyes, and a something sweet and touching in her native accent which charms her many friends — "Give me my thatched cottage" as she sang grew so earnest she seemed half lost in song and for a transient time I fancied she *had* found it and would be seen "na mair," and then her foreign accent made her again a wanderer — we will talk about her sometime when you come — Father sat all the evening looking *mad,* and *silly,* and yet so much amused you would have *died* a laughing — when the performers bowed, he said "Good evening Sir" — and when they retired, "very well — that will do," it was'nt *sarcasm* exactly, nor it was'nt *disdain,* it was infinitely funnier than either of those virtues, as if old Abraham had come to see the show, and thought it was all very well, but a little excess of *Monkey!* She took 4000 $ / *mistake* arithmetical/ for tickets at Northampton aside from all expenses. I'm glad you took a seat opposite Lord Mayor — if he had sat in your lap it had pleased me even better — it must seem pretty grand to be a city officer and pat the

Sheriff's back, and wink to the Policemen! I'm sorry you got so tired, and would suggest respectfully a Rose in every thorn!

We are all pretty comfortable, and things get along well – Bowdoin has gone home haying – the Tutors are hanging on – Francis March is here, had not been *seen* at the latest – the Exhibition came, and *went* for all that I know – choosing not to "tend." Sanford – Valedictorian – Stebbins – Salutatorian – Carr [Karr] – Oratio Philosophico – I do not know the rest, except that Wm Washburn has a Dissertation from the delivery of which he is "respectfully excused."

About our coming to Boston – we think we shall probably *come* – we want to see our friends – yourself and Aunt L's family – we dont care a fig for the *museum*, the stillness, or Jennie Lind. We are not going to stay long – not more than a week – are sorry Emily is gone, but she shall come to see us – how long will Joel be gone – we have talked of Thursday or Friday as the earliest that we should come – perhaps not until Monday – can you write a line and send to us tomorrow, how long Joe will be gone? Give our love to our friends, and tell them we will write them and let them know our plans as soon as we hear from you – Thank them if you please for their kind invitation, and tell them we are coming not to see *sights* but *them*, and therefore all the stillness will not incommode us. I saw Martha Friday – she inquired all about you, and said she was going to write, and Susie too that I could send next time – it has rained ever since then and it is raining now, now so I disappoint you – have patience Austin, and they shall come next time. Father says your letters are altogether before Shakespeare, and he will have them published to put in our library. Emily Fowler's regards – Love from us all – dont know what I say I write in such a hurry.

Your aff Sister

Emily

Manuscript: AC. Ink. Dated: Sunday afternoon.

Publication: L (1894) 81–83, in part; L (1931) 80–83, in part; *Home* 150–153, entire.

The churches were generally the only meeting places in New England towns large enough to hold such an audience as Jenny Lind could draw. ED never heard any other singer or instrumental musician of note.

47

To Austin Dickinson   *13 July 1851*

You must'nt *care* Dear Austin, Vinnie and I cant come — it is'nt any matter, I hope you a'nt troubled about it. We *were* disappointed at first, because not very well, and thinking while at Boston we would see Aunt Lavinia's physician; we did'nt want to tell *you why* we were bent on coming, thinking now you were *gone* you might feel anxious about us — we knew it would worry you and therefore made our plans to come now and see you, and saying not a word to any but Aunt L — follow the advice of her Homeopathic physician. If we had told our reasons for coming at this time we should have seemed more reasonable in wishing so much to come, and we knew you would have us *at once* tho' it might not be convenient.

We are not very sick, we work and go out and have company, but neither of us are well — Dr Brewster has fussed until we are satisfied that he does'nt know what ails us, and we are tired and wearied of being under his care. Father has great confidence in Dr Dean of Greenfield, and thinks sometime this week we may ride up and see him. If he cant tell what ails us, nor do us any good, then we will come in the autumn and see the other man.

Do not feel anxious for us — I think we will soon be well — we have been ailing sometime but not very seriously, and Dr Brewster has tried one thing after another till we are most discouraged, and sometimes we think to ourselves that we shant ever get well, but I guess we shall. I long so to see you Austin, and hear your happy voice, it will do us all more good than any other medicine. Do not blame yourself for what you said and did, and do not allow our friends to reproach themselves at all — we knew you had kindest reasons and thank you and them for so kindly consulting our pleasure.

When you go back in the autumn we can see you then, and you must'nt think anything about it, or care for what you wrote. I dont know what Father said — did know not he was going to write you — your sorrowful letter was our first intimation that ever he had written, and I guess we felt as badly to get such a letter from *you*, as you did or *could* at what you heard from Father. I feel so grieved, dear Austin, if Father has blamed *you*, *Viny and me* are the ones if there is fault *anywhere* — we should have told you frankly why we wished to come—but we did'nt want to worry you as we feared we should. Never mind it Austin—we shall see you soon and tell you all those things which seem obscure when written. Tell all our friends and Joel that we would love to see them but think we will stay at home and come some other time—much love to them all. Joel must'nt look in any of the Depots for he wont find us there, and it would give him trouble. You must'nt think of such a thing as seeing us now, for we have *decided,* and think not best to come.

Vinnie will write you soon—sends her love—mine too. Mother sends her love and a little curl of her hair "to put you in mind of your affectionate mother"—Sue and Martha send love. Bowdoin is haying yet—we expect him soon—take good care of yourself Austin, we shall all be so happy to see your face at home.

It is late—Goodnight—Vinnie is snoring!

Manuscript: AC. Ink. Dated: Sunday night.
Publication: *Home* 153–155.

48

To Austin Dickinson   20 July 1851

Seems to me you are hardly *fair,* not to send me any letter—I was somewhat disappointed to be thus overlooked—my note from you once a week, had come so very punctually I *did* set my heart on getting a *little something*—even a *word* of love, a *line* not *quite* unmindful, and I had from my heart fully and freely forgiven you, but now I am very angry—you shall not have a tender mercy—as I live saith me, and as my inkstand liveth you shall have no peace until all is fulfilled. If I thought you would *care* any I would hold my tongue so tight that Inquisition *itself* should'nt wring a sentence from me—but t'would only punish *me* who would fain get off *un*punished, therefore *here I am, a'nt* you happy to see me? Since you did'nt write to *me* I pocketed my sorrows, and I hope they are being sanctified to my *future* good—that is to say—I shall "know what to expect, ["] and my "expectations will *not* be realized," you will pardon the freedom I use with your remarks. How it made us laugh—Poor little Sons of Erin—I should think they would rue the day that ever you

[124]

came among them. Oh how I wish I could see your world and it's little kingdoms, and I wish I could see the King — Stranger — he was my *Brother*! I fancy little boys of several little sizes, some of them clothed in *blue* cloth, some of them clad in *gray* — I seat them round on benches in the schoolroom of my mind — then I set them all to shaking — on peril of their lives that they move their lips or whisper — then I clothe you with authority and empower you to punish, and to enforce the law, I call you "Rabbi – Master," and the picture is complete! It would seem very funny, say for Susie and me to come round as Committee — we should enjoy the terrors of 50 little boys and any specimens of *discipline* in your way would be a rare treat for us. I should love to know how you managed — whether government as a *science* is laid down and executed, or whether you *cuff and thrash* as the occasion dictates — whether you use *pure law* as in the case of *commanding*, or whether you *enforce* it by means of sticks and stones as in the case of *agents* — I suppose you have authority bounded but by their lives, and from a remark in one of your earliest letters I was led to conclude that on a certain occasion you *hit the boundary line*! I should think you'd be tired of school and teaching and such hot weather, I really wish you were *here* and the Endicot school where you *found* it — whenever we go to ride in our beautiful family carriage, we think if "wishes were horses" we *four* "beggars would ride." We shall enjoy brimfull everything *now* but *half* full, and to have you home once more will be like living *again!*

We are having a pleasant summer — without one of the five it is yet a *lonely* one — Vinnie says sometimes — Did'nt we have a *brother* — it seems to me we *did* — his name was Austin — we call, but he answers not again — Echo — where is Austin — laughing — "where *is* Austin"? I do hope you'll be careful so as to come home *well*. I wish they need not *exhibit* just for once in the year, and give you up on *Saturday* instead of the next week Wednesday, but keep your courage up and show forth those Emerald Isles till School Committees and Mayors are *blinded* with the dazzling! Would'nt I love to be there with certain *friends* of mine — *Toilet Cushions*, and *"Carpets,"* &c, is what I mean! If this should seem *obscure* let me recommend *West St* as an appropriate "Pony" together with *other* ponies, such as Mr and Mrs Cutler! Susie is at home – Martha is in Burlington seeing a friend of her's. I see more of Susie than of any other girl. She said the last time I saw her, she had'nt had a "talk since Austin went away" — she and Martha too seem to miss you much, and talk a great deal of seeing you. Abby Wood has gone to visit Miss Peck in New Haven — the rest of the girls are at home. Sprague's *shop* was set on fire one night last week, and came very near burning up — the roof was burnt off, and it met some other injuries — a process is going on to find out the offenders. John Emerson has come, and has entered himself as a student in Father's office — he carries about the sail of a good sized British vessel, when he has oped his mouth I *think* no dog has barked. Root spent with us Friday evening — inquired for you with interest, and said he'd be glad to see you.

Our apples are ripening fast — I am fully convinced that with *your* approbation they will not only *pick themselves*, but arrange one another in baskets, and present themselves to be eaten.

Love from all to all there — to *Joel* — hope he is better.

Emilie.

Mother and Vinnie send their love. We all want to see you. Mrs S. E. Mack, and Mrs James Parsons want to see you. John Sanford acts like a simpleton since he got the valedictory, he is so delighted, he dont know what to do.

MANUSCRIPT: AC. Ink. Dated: Sunday Evening.
PUBLICATION: L (1894) 83–85, in part; L (1931) 83–84, in part; *Home* 155–157, entire.
Cornelia (Nellie) Peck later married J. Howard Sweetser. The wheelwright shop of Sprague and Perkins burned on 15 July. John Emerson was an admirer of Eliza Coleman.

49

To Austin Dickinson 27 *July 1851*

"I will never desert Micawber" however *he may* be forgetful of the "Twins" and me, I promised the Rev Sir to "cherish" Mr Micawber, and cherish him I *will*, tho Pope or Principality, endeavor to drive me from it — the "Twins" cling to him *still* — it would quite break his heart abandoned tho' he be, to hear them talk about him. Twin *Martha* broke her heart and went to the Green Mountain, from the topmost cliff of which she flings the *pieces* round. Twin *Susan* is more calm, tho' in *most deep* affliction. You'd better not come home, I say the *law* will have you, a *pupil* of the law, o'ertaken *by* the law, and brought to "condign punishment" — scene for angels and men — or rather for *Archangels* who being a little *higher* would seem to have a 'vantage so far as view's concerned! *"Are* you pretty comfortable tho," and are you deaf and dumb and gone to the asylum where such afflicted persons learn to hold their tongues?

The next time you a'nt going to write me I'd thank you to let me know — this kind of *protracted* insult is what no man can bear — fight with me like a man — let me have fair shot, and you are "caput mortuum" et "cap a pie," and that ends the business! If you really think I so deserve this silence tell me why — how — I'll be a *thorough* scamp or else I wont be *any,* just which you prefer!

[Horace] Taylor of Spencer's class went to Boston yesterday, it was in my heart to send an *apple* by him for your private use, but Father overheard some of my intentions and said they were "rather small" — whether this remark was intended for the *apple,* or for my noble self I did not think to ask him — I rather think he intended to give us *both* a cut — however, he may go!

You are coming home on Wednesday, as perhaps you know, and I am very happy in prospect of your coming, and hope you want to see us as much as we do you. Mother makes nicer pies with reference to your coming, I arrange my tho'ts in a convenient shape, Vinnie grows only *perter* and *more* pert day by day.

The Horse is looking finely, better than in his life, by which you may think him *dead* unless I add *before.* The carriage stands in state all covered in the chaise-house — we have *one foundling hen* into whose young mind I seek to instill the fact that "Massa is a comin!" The garden is amazing — we have beets and beans, have had *splendid potatoes* for three weeks now. Old Amos weeds and hoes and has an oversight of all thoughtless vegetables. The apples are fine and large in spite of my impression that *Father* called them "small."

Yesterday there was a *fire* — at about 3. in the afternoon Mr Kimberly's barn was discovered to be on fire — the wind was blowing a gale directly from the west, and having had no rain, the roofs [were] as dry as stubble. Mr Palmer's house was cleared — the *little house* of Father's, and Mr Kimberly's also. The engine was broken and it seemed for a little while as if the whole street must go. The Kimberly barn was burnt down, and the house much charred and injured, tho not at all destroyed. Mr Palmer's barn took fire and Dea Leland's also, but were extinguished with only part burned roofs. We all feel very thankful at such a narrow escape. Father says there was never such imminent danger, and such miraculous escape. Father and Mr Frink took charge of the fire, or rather of the *water*, since fire *usually* takes care of *itself*. The men all worked like heroes, and after the fire was out Father gave commands to have them march to Howe's where an entertainment was provided for them — after the whole was over, they gave "three cheers for Edward Dickinson, and three more for the Insurance Company"!

On the whole it is very wonderful that we did'nt all burn up, and we ought to hold our tongues and be very thankful. If there *must be* a fire I'm sorry it couldnt wait until you had got home, because you seem to enjoy such things so very much.

There is nothing of moment now which I can find to tell you except a case of measles in Hartford. The Colemans were here last week, passed a night here – they came to get John Emerson to travel with Wm Flint. John went to Monson Saturday, and starts with Wm Flint for the White Mts today.

This is one more feather in the Valedictorian's cap, I guess he thinks he will certainly have her now — I mean will have *Eliza*. If *I* loved a girl to disstraction, I think it would take some coaxing before I would act as footman to her crazy friends – yet love is *pretty solemn*. I dont know as I blame John. He is going to be Tutor next year. Vinnie and I made Currant Wine one day last week, I think it will suit you finely.

You remember James Kellogg's Dogs — the one they kept for a watch dog was poisoned by someone and died last week. Chauncey Russell, Frank Pierce, and George Cutler are somewhere on the coast catching fur and fishes, but principally the *former*. Perhaps they have called on you during their travels sometime tho' I dont know their route exactly. Would'nt I love to take a peep at Old Fanueil and all the little Irish, the day of the city fair?

Goodbye Sir — Fare you well, my benison to your school.

The folks all send their love. My compliments to Joel.

MANUSCRIPT: AC. Ink. Dated Sunday night. Envelope addressed: Austin Dickinson./Care of Loring Norcross Esq./Boston./Mass.

PUBLICATION: L (1894) 109–111, in part; L (1931) 104–106, in part; *Home* 157–159, entire.

The houses on the east side of the common were close together, and a fire in one endangered a large section. According to the records of the Hampshire County registry of deeds, Edward Dickinson purchased from Nathan Dickinson, 16 March 1840, a house on the east side of the common. William Flynt, a cousin from Monson, had been ill. Henry Frink was landlord of the newly opened Hygeian Hotel (American House).

50

To Abiah Root   *19 August 1851*

"Yet a little while I am with you, and again a little while and I am *not* with you" because you go to your mother! Did she not tell me saying, "yet a little while ye shall see me and again a little while and ye shall *not* see me, and I would that where I am, there *ye* may be also" – but the virtue of the text consists in *this* my dear – that "if I *go*, I *come* again, and ye shall be with me where I *am*;" that is to say, that if you come in *November* you shall be mine, and I shall be thine, and so on "vice versa" until "ad infinitum" which isn't a *great* way off! While I think of it my dear friend, and we are upon these subjects, allow me to remark that you have the funniest manner of popping into town, and the most *lamentable* manner of popping *out* again of any one I know.

It really becomes to me a matter of serious moment, this propensity of your's concerning your female friends – the "morning cloud and the early dew" are not more evanescent.

I think it was *Tuesday evening* that we were so amused by the oratorical feats of three or four young gentlemen – I remember I sat by you and took great satisfaction in such seat and society – I remember further our mutual Goodnights, our promises to meet again, to tell each other tales of our own heart and life, to seek and find each other after so long a time of distant separation – I can hardly realize Abiah that these are *recollections*, that our happy *today* joins the great band of *yesterdays* and marches on to the dead – too quickly *flown* my

[129]

Bird, for me to satisfy me that you *did* sit and sing beneath my chamber window! I only went out *once* after the time I saw you — the morning of Mr Beecher, I looked for you in vain – I discovered your Palmer cousins, but if you indeed were *there* it must have been in a form to my gross sense impalpable. I was *disappointed* Abiah – I had been hoping much a little visit from you – when will the hour *be* that we shall sit together and talk of what we were, and what we *are* and may be — with the shutters *closed,* dear Abiah and the balmiest little breeze stealing in at the window? I *love* those little fancies, yet I would love them *more* were they not *quite so fanciful* as they have seemed to be – I have fancied so many times and so many times gone home to find it was *only* fancy that I am half afraid to *hope* for what I *long* for. It would seem my dear Abiah that out of all the moments crowding this little world a *few* might be vouchsafed to spend with those we love — a *separated* hour — an hour more pure and true than *ordinary* hours, when we could *pause* a moment before we journey on – we had a *pleasant* time talking the other morning – had I known it was *all my portion,* mayhap I'd *improved* it more – but it never'll come back again to try whether or no. Dont you think sometimes these brief imperfect meetings have a tale to tell – perhaps but for the sorrow which accompanies *them* we would not be reminded of brevity and change – and would build the dwelling *earthward* whose site is in the skies – perhaps the treasure *here* would be *too dear* a treasure – could'nt "the moth corrupt, and the thief break thro' and steal" – and this makes me think how I *found* a little moth in my stores the other day — a very *subtle* moth that had in ways and manners to me and mine unknown, contrived to hide itself in a favorite worsted basket – how long my little treasurehouse had furnished an arena for it's destroying labors it is not *mine* to tell – it had an *errand* there – I trust it fulfilled it's mission; it taught me dear Abiah to have no treasure *here,* or rather it tried to tell me in it's little mothy way of another *enduring* treasure, the robber cannot steal which, nor time waste away. How many a lesson learned from lips of such tiny teachers – dont it make you think of the Bible – "not many mighty – not wise"?

You met our dear Sarah Tracy after I saw you here – her sweet face is the same as in those happy school days – and in vain I search for wrinkles brought on by many cares – we all love Sarah dearly, and shall try to do all in our power to make her visit happy. Is'nt it very remarkable that in so many years Sarah has changed so little – not that she has stood still, but has made such *peaceful* progress – her thot's tho' they are *older* have all the charm of youth – have not yet lost their freshness, their innocence and peace – she seems so pure in heart – so sunny and serene, like some sweet Lark or Robin ever soaring and singing – I have not seen her much – I want to see her more – she speaks often of *you*, and with a warm affection – I hope no change or time shall *blight* these loves of ou[r]'s, I would bear them all in my arms to my home in the glorious heaven and say "here am I my Father, and those whom thou hast given me." If the life which is to come is better than dwelling *here*, and angels are there and our friends are glorified and are singing there and praising there need we fear to go – when spirits beyond *wait* for us – I was meaning to see you more and talk about such things with you – I want to know your views and your *eternal* feelings – how things *beyond* are to you – Oh there is much to speak of in meeting one you love, and it always seems to me that I might have spoken more, and I almost always think that what *was* found to say might have been left unspoken.

Shall it *always* be so Abiah – is there no *longer* day given for our communion with the spirits of our love? – writing is brief and fleeting – conversation will come again, yet if it *will*, it hastes and must be on it's way – earth is short Abiah, but Paradise is *long* there must be many moments in an eternal day – then *sometime we* shall tarry, while time and tide *roll on*, and till then Vale!

Your own dear

Emilie

MANUSCRIPT: HCL (ARS 9). Ink. Dated: Tuesday Evening.
PUBLICATION: L (1894) 53–57, in part; L (1931) 46–50, in part.
ED had seen Abiah unexpectedly during commencement activities on 12 August. Next morning Henry Ward Beecher delivered an address on "Imagination." Graduation was held on Thursday. Probably this letter was written the following Tuesday. The first quotation recalls John 16.16; the second, Matthew 6.19; the third, I Corinthians 1.26. The last, from John 17.24, is also quoted in letter no. 785.

51

To Austin Dickinson   *Boston, 8 September 1851*

You are very thoughtful Austin to make so many plans for our pleasure and happiness, and yet it is so hot we hardly feel like going out. We had a very pleasant evening, and will tell you something when you come. Will you come after school this morning? It seems a great while since we've seen you. We are very warm indeed, but quite happy — we will be very much so if you will be sure to come. Vinnie and I like your friend very much.

You must'nt feel disappointed for yourself or for us, because it is so hot that we dont think we can come — it will be cooler sometime. Vinnie is comfortable — did you rest well last night, and have a nice breakfast this morning.

Sure to come!

Emily

Fanny sends her love

MANUSCRIPT: AC. Pencil. Addressed on the fold: Austin Dickinson./ Endicot school.

PUBLICATION: *Home* 163.

In September Emily and Lavinia made their long anticipated visit to Boston, staying with the Norcrosses from 6 to 26 September. This note, written then, was delivered by hand at the school. Fanny Norcross was now four years old.

52

To Austin Dickinson   *23 September 1851*

We have got home, dear Austin — it is very lonely here — I have tried to make up my mind which was better — home, and parents, and country; or city, and smoke, and dust, shared with the only being I can call my Brother — the scales dont poise very evenly, but so far as I can judge, the balance is in your favor. The folks are much more lonely than while we were away — they say they seemed to feel that we were straying together, and together would return, and the *un-attended* sisters seemed very sad to them. They had been very well indeed, and got along very nicely while we were away. When Father was gone at night, Emeline [Kellogg] stayed with mother. They have had a number of friends to call, and visit with them. Mother never was busier than while we were away — what with fruit, and plants, and chickens, and sympathizing friends, she really was so hurried she hardly knew what to do.

Vinnie and I came safely, and met with no mishap — the boquet was not withered, nor was the bottle cracked. It was fortunate for the freight car, that Vinnie and I were there, our's being the only baggage passing along the line. The folks looked very funny, who travelled with us that day — they were dim and faded like folks passed away — the conductor seemed so grand with about *half a dozen* tickets, which he dispersed, and demanded in a very small space of time — I judged that the *minority* were travelling that day, and could'nt hardly help smiling at our ticket friend, however sorry I was at the small amount of people, passing along his way. He looked as if he wanted to make an apology for not having more travellers to keep him company.

The route and the cars seemed strangely — there were no boys with fruit, there were no boys with pamphlets — one fearful little fellow ventured into the car with what appeared to be publications and tracts — he offered them to no one, and no one inquired for them, and he seemed greatly relieved that no one wanted to buy them.

At Sunderland, we happened to think that we might find John Thompson, and find John Thompson we did, just sitting down to dinner — he seemed overjoyed to see us — wants very much to see you — asked many questions about yourself and school, all of which we answered in a most glowing manner, and John's countenance fell — we asked him if he was happy — "why, *pretty* happy" — they promised him "35." according to his own story — only 25. of whom have yet made their appearance — he thinks he will not stay more than half a term, and wonders "how in the world" you contrived to be so happy, and like Sunderland people so exceedingly well. He says he has no plan, should he not remain there — seems to be somewhat sober at the little he finds to do — studies law in his leisure. "The Elder" had gone to dinner — Mr Russell was there, seemed quite pleased to see us for our brother's sake — he asked us all about you, and expressed his sincere pleasure in your present prosperity — "wished they had had you *there*," when Thompson was not present! There has been nothing said about Mr

[133]

Russell lately, as Landlord of the Hygeian — Frink is there himself, and seems to like it well, and probably will keep it, I judge from what they say. They have a great deal of company, and everything goes on well.

You wanted us to tell you about the Pelham Picnic — the folks did'nt know that there had ever been any, so I cannot give you any information there. I suspect if there *was* a party, it was composed of persons whom none of us know. Calvin Merrill is married, you *know* — he had a great wedding party at the residence of his bride, the blooming Mrs Benjamin — Tim Henderson and "suite," and Cotton Smith and suite were among the guests, and were suitably honored. Mr Merrill resides with the recent *Mrs* Merrill, alias Mrs Benjamin, *more* alias, Mrs Thompson — for the sake of the widowed lady for the third time a *bride*. I hope her buried Lords are buried very low, for if on some fine evening they should fancy to *rise* I fear their couple of angers might accompany them, and exercise themselves on grooms who erst were widowers, and widows who are brides.

Bowdoin has gone home on account of his eye — he has'nt been able to use it since we went away — the folks are afraid he will never have the use of it — he dont know when he'll come back — probably not, till it gets well, which we fear may not soon be — at present his father is sick — pretty sick with the dysentery. Howland is here with father — will stay a while I guess. They go to Northampton together, as it is court there now and seem very happy together in the law. Father likes Howland grandly, and they go along as smoothly as friendly barks at sea — or when harmonious stanzas become one melody. Howland was here last evening — is jolly and just as happy — really I cant think now what *is* so happy as he. He wants to see you, says he is going to write you. Sanford is in town, but as yet we hav'nt seen him. Nobody knows what the fellow is here for.

You remember [John] Lord the Historian who gave some lectures here — he has come round again, and is lecturing now on the "Saints and Heroes." He gives them at the chapel — I guess all of us shall go — tho' we were too tired last evening. Prof Jewett has come and is living with his wife east of Gen Mack and *his* wife. Pretty perpendicular times, I guess, in the ancient mansion. I am glad we dont come home as we used, to this old castle. I could fancy that skeleton cats ever caught spectre rats in dim old nooks and corners, and when I hear the query concerning the pilgrim fathers — and imperturbable Echo merely answers *where*, it becomes a satisfaction to know that they are there, sitting stark and stiff in Deacon Mack's mouldering arm chairs. We had'nt been home an hour, when Martha came to see us — she was here on Saturday after the stage came in, and was dreadfully disappointed because we did not come. She has'nt changed a bit, and I love her dearly. She was so indignant about her sweet boquet — she said it was kind and fragrant, and would have comforted you in the first few days of exile. I showed her all my treasures — I opened the little box containing the scented beads — I tried it on my wrist, she exclaimed it was how beautiful — then I clasped it on her own, and while she praised it's workmanship and turned it o'er and o'er, I told her it was her's, and you did send it to her — then that sweet face grew radiant, and joyful that blue eye, and Martha seemed so happy to know you'd tho't of her, it would have made you happy — *I* know! She said she should write you — if she has not, she will directly — she has had a letter from Sue — she is situated very pleasantly, and tells her sisters here that she can see no reason why she should not be happy — they are very kind to her — she loves some of her scholars. I hav'nt seen Martha long enough to ask but a very little, but I will find out everything before I write again. It has rained very hard all day, it has been "dark and dreary" and winds "are never weary."

Mother has three shirts which she is going to send you besides the ones we bro't — also a pair of bosoms which her forgetful son failed to carry away. She will send you the whole by the first good opportunity, and we shall send some fruit as soon as we have a chance. It is beautiful — *beautiful!!* Mother sends much love and Vinnie.

Your lonely

Sister Emily

Father has just home come, having been gone today. I have therefore not till now got a glimpse of your letter. Sue's address is, Care of Mr Archer — 40. Lexington St. I will keep the note till I see, or send, to Bowdoin. I answer all the questions in your note but *one — that* I cannot do till they let you come home — that will be *soon,* dear Austin — do not despair — we're "with you alway, even unto the end"! Tho' absence be not for "the present, joyous, but grievous, ["] it shall work out for us a far more exceeding and "eternal weight" of *presence!*

Give our love to our Boston friends — tell them we are well and got home very nicely. Vinnie found the shawls very comfortable and thanks them much for them.

Speaking of *fireworks*, tell Joe we wont ever forget him – *forget him? – never – "*let April tree forget to bud" – etc!

Will Aunt Lavinia sometime tell Mrs Greely how beautifully the boquet came, and how much it has been admired?

You may if you would like, remember both of your sisters to Misses Knight, and French, also tell Mr Nurse we are very sorry for him!

MANUSCRIPT: AC. Ink. Dated: Tuesday Evening. Envelope addressed: Wᵐ Austin Dickinson./Care of Joel Norcross./Boston./Mass. Postmarked: Amherst Ms./Sep 24.

PUBLICATION: L (1894) 87–89, in part; LL 160–161, in part; L (1931) 86–87, in part; *Home* 165–168, entire.

On the journey home from Boston the girls traveled by the Vermont & Massachusetts Railroad to Grout's Corner (Miller's Falls) and then fifteen miles by stage, through Sunderland. John Thompson, whom they saw there, had taken Austin's place as teacher in the Sunderland school. To support herself, Susan Gilbert left Amherst in September against family opposition to teach at a private school in Baltimore, conducted by Robert Archer.

53

To Austin Dickinson   *1 October 1851*

We are just thro' dinner, Austin, I want to write so much that I omit digestion, and a *dyspepsia* will probably be the result. I want to see you more than I ever did before – I should have written again, before I got your letter, but thought there might be something which I should love to tell you, or if you should ask any questions I would want to answer those. I received what you wrote, at about 2½ oclock yesterday. Father brought home the same, and waited himself in order to have me read it – I reviewed the contents hastily – striking out all suspicious places, and then very *artlessly* and unconsciously began. My heart went "pit a pat" till I got safely by a remark concerning Martha, and my stout heart was *not* till the manuscript was over. The allusion to Dick Cowles' grapes, followed by a sarcasm on Mr Adams' tomatoes, amused father highly. He quite *laid it to heart,* he thot, it was so funny. Also the injunction concerning the college tax, father took occasion to say was "quite characteristic."

You say we must'nt trouble to send you any fruit, also your clothes must give us no uneasiness. I dont ever want to have you say any more such things. They make me feel like crying. If you'd only *teased* us for it, and declared that you *would* have it, I should'nt have cared so much that we could find no way to send you any, but you resign so cheerfully your birthright of purple grapes, and do not so much as *murmur* at the departing peaches, that I hardly can taste the one or drink the juice of the other. They are so *beautiful* Austin — we have such an *abundance* "while *you* perish with hunger."

I do hope someone will make up a mind to go before our peaches are quite gone. The world is full of people travelling *everywhere,* until it occurs to you that you will send an errand, and then by "hook or crook" you cant find any traveller, who for money or love can be induced to go and convey the opprobrious package! It's a very selfish age, that is all I can say about it! Mr storekeeper Sweetser has been "almost persuaded" to go, but I believe he has put it off "till a more convenient season," so to show my disapprobation, I shant buy any more gloves at Mr. Sweetser's store! Dont you think it will seem very cutting to see me pass by his goods, and purchase at Mr Kellogg's? I dont think I shall *retract* should he regret his course, and decide to go *tomorrow,* because it is the *"principle"* of disappointing people, which I disapprove!

You must not give it up, but that you will *yet* have some, there *may* be some good angel passing along your way, to whom we can entrust a snug little bundle — the peaches are very large — one side a *rosy* cheek, and the other a *golden,* and that peculiar coat of velvet and of down, which makes a peach so beautiful. The grapes too are fine, juicy, and *such* a purple — I fancy the robes of kings are not a *tint* more royal. The vine looks like a kingdom, with ripe round grapes for kings, and hungry mouths for subjects — the first instance on record of subjects devouring kings! You *shall* have some grapes dear Austin, if I have to come on foot in order to bring them to you.

The apples are very fine — it is'nt quite time to pick them — the cider is almost done — we shall have some I guess by Saturday, at *any rate Sunday noon!* The vegetables are not gathered, but will be before very long. The horse is doing nicely, he travels "like a bird," to use a favorite phrase of your delighted mother's. You ask about the leaves — shall I say they are falling? They had begun to fall before Vinnie and I came home, and we walked up the steps through "little brown ones rustling." Martha and I were talking of you the other night, how we wished you were here to see the autumn sun set, and walk and talk with us among the fading leaves.

Martha is very long talking of you and Susie, she seems unreconciled to letting you go away. She is down here most every day — she brings Sue's letters and reads them. It would make you laugh to hear all which she has to tell — she writes in excellent spirits, tho' Martha and I think they are "*unnatural*," we think she is so gay because she feels so badly and fancies we shant know. Susie asks in every letter why she dont hear from you — she says "Emily and Austin were going to write *so soon*, and I'll warrant I wont hear from either of them, for *one while*." I sent her a letter Monday — I hope if you have not written, you *will* do very soon, for Susie is so far off, and wants so much to have you. Martha wants to see you very much indeed, and sends her love to you. Emily Fowler has gone travelling somewhere with her father — New Haven and New York are to be the stopping places. Charlie has yet no school. I suspect he needs *your aid* in passing himself off somewhere. I have smiled a good many times at that fruitful ride to Sunderland, and the blessings and favors which accompanied it, to Charles. Vinnie tells me *she* has detailed the *news* — she reserved the *deaths* for me, thinking I might fall short of my usual letter somewhere. In accordance with her wishes, I acquaint you with the decease of your aged friend — Dea Kingsbury. He had no disease that we know of, but gradually went out. Martha Kingman has been very sick, and is not yet out of danger. Jane Grout is slowly improving, tho' very feeble yet. "Elizy" has been in Boston, she came home Tuesday night. She asked her friends, and they endeavored to find you, but could not.

She says she told you when you were at home that she should go in *October*, and you were coming to see her, but as she changed her mind and went *earlier*, she did not suppose of course, that you would know she was there. She was very sorry not to be able to find you.

Father has written to Monson to have them all come up here and make us a family visit — I hardly think they will come. If they dont, sometime, next week mother means to go to Monson, and make *them*

[138]

a little visit. Bowdoin's eye is better, and he has got back to the office — Howland has gone to Conway – will probably be here again in the course of two or three weeks. Did Vinnie tell you that she went with him to Ware, and how it made a hubbub in the domestic circle?

Emeline and Henry are just learning to say *"we,"* I think they do very well for such "new beginners." There was quite an excitement in the village Monday evening. We were all startled by a violent church bell ringing, and thinking of nothing but fire, rushed out in the street to see. The sky was a beautiful red, bordering on a crimson, and rays of a gold pink color were constantly shooting off from a kind of sun in the centre. People were alarmed at this beautiful Phenomenon, supposing that fires somewhere were *coloring the sky.* The exhibition lasted for nearly 15. minutes, and the streets were full of people wondering and admiring. Father happened to see it among the very first and rang the bell *himself* to call attention to it. You will have a full account from the pen of Mr Trumbell, whom I have not a doubt, was seen with a large lead pencil, a noting down the sky at the time of it's highest glory. Father will write you soon — the day that your letter came with a list of our expenses — he seemed very busy, so I did'nt read *that* part, and his hands have been so full that I have seen no time when I could show it to him — however he knows of all our expenditures, and will make everything right when you next come home — you dont like to have us ever speak of such things, but father wrote to know, and I tho't you might think it strange he should not write about it after your letter came. You will be here now *so soon* — we are impatient for it — we want to see you, Austin, how much I cannot say here.

Your aff
Emily

Your clothes are in beautiful order, everything in waiting to have some way to send. I have heeled the lamb's wool stockings, and now and then repaired some imperfections in the destined shirts — when you *wear* them, you must'nt forget these things. You made us very happy while we were away. Love from all the folks, with a how I do want to see you!

MANUSCRIPT: AC. Ink. Dated: Wednesday noon. Envelope addressed: William Austin Dickinson./Care of Joel Norcross./Boston./Mass. Postmarked: Amherst Ms Oct 2.

PUBLICATION: *L* (1894) 90–93, in part; *LL* 162–164, in part; *L* (1931) 90–92, in part; *Home* 169–172, entire.

An account of the aurora borealis was published in the *Hampshire and Franklin Express* on 3 October. Each of the two Howland brothers, William and George, was for a time a special friend of Lavinia's. Emeline Kellogg and Henry Nash were married four years later. Samuel Kingsbury died, September 27, aged 88. On Jane Grout, see letter no. 60.

54

To Austin Dickinson   *5 October 1851*

I dont know why, dear Austin, there is'nt much to say which will interest you, but somehow I feel bound to let nobody escape me who may by any accident happen to light on *you.*

I take great satisfaction in the consciousness that no one eludes my vigilance, nor can by any means rid themselves of whatever bag or bundle I am disposed to send — and again, Austin, "when the day is dark and drear and the wind is never weary," a slight recollection may be of some avail in lighting the heart up. It is such a day *today* — nothing but rain and shower, and shower after shower of chilly pelting rain. I am at home from meeting on account of the storm and my *slender constitution*, which I assured the folks, would not permit my accompanying them today.

It is Communion Sunday, and they will stay a good while – what a nice time pussy and I have to enjoy ourselves! Just now the sun peeped out. I tell you I chased it back again behind the tallest cloud, it has not my permission to show its face again till after all the meeting, *then* it may shine and shine, for all pussy and I care!

I was glad to hear from you Austin, and again I was very sorry, if you can reconcile a story so inconsistent. Glad to know you were better — better *physically*, but who cares for a *body* whose *tenant* is ill at ease? Give me the aching *body*, and the spirit glad and serene, for if the gem shines on, forget the mouldering casket! I think you are better now — I fancy you *convalescent* during this rainy day. I am sure that long before *this time* that "hour" has passed away, and the "daughter of the dawn" has touched a note more gay, with her slight "rosy fingers." "No Rose but has a thorn," recollect this, dear Austin, and you will derive a faith rosier than *many* roses, which will quite compensate you for now and then a thorn! It expresses *worlds* to me, "some one to see who cares for [you], and for whom you care," and I think I laughed at the phrase "my own selve's company," as conveying a meaning very clear to me. I dont wonder that little room seems small and lonely, and I dont wonder the folks there seem *smaller still* — I *know* they are very little, very small indeed, I know that scores might vanish and nobody would miss them, they fill so small a crevice in a world full of life; how much you feel the need of a companion there. I wish a smiling fortune would send you such an one, but if you talk with no one, you are amassing thoughts which will be bright and golden for those you left at home — *we* meet our friends, and a constant interchange *wastes tho't* and feeling, and we are then obliged to *repair* and *renew* – there is'nt the *brimfull* feeling which one gets *away*.

Why when Vinnie and I came home, we were *rich* in conversation — we were rich in disdain for Bostonians and Boston, and a coffer fuller of *scorn, pity, commisseration*, a miser hardly had.

Sometimes, I am afraid it will hurt you to stay there. I'm afraid the year you teach will become so embittered that all this blessed country cannot wash it away. Oh I hope not — if indeed no joy is added during one long year, I pray that there be no cankers which shall corrode away! I long for this Boston year to fall from out the circle, to perish and flee away, and be forever gone — your being where you are is a *mutual* trial — both yourself, and us, are for the time bereaved — yet your lot is the hardest, in that while *four anticipate*, in *your* case there's but one — we can gather together and say we are very lonely, and it would be so happy if we were all at home — yet one sustains the other — Vinnie and I console and comfort father and mother — I encourage *Vinnie*, Vinnie in turn cheers *me* — but one and alone, you are indeed dependant, in any pensive hour, dependant on *yourself* too, the very one of *all* least likely to sustain you — if it were not *hope*, it would not be *endurance*! Thank God there is *one* bird that singeth for *forever* and builds her nest anew in the boughs of paradise! You will have several friends to see you in the course of the week. Wm Kellogg is going tomorrow — also Ebenezer Burgess of the senior class — Burgess called on Friday evening and offerred to carry anything which we would like to send — he says he shall see you often — I believe he's an Alpha Delta, and I hope you'll be glad to see him, tho' I dont know enough about him to know whether you will or not.

Council Cutler was there last week, and said he would like to see you if he could get time — we told him where you were, but he came Saturday night and we hav'nt yet found out whether he saw you or not. How funny it seems to me to have you live in Boston, and be having calls from our country tradesmen!

Whatever else you forget, Austin, dont cease to remember *Smith*, who made such a plunge at you on a certain evening — keep *his* memory green, whatever else betides! I will use my utmost influence to keep him at home during the rest of your absence, and I'm sure you will wish me well in so needful an enterprise. Vinnie's love. Mother sends her love and your waistcoat, thinking you'll like the one, and quite likely *need* the other. All of the other clothes can go any time after Tuesday.

Your aff Sister

MANUSCRIPT: AC. Ink. Dated: Sunday morning. Envelope addressed: Wm Austin Dickinson./Boston./Mass.

PUBLICATION: L (1894) 90, one sentence only; L (1931) 88–90, in part; *Home* 181–183, entire.

The letter, without stamp or postmark, was delivered by hand, perhaps by Ebenezer Burgess, who is mentioned as the undergraduate who would probably see Austin. The quotation in the second paragraph attempts to recall the opening lines of Longfellow's "The Rainy Day": "The day is cold, and dark, and dreary;/It rains, and the wind is never weary." (See letter no. 36.)

55

To Austin Dickinson   *7 October 1851*

Dear Austin.

Father has just decided to go to Boston. I have no time to write. We send you a few of our grapes — wish they were nicer — wish too we had some peaches. I send one remaining one — only a frost one. It expresses my feelings — that is pretty much all.

Was so glad to hear from you — even a word is valued.

I know how busy you are, I dont think it strange not to hear more. Howland was here yesterday. Gone today. Thompson was here Saturday — drank tea with us — dont mean to teach in Sunderland after this week. I have tried Dr Jackson's prescription and find myself better for it. I have used it all up now, and wish you would get me some more at the same place if you can. Father has the Recipe, and will give it to you. I should like to have you get *three or four* times the quantity contained in the Recipe, as it is so good an opportunity, and I think it benefits me much. Martha sends her love — is well. Bowdoin is better and back again. Spencer is very sick, and will probably not live long.

You will be here soon dear Austin, and then away with my pen. Dont get sick these cool days when fevers are around! Vinnie's love — not that she cares particularly about *seeing* Edmund Converse, but after what was said, she only wanted to be polite, that's all. Our regards to Mr McCurdy, if you are a mind to give them. Love —

Emily

Manuscript: AC. Pencil. Dated: Tuesday noon. Lavinia has added a note on the same sheet.
Publication: *Home* 183–184.
The girls had not met Edmund W. Converse, a Boston acquaintance of Austin's, when they visited Austin in September. John Laurens Spencer died, 12 October 1851, aged 33.

56

To Susan Gilbert (Dickinson)   *9 October 1851*

I wept a tear here, Susie, on purpose for *you* — because this "sweet silver moon" smiles in on me and Vinnie, and then it goes so far before it gets to you — and then you never told me if there *was* any moon in Baltimore — and how do *I* know Susie — that you see her sweet face at all? She looks like a fairy tonight, sailing around the sky in a little silver gondola with stars for gondoliers. I asked her to let me ride a little while ago — and told her I would *get out* when she got as far as Baltimore, but she only smiled to herself and went sailing on.

I think she was quite ungenerous – but I have learned the lesson and shant ever ask her again. To day it rained at home – sometimes it rained so hard that I fancied you could hear it's patter – patter, patter, as it fell upon the leaves – and the fancy pleased me so, that I sat and listened to it – and watched it earnestly. *Did* you hear it Susie – or was it *only* fancy? Bye and bye the sun came out – just in time to bid us goodnight, and as I told you sometime, the moon is shining now.

It is such an evening Susie, as you and I would walk and have such pleasant musings, if you were only here – perhaps we would have a "Reverie" after the form of "Ik Marvel," indeed I do not know why it would'nt be just as charming as of that lonely Bachelor, smoking his cigar – and it would be far more profitable as "Marvel" *only* marvelled, and you and I would *try* to make a little destiny to have for our own. Do you know that charming man is dreaming *again,* and will wake pretty soon – so the papers say, with *another* Reverie – more beautiful than the first?

Dont you hope he will live as long as you and I do – and keep on having dreams and writing them to us; what a charming old man he'll be, and how I envy his grandchildren, little "Bella" and "Paul"! We will be willing to die Susie – when such as *he* have gone, for there will be none to interpret these lives of our's.

Longfellow's "golden Legend" has come to town I hear – and may be seen *in state* on Mr. Adams' bookshelves. It always makes me think of "Pegasus in the pound" – when I find a gracious author sitting side by side with "Murray" and "Wells" and "Walker" in that renowned store – and like *him* I half expect to hear that they have *"flown"* some morning and in their native ether revel all the day; but for our sakes dear Susie, who please ourselves with the fancy that we are the only poets, and everyone else is *prose,* let us hope they will yet be willing to share our humble world and feed upon such aliment as *we* consent to do!

You thank me for the Rice cake – you tell me Susie, you have just been tasting it – and how happy I am to send you anything you love – how hungry you must grow before it is noon there – and then you must be faint from teaching those stupid scholars. I fancy you very often descending to the schoolroom with a plump Binomial Theorem struggling in your hand which you must dissect and exhibit to your incomprehending ones – I hope you whip them Susie – for *my* sake

[144]

–whip them *hard* whenever they dont behave just as you want to have them! I know they are very dull – sometimes – from what Mattie says – but I presume you encourage them and forgive all their mistakes. It will teach you *patience* Susie – you may be sure of that. And Mattie tells me too of your evening carousals – and the funny frights you give in personating the Master – just like you Susie – like you for all the world – how Mr Payson would laugh if I could only tell him, and then those great dark eyes – how they would glance and sparkle! Susie – have all the fun wh' you possibly can – and laugh as often and sing, for tears are plentier than smiles in this little world of our's; only dont be so happy as to let Mattie and me grow dimmer and dimmer and finally fade away, and merrier maids than we smile in our vacant places!

Susie, *did* you think that I would never write you when you were gone away – what made you? I am sure you know my promise far too well for that – and had I never said so – I should be *constrained* to write – for what shall separate us from any whom we love – not "*hight* nor depth" . . .

MANUSCRIPT: HCL (L 5). Ink. Dated: Thursday Evening. End of letter missing.

PUBLICATION: FF 205–208.

According to ED's letter to Austin of 1 October, she had written to Sue once before, on 29 September. *Reveries of a Bachelor* (1850) by Ik Marvel (Donald G. Mitchell) was a bestseller. Longfellow's *Golden Legend* had recently been published. Lindley Murray, William Harvey Wells, and John Walker were compilers of language texts.

57

To Austin Dickinson   *10 October 1851*

Dear Austin.

Father says he came down upon you so unexpectedly that you hardly had time to recover from your surprise before he was *off again* – he says you were so astonished that you hardly knew what to say – he thinks you are not very well, and I feel so anxious about you that I cannot rest until I have written to you and given you some advice. They say Mr Sweetser is going – he may not and he may. I will conclude to risk him. I am very sorry indeed that your eyes have been so troublesome. I really hope they are better and will trouble you no more. You ought to be very careful about using them *any* now – I do not care if you *never* write me a letter, if you'll only spare your eyes until they have got better. I would not spend much strength upon those little school boys – you will need it all for something better and braver, after you get away. It would rejoice my heart, if on some pleasant morning you'd turn the schoolroom key on Irish boys – *Nurse* and all, and walk away to freedom and the sunshine here at home. Father says all Boston would not be a temptation to you another year – I wish it would not tempt you to stay another day. Oh Austin, it is wrong to tantalize you so while you are braving *all things* in trying to fulfill duty. Duty is black and brown – home is bright and shining, "and the spirit and the bride say *come*, and let him that" wandereth come – for "behold all things are ready"! We are having such lovely weather – the air is as sweet and still, now and then a gay leaf falling – the crickets sing all day long – high in a crimson tree a belated bird is singing – a thousand little painters are ting[e]ing hill and dale. I admit *now*, Austin, that autumn is *most* beautiful, and spring is but the least – yet they "differ as *stars*" in their distinctive glories. How happy if you were here to share these pleasures with us – the fruit should be more sweet, and the dying day more golden – merrier the falling nut, if with you we gathered it and hid it down deep in the abyss of basket; but you complain not – wherefore do we? I had a long letter from Sue last Tuesday evening and Mat had one that day and came down here to read it – we had a beautiful time reading about Susie and talking of [*words erased*] the good times of last summer – and we anticipated – boasted ourselves of tomorrow [*one line erased*] the future we created, and all of us went to ride in an air bubble for a carriage. We have made all our plans for you and us [*words erased*] in another year – we cherish all the past – we glide adown the present, awake, yet dreaming, but the *future* of ours *together* – there the birds sing *loudest*, and the sun shines *always* there.

Martha and I are very much together – we fill each niche of time with statues of you and Sue and in return for this, they smile beautiful smiles down from their dwelling places. Martha wears the charm when she goes out calling, and many a eulogium is passed upon your gift. Sue says in her letter she has had a "brief letter from you" –

[146]

wont you write her a longer? Father says you wear a white hat, cocked up at the sides — know I shall like it's looks and want so much to see it — as for the *wearer*, I want to see him too — but which the *most*, prithee?

Father says you ate little dinner when you dined with him — he did'nt know whether you were not hungry, or whether it was *astonishment* at encountering him — I *hope* the latter. You must get better fast — we shall have a busy day for you on Cattle Show day. We have had some sweet cider — I drank your health. I thank you for the vial. I had a dissertation from Eliza Coleman a day or two ago — dont know which was the author — Plato, or Socrates — rather think Jove had a finger in it. Abby Wood has not come — Emerson and Dickinson have been threatened with fevers, but are better now. Spencer is still alive, but cannot linger long. He is sick at Dea Haskell's — his mother is here. Mother came home yesterday — had a pleasant visit at Monson. They all send their love. Vinnie sends her's. How soon you will be here! Days, flee away — "lest with a whip of *scorpions* I overtake your lingering!"

I am in a hurry — this pen is too slow for me — "it hath done what it could."

Your aff

Emily

MANUSCRIPT: AC. Ink. Dated: Friday morning. Envelope addressed: William Austin Dickinson./Care of Joel Norcross./31 — Milk St./Boston./Mass./Mr Sweetser./[*in another hand*: American House].

PUBLICATION: L (1894) 93–95, in part; L (1931) 92–93, in part; *Home* 184–186, entire.

The passages dealing with Sue were at some time badly mutilated. For the quoted lines near the end, see letter no. 17.

58

To Austin Dickinson   *17 October 1851*

We are waiting for breakfast, Austin, the meat and potato and a little pan of your favorite brown bread are keeping warm at the fire, while father goes for shavings.

While we were eating supper Mr Stephen Church rang the door

bell very violently and offerred to present us with *three barrels of shavings*. We are much overcome by this act of magnanimity and father has gone this morning to claim his proffered due. He wore a palm leaf hat, and his pantaloons tucked in his boots and I could'nt help thinking of *you* as he strode along by the window.

I dont think "neglige" quite becoming to so mighty a man. I had rather a jacket of green and your barndoor apparrel, than all the mock simplicity of a lawyer and a man. The breakfast is so warm and pussy is here a singing and the teakettle sings too as if to see which was loudest and I am so afraid lest kitty should be beaten — yet a *shadow* falls upon my morning picture — where is the youth so bold, the bravest of our fold, a seat is empty here — spectres sit in your chair and now and then nudge father with their long, bony elbows. I wish you were here dear Austin — the dust falls on the bureau in your deserted room and gay, frivolous spiders spin away in the corners. I dont go there after dark whenever I can help it, for the twilight seems to pause there and I am half afraid, and if ever I have to go, I hurry with all my might and never look behind me for I know who I should see.

Before next Tuesday — Oh before the coming stage will I not brighten and brush it, and open the long closed blinds, and with a sweeping broom will I not bring each spider down from its home so high and tell it it may come back again when master has gone — and oh I will bid it to be a tardy spider, to tarry on the way, and I will think my eye is fuller than sometimes, tho' *why* I cannot tell, when it shall rap on the window and come to live again. I am so happy when I know how soon you are coming that I put away my sewing and go out in the yard to think. I have tried to delay the frosts, I have coaxed the fading flowers, I thought I *could* detain a few of the crimson leaves until you had smiled upon them, but their companions call them and they cannot stay away — you will find the blue hills, Austin, with the autumnal shadows silently sleeping on them, and there will be a glory lingering round the day, so you'll know autumn has been here, and the *setting sun* will tell you, if you dont get home till evening. How glad I am you are well — you must try hard to be careful and not get sick again. I hope you will be better than ever you were in your life when you come home *this time*, for it never seemed so long since we have seen you. I thank you for such a long letter, and yet if I might choose, *the next* should be a longer. I think a letter just about

three days long would make me happier than any other kind of one —
if you please, dated at Boston, but thanks be to our Father, you may
conclude it *here*. Everything has changed since my other letter — the
doors are shut this morning, and all the kitchen wall is covered with
chilly flies who are trying to warm themselves — poor things, they do
not understand that there are no summer mornings remaining to them
and me and they have a bewildered air which is really very droll,
did'nt one feel *sorry* for them. You would say t'was a gloomy morning
if you were sitting here — the frost has been severe and the few lingering leaves seem anxious to be going and wrap their faded cloaks more
closely about them as if to shield them from the chilly northeast wind.
The earth looks like some poor old lady who by dint of pains has
bloomed e'en till *now*, yet in a forgetful moment a few silver hairs
from out her cap come stealing, and she tucks them back so hastily
and thinks nobody *sees*. The cows are going to pasture and little boys
with their hands in their pockets are whistling to try to keep warm.
Dont think that the sky will frown so the day when you come home!
She will smile and look happy, and be full of sunshine *then* — and
even *should* she frown upon her child returning, there is *another* sky
ever serene and fair, and there is *another* sunshine, tho' it be darkness
there — never mind faded forests, Austin, never mind silent fields —
here is a little forest whose leaf is ever green, here is a *brighter* garden,
where not a frost has been, in its unfading flowers I hear the bright bee
hum, prithee, my Brother, into *my* garden come!

Your very aff
Sister.

MANUSCRIPT: AC. Ink. Dated: Friday morning. Envelope addressed:
Wᵐ Austin Dickinson/Care of Joel Norcross – 31 – Milk St./Boston./Mass.
Postmarked: Amherst Ms. Oct 17. Enclosed with the letter is a slip of paper
to which is attached a pressed leaf, with the note: "We'll meet again as
heretofore some summer's morning."

PUBLICATION: L (1894) 95–97; LL 165–167, in part; L (1931) 93–96;
Home 190–191.

Austin was planning to come to Amherst for the annual "Cattle Show,"
to be held on October 22, and to bring with him his friend Edmund W.
Converse. To many of the people of Amherst the autumn fair was the most
important public event of the year, and the Dickinsons participated fully
in it. On this occasion a dinner was served to two hundred and seventy-

five people at the Amherst House, after which Edward Dickinson gave a history of the Hampshire Agricultural Society. The poem at the end of the letter is printed here, as ED wrote it, in prose form.

59

To Austin Dickinson   *25 October 1851*

Dear Austin.

I've been trying to think this morning how many weeks it was since you went away – I fail in calculations – it seems so long to me since you went back to school that I set down days for years, and weeks for a *score* of years – not reckoning time "by minutes" I dont know what to think of such great discrepancies between the *actual* hours and those which "seem to be." It may seem long to *you* since you returned to Boston – how I wish you could stay and never go back again. Everything is so still here, and the clouds are cold and gray – I think it will rain soon – Oh I am so lonely!

We had a beautiful visit, but it was all too short for we brothers and sisters, and Vinnie and I are dwelling upon the one to come. Thanksgiving is but four weeks, or a little more than four weeks and yet it seems to be a very great way off, when I look forward to it. I have thought you were very sober, since you went away, and I did when you were here, but now you are out of sight, I remember it more frequently, and wonder I did'nt ask you if anything troubled you. I hope you are better now. I waked up this morning, thinking that this was the very morning your eyes were to be well, and I really hope that oculist has'nt broken his promise. You must'nt use them much until they get very strong – you need'nt write to us except on a slip of paper, telling us how you are, and whether you are happy – and I would'nt write at all, until they were perfectly well.

You had a windy evening going back to Boston, and we thought of you many times and hoped you would not be cold. Our fire burned so cheerfully I could'nt help thinking of how many were *here* and how many were *away*, and I wished so many times during that long evening that the door would open and you come walking in. Home is a holy thing – nothing of doubt or distrust can enter it's blessed portals. I feel it more and more as the great world goes on and one and another forsake, in whom you place your trust – here seems indeed to

[150]

be a bit of Eden which not the sin of *any* can utterly destroy — smaller it is indeed, and it may be less fair, but fairer it is and *brighter* than all the world beside. I hope this year in Boston will not impair your health, and I hope you will be as happy as you used to be before. I dont wonder it makes you sober to leave [this] blessed air — if it were in my power I would on every morning transmit it's purest breaths fragrant and cool to you. How I wish you could have it — a thousand little winds waft it to me this morning, fragrant with forest leaves and bright autumnal berries. I would be *willing* to give you my portion for today, and take the salt sea's breath in it's bright, bounding stead. Now Austin — you have no friend there — why not see Converse often, and laugh and talk with *him?* I think him a noble fellow — it seems to me so pleasant for you to talk with somebody, and he is much like you in many thoughts and feelings. I know he would love to have you for a comrade and friend, and I would be with him a good deal if I were you. Mother feels quite troubled about those little boys — fears you will kill one sometime when you are punishing him — for *her sake* be careful! Emily Fowler and Mat were here all afternoon yesterday — never saw Emily F—— when she seemed more sincere — shall go and see her soon — Mat misses *you* so much, and her dear sister Susie. Henry Root was here all evening. Mother's and Vinnie's love. Remember us to Converse — take care of *yourself* —

Your aff
Emily

MANUSCRIPT: AC. Ink. Dated: Saturday noon. Addressed on the fold: For my brother Austin.
PUBLICATION: L (1894) 89–90, in part; L (1931) 87–88, in part; *Home* 193–194, entire.

Austin's visit at home lasted only two days, and he and his friend Converse left on October 23.

60

To Austin Dickinson   *30 October 1851*

Dear Austin.

Something seems to whisper "he is thinking of home this evening," perhaps because it rains — perhaps because it's evening and the orches-

[151]

tra of winds perform their strange, sad music. I would'nt wonder if home were thinking of him, and it seems so natural for one to think of the other — perhaps it is no superstition or omen of this evening — no omen "at all – at all" as Mrs Mack would say.

Father is staying at home the evening is so inclement. Vinnie diverts his mind with little snatches of music, and mother mends a garment to make it snugger for you – and what do you think *I* do among this family circle — I am thinking of you with all my heart and might, and it just occurs to me to note a few of my tho'ts for your own inspection. "Keeping a diary" is not familiar to me as to your sister Vinnie, but her own bright example is quite a comfort to me, so I'll try.

I waked up this morning thinking for all the world I had had a letter from you — just as the seal was breaking, father rapped at my door. I was sadly disappointed not to go on and read, but when the four black horses came trotting into town, and their load was none the heavier by a tiding for me — I was not disappointed then — it was harder to me than had I been disappointed. I have got over it now tho'. I have been thinking all day of how I would break the seal and how gallantly I would read when my letter came, and when it *did'nt* come, I found I had made no provision for any such time as that, but I wont chide you Austin. I know you will write me soon — perhaps your eyes disturb you and will not let you write. I should be unkind to have so much importunity. Dont you wish you were here tonight? — Oh I know *I* wish so, and all the rest of them too. I find I miss you more "when the lamps are lighted," and when the winds blow high and the great angry raindrops clamor against the window. Your room is snug and cozy thro' these chilly evenings — I really hope it is — and I hope the stove is singing the merry song of the wood, and how are the cigars — "pretty comfortable" say, now? The weather has been unpleasant ever since you went away. Monday morning we waked up in the midst of a furious snow storm — the snow was the depth of an inch — oh it looked so wintry — bye and bye the sun came out, but the wind blew violently and it grew so cold that we gathered all the quinces — put up the stove in the sitting room, and bade the world Good bye. Kind clouds came on at evening, still the sinking thermometer gave terrible signs of what would be on the morning — at last the morning came laden with mild south winds, and the winds have brought the rain — so here we are. I hope your eyes are better. I have been feeling anxious since we have heard from you lest they might not be as well and had prevented your writing. Your very hasty letter just at your return rejoiced us — that you were "better — happier — heartier" — what made you think of such beautiful words to tell us how you were, and how cheerful you were feeling? It did us a world of good — how little the scribe thinks of the value of his line — how many eager eyes will search it's every meaning — how much swifter the strokes of "the little mystic clock, no human eye hath seen, which ticketh on and ticketh on, from morning until e'en." If it were not that I could write you — you could not go away, *therefore* —— pen and ink are very excellent things!

We had new *brown bread* for tea — when it came smoking on and we sat around the table, how I did wish a slice could be reserved for you. I fell at once to thinking perhaps *Mrs Reed* had brown bread, and oh I *hoped* she had, and I hoped you were well and hungry so that you could enjoy it. You shall have as many loaves as we have eaten *slices* if you will but come home. This suggests Thanksgiving — you will soon be here — then I cant help thinking of how when we re- joice — so many hearts are breaking, next Thanksgiving day. What will you say, Austin, if I tell you that Jennie Grout and merry Martha King- man will spend the day above? They are not here — "while we delayed to let them forth, angels beyond stayed for them."

It *cannot* be — yet it is so — Jennie Grout was buried yesterday — Martha Kingman died at four o,clock this morning — one and another, and another — how we pass away! Did you know that Merrick in Mr Colton's shop was engaged to Jane Grout? The poor fellow is quite heart broken — he walked to the grave with her parents, and was prayed for as one deeply afflicted in the funeral prayer. I dont know of any one very sick just now. Did you know that *Helen Humphry* was go- ing to be married soon to Mr Stoddard of the "Stoddard and Lathrop" firm — Northampton — it is so! Mother and Vinnie and Martha send you their love. Will you remember us to Mr Converse — will you tell your friend McCurdy how sorry [we were] he could'nt come? Now Austin, mark me, in four weeks from today we are all happy again!

Your aff
Emily

Manuscript: AC. Ink. Dated: Thursday Evening. Envelope addressed: Wm Austin Dickinson./Care of Joel Norcross./31 – Milk St./Boston./ Mass. Postmarked: Amherst Ms Oct 31.

Publication: L (1894) 97–99, in part; LL 168–169, in part; L (1931) 96–97, in part; Home 194–196, entire.

For Mrs. Mack, see Appendix 2. Jane B. Grout died, 27 October 1851, aged 19. A poem, "The Life Clock," translated from the German, was published in the *Hampshire Gazette* (4 August 1846) and in the *Northampton Courier* (14 July 1847). The first stanza reads:

> There is a little mystic clock,
> No human eye hath seen,
> That beateth on and beateth on
> From morning until e'en.

61

To Emily Fowler (Ford) *about 1851*

It has been a long week dear Emily, for I have not seen your face, but I have contrived to think of you very much indeed, which has half reconciled me to not seeing you for so long. I was coming several times, but the snow would start the first, and then the paths were damp, and then a friend would drop in to chat, and the short afternoon was gone, before I was aware. Did Mr Dickinson give you a message from me? He promised to be faithful, but I dont suppose Divines think *earthly* loves of much consequence. My flowers come in *my* stead, today, dear Emily. I hope you will love to see them, and whatever word of love, or welcome kindly, you would extend to *me*, "do even so to *them*." They are small, but *so* full of meaning, if they only mean the *half* of what I bid them.

Very affy,
Emily.

Manuscript: NYPL. Ink. Dated: Saturday noon.
Publication: L (1894) 136; L (1931) 135–136.
The date is conjectured from the handwriting. Delivered by hand, the note is inscribed on the outer fold: Dear Emily. William Cowper Dickinson, here mentioned, was a tutor at Amherst College.

The house on Pleasant Street

The Dickinson homestead

William Austin Dickinson

Susan Huntington Gilbert (Dickinson)

Lavinia Norcross Dickinson

Martha Isabella Gilbert (Smith)

John L. Graves

Elizabeth Chapin Holland

62

To Austin Dickinson   *11 November 1851*

I cant write but a word, dear Austin, because its already noon and Vinnie is waiting to go to the office for me, and yet a *single word* may be of comfort to you as you go travelling on. It should be a word big and warm and full of sweet affection if I could make it so — Oh it should fill that room, that small and lonely chamber with a thousand kindly things and precious ministrations – I wonder if it *will*, for know that if it *does* not, it is bad and disobedient and a most unworthy type of its affectionate mistress! I was to write last night, but company detained me – Martha came this morning and spent the forenoon with us, or I had written more than I'm afraid I *can* now, the time flies so fast. I said to Martha this morning that I was going to write and we decided between us that it would make you happier to have us talk about you and wish you could be here, and write you more again. Mattie sends you her love — she thinks a great deal of you — I enjoy seeing her so much, because we are both bereaved, and can sorrow on together, and Martha loves you, and we both love Susie, and the hours fly so fast when we are talking of you.

I watched the stage coach yesterday until it went away, and I hoped you would turn around, so to be sure and see me – I did'nt mind the rain which sometimes pelted me with a big drop, nor the sharp westerly wind. I only thought to me that should you turn around for a last look at home and I should not be there, I never could forgive me. I thought you saw me once, the way I told was *this*. You know your cap was black, and where it had been black, it all at once grew *white*, and I fancied *that* was *you*.

How lonely it was last night when the chilly wind went down, and the clear, cold moon was shining — it seemed to me I could pack this little earthly bundle, and bidding the world Goodbye, fly away and away, and never come back again to be so lonely here, and then I thought of "Hepzibah" how sorrowful *she* was, and how she longed to sleep, because the grave was peaceful, yet for affection's sake, and for the sake of "Clifford" she wearied on, and bye and bye, kind angels took both of them home, and it seemed almost a lesson, given us to learn. I dont mean that you are *him*, or that Hepzibah's *me* except in a relative sense, only I was reminded.

You are not alone, dear Austin, warm hearts are beating for you, and at mention of your name, brighter beams the eye — you *must not* be despondent — no, Austin, I cannot have you — dont think of the present — the present is unkind, but the future loves you — it sees you a great way off and runs to meet you — "my son was dead, and lives again -- he was lost and is found!" I was thinking of you last night — I dropped asleep thinking of you. Lo, I *dreamed*, and the world was no more *this* world, but a world bright and fair — no fading leaves, no dying friends, and I heard a voice saying there shall be no more tears, neither any crying, and they answered, *nevermore*, and up from a thousand hearts went a cry of praise and joy and great thanksgiving, and I awoke, yet I know the place was heaven, and the people singing songs were those who in their *lifetimes* were parted and separated, and their joy was because they should never be so any more. Good bye, dear Austin, yet why Good bye, are you not with me always — whether I wake or sleep? "And tho *all others* do, yet will not *I* forsake thee"!

Emilie

MANUSCRIPT: AC. Ink. Dated: Tuesday noon. Envelope addressed: Wm Austin Dickinson./Care of Joel Norcross./31 – Milk St. Boston./Mass. Postmarked: Amherst Ms. Nov 11.

PUBLICATION: *Home* 198–199.

Austin came unexpectedly to Amherst to vote on election day, Monday, November 10, and returned to Boston that afternoon. Hawthorne's *The House of the Seven Gables*, in which Clifford Pyncheon and his sister Hepzibah are principal characters, was published in the spring of 1851.

63

To Austin Dickinson   *16 November 1851*

Dear Austin.

We have just got home from meeting — it is very windy and cold — the hills from our kitchen window are just crusted with snow, which with their blue mantillas makes them seem so beautiful. You sat just here last Sunday, where I am sitting now and our voices were nimbler than our pens can be, if they try never so hardly. I should be quite sad today, thinking about last Sunday did'nt another Sabbath smile at me so pleasantly, promising me on it's word to present you here again when "six days work is done."

Father and mother sit in state in the sitting room perusing such papers only, as they are well assured have nothing carnal in them. Vinnie is eating an apple which makes me think of gold, and accompanying it with her favorite [New York] Observer, which if you recollect, deprives us many a time of her sisterly society. Pussy has'nt returned from the afternoon assembly, so you have us all just as we are at present. We were very glad indeed to hear from you so soon, glad that a cheerful fire met you at the door. I *do* well remember how chilly the west wind blew, and how everything shook and rattled before I went to sleep, and I often tho't of you in the midnight car, and hoped you were not lonely. I wished that "Jim" was there to keep you pleasant company, or rather that you were *here*, soundly asleep and adream.

How farcical it seems to sit here a writing, when another Sunday's sun shall shine upon us all in each other's society, and yet thanks to a being inventing paper and pen, they are better far than nothing! By means of them indeed, 'tis little I can tell you, but I can tell how much I would if I could, and there's something comforting in it. We are thinking most of Thanksgiving, than anything else just now — how full will be the circle, less then by none — how the things will smoke, how the board will groan with the thousand savory viands — how when the day is done, Lo the evening cometh, laden with merrie laugh, and happy conversation, and then the sleep and the dream each of a knight or "Ladie" — how I love to see them, a beautiful company, coming down the hill which men call the Future, with their hearts full of joy, and their hands of gladness. Thanksgiving *indeed*, to a family united, once more together before they go away! "Both together" it says, "one taken, the other left."

Col' Kingman's other daughter died yesterday — her funeral is tomorrow. Oh what a house of grief must be their's today — the grass not growing green above the grave of Martha, before little Ellen is laid close beside. I dont know but they are the happier, and we who longer stay the more to be sorrowed for.

Mr [William] Tyler preached this PM — a sermon concerning Spencer, of which you heard us speak when you were here. A beautiful memorial of his life and character, and preached by the request of Spencer's friends in the village. Martha was here on Friday and we had a beautiful hour to sit and talk together. Martha becomes far dearer to me with every week and day — her's is a spirit as beautiful and pure as one will seldom meet in a world like our's, and it is all the lovelier because it is so *rare*. Martha inquired for you, as she never comes *without* doing, and sends the weekly love which I always bring, and which I love to bring, if it makes you happier. I hope you are encouraged since you were at home — *do not* be lonely. Susie is lonely, and Martha, and I am lonely too, and this is a lonely world, in the cheerfullest aspects of it. We will not live here always — but [?] will dwell together beyond the bright blue sky, where "they live whom we call dear." The winter will fly swiftly, then will be the spring — think of nothing but hope — heed nothing but anticipation — "the griefs of the present moment are not to be compared with the joys which are hereafter." Bye and bye you are coming home — so is Susie — so is joy and gladness, which have been staying away just as long as you have. Dont mind the days — some of them are long ones but who cares for length when breadth is in store for him, or who minds the cross, who *knows* he'll have a crown? I wish I could imbue you with all the strength and courage which can be given men — I wish I could assure you of the constant remembrance of those you leave at home — I wish, but Oh how vainly, that I could bring you back again, and never more to stray! You are tired *now* Dear Austin, with my incessant din, but I cant help saying any of these things.

The very warmest love from Vinnie and every one of us. I am *never* ready to go —

Reluctant Emily

Manuscript: AC. Ink. Dated: Sunday afternoon. Envelope addressed: Wᵐ Austin Dickinson./Care of Joel Norcross./Boston./Mass. Postmarked: Amherst Ms. Nov 17.

Publication: L (1894) 100–101, in part; L (1931) 98–99, in part; *Home* 199–201, entire.

Martha Kingman died on October 30, and Ellen on November 15. The last quotation echoes Romans 8.18.

64

To Austin Dickinson   *20 November 1851*

I cant write but a syllable, Austin, my letter ought to be in — it is
2'o'clock even now, but I do want to thank you for what I read last
evening — I want you to know we think of you every morning and
noon, I want to tell you that Father is not at home this week, therefore you do not hear concerning your plans from him. He went to
Greenfield Monday, uncertain whether he'd get home *that* day, or
two days after. We had a letter yesterday saying he will come home
today, and I presume he will write you immediately upon his getting
home. If I am *selfish* Austin, I tell you you *must come home* — it
seems a good many days to take from your little visit, but *you* know
better than I what is best about it. Father will be at Boston, and I
think he seems inclined to have you wait the Convention. I hope and
Vinnie hopes, you wont decide to stay. Are you willing to get me
once more, *two or three times this prescription,* and bring it when you
come? I have seen much of Mattie since you went away — she is here
most every day. Susie has sent me a letter which has been lost on
the way — I have had a note from her this week. So many things to
tell you, but will not write them now — *rather* — *tell* them — dear
Austin, it will be soon!

Love from all and me more
Emily

MANUSCRIPT: AC. Ink. Dated: Thursday noon. Envelope addressed:
Wm Austin Dickinson/Care of Joel Norcross./Boston./Mass. Postmarked:
Amherst Ms Nov 20.
PUBLICATION: *Home* 202.
Edward Dickinson was a delegate to the Whig Convention on Novem-
ber 25. Austin, at his father's desire, stayed in Boston for the occasion, and
went home on November 26, the day before Thanksgiving.

65

To Austin Dickinson   *15 December 1851*

Did you think I was *tardy*, Austin? For two Sunday afternoons,
it has been so cold and cloudy that I did'nt feel in my very happiest

mood, and so I did not write until next monday morning, determining in my heart never to write to you in any but cheerful spirits.

Even this morning Austin, I am not in merry case, for it snows slowly and solemnly, and hardly an outdoor thing can be seen a stirring — now and then a man goes by, with a large cloak wrapped around him and shivering at that, and now and then a stray kitten out on some urgent errand creeps thro' the flakes, and crawls so fast as *may* crawl half frozen away. I am glad for the sake of your body that you are not here this morning, for it is a trying time for fingers and toes, for for the heart's sake, I would verily have you *here* — you know there *are* winter mornings when the cold *without* only adds to the warm *within*, and the more it snows and the harder it blows, brighter the fires blaze, and chirps more merrily the "cricket on the hearth"; it is hardly cheery enough for such a scene this morning, and yet methinks it *would* be if you were only here. The future full of sleighrides would chase the gloom from our minds, which only deepens and darkens with every flake that falls.

Black Fanny would "toe the mark" if you should be here tomorrow, but as the prospects are, I presume Black Fanny's hoofs will not attempt to fly. Do you have any snow in Boston? Enough for a ride, I hope, for the sake of "Auld Lang Syne." Perhaps the "Ladie" of curls, would not object to a drive. So you took Miss Mary to The Mercantile — Vinnie is quite excited about her going to Boston, and things are turning out "just as she expected." Father remarked "he was very glad of it — he thought it would please the *old folks* to have the school master pay respect to their darter." I think that "heavy cold" must be making progress as that devoted family have not yet been seen, or what is *more* suspicious, heard of.

I am glad you like Miss Nichols, it must be so pleasant for you to have somebody to care for, in such a cheerless place — dont shut yourself away from anyone whom you like, in order to keep the faith to those you leave behind! Your friends here are much happier in fancying *you* happy, than if in a pledge so stern you should refuse all friendliness. Truth to the ones you leave does not demand of you to refuse those whom you find, or who would make your exile a less desolate thing in their cheerful circles. On the contrary, Austin, I am very sure that seclusion from everyone there would make an ascetic of you, rather than restore you brighter and truer to *them*. We miss you more and more, we do not become accustomed to separation from you. I almost wish sometimes we need'nt miss you so much, since duty claims a year of you entirely to herself, and then again I think that it is pleasant to miss you if you must go away, and I would not have it otherwise, not even if I could. In every pleasure and pain you come up to our minds so wishfully, we know you'd enjoy our joy, and if you were with us Austin, we could bear little trials more cheerfully — then when we have any dainty, someone is sure to say "it is such as *Austin* loves." When I know of anything funny, I am just as apt to cry, far *more* so than to *laugh*, for I know who *loves jokes best*, and who is not here to enjoy them. We dont *have* many jokes tho' *now*, it is pretty much all sobriety, and we do not have much poetry, father having made up his mind that its pretty much all *real life*. Fathers real life and *mine* sometimes come into collision, but as yet, escape unhurt! I give all your messages to Mat — she seems to enjoy every one more than the one before — she was here three afternoons last week, one evening she took tea here with Abby and Abiah Root, and we had such a pleasant time; how I did wish you were here, and so did all the girls — every one of them spoke of it. Did you know that Jane Humphrey's sister [Martha], that you saw at S. Hadley once was dead? They have sent for Jane to come home, I dont know whether she will, she is so far from home. I am so glad you are well, and in such happy spirits — both happy and well is a great comfort to us when you are far away.

Emilie.

Thank you for the music Austin, and thank you for the books. I have enjoyed them very much. I shall learn my part of the Duett, and try to have Vinnie her's. She is very much pleased with Charity.

She would write you now but is busy getting her lesson.

Mother is frying Doughnuts — I will give you a little platefull to have warm for your tea! *Imaginary* ones — how I'd love to send you *real* ones.

MANUSCRIPT: AC. Ink. Dated: Monday morning. Envelope addressed: Wm Austin Dickinson./Boston./Mass. The letter was delivered by hand.

PUBLICATION: L (1894) 102–104, in part; LL 172–173, in part; L (1931) 100–101, in part; Home 208–210, entire, where it is dated January 12.

Austin returned to Boston on Monday, December 1. The second Monday after his departure is recorded in Lavinia's diary as a "snowy, gloomy day." During the interval Abiah Root had been visiting her cousins the Palmers. The evening she spent at the Dickinsons' with Abby Wood and Martha Gilbert was Emily's twenty-first birthday. "Miss Mary" was Mary Warner. Martha Humphrey died on 10 December, aged twenty.

66

To Austin Dickinson   *24 December 1851*

Dont tell them, *will* you Austin; they are all asleep soundly and I snatch the silent night to speak a word to you. Perhaps *you* are sound asleep, and I am only chatting to the *semblance* of a man ensconced in warmest blankets and deep, downy pillows. I am afraid not, dear Austin, I'm afraid that dreadful pain will keep you wide awake all this dreary night, and *so* afraid am I, that I steal from happy dreams and come to sit with you. Since your letter came, we have thought *so* much about you, Oh more, *many* more than pen and ink can tell you — we are thinking of you *now* midst the night so wild and stormy. Austin, I hav'nt a doubt that Vinnie and mother are dreaming *even now* of you, tho' Vinnie was *so* sleepy the last time she opened her eye, and mother has had a very fatiguing day. And you know that *I* do, *dont* you, or I should'nt incur such perils for the sake of seeing you. Hav'nt you taken cold, or exposed yourself in some way, or got too tired, teaching those useless boys? — I am so sorry for you. I do wish it was *me*, that you might be well and happy, for I have no profession, and have such a snug, warm home that I had as lief suffer some, a great deal rather than not, that by doing so, you were exempted from it. May I change places, Austin? *I* dont care how sharp the pain is, not if it dart like arrows, or pierce bone and bone like the envenomed barb, I should be twice, *thrice* happy to bear it in your place. Dont try to teach school at all, until you get thoroughly well! The committee will excuse you, I *know* they will, they *must*; tell them if they dont I will tell the Mayor of them and get them all turned out! I am glad to know you are prudent in consulting a physician; I hope he will do you good; has anyone with neuralgia, tried him, that recommended him to you? I think that warmth and rest, cold water and care, are the best medicines for it. I know you can get all these, and be your own physician, which is far the better way.

Now Austin, I cant come, I have no horse to fetch me, I can only advise you of what I think is good, and ask you if you will do it. Had I the art and skill of the greatest of all physicians, and had under my care whole hospitals of patients, I could'nt feel more anxious than in this single case; I do feel so desirous of a complete recovery!

But lest I harm my patient with too much conversation on sickness and pain, I pass to themes more cheerful and reminiscence gay. I know it would make you laugh to see Vinnie sleeping as soundly as a poker, and shovel and pair of tongs, and Cousin Emily Norcross bringing up the rear in a sleep twice as sound and full twice as sonorous, and there come snatches of music from away in mother's room, which wake a funny response in my amused being. I can think of nothing funnier than for intelligent beings to bid the world good night, and go out with their candles, and there's nothing that I enjoy more than rousing these self-same beings and witnessing their discomfiture at the *bare idea* of morning, when they're *so* sleepy yet!

Vinnie thinks me quite savage, and frequently suggests the propriety of having me transported to some barbarous country, where I may meet with those of a similar nature, and allow her to spend her days — that is, such small remainder as my inhumanity spares — in comparative ease and quietness!

She thinks ancient martyrs very trifling indeed and would *welcome* the stake in preference to the sunrise, and that shrill morning call she may be sure to hear!

A'nt you sorry for her; she thinks of your sympathies often, and thinks they would all be hers, if they were nearer home.

Father will come tomorrow, and I will take care of Mat. Had a "merry Christmas" from Sue, besides some beautiful gifts for Vinnie and me, Monday evening. We are having a cozy, rosy, posy little visit with Cousin Emily — enjoy it very much, would love to have you here, if it might be possible. I was glad you remembered Emily, it pleased her very much. Why did you apologize for any of your letters? Coming from you, Austin, they never can be otherwise than delightful to us; better than that you give us, we shall never desire.

[163]

Write to us very soon, and say how you are, and be very careful indeed, and dont write but a little, if you find it pains you. Much love.

Emily.

MANUSCRIPT: AC. Ink. Dated: Wednesday night. 12 o'clock. Envelope addressed: Wm Austin Dickinson/Care of Joel Norcross. 31. Milk St./ Boston./Mass. Postmarked: Amherst Ms. Dec 25.
PUBLICATION: *Home* 204–206.

ED's Mount Holyoke roommate, Emily Norcross, was the cousin now visiting them. Edward Dickinson was in Monson, the home of the Norcross family.

67

To Austin Dickinson   *31 December 1851*

Late at night, dear Child, but I cant help thinking of you, and am so afraid you are sick — come home tomorrow, Austin, if you are not perfectly sure that you shall be well right away, for you must not suffer there — Vinnie has got her message — We did not get the answer from you — I must not write another word, but Austin, come home, remember, if you are not better right away. Love for you.

Emilie.

MANUSCRIPT: AC. Pencil. Envelope addressed: Wm Austin Dickinson./ Care of Joel Norcross/31. Milk Street/Boston/Mass. Postmarked: Amherst Ms Jan 1 1852.
PUBLICATION: *Home* 207.

68

To Austin Dickinson   *5 January 1852*

I will write a word to you, Austin, to send by Mr Watson. I've found your Gaitor shoes, and send them as you desired.

Mary Warner was here on Thursday, has only just got out; influenza is prevalent here — how lucky they took it in Boston, it would have been so vulgar to have imbibed it *here* among the pools and pastures! Mary said she had finished "Kavanagh," and would return it immediately, which she has *not* done, or you would receive it now. I should go for it this morning, but it storms and is so icy, that I dare not venture out. You shall have it tho, by the next good opportunity. Mr. *Goodale* left for California, this morning, George Godfrey meets him in New York, Tuesday.

Emiline Kellogg is quite sick — they have very much feared a fever, but she's rather more comfortable now.

You remember our telling you of a Cousin George Dickinson, from New York, who came to Amherst last summer, when you were away. He passed the Sabbath in town, took tea here, and passed the evening, is a fine fellow, and has a great desire to see you. We had a very quiet New Year's, I had as a gift from Mattie, an exquisite "piece of carpeting," similar to one Sue gave you, sometime ago!

I dont know anything of the railroad tho' I fancy "things is workin," and so soon as "things *has* worked" I promise to let you know. I am very glad indeed that you've called upon the Lymans — I think Mary a beautiful person, and will certainly go and see her as soon as she comes to town. I have never known Charlotte at all. Vinnie will tell the Jones' some day when she's out this week.

Mrs Howe has heard from Sabra, she is very happy indeed. Mrs Howe was perfectly delighted with your visit there, the last time you were at home — also Mrs Hartly, and all the tavern gang — have spoken of it frequently, and with much evident pleasure. Goodbye, Austin, hope you are happy and well, and would write much more, but your stockings call me.

Aff yr sister,
Emilie

Manuscript: AC. Ink. Dated: Monday morning. Addressed on the fold: Wm Austin Dickinson.

Publication: *Home* 207–208.

ED's familiarity with *Kavanagh* has already been noted. (See letter no. 38.) The book seems to have belonged to Austin. The charter for the Amherst and Belchertown Railroad, to connect Amherst with lines already laid through Palmer, was granted on 24 May 1851.

69

To Abiah Root   *about January 1852*

My very dear Abiah,

I love to sit here alone, writing a letter to you, and whether your joy in reading will amount to as much or more, or even less than mine in penning it to you, becomes to me just now a very important problem — and I will tax each power to solve the same for me; if as happy, indeed, I have every occasion for gratitude — more so, my absent friend, I may not hope to make you, but I do hope most earnestly it may not give you *less*. Oh, I do know it will not, if school-day hearts are warm and school-day memories precious! As I told you, it is Sunday to-day, so I find myself quite curtailed in the selection of subjects, being myself quite vain, and naturally adverting to many worldly things which would doubtless grieve and distress you: much more will I be restrained by the fact that such stormy Sundays I always remain at home, and have not those opportunities for hoarding up great truths which I would have otherwise. In view of these things, Abiah, your kind heart will be lenient, forgiving all empty words and unsatisfying feelings on the Sabbath-day ground which we have just alluded to. I rejoice in one theme appropriate to every place and time — indeed it cannot intrude in the hour most unseemly for every other thought and every other feeling; and sure I am to-day, howe'er it may be holy, I shall not break or reproach by speaking of the links which bind us to each other, and make the very thought of you, and time when I last saw you, a sacred thing to me. And I have many memories, and many thoughts beside, which by some strange entwining, circle you round and round; if you please, a vine of fancies, towards which dear Abiah sustains the part of oak, and as up each sturdy branch there climbs a little tendril so full of faith and confidence and the most holy trust, so let the hearts do also, of the dear "estray"; then the farther we may be from home and from each other, the nearer by that faith which "overcometh all things" and bringeth us to itself.

Amherst and Philadelphia, separate indeed, and yet how near, bridged by a thousand trusts and a "thousand times ten thousand" the travellers who cross, whom you and I may not see, nor hear the trip of their feet, yet faith tells us they are there, ever crossing and re-crossing. Very likely, Abiah, you fancy me at home in my own little chamber, writing you a letter, but you are greatly mistaken. I am on the blue Susquehanna paddling down to you; I am not much of a sailor, so I get along rather slowly, and I am not much of a mermaid, though I verily think I shall be, if the tide overtakes me at my present jog. Hardhearted girl! I don't believe you care, if you did you would come quickly and help me out of this sea; but if I drown, Abiah, and go down to dwell in the seaweed forever and forever, I will not forget your name, nor all the wrong you did me!

Why did you go away and not come to see me? I felt so sure you would come, because you promised me, that I watched and waited for you, and bestowed a tear or two upon my absentee. How very sad it is to have a confiding nature, one's hopes and feelings are quite at the mercy of all who come along; and how very desirable to be a stolid individual, whose hopes and aspirations are safe in one's waistcoat pocket, and *that* a pocket indeed, and one not to be picked!

Notwithstanding your faithlessness I should have come to see you, but for that furious snow-storm; I did attempt in spite of it, but it conquered in spite of me, and I doffed my hood and shawl, and felt very crestfallen the remainder of the day. I did want one more kiss, one sweet and sad good-by, before you had flown away; perhaps, my dear Abiah, it is well that I go without it; it might have added anguish to our long separation, or made the miles still longer which keep a friend away. I always try to think in any disappointment that had I been gratified, it had been sadder still, and I weave from such supposition, *at times*, considerable consolation; consolation upside down as I am pleased to call it.

. . . Shall I have a letter soon — oh, may I very soon, for "some days are dark and dreary, and the wind is never weary."

Emily E.

but my dear child, you know that I do not feel well at sometimes, and when my feelings come, I permit them to overcome me when perhaps I ought not — yet *at the time* submission seems almost inevitable. I will try to get stout and well before you come again, and who says the past shall not be forgiven by the day to come? I say she *shall* be, and that the deeper the crimson, the purer and more like snow the heart repentant, when penitence can come.

MANUSCRIPT: missing. See note 3 in "Notes on the Present Text." All of the letter above the signature has been published; all below it is unpublished.

PUBLICATION: *L* (1894) 57–60; *L* (1931) 50–52, dated (presumably by ED): Sunday Evening.

Abiah Root was in Philadelphia from January to June 1852 (see the letter from Mrs. Strong to Mrs. Todd written in 1892 – *AB* 207). She had been visiting her cousins the Palmers in Amherst, and ED is complaining that Abiah did not pay her a goodbye visit. The letter closes with lines which attempt to recall Longfellow's "The Rainy Day" (see letter no. 36).

70

To Susan Gilbert (Dickinson)   *21 January 1852*

Will you forgive me, Susie, I cannot stay away; and it is not *me only* – that writes the note today – dear Mattie's *heart* is here, tho' her *hand* is not quite strong enough to hold a pen today. I have just come from your home, and I promised Mattie I would write you, and tell you about her. Now dont feel anxious, dear Susie, Mattie is only sick *a little* and Dr Smith and I, are going to cure her right away in a day, and she will be so much stronger than she was before. She has a disordered stomach, and coughs some, which Dr Smith says is owing to the stomach — and more immediately, to a cold she has taken; he says she will soon be well, and she looks so sweet and happy — that could you *see* her, Susie — you would think she was *playing* sick — just to lie in the grand french bedstead and have dear little vials sitting on the stand. I told Mattie this morning — she looked so sweet and patient, and willing to be sick; Mattie looked up so funny, and said she *"was'nt willing"* and I need'nt have any such little notions in reference to her; so my dear Susie, you see she is quite herself, and will be very strong and well in a day or two.

She has'nt got your letter, owing she thinks to the great snow storm, which blocked up all the railroads, and dont give us any mail — and Susie — I am so credulous, and so easily deluded by this fond heart of mine — that I am supposing snow storms have got *my* letter too, and I shant lay it to *you*, but to the wicked *snow storm*, if mine does not come *too*! I told Mattie this morning, that I felt all taken away, without her, or Susie, and indeed I have thought today of what would

[168]

become of me when the "bold Dragon" shall bear you both away, to live in his high mountain — and leave me here alone; and I could have wept bitterly over the only *fancy* of ever being so lone — and then Susie, I thought how these short adieus of our's might — Oh Sue, they *might* grow sadder and longer, and that bye and bye they would not be said any more, not any more *forever*, for that of our precious band, some *one* should pass away.

Such thoughts will come and come — now you are gone away — and I watch your letters Susie, to see if they grow saintlier, and more like Susie *Spirit*, than my dear earthly child. Forgive me a smile, Susie, on a subject near my heart, but for the last few weeks and days — they *are* so evanescent that I cant see them *at all*; dear Susie, *please* be corporal, it would so comfort me! The days dont go very fast — I shall certainly have to *poke* them — if they dont go along; yet they *do* move a *little*, and bounding o'er them all — I meet the glad July — and have you in my arms — Oh Susie — you *shall* come, tho the time be *ever* so long, and go ever so slowly — and I should get *so* tired, if it was'nt for faith. *You* may have faith *too* Susie — I will not take it all, and *besides*, "eno' and to spare" for Vinnie and Mattie. Susie, dont worry a bit, for Mattie — she is'nt sick but *a little*, and I will write again in two or three days — to tell you she has got well; and when you would love, dear Susie, so would *I better*, to have letter from you.

Emilie

Love, much love!

MANUSCRIPT: HCL (L 15). Ink. Dated: Wednesday noon. Envelope (YUL) addressed: Miss Susan H Gilbert./Care of Mr Archer./40 – Lexington St./Baltimore./Md. Postmarked: Amherst Ms Jan 22.

PUBLICATION: FF 209–211, in part.

On January 14 Mattie contracted influenza, then unusually prevalent. She was ill for several weeks, and this letter was written with the purpose of allaying Sue's apprehensions (see no. 71).

71

To Austin Dickinson   *28 January 1852*

I have just got your letter, Austin, and have read and sat down to answer it almost in a breath, for there's so much I want to say, and so little time to say it, that I must be very spry to write you tonight at all.

It has been a long, lonely winter; we do need you at home, and since you have been sick and are away from us, the days seem like *ages*, and I get tired of ever hoping to see you again. It seems to me it would do you a great deal of good to leave school a few days, and come home. We are very anxious to see you, the journey would do you good, and the pure air here, and seeing your old friends would quite restore you. Cant you, Austin? I do wish you would; never mind the boys; if they cant fill your place for a week, just let it be *un*filled. I dont believe the boy's minds would suffer, or run to waste in such a short space of time, and I do think your health requires it. You may feel so well by the time you get this that you wont think it worth the while in a *hea*[*l*]*th* view[?] — but it's a long while since Thanksgiving, and we should like to see you, and perhaps you would like to come. Wont you think of it tonight and follow my good advice into the Fitchburgh Depot, where you will find a ticket to take you home to-morrow? How glad we should all be to see you! I am rejoiced that your face is better, hope it is now well, as t'will be almost three days from the time you wrote to me, when this reaches you.

I dont understand your being troubled with the palpitation so much, but think it must be owing to a disordered system, and too violent exertions in your school, which I would modestly wish at the bottom of the sea, before ever you were engaged in it. I think you need rest, and riding, and perfect freedom from care — *that* you will find here, and Vinnie and I will do everything we *can* to make you happy, if you will make *us* happy by deciding to come. *Generous*, isn't it, offerring to make *you* happy, if you'll make *us* so *first*; but in the end, we should *all* be happy, I guess. Poor Mat has been pretty sick, but is recovering now; just a fortnight today since she was taken down.

I am down there a great deal, and spend most all my time in going to see her, thinking of something to carry her, or writing letters to Sue, telling her all about Martha. I had a long letter from Sue last Thursday, and wrote her that day of Mat's sickness, at Mat's request; told her Mat was'nt much sick, had a touch of the influenza and would be out again soon. Poor Sue thought otherwise, concluded Mat was very sick and I had written not so for fear I should alarm her; so yesterday I had the most anxious note from her — she seemed almost distracted lest Mat was sick very, and we were keeping it from her; but

I wrote her immediately, stating how Mat was, and Mrs C[utler] wrote too, so Sue will soon be relieved. You are gone, and Sue; Mat's sickness deprives me of her, and on the whole, Austin, I do feel rather lonely, but you'll all get back at sometime, and if I live till then, I mean to be happy enough to make up for all this lost time. Emiline is still very feeble, sits up only a little, cannot bear the light at all on account of her head, and tho' slowly recovering, is very feeble yet. I went up to see her today — her room is kept so dark that I could'nt see where she was for some time — at last I heard a little faint voice way out in the corner, and found poor Em' out there — she inquired for you — I told her you had been shut up with your face, and she smiled and said "we are all sick at a time." It is five weeks today, since she was taken sick, a long and tedious sickness, but I hope she will soon get well. Her hair is all cut off, and to see her propped up with pillows, you would'nt hardly know her.

Mary Warner and Thurston are getting along nicely, spent last Monday evening, sliding down Boltwood's hill — the very last phase of flirtation. Mary dont seem very flourishing just now — everybody seems to get the idea that she's a little gone by, and faded. Dont be roused by this into the former furie, for Mary and Vinnie and I are on the pleasantest terms in the world. Emily Fowler is visiting Liz Tyler. Abby Wood is as usual; Mr Bliss is confined to the house with one of his old attacks, so the work at "Shanghi" I suppose cannot go forward! Abby brought her work down and staid all Monday forenoon; said she wrote a letter of 16 pages to Eliza Coleman last week, and had just received one of *ten* in return. Dear me, I'm glad I have no such hot correspondents! Only think of it, Abby Wood and Eliza C. Where is Charles Dickens, is all I have tongue to say? Mary Lyman has not come — Mary French is visiting her coz' in Oxford. Prof Haven gave a Lyceum Lecture last evening, upon the deaf and dumb, and the manner of teaching them — it was called very interesting — he gives one at Northampton tonight — the President [Hitchcock] lectures at Springfield this evening, so you see Lyceum Lectures are pretty plenty around here.

Dr Wesselhoeft's bill is correct I presume. He sent Vinnie medicine three or four times, and me twice — and although we were not benefited by it, he probably did the best he could for us, and I'd rather you would pay it, without any words about it, and Vinnie and I will pay you, when you get home. I dont want any fuss with him. Vinnie and I have tried him and are satisfied that for us the medicine has no power, but I am glad we tried him; we should'nt have *known* without. Go and see him as soon as you can conveniently, Austin; I dont like an unpaid bill.

Mother seems quite delighted at what you said to her about making you a visit — I should'nt be at all surprised should she conclude to go and see you, though of course she has not had time to think at all about it.

I think she is very happy at your mention of her, and desire to see her. I mean she shall go. Vinnie and I have been there so recently, it is not best for us to think of it, but you are very kind, Austin, you do not know how much we all think of you, how much you are missed at home.

I thank you for your letter, it sounds like old times — and makes me feel quite happy, except where you are sick. Mother and Vinnie send their love, and father says he thinks you had better come home for a few days unless you are very much better.

Emilie E.

You sent us the *Duett*, Austin. Vinnie cannot learn it, and I see from the outside page, that there is a piece for *two* hands.

Are you willing to change it. Dont be in haste to send it; any time will do! Shall write when I hear from you, more fully.

MANUSCRIPT: AC. Ink. Dated: Wednesday Evening. Envelope addressed: Wm Austin Dickinson./Care of Joel Norcross./31 – Milk Street./ Boston/Mass. Postmarked: Amherst Ms Jan 29. The two final paragraphs of the letter are on a separate slip of paper.

PUBLICATION: *Home* 211–214.

Both Benjamin E. Thurston and Daniel Bliss were seniors in Amherst College. Bliss, who was nearly thirty years old, married Abby Wood in 1855, and went as a missionary to Syria, not to China. Haven's lecture, "The Art of Instructing the Deaf and Dumb," was given on January 27. Dr. William Wesselhöft (1794–1858) was a well-known physician from Germany who practiced medicine in Boston from 1841 until his death.

72

To Austin Dickinson   *6 February 1852*

Austin.

I have never left you so long before, since you first went away, but we have had such colds that we could not use our eyes so long as to write a letter, and the privation on our part has been greater, I dare say, than it possibly could — on your's.

I have received both your letters, and enjoyed them both very much; *particularly* the notes on the agricultural convention. Miss Kelly's part of the performance was very fine indeed, and made much fun for us. Should think you must have some *discipline* in order to write so clearly amidst so much confusion. Father seemed specially pleased with the story of the farmer. I am so glad you are better — I wish you might have been spared just for a little visit, but we will try and wait if you dont think best to come, and shall only be the gladder to see you at last. I hope you will be very careful and not get sick again, for it seems to me you've had so much miserable health since you have lived in Boston; if it dont ruin your constitution, I shall be very glad. I am very sorry to hear of the illness of the teachers; I should think you must miss them, they have been with you so long. You will tell us if they are better, when you write home again.

Since we have written you, the grand Rail Road decision is made, and there is great rejoicing throughout this town and the neighboring; that is Sunderland, Montague, and Belchertown. Every body is wide awake, every thing is stirring, the streets are full of people talking cheeringly, and you really should be here to partake of the jubilee. The event was celebrated by D. Warner, and cannon; and the silent satisfaction in the hearts of all is it's crowning attestation.

Father is realy *sober* from excessive satisfaction, and bears his honors with a most becoming air. Nobody *believes* it yet, it seems like a fairy tale, a most *miraculous* event in the lives of us all. The men begin working next week, only think of it, Austin; why I verily believe we shall fall down and worship the first "Son of Erin" that comes, and the first sod he turns will be preserved as an emblem of the struggles and victory of our heroic fathers. Such old fellows as Col' Smith *and his wife*, fold their arms complacently, and say, "well, I declare, we have got it after all" — *got it*, you good for nothings! and so we *have*, in spite of sneers and pities, and insults from all around; and we will *keep* it too, in spite of earth and heaven! How I wish you were here, it is really too bad, Austin, at such a time as now — I miss your big Hurrahs, and the famous stir you make, upon all such occasions; but it is a comfort to know that you are here — that your whole soul is here, and tho' apparently absent, yet present in the highest, and the truest sense. I have got a great deal to say, and I fancy I am saying it in rather a headlong way, but if you can read it, you will know what it means. Martha gets along nicely, was able to have her dress on, and go in the dining room for the first time yesterday. She sends you her love, and will write to you just as soon as [she] is able.

Mother has not decided yet, about going to Boston — seems to think if you are better it is hardly best to go. I will tell you more decide[d]ly when I write again — she would love to do so dearly, but it's a good deal of effort to go away from home at this season, and I hardly know what she will do. Emiline improves slowly. Tutor Howland appeared on Wednesday, and remained in town till today — took tea here Wednesday evening — took Vinnie to ride yesterday morning, spent most of the afternoon here, and is just shutting the gate upon his last farewell, as I write this morning. I have been to ride twice since I wrote you, once with a party, manned by Root & Co. and last evening with *Sophomore Emmons,* alone; will tell you all about it when I write again, for I am in such a hurry that I cannot stop for breath. Take good care of yourself, Austin, and think much of us all, for we do so of you.

Emilie

I send you my prescription again. Will it trouble you too much to get me another bottle, of the same size as the others, namely *twice the quantity,* and send to me by the first person who comes? You are kind very, Austin, to attend to all my little wants, and I'm sure I thank you for it.

April is'nt far off, and then — and then, we are the "merrie men"!

Vinnie sends her love, and mother. Vinnie says she thinks you dont pay much attention to her.

MANUSCRIPT: AC. Ink. Dated: Friday morning. Envelope addressed: Wᵐ Austin Dickinson./Care of Joel Norcross./31 – Milk St./Boston./ Mass. Postmarked: Amherst Ms. Feb 6. The final three paragraphs are written on a separate strip of paper and on the inside of the envelope flap.

PUBLICATION: *Home* 217–218.

The *Hampshire and Franklin Express* announced on February 6 that the stock of the Amherst and Belchertown Railroad had been fully subscribed. Luke Sweetser was elected president and Edward Dickinson one of the directors.

73

To Susan Gilbert (Dickinson)   *about 6 February 1852*

Will you let me come dear Susie — looking just as I do, my dress soiled and worn, my grand old apron, and my hair — Oh Susie, time would fail me to enumerate my appearance, yet I love you just as dearly as if I was e'er so fine, so you wont care, will you? I am so glad dear Susie — that our hearts are always clean, and always neat and lovely, so not to be ashamed. I have been hard at work this morning, and I ought to be working now — but I cannot deny myself the luxury of a minute or two with you.

The dishes may wait dear Susie — and the uncleared table stand, *them* I have always with me, but you, I have "not always" — *why* Susie, Christ hath saints *manie* — and I have *few*, but thee — the angels shant have Susie — no – no no!

Vinnie is sewing away like a *fictitious* seamstress, and I half expect some knight will arrive at the door, confess himself a *nothing* in presence of her loveliness, and present his heart and hand as the only vestige of him worthy to be refused.

Vinnie and I have been talking about growing old, today. Vinnie thinks *twenty* must be a fearful position for one to occupy — I tell her I dont care if I am young or not, had as lief be thirty, and you, as most anything else. Vinnie expresses her sympathy at my "sere and yellow leaf" and resumes her work, dear Susie, tell me how *you* feel — ar'nt there days in one's life when to be old dont seem a thing so sad —

I do feel gray and grim, this morning, and I feel it would be a comfort to have a piping voice, and broken back, and scare little children. Dont *you* run, Susie dear, for I wont do any harm, and I do love you dearly tho' I do feel so frightful.

Oh my darling one, how long you wander from me, how weary I grow of waiting and looking, and calling for you; sometimes I shut my eyes, and shut my heart towards you, and try hard to forget you because you grieve me so, but you'll never go away, Oh you never will — say, Susie, promise me again, and I will smile faintly — and take up my little cross again of sad — *sad* separation. How vain it seems to *write*, when one knows how to feel — how much more near and dear to sit beside you, talk with you, hear the tones of your voice; so hard to "deny thyself, and take up thy cross, and follow me" — give me strength, Susie, write me of hope and love, and of hearts that *endured,* and great was their reward of "Our Father who art in Heaven." I dont know how I shall bear it, when the gentle spring comes; if she should come and see me and talk to me of you, Oh it would surely kill me! While the frost clings to the windows, and the World is stern and drear; this absence is easier; the *Earth* mourns too, for all her little birds; but when they all come back again, and she sings and is so merry — pray, what will become of me? Susie, forgive me, forget all what I say, get some sweet little scholar to read a gentle hymn, about Bethleem and Mary, and you will sleep on sweetly and have as peaceful dreams, as if I had never written you all these ugly things. Never mind the letter Susie, I wont be angry with you if you dont give me any at all — for I know how busy you are, and how little of that dear strength remains when it is evening, with which to think and write. Only *want* to write me, only sometimes sigh that you are far from me, and that will do, Susie! Dont you think we are good and patient, to let you go so long; and dont we think you're a darling, a real beautiful hero, to toil for people, and teach them, and leave your own dear home? Because we pine and repine, dont think we forget the precious patriot at war in other lands! Never be mournful, Susie — be happy and have cheer, for how many of the long days have gone away since I wrote you — and it is almost noon, and soon the night will come, and then there is one less day of the long pilgrimage. Mattie is very smart, talks of you *much,* my darling; I must leave you now — "one little hour of Heaven," thank who did give it me, and will he also grant me one longer and *more* when it shall please his love — bring Susie home, ie! Love always, and ever, and true!

Emily —

MANUSCRIPT: HCL (L 10). Ink. Dated: Friday forenoon.
PUBLICATION: FF 182–184, in part.
The exact date of the letter is uncertain, but its report on Mattie's condition is similar to that of the same date in the preceding letter to Austin, and no other Friday in the month seems to apply as well.

74

To Susan Gilbert (Dickinson)   *about February 1852*

It's a sorrowful morning Susie — the wind blows and it rains; "into each life some rain must fall," and I hardly know which falls fastest, the rain without, or within – Oh Susie, I would nestle close to your warm heart, and never hear the wind blow, or the storm beat, again. Is there any room there for me, or shall I wander away all homeless and alone? Thank you for loving me, darling, and *will* you "love me more if ever you come home"? — it is enough, dear Susie, I know I shall be satisfied. But what can I do towards you? — *dearer* you *cannot* be, for I love you so already, that it almost breaks my heart — perhaps I can love you *anew*, every day of my life, every morning and eve- ning – Oh if you will let me, how happy I shall be!

The precious billet, Susie, I am wearing the paper out, reading it over and o'er, but the dear *thoughts* cant wear out if they try, Thanks to Our Father, Susie! Vinnie and I talked of you all last evening long, and went to sleep mourning for you, and pretty soon I waked up say- ing "Precious treasure, thou art mine," and there you were all right, my Susie, and I hardly dared to sleep lest some one steal you away. Never mind the letter, Susie; you have so much to do; just write me every week *one line*, and let it be, "Emily, I love you," and I will be satisfied!

Your own Emily
L'ove to Hattie from us all. Dear Mattie is almost well.
Vinnie's love – Mother's –

MANUSCRIPT: HCL (L 22). Ink. Dated: Wednesday morn. Addressed on the fold: Susie. Unpublished.
The first quotation is from Longfellow's "The Rainy Day." (See letter no. 36.)

75

To Austin Dickinson *about February 1852*

Had a beautiful letter from Sue, on Friday. Wᵐ Whn' [Washburn] is here yet, strange in so big a world there seems to be no corner for him!

"Dream Life" is not near so great a book as the "Reveries of a Bachelor["], yet I think it full of the very sweetest fancies, and more exquisite language I defy a man to use; on the whole I enjoy it very much, tho' I cant help wishing all the time, that he had been *translated* like Enoch of old, after his Bachelors Reverie, and the "chariot of fire, and the horses thereof," were all that was seen of him, after that exquisite writing.

MANUSCRIPT: HCL (B 171). Ink.
PUBLICATION: LL 82, in part.

Dream Life, by Ik Marvel (Donald G. Mitchell), was published in December 1851. Mrs. Bianchi said (in *LL*) that this letter was written after receiving a copy of the book from Austin. The location of the copy, if it survives, is not known. For an identification of Washburn, see Appendix 1. In her scripture allusion, ED combined the translation of Enoch with that of Elijah: ". . . behold, there appeared a chariot of fire, and horses of fire, . . . and Elijah went up by a whirlwind into heaven" (2 Kings 2.11).

76

To Austin Dickinson *18 February 1852*

Austin.

We received your letters last evening — or Father and Vinnie did, for I did'nt seem to have any; Vinnie cant write today on account of those metaphysics, to which you so touchingly allude. Father also is very busy, so perhaps you wont object to an article from me.

We are all pretty well at home — Martha is getting better, and Emeline, very slowly. Mat sends her love to you and says she shall write you a letter as soon as she is strong enough to keep letters on the line — she sits up most of the day now, but is not able to confine her attention to anything but a little while at a time, and has not yet been out. I have heard from Sue three times, since I have written you — she is well, and in usual spirits. I think it would make Mat very happy to have a letter from you should you find a leisure hour, although she did not tell me to say so — they always inquire for you at Mrs W^m C[utler]'s, and Mat would have written you a long time ago had she been able to do so.

Abby Wood is quite sick this week, but I think will be better soon.

Mr Sweetser's house took fire Monday evening and was with great difficulty extinguished — the family did not lie down all night, and the escape was narrow — very. The chimney had been on fire during the day, but no danger was apprehended, and sometime the last of the evening, Mrs Sweetser in going up stairs to give Abby her medicine, thought she smelt smoke in the room. Abby had not perceived it. Mrs S. then opened a door in another direction and the smoke seemed to increase – upon opening the garret door, she saw the flames bursting out from the big timbers near the chimney. Mr Sweetser was at the store — Mrs S. with great presence of mind closed the door, sent at once for Mr. Sweetser, and the family themselves worked until it was morning, pouring water, and sawing away great pieces of timber, until the flames were subdued. The house is a good deal injured, but it is such a miracle that they were not all destroyed that they dont care much for damages. Who did you send your letters and Vinnie's music by? We heard accidentally that there was something for us at Wm Kellogg's store, and there they were — we dont know whence — or by whom, tho' we have suspicions of one Oliver Watson! The vial and flannel came safely, and are just the things desired. I thank you *always* for all you do for me, and would love to send you something did I know what you would like. I was on the point one day of buying a pound of *peanuts* and sending them to you in memory of college days, but Vinnie laughed me out of it — if you will like them tho', and will let me know you shall certainly have them.

Vinnie sends her love to you, and thanks you very much for her music — it is correct. Mother wont come to Boston, probably, this spring — she wants to see you very much, and did think about going some, at the time you were so unwell, but now you are better, and will be at home so soon, she will not think it worth while.

We are all very happy to have you well and happy, and hope you may not be sick in all the rest of the time that you remain in

[179]

Boston. We have never told you that Pussy has gone – she disappeared about four weeks ago, and we can find nothing of her, so we presume she is dead. We miss her very much, and I think you will miss her, when you come home.

April dont seem quite so far off as it used to, last December – I can almost count the days now, before you are coming home, they seem so few. There are a good many lectures here now, before the Lyceum. Mr Mt Pleasant-Nash, is giving a course of Agricultural ones, twelve in all – and besides a lecture from him once or twice in a week, there is also another from some other gentlemen, on some literary subject. Prof Fowler gave one upon Adam Smith, last evening. Tutor Edwards will give the next. Emmons passed the evening here, and Vinnie and I staid at home – mother went out with Father, but thought the lecture too high for her unobtrusive faculties. I shall love to get a letter when you have the time.

Emily.

Mother wants me to add a word in relation to her coming – you will see what she thinks about in the longer sheet – besides the other reasons, there given – Father will be away at Court for three or four weeks to come, most all of the time – *this* mother thinks an objection, as should she go away too we should be quite alone, and the folks would'nt think that safe. Then she thinks you are very busy, and however happy to see her, and desirous to have her come, yet her visit would necessarily occupy much of your time, and as she will see you so soon at home, she wants me to ask you if you dont agree with her in its not being just the thing, for her to visit you now? Kate Hitchcock is to be married in March. I dont envy her that Storrs. Root, Harrington, Storrs, Emmons, Graves, and the Tutors, come in quite often to see us. Emily Fowler was here Monday afternoon – inquired particularly for you – says Charles is "doing nicely." March is at Harvard – and writes encouragingly in reference to himself. Emily has much to make her sad – I wonder how she endures all her numberless trials. The railroad goes on swimmingly – everything is stir and commotion. The Godfreys have heard from George – he has reached the Isthmus, suffered all things, according to his account, and thinks going to California, quite a little undertaking! He has probably reached the mines before now. Much love from us all.

MANUSCRIPT: AC. Ink. Dated: Wednesday morn. Envelope addressed:
Wm Austin Dickinson/Care of Joel Norcross./31 – Milk St./Boston/Mass.
Postmarked: Amherst Ms. Feb 18.
PUBLICATION: *Home* 219–221.
"Mr Mt Pleasant-Nash" was the Reverend John Adams Nash, principal
of Mount Pleasant Institute. Catharine Hitchcock married Henry Storrs,
9 March 1852.

77

To Susan Gilbert (Dickinson)   *about February 1852*

Thank the dear little snow flakes, because they fall *today* rather
than some vain *weekday*, when the world and the cares of the world
try so hard to keep me from my departed friend – and thank you, too,
dear Susie, that you never weary of me, or never *tell* me so, and that
when the world is cold, and the storm sighs e'er so piteously, I am sure
of one sweet shelter, *one* covert from the storm! The bells are ringing,
Susie, north, and east, and south, and *your own* village bell, and the
people who love God, are expecting to go to meeting; dont *you* go
Susie, not to *their* meeting, but come with me this morning to the
church within our hearts, where the bells are always ringing, and the
preacher whose name is Love – shall intercede there for us!

They will all go but me, to the usual meetinghouse, to hear the
usual sermon; the inclemency of the storm so kindly detaining me;
and as I sit here Susie, alone with the winds and you, I have the old
king feeling even more than before, for I know not even the *cracker
man* will invade *this* solitude, this sweet Sabbath of our's. And thank
you for my dear letter, which came on Saturday night, when all the
world was still; thank you for the love it bore me, and for it's golden
thoughts, and feelings so like gems, that I was sure I *gathered* them in
whole baskets of pearls! I mourn this morning, Susie, that I have no
sweet sunset to gild a page for *you*, nor any bay so blue – not even a
little chamber way up in the sky, as your's is, to give me thoughts of
heaven, which *I* would give to you. You know how I must write you,
down, down, in the terrestrial; no sunset here, no stars; not even a bit
of *twilight* which I may poetize – and send you! Yet Susie, there will
be romance in the letter's ride to you – think of the hills and the dales,

[181]

and the rivers it will pass over, and the drivers and conductors who will hurry it on to you; and wont that make a poem such as can ne'er be written? I think of you dear Susie, *now*, I dont know how or why, but more dearly as every day goes by, and that sweet month of promise draws nearer and nearer; and I view July so differently from what I used to — once it seemed parched, and dry — and I hardly loved it *any* on account of it's heat and dust; but *now* Susie, month of all the year the best; I skip the violets — and the dew, and the early Rose and the Robins; I will exchange them *all* for that angry and hot noonday, when I can count the hours and the *minutes* before you come — Oh Susie, I often think that I will try to tell you how very dear you are, and how I'm watching for you, but the words wont come, tho' the *tears* will, and I sit down disappointed — yet darling, you know it all — then why do I seek to tell you? I do not know; in thinking of those I love, my reason is all gone from me, and I do fear sometimes that I must make a hospital for the hopelessly insane, and chain me up there such times, so I wont injure you.

Always when the sun shines, and always when it storms, and *always always*, Susie, we are remembering you, and what else besides *remembering*; I shall not *tell* you, because you know! Were it not for dear Mattie, I dont know what we would do, but she loves you so dearly, and is never tired of talking about you, and we all get together and talk it oer and oer, and it makes us more resigned, than to mourn for you *alone*. It was only yesterday, that I went to see dear Mattie, intending in my heart to stay a little while, only a *very* little one, because of a good many errands which I was going to do, and will you believe it, Susie, I was there an hour — and an hour, and half an hour besides, and would'nt have supposed it had been minutes so many — and what do [you] guess we talked about, all those hours long — what would you give to know — give me one little glimpse of your sweet face, dear Susie, and I will tell you all — we did'nt talk of statesmen, and we did'nt talk of kings — but the time was *filled full*, and when the latch was lifted and the oaken door was closed, why, Susie, I realized as never I did before, how much a *single cottage* held that was dear to me. It is sweet — and like home, at Mattie's, but it's *sad* too — and up comes little memory and paints – and paints – and paints – and the strangest thing of all, her canvass is never full, and I find her where I left her, every time that I come — and who is she painting – Ah,

[182]

Susie, "dinna choose to tell" — but it is'nt Mr Cutler, and it is'nt Daniel Boon, and I shant *tell* you any more – Susie, what will you say if I tell you that Henry Root is coming to see me, some evening of this week, and I have promised to read him some parts of all your letters; now you wont care, dear Susie, for he wants so much to hear, and I shant read him anything which I know you would not be willing – just some little places, which will please him so – I have seen him several times lately, and I admire him, Susie, because he talks of *you* so frequently and beautifully; and I know he is so true to you, when you are far away – We talk more of you, dear Susie, than of any other thing – he tells me how wonderful you are, and I tell him how true you are, and his big eyes beam, and he seems so delighted – I know you would'nt care, Susie, if you knew how much joy it made – As I told him the other evening of all your letters to me, he looked up *very* longingly, and I knew what he would say, were he enough acquainted — so I answered the question his heart wanted to ask, and when some pleasant evening, before this week is gone, you remember home and Amherst, then know, Loved One — that *they* are remembering *you*, and that "two or three" are gathered in your name, loving, and speaking of you — and will you be there in the midst of them? Then I've found a beautiful, new, friend, and I've told him about dear Susie, and promised to let him know you so soon as you shall come. Dear Susie, in all your letters there are things sweet and many about which I would speak, but the time says no — yet dont think I forget them — Oh no — they are safe in the little chest which tells no secrets — nor the moth, nor the rust can reach them — but when the time we dream of, comes, *then* Susie, I shall bring them, and we will spend long hours chatting and chatting of them — those precious thoughts of friends — how I loved them, and how I love them now — nothing but Susie *herself* is *half* so dear. Susie, I have not asked you if you were cheerful and well — and I cant think why, except that there's something *perrennial* in those we dearly love, immortal life and vigor; why it seems as if any sickness, or harm, would flee away, would not dare do them wrong, and Susie, while you are taken from me, I class you with the *angels*, and you know the Bible tells us — "there is no sickness there." But, dear Susie, *are* you well, and *peaceful*, for I wont make you cry by saying, are you *happy*? Dont see the *blot*, Susie. It's because I *broke the Sabbath!*

[183]

Susie, what shall I do — there is'nt room enough; not *half* enough, to hold what I was going to say. Wont you tell the man who makes sheets of paper, that I hav'nt the *slightest respect* for him!

And when shall I have a letter — when it's convenient, Susie, not when tired and faint — *ever!*

Emeline gets well so slowly; poor Henry; I guess he thinks true love's course does'nt run very smooth —

Much love from Mother and Vinnie, and then there are *some others* who do not dare to send —

Who loves you most, and loves you best, and thinks of you when others rest?

T'is Emilie —

MANUSCRIPT: HCL (L 9). Ink. Dated: Sunday morning.
PUBLICATION: *FF* 177–181, in part.
The beautiful new friend was probably Henry Vaughan Emmons. In a recent letter to Austin (no. 72) she spoke of having taken a ride with him alone. Henry Nash and Emeline Kellogg were married three years later (see letter no. 53).

78

To Emily Fowler (Ford)   *about 1852*

Dear Emily,

I cant come in this morning, because I am so cold, but you will know I am here — ringing the big front door bell, and leaving a note for you.

Oh I *want* to come in, I have a great mind *now* to follow little Jane into your warm sitting room; are you there, dear Emily?

No, I resist temptation, and run away from the door just as fast as my feet will carry me, lest if I once come in, I shall grow so happy, *happy*, that I shall stay there *always*, and never go home at *all!* You will have read this quite, by the time I reach the office, and you cant think how fast I run!

Aff
Emily.

P.S. I have just shot past the corner, and now all the wayside houses, and the little gate flies open to see me coming home!

MANUSCRIPT: NYPL. Ink. Dated: Thursday morn. Addressed on the fold: Miss Emily E. Fowler.
PUBLICATION: L (1894) 135; LL 136–137; L (1931) 135.
The date is conjectured from the handwriting.

79

To Austin Dickinson   *2 March 1852*

Only a word, Austin, to tell you how we are. I presume you were quite surprised to receive an anonymous bundle, which you must have done today, if Mr Graves did his duty. I did'nt mean it should go without a letter in it, of some considerable length. I wanted to write you yesterday more than I ever did in my life, and will tell you now, why I did'nt. But first, I will write how we *are,* since I promised you that, beforehand.

Father has been shut up with the rheumatism, since Saturday — is rather better today, and hopes to be out tomorrow — the rest of us are as well as could possible be expected! Our *minds* are not well, *mine* especially, has quite a number of symptoms — and I apprehend a *result!* On the whole, however; we bear it with a good deal of fortitude.

I would have given most anything to have had you here, last evening — the scene was indeed too rich, to be detailed by my pen, and I shall ever regret that the *world* has lost such a chance to laugh. Let me add as I go along, that father's frame of mind is *as usual* the *happiest,* developing itself in constant acts of regard, and *epithets of tenderness!*

Soon after tea, last night, a violent ring at the bell – Vinnie obeys the summons – Mr Harrington, Brainerd, would like to see me at the door. I come walking in from the kitchen, frightened almost to death, and receive the command from father, "not to stand at the door" — terrified beyond measure, I advance to the outside door — Mr. H. has an errand — will not consent to come in, on account of my father's sickness — having dismissed him hastily, I retreat again to the kitchen — where I find mother and Vinnie, making most desperate efforts to control themselves, but with little success — once more breathe freely, and conclude that my lungs were given me, for only the best of purposes. Another ring at the door — enter W^m [Cowper] Dickinson —

[185]

soon followed by Mr Thurston! I again crept into the sitting room, more dead than alive, and endeavored to *make conversation*. Father looked round triumphantly. I remarked that "the weather was rather cold" today, to which they all assented – indeed I *never witnessed such wonderful unanimity*. Fled to my mind again, and endeavored to procure something equally agreeable with my *last happy remark*. Bethought me of Sabbath day, and the Rev. Mr Bliss, who preached upon it – remarked with wonderful emphasis, that I thought the Rev. gentleman a very remarkable preacher, and discovered a strong resemblance between himself & Whitfield, in the way of remark – I confess it *was rather* laughable, having never so much as seen the *ashes* of that gentleman – but oh such a look as I got from my rheumatic sire. You should have seen it – I never can find a language vivid eno' to portray it to you – well, pretty soon, another pull at the bell – enter *Thankful Smith*, in the furs and robes of her ancestors, while *James* brings up the rear.

Austin, my cup was full – I endeavored to shrink away into primeval nothingness – but sat there large as life, in spite of every effort. Finally Father, accompanied by the cousins, adjourned to the kitchen fire – and Vinnie and I, and our friends enjoyed the rest of the evening.

How much I have said about nothing, and yet if you were *here*, I should take so much comfort in telling you all these things, that I try to forget you are gone, and to talk as if it *were* so; and how I wish it *was*, and that brings me back again to the feet of the smiling April; oh April, April, wilt thou not soon be here?

Dear Austin, are you well, and are y'r spirits cheerful? How I do want to see you – Oh yes – *indeed* I do, and so do we all! Mother did'nt send *all* the clothes because it is'nt the washing week, but she tho't you might like these now, and the rest will be done next Monday, to send by the first who goes. They were delighted with the Gimp, at Mrs. Warner's. Mrs Warner says "Austin has such a *perfect* taste" – Dont tell Emily Norcross – Vinnie and I, kept dark! No more now from

Emilie

Much love from us all – take good care of yourself. Love to E Norcross – and all.

MANUSCRIPT: AC. Ink. Dated: Tuesday noon. Envelope addressed: Wm Austin Dickinson/Care of Joel Norcross./31 – Milk St. Boston/Mass. Postmarked: Amherst Ms. Mar 3.
PUBLICATION: *Home* 222–223.
George Whitefield, the noted evangelist, had visited Jonathan Edwards at Northampton in 1740.

80

To Austin Dickinson   *7 March 1852*

I will write while they've gone to meeting, lest they stop me, when they get home. I stayed to Communion this morning, and by that way, bought the privilege of not going this afternoon, and having a talk with you, meanwhile.

It's a glorious afternoon – the sky is blue and warm – the wind blows just enough to keep the clouds sailing, and the sunshine, Oh *such* sunshine, it is'nt like gold, for gold is dim beside it; it is'nt like anything which you or I have seen! It seems to me "Ik Marvel" was born on such a day; I only only wish you were here. Such days were made on purpose for Susie and you and me, then what in the world are you gone for, Oh dear, I do not know, but this I *do* know, that if *wishing* would bring you home, you were here today. Is it pleasant in Boston? Of *course* it is'nt, tho', I might have known more than to make such an inquiry. No doubt the streets are muddy, and the sky some dingy hue, and I can think just how every thing bangs and rattles, and goes rumbling along thro' stones and plank and clay! I dont feel as if I could have you there, possibly, another day. I'm afraid you'll turn into a bank, or a Pearl Street counting room, if you have not already, assumed some monstrous shape living in such a place.

Let me see – April – three weeks until April – the very *first* of April, well, perhaps that will do, only be sure of the week, the *whole* week, and nothing but the week; if they make new arrangements, give my respects to them, and tell them *old* arrangements are good enough for you, and you will have them, then if they raise the wind, why let it blow – there's nothing more excellent than a breeze now and then!

[187]

What a time we shall have Fast day, after we get home from meeting—why it makes me *dance* to think of it; and Austin, if I dance so many days beforehand what will become of me when the hour really arrives? I dont know, I'm sure, and I dont care, much, for that, or for anything else, but get you home! We will call on [*half a page cut out*]

I have been hunting all over the house, since the folks went to meeting, to find a small tin box, to send her flowers in [*lines missing*] very often and [*line erased*]. Abby is getting well, is coming down stairs this week. Emiline, too is gaining—we will have them all cured before you get here. I'm so glad you are well and happy, it half reconciles me to having you away—the *smallest* half! Kate Hitchcock and Storrs, are coming off tomorrow evening. Dont know whether they will have a wedding, or not, presume the *faculty* will be present in robes. I am more and more convinced, that this is a great country! Emily Fowler was here yesterday afternoon—inquired for, and sent [*verso of half-page cut out*]

out of the house. Dont know where they are going—guess they will have to live on College Tower, for the houses are pretty full [*five lines missing*]. There's a great demand for Houses, and Father looks very grand, and carries his hands in his pockets in case he should meet a *Northampton man*. The Tyler's are going to Pawtucket this spring, to live.

Henry [Nash] has whiskers. Wells Newport has disappeared, and our horse is now under the care of Jeremiah Holden, who seems a faithful hand. There are many things to say, but meeting is out, and all the folks are coming.

Sunday evening—

Much Love from Mother and Vinnie—we are now pretty well, and our hearts are set on April, the *very first* of April!

Emilie

Love to Miss Nichols—E. Norcross, if still there, and all the relatives. Sorry he did'nt see Sue.

Liked your letter very much, and hope I shall have another one pretty soon.

Vinnie went to South Hadley with Henry Root, Wednesday to call on Jane [Hitchcock].

Father has got well. John Emerson's going [to give a] lecture, Tues[day].

[188]

MANUSCRIPT: AC. Ink. Dated: Sunday afternoon. Envelope addressed by Edward Dickinson: Mr. Austin Dickinson/Boston. The mutilations of this letter, like those in other letters written to Austin, were probably made at some later date to expunge references to Sue.

PUBLICATION: L (1894) 78–79, in part; L (1931) 75–76, in part; Home 226–232, entire, with facsimile reproduction.

The New England Puritans established a Fast Day in March or April, celebrated by proclamation of the magistrates of each province or colony; the custom survived as a holiday in Massachusetts well into the nineteenth century. In 1852 it fell on April 8.

81

To Jane Humphrey   *23 March 1852*

Thank you for the Catalogue, dear Jennie — why did you run away from N. England and Vinnie and me?

Jennie did'nt answer the letter I sent her a long ago, but I am not angry with her. The snows have covered Abby in her sweet churchyard rest. I was going to pick a leaf from the tree nearest her grave and send it in here, Jennie, but I thought I might disturb her — and besides the leaves are faded and would only make you cry. Your sister Helen will be very near us Jennie. I shall hope to see her sweet face when I go to Northampton with father.

Now Jennie, dont forget me and I will remember you and some sweet summer's day in the future I shall meet you — if not on earth, Jennie, I *will* somewhere else — you know where!

The folks at the West must be kind to you — tell them to be for *my* sake — they *will* not refuse me.

I send you a taste Jennie, of E. Kellogg's wedding cake — you remember her, dont you? Eat it tearfully, Jennie, for it came all the way from me!

                                                  Your aff
                                                  Emilie

MANUSCRIPT: Rosenbach 1170/17 (3). Ink. Envelope, partly torn away, addressed: Miss Jane T. H.../Wi.../La... Postmarked: Amherst Ms. Mar 24. Unpublished.

Jane Humphrey was teaching at Willoughby, Ohio. Abby Haskell died 19 April 1851. Eliza Kellogg married Hanson Read, 25 November 1851.

82

To Austin Dickinson   *24 March 1852*

You would'nt think it was spring, Austin, if you were at home this morning, for we had a great snow storm yesterday, and things are all white, this morning. It sounds funny enough to hear birds singing, and sleighbells, at a time. But it won't last any, so you need'nt think 'twill be winter at the time when you come home.

I waited a day or two, thinking I might hear from you, but you will be looking for me, and wondering where I am, so I shant wait any longer. We're rejoiced that you're coming home — the first thing we said to father, when he got out of the stage, was to ask if you were coming. I was sure you would all the while, for father said "of course you would," he should "consent to no other arrangement," and as you say, Austin, what father *says*, "he means." How very soon it will be now — why when I really think of it, how near, and how happy it is, my heart grows light so fast, that I could mount a grasshopper, and gallop around the *world*, and not fatigue him any! The sugar weather holds on, and I do believe it will stay until you come.

Mat came home from meeting with us last Sunday, was here Saturday afternoon when father came, and at her special request, was secreted by me in the *entry*, until he was fairly in the house, when she escaped, *unharmed*.

She inquired all about you, and is delighted enough, that you are coming home. I think Mat's got the notion that you dont care much for home or old friends, but have found their better substitutes in Boston, tho' I do my very best to undelude her. But you will be here soon, and you, of all others, know best how to convince her. I had a letter from Sue last week, at Washington — am expecting another to-day. Dwight Gilbert wrote Mat, that "the Pres' gave a Levee, as soon as he heard of their arrival." The "M C" remind Sue vividly of little boys at school, squabbling, and quarrelling — a very apt illustration! We had a visit from Uncle Bullard, while father was gone — he appeared Friday night, at teatime, and left us Saturday morning, had a very pleasant time. Abby Wood has got well. Emiline is able to ride out, which she did last week, with Henry, to his infinite exultation. Mat is well as ever; Jane Greely is sick with the quinzy — quite sick. Jane Gridley's husband is sick. "Mrs Skeeter" is very feeble, "cant bear

Allopathic treatment, cant have Homeopathic" — dont want Hydro-pathic — Oh what a pickle she is in – should'nt think she would deign to *live* — it is so decidedly vulgar! They have not yet concluded where to move — *Mrs W.* will perhaps obtain board in the "celestial city," but I'm sure I cant imagine what will become of the rest. Here comes Mattie!

She has just gone away, after staying with me two hours. We have had a beautiful time — Mat anticipates so much in seeing you. Do make the days fly, wont you? Here's her love!

Most everybody is going to move. Jane Gridley has bought the old Simeon S[t]rong place — and is going to move there soon. Frank Pierce, the Montague place, up north — Foster Cook, Mr. Harrington's house – Mr Harrington will move into the Colburn place, until his new house is done &c. This is practical enough. I never tho't I should come to it! Keep well, and happy, Austin – 13 – days, and you shall come!

Much love from us all.

Emilie.

Manuscript: AC. Ink. Dated: Wednesday morn. Envelope addressed: Wᵐ Austin Dickinson/Care of Joel Norcross./31 – Milk St./Boston/Mass. Postmarked: Amherst Ms. Mar 24.

Publication: L (1894) 106–107, in part; L (1931) 102–103, in part; *Home* 232–233, entire.

Jane L. Gridley (b. 1829), daughter of Dr. Timothy Gridley, married Dr. George S. Woodman, 17 September 1849.

83

To Austin Dickinson   *30 March 1852*

Austin — have you plenty of time before you come home, to try and match this bit of calico, and get me 10. yards of it? It is but a 12½ ct. calico, but very pretty indeed, and as Vinnie has one, I think I would like to have one.

You used to like her's, I remember. Dont look, unless you have time – and dont get anything unless you can find this same. Everybody sends their love, and we're all longing to see you. Mary Warner sends her love — I saw her yesterday.

Never mind the calico, Austin, should it give you any trouble.

Affy.
Emilie.

MANUSCRIPT: AC. Ink. Envelope addressed: Wm Austin Dickinson./ Care of Joel Norcross./31 – Milk St./Boston/Mass. Postmarked: Amherst Ms. Mar 30.

PUBLICATION: *Home* 235–236.

This note, addressed by ED, was added at the end of a letter from Lavinia.

84

To Austin Dickinson   31 *March 1852*

Dear Austin

You speak of not coming home, and I cant help writing one word, tho' I have but a moment of time.

I am so surprised and astonished, at the bare supposition that you are not coming, that I hardly know what to say. I am sure you are not in earnest, you cannot mean what you say. If I supposed you did, I should rather speak, than write, and rather cry, than either. We have tho't of nothing else and talked of nothing else, all winter and spring, and now the time is so near, I dont believe you will disappoint us. The winter was long and lonely, and without Susie and you, *spring* is so, but whenever the time seemed long, I looked away to April, and was sure of happiness then. I dont wonder you cant think how we look — I know just exactly how you look.

Do you wear a Kossuth Hat? I somehow tho't you did. Austin, you know mother is not in the habit of writing — she talks a great deal about you, and so does Vinnie. Are you willing to get the bottle filled again with my medicine?

We all send you our love, and shall not hear a word to your not coming in April.

Affy
Emily.

Mr Ford was in town yesterday. He called here with Emily & inquired much for you.

MANUSCRIPT: AC. Pencil. Dated: Wednesday. Enclosed in a letter written by Lavinia. An attempt has been made to erase the words "Susie and" in the second paragraph.
PUBLICATION: *Home* 236.
Louis Kossuth visited the United States in the winter and spring of 1852, and was received with great enthusiasm. His pictures show him wearing a hat with a flat-topped crown, wide brim, with a plume attached to one side. The sales of the American copies were enormous.

Gordon Ford and Emily Fowler were married late in 1853. Austin came home on April 7 and stayed five days.

85

To Susan Gilbert (Dickinson)   *5 April 1852*

Will you be kind to me, Susie? I am naughty and cross, this morning, and nobody loves me here; nor would *you* love me, if you should see me frown, and hear how loud the door bangs whenever I go through; and yet it is'nt anger — I dont believe it is, for when nobody sees, I brush away big tears with the corner of my apron, and then go working on — bitter tears, Susie — so hot that they burn my cheeks, and almost schorch my eyeballs, but *you* have wept much, and you know they are less of anger than *sorrow*.

And I do love to run fast — and hide away from them all; here in dear Susie's bosom, I know is love and rest, and I never would go away, did not the big world call me, and beat me for not working.

Little *Emerald Mack* is washing, I can hear the warm suds, splash. I just gave her my pocket handkerchief — so I cannot cry any more. And Vinnie sweeps — sweeps, upon the chamber stairs; and Mother is hurrying round with her hair in a silk pocket handkerchief, on account of dust. Oh Susie, it is dismal, sad and drear eno' — and the sun dont shine, and the clouds look cold and gray, and the wind dont blow, but it *pipes* the shrillest roundelay, and the birds dont sing, but twitter — and there's nobody to smile! Do I paint it *natural* — Susie, so you think how it looks? Yet dont you care — for it wont last so always, and we love you just as well—and think of you, as dearly, as if it were not so. Your precious letter, Susie, it sits here now, and smiles so kindly at me, and gives me such sweet thoughts of the dear writer. When you come home, darling, I shant have your letters, shall I, but I shall have *yourself*, which is more—Oh more, and better, than I can even think! I sit here with my little whip, cracking the time away, till not an hour is left of it—then you are here! And *Joy* is here—joy now and forevermore!

Tis only a few days, Susie, it will soon go away, yet I say, go now, this very moment, for I need her—I must have her, Oh give her to me!

Mattie is dear and true, I love her very dearly—and Emily Fowler, too, is very dear to me–and Tempe–and Abby, and Eme', I am sure– I love them all–and I hope they love me, but, Susie, there's a great corner still; I fill it with that is gone, I hover round and round it, and call it darling names, and bid it speak to me, and ask it if it's Susie, and it answers, Nay, Ladie, Susie is stolen away!

Do I repine, is it all murmuring, or am I sad and lone, and cannot, cannot help it? Sometimes when I do feel so, I think it may be wrong, and that God will punish me by taking you away; for he is very kind to let me write to you, and to give me your sweet letters, but my heart wants *more*.

Have you ever thought of it Susie, and yet I know you have, how much these hearts claim; why I dont believe in the whole, wide world, are such hard little creditors—such real little *misers*, as you and I carry with us, in our bosoms every day. I cant help thinking sometimes, when I hear about the ungenerous, Heart, keep very still—or someone will find you out!

I am going out on the doorstep, to get you some new–green grass– I shall pick it down in the corner, where you and I used to sit, and have long fancies. And perhaps the dear little grasses were growing all the while—and perhaps they heard what we said, but they cant *tell*! I have come in now, dear Susie, and here is what I found—not quite so glad and green as when we used to sit there, but a sad and pensive grassie—mourning o'er hopes. No doubt some spruce, young *Plantain leaf* won its young heart away, and then proved false—and dont you wish *none* proved so, but little Plantains?

I do think it's wonderful, Susie, that our hearts dont break, *every day*, when I think of all the whiskers, and all the gallant men, but I

[194]

guess I'm made with nothing but a hard heart of stone, for it dont break any, and dear Susie, if mine is stony, your's is stone, upon stone, for you never yield *any*, where *I* seem quite beflown. Are we going to *ossify* always, say, Susie — how will it be? When I see the Popes and the Polloks, and the John-Milton Browns, I think we are *liable*, but I dont know! I am glad there's a big *future* waiting for me and you. You would love to know what I read – I hardly know what to tell you, my catalogue is so small.

I have just read three little books, not great, not thrilling — but sweet and true. "The Light in the Valley," "Only," and A "House upon a Rock" – I know you would love them all — yet they dont *bewitch* me any. There are no walks in the wood — no low and earnest voices, no moonlight, nor stolen love, but pure little lives, loving God, and their parents, and obeying the laws of the land; yet read, if you meet them, Susie, for they will do one good.

I have the promise of "Alton Lock" — a certain book, called "Olive," and the "Head of a Family," which was what Mattie named to you. Vinnie and I had "Bleak House" sent to us the other day — it is like him who wrote it — that is all I can say. Dear Susie, you were so happy when you wrote to me last – I am so glad, and you will be happy *now*, for *all* my sadness, *wont* you? I cant forgive me ever, if I have made you sad, or dimmed your eye for me. I write from the Land of Violets, and from the Land of Spring, and it would ill become me to carry you nought but sorrows. I remember you, Susie, *always* – I keep you ever here, and when *you* are gone, then I'm gone — and we're 'neath one willow tree. I can only thank "the Father" for giving me such as you, I can only pray unceasingly, that he will bless my Loved One, and bring her back to me, to "go no more out forever." "Herein is Love." But *that* was Heaven — *this* is but *Earth*, yet Earth so *like* to heaven, that I would hesitate, should the true one call away.

Dear Susie — adieu!

Emilie –

Father's sister is dead, and Mother wears black on her bonnet, and has a collar of crape. A great deal of love from Vinnie, and she wants that *little* *note*. Austin comes home on Wednesday, but he'll only stay two days, so I fancy we shant go sugaring, as "we did last year." *Last year* is *gone*, Susie, did you ever think of *that*? Joseph [Lyman] is out south somewhere, a very great way off, yet we hear from him –

MANUSCRIPT: HCL (L 13). Ink. Dated: Monday morning.
PUBLICATION: FF 197–200, in part.
"Emerald" was used to distinguish Mrs. Mack, the Irish washerwoman, from members of the family of Deacon David Mack. In "the Popes and the Polloks and the John-Milton Browns" ED is characterizing the young men of her acquaintance. The works of Alexander Pope were studied in schools as models of English verse; Robert Pollock, a Scottish poet, wrote *The Course of Time* (1827), which had great contemporary reputation. Perhaps she intends the ambiguity of "John-Milton Brown." Of the several John Browns known at the time, the best known was the Scottish divine (1784–1858), who wrote voluminously on religious subjects.

The books mentioned are as follows: *The Light in the Valley*, a memorial of Mary Elizabeth Stirling, who died at Haddonfield, New Jersey, 30 January 1852 (Philadelphia, American Baptist Publication Society, 1852); *Only*, by Matilda Anne Mackarness (Boston & Cambridge, J. Monroe, 1850); *idem, A House upon a Rock* (1852); *Alton Locke*, by Charles Kingsley (1850); *Olive*, by Dinah Maria Craik (Miss Mulock) (1850); *idem, Head of a Family* (1851). Dickens' *Bleak House* was published in monthly parts in 1852–1853.

Edward Dickinson's sister Mary (Mrs. Mark Newman) died 30 March 1852.

86

To Jane Humphrey   *about April 1852*

And what will dear Jennie say, if I tell her that selfsame minister preached about her again *today*, text and sermon, and all; morning and afternoon: why, the minister must be mad, or else *my* head is turned, I am sure I dont know which — a little of both, may be! Yet it is'nt Sunday *only*, it's all the days in the week, the *whole seven* of them, that I miss Jennie and remember the long, sweet days when she was with me here. I think I love you *more* when spring comes — you know we used to sit in the front door, afternoons after school, and the shy little birds would say chirrup, chirrup, in the tall cherry trees, and if our dresses rustled, hop frightened away; and there used to be some farmer cutting down a tree in the woods, and you and I, sitting there, could hear his sharp ax ring. You wont forget it, Jennie, Oh no, I'm sure you wont, for when you are old and gray, it will be a sweet thing to think of, through the long winter's day! And I *know* *I'll* remember it, for it's so precious to me that I doubt if I *could* forget it, even if I should try.

Thank you for the letter, Jennie; it was very sweet and cheering to hear your voice once more, and it was *sad too*, for I was quite sure then, that you were indeed in Willoughby, in the far state Ohio. I had heard of it all before, but not from *you*, and I did'nt want to believe it, so I made up my mind straightway, that it was'nt at all true – but Jennie, I dont doubt *you*, for you never deceived me. Why so *far*, Jennie, was'nt there room enough for that young ambition, among New England hills, that it must spread it's wings, and fly away, and away, till it paused at Ohio? *Sometimes* think my dear Jennie was a *wee bit uneasy* in her own home and country, or she never had strolled so far, but wont reproach her any, for it's sad to be a stranger, and she *is* now. Why, I cant think what would tempt me to bid my friends Good bye. I'm afraid I'm growing *selfish* in my dear home, but I do love it so, and when some pleasant friend invites me to pass a week with her, I look at my father and mother and Vinnie, and all my friends, and I say no – no, cant leave them, what if they die when I'm gone; Kind Friend – "I pray thee have me excused!" Your home is broken, Jennie; my home is whole; that makes a sad, sad difference, and when I think of it more, it dont seem strange to me, as it did at first, that you could leave it.

If God should choose, Jennie, he could take *my* father, too, and my dear Vinnie, and put them in his sky, to live with him forever, but I shall pray to him every day of my life, not to take them.

It does'nt seem one bit as if *my* friends would die, for I do love them so, that even should death come after them, it dont seem as if they'd go; yet there is Abbie, and Mr. Humphrey, and many and many a dear one, whom I loved just as dearly, and *they* are not upon Earth, this lovely Sabbath evening. Bye and bye we'll be all gone, Jennie, *does* it *seem* as if we would? The other day I tried to think how I should look with my eyes shut, and a little white gown on, and a snow-drop on my breast; and I fancied I heard the neighbors stealing in so softly to look down in my face – so fast asleep – so still – Oh Jennie, will you and I really become like this? Dont mind what I say, Darling, I'm a naughty, bad girl to say sad things, and make you cry, but I think of the grave very often, and how much it has got of mine, and whether

I can ever stop it from carrying off what I love; that makes me sometimes speak of it when I dont intend.

Since I wrote you last, it is spring — the snow has almost gone, and the big, brown Earth is busy, arraying herself in green — first she puts on pantalettes, then little petticoats, then a frock of all colors, and such sweet little stockings and shoes — no, they are not shoes, they are least little bits of gaiters, laced up with blossoms and grass. Then her *hair*, Jennie, perfectly *crowned* with flowers – Oh she'll be a comely maid, by May Day, and she shall be *queen*, if she can! I do wish I could tell you just how the Robins sing — they dont sing now, because it is past their bedtime, and they're all fast asleep, but they *did* sing, this morning, for when we were going to church, they filled the air with such melody, and sang so deliciously, that I tho't really, Jennie, I never should get to meeting. I did want to fly away, and be a Robin too! Spring may be earlier, with you, but *she* cant be any sweeter, I know, and it wont make you angry if I say little birds there, cant sing *half so well*, for I dont believe they can! It is'nt *quite* a year since we laid Abbie to rest, sweet child, she gathers flowers in the *immortal* spring, and they dont fade, tho' she picks them all morning, and holds in her hand till noon; would'nt you and I love such violets, and Roses that never fade – Ah Jennie!

My paper *will* go away, my minutes will go with it, naughty paper — and naughty time — what shall I do *unto* you, how shall I punish you? You shall work for me again, when Jennie has answered my letter, and you wont like that, I *know*! The sooner you write me, therefore, the sooner I'll punish *them*, and you know they ought to be whipped — just as truly as *I* do!

Seems to me I could write all night, Jennie, and then not say the half, nor the *half of the half* of all I have to tell you, but its well I may not do so – since it would weary you. Jennie, be well, and be happy, and sometimes think of me, and how dearly I loved you, and love you still!

Aff –

Emilie –

Manuscript: Rosenbach 1170/17 (4). Ink. Dated: Sunday Evening. Unpublished, except for sentences 3–6 in the first paragraph which were published in Whicher, *This Was a Poet* (1938), 44.

[198]

This letter follows the letter written in March (no. 81) and replies to an answer to it recently received. The opening echoes that moment in *David Copperfield* when David sits in church and imagines the preacher talking about Dora (chapter 26). Jane's father had been dead for two years. The "Mr Humphrey" here mentioned is Leonard Humphrey.

87

To Austin Dickinson   *21 April 1852*

Austin –

I wanted to write you Sunday – I was much disappointed not to, but we have had a long, and unexpected visit from some cousins in Syracuse, and I've had so much to do that I could not write before, but I have thought of you very often during this dismal storm – and hoped you were well, and not unhappy. It storms furiously now – and the rain and hail take turns beating the windows. The sun has'nt shone since Saturday, all that time the wind's blown almost a constant gale, and it has been drear enough. Vinnie said to me this morning, that "things had'nt seemed natural since Austin went away" – and I dont think they have, but I hope you are happy, and dont miss us much now. I dont think I should mind the weather if Susie, and you were here, but I feel so very lonely now, when it storms – and the wind blows. I will tell you about the cousins. You have heard father speak of his cousin, Pliny Dickinson, of Syracuse. He has had two daughters in Hanover, at Mrs Austin Dickinson's school – there is a vacation there, and he has been on to Hanover for the girls. Cousin Harriet heard he was coming, and she and Zebina wrote – urging him and his daughters to visit them. They arrived on Saturday noon, passed that night at Cousin Harriet's, and then proposed coming here. Of course, we told them they might – and having got our permission, they came home with us from meeting – and stayed until yesterday noon, when they went back to Cousin Harriet's.

Cousin Pliny says he "might stay around a month, visiting old acquaintances – if it was'nt for his business."

Fortunate for us indeed, that his business feels the need for him, or I think he would *never* go. He is a kind of compound of Deacon Haskell, Calvin Merrill, and Morton Dickinson, so you will easily guess how much we enjoy his society. The girls are pretty girls, very simple hearted and happy — and would be very interesting, if they had any body to teach them. The oldest, Lizzie, is nineteen — looks exactly Sarah Pynchon, and is very lively and bright, Sarah, the younger — fifteen, a sober little body — and has quite a pensive air, and a cough.

They will stay until May sometime, in Hatfield with their Grand-mother — and then go back to Hanover.

Mattie is very well, was with us yesterday morning — inquired particularly for you, and sent her love to you. I have not heard from Sue, since you went away, but think I shall today. Mrs Bishop Tyler spent the day with us, last Friday — we enjoyed it very much. She has now gone to Pawtucket, and Lizzie is going today. Mary Lyman came Saturday — and I shall go and see her just as soon as it clears off, for it's stormed ever since she came. She has been in Hanover — at the same school with these cousins — attending to French and music, and they have told us how much she said about you. Lizzie says "Miss Lyman thinks there never *was* such a fellow," and the girls admire her so much, that they think you must be most perfect — so to have won her regard.

The Fowler House is shut up, and E – and Willie are at Mrs Ferry's; I believe the Professor has gone.

I send you a schedule of yesterday — the Exhibition is said to have been a very fine one, tho' Mat and I *did'nt* go! We are thinking a great deal about May, and your coming home to see us. I hope we shall live and be well. I shall not allow *Mrs Aiken* to visit home at that time. I think she and David, can come some other time. I enclose my pre-scription, Austin, and if you can have the vial filled, and send it by Mr Watson, I should be very glad to have you, tho' dont, unless it's convenient. Wm Dickinson will take the valise — it is not certain whether he will go tomorrow, or Friday. We think a great deal about you, and all send you much love. You must write when you get the time.

Your very aff

Emilie –

MANUSCRIPT: HCL (L 23). Ink. Dated: Wednesday morn.
PUBLICATION: *LL* 34, three sentences only.

Cousins Harriet and Zebina Montague were sister and brother, he an invalid. Professor Fowler sailed for Europe, April 29. Pliny Dickinson, from Syracuse, and his daughters, left Amherst on April 21 (Lavinia's diary – HCL). Mrs. Aiken, who has not been identified, is referred to again in letter no. 113.

88

To Susan Gilbert (Dickinson)   *late April 1852*

So sweet and still, and Thee, Oh Susie, what need I more, to make my heaven whole?

Sweet Hour, blessed Hour, to carry me to you, and to bring you back to me, long enough to snatch one kiss, and whisper Good bye, again.

I have thought of it all day, Susie, and I fear of but little else, and when I was gone to meeting it filled my mind so full, I could not find a *chink* to put the worthy pastor; when he said "Our Heavenly Father," I said "Oh Darling Sue"; when he read the 100th Psalm, I kept saying your precious letter all over to myself, and Susie, when they sang – it would have made you laugh to hear one little voice, piping to the departed. I made up words and kept singing how I loved you, and you had gone, while all the rest of the choir were singing Hallelujahs. I presume nobody heard me, because I sang *so small*, but it was a kind of a comfort to think I might put them out, singing of you. I a'nt there this afternoon, tho', because I am here, writing a little letter to my dear Sue, and I am very happy. I think of ten weeks – Dear One, and I think of love, and you, and my heart grows full and warm, and my breath stands still. The sun does'nt shine at all, but I can feel a sunshine stealing into my soul and making it all summer, and every thorn, a *rose*. And I pray that such summer's sun shine on my Absent One, and cause her bird to sing!

You have been happy, Susie, and now are sad – and the whole world seems lone; but it wont be so always, "some days *must* be dark and dreary"! You wont cry any more, will you, Susie, for my father will be your father, and my home will be your home, and where you go, I will go, and we will lie side by side in the kirkyard.

I have parents on earth, dear Susie, but your's are in the skies, and I have an earthly fireside, but you have one above, and you have a "Father in Heaven," where I have *none* — and *sister* in heaven, and I know they love you dearly, and think of you every day.

Oh I wish I had half so many dear friends as you in heaven — I could'nt spare them now — but to know they had got there safely, and should suffer nevermore – Dear Susie!

I know I was very naughty to write such fretful things, and I know I could have helped it, if I had tried hard enough, but I thought my heart would break, and I knew of nobody here that cared anything about it — so I said to myself, "We will tell Susie about it." You dont know what a comfort it was, and you wont know, till the big cup of bitterness is filled brimfull, and they say, "Susie, drink it!" Then Darling, let me be there, and let me drink the half, and you will feel it all!

I am glad you have rested, Susie. I wish the week had been *more*, a whole *score* of days and joys for you, yet again, had it lasted longer, then had you not come so soon and I had been lonelier, it is right as it is! Ten weeks, they will seem short to you — for care will fill them, but to Mattie and me, long. We shall grow tired, waiting, and our eyes will ache with looking for you, and with now and then a tear. And yet we have *hope* left, and we shall keep her busy, cheering away the time. Only think Susie, it is vacation now — there shall be no more vacation until ten weeks have gone, and no more snow; and how very little while it will be now, before you and I are sitting out on the broad stone step, mingling our lives together! I cant talk of it now tho', for it makes me long and yearn so, that I cannot sleep tonight, for thinking of it, and you.

Yes, we did go sugaring, and remembered who was gone — and who was there last year, and love and recollection brought with them Little Regret, and set her in the midst of us.

Dear Susie, Dear Joseph; why take the best and dearest, and leave our hearts behind? While the Lovers sighed; and twined oak leaves, and the *anti* enamored ate sugar, and crackers, in the house, I went to see what I could find. Only think of it, Susie; I had'nt any appetite, nor any Lover, either, so I made the best of fate, and gathered antique stones, and your little flowers of moss opened their lips and spoke to me, so I was not alone, and bye and bye Mattie and me might have been seen sitting together upon a high – gray rock, and we might have been heard talking, were anyone very near! And did thoughts of that dear Susie go with us on the rock, and sit there 'tween us twain? Loved One, thou knowest!

I gathered something for you, because you were not there, an acorn, and some moss blossoms, and a little shell of a snail, so whitened by the snow you would think 'twas a cunning artist had carved it from alabaster — then I tied them all up in a leaf with some last summer's grass I found by a brookside, and I'm keeping them all for you.

I saw Mattie at church today, tho' could not speak to her. Friday evening I saw her, and talked with her besides. Oh I do love her — and when you come if we all live till then, it will be *precious*, Susie. You speak to me of sorrow, of what you have "lost and loved," say rather, of what you have loved and *won*, for it is *much*, dear Susie; I can count the big, true hearts by *clusters*, full of bloom, and bloom amaranthine, because *eternal*!

Emilie —

I have heard all about the journal. Oh Susie, that you should come to this! I want you to get it bound — at my expense — Susie — so when he takes you from me, to live in his new home, I may have *some* of you. I am sincere.

Mother sends her best love to you. It makes her look so happy when I give your's to her. Send it always, Susie, and send your respects to father! And much from Vinnie. She was so happy at her note. After she finished reading it, she said, "I dont know but it's wrong, but I love Sue better — than Jane, and I love her and Mattie better than all the friends I ever had in my life." Vinnie hopes to be like you, and to do as you do.

MANUSCRIPT: HCL (L 18). Ink. Dated: Sunday afternoon.
PUBLICATION: LL 20, three sentences in part; FF 213–215, in part.

Sue had been spending her spring holiday of ten days at Havre de Grace, Maryland, with her friend Harriet Hinsdale, at the home of the latter's sister, Mrs. Armon Davis. Joseph Lyman was the young man whose name Emily couples with Sue's as another distant friend. At the end of the fifth from the last paragraph ED wrote, upside down: *Hattie!* On the quotation from Longfellow's "The Rainy Day" in the fourth paragraph, see the note to letter no. 36.

To Austin Dickinson   *10 May 1852*

Dear Austin.

I have made the fires, and got breakfast, and the folks wont get up, and I dont care for it because I can write to you. I did not write yesterday, because mother was sick, and I thought it would trouble you. She was attacked Friday, with a difficulty in her face, similar to the one which you have, and with which you suffer so much once or twice in a year. She had her face lanced˙yesterday, and was much more comfortable last evening, so I'think she'll get well right away.

Vinnie and I have had to work pretty hard on account of her sickness, so I'm afraid we shant write you anything very refreshing this time. Vinnie will tell you all the news, so I will take a little place to describe a thunder shower which occurred yesterday afternoon — the very first of the season. Father and Vinnie were at meeting, mother asleep in her room, and I at work by my window on a "Lyceum Lecture." The air was really scorching, the sun red and hot, and you know just how the birds sing before a thunder storm, a sort of hurried, and agitated song — pretty soon it began to thunder, and the great "cream colored heads" peeped out of their windows — then came the wind and rain and I hurried around the house to shut all the doors and windows. I wish you had seen it come, so cool and so refreshing — and everything glistening from it as with a golden dew — I tho't of you all the time, and I thought too, of Susie; I did wish you both here through all that blessed shower.

This morning is fair and delightful — you will awake in dust, and amidst the ceaseless din of the untiring city, would'nt you change your dwelling for my palace in the dew? I hear them coming, Austin. Goodbye for now. I shall see you so soon.

E.

MANUSCRIPT: AC. Ink. Dated: Monday morning. 5.oc. Envelope addressed: Wᵐ Austin Dickinson./Care of Joel Norcross/31 – Milk St./ Boston./Mass. Postmarked: Amherst Ms. May 10.

PUBLISHED: L (1894) 107, in part; L (1931) 103–104, in part; *Home* 238, entire.

To Austin Dickinson   *13 May 1852*

Dear Austin.

I have wanted to write you a long letter all the week, but you know Mother has been sick, and I have had more to do; but I've tho't of you all the time, and thought too how happy we should be if you were living at home.

It is very hard to have it so, but I try to be as happy and as cheerful as I can to keep father and mother from feeling so very lonely as they must all the while.

Mattie was with me most all the afternoon — we had a long, sad talk about Sue and Michigan, and Life, and our own future, and Mattie cried and I cried, and we had a solemn time, and Mat said she had a beautiful letter from you last night. She was going to send you some flowers in a box, the other day, but you had'nt then answered her letter, and Mat is very shy, so you see why you did'nt get them. John Thompson brought us the books — he arrived Monday — no, it was Tuesday evening — I have read "Ellen Middleton" and now Mat has it.

I need'nt tell you I like it, nor need I tell you more, for you know already.

I thank you more and more for all the pleasures you give me — I can give you nothing Austin, but a warm and grateful heart, that is your's now and always. Love from all, and Mat.

                                   Emilie

Only think, you are coming Saturday! I dont know why it is that it's always *Sunday* immediately you get home — I will arrange it differently. If it was'nt 12 o'clock I would stay longer.

MANUSCRIPT: AC. Pencil. Dated: Thursday night. Addressed on the fold: Austin. An attempts has been made at some time to erase the words "Sue and" in the third paragraph.

PUBLICATION: L (1894) 79–80, in part; L (1931) 77, in part; *Home* 243, entire.

A draft of a letter from Austin to Martha Gilbert, dated 11 May 1852, is in *Home* 240–242. Lady Georgiana Fullerton's novel *Ellen Middleton*, which attracted W. E. Gladstone's attention when it first appeared in the *English Review*, was published in an American edition in 1849.

To Abiah Root   *about May 1852*

I love to link you, A. and E., I love to put you together and look at you side by side – the picture pleases me, and I should love to watch it until the sun goes down, did I not call to mind a very precious letter for which I have not as yet rendered a single farthing, so let me thank you that midst your many friends and cares and influenzas, you yet found time for me, and loved me. You remarked that I had written you more affectionately than wont – I have thought that word over and over, and it puzzles me now; whether our few last years have been cooler than our first ones, or whether I write indifferently when I truly know it not, the query troubles me. I do believe sincerely, that the friendship formed at school was no warmer than now, nay more, that *this* is warmest – they differ indeed to me as morning differs from noon – one may be fresher, cheerier, but the other fails not.

You and I have grown older since school-days, and our years have made us soberer – I mean have made *me* so, for you were always dignified, e'en when a little girl, and *I* used, now and then, to cut a timid caper. That makes me think of you the very first time I saw you, and I can't repress a smile, not to say a hearty laugh, at your little girl expense. I have roused your curiosity, so I will e'en tell you that one Wednesday afternoon, in the days of that dear old Academy, I went in to be entertained by the rhetoric of the gentlemen and the milder form of the girls – I had hardly recovered myself from the dismay attendant upon entering august assemblies, when with the utmost equanimity you ascended the stairs, bedecked with dandelions, arranged, it seemed, for curls. I shall never forget that scene, if I live to have gray hairs, nor the very remarkable fancies it gave me then of you, and it comes over me now with the strangest bygone funniness, and I laugh merrily. Oh, Abiah, you and the early flower are forever linked to me; as soon as the first green grass comes, up from a chink in the stones peeps the little flower, precious "leontodon," and my heart fills toward you with a warm and childlike fullness! Nor do I laugh now; far from it, I rather bless the flower which sweetly, slyly too, makes me come nearer you.

But, my dear, I can't give the dandelion the privilege due to you, so good-by, little one!

I would love to see you, Abiah, I would rather than write to you, might I with equal ease, for the weather is very warm, and my head aches a little, and my heart a little more, so taking me *collectively*, I seem quite miserable, but I'll give you the sunny corners, and you must'nt look at the shade. You were happy when you wrote me; I hope so now, though I would you were in the country, and could reach the hills and fields. I can reach them, carry them home, which I do in my arms daily, and when they drop and fade, I have only to gather fresh ones. Your joy would indeed be full, could you sit as I, at my window, and hear the boundless birds, and every little while feel the breath of some new flower! Oh, do you love the spring, and isn't it brothers and sisters, and blessed, ministering spirits unto you and me, and us all?

I often see Abby — oftener than at sometimes when friendship drooped a little. Did you ever know that a flower, once withered and freshened again, became an immortal flower, – that is, that it rises again? I think resurrections here are sweeter, it may be, than the longer and lasting one – for you expect the one, and only hope for the other. . . . I will show you the *sunset* if you will sit by me, but I cannot bring it there, for so much gold is heavy. Can you see it in Philadelphia?

Abby's health does not change – I fear the wide world holds but little strength for her – I would it were otherwise. Abby is sweet and patient, does n't it ever seem as if her lovely patience was shriving her for God? We cannot tell, but I trust that her sweet face may not be hidden yet. Dear Abiah, do write me whenever you love to do, yet *oftener* I am not confident I ever would hear at all, should I conclude the bargain.

Emilie.

MANUSCRIPT: missing. See note 3 in "Notes on the Present Text." All of the letter, except the concluding paragraph, has been published.

PUBLICATION: L (1894) 60–63; L (1931) 52–54, dated (presumably by ED): Sabbath Day.

Abiah remained in Philadelphia until June (see letter no. 69).

92

To Susan Gilbert (Dickinson)   *about May 1852*

Precious Sue – Precious Mattie!

All I desire in *this* life – all I pray for, or hope for in that long life to come!

Dear Mattie just left me, and I stand just where we stood smiling and chatting together a moment ago. Our last words were of you, and as we said Dear Susie, the sunshine grew so warm, and out peeped prisoned leaves, and the Robins answered Susie, and the big hills left their work, and echoed Susie,, and from the smiling fields, and from the fragrant meadows came troops of *fairy* Susies, and asked "Is it me"? No, Little One, "Eye hath not seen, nor ear heard, nor can the heart conceive" *my* Susie, whom I love.

These days of heaven bring you nearer and nearer, and every bird that sings, and every bud that blooms, does but remind me more of that garden *unseen*, awaiting the hand that tills it. Dear Susie, when you come, how many boundless blossoms among those silent beds! How I do count the days – how I do long for the time when I may count the *hours* without incurring the charge of Femina insania! I made up the Latin – Susie, for I could'nt think how it went, according to Stoddard and Andrew!

I want to send you *joy*, I have half a mind to put up one of these dear little Robin's, and send him singing to you. I know I would, Susie, did I think he would live to get there and sing his little songs.

I shall keep everything singing tho', until Dear Child gets home – and I shant let anything *blossom* till then – either.

I have got to go out in the garden now, and whip a Crown-Imperial for presuming to hold it's head up, until you have come home, so farewell, Susie – I shall think of you at sunset, and at sunrise, again; and at noon, and forenoon, and afternoon, and always, and evermore, till this heart stops beating and is still.

                                                                     Emilie

MANUSCRIPT: HCL (B 173). Ink. Dated: Wednesday.
PUBLICATION: LL 27, in small part, somewhat altered.
Solomon Stoddard and Ethan Allen Andrews compiled *A Grammar of the Latin Language for Schools and Colleges* (Boston, 1837). ED's quota-

tion paraphrases 1 Corinthians 2.9: "Eye hath not seen, nor ear heard, neither have entered into the heart of man, the things which God hath prepared for them that love him."

93

To Susan Gilbert (Dickinson)   *early June 1852*

They are cleaning house today, Susie, and I've made a flying retreat to my own little chamber, where with affection, and you, I will spend this my precious hour, most precious of all the hours which dot my flying days, and the one so dear, that for it I barter everything, and as soon as it is gone, I am sighing for it again.

I cannot believe, dear Susie, that I have stayed without you almost a whole year long; sometimes the time seems short, and the thought of you as warm as if you had gone but yesterday, and again if years and years had trod their silent pathway, the time would seem less long. And now how soon I shall have you, shall hold you in my arms; you will forgive the tears, Susie, they are so glad to come that it is not in my heart to reprove them and send them home. I dont know why it is — but there's something in your name, now you are taken from me, which fills my heart so full, and my eye, too. It is not that the mention *grieves* me, no, Susie, but I think of each "sunnyside" where we have sat together, and lest there be no more, I guess is what makes the tears come. Mattie was here last evening, and we sat on the front door stone, and talked about life and love, and whispered our childish fancies about such blissful things — the evening was gone so soon, and I walked home with Mattie beneath the silent moon, and wished for you, and Heaven. You did not come, Darling, but a bit of Heaven did, or so it *seemed* to us, as we walked side by side and wondered if that great blessedness which may be our's sometime, is granted now, to some. Those unions, my dear Susie, by which two lives are one, this sweet and strange adoption wherein we can but look, and are not yet admitted, how it can fill the heart, and make it gang wildly beating, how it will take *us* one day, and make us all it's own, and we shall not run away from it, but lie still and be happy!

You and I have been strangely silent upon this subject, Susie,

[209]

we have often touched upon it, and as quickly fled away, as children shut their eyes when the sun is too bright for them. I have always hoped to know if you had no dear fancy, illumining all your life, no one of whom you murmured in the faithful ear of night — and at whose side in fancy, you walked the livelong day; and when you come home, Susie, we must speak of these things. How dull our lives must seem to the bride, and the plighted maiden, whose days are fed with gold, and who gathers pearls every evening; but to the *wife*, Susie, sometimes the *wife forgotten*, our lives perhaps seem dearer than all others in the world; you have seen flowers at morning, *satisfied* with the dew, and those same sweet flowers at noon with their heads bowed in anguish before the mighty sun; think you these thirsty blossoms will *now* need naught but – *dew?* No, they will cry for sunlight, and pine for the burning noon, tho' it scorches them, scathes them; they have got through with peace – they know that the man of noon, is *mightier* than the morning and their life is henceforth to him. Oh, Susie, it is dangerous, and it is all too dear, these simple trusting spirits, and the spirits mightier, which we cannot resist! It does so rend me, Susie, the thought of it when it comes, that I tremble lest at sometime I, too, am yielded up. Susie, you will forgive me my amatory strain — it has been a very long one, and if this saucy page did not here bind and fetter me, I might have had no end.

I have got the letter, Susie, dear little bud, and all – and the tears came again, that alone in this big world, I am not *quite* alone. Such tears are showers – friend, thro' which when smiles appear, the angels call them rainbows, and mimic them in Heaven.

And now in four weeks more – you are mine, *all* mine, except I *lend* you a little occasionally to Hattie and Mattie, if they promise not to lose you, and to bring you back very soon. I shall not count the days. I shall not fill my cups with this expected happiness, for perhaps if I do, the angels, being thirsty, will drink them up – I shall only *hope*, my Susie, and *that* tremblingly, for hav'nt barques the fullest, stranded upon the shore?

God is good, Susie, I trust he will save you, I pray that in his good time we once more meet each other, but if this life holds not another meeting for us, remember also, Susie, that it had no *parting* more, wherever that hour finds us, for which we have hoped so long, we

shall not be separated, neither death, nor the grave can part us, so
that we only *love*!

Your Emilie –

Austin has come and gone; life is so still again; why must the storm
have calms? I hav'nt seen Root this term, I guess Mattie and I, are
not sufficient for him! When will you come again, in a week? Let it
be a *swift* week!

Vinnie sends much love, and Mother; and might I be so bold as to
enclose a *remembrance*?

MANUSCRIPT: HLC (L 20). Ink. Dated: Friday morning.
PUBLICATION: *LL* 43, in part.
Sue returned home early in July.

94

To Susan Gilbert (Dickinson)   *11 June 1852*

I have but one thought, Susie, this afternoon of June, and *that*
of you, and I have one prayer, only; dear Susie, *that* is *for* you. That
you and I in *hand* as we e'en *do* in heart, might ramble away as children, among the woods and fields, and forget these many years, and
these sorrowing cares, and each become a child again – I would it
were so, Susie, and when I look around me and find myself alone, I
sigh for you again; little sigh, and vain sigh, which will not bring
you home.

I need you more and more, and the great world grows wider, and
dear ones fewer and fewer, every day that you stay away – I miss my
biggest heart; my own goes wandering round, and calls for Susie –
Friends are too dear to sunder, Oh they are far too few, and how soon
they will go away where you and I cannot find them, *dont* let us forget these things, for their remembrance *now* will save us many an
anguish when it is *too late* to love them! Susie, forgive me Darling,
for every word I say — my heart is full of you, none other than you
in my thoughts, yet when I seek to say to you something not for the
world, words fail me. If you were here — and Oh that you were, my
Susie, we need not talk at all, our eyes would whisper for us, and

your hand fast in mine, we would not ask for language – I try to bring
you nearer, I chase the weeks away till they are quite departed, and
fancy you have come, and I am on my way through the green lane
to meet you, and my heart goes scampering so, that I have much ado
to bring it back again, and learn it to be patient, till that dear Susie
comes. Three weeks – they cant last always, for surely they must go
with their little brothers and sisters to their long home in the west!

I shall grow more and more impatient until that dear day comes,
for till now, I have only *mourned* for you; now I begin to *hope* for
you.

Dear Susie, I have tried hard to think what you would love, of
something I might send you – I at last saw my little Violets, they
begged me to let *them* go, so here they are – and with them as Instructor, a bit of knightly grass, who also begged the favor to accompany them – they are but small, Susie, and I fear not fragrant now,
but they will speak to you of warm hearts at home, and of the something faithful which "never slumbers nor sleeps" – Keep them 'neath
your pillow, Susie, they will make you dream of blue-skies, and
home, and the "blessed countrie"! You and I will have an hour with
"Edward" and "Ellen Middleton", sometime when you get home –
we must find out if some things contained therein are true, and if
they are, what you and me are coming to!

Now, farewell, Susie, and Vinnie sends her love, and mother
her's, and I add a kiss, shyly, lest there is somebody there! Dont let
them see, *will* you Susie?

Emilie –

Why cant *I* be a Delegate to the great Whig Convention? – dont
I know all about Daniel Webster, and the Tariff, and the Law? Then,
Susie I could see you, during a pause in the session – but I dont like
this country at all, and I shant stay here any longer! "Delenda est"
America, Massachusetts and all!

open me carefully

Manuscript: HCL (L 2). Ink. Dated: Friday afternoon. Addressed
on the fold: Miss Susan H. Gilbert./40–Lexington St./Baltimore./Md–
Publication: FF 215–217, in part.
Edward Dickinson was a delegate to the national Whig convention,
which met in Baltimore on 16 June 1852. He delivered the letter.

95

To Austin Dickinson   *20 June 1852*

Your last letter to us, Austin, was very short and very unsatisfying — we do not feel this week that we have heard anything from you
for a very great while, and father's absence, besides, makes us all very
lonely.

I infer from what you said, that my last letter did'nt suit you, and
you tried to write as bad a one as you possibly could, to pay me for
it; but before I began to write, Vinnie said *she* was going to, and
I must'nt write any news, as she was depending upon it to make her
letter of, so I merely talked away as I should if we'd been together,
leaving all the matter o'fact to our practical sister Vinnie — well, we
had calls Sunday evening, until too late to write, and Vinnie was
sound asleep when the mail went out in the morning. I was determined to send you *my* letter, that very day, so Vinnie's note of news,
for which I had starved my own, is as yet unwritten. We have looked
every day for a long letter from you, and really felt sadly enough
when Saturday came without it. I should have written you sooner,
but we have had Miss Bangs cutting dresses for us this week, and
have been very busy, so I could'nt possibly write, but we have all
thought of you, and *that* is better than writing. Father has not got
home, and we dont know when to expect him. We had a letter from
him yesterday, but he did'nt say when he should come. He writes
that he "should think the whole world was there, and some from
other worlds" — he says he meets a great many old friends and acquaintances, and forms a great many new ones — he writes in very
fine spirits, and says he enjoys himself very much. I think it will do
him the very most good of anything in the world, and I do feel happy
to have father at last, among men who sympathize with him, and
know what he really is. I wish you could have gone with him, you
would have enjoyed it so, but I did'nt much suppose that selfish old
school would let you. Father writes that he's called on Sue, twice,
and found her very glad to see him. She will be home in a fortnight —
only think of that!

Mattie gets along nicely — she sends her love to you — she is down
here most every day. Abby Wood had a little party, week before last —
a very pleasant one. Last week, the Senior Levee came off at the Presi-

dent's. Vinnie went to the Levee, and I went to walk with Emmons. Vinnie had a nice time — said everything went off pleasantly, and very much as usual. I believe Prof. Haven is to give one soon — and there is to be a Reception at Prof. Tyler's, next Tuesday evening, which I shall attend. You see Amherst is growing lively, and by the time you come, everything will be in a buzz.

Uncle Samuel's family are here, boarding at Mr Palmer's. Uncle Samuel was here himself, about a week, and is now in New York. Arthur, the oldest one, is going to work on a farm this summer, so as to grow stout and strong, before entering college. Porter Cowles is going to take him. Mr Bowdoin is here still — comes round with the news every day — he has formed quite a fancy for Mat, since Mary became so feeble — has called on her two or three times, been to walk with her once, and walked home with her from the President's. Mat smiles and looks very peculiarly when we mention Mr Bowdoin. I hav'nt seen Mary Warner since you went away — the last time I *heard* of her, she had Thurston and Benjamin, *weeding her flower garden. That's* romantic, is'nt it — she better have her heart wed, before she weeds her garden!

As father has'nt come, Mother cant say certainly how soon you will see her in Boston; just as soon as he comes, she will go, tho, and we shall let you know. She has got her new teeth in, and I think they look very nicely. We all send you our love.

Emilie.

I hope you will write me a letter as soon as you possibly can.

MANUSCRIPT: AC. Ink. Dated: Sunday morning. Envelope addressed: Wᵐ Austin Dickinson/Care of Joel Norcross./31 – Milk St./Boston. Postmarked: Amherst Ms. Jun 21.

PUBLICATION: L (1894) 108, in part; L (1931) 104, in part; *Home* 246–247, entire.

The *Hampshire and Franklin Express,* 10 September 1852, reported that Edward Dickinson "had the honor to represent the old Sixth District in the National nominating Convention. To that convention he carried a firm and unwavering friendship to Daniel Webster, which led him to stand by the great statesman through the fifty-five ballots of that body."

96

To Susan Gilbert (Dickinson)   *27 June 1852*

My Susie's last request; yes, darling, I grant it, tho' few, and fleet the days which separate us now — but six more weary days, but six more twilight evens, and my lone little fireside, my *silent* fireside is once more full.

"We are seven, and one in heaven," we are *three* next Saturday, if *I* have *mine* and heaven has none.

Do not mistake, my Susie, and rather than the car, ride on the golden wings where you will ne'er come back again — do not forget the lane, and the little cot that stands by it, when people from the clouds will beckon you, and smile at you, to have you go with them — Oh Susie, my child, I sit here by my window, and look each little while down towards that golden gateway beneath the western trees, and I fancy I see you coming, you trip upon the green grass, and I hear the crackling leaf under your little shoe; I hide behind the chair, I think I will surprise you, I grow too eager to see you, I hasten to the door, and start to find me that you are not there. And very, very often when I have waked from sleep, *not quite* waked, I have been sure I saw you, and your dark eye beamed on me with such a look of tenderness that I could only weep, and bless God for you.

Susie, will you indeed come home next Saturday, and be my own again, and kiss me as you used to? Shall I indeed behold you, not "darkly, but face to face" or am I *fancying* so, and dreaming blessed dreams from which the day will wake me? I hope for you so much, and feel so eager for you, feel that I *cannot* wait, feel that *now* I must have you — that the expectation once more to see your face again, makes me feel hot and feverish, and my heart beats so fast — I go to sleep at night, and the first thing I know, I am sitting there wide awake, and clasping my hands tightly, and thinking of next Saturday, and "never a bit" of you.

Sometimes I must have Saturday before tomorrow comes, and I wonder if it w'd make any difference with God, to give it to me *today*, and I'd let him have Monday, to make him a Saturday; and then I feel so funnily, and wish the precious day would'nt come quite so soon, till I could know how to feel, and get my thoughts ready for it.

Why, Susie, it seems to me as if my absent Lover was coming

home so soon — and my heart must be so busy, making ready for him.

While the minister this morning was giving an account of the Roman Catholic system, and announcing several facts which were usually startling, I was trying to make up my mind wh' of the two was prettiest to go and welcome *you* in, my fawn colored dress, or my blue dress. Just as I had decided by all means to wear the blue, down came the minister's fist with a terrible rap on the counter, and Susie, it scared me so, I hav'nt got over it yet, but I'm glad I reached a conclusion! I walked home from meeting with Mattie, and *incidentally* quite, something was said of you, and I think one of us remarked that you would be here next Sunday; well — Susie — what it was *I* dont presume to know, but my gaiters seemed to leave me, and I seemed to move on wings — and I move on wings now, Susie, on wings as white as snow, and as bright as the summer sunshine — because I am with you, and so few short days, you are with me at home. Be patient then, my Sister, for the hours will haste away, and Oh *so* soon! Susie, I write most hastily, and very carelessly too, for it is time for me to get the supper, and my mother is gone and besides, my darling, so near I seem to you, that I *disdain* this pen, and wait for a *warmer* language. With Vinnie's love, and my love, I am once more

Your Emilie —

Manuscript: HCL (L 7). Ink. Dated: Sunday afternoon.
Publication: FF 217–219, in part.

After ED's father returned from Baltimore, her mother went to Boston to visit Austin, and probably stayed with the Norcrosses. Sue was to return to Amherst on July 3. Austin completed the school year in Boston, and came home on July 26. Since the principal correspondents were now both at home, a gap of several months appears before the next letter. The quotation in the second paragraph alludes to Wordsworth's poem "We Are Seven," though it is two of the children who are in heaven, not one.

97

To Susan Gilbert (Dickinson)   *early December 1852*

Dear Friend.

I regret to inform you that at 3. oclock yesterday, my mind came to a stand, and has since then been stationary.

Ere this intelligence reaches you, I shall probably be a snail. By this untoward providence a mental and moral being has been swept ruthlessly from her sphere. Yet we should not repine — "God moves in a mysterious way, his wonders to perform, he plants his foot upon the sea, and rides upon the storm," and if it be his will that I become a *bear* and bite my fellow men, it will be for the highest good of this fallen and perishing world. If the gentleman in the air, will please to stop throwing snowballs, I may meet you again, otherwise it is uncertain. My parents are pretty well — Gen Wolf is here — we're looking for Major Pitcairn in the afternoon stage.

We were much afflicted yesterday, by the supposed removal of *our Cat* from time to Eternity.

She returned, however, last evening, having been detained by the storm, beyond her expectations.

I see by the Boston papers that Giddings is up again — hope you'll arrange with Corwin, and have the North all straight.

Fine weather for sledding — have spoken for 52 cord black walnut. We need some paths our way, shant you come out with the team?

Yours till death –

Judah

MANUSCRIPT: HCL (B 176). Ink. Dated: Friday noon.

PUBLICATION: LL 55, in part, and altered.

Sue was in Amherst. In the autumn of 1852, Edward Dickinson was the Whig candidate for Congress from the tenth district, and was elected in December. The gentlemen identified with the historic figures General Wolfe (who died victorious at Quebec) and Major Pitcairn (fatally wounded at Bunker Hill) were probably political visitors, calling on Edward Dickinson. Joshua Reed Giddings broke with the Whig party in 1848. Thomas Corwin, Fillmore's Secretary of the Treasury, had also opposed the Fugitive Slave Law endorsed by the Whig convention. The quotation from William Cowper's "Light Shining out of Darkness," with which ED would be especially familiar from its hymn setting, seems to have been from memory, since it alters the third line, which reads: "He plants his footsteps in the sea." The historical associations with the name Judah are so many that the private association for which ED uses it as a signature makes any conjecture about its intent in this letter, largely a *jeu d'esprit*, pure guesswork.

To Emily Fowler (Ford)   *about 13 January 1853*

Dear Emily –

I fear you will be lonely this dark and stormy day, and I send this little messenger to say you must not be.

The day is long to me, because I have no Vinnie, and I think of those today who never had a Vinnie, and I'm afraid they are lone. I have wanted to come and see you – I have tried earnestly to come, but always have been detained by some ungenerous care, and now this falling snow, sternly, and silently, lifts up its hand between.

How glad I am affection can always leave and go – How glad that the drifts of snow pause at the outer door, and go no farther, and it is as warm within as if no winter came! Dear Emily, do not sorrow, upon this stormy day — "into each life some '*flakes*' must fall, some days must be dark and dreary." Let us think of the pleasant summer whose gardens are far away, and whose Robins are singing always!

If it were not for blossoms we know that we shall see, and for that brighter sunshine above – beyond – away – these days were dark indeed, but I try to keep recollecting that we are away from home — and have many brothers and sisters who are expecting us. Dear Emilie — dont weep, for you will both be so happy, where "sorrow cannot come."

Vinnie left her Testament on a little stand in our room, and it made me think of her, so I thought I w'd open it, and the first words I read were in those sweetest verses — "Blessed are the poor – Blessed are they that mourn – Blessed are they that weep, for they shall be comforted." Dear Emily, I thought of you, and I hasted away to send this message to you.

Emilie –

MANUSCRIPT: NYPL. Ink. Dated: Thursday evening.

PUBLICATION: L (1894) 134–135, in part; L (1931) 134, in part.

The year is conjectured from the handwriting. There was a heavy snowstorm on January 13. Professor Fowler was still in Europe. Lavinia was presumably making one of her customary visits to Boston. The quoted lines in the third paragraph paraphrase Longfellow's "The Rainy Day" (see letter no. 36).

To Emily Fowler (Ford)   *early 1853?*

Dear Emily,

I said when the Barber came, I would save you a little ringlet, and fulfilling my promise, I send you one today. I shall never give you anything again that will be half so full of sunshine as this wee lock of hair, but I wish no hue more sombre might ever fall to you.

All your gifts should be rainbows, if I owned *half* the skies, and but a bit of sea to furnish raindrops for me. Dear Emily — this is all — It will serve to make you remember me when locks are crisp and gray, and the quiet cap, and the spectacles, and "John Anderson my Joe" are all that is left of me.

I must have one of yours – Please spare me a little lock sometime when you have your scissors, and there is one to spare.

Your very aff
Emilie –

MANUSCRIPT: NYPL. Pencil. Addressed on the outer fold: Emilie.
PUBLICATION: *L* (1894) 133; *L* (1931) 132–133.

ED was wearing her hair short at the time. In the late summer of 1852 Lavinia wrote to Austin: "Emilie's hair is cut off & shes very pretty." (*Home* 248). Mrs. Ford's collection of her friends' hair is in NYPL, but ED's ringlet is missing.

100

To John L. Graves   *about February 1853*

Cousin John.

I thought perhaps you and your friend would come in to drink *wine* this evening, as I asked you to do, after Vinnie got home, but I want to tell you something.

Vinnie and I are asked out this evening, and Vinnie's obliged to go. It will not be as pleasant when she is absent from home, and now I want to know if you will be busy *next* week, and if not, wont you save an evening, or an hour of one, when you will come and see us, and taste the currant wine?

Please tell your friend — Mr Emmons, and invite him to come with you upon another evening.

Vinnie and I are sorry, but fortune is unkind.

Your Cousin Emily.

MANUSCRIPT: HCL (G 5). Ink. Dated: Friday afternoon.
PUBLICATION: *Home* 224–225.

John Graves, now a sophomore at Amherst College, had introduced his friend Henry Vaughan Emmons to the Dickinson girls a year earlier. ED counted Graves as her friend, yet the formal address was customary. Vinnie had been away in January.

101

To John L. Graves   *about February 1853*

I wonder if Cousin John has a lesson to learn this evening?

Emilie –

MANUSCRIPT: HCL (G 9). Pencil. Addressed: Cousin John. Unpublished.

ED here suggests that John might call this evening, if he is free to do so.

102

To Susan Gilbert (Dickinson)   *24 February 1853*

The sun shines warm, dear Susie, but the *sweetest* sunshine's gone, and in that far off Manchester, all my blue sky is straying this winter's afternoon. Vinnie and I are here — just where you always find us when you come in the afternoon to sit a little while – We miss your face today, and a tear fell on my work a little while ago, so I put up my sewing, and tried to write to you. I had rather have *talked,* dear Susie — it seems to me a long while since I have seen you much — it is a long while Susie, since we have been together — so long since we've spent a twilight, and spoken of what we loved, but you will come back again, and there's all the *future* Susie, which is as yet untouched! It is the brightest star in the firmament of God, and I look in it's face the oftenest.

[220]

I ran to the door, dear Susie – I ran out in the rain, with nothing but my slippers on, I called "Susie, Susie," but you did'nt look at me; then I ran to the dining room window and rapped with all my might upon the pane, but you rode right on and never heeded me.

It made me feel so lonely that I could'nt help the tears, when I came back to the table, to think I was eating breakfast, and *you* were riding away – but bye and bye I thought that the same ugly coach which carried you away, would have to bring you *back again* in but a little while, and the spite pleased me so that I did'nt cry any more till the tear fell of which I told you. And now, my absent One, I am hoping the days away, till I shall see you home – I am sewing as fast as I can, I am training the stems to my flowers, I am working with all my might, so as to pause and love you, as soon as you get home.

How fast we will have to talk then – there will be those farewell gaieties – and all the days before, of which I have had no fact, and there will be your absence, and your *presence*, my Susie dear, sweetest, and brightest, and best of every and all the themes. *It is sweet* to talk, dear Susie, with those whom God has given us, lest we should be alone – and you and I have *tasted it*, and found it *very sweet*; even as fragrant flowers, o'er which the bee hums and lingers, and hums *more* for the lingering.

I find it very lonely, to part with *one of mine*, with mine *especially*, and the days will have more *hours* while you are gone away.

They played the trick yesterday – they dupe me again today.

Twelve hours make *one – indeed* – Call it *twice* twelve, three times twelve, and add, and add, and add, then multiply again, and we will talk about it.

"At Dover dwells George Brown Esq – Good Carlos Finch and David Fryer" – Oh Susie! How much escapes me, mine; whether you reached there safely, whether you are a stranger – or have only just *gone home* – Whether you find the friends as you fancied you should find them, or dearer than you expected?

All this, and more, Susie, I am eager to know, and I *shall* know soon, shant I? I love to *think* I shall. Oh Susie, Susie, I must call out to you in the old, old way – I must say how it seems to me to hear the clock so silently tick all the hours away, and bring me not my gift – my own, my own!

Perhaps you cant read it, Darling, it is incoherent and blind; but the recollection that prompts it, is very distinct and clear, and reads easily. Susie, they send their love — my mother and my sister — *thy* mother and thy sister, and the Youth, the Lone Youth, Susie, you know the rest!

Emilie —

Tell me when you write Susie, if I shall send my love to the Lady where you stay!

MANUSCRIPT: HCL (L 11). Ink. Dated: Thursday afternoon.
PUBLICATION: *FF* 220–223, in part, with alterations.
Sue was in Manchester, New Hampshire, visiting Mrs. Samuel C. Bartlett, the sister of Julius Learned, Mary Gilbert's widower. The source of ED's couplet is Longfellow's *Kavanagh*: "At Dover dwells George Brown, Esquire,/Good Christopher Finch, and Daniel Friar." The lines form a device used to reckon the day of the week on which the first of each month will fall. The twelve words represent the months of the year in sequence, and the seven initial letters, A B C D E F G, stand for the days of the week. The day on which January 1 falls in any specific year will be represented by "A" in "At." It then is simple to discover on what days the other eleven months will begin.

103

To Susan Gilbert (Dickinson)   *5 March 1853*

I know dear Susie is busy, or she would not forget her lone little Emilie, who wrote her just as soon as she'd gone to Manchester, and has waited so patiently till she can wait no more, and the credulous little heart, fond even tho' forsaken, will get it's big black inkstand, and tell her once again how well it loves her.

Dear Susie, I have tried so hard to act patiently, not to think unkind thoughts, or cherish unkind doubt concerning one not here, I have watched the stages come in, I have tried to look indifferent, and hum a snatch of tune when I heard Father and Austin coming, and knew how soon they'd bring me a dear letter from you, or I should look in the hat, and find it all empty — and here comes Saturday, and tomorrow the world stands still, and I shall have no message from my dear Susie!

Why dont you write me, Darling? Did I in that quick letter say anything which grieved you, or made it hard for you to take your usual pen and trace affection for your bad, sad Emilie?

Then Susie, you must forgive me before you sleep tonight, for I will not shut my eyes until you have kissed my cheek, and told me you would love me.

Oh it has been so still, since when you went away, nothing but just the ticking of the two ceaseless clocks — swiftly the "Little mystic one, no human eye hath seen," but slowly and solemnly the tall clock upon the mantel — you remember *that* clock, Susie. It has the oddest way of striking twelve in the morning, and six in the afternoon, just as soon as you come. I am trying to teach it a few of the proprieties of life, now you are gone away, and the poor thing does indeed seem quite obedient, and goes slowly eno', but as soon as you're back again, Susie, it will be the same graceless one it ever used to be, and only gallop with accelerated speed, to make up for resting now.

Dear Susie, it is harder to live alone than it was when you were in Baltimore, and the days went slowly, *then* — they go e'en slower than they did while you were in the school — or else I grow impatient, and cannot brook as easily absence from those I love. I dont know which it is — I only know that when you shall come back again, the Earth will seem more beautiful, and bigger than it does now, and the blue sky from the window will be all dotted with gold — though it may not be evening, or time for the stars to come.

It is pleasant to talk of you with Austin — and Vinnie and to find how you are living in every one of their hearts, and making it warm and bright there — as if it were a sky, and a sweet summer's noon. Austin has gone this morning — the last little thing I did for him was while they were at breakfast, to write on four envelopes for him to send to you —

It made me smile, Susie, to think how Little Argus was cheated after all — and I smiled again, at thinking of something holier, of something from the skies, come Earthward.

Dear Susie, I dont forget you a moment of the hour, and when my work is finished, and I have got the tea, I slip thro' the little entry, and out at the front door, and stand and watch the West, and remember all of mine — yes, Susie — the golden West, and the great, silent Eternity, for ever folded there, and bye and bye it will open it's everlasting, arms, and gather us all – all; Good bye, dear Susie – they all send you their love –

Emilie –

Susie – will you give my love to Mrs Bartlett, and tell her the fortnight is out next Wednesday, and I thought she m't like to know!

MANUSCRIPT: HCL (L 8). Ink. Dated: Saturday morning.
PUBLICATION: FF 188–189, in part.

Austin left on March 5 for Cambridge, to enter the Harvard Law School; the term had already begun two days earlier. The four envelopes ED addressed for him to send Sue indicate that his courtship is developing. For an explanation of the "Little mystic one," see the note for letter no. 60.

104

To Austin Dickinson   *8 March 1853*

Dear Austin.

Dont feel lonely, for we think of you all the time, and shall love you and recollect you all the while you are gone. Your letter made us all feel sadly, and we had a sober evening thinking of you at Cambridge, while we were all at home.

I hope you are better now, and like the looks of things better than you thought you should at first. You were perfectly tired out when you went away from home and I thought you'd feel rather lonely until you got rested a little and then things would look bright again. I am glad you think of us, and think you would like to see us, for I've thought a good many times that you would soon forget us, on going away from home. I dont think you can miss us more than we do you, Austin, and dont think we have forgotten you, because you are away.

I am glad you found a letter waiting for you from Sue for I think it must have made things seem a little more like home.

I hav'nt heard from her yet. I dont much expect to now – though I wrote her again on Saturday. I had a letter for Sue directed to my care last evening – the outside envelope in Mr Learned's hand, and containing one from Martha. I shall send it to Sue today.

Father went to New York, this morning – he thinks he shall come home Thursday, tho' he dont know certainly.

We have sent you a *table cover* this morning by Mr Green — also two little wash cloths, which we found and thought you would like. Mother wants me to tell you if there's anything else you would like, that you must let us know and we will send it to you by the first opportunity — also to send your washing home every time you can find a chance, and your clothes shall be well taken care of. Above all things, take care of yourself, and dont get sick away, for it would be very lonely for you to be sick among strangers, and you're apt to be careless at home. What a time you must have had getting on in the snow storm! We felt very anxious about you — mother, particularly, and wondered how you would get through, and yet I knew you never had any trouble anywhere, and I really did'nt think that with you on board the cars, there could anything happen. But Austin, you are there — the time will soon be over, and we shall all be together again as we were of old — you know how fast time *can* fly, if we only let it go — then recollect dear Austin, that none of us are gone where we cannot come home again, and the separations *here* are but for a little while. We will write again very soon.

Emilie.

Mother and Vinnie send much love, and say you must'nt be lonely. I have done what you wanted me to.

Manuscript: AC. Ink. Dated: Tuesday morning. An attempt has been made to erase the words "from Sue" in the third paragraph.

Publication: *Home* 260–261.

During the rest of the year ED and other members of the family, in writing to Austin, used envelopes addressed and franked by Edward Dickinson who learned, after he went to Washington in December, that the privilege did not extend so far.

The news about the Newman family in letter no. 106 makes clear that Edward Dickinson's trip to New York was made in connection with their affairs. His sister Mary, and her husband Mark Newman, had both died within the year, and Edward Dickinson was guardian of their son and four daughters. Martha Gilbert was living with her brother at Grand Haven, Michigan.

105

To Susan Gilbert (Dickinson)   *about March 1853*

Write! Comrade, write!

On this wondrous sea
Sailing silently,
Ho! Pilot, ho!
Knowest thou the shore
Where no breakers roar –
Where the storm is oer?

In the peaceful west
Many the sails at rest –
The anchors fast –
Thither I pilot *thee* –
Land Ho! Eternity!
Ashore at last!

                                        Emilie –

MANUSCRIPT: HCL (B 73). Pencil. Addressed: Susie.
PUBLICATION: *Poems* (1955) 6–7.
This note in verse was enclosed in one of the letters written at this time.
ED wrote Austin on March 18: "I've written her three times." The message
may say more than "Write me a letter." ED had begun writing poetry and
was probably encouraging Sue to do the same.

106

To Austin Dickinson   *12 March 1853*

Dear Austin.

I am afraid you think that we have all forgotten you, we hav'nt
written now for so many days, but we hav'nt, and I will tell you why
we have kept still so long. We thought from your first letter that you'd
probably write us again in a day or two, and there might be some
thing which you would want to know, so we waited to hear from
you – well, you did not seem to write so soon as we expected, and I

thought Wednesday morning I would'nt wait any longer, but we know not what is before us.

A little while after breakfast Vinnie went over to Mr Kellogg's on an errand — was'nt going to stay but a minute — well, two hours had passed away and nothing was seen of Vinnie, and I had begun to wonder what had become of her, when Emmeline walked in with her, and helped her onto the Lounge. Her right hand was all done up, and she looked so faint I thought somebody had killed her. It seems she went to the door and found the Dog lying there, and thought she would pat him a little so that he would'nt growl, but he did growl terribly, then snapped at her hand, and bit the thumb on her right hand, almost thro from one side to the other. Her hand pained her so much that she fainted constantly, and as soon as she was able Emmeline came home with her. Mr Kellogg's folks felt dreadfully about it, they did everything they could — Em went for Dr Woodman, and we had quite a time — this was when father was gone, and of course it frightened us more, but you need'nt be scared any longer Austin, for she's doing nicely now. She cant comb her hair or dress her, or help herself at all, so you see I have my hands full, for besides doing all this, I have to do her usual work. *That's* the reason I hav'nt written you Austin, many a time before. I could'nt get time to do it, but I've thought of you just as much, and more, than if I c'd have written, and we all miss you every day, and want to see you more than I can possibly tell you. I am so glad to know you're happier, and that Cambridge looks brighter to you. We enjoyed your letter very much and laughed heartily at it — *father* particularly, seemed to think it "uncommon" fine. He got home Thursday night, at about 12 o clock.

The Newman family are coming here about the middle of April — another fact which will please you. Uncle Sweetser and his wife are going to Europe in May, and Elisabeth and their children are coming to Amherst to board at Mr Newman's for the summer! Such intelligence needs no comments. I have telegraphed to Sue. Dont say anything about it in the letter you write me next, for father reads all your letters before he brings them home, and it might make him feel unpleasantly.

I hope we shall all be spared to have one *kitchen meeting*, and express our several minds on this infamous proceeding, but I wont trouble you. You asked about the Paper. Daniel Webster of Deerfield cant come on account of the limited salary — Mr [Samuel] Nash, on account of his eyes, and as Mr Trumbull has gone, they got Mr Sydney Adams, with the *assistance of others* to get out the this weeks one. Bowdoin "moves on" like snails. I have heard once from Susie — not much tho'. We will hem the crash, and send it to you by the first opportunity. Mother wants you to get a cheap Comforter and put on the palmleaf mattress; — she says t'will be easier to you.

We all send you our love. Vinnie says she will write as soon as she uses her hand. Write us soon.

Aff
Emilie

MANUSCRIPT: AC. Pencil. Dated: Saturday morning. Postmarked: Mar. 12.

PUBLICATION: *Home* 263–264.

Edward Dickinson's guardianship of the Newman girls put the whole family in a difficult position. Though Newman had left a comfortable estate, he bequeathed most of it to missionary societies. The girls came to Amherst accompanied by their father's sister, Mrs. Fay, and lived in the house owned by Dickinson, on the east side of the common. The Sweetser children were to be cared for during the summer by their aunt Elizabeth, the still unmarried youngest Dickinson sister, who divided her time among various members of the family. The "Paper" alluded to was the *Hampshire and Franklin Express*, which was undergoing a change of management under the ownership of the Adams family; J. R. Trumbull no longer served as editor.

107

To Susan Gilbert (Dickinson)   *12 March 1853*

Dear Susie —

I'm so amused at my own ubiquity that I hardly know what to say, or how to relate the story of the wonderful correspondent. First, I arrive from Amherst, then comes a ponderous tome from the learned Halls of Cambridge, and again by strange metamorphosis I'm just from Michigan, and am Mattie and Minnie and Lizzie in one wondering breath — Why, dear Susie, it must'nt scare you if I loom up from Hindoostan, or drop from an Appenine, or peer at you suddenly

[228]

from the hollow of a tree, calling myself King Charles, Sancho Panza, or Herod, King of the Jews – I suppose it is all the same.

"Miss Mills," that is, Miss Julia, never *dreamed* of the depths of *my clandestiny*, and if *I* stopped to think of the figure I was cutting, it would be the last of me, and you'd never hear again from you poor Jeremy Bentham –

But I say to my mind, "tut, tut," "Rock a bye baby" conscience, and so I keep them still!

And as for the pulling of wool over the eyes of Manchester, I trust to the courtesy of the Recording Angel, to say nothing of *that*. One thing is true, Darling, the world will be none the wiser, for Emilie's omnipresence, and two big hearts will beat stouter, as tidings from *me* come in. I love the opportunity to serve those who are mine, and to soften the least asperity in the path which ne'er "ran smooth," is a delight to me. So Susie, I set the trap and catch the little mouse, and love to catch him dearly, for I think of you and Austin – and know it pleases you to have my tiny services. Dear Susie, you are gone – One would hardly think I had lost you to hear this revelry, but your absence insanes me so – I do not feel so peaceful, when you are gone from me – All life looks differently, and the faces of my fellows are not the same they wear when you are with me. I think it is this, dear Susie; you sketch my pictures for me, and 'tis at their sweet colorings, rather than this dim real that I am used, so you see when you go away, the world looks staringly, and I find I need more vail – Frank Peirce thinks I mean *berage* vail, and makes a sprightly plan to import the "article," but dear Susie knows what I mean. Do you ever look homeward, Susie, and count the lonely hours Vinnie and I are spending, because that you are gone?

Yes, Susie, very lonely, and yet is it very sweet too to know that you are happy, and to think of you in the morning, and at eventide, and noon, and always as smiling and looking up for joy – I could not spare you *else*, dear Sister, but to be sure your life is warm with such a sunshine, helps me to chase the shadows fast stealing upon mine – I *knew* you would be happy, and you know now of something I had told you.

There *are* lives, sometimes, Susie – Bless God that we catch faint glimpses of his brighter Paradise from *occasional* Heavens *here*!

Stay, Susie; yet *not* stay! I cannot spare your sweet face another hour more, and yet I want to have you gather more sheaves of joy — for bleak, and waste, and barren, are most of the fields found here, and I want you to *fill* the *garner. Then* you may come, dear Susie, and ᶠrom our silent home, Vinnie and I shall meet you. There is much to tell you, Susie, but I cannot bring the deeds of the rough and jostling world into that sweet inclosure; they are fitter *fonder, here* — but Susie, I do bring you a Sister's fondest love — and gentlest tenderness; little indeed, but "a'," and I know you will not refuse them. Please remember me to your friend, and write soon to

your lonely
Emilie —

Vinnie sends you her love – She would write, but has hurt her hand – Mother's love too – Oh Susie!

MANUSCRIPT: HCL (L 4). Ink. Dated: Saturday noon.
PUBLICATION: FF 190–192, in part.

In the first paragraph ED alludes to the various envelopes addressed in her hand: first her own letters to Sue; then Austin's, in the envelopes she addressed for him; and finally those sent in her care and forwarded to Sue from her relatives in Michigan, her sister Martha and the two sisters-in-law. Julia Mills, in *David Copperfield,* was the bosom friend of Dora Spenlow, and described as "interested in others' loves, herself withdrawn." It is Austin who is identified with the philosopher and jurist Bentham.

108

To Austin Dickinson   *18 March 1853*

Dear Austin.

I presume you remember a story Vinnie tells of a Breach of promise Case where the correspondence between the parties consisted of a reply from the girl to one she had never received, but was daily expecting — well *I* am writing an answer to the letter I hav'nt had, so you will see the force of the accompanying anecdote. I have been looking for you ever since despatching my last, but this is a fickle world, and it's a great source of complacency that t'will all be burned up bye and bye. I should be pleased with a line when you've published your work to Father, if it's perfectly convenient. Your letters are very funny indeed

[230]

— about the only jokes we have, now you and Sue are gone, and I hope you will send us one as often as you can. Father takes great delight in your remarks to him — puts on his spectacles and reads them o'er and o'er as if it was a blessing to have an only son.

He reads all the letters you write as soon as he gets, at the post office, no matter to whom addressed. I presume when Sue gets back, and has directed to her, he will take them and read them first. Well, I was telling you, he reads them once at the office, then he makes me read them loud at the supper table again, and when he gets home in the evening, he cracks a few walnuts, puts his spectacles on, and with your last in his hand, sits down to enjoy the evening. He remarked in confidence to me this morning, that he "guessed you saw through things there" — of course I answered "yes sir," but what the thought conveyed I remained in happy ignorance. Whether he meant to say that you saw through *the Judges*, overcoats and all, I could not quite determine but I'm sure he designed to compliment you very highly.

I do think it's so funny — you and father do nothing but "fisticuff" all the while you're at home, and the minute you are separated, you become such devoted friends; but this is a checkered life.

I believe at this moment, Austin, that there's no body living for whom father has such respect as for you, and yet your conduct together is quite peculiar indeed. But my paper is getting low, and I must hasten to tell you that we are very happy to hear good news from you — that we hope you'll have pleasant times, and learn a great deal while you're gone, and come back to us greater and happier for the life lived at Cambridge. We miss you more and more. I wish that we could see you, but letters come the next — write them often, and tell us everything!

Aff
Emilie.

Dear Austin, I've just decided that my yarn is not quite spun, so I'll spin it a little longer.

Vinnie's hand is getting well, tho' she cant sew or write with it. She sends her love to you, and says she shall write a note, as soon as her hand gets able.

Anna Warner's a little better, tho' the *medical faculty* dare as yet give little encouragement of her return thitherward. Mary is at present incarcerated, and becomes in the public eye, more and more of a martyr daily. The Quinsy approached Miss Goudy [?], but was dexterously warded off by homeopathic glances from a certain Dr Gregg, of whom you may hear in Boston. Professor Warner, and consort, and surviving son, are much as usual. Father's Cummington friend, late from State's prison in Brooklyn, took tea with us this week. He has *advanced* somewhat since we children have seen him.

Jerry [Holden?] and Mrs Mack inquire for "Mr Austin." Most all of the folks we asked here have made their "party call," and we have had our hands full in entertaining them. You must tell us about the party which you attend at Miss C's. I have not heard from Sue again, tho' I've written her three times. I suppose she'll be coming home Saturday, and I'll tell you something funny the next time I write.

We all send you much love, and wish you were here today, so we could talk with you.

Emilie again.

MANUSCRIPT: AC. Pencil. Dated: Friday morning. Postmarked: Mar 18. An attempt has been made at some time to erase the words "and Sue" in the first paragraph. ED's postscript is written on a separate sheet.

PUBLICATION: L (1894) 112–113, in part; L (1931) 107–109, in part; Home 265–267, entire.

Anna Warner was the younger sister of Mary Warner, one of ED's close friends (see letter no. 118). Jerry, whose name appears several times in the letters of 1853–54, was probably the "faithful hand," Jeremiah Holden, mentioned in letter no. 80. For further details about Mrs. Mack, see Appendix 2.

109

To Austin Dickinson   24 March 1853

Dear Austin.

How much I miss you, how lonely it is this morning—how I wish you were here, and how very much I thank you for sending me that long letter, which I got Monday evening, and have read a great many times, and presume I shall again, unless I soon have another.

I find life not so bright without Sue and you, or Martha, and for a little while I hav'nt cared much about it. How glad I was to know that you had'nt forgotten us, and looked forward to home, and the rustic seat, and summer, with so much happiness. You wonder if we think of you as much as you of us – I guess so, Austin – it's a great deal anyhow, and to look at the empty nails, and the empty chairs in the kitchen almost obscures my sight, if I were used to tears. But *I* think of the rustic seat, and I think of the July evening just as the day is done, and I read of the one come back, worth all the "ninety and nine" who have not gone from home, and these things strengthen me for many a day to come.

I'm so glad you are cheerful at Cambridge, for cheerful indeed one must be to write such a comic affair as your last letter to me. I believe the message to Bowdoin, w'd have killed father outright if he had'nt just fortified nature with two or three cups of tea. I could hardly contain myself sufficiently to read a thing so grotesque, but it did me good indeed, and when I had finished reading it, I said with a pleasant smile, "then there is something left"! I have been disgusted, ever since you went away, and have concluded several times that it's of no use minding it, as it is only a puff ball. But your letter so raised me up, that I look round again, and notice my fellow men.

I think you far exceed Punch – much funnier – much funnier, cant keep up with you at all!

I suppose the young lady will be getting home today – how often I thought of you yesterday afternoon and evening. I did "drop in at the Revere" a great many times yesterday. I hope you have been made happy. If so I am satisfied. I shall know when you get home.

I have been to see Mrs Cutler several times since Sue has been gone. *Mr Cutler* has missed her dreadfully, which has gratified me much. What I was going to tell you was that Mr Cutler's folks had written Sue to meet *Mr Sweetser* in Boston last week, and come to Amherst with him. I knew she would'nt come, and I couldnt help laughing to think of him returning to town alone – that's all! Sue's outwitted them all – ha-ha! just imagine me giving three cheers for American Independence!

I did get that little box, and do with it as you told me. I wrote you so at the time, but you must have forgotten it. Write again soon, Austin, for this is a lonely house, when we are not all here.

Emilie.

Mother says "tell Austin I think perhaps I shall write him a letter myself."

Mother sends her love, and is very much obliged to you for the message to her, and also for the comb, which you told us was coming. She wants you to send your clothes home just as soon as you can, for she thinks you must certainly need some by this time. We hav'nt had much maple sugar yet, but I shall send you some when Mr Green goes back. We have had some maple molasses. I know you would love some, if you were here – how I do wish you were here! I read the proclamation, and liked it very much. I had a letter from Mat, last night – she said a great deal of Sue and you, and *so* affectionately. If Sue thinks Mat would be willing, I will send the letter to you, the next time I write.

MANUSCRIPT: AC. Pencil. Dated: Thursday morning. Postmarked: Mar 24. An attempt has been made throughout to erase Sue's name.

PUBLICATION: *Home* 269–270.

According to a carefully contrived plan between Austin and Sue, the latter returned from Manchester by way of Boston. The correspondence that follows indicates that they became engaged at this time. Sue arrived in Amherst on March 24. Lavinia's hand had recovered sufficiently for her to write a note to Austin that was enclosed with Emily's.

110

To Austin Dickinson   *27 March 1853*

Oh my dear "Oliver," how chipper you must be since any of us have seen you? How thankful we should be that you have been brought to Greenville, and a suitable frame of mind! I really had my doubts about your reaching Canaan, but you relieve my mind, and set me at rest completely. How long it is since you've been in this state of complacence towards God and your fellow men? I think it must be sudden, hope you are not deceived, would recommend "Pilgrim's Progress," and "Baxter upon the will." Hope you have enjoyed the Sabbath, and sanctuary privileges – it is'nt *all* young men that have the preached word.

Trust you enjoy your closet, and meditate profoundly upon the

Daily Food! I shall send you Village Hymns, by earliest opportunity.

I was just this moment thinking of a favorite stanza of your's, "where congregations ne'er break up, and Sabbaths have no end."

That must be a delightful situation, certainly, quite worth the scrambling for!

Quite likely you have *tickets* for your particular friends – hope I should be included, in memory of "old clothes."

And Austin is a Poet, Austin writes a psalm. Out of the way, Pegasus, Olympus enough "to him," and just say to those "nine muses" that we have done with them!

Raised a living muse ourselves, worth the whole nine of them. Up, off, tramp!

Now Brother Pegasus, I'll tell you what it is – I've been in the habit *myself* of writing some few things, and it rather appears to me that you're getting away my patent, so you'd better be somewhat careful, or I'll call the police! Well Austin, if you've stumbled through these two pages of folly, without losing your hat or getting lost in the mud, I will try to be sensible, as suddenly as I can, before you are quite disgusted. *Mademoiselle* has come, quite to the surprise of us all. I concluded you had concluded to sail for Australia. Sue's very sober yet, she thinks it's pretty desolate without old Mr Brown.

She seems to be absent, sometimes, on account of the "old un," and I think you're a villainous rascal to entrap a young woman's "phelinks" in such an awful way.

You deserve, let me see; you deserve hot irons, and Chinese Tartary; and if I were Mary Jane, I would give you one such "mitten" Sir. as you never had before! I declare, I have half a mind to *throw a stone* as it is, and kill five barn door fowls, but I wont, I'll be considerate! Miss Susie was here on Friday, was here on Saturday, and Miss Emilie, there, on Thursday. I suppose you will go to the "*Hygeum*" as usual, this evening. Think it a dreadful thing for a young man under influences to frequent a hotel, evenings! Am glad our Pilgrim Fathers got safely out of the way, before such shocking times! Are you getting on well with "the work," and have you engaged the Harpers? Shall bring in a bill for my Lead Pencils, 17, in number, disbursed at times to you, as soon as the publishment. Also, two envelopes daily, during *despatch of proofs*, also Johnnie Beston, also David Smith, and services from same!

Dear Austin, I am keen, but you are a good deal keener, I am *something* of a fox, but you are more of a hound! I guess we are very good friends tho', and I guess we both love Sue just as well as we can. You need'nt laugh at my letter — it's a few *Variations* of *Greenville* I thought I would send to you.

Affy
Emilie.

Love from us all. Monday noon. Oh Austin, Newton is dead. The first of my own friends. Pace.

MANUSCRIPT: AC. Ink. Dated: Sabbath evening. Postmarked: Amherst Ms Mar 28. An attempt has been made to erase "Sue" in the second paragraph above the signature.

PUBLICATION: L (1931) 109–110, in part; *Home* 271–273, entire.

The salutation "Oliver" may be an oblique congratulation on Austin's recent and still secret engagement to Sue, suggested by Oliver's comment on his love for Celia (*As You Like It*, V, ii): ". . . my sudden wooing . . . her sudden consenting." ED applies the name again in letter no. 113. The letter from Austin to which this is a reply had enclosed a poem of his own composition, and the "*Variations* of *Greenville*" may allude to it. On the whole she treats his verses with more politeness than enthusiasm. Benjamin Newton died at Worcester, 24 March 1853 (see letter no. 153). Johnnie Beston was a youthful handyman; so probably was David Smith.

111

To Emily Fowler (Ford)   *spring 1853*

Dear Emily,

I come and see you a great many times every day, though I dont bring my body with me, so perhaps you dont know I'm there. But I love to come just as dearly, for nobody sees me then, and I sit and chat away, and look up in your face, and no matter who calls, if its "my Lord the King," he does'nt interrupt me. Let me say, dear Emily, *both* mean to come at a time, so you shall be very sure I am sitting by your side, and not have to trust the fancy.

I want very much to be with you a long while at a time, to talk as

[236]

we used, "Lang Syne," and during this long spring I'm very sure I shall see you, and make up the winter's loss.

I hope you are better today, dear Emilie –

Aff

E –

MANUSCRIPT: NYPL. Pencil. Dated: Tuesday noon. Addressed: Emilie.

PUBLICATION: L (1894) 134, in part; L (1931) 133–134, in part. The date is conjectured from the handwriting.

112

To Emily Fowler (Ford)   spring 1853

Gladly, dear Emily –
Only see how the sun shines.

Emilie –

MANUSCRIPT: NYPL. Pencil. Unpublished.
Emily may have responded to ED's last note by suggesting they go for a walk.

113

To Austin Dickinson   2 April 1853

Dear Austin.

I rather thought from your letter to me that my essays, together with the Lectures at Cambridge, were rather too much for you, so I thought I would let you have a little vacation; but you must have got rested now, so I shall renew the series. Father was very severe to me; he thought I'd been trifling with you, so he gave me quite a trimming about "Uncle Tom" and "Charles Dickens" and these "modern Literati" who he says are *nothing*, compared to past generations, who flourished when *he was a boy*. Then he said there were "somebody's *rev-e-ries*," he did'nt know whose they were, that he thought were very ridiculous, so I'm quite in disgrace at present, but I think of that "pinnacle" on which you always mount, when anybody insults you, and that's quite a comfort to me.

We are all pretty well at home, and it seems a great while, Austin, since we have heard from you. The correspondence from "Oliver" did'nt seem to say a great deal of how you were getting along, or of yourself, at Cambridge, and I am waiting patiently for one of those grand old letters you used to send us when you first went away.

I have got a nice cake of Sugar, to send you by Mr Green, and shall put in some big, sound Apples, if there is any room. Vinnie would have written you this week, but has had quite a cold, which settled in her eyes, and she has not used them much. She will write you the first of next week. Vinnie and Sue walked down to mill yesterday. Sue comes down here most every day [*one line erased*]. Emily Fowler spent yesterday afternoon here. She *inquired for you*. The girls "Musical" met here on Tuesday evening, and we had as pleasant a time as could have been expected, in view of the individuals composing the society. Dr Brewster was in town yesterday, and took tea here. He asked a great deal about you, and said he was going to write you to come and make him a visit. I told him I "presumed you'd go." Mary Aiken is in town with her children, and is going to stay a fortnight. I wonder she did'nt wait, and meet *you* here in May. Thurston and Benjamin are in town on a visit.

Rufus Cowles gave us a call last evening. He is quite a young man! Mr Godfrey's folks have gone, and Mr and Mrs Pierce have moved into the house. The second generation spend most of their time in our door yard.

This is all the news I can think of, but there is one *old story*, Austin, which you may like to hear — it is that we think about you the whole of the livelong day, and talk of you when we're together, and [*several words erased*] of the golden link which binds us all together.

And you can recollect when you are busy studying, that those of us [at] home not so hard at work as you are, get much time to be with you. We all send our love to you, and hope you will be very careful, and take good care of yourself.

Emilie.

That *was* a "grand old letter," Austin, and I shall answer it soon, but I cannot today, for I feel more like writing that little note of mine, and talking of you.

Oh how much it pleased Father, and how it made us all laugh, tho'
I did'nt laugh so hard as the rest, on account of *my note.* There's a
beautiful verse in the Bible — "Let not your heart be troubled" — so
believe in [Sue ?], believe also in me!

Emilie.

MANUSCRIPT: AC. Pencil. Dated: Saturday noon. Envelope franked
and addressed by Edward Dickinson. Postmarked: Amherst Ms Apr [?].

PUBLICATION: *L* (1894) 122–123, in part; *L* (1931) 120–121, in part;
Home 273–275, entire.

One word in the last sentence is altered and illegible.

"Somebody's *rev-e-ries*" of course refers to Ik Marvel's *Reveries of a
Bachelor.*

ED and her friends occasionally gathered for an evening of music (see
letters no. 118 and 202).

114

To Austin Dickinson   *8 April 1853*

Dear Austin.

I've expected a letter from you every day this week, but have been
disappointed — and last night I thought I should have one as surely
as I lived, but I did not. I'm sure you are very busy, or I should have
had a note, but I will "bide and see." It seems as if you'd been gone
several hundred years, and it had been some centuries since we had
heard from you, and I should like to know when you were coming
home, for if it is'nt probable that you are coming *some time,* I think
I shall take the stage, or run away myself. I asked you this same question in my last Saturday's letter, but you make me no reply. I cant
help wondering sometimes if you think of us as often as we all do of
you, and want to see us *half* as much. I think about this a great deal,
and tho' I dont talk with Vinnie or Sue, about it, yet it often troubles
me. I think we miss each other more every day that we grow older,
for we're all unlike most everyone, and are therefore more dependent
on each other for delight.

Last evening Sue and I walked down to the Old Oak Tree, and sat
there and talked a long while, principally of you, and ourselves. Sue

[239]

said she guessed you were writing us, as we sat there talking, and we both wished you were there. Last Saturday evening I spent with Sue in her room — she read me some funny things which you had just written her, concerning her sorry suitors, and your *excellent suggestions* to prevent future accidents! I think you are rather hard upon unfortunate gentlemen — presume they would like to shoot you, if they knew you had won the bird.

Sue was here to supper last night, and I could'nt but think of a great many things, which we will talk about sometime, if you ever come home.

Mrs Scott is ironing here today — we shall have all your clothes in nice order to send by Mr Green. When is the good man coming? I get quite out of patience, waiting to send your sugar. I hope some country friend has given you a taste long before this time, for you must miss such little luxuries, you always get at home.

Have you had any maple molasses, or any Graham Bread, since you have been away? Every time a new loaf comes smoking on to the table, we wonder if you have any where you have gone to live.

I should love to send you a loaf, dearly, if I could. Vinnie sends her love to you, and thanks you very much for the Rubber. She finds it "capital," she says, and she will write you a letter, when the valise goes back. Mother sends her love, and says she thinks very often she shall certainly write to you, but she knows that we write so often she thinks we say all there is, and so she recollects you, but says nothing about it. I have mended your gloves, Austin, and Vinnie, all the clothes which were out of repair. I have written you in a hurry. I shall never write any more grand letters to you, but all the *little* things, and the things called *trifles*, and the crickets upon the hearth, you will be sure to hear.

Emilie.

Wont you write to me pretty soon? I send that letter of Mat's, wh' I said I would. Much love from all. We have charming weather here. I know you would be so happy, if you were at home – but you'll come soon and we shall be glad to see you.

Jerry inquires for you.

MANUSCRIPT: AC. Pencil. Dated: Friday noon. Envelope franked and addressed by Edward Dickinson. Postmarked: Amherst Ms Apr 9.

PUBLICATION: *Home* 275–276.
ED is writing to her brother with such frequency during these months that, as she here notes, her letters are largely concerned with the minutiae of daily living.

115

To Austin Dickinson   *12 April 1853*

Dear Austin.

You asked me in your Sat morning's letter to write you so you'd hear from me yesterday, but your letter did'nt get here until last evening, so you see I could not very well; but I must write a word this noon, to tell you that they've both come, tho' they tarried upon the way.

I thanked you for the long one in my letter of Saturday, but I want to thank you again, it was such a beautiful one, and too, for yesterday's wh' I did not expect. Sue was here when it came, and we read it together. I staid with her Saturday evening, and we spent part of it reading your long letter to me, and talking of what it made us both think of, and of you. Sue thought t'was the most beautiful letter she ever heard.

I have taken *your place* Saturday evening, since you have been away, but I will give it back to you as soon as you get home. *Get home* dear Austin — how soon now you are coming, and how happy we are in the thought of seeing you! I cant realize that you will come — it is so still and lonely, that it dont seem possible it can be otherwise, but we shall see, when the nails hang full of coats again, and the chairs hang full of hats, and I can count the slippers under the kitchen chair. Oh Austin, how we miss them, and more than them, somebody who used to hang them there, and get many a hint ungentle, to carry them away. Those times seem far off now, a great way, as things we did when children. I wish we were children now. I wish we were *always* children, how to grow up I dont know.

We had company to tea last evening, Mr and Mrs Jewett, and little Henry, then Mr Haven, and Sue — it seems much more like *home* to have her with us *always*, than to have her away. We had a delightful evening. How often we thought of you, and wished you were not away!

[241]

Father went home with Sue. I think he and mother both think a great deal of her, and nobody will make me believe that they dont think she is their's, just as much as Vinnie or you or me. Perhaps I am mistaken, but I can most always tell anything that I want to. Emmons brought me a beautiful boquet of Arbutus, last evening — it's the first I have seen this year. Cousin John has made us an Aeolian Harp, which plays beautifully, alone, whenever there is a breeze.

Austin, you must'nt care if your letters do not get here just when you think they will — they are always new to us, and delightful always, and the more you send us, the happier we shall be. We all send our love to you, and think much and say much, of seeing you again — keep well till you come, and if knowing that we all love you, makes you happier, then Austin, you may sing the whole day long!

Aff
Emilie.

We now expect to send your valise in a day or two, by Mr Wm Cutler.

MANUSCRIPT: AC. Pencil. Dated: Tuesday noon. Envelope franked and addressed by Edward Dickinson. Postmarked: Amherst Ms Apr 12.

PUBLICATION: *L* (1894) 111–112, in part; *L* (1931) 106–107, in part; *Home* 276–277, entire.

An attempt has been made throughout to erase the name "Sue." For a later reference to the aeolian harp, see letter no. 137.

116

To Austin Dickinson *16 April 1853*

Dear Austin.

You make me happy, when you write so affectionately, happier than you know, and I always want to write to you as soon as your letters come, but it is not very often convenient that I can. Yet I *will* the morning after, as I do today. I am all alone, Austin. Father has gone to New York, Vinnie to Northampton, and mother is cutting out apples in the kitchen. I had forgotten *Pussy*, tho'; she's sitting on the mat, looking up in my face as if she wondered who I was writing to — if she knew it was "Master Austin" I guess she would send some word, for I know Pussy remembers you, and wonders where you are. Sometimes when she's more intelligent, I've half a mind to tell her how you have gone to Cambridge, and are studying the law, but I dont believe she'd understand me.

You cant think how delighted father was, with the account you gave of northerners and southerners, and the electioneering — he seemed to feel so happy to have you interested in what was going on at Cambridge — he said he "knew all about it — he'd been thro' the whole, it was only a little specimen of what you'd meet in life, if you lived to enter it." I could'nt hardly help telling him that I thought his idea of life rather a boisterous one, but I kept perfectly still.

I dont love to read your letters all out loud to father – it would be like opening the kitchen door when we get home from meeting Sunday, and are sitting down by the stove saying just what we're a mind to, and having father hear. I dont know why it is, but it gives me a dreadful feeling, and I skipped about the wild flowers, and one or two little things I loved the best, for I could'nt read *them* loud to anybody [*several words erased*]. I shant see her this morning, because she has to *bake* Saturday, but she'll come this afternoon, and we shall read your letter together, and talk of how soon you'll be here [*seven lines erased*].

I shall think of you taking tea at Aunt Lavinia's tonight, and we shall take tea alone, how pleasant it would be to have you with us while father is away, but it is'nt *May* yet. Thank you for remembering me when you found the wild flowers, and for wanting me to stay a week with you. These things are very kind, and I will not forget them. The birds sing beautifully, Pussy is trying to beat them. Dont work too hard Austin, dont get too tired, so that you cannot sleep, we always think of you. Love from us all.

Emilie.

John Thompson is in the office of Mr Vose, in Springfield.

MANUSCRIPT: AC. Pencil. Dated: Saturday noon. Envelope addressed by ED in ink: Wm Austin Dickinson/Law School./Cambridge./Mass. Postmarked: Amherst Ms Apr 16.

PUBLICATION: L (1931) 111–112, in part; *Home* 278–279, entire, except for mutilated parts.

John Thompson, a college classmate of Austin's, later practiced law in Chicago.

117

To John L. Graves *spring 1853*

A little poem we will write unto our Cousin John,
to tell him if he does not come and see us very soon,
we will immediately forget there's any such a man,
and when he comes to see us, we will not be "at home."

Emilie – Vinnie –

MANUSCRIPT: HCL (G 8). Pencil. Dated: Thursday morn. Addressed on the fold: Cousin John. Unpublished.

The date is conjectured from the handwriting. Graves had made the harp for ED early in April (see letter no. 115). Perhaps this was written later in the month.

118

To Austin Dickinson *21 April 1853*

Dear Austin.

We could hardly eat any supper last night, we felt so badly to think you had'nt got the valise, and we talked all the time about it while we sat at the table, and called Mr Cutler names – Father says he "would like to reach him just long enough to cuff his ears." We do feel so badly about it, we dont know what to do.

There were all your clothes in such beautiful order, and a cake of new maple sugar, and mother had with her own hand selected and polished the apples, she thought it would please you so. It is too bad – too bad. We do feel vexed about it. Mother thinks it is lost – she says you will never see it. Father thinks he would'nt *dare* to lose it, but is too selfish to trouble himself by sending you any word. Mother is so afraid that you will need the clothes, and wont know what to do without them, and Vinnie and I keep hoping, and trying to persuade her that you've got them before now.

We have all been thinking how much you'd enjoy the sugar, and how nice the apples would taste after studying all day long, and "living very sparingly," but this [is] a vexing world, and things "aft gang

[244]

aglay." I wont talk any more of this, for I know you are disappointed as much as any of us, and want to hear something sunnier — and there is something sunnier. I was with dear Susie last evening, and she told me how on Monday she walked out in the fields, carrying your letter with her, and read it over and over, "sitting on the stile," and pausing as she read, to look at the hills and the trees and the blue, blue home beyond.

Susie talked much of you, and of her lonely life when you were gone away, and we said you would soon be here, and then we talked of *how* soon, and of many and many a sunlight and many and many a shade which might steal upon us ere then. How I wish you were here, dear Austin, how I do wish for you so many times every day, and I miss the long talks most, upon the *kitchen stone hearth*, when the just are fast asleep. I ask myself many times if they will come back again, and whether they will stay, but we dont know.

Father wont go to Boston this week, as he had intended to, for he finds a great deal to do in starting the Newman family. I think now he will go *next week*, tho' I dont know what day. The Newmans all board at Mrs Merrill's until they get into their house, which will be by Saturday, certainly. Their Irish girl stays here, for Mrs Merrill was afraid she would not agree with *her* girl. The Newmans seem very pleasant, but they are not *like us*. What makes a few of us so different from others? It's a question I often ask myself. The Germanians gave a concert here, the evening of Exhibition day. Vinnie and I went with John. I never heard [such] *sounds* before. They seemed like *brazen Robins,* all wearing broadcloth wings, and I think they were, for they all flew away as soon as the concert was over. I tried so hard to make Susie go with us, but she would'nt consent to it. I could not bear to have her lose it.

Write me as soon as this comes, and say if you've got the valise.

Emilie

Anna Warner died Tuesday night, and will be buried tomorrow, I suppose. They seem to feel very badly. She has been sick a great while now. You will not be surprised at hearing it. Mother wants me to tell you *from her* to get all the clothes you need at some good place in Boston, should you not find the valise. I hope you have got it before now. I should'nt think he *would lose* it, after all you have done for him. Mother says she can never look upon him again.

MANUSCRIPT: AC. Pencil. Dated: Thursday noon. Envelope franked and addressed by Edward Dickinson. Postmarked: Amherst Ms [?]

PUBLICATION: L (1894) 122, in part; L (1931) 120, in part; Home 280–281, entire.

Edward Dickinson enclosed a brief note saying that he must postpone his trip to Boston. The missing valise probably turned up, for it is not mentioned again. John Graves's invitation to the girls may have followed ED's reminder (no. 117) that he had not called recently. Anna Charlotte Warner was the eleven-year-old daughter of Professor Aaron Warner. On the Newmans, see letters no. 104 and 106.

The Germania orchestra, conducted by Carl Bergmann, came to the United States from Berlin in 1848. During the six years it lasted, the orchestra gave nine hundred concerts in all parts of the country, often in collaboration with local choral societies. The Spring Exhibition at Amherst College took place on April 19, and was concluded with a concert by the Germania Serenade Band.

119

To Henry V. Emmons   *spring 1853*

Mr Emmons –

Since receiving your beautiful writing I have often desired to thank you thro' a few of my flowers, and arranged the fairest for you a little while ago, but heard you were away –

I have very few today, and they compare but slightly with the immortal blossoms you kindly gathered me, but will you please accept them – the "Lily of the field" for the blossoms of Paradise, and if 'tis ever mine to gather those which fade not, from the garden we have not seen, you shall have a brighter one than I can find today.

Emilie E. Dickinson

MANUSCRIPT: HCL (E 1). Pencil.
PUBLICATION: NEQ XVI (1943) 366–367.

Although the nature of Emmons's "beautiful writing" is not specified, it is possible he had lent ED a copy of his dissertation "Sympathy in Action," presented at the Spring Exhibition on April 19. The two notes to Emmons that follow this appear to form a sequence, and since there is no way to date them exactly, they have been placed here together.

[246]

120

To Henry V. Emmons   *spring 1853*

Ungentle "Atropos"! And yet I dare not chide her, for fear those saucy fingers will ply the shears again.

Perhaps she suspects the *wine!* Please tell her it's only *Currant Wine*, and would she be so kind as to lend me her shears a little, that I might cut a thread?

Vinnie and I wait patiently the coming of our friends, and trust a brighter evening will soon reward us all for the long expectation.

Your friends,
Emilie & Vinnie Dickinson –

MANUSCRIPT: HCL (E 6). Ink.
PUBLICATION: *NEQ* XVI (1943) 370.
The friend included in the invitation is John Graves.

To Henry V. Emmons   *spring 1853*

Thank you, indeed, Mr Emmons, for your beautiful acknowledgment, far brighter than my flowers; and while with pleasure I *lend* you the little manuscript, I shall beg leave to claim it, when you again return. I trust you will find much happiness in an interview with your friend, and will be very happy to see you, when you return.

Emilie E. Dickinson

MANUSCRIPT: HCL (E 2). Pencil.
PUBLICATION: *NEQ* XVI (1943) 367.
There is no clue to the nature of the manuscript which ED lent Emmons. Since the friendship of the two was based on a shared interest in literature, one may surmise that she loaned him a gathering of her own poems. For a probable identification of the "friend," see letter no. 136.

To Austin Dickinson   *7 May 1853*

Dear Austin.

A week ago, we were all here — today we are not all here — yet the bee hums just as merrily, and all the busy things work on as if the same. They do not miss you, Child, but there is a humming bee whose song is not so merry, and there are busy ones who pause to drop a tear. Let us thank God, today, Austin, that we can love our friends, our brothers and our sisters, and weep when they are gone, and smile at their return. It is indeed a joy which we are blest to know. Today is very beautiful — just as bright, just as blue, just as green and as white, and as crimson, as the cherry trees full in bloom, and the half opening peach blossoms, and the grass just waving, and sky and hill and cloud, can make it, if they try. How I wish you were here, Austin — you thought *last* Saturday beautiful — yet to this golden day, 'twas but one single gem, to whole handfuls of jewels. You will ride today, I hope, or take a long walk somewhere, and recollect us all, Vinnie and me, and Susie and Father and mother and home. Yes, Austin, every one of us, for we all think of you, and bring you to recollection many times each day — not *bring* you to recollection, for we never put you away, but keep recollecting on. Was'nt you very tired when you got back to Cambridge? I thought you would be, you had so much to do, the morning you went away. I hope you do not cough mornings, as you did when you were at home. If you do, go and see that Apothecary who gave you something before, and get something to cure it. And Austin, dont you care about anything else that troubles you — It isn't anything — It is too slight, too small, to make you worry so — dont think any more about it. We all love you very much — wont you remember *that* when anything worries you, and you wont care then.

I dont feel as if you'd been here — the time was so very short — how I wish today was last Saturday, and last Saturday was today, so we could see you. Shant you write us pretty soon? We have looked for a note before. Susie and I walked together all last Tuesday evening, talking of you and the visit, and wishing you were here, and would not go away again. I love her more and more. She looks very lovely in colors — she dont wear mourning now.

You must think of us tonight, while Mr Dwight takes tea here, and we will think of you far away, down in Cambridge. Dont mind the law, Austin, if it is rather dry, dont mind the daily road, tho' it is rather dusty, but remember the brooks and the hills, and remember while you're *but one*, we are *but four* at home!

Emilie.

You *must* come home in the recess.

MANUSCRIPT: AC. Pencil. Dated: Saturday noon. Envelope franked and addressed by Edward Dickinson. Postmarked obliterated.

PUBLICATION: L (1894) 123–124, in part; L (1931) 121–122, in part; *Home* 283–284, entire.

With ED's letter was enclosed one from Lavinia (*Home* 282–283). Austin had been home for a short visit, from April 29 until May 2. It seems probable that Austin's worry rose out of his fear that the family would object to his plan to have his hair cut short (see letters no. 126 and 132).

123

To Austin Dickinson   *16 May 1853*

"Strikes me" just so, dear Austin, but somehow I have to work a good deal more than I used to, and harder, and I feel so tired when night comes, that I'm afraid if I write you, 'twill be something rather bluer than you'll be glad to see — so I sew with all my might, and hope when work is done to be with you much oftener than I have lately been.

Somehow I am lonely lately — I feel very old every day, and when morning comes and the birds sing, they dont seem to make me so happy as they used to. I guess it's because you're gone, and there are not so many of us as God gave for each other. I wish you were at home. I feel very sure lately that the years we have had together are more than we shall have — I guess we shall journey separately, or reach the journey's end, some of us — but we don't know. We all love you very much. I don't believe you guess how much home thinks and says of it's only absent child — yes, Austin, home is faithful, none other is so true [*three lines erased*].

You must'nt mind what I say about feeling lonely lately. It is'nt any matter, but I thought I would tell you, so you'd know why I did'nt write more. Vinnie and I thank you very much for your letters — we always thank you, and your letters are dearer than all the rest that come. Vinnie did the errand which you wanted her to, but the stage did'nt come over from Northampton at noon, and she could'nt send till today. She sends her love to you, and will write to you very soon. Susie says her letter was safely delivered, and she seemed very grateful — she has not yet received your week before last letter — she thinks someone here has got it. Susie and I went to meeting last evening and Father went home first with Susie and then with me. I thought the folks would stare. I think Father feels that she appreciates him, better than most anybody else — How pleasant it is, is'nt it?

She is a dear child to us all, and we see her every day.

We had a very pleasant visit from the Monson folks — they came one noon and stayed till the next. They agree beautifully with Father on the "present generation." They decided that they hoped every young man who smoked would take fire. I respectfully intimated that I thought the result would be a vast conflagration, but was instantly put down.

We are very glad Joel is better, and shall be glad to see him. Take good care of yourself, Austin — now the days grow warm, and dont study too hard. I want to have you tell me how soon you're coming home. You must think of nothing but coming!

Emilie.

While I write, the whistle is playing, and the cars just coming in. It gives us all new life, every time it plays. How you will love to hear it, when you come home again! How soon is the recess? We are anxious to know, and you must come home, *of course.* You must write us pretty soon, and tell us when you are coming — so we can anticipate it. Mr Dwight has finished preaching, and it now remains to be seen if the people ask him to stay. We are all charmed with him, and I'm sure he will have a call. I never heard a minister I loved half so well, so does Susie love him, and we all — I wish you were at meeting every time he preaches.

The term has commenced, and there were a great many students to hear him yesterday. We all send our love to you. Mother says she shall send your stockings by the first opportunity. Have you received the package sent by Wm Kellogg? I have written so very fast, but I hope you can read what I write.

MANUSCRIPT: A.C. Pencil. Dated: Monday noon. Envelope franked and addressed by Edward Dickinson. Postmarked: Boston May 17. An attempt has been made throughout to erase the name "Sue."

PUBLICATION: L (1931) 112–113, in part; Home 287–289, entire, except for mutilated parts.

The "Monson folks" presumably included Mrs. Dickinson's stepmother, Sarah Vaill Norcross. The first regular trip of a passenger train on the Amherst and Belchertown Railroad was made on May 9. On May 24 the First Church voted to invite the Reverend Edward S. Dwight to become their pastor. He accepted the call in August.

124

To Emily Fowler (Ford)   *about June 1853*

The Buds are small, dear Emily, but will you please accept one for your Cousin and yourself? I quite forgot the *Rosebugs* when I spoke of the buds, last evening, and I found a family of them taking an early breakfast on my most precious bud, with a smart little worm for Landlady, so the sweetest are gone, but accept my love with the smallest, and I'm

Lovingly,
Emilie.

MANUSCRIPT: NYPL. Pencil.
PUBLICATION: L (1894) 133; L (1931) 133.
The cousin was Julia Jones of Bridgeport, Connecticut.

125

To Austin Dickinson   *5 June 1853*

Dear Austin.

It is Sunday, and I am here alone. The rest have gone to meeting, to hear Rev Martin Leland. I listened to him this forenoon in a state of mind very near frenzy, and feared the effect too much to go out this afternoon. The morning exercises were perfectly ridiculous, and we spent the intermission in mimicking the Preacher, and reciting extracts from his most memorable sermon. I never heard father so funny.

How I did wish you were here. I know you'd have died laughing. Father said he didn't dare look at Sue — he said he saw her bonnet coming round our way, and he looked "straight ahead" — he said he ran out of meeting for fear somebody would ask him what he tho't of the preaching. He says if anyone asks him, he shall put his hand to his mouth, and his mouth in the dust, and cry, Unclean — Unclean!! But I hav'nt time to say more of Martin Leland, but I wish you were here today, Austin, and could hear father talk, and you would laugh so loud they would hear you way down in Cambridge. Vinnie and I got your letters just about bedtime last evening. I had been at Sue's all the evening and communicated to her the fact that they had not come. She had felt all the time she said, perfectly sure that [*remainder of letter missing, Postscript on first page*]: All send love to you Austin — write us again very soon – I am glad for "The Honeysuckle."

MANUSCRIPT: AC. Pencil. Dated: Sunday afternoon. Envelope franked and addressed by Edward Dickinson. Postmarked: Amherst Ms Jun 6. The letter has been torn in half, and an attempt has been made throughout to erase or alter the name "Sue."
PUBLICATION: *Home* 292.

126

To Austin Dickinson 9 *June 1853*

Dear Austin.

I got your letter — I delivered the one to Sue. Jerry stood ready to act at moment's notice, and all was as you wished, but Sue thought not best, so I suppose you'll receive a telegraphic despatch, and Susie and I shall not see you this evening.

Your letter troubled me a good deal for a moment, I tho't something dreadful had happened; you were about to be killed and were coming to bid us Goodbye, or something of the kind, but I know the whole now.

Whenever you want help, Austin, just call on Jerry and me, and we will take care of you, and perhaps we'll *help a little*. I hope you wont trouble yourself about any remarks that are made – they are not worth the thought of — certainly not the care for. Dont mind them.

Nobody'll dare to harm dear Susie, nobody'll dare to harm you. You are too far from them; dont fear them. I hope the hair is off — you must tell me about it as soon as you write again, and write us soon. We are pretty well now. I rode with Emmons last evening, and had a beautiful ride. New London is coming today, but I dont care, I dont think folks are much. I do wish you were here. Dear Austin, now remember not to care for these foolish things, for they cant reach Sue.

Love from us.

Emilie

MANUSCRIPT: AC. Pencil. Dated: Thursday morning. Envelope franked and addressed by Edward Dickinson. Postmarked: Amherst Ms Jun 9. An attempt has been made throughout to erase or alter the name "Sue."

PUBLICATION: *Home* 293.

In celebration of the opening of the Amherst and Belchertown Railroad, an excursion was arranged at the joint invitation of the railroad and the New London, Willimantic and Palmer line, to bring the people of New London by special train to Amherst. Austin's worry seems to have to do with people's remarks about him and Sue. On his concern about his hair, see letters no. 122 and 132.

127

To Austin Dickinson   *13 June 1853*

My dear Austin.

I dont know where to begin. There has been considerable news since I have written much to you, and yet of such a kind as I dont think you would care for. I will tell you first how glad I am you are better, and are not going to be sick, as I was afraid when you wrote me. Do be careful, very careful, Austin, for you are from us all, and if anything happens to you, we cannot find it out and all·take care of you as we can when you're at home. I dont think you'd better study any for a day or two, until you feel perfectly well. I wont say any more about it, if you dont want to have me, lest I make you sick by talking, as you said you should be if I told anybody, and folks wrote letters to you; but just come home the moment whenever you are sick, or think you are going to be sick, and you shall have Vinnie and me and Somebody nearer than either of us to take care of you, and make you well. I sent the White Hat as you wished, and you've probably received it before this. I sent it on Saturday, with special instructions to Driver, and presume it has got there safely.

I will send *the other* directly, if you would like to have me.

The New London Day passed off grandly – so all the people said – it was pretty hot and dusty, but nobody cared for that. Father was as usual, Chief Marshal of the day, and went marching around the town with New London at his heels like some old Roman General, upon a Triumph Day. Mrs Howe got a capital dinner, and was very much praised. Carriages flew like sparks, hither, and thither and yon, and they all said t'was fine. I spose it was – I sat in Prof Tyler's woods and saw the train move off, and then ran home again for fear somebody would see me, or ask me how I did. Dr Holland was here and called to see us – seemed very pleasant indeed, inquired for you, and asked mother if Vinnie and I might come and see them in Springfield.

Last week was beautiful, tho' very warm and dry. I was very happy last week, for we were at Susie's house, or Susie was at our house most all the time, and she always makes us happy. Vinnie is down there now.

The stories are all still, Austin. I dont hear any now, and Susie says she dont care now the least at all for them. They must not trouble you – they are very low – of the earth – they cannot reach our heaven if they climb never so high. I will attend to Bowdoin.

Mr Ford sat with us in church yesterday, and took tea at our house last night. I think he's a popinjay.

We had a visit from Joel. Ego, mitie, me. We all go down to the grove often. Father and mother together walked down there yesterday morning. I think they will all live. Father thinks so. We all send you our love.

Emilie.

I have had a letter from Mat, and she sent her love to you, and will write you very soon.

I will find out accurately what "the expenses" are, and let you know next time. We did the best we c'd, and everything very safely.

I gave Jerry your messages, at which his teeth increased, and his countenance expanded—he laughed also for some time, as if taking the joke moderately and wasting none of it.

Austin—there's nothing in the world that Jerry wont do for you. I believe he thinks you are finer than anybody else, and feels quite consequential to think of serving you. Send him a word sometimes, for it affects him so. Mrs Mack too inquires for you with unabating interest. It's pleasant to be liked by such folks, and I love to hear them speak of you with interest. Mr Dwight has not given an answer. I feel a good deal afraid, but try to hope for the best. 'Twill be dreadful if we dont get him. You dont tell us about your hair—wont you next time, Austin, for your peace is our's. Write us often, and we will, and think that if we all live we shall again meet together during these summer days. I shall be glad to see the Poems.

MANUSCRIPT: AC. Pencil. Dated: Monday morning. Envelope franked and addressed by Edward Dickinson. Postmarked: Amherst Ms Jun 14. An attempt has been made throughout to erase all passages mentioning the name of Sue.

PUBLICATION: L (1894) 116, in part; L (1931) 114–115, in part; Home 295–296, entire.

The Reverend E. S. Dwight did in fact accept the call to the First Church later in the summer (see letter no. 123). On Jerry Holden, see letter no. 108. In ED's previous letter to Austin she indicates that he anticipated family opposition were he to have his hair cut short, as he seemed to wish. He finally concluded to have it done (see letter no. 132).

The greater part of the letter gives details on the New London influx. A morning train brought 325 people, on the ninth. They were provided a dinner at noon at the Amherst House, of which Mrs. Albin P. Howe was the landlady, and welcomed by Edward Dickinson.

For the allusion to Poems, in the last sentence, see the following letter.

128

To Austin Dickinson   *19 June 1853*

Do you want to hear from me, Austin? I'm going to write to you altho' it dont seem much as if you would care to have me. I dont know why exactly, but things look blue, today, and I hardly know what to do, everything looks so strangely, but if you want to hear from me, I shall love very much to write – Prof Tyler has preached today, and I have been all day – Susie walked home from meeting with us, and was so disappointed at having no letter from you – It really seems very unsafe to depend upon Judge Conkey, and that Mr Eaton too, I should think quite hazardous – Dont wait for them next time. We received your notes and the Poems, for which we thank you, last week – Father seemed much pleased with his letter, and all of us laughed a little – The remark concerning Mr Ford seemed to please father mightily – I dont dont [sic] mean what I said, but your opposition to me – He told me you'd "hit me off nicely." You make me think of Dickens, when you write such letters as that – I am going to read it to Sue – I should have done before, but the afternoon it came, we had terrible thunder showers, and it rained all evening long, and yesterday afternoon Father wanted us all to ride, so I have not had opportunity – I walked with her last evening – She wore her new things today, and looked beautifully in them – a white straw hat, trimmed with Rouches – mantilla of fawn colored silk, very handsomely finished, and white Dress. She is going after Miss Bartlett tomorrow morning at 5 – and begins her Dressmaking tomorrow –

She says she shall just get thro' by the time you get home –

So shall Vinnie and I – there must be no sewing then – We are all pretty well, and the weather is beautiful – If you were here I think you would be very happy, and I think we should, but time has wings, and you will be with us soon. We have been free from company by the "Amherst and Belchertown Railroad" since Joel went home, tho' we live in constant fear of some other visitation –

"Oh would some power the giftie gie" folks, to see themselves as we see them. Burns. I have read the poems, Austin, and am going to read them again, and will hand them to Susie – They please me very much, but I must read them again before I know just [what] I think of "Alexander Smith" – They are not very coherent, but there's good deal of exquisite frensy, and some wonderful figures, as ever I met in my life – We will talk about it again – The grove looks nicely, Austin, and we think must certainly grow – We love to go there – it is a charming place. Everything is singing now, and everything is beautiful that *can* be in it's life.

So Joel did'nt have a remarkable trip up here — wonder which enjoyed it the most — the pestilence, or the victims – Dont tell him what I said – And think besides Aunt Lavinia must be very busy – Guess "Father will be tired" when they next visit here.

Jerry gets along nicely, takes first-rate care of the horse, and seems unusually grand after having a message from you. It has the same effect as a big mug of cider, and *looks* a good deal better. I am glad your eye has got well. You must use it carefully, for a little while – I hope you received your hat – I had not time to write you with it, for I did it up late at night, after having folks here all the evening, and I hope it did not seem strange to you –

The time for the New London trip has not been fixed upon –

I sincerely wish it may wait until you get home from Cambridge, if you would like to go –

The cars continue thriving – a good many passengers seem to arrive from somewhere, tho' nobody knows from where – Father expects his new Buggy to come by the cars, every day now, and that will help a little – I expect all our Grandfathers and all their country cousins will come here to pass Commencement, and dont doubt the stock will rise several percent that week. If we children and Sue could obtain board for the week in some "vast wilderness," I think we should have good times. Our house is crowded daily with the members of this world, the high and the low, the bond and the free, the "poor in this world's goods," and the "almighty dollar,["] and "what in the world are they after" continues to be unknown – But I hope they will pass away, as insects on vegetation, and let us reap together in golden harvest time — that is you and Susie and me and our dear sister Vinnie must have a pleasant time to be unmolested together, when your school days end. You must not stay with Howland after the studies cease — We shall be ready for you, and you must come home from school, not stopping to play by the way! Mother was much amused at the feebleness of your hopes of hearing from her – She got so far last week once, as to take a pen and paper and carry them into the kitchen, but her meditations were broken by the unexpected arrival of *Col Smith* and his wife, so she must try again – I'm sure you will hear from her soon. We all send our love to you, and miss you very much, and think of seeing you again very much, and love dear Sue constantly. Write me again soon. I have said a good deal today.

Emilie.

MANUSCRIPT: AC. Pencil. Dated: Sunday afternoon. Envelope franked and addressed by Edward Dickinson. Postmarked: Amherst Ms Jun 20.

PUBLICATION: L (1894) 114–115, in part; L (1931) 113–114, in part; Home 298–300, entire.

After the visit of the New London citizens, it was proposed that the Amherst people should take a similar excursion to New London.

Austin's last letter had evidently asked whether Emily would care to read the poems of the young Scottish poet Alexander Smith (1830–1867). She said that she would (letter no. 127), and the copy he sent of Smith's *A Life Drama and Other Poems* (1853) is in the Dickinson collection (HC).

129

To Austin Dickinson   *26 June 1853*

I shall write you a little, Austin, to send by Father tomorrow, tho' you havnt yet answered my long letter which went to you last Monday, and I've been looking for something from you for a good many days. The valise did'nt get to us till a long time after you sent it, and so 'twas a good while Austin, before you heard from us, but you know all about it now, and I hope you dont care. But we felt so sorry to disappoint you by not sending the things which you requested to have us. Sue did'nt hear yesterday, so we are all in a tantrum to know the meaning of that.

If you ever get where we are again, we shall tell you how many letters are missing by the way, and never reach you, and we shall ask you too how many have gone to us, which we have not received.

It is cold here today, Austin, and the west wind blows — the windows are shut at home, and the fire burns in the kitchen. How we should love to see you, how pleasant it would be to walk to the grove together. We will walk there, when you get home. We all went down this morning, and the trees look beautifully. Every one is growing, and when the west wind blows, the pines lift their light leaves and make sweet music. Pussy goes down there too, and seems to enjoy much in her own observations. Mr Dwight has not answered yet — he probably will this week. I do think he will come Austin, and shall be so glad if he will.

Did Susie write you how Vinnie went to South Hadley with Bowdoin, and she came to stay with me? And how we sewed together, and talked of what would be? We did sew and talk together, and she said she should tell you what a sweet time we had. Emmons asked me to ride yesterday afternoon, but I'd promised to go somewhere else, so he asked me to go this week, and I told him I would. Has father written you that Edwin Pierce, our neighbor, was arrested last week, for beating a servant girl, tried, and fined two dollars and costs? Vinnie and I heard the whipping, and could have testified, if the Court had called upon us. Also Dea Cowan's son George was detected while breaking into the Bonnet Shop, the other night, and is to be tried next Wednesday. Mr Frank Conkey is absent, and the criminal desiring his services, the parties consent to wait.

What do you think of Amherst? Dont you think your native place shows evident marks of progress? Austin — home looks beautifully — we all wish you here always, but I hope 'twill seem only dearer for missing it so long. Father says you will come in three weeks — that wont be long now. Keep well and happy, Austin, and remember us all you can, and much love from home

and Emilie.

Austin — are you willing to get me another bottle of medicine, if it wont trouble you too much, and send it to me by father? I enclose the prescription. You can get it at Mr Burnett's, but dont get it, Austin, unless it's convenient for you.

Mr and Mrs Godfrey have moved into the Baker house, across the road, and we're so glad to get them back again.

MANUSCRIPT: AC. Pencil. Dated: Sunday afternoon. An attempt has been made to erase the name "Sue."

PUBLICATION: L (1894) 117–118, in part; L (1931) 116, in part; Home 300–302, entire.

George Godfrey's wife was a seamstress who ran a boarding house.

130

To Austin Dickinson   *1 July 1853*

Dear Austin —

I'm sorrier than you are, when I cant write to you — I've tried with all my might to find a moment for you, but time has been so short, and my hands so full that until now I could not. Perhaps you do not know that Grandmother has been making a visit this week, and has just gone this noon – She has, and we are tired, and the day very warm, but write to you I will, before a *greater* happens.

Some of the letters you've sent us we have received, and thank you for affectionately – Some, we have not received, but thank you for the memory, of which the emblem perished. Where all those letters go – our's and your's, and Susie's, somebody surely knows, but we do not.

The note which came to Susie in the last evening's letter, was given her – She does not get the letters you say you send to her, and she sends others which you do not receive. Austin, if we four meet again we'll see what this all means. I tell Susie you write to her, and she says she *"knows* so" notwithstanding they do not often come – There's a new Postmaster today, but we dont know who's to blame. You never wrote me a letter, Austin, which I liked half so well as the one Father brought me, and you need'nt fear that we dont always love you, for we always do – We think of your coming home with a great deal of happiness, and are glad you want to come –

Father said he never saw you looking in better health, or seeming in finer spirits. He did'nt say a word about the Hippodrome or the museum, and he came home so stern that none of us dared to ask him, and besides Grandmother was here, and you certainly dont think I'd allude to a *Hippodrome* in the presence of that lady! I'd as soon think of popping fire crackers in the presence of Peter the Great! But you'll tell us when you get home – how soon – how soon! [*several words erased.*]

We are glad you're so well, Austin. We're glad you are happy too, and how often Vinnie and I wonder concerning something of which you never speak. We are pretty well, but tired, the weather too so warm that it takes the strength away. I am glad you are glad that I went to ride with Emmons. I went again with him one evening while father was gone, and had a beautiful ride.

I thank you for what you sent me, and for your kindness in saying what you did. I sent your little brush. I admire the Poems very much. We all send our love to you – shall write you again, Sunday.

Emilie –

MANUSCRIPT: AC. Pencil. Dated: Friday afternoon. Envelope franked and addressed by Edward Dickinson. Postmarked: Amherst Ms Jul 2.

PUBLICATION: L (1894) 116–117, in part: L (1931) 115–116, in part; Home 303–304, entire.

The grandmother visiting the Dickinsons was Sarah Vaill Norcross, Mrs. Dickinson's stepmother. The comment on lost letters implies criticism of Seth Nims, the postmaster (see letter no. 16). The poems that ED admires are those of Alexander Smith (see letter no. 128).

131

To Austin Dickinson   *8 July 1853*

Dear Austin –

I must write you a little before the cars leave this noon – just to tell you that we got your letter last evening, and were rejoiced to hear from you after so long a time, and that we want to see you, and long to have you come, much more than I can tell you –

We did'nt know what to make of it that we did'nt hear from you, but owed it to the post masters on the way, and not to you, but now we know you've had company, you are rather more excusable –

Susie was here last night, saying she'd had a letter, and that we should have one at home before bedtime, which we did about 10 – o'clock, when father came home from the office. Now Austin – we hav'nt written you oftener, because we've had so much company, and so many things to do. We want to get all our work done before you come home, so as not to be busy sewing when we want to see you; that's why we dont write oftener. You dont know how much we think of you, or how much we say, or how wish you were here every hour in the day, but we have to work very hard, and cannot write half as often as we want to to you. We think you dont write to us any, and we must all be patient until you get home, and then I rather think we shall wipe out old scores in a great many good talks. You say it is hot and dry. It is very dry here, tho' now for two or three days the air is fine and cool – Everything is so beautiful, it's a real Eden here; how happy we shall be roaming round it together! The trees are getting over the effect of the Canker worm, and we hope we may have some apples yet, tho' we cant tell now – but we feel very thankful that the leaves are not all gone, and there's a few green things which hav'nt been carried away – Mother expects to go to Monson tomorrow afternoon, to spend the Sabbath – They want very much to have her, and we think she had better go – She will come home Monday afternoon –

Vinnie will write what she thinks about Mary Nichols' coming in her next. What would please you about it? I want you should all do what will make you the happiest — after that I dont care.

I am glad you have enjoyed seeing Gould – About something for Mother – I think it would please her very much if you should bring her something, tho' she would'nt wish you to get anything very expensive –

Vinnie and I will think of something and write you *what* next time – I hope to send father's Daguerreotype before you come, and will if I can get any safe opportunity. We shall write you again in a day or two, and all send our love –

Your aff sister
Emilie –

MANUSCRIPT: AC. Pencil. Dated: Friday noon. The envelope, not franked, is addressed by ED: Wm Austin Dickinson./Law School./Cambridge./Mass. Postmarked: Amherst Ms Jul 9.

PUBLICATION: *Home* 305–306.

Mary Nichols was a Boston friend of Austin's. The daguerreotype of Edward Dickinson is not now known to be in existence.

132

To Austin Dickinson   10 *July* 1853

[*first page missing*]

. . . are so glad it's off, and you are you at last. I will not tell the folks, if you dont want to have me. Dr Holland and his wife, spent last Friday with us — came unexpectedly — we had a charming time, and have promised to visit them after Commencement. They asked all about you, and Dr Holland's wife expressed a great desire to see you — He said you would be a Judge – there was no help for it — you must certainly be a Judge! We had Champagne for dinner, and a very fine time – We were so sorry you were not here, and Dr and Mrs Holland

expressed their regret many times – Mother's coming home Monday –
It seems very queer indeed to have her gone over Sunday, but we get
along very well. It rained beautifully Saturday.

Susie is here or we there, pretty much all of the time now – We
walked home from church together, and she said she was going to write
you today – Mrs Cutler is going to Hardwick next week for a visit,
and Sue is going to keep house – Perhaps you will go and see her, in
case you should be in town! I cannot realize that you will come so
soon, but I'm so glad, and we all are – Never mind the hair, Austin,
we are glad, and that's all we care, and all Susie cares is, that you
should *suspect* she should care – Love till you come –

Emilie –

As you are coming home Austin, and it's a good opportunity, I
think I had better have another bottle of medicine, tho' I hav'nt used
up the other yet – But dont you get it for me if you are very busy, or
have other errands to do which will take all your time. You can do
nothing for me, for which I thank you so much.

MANUSCRIPT: AC. Pencil. Envelope franked and addressed by Edward
Dickinson. Postmarked: Amherst Ms Jul 11. With the letter is one enclosed from Lavinia (*Home* 308). The paragraph following the signature
is on a separate sheet addressed on the verso: Austin.

PUBLICATION: *LH* 31–32, in part; *Home* 308–309, entire.

The first sentence, from which the beginning has been torn away,
refers to Austin's hair (see letters no. 122 and 126). Austin came home on
July 14 for a six-weeks vacation. The unexpected visit from Dr. Holland
and his wife marks the beginning of the friendship between ED and Mrs.
Holland, who met for the first time on this occasion. Holland's connection
with the *Springfield Republican* brought him often to Amherst.

133

To Dr. and Mrs. J. G. Holland   *autumn 1853*

Dear Dr. and Mrs Holland – dear Minnie – it is cold tonight, but
the thought of you so warm, that I sit by it as a fireside, and am never
cold any more. I love to write to you – it gives my heart a holiday and
sets the bells to ringing. If prayers had any answers to them, you were
all here to-night, but I seek and I don't find, and knock and it is not

[263]

opened. Wonder if God is just — presume he is, however, and t'was only a blunder of Matthew's.

I think mine is the case, where when they ask an egg, they get a scorpion, for I keep wishing for you, keep shutting up my eyes and looking toward the sky, asking with all my might for you, and yet you do not come. I wrote to you last week, but thought you would laugh at me, and call me sentimental, so I kept my lofty letter for "Adolphus Hawkins, Esq."

If it wasn't for broad daylight, and cooking-stoves, and roosters, I'm afraid you would have occasion to smile at my letters often, but so sure as "this mortal" essays immortality, a crow from a neighboring farm-yard dissipates the illusion, and I am here again.

And what I mean is this — that I thought of you all last week, until the world grew rounder than it sometimes is, and I broke several dishes.

Monday, I solemnly resolved I would be *sensible*, so I wore thick shoes, and thought of Dr Humphrey, and the Moral Law. One glimpse of *The Republican* makes me break things again — I read in it every night.

Who writes those funny accidents, where railroads meet each other unexpectedly, and gentlemen in factories get their heads cut off quite informally? The author, too, relates them in such a sprightly way, that they are quite attractive. Vinnie was disappointed to-night, that there were not more accidents — I read the news aloud, while Vinnie was sewing. *The Republican* seems to us like a letter from you, and we break the seal and read it eagerly. . . .

Vinnie and I talked of you as we sewed, this afternoon. I said — "how far they seem from us," but Vinnie answered me "only a little way" . . . I'd love to be a bird or bee, that whether hum or sing, still might be near you.

Heaven is large — is it not? Life is short too, isn't it? Then when one is done, is there not another, and — and — then if God is willing, we are neighbors then. Vinnie and mother send their love. Mine too is here. My letter as a bee, goes laden. Please love us and remember us. Please write us very soon, and tell us how you are. . . .

Affy,
Emilie.

MANUSCRIPT: missing. The text is from *Letters* (1894), which reproduces in facsimile the first paragraph (showing the letter to be dated: Tuesday Evening), and the signature: Affy, Emilie.

PUBLICATION: L (1894) 157–158; LL 185–186; L (1931) 156–157; LH 32–34.

Emily and Vinnie visited the Hollands in September, pursuant to plans made in July. Mrs. Holland's sister Amelia (Minnie) Chapin lived with the Hollands until her marriage in 1856. Dr. Heman Humphrey, president of Amherst College from 1823 until 1845, had taught moral philosophy. Adolphus Hawkins, in Longefellow's prose romance *Kavanagh*, is a character whose writings satirize the effusions of the village poet. The scripture paraphrase in the first paragraph is from Matthew 7. 7–8; that in the second, from Luke 11. 12: "Or if he shall ask an egg, will he offer him a scorpion?"; that in the third, from I Corinthians 15. 53.

134

To Susan Gilbert (Dickinson)   *October 1853*

Dear Susie —

I send you a little air — The "Music of the Spheres." They are represented above as passing thro' the sky.

MANUSCRIPT: HCL (B 75). Pencil. Addressed: Susie. ED made a sketch of ascending musical notations and puffs of ascending clouds.
PUBLICATION: FF 185.
Sue was visiting in New York at this time.

135

To Susan Gilbert (Dickinson)   *about October 1853*

It's hard to wait, dear Susie, though my heart is there, and has been since the sunset, and I knew you'd come – I'd should have gone right down, but Mother had been at work hard, as it was Saturday, and Austin had promised to take her to Mrs Cobb's, as soon as he got home from Palmer — then she wanted to go, and see two or three of the neighbors, and I wanted to go to you, but I thought it would be unkind — so not till tomorrow, Darling — and all the stories Monday —

except short sketches of them at meeting tomorrow night. *I* have stories to tell – very unusual for me – a good many things have happened – Love for you Darling – How can I sleep tonight?

> Ever Emilie –

So precious, my own Sister, to have you here again – *Somebody loves you* more – or I were there this evening –

Mother sends her love – She spoke of it this morning, what a day Susie would have –

MANUSCRIPT: HCL (B 152). Pencil. Dated: 6 o'clock. Addressed: Susie.
PUBLICATION: FF 220, in part.
Probably this note welcomes Sue home from her New York trip.

136

To Henry V. Emmons   *autumn 1853*

I send you the book with pleasure, for it has given me happiness, and I love to have it busy, imparting delight to others.

Thank you for the beautiful note – It is too full of poesy for a Saturday morning's reply, but I will not forget it, nor shall it fade as the leaves, tho' like them gold and crimson –

I send a note for your friend – Please remember me to her, with a sincere affection –

I am happy that she is with you – I have not read the book of which you speak – I will be happy to whenever agreable [sic] to you – and please give me an opportunity to see you "sirrah" very soon –

> Your friend
> Emily E. Dickinson

MANUSCRIPT: HCL (E 3). Pencil. Dated: Saturday morn.
PUBLICATION: NEQ XVI (1943) 368.
The friend here mentioned is not Susan Phelps, to whom Emmons became engaged in the following year (see letters no. 168 and 169). ED had not yet met her. The person referred to is probably Eliza Judkins, formerly a teacher at Amherst Academy (see letter no. 163).

137

To John L. Graves   *late 1853*

In memory of Æolus.

Cousin John – ,

I made these little Wristlets. Please wear them for me. Perhaps
they will keep you warm.

Emilie.

MANUSCRIPT: HCL (G 6). Pencil. Addressed on the fold: Mr John L
Graves/Present. Unpublished.

At the top ED sketched a grave, with head and foot stones. The wristlets were sent as a gift in return for the aeolian harp which Graves had
made and presented ED in April (see letter no. 115). They were gaily
striped and survived for many years, "shown to his children long ago, as
Emily's handiwork" (letter from Miss Louise B. Graves, 12 August 1951,
to the editor).

138

To Henry V. Emmons   *late 1853*

Friend –

Which of us is mistaken?

E. E. D.

MANUSCRIPT: HCL (E 8). Pencil. Dated Tuesday noon.
PUBLICATION: NEQ XVI (1943) 371.

ED's friendship with Emmons stemmed from their interest in books.
This note may have something to do with reading.

139

To Austin Dickinson   *8 November 1853*

Dear Austin –

It seems very lonely without you. Just as I write it snows, and we
shall have a storm. It makes me think of Thanksgiving, when we are

all here again. Sue was with us yesterday afternoon, and as usual walked up to Miss Baker's with Vinnie –

I got my plants in yesterday, and it was so cold last night that the squashes all had to be moved.

We shall move the table into the sitting room today, and with a cheerful fire, and only one thing wanting, you can think just how we look. I guess things at the house are getting along pretty well, tho' father said this morning he almost wished he'd persuaded you to stay until after Thanksgiving. Father went away, bidding us an affectionate good bye yesterday morning, having business in Springfield which would detain him all day, and perhaps until the next day, and returned at dinner time, just as the family were getting *rather busy* – Of course, we were delighted to be together again! After our long separation! Had a letter from Mat, last night, which I would enclose to you, but have just sent it to Sue. She spoke of you very affectionately, sent her love, and wanted you to write her. She enclosed a private letter to Sue. I hope you have got there safely, and found a pleasant home. It looks so bleak this morning that if you were me, at all, you might be inclined to be homesick; as you are not, I hope you're not.

I must not write any more, for there is'nt a moment to spare before this goes in the mail.

I'm afraid you cant read it now, I have written in such a hurry – We all send you our love, and hope you are happy, and think much of seeing you again.

Affy,
Emily.

PS. Pussy is well –

MANUSCRIPT: AC. Pencil. Dated: Tuesday morning. Envelope addressed and franked by Edward Dickinson. Postmarked: Amherst Ms Nov 8.

PUBLICATION: *Home* 311.

Austin remained at home until after the Cattle Show, October 26, returning to law school some days after the fall term began. "Mat" is Martha Gilbert.

To Austin Dickinson   *10 November 1853*

Dear Austin –

I was so glad to get your letter, and thank you for writing so soon. It does seem so strange without you, but we try to make the most of us, and get along pretty well.

The weather is very cold here. Day before yesterday, we had a snow storm — yesterday a terrible rain, and today the wind blows west, and the air is bitter cold. I am so glad you got there pleasantly, and feel so much at home. Mr Dwight preached beautifully Sunday, and I knew you w'd miss him.

Mrs Fay is moving today, and Father is so solemn –

I do wish he would "look more cheerful" – I think the Artist was right –

Sue was here day before yesterday, but it stormed and blew so yesterday, no one could get out, and therefore we did not see her.

Father remarked yesterday that he would like it very well if you were here to vote. For all you differ, Austin – he cant get along without you, and he's been just as bleak as a November day, ever since you've been gone. You asked me about the railroad — Everybody seems pleased at the change in arrangement. It sounds so pleasantly to hear them come in twice. I hope there will be a bell soon. We were talking about it this morning. Write very often, Austin. You are coming next week Saturday, you know, and the Roosters are ripening!

The family party is to be at "Miss Willim's"!

Good bye.
Emilie.

MANUSCRIPT: AC. Pencil. Dated: Thursday morn. Envelope franked and addressed by Edward Dickinson. Postmarked: Amherst Ms Nov 10. An attempt has been made to alter the reference to Sue.

PUBLICATION: *Home* 311–312.

Mrs. Samuel A. Fay, an aunt of the Newman girls, kept house for them when they moved to Amherst (see letter no. 106). Enclosed with this letter was one from Lavinia (*Home* 312–313).

Dear Austin.

You did'nt come, and we were all disappointed, tho' none so much as father, for nobody but father really believed you would come, and yet folks are disappointed sometimes, when they dont expect anything. Mother got a great dinner yesterday, thinking in her kind heart that you would be so hungry after your *long ride*, and the table was set for you, and nobody moved your chair, but there it stood at the table, until dinner was all done, a melancholy emblem of the blasted hopes of the world. And we had new custard pie, too, which is a rarity in days when hens dont lay, but mother knew you loved it, and when noon really got here, and you really did not come, then a big piece was saved in case you should come at night. Father seemed perfectly sober, when the afternoon train came in, and there was no intelligence of you in any way, but "there's a good time coming"! I suppose Father wrote you yesterday that Frank Conkey was chosen Representative. I dont know whether you will care, but I felt all the while that if you had been here, it w'd not have been so.

I wonder if you voted in Cambridge, I did'nt believe you would come. I said so all the while, and tho' I was disappointed, yet I could'nt help smiling a little, to think that I guessed right. I told Father I *knew* you w'd vote somehow in Cambridge, for you always did what you wanted to, whether 'twas against the law or not, but he would'nt believe me, so when he was mistaken, I *was* a little gratified. Sue "spent the afternoon, and took tea" at Dea [John] Leland's yesterday. I was with her last evening, and she came half way home with me. She did'nt think you would come. George Allen remarked at their table yesterday, that for his part, he hoped Frank Conkey would be chosen representative, for he was a very smart fellow, and the finest Lawyer in Amherst—also that he was said to present his cases in court much finer than any other, and should *he himself* George Allen, have any difficult business, he should surely entrust it to him!

If that is'nt the apex of human impudence, I dont know anything of it. She remarked in her coolest, most unparralled way, that she wanted to open the door, and poke him out with the poker!

So much for the Amherst youth! I should recommend a closet, and self examination, accompanied with bread and water, to that same individual, till he might obtain faint glimpses of something like common sense. If Joseph Addison were alive, I should present him to him, as the highest degree of absurdity, which I had yet discerned, as it is, I will let him alone in the undisturbed possession of his remarkable folly.

Mr James Kellogg's brother from New York, with a family of nine, are here for a little while, and board at the Amherst House. Quite an affair to the town, and to the Landlord's purse. I'm telling all the news, Austin, for I think you will like to hear it. You know it's quite a sacrifice for *me* to tell what's going on.

We want to see you, all of us — we shall be very happy when you come. I hope you'll get home on Saturday. Prof Park will preach in Amherst next Sunday. I know you will want to hear him.

I send my prescription, Austin, and would be glad to have you attend to it for me, if you have time, but if it is inconvenient, no matter now. Mother sends much love — father is gone away. Vinnie has written herself, and I am today and always,

> your aff
> Sister Emily.

MANUSCRIPT: AC. Pencil. Dated: Monday morning. Envelope franked and addressed by Edward Dickinson. Postmark obliterated.

PUBLICATION: *Home* 313–314.

James Kellogg, a prominent Amherst manufacturer, was the father of ED's friend Emeline Kellogg. The Reverend Edwards Amasa Park, a professor at Andover Theological Seminary, was one of the distinguished preachers of his day. Offered the presidency of Amherst in 1844, he declined it. With this letter, as with the preceding, was enclosed one from Lavinia (*Home* 315).

142

To Austin Dickinson   21 November 1853

Dear Austin.

I should have written you long ago, but I tho't you would certainly come Saturday, and if I sent a letter, it w'd not get to you. I was so glad to get your letter. I had been making calls all Saturday afternoon, and came home very tired, and a little disconsolate, so your letter was more than welcome.

I felt so sorry I did not write again, when I found you were not coming home, and w'd look for a line on Friday, but you must'nt feel disappointed, Thanksgiving will come so soon.

Oh Austin, you dont know how we all wished for you yesterday. We had such a splendid sermon from that Prof Park — I never heard anything like it, and dont expect to again, till we stand at the great white throne, and "he reads from the book, the Lamb's book." The students and chapel people all came, to our church, and it was very full, and still – so still, the buzzing of a fly would have boomed like a cannon. And when it was all over, and that wonderful man sat down, people stared at each other,. and looked as wan and wild, as if they had seen a spirit, and wondered they had not died. How I wish you had heard him. I thought of it all the time, and so did Sue and Vinnie, and father and mother spoke of it as soon as we got home. But — it is over. Sawyer spent last evening here, but I was at meeting, and had only an opportunity to bid him Good night as I came in.

I suppose that Thanksgiving party is to take place as surely as any stated Fast, and it is quite as cheerful, as those occasions to me. It will have to happen this year, but *we* wont go again. I know it is too bad, but we will make the best of it, and from this time henceforth, we'll have no more to do with it.

No Austin – you're very kind, but there is nothing more we shall want you to do for us than we have spoken of. I wish you might come sooner, but come just as soon as you can —

Susie is all worn out sewing. She seems very lonely without you, and I think seems more depressed than is usual for her. I am so glad you are coming. I think a great many things need you. I will write no more – We shall soon see you, and can say all we please – Remember us to Mr Clark cordially – Take care of yourself, and get here early Wednesday.

Affy
Emilie.

MANUSCRIPT: AC. Pencil. Dated: Monday morning. Envelope franked by Edward Dickinson but addressed by ED: William Austin Dickinson/

Law School/Cambridge/Mass. Postmark obliterated. An attempt has been made to erase and alter the name "Sue."

PUBLICATION: *L* (1894) 102, in part; *L* (1931) 99, in part; *Home* 316–317, entire.

Stephen Greely Clarke, of Manchester, New Hampshire, was a friend of Austin's at Harvard Law School. On Professor Park, see the note in the preceding letter. With this letter, as with the two preceding, was enclosed one from Lavinia (*Home* 317–319).

143

To Emily Fowler (Ford)   *23 November 1853?*

Dear Emily –

I think of you a great deal, tho' I have not been to see you, and my heart runs in every day to see if it cannot comfort you.

I was coming Saturday Evening, but heard you had company. I do hope after Thanksgiving that I can come and see you a great many times and stay a long while, and I hope you will do so here. I have only a little space left to wish you a sweet Thanksgiving.

Aff
Emilie

MANUSCRIPT: YUL. Pencil. Unpublished. Dated: Wednesday noon. Addressed: Emilie.

If the letter was written in 1853, as the handwriting suggests, it was probably written on November 23. Thanksgiving was the following day.

144

To Austin Dickinson   *13 December 1853*

It's quite a comfort, Austin, to hear that you're *alive*, after being for several days in ignorance of the fact — and when I tell you honestly that Vinnie and George Howland would have gone to Northampton yesterday to *telegraph* to you, if we had'nt heard yesterday noon, you can judge that we felt some alarm.

We supposed you had either been *killed*, in going from Cambridge to Boston, for the sake of your watch, or had been very sick and were at present *delirious* and therefore could not write. Mother and Vinnie, Sue and me, were about as disconsolate last Saturday night at sundown, as you would often see. Sue spent the evening here and I went home with her, each feeling perfectly sure that you were not in this world, neither in that to come, and worrying ourselves to fevers in wondering where you were, and why you did'nt write something to some of us. Oh how you would have laughed to have seen us flying around — dodging into the post office and insisting upon it we had a letter there, notwithstanding poor Mr Nims declared there was nothing there — then chasing one another down to our office to Bowdoin, and telling him we knew all about it — he had got the letter and was hiding it, and when he took oath he had not, plunging into the street again, and then back to the house to communicate the result of our forlorn proceedings — and mother — oh she thought the bears in the wood had devoured you, or if you were not eaten up, you were such a monster of thoughtlessness and neglect! but it's all over now, and Thank God you are safe! We are all here, dear Austin — still getting cheerfully on — still missing you, and wishing for you, and knowing you cannot come — Oh for the pleasant years when we were young together, and this was *home — home*!

Poor Susie hears nothing from you — She knows you have written tho'. Sue and I walked to Plainville to meeting Sunday night, and walked back again — Mr Dwight was there — I presume it will make you laugh. Mother could'nt find that Collar Pattern, but you left a Collar in the kitchen cupboard, which you said was just right, and I've ripped it, and cut a pattern from that, and the next time you write if you'll tell me if it's the correct one, Vinnie'll take it up to Miss Baker. We hear from Father often — in better spirits now — When are you coming home. We do want to see you — Much love for you. Write soon —

Your aff Sister,

Emily.

Manuscript: AC. Pencil. Dated: Tuesday morning. Envelope franked by Edward Dickinson but addressed by Lavinia, who enclosed with this a letter of her own (*Home* 329). Postmarked: Amherst Ms Dec 13.

Publication: *Home* 328–329.

[274]

Plainville was a settlement west of Amherst. Congress convened on December 5, and Edward Dickinson had been in Washington since the first of the month. This letter is written on embossed stationery showing the Capitol, and on the fourth page ED drew a chimney with escaping smoke, and approaching the door a striding Indian whose feathered headdress is labeled "Member from the 10th."

145

To Austin Dickinson   *20 December 1853*

Well Austin — dear Austin — you have got back again, Codfish and Pork and all — *all* but the *slippers*, so nicely wrapped to take, yet found when you were gone, under the kitchen chair. I hope you wont want them — Perhaps you have some more there — I will send them by opportunity – should there be such a thing. Vinnie proposed *franking* them, but I fear they are rather large! What should you think of it. It is'nt *every* day that we have a chance to sponge Congress — I wish Vinnie could go as a member — She'd save something snug for us all, besides enriching herself, but Caesar is such "an honorable man" that we may all go to the Poor House, for all the American Congress will lift a finger to help us —

Sue went round collecting for the charitable societies today, and calling on *Miss Kingsbury* in the exercise of that function, the gentle miss remarked that she "would'nt give a cent, nobody gave *her* anything, and she would'nt give them anything," i.e. nobody — she "had to do all the work,["] besides taking care of *"her"* referring Sue supposed to the proprietor of a huge ruffled night cap, protruding from a bed in their spacious apartment. Sue said the gate went "shang, wang, wang" as she passed out of it.

The usual rush of callers, and this beleaguered family as yet in want of time — I do hope immortality will last a little while, but if the Adams' should happen to get there first, we shall be driven there. Vinnie has the headache today. She intends to increase the friction, and see what that will do! She dont believe a word of the man without any action — thinks it is one of your hoaxes — Vinnie went down yesterday to see about the Horse, and found everything right.

[275]

We heard from Father last night and again tonight. He is coming home on Thursday. He alludes to you several times.

We were real glad to get your note, and to know that all was well. Sue shall have hers early tomorrow morning — Will that be soon enough? She has been here this afternoon. She is going to send the letters you spoke of, directly. Well Austin — you are gone, and the wheel rolls slowly on — nobody to laugh with — talk with, nobody down in the morning to make the fun for me! Take care of your lungs, Austin — take that just as I told you, and pretty soon you'll be well.

Emilie —

Hope you can read it. I have written to Clark, today, so will Vinnie — Write me just as soon as you can. Mother's love, and Vinnie's.

6 o'clock   Wednesday morn

Dear Austin — I add a word to say that I've got the fires made and waked the individuals, and the Americans are conquering the British on the teakettle. Hope you are happy this morning — hope you are well — Have you taken your medicine yet? Write the effect of it. Will now proceed to get breakfast consisting of hash and brown bread — Dessert — *A. Sauce.* I shall have to employ a Reporter. Wish you a merry breakfast — wish you were here with me. The bath goes briskly on —

MANUSCRIPT: AC. Pencil. Dated: Tuesday Evening. Envelope franked and addressed by Edward Dickinson. Postmarked: Amherst Ms Dec 21.

PUBLICATION: L (1894) 119, in part; L (1931) 117–118, in part; *Home* 330–331.

Austin had been in Amherst on December 16 to attend the wedding of Emily Fowler and Gordon Ford.

146

To Emily Fowler Ford   *21 December 1853*

Dear Emily,

Are you there, and shall you always stay there, and is it not dear Emily any more, but Mrs. Ford of Connecticut, and must we stay alone, and will you not come back with the birds and the butterflies, when the days grow long and warm?

Dear Emily, we are lonely here. I know Col. S[mith] is left, and Mr. and Mrs. K[ellogg], but pussy has run away, and you do not come back again, and the world has grown so long! I knew you would go away, for I know the roses are gathered, but I guessed not yet, not till by expectation we had become resigned. Dear Emily, when it came, and hidden by your veil you stood before us all and made those promises, and when we kissed you, all, and went back to our homes, it seemed to me translation, not any earthly thing, and if a little after you'd ridden on the wind, it would not have surprised me.

And now five days have gone, Emily, and long and silent, and I begin to know that you will not come back again. There's a verse in the Bible, Emily, I don't know where it is, nor just how it goes can I remember, but it's a little like this—"I can go to her, but she cannot come back to me." I guess that isn't right, but my eyes are full of tears, and I'm sure I do not care if I make mistakes or not. Is it happy there, dear Emily, and is the fireside warm, and have you a little cricket to chirp upon the hearth?

How much we think of you—how dearly love you—how often hope for you that it may all be happy.

Sunday evening your father came in—he stayed a little while. I thought he looked solitary. I thought he had grown old. How lonely he must be—I'm sorry for him.

Mother and Vinnie send their love, and hope you are so happy. Austin has gone away. Father comes home to-morrow. I know father will miss you. He loved to meet you here.

> "So fades a summer cloud away,
>   So smiles the gale when storms are o'er
> So gently shuts the eye of day,
>   So dies a wave along the shore."

Kiss me, dear Emily, and remember me if you will, with much respect, to your husband. Will you write me sometime?

Affectionately,

Emily.

MANUSCRIPT: missing.

PUBLICATION: L (1894) 145–146; L (1931) 143–144, dated (presumably by ED): Wednesday Eve.

Emily Fowler married Gordon L. Ford, 16 December 1853. The stanza quoted is from the Barbauld hymn beginning "How blest the righteous when he dies," but it is evidently quoted from memory, since the second word of the second line actually is *sinks*.

147

To Austin Dickinson   *27 December 1853*

I will write to you Austin, tho' everything is so busy, and we are all flying round as if we were distracted. We send you a little box, containing some good things to help you on your way, and I hope they will please you.

Take good care of yourself, Austin until you get home again, and then we will take care of you – You must have a good time with father – He seems very happy at home, and I guess is happy at Washington – [Sue was with me?] yesterday – I found a – I wont tell you tho' till you get home, I guess — as there are particulars – We think always of you, and hope you are always glad. Father is going now. They have just finished oysters – I wish you could have some.

Love –
Emilie.

Mother wants you to save the box – I have written Emilie Ford. If Clark has come, give our love to him –

MANUSCRIPT: AC. Pencil. Dated: Tuesday noon.
PUBLICATION: *Home* 331–332.
Edward Dickinson came home for the Christmas recess, December 22. He went to Boston to see Austin and carried ED's note with him.

148

To Austin Dickinson   *27 December 1853*

Austin.

If it wont trouble you too much, are you willing to get me another bottle of my medicine, at Mr Joseph Burnett's, 33 – Tremont Row? I did not like to ask Father, because he's always in such a hurry — I hope it wont trouble you —

MANUSCRIPT: AC. Pencil. The envelope is franked by Edward Dickinson M. C., but addressed in ED's hand: William Austin Dickinson./Law School/Cambridge/Mass. Postmarked: Amherst Ms Dec 27.
PUBLICATION: *Home* 332.
Enclosed is a prescription for glycerin and water, one part to three parts (ounces), on which ED has written: "Mr Burnett, 33. Tremont row. Please send *twice* the amount prescribed."

ED's "medicine" is a simple skin lotion, prescribed even today for rough or chapped hands.

149

To Dr. and Mrs. J. G. Holland 2 *January 1854*

May it come *today?*
Then New Year the sweetest, and long life the merriest, and the Heaven highest — by and by!

Emilie.

MANUSCRIPT: missing.
PUBLICATION: *L* (1894) 162; *LL* 189; *L* (1931) 159; *LH* 35: dated (presumably by ED): January 2d.
The first chapter of Holland's *History of Western Massachusetts* appeared in the *Springfield Republican* on 2 January 1854. The *History* ran serially in weekly installments, and was published in book form in 1855. Mrs. Todd's note reads: "Enclosing some leaves, 1854."

150

To Henry V. Emmons *early January 1854*

I will be quite happy to ride tomorrow, as you so kindly propose, tho' I regret sincerely not to see you this evening —

Thank you for remembering Father. He seems much better this morning, and I trust will soon be well. I will ride with much pleasure tomorrow, at any hour in the afternoon most pleasant to yourself —

Please recollect if you will two little volumes of mine which I thought Emily lent you –

> Your friend
> E. E. D –

MANUSCRIPT: HCL (E 4). Pencil.
PUBLICATION: *NEQ* XVI (1943) 368–369.
On his return from Boston on 29 December 1853, Edward Dickinson was in a train that was stalled by heavy snow for twenty hours near Framingham.

151

To Henry V. Emmons   *early January 1854*

Cousin John & Mr Emmons please not regret the little mishap of last evening, for Vinnie and I quite forgot Mr Saxe, in our delightful ride, and were only disappointed lest you should *think* us so.

Will you please receive these blossoms – I would love to make *two garlands* for certain friends of mine, if the summer were here, and till she comes, perhaps one little cluster will express the wish to both. Please share it together, and come in for an evening as soon as college duties are willing you should do.

> Your friends, Emilie
> and Vinnie –

MANUSCRIPT: HCL (E 5). Ink. Dated: Wednesday morn.
PUBLICATION: *NEQ* XVI (1943) 369–370.
The letter was sent to both Emmons and John Graves. The currently popular poet John Godfrey Saxe lectured at Easthampton on Tuesday, January 2. There is no record of an engagement in Amherst at the time, yet he seems to have been speaking somewhere within easy reach.

152

To Austin Dickinson   *5 January 1854*

Austin –

George Howland has just retired from an evening's visit here, and

I gather my spent energies to write a word to you – "Blessed are they that are persecuted for righteousness' sake, for they shall have their reward"! Dear Austin – I dont feel funny, and I hope you wont laugh at anything I say. I am thinking of you and Vinnie, what nice times you are having, sitting and talking together, while I am lonely here, and I *wanted* to sit and think of you, and fancy what you were saying, all the evening long, but —— ordained otherwise. I hope you will have grand times, and dont forget the *unit* without you, at home.

I have had some things from you, to which I perceived no meaning. They either were very vast, or they did'nt mean anything, I dont know certainly which. What did you mean by a note you sent me day before yesterday? Father asked me what you wrote and I gave it to him to read – He looked very much confused and finally put on his spectacles, which did'nt seem to help him much – I dont think a *telescope* would have assisted him.

I hope you will write to me – I love to hear from you, and now Vinnie is gone, I shall feel very lonely. Susie has been with me today – she is a dear sister to me – She will write and enclose with mine.

Father and Mother are going to South Hadley tomorrow, to be gone all day, and Sue I guess will come to spend the day with me. Prof. Haven will give a Lyceum Lecture next Monday Eve – Subject – Power Ottoman in Europe. There will be a Temperance Lecture in the Hall tomorrow evening. The Academy and Town Schools have been riding "En Masse" this afternoon, and have got home this evening, singing as they came. Well – we were all boys once, as Mrs. Partington says.

Jerry has been to ride today – Left home at Eight this morning – Goal – South Hadley Falls –

Suppose he will return sometime during the evening –

He takes good care of the horse – When shall you come home Austin? We do want to see you again – You must come as soon as you and Vinnie think best, for she will want you some – Dont mind the writing, Austin – for I'm so tired tonight, I can hardly hold my pencil. Love for them all, if there are those to love and think of me, and more and most for you, from

Emily.

If it's perfectly convenient, when you come, I should like the vial filled, which you took away with you –

MANUSCRIPT: AC. Pencil. Dated: Thursday Evening. Envelope missing. Much of the third paragraph has been erased, but all of it can be read.

PUBLICATION: *L* (1894) 118–119, in part; *L* (1931) 116–117, in part; AB 98, in part; *Home* 337–338, entire.

Lavinia either went to Boston with her father, or followed alone a few days later. George Howland was her friend. The word "ride" refers to driving or sleighing. Horseback riding is specifically so named.

153

To Edward Everett Hale   *13 January 1854*

Rev Mr Hale –

Pardon the liberty Sir, which a stranger takes in addressing you, but I think you may be familiar with the last hours of a Friend, and I therefore transgress a courtesy, which in another circumstance, I should seek to observe. I think, Sir, you were the Pastor of Mr B. F. Newton, who died sometime since in Worcester, and I often have hoped to know if his last hours were cheerful, and if he was willing to die. Had I his wife's acquaintance, I w'd not trouble you Sir, but I have never met her, and do not know where she resides, nor have I a friend in Worcester who could satisfy my inquiries. You may think my desire strange, Sir, but the Dead was dear to me, and I would love to know that he sleeps peacefully.

Mr Newton was with my Father two years, before going to Worcester – in pursuing his studies, and was much in our family.

I was then but a child, yet I was old enough to admire the strength, and grace, of an intellect far surpassing my own, and it taught me many lessons, for which I thank it humbly, now that it is gone. Mr Newton became to me a gentle, yet grave Preceptor, teaching me what to read, what authors to admire, what was most grand or beautiful in nature, and that sublimer lesson, a faith in things unseen, and in a life again, nobler, and much more blessed –

Of all these things he spoke – he taught me of them all, earnestly, tenderly, and when he went from us, it was as an elder brother, loved indeed very much, and mourned, and remembered. During his life in Worcester, he often wrote to me, and I replied to his letters – I always asked for his health, and he answered so cheerfully, that while I knew he was ill, his death indeed surprised me. He often talked of God, but I do not know certainly if he was his Father in Heaven – Please Sir, to tell me if he was willing to die, and if you think him at Home, I should love so much to know certainly, that he was today in Heaven. Once more, Sir, please forgive the audacities of a Stranger, and a few lines, Sir, from you, at a convenient hour, will be received with gratitude, most happy to requite you, sh'd it have opportunity.

Yours very respectfully,
Emily E. Dickinson

P.S. Please address your reply to Emily E. Dickinson – Amherst – Mass –

MANUSCRIPT: Lilly. Ink. Dated: Amherst. Jan 13th.
PUBLICATION: T. F. Madigan's catalog, *The Autograph Album* I (1933) 50, in part; *American Literature* VI (1935) 5, entire; G. F. Whicher, *This Was a Poet* (1938), 84–85, in part.

Hale's reply is not known to survive. ED referred to Newton on at least four other occasions. Her earliest comment is in a letter written to Austin on 27 March 1853, three days after Newton's death (no. 110): "Oh Austin, Newton is dead. The first of my own friends. Pace." Three later allusions, almost certainly to Newton, are in letters to Higginson. The first, in a letter written in 1862 (no. 261), says: "When a little Girl, I had a friend, who taught me Immortality – but venturing too near, himself – he never returned." The second, written in the same year (no. 265), comments: "My dying Tutor told me that he would like to live till I had been a poet. . ." The third, written fourteen years later (no. 457), indicates how vivid the memory of Newton continued to remain: "My earliest friend wrote me the week before he died 'If I live, I will go to Amherst – if I die, I certainly will.'"

None of the correspondence between ED and Newton has ever been found, and the assumption therefore is that important letters revealing the development of Emily Dickinson as a poet have long since been destroyed (see letter no. 30).

154

To Susan Gilbert (Dickinson)   *15 January 1854*

I'm just from meeting, Susie, and as I sorely feared, my "life" was made a "victim." I walked – I ran – I turned precarious corners – One moment I was not — then soared aloft like Phoenix, soon as the foe was by – and then anticipating an enemy again, my soiled and drooping plumage might have been seen emerging from just behind a fence, vainly endeavoring to fly once more from hence. I reached the steps, dear Susie – I smiled to think of me, and my geometry, during the journey there – It would have puzzled Euclid, and it's doubtful result, have solemnized a Day. How big and broad the aisle seemed, full huge enough before, as I quaked slowly up — and reached my usual seat!

In vain I sought to hide behind your feathers – Susie – feathers and *Bird* had flown, and there I sat, and sighed, and wondered I was scared so, for surely in the whole world was nothing I need to fear – Yet there the Phantom was, and though I kept resolving to be as brave as Turks, and bold as Polar Bears, it did'nt help me any. After the opening prayer I ventured to turn around. Mr Carter immediately looked at me – Mr Sweetser attempted to do so, but I discovered *nothing*, up in the sky somewhere, and gazed intently at it, for quite a half an hour. During the exercises I became more calm, and got out of church quite comfortably. Several roared around, and, sought to devour me, but I fell an easy prey to Miss Lovina Dickinson, being too much exhausted to make any farther resistance.

She entertained me with much sprightly remark, until our gate was reached, and I need'nt tell you Susie, just how I clutched the latch, and whirled the merry key, and fairly danced for joy, to find myself *at home*! How I did wish for you — how, for my own dear Vinnie — how for Goliah, or Samson — to pull the whole church down, requesting Mr Dwight to step into Miss Kingsbury's, until the dust was past!

Prof Aaron Warner, late propounder of Rhetoric to youth of Amherst College, gave us the morning sermon. Now Susie, you and I, admire Mr Warner, so my felicity, when he arose to preach, I need not say to you. I will merely remark that I shall be much disappointed if the Rev Horace Walpole does'nt address us this evening.

You can see how things go, dear Susie, when you are not at home. If you stay another Sunday, I hav'nt any doubt that the "Secretary of War" will take charge of the Sabbath School — yet I would not alarm you!

The singing reminded me of the Legend of "Jack and Gill," allowing the Bass Viol to be typified by *Gill*, who literally tumbled after, while Jack — i e the choir, galloped insanely on, "nor recked, nor heeded" him.

Dear Sister, it is passed away, and you and I may speak of dear things, and little things — some of our *trifles* Susie – There's Austin — he's a trifle — and trifling as it is that he is coming Monday, it makes my heart [beat] faster — Vinnie's a trifle too — Oh how I love such trifles. Susie, under that black spot, technically termed a *blot*, the word *beat* may be found – My pen fell from the handle — occasioning the same, but life is too short to transcribe or apologize – I dont doubt Daniel Webster made many a blot, and I think you said, *you* made one, under circumstances quite aggravating! But of Austin and Vinnie – One is with me tomorrow noon, and I shall be so happy.

The one that returns, Susie, is dearer than "ninety and nine" that did not go away. To get you all once more, seems vague and doubtful to me, for it would be so dear. Did you ever think, Susie, that there had been no grave here? To me there are three, now. The longest one is Austin's – I must must plant brave trees there, for Austin was so brave — and Susie, for you and Vinnie I shall plant each a rose, and that will make the birds come.

Sister, I hav'nt asked if you got to Manchester safely, if all is happy, and well, and yet I'm sure it is — if it were not, you would have told me. Susie, the days and hours are very long to me, but you must not come back until it is best and willing.

Please remember me to your friends, with respect and affection, leaving only affection for you — from your own

Emily —

Remember the hint, Susie!
Mother asks if I've given her love.

MANUSCRIPT: HCL (L 19). Ink. Dated: Sabbath Day.
PUBLICATION: LL 31, in part, and altered.

Sue visited Mrs. Samuel C. Bartlett in Manchester, New Hampshire, between January 10 and 24. With her sister and father away, ED felt unprotected. Professor Aaron Warner had resigned on 21 November 1853, because the trustees had adopted a report severely critical of his work without hearing his side of the case. Austin came home shortly after this letter was written — possibly the next day — to stay until March 1.

155

To Henry V. Emmons   *17 February 1854*

         Please, Sir, to let me
         be a *Valentine* to Thee!

MANUSCRIPT: HCL (E 9). Ink. Dated: Febuary 17th.
PUBLICATION: *NEQ* XVI (1943) 372.
The message is written in the center of a small elaborately embossed sheet of stationery, evidently made for the purpose.

156

To Austin Dickinson   *14 March 1854*

Dear Austin.

It is getting late now, but I guess you'll "have occasion," so I write a word from home —

After you went away yesterday, I washed the dishes, and tried the Drainer — It worked admirably, and reminded me much of you. Mother said I must tell you. Then I worked until dusk, then went to Mr Sweetser's to call on Abiah Root, then walked around to Jerry's and made a call on him — then hurried home to supper, and Mother went to the Lyceum, while John Graves spent the evening with Vinnie and I until past 10 — Then I wrote a long letter to Father, in answer to one we had from him yesterday — then crept to bed softly, not to wake all the folks, who had been asleep a long time — I rose at my usual hour, kindled the "fires of Smithfield," and missed you very much in the lower part of the house — you constituting my principal society, at that hour in the day. My family descended after taking their bath, and we breakfasted *frugally*. Mother and Vinnie were quite silent, and there was nobody to make fun with me at the table.

Today has passed as usual — Sue came this afternoon, and we gave her all her things. The note was quite unexpected. I had a letter from Garrick [?] Mallery this evening. Sue and I went up to Mr — Sweetser's to see Abiah — then I went home with her, and had a pleasant time — She said she meant to have you get her letter first, but I ad-

[286]

vised not to quarrel on so minute a point — Father wrote a very pleasant letter — said he hoped you had got well. Prof Fowler, was very interesting — so mother said, and had a very good audience — Did'nt you find it very lonely, going back to Mrs Ware's? We speak of it very often.

I would'nt sit up late, if I were you, or study much evenings. Vinnie has been to see Mrs Mack about the house — Mrs Mack says John White is a nice man to be in the house — neat, orderly, clean, and so is his wife — does not drink, she says, and "has took the pledge." Mrs Mack says the only thing is whether he can pay the rent, and he *thinks* he can pay it. Mrs Mack would like to have him there — "a great deal better than Morrison." You must do as you think best.

Mr Field's daughter is dead.

I dont think you left anything — Should I find such, I shall direct it to the "Honorable Edward Dickinson" and send it on!

I hope you wont be lonely in Cambridge — you must think of us all when you are.

And if the cough troubles you follow my prescription, and it will soon get well. You must write whenever you can.

You know you can *telegraph* to Father if you would like to — you are not confined to the pen! It seems pretty still here, Austin, but I shant tell you about it, for twill only make you lonely — Love from Mother. Remember us to Clark. Goodnight —

Emilie —

MANUSCRIPT: AC. Pencil. Dated: Tuesday Evening. Envelope addressed: Wm Austin Dickinson./Law School./Cambridge/Mass. Postmarked: Amherst Ms Mar 15.

PUBLICATION: *Home* 342–343.

Austin had delayed his return to Cambridge until March 13 because of illness. Sarah E. Field died of consumption, March 14, aged seventeen.

157

To Austin Dickinson   *16 March 1854*

Dear Austin.

Cousin John has passed part of the evening here, and since he took his hat, I have written a letter to Father, and shall now write to

[287]

you. Your letter came this noon – Vinnie went after it before we sat down to dinner. You are very kind to write so soon. Dont think we miss you any – hey? Perhaps you know nothing about it. We are indeed very lonely, but so very hard at work that we havnt so much time to think, as you have. I hope your room will seem more cheerful when you've been there a little while.

You must'nt think anything about Mrs Ware. Since you went back to Cambridge, the weather has been wonderful, the thermometer every noon between 60 and 70°. above zero, and the air full of birds.

Today has not seemed like a day. It has been most unearthly – so mild, so bright, so still, the kitchen windows open, and fires uncomfortable.

Since supper it lightens frequently – In the South you can see the lightning, in the North the Northern Lights. Now a furious wind blows, just from the north and west, and winter comes back again.

Sue was here yesterday and today – spent a part of both afternoons with us. Seems much like old times. We gave her the letter. Vinnie's bundle came today, after giving her great suspense. Mr Potter brought it to the house himself, and seemed very pleasant indeed. I went to the door – I liked him. Mary Warner and her friend Abbie Adams, made a call of about an hour, here this forenoon. They had been *taking a walk*. I think any sentiment must be consecrated by an interview in the mud. There would be certainly, a correspondence in *depth*.

There is to be a Party at Prof Haven's tomorrow night, for married people merely. Celibacy excludes me and my sister. Father and mother are invited. Mother will go.

Emiline and Jennie Hitchcock were both here this afternoon.

Mrs Noyes is sewing up stairs. Jerry went for her with our horse. Mr Cabot said there was no danger and Jerry drove very carefully. Jerry asked us yesterday when we were writing to Mr Austin, to tell him Fanny was much improved by recent exercise, and looked finer than ever. Jerry is so kind and pleasant that I cant bear the thought of his going away.

He speaks of you with great admiration. We are going to send two little cakes of maple sugar to Father tomorrow. We thought it would please him.

Miller came here yesterday to see if Father wanted to hire him this summer – said he had had a fine offer, and before accepting it, would like to know if he was needed here. He wanted us to ask you when we wrote. I think he is a humbug. I hope you wont employ him.

I have more to say, but am too tired to now. Mother and Vinnie send love – They are both getting ready for Washington. Take care of yourself Austin, and dont get melancholy. Remember Clark.

Emilie –

MANUSCRIPT: AC. Ink. Dated: Thursday Evening. Envelope addressed: Wm Austin Dickinson./Law School./Cambridge/Mass. Postmarked: Amherst Ms Mar 17.

PUBLICATION: L (1894) 120, in part; L (1931) 118–119, in part; Home 344–345, entire.

It has been generally assumed until now that ED accompanied her brother, mother, and sister to Washington in April 1854. Evidence now leads to the conclusion that she did not go until February 1855. The final paragraph of this letter makes clear that she intends to remain home at this time. A letter from Edward Dickinson to Austin, written March 13 (Home 339) says:

I have written home, to have Lavinia come with yr mother & you – & Emily too, if she will – but that I will not insist upon her coming.

ED's letter of March 19 (no. 158) to Austin tells him that "Cousin John is going to stay here at night when they are away, and wants to know quite eagerly 'when it is to come off.'" Austin heard from his father again on the twenty-fourth (Home 354):

I hear from home that yr mother & Lavinia are getting ready as fast as possible, to come here. I should like to have you all come as early in April as you can.

On March 26 ED comments to Austin (letter no. 159): "The sewing is moving on – I guess the folks will be ready by next week Tuesday." But the final direct evidence that ED remained home at this time is contained in a letter (Dartmouth College – Bartlett papers) written by Susan Gilbert to her friend Mrs. Samuel C. Bartlett, in April:

I forgot to tell you – I am keeping house with Emily, while the family are in Washington – We frighten each other to death nearly every night – with that exception, we have very independent times.

For further data, see the notes to letters no. 178 and 179.

158

I have just come from meeting, Austin – Mr Luke Sweetser presided, and young Mr Hallock made a prayer which I dont doubt you heard in Cambridge – It was really very audible – Mr Dwight was not there – Sue did not go – Tempe Linnell sat by me – I asked her if she was engaged to Sam Fiske, and she said *no*, so you can tell Mrs Jones she was slightly mistaken. Have you had a pleasant day, Austin? Have you been to meeting today? We have had a lovely Sunday, and have thought of you very much. Mr Dwight preached all day. Mr Williston and [William S.] Clark were at our church this morning – There was a letter read from the Congregational c'h in Washington – D C, requesting the company of the Pastor and a Delegate, at the ordination of that Rev Mr Duncan, who was so much admired by Father when he was at home before – Father was chosen Delegate, but whether Mr Dwight will go or not, I dont know –

Tuesday morning –

Austin – I had'nt time to finish my note Sunday night – I shall do so now – Received your note last evening, and laughed all night till now – You must not be so facetious – It will never do. Susie was here when the note arrived, and we just sat and screamed. I shall keep the letter always. Marcia is here this morning – the work goes briskly on –

We are almost beside ourselves with business, and company – "Lysander" has not yet called – Emmons spent Friday evening here. I went with Cousin John last evening to call on Sue – stayed till most 11 – and had a splendid time – Sue seemed her very finest – She sends this little note.

Was at Mr Dwight's yesterday – they had a great deal to say about you and Susie and how happy Vinnie and I must be to have such a beau[tiful sister?]

We had two letters from Father last night – one to mother and one to me – I shall telegraph to him soon! Charlie sings every day – Everybody admires him – You must tell Aunt Lavinia –

How did Mr Bourne bear the announcement that both the black eyes were disposed of? It must have been quite a shock to him. Mrs Noyes has gone home – Helped us a great deal – Cenith has just arrived, so between her and "Judah" and Marcia and Miss Cooly, I guess the folks will go – Cousin John is going to stay here at night when they are away, and wants to know quite eagerly "when it is to come off." I am glad you have got settled and are not afraid of ghosts. You must have pleasant times with Clark.

We all send our love to you – Wont you write soon about John White – He is anxious to know, and Mrs Mack wants very much to have him come in there. Good bye Austin – Great hurrah – Remember us always to Clark –

Emily –

MANUSCRIPT: AC. Pencil. Dated: Sunday Evening. Envelope addressed (in ink): Wm Austin Dickinson./Law School./Cambridge./Mass. Postmarked: Amherst Ms Mar 22.

PUBLICATION: *Home* 346–351, with facsimile 347–350.

An attempt has been made to alter every reference to Sue. The women named in the paragraph next to the last evidently were seamstresses and other helpers called in to assist Mrs. Dickinson and Lavinia to prepare for their impending trip to Washington.

159

To Austin Dickinson   *26 March 1854*

Well Austin – it's Sunday evening – Vinnie is sick with the ague – Mother taking a tour of the second story as she is wont Sabbath evening – the wind is blowing high, the weather very cold, and I am rather cast down, in view of all these circumstances. Vinnie's face began to ache Friday – that night, and yesterday, and last night, she suffered intensely, and nothing seemed to relieve her. Today she is better – has sat up in the big rockingchair most of the time, and seems quite bright this evening. I guess she'll be smart tomorrow. She sends her love to you and says you will sympathize with her. I went to meeting alone all day. I assure you I felt very solemn. I went to meeting five minutes before the bell rang, morning and afternoon, so not to have to go in after all the people had got there. I came home with Sue from meeting. She said she wished you had heard Mr Dwight's sermons today. He has preached wonderfully, and I thought all the afternoon how I wished you were there.

[291]

The sewing is moving on — I guess the folks will be ready by next week Tuesday. That is the day fixed now. I have to work very hard. I dont write to you very often now, and I cant till all this is over. I should love to see you this evening. I told Vinnie a few minutes ago that it seemed very funny not to see you putting on your surtout, and asking us if we would like to call at Mrs Jones'! I received several notes, or paragraphs, from you, in the course of the week, for which I am much obliged. The wind has blown a gale for the last week, in Amherst.

Sue and I went to the Depot yesterday to get "Vinnie's Express," and we had to hold our bonnets on and take hold of each other too, to keep from blowing away. We had a snow storm here last week, and there's a covering of snow on the ground now.

Mr Sweetser's family went to meeting in a sleigh, so you can see there's a little. Sam Fiske called here this evening. I will tell you something funny. You know Vinnie sent Father a box of maple sugar — She got the box at the store and it said on the outside of it, "1 Doz Genuine Quaker Soap." We did'nt hear from the box, and so many days had passed, we began to feel anxious lest it had never reached him, and Mother writing soon, alluded in her letter to the "sugar sent by the girls," and the funniest letter from Father, came in answer to her's. It seems the box went straightway, but father not knowing the hand, merely took off the papers in which the box was wrapped, and the Label "Quaker Soap" so far imposed upon him, that he put the box in a drawer with his *shaving materials*, and supposed himself well stocked with an excellent Quaker soap, until mother gave him the hint, which led to the discovery. He said he really supposed it a plan for the progress of soap, until he had mother's letter. We all send our love to you, and want you should write us often.

Good night — from
Emilie —

I spelt a word wrong in this letter, but I know better, so you need'nt think you have caught me.

MANUSCRIPT: AC. Ink. Dated: Sunday Evening. Envelope addressed: Wm Austin Dickinson./Law School./Cambridge/Mass. Postmarked: Amherst Ms. Mar 27.

PUBLICATION: L (1894) 121–122, in part; L (1931) 119–120, in part; *Home* 356–357, entire.

To John L. Graves   *spring 1854?*

Dear John –

Be happy –
Emily –
Early Monday morning –

MANUSCRIPT: HCL (G 7). Pencil. Addressed: Cousin John.
PUBLICATION: *Home* 400.

See letter no. 170.

To Emily Fowler Ford   *spring 1854*

I have just come home from meeting, where I have been all day, and it makes me so happy to think of writing you that I forget the sermon and minister and all, and think of none but you. . . . I miss you always, dear Emily, and I think now and then that I can't stay without you, and half make up my mind to make a little bundle of all my earthly things, bid my blossoms and home good-by, and set out on foot to find you. But we have so much matter of fact here that I don't dare to go, so I keep on sighing, and wishing you were here.

I know you would be happier amid this darling spring than in ever so kind a city, and you would get well much faster drinking our morning dew – and the world here is so beautiful, and things so sweet and fair, that your heart would be soothed and comforted.

I would tell you about the spring if I thought it might persuade you even now to return, but every bud and bird would only afflict you and make you sad where you are, so not one word of the robins, and not one word of the bloom, lest it make the city darker, and your own home more dear.

But nothing forgets you, Emily, not a blossom, not a bee; for in the merriest flower there is a pensive air, and in the bonniest bee a sorrow – they know that you are gone, they know how well you loved them, and in their little faces is sadness, and in their mild eyes, tears. But another spring, dear friend, you must and shall be here, and nobody can take you away, for I will hide you and keep you — and who would think of taking you if I hold you tight in my arms?

Your home looks very silent — I try to think of things funny, and turn the other way when I am passing near, for sure I am that looking would make my heart too heavy, and make my eyes so dim. How I do long once more to hear the household voices, and see you there at twilight sitting in the door — and I shall when the leaves fall, sha'n't I, and the crickets begin to sing?

You must not think sad thoughts, dear Emily. I fear you are doing so, from your sweet note to me, and it almost breaks my heart to have you so far away, where I cannot comfort you.

All will be well, I know, and I know all will be happy, and I so wish I was near to convince my dear friend so. I want very much to hear how Mr. Ford is now. I hope you will tell me, for it's a good many weeks since I have known anything of him. You and he may come this way any summer; and how I hope he may — and I shall pray for him, and for you, and for your home on earth, which will be next the one in heaven.

Your very affectionate,
Emilie.

I thank you for writing me, one precious little "forget-me-not" to bloom along my way. But one little one is lonely — pray send it a blue-eyed mate, that it be not alone. Here is love from mother and father and Vinnie and me. . . .

MANUSCRIPT: missing.

PUBLICATION: L (1894) 142–144; L (1931) 141–143, dated (presumably by ED): Sunday Afternoon.

Before moving to Brooklyn, New York, where they permanently resided, the Gordon Lester Fords lived briefly in New London, Connecticut.

162

To Henry V. Emmons *about 1854*

Friend.

I look in my casket and miss a pearl — I fear you intend to defraud me.

Please not forget your promise to pay "mine own, with usury."

I thank you for Hypatia, and ask you what it means?

Have you heard from your friend, Miss Judkins, recently? I desire to write to her, but have not her address, and will you please tell Johnny if a little note to her would make your next too heavy.

Your Friend

Emilie –

MANUSCRIPT: HCL (E 12). Pencil. Dated: Tuesday morn.

PUBLICATION: *NEQ* XVI (1943) 372.

Kingsley's *Hypatia* was published in 1853. Eliza Maria Judkins had taught drawing, painting, and penmanship at Amherst Academy in 1841–1842, and had probably been one of ED's teachers. The first sentence of the letter may be a reminder that Emmons still has not returned the book which ED had lent him (see letter no. 150). Johnny Beston was a youthful handyman.

163

To Henry V. Emmons   *May 1854?*

Friend –

I said I should send some flowers this week. I had rather not until next week – My Vale Lily asked me to wait for her. I told her if you were willing – Please say by little Johnnie if next week is acceptable –

Your friend,

Emilie –

MANUSCRIPT: HCL (E 10). Pencil.

PUBLICATION: *NEQ* XVI (1943) 372.

164

To Henry V. Emmons   *May 1854?*

Receive us –

MANUSCRIPT: HCL (E 11). Pencil.

PUBLICATION: *NEQ* XVI (1943) 372.

The note probably accompanied flowers.

165

To Austin Dickinson   *early June 1854*

Well Austin –

Sunday has come again, and it really seems to me you have been gone a good while.

I hope you will get home before a great many Sundays – It seems quite lonely here, and when I think Sue is going, I confess things seem too solitary, but so we go –

I went home from meeting with Sue, and stayed in her room some-time – She wondered she did'nt hear from you Saturday – so did we – Sue is afraid you are sick – I say you are hard at work, and that's why we dont hear from you. Sue is well – we see her every day – How we shall miss her!

I went out before tea tonight, and trained the Honeysuckle – it grows very fast and finely.

Both of them are full of buds. I take good care of the tree – give it a pail of water every day, and certainly it looks stouter, and we all think it will live.

Your grove looks beautifully too – I went down there tonight.

John Emerson just went away from here – he has been spending the evening, and I'm so tired now, that I write just as it happens, so you must'nt expect any style.

This is truly extempore, Austin – I have no notes in my pocket.

Vinnie has gone to bed – Mother is giving the finishing stroke to a letter to Father, out on the kitchen stand – so you see I am all alone.

We have called upon Mary Lyman – had a very pleasant call – she spoke of you very admiringly.

Emily Fowler is here still – will leave in a day or two. We have been to see her, and she has been to see us – She seems very sincere and affectionate – Mr Ford is spending the Sabbath here – Little Pat holds on yet, tho' I expect every morning he'll be bound out for life, and we shall be in the lurch again. He asked me tonight if I had a newspaper – Why, said I, "Pat, can you read"? "Yes marm" he an-swered – I asked him what kind of a one he thought he should like – "Oh" said he with the utmost gravity "I want to read the *newses*." I gave him two *Lawrence Couriers*, at which he seemed quite overcome – I presume it was a munificence very grand to him – Horace works finely, and seems to feel just as much interest, as if it was all his own – We hear from Father about every day – he is fast getting well, and writes in good spirits –

We cleaned house all last week – that is to say – Mother and Vinnie did, and I scolded, because they moved my things – I cant find much left anywhere, that I used to wear, or know of. You will easily conclude that I am surrounded by trial.

Austin – Mrs Fay wants very much to have you purchase a few articles for their parlor, before you come, if you are willing to. She said she asked Father about it, and he told her you got everything of the sort here, and if you had the time, you would be willing to get a few things for her – She wants a large Rocking Chair – a WhatNot – One or two Ottomans – and a little article of the Tete a Tete fashion. She will leave it all to your taste, and thank you very much if you will do it for her.

I hope it wont trouble you – Sue says she guesses it wont – Sue says you can step into a furniture store – order what you want, and have it packed and forwarded, without farther trouble to you. There's no more room tonight, Austin – Much love for you – Write.

Emilie –

MANUSCRIPT: HCL (L 11). Ink. Dated: Sunday Evening.
PUBLICATION: FF 192–195, in part.

When this letter was written, Austin was within a few weeks of his Law School examination and admission to the Massachusetts bar. Susan Gilbert had been planning to join her sister Martha at Geneva, New York, shortly, but she was not able to go before August. Horace Church had recently been put in charge of the Dickinson grounds. For a note on little Pat, see Appendix 2. Emily Fowler Ford had come home for a visit, as ED hoped when she wrote to her earlier in the spring.

166

To Abiah Root   *about 25 July 1854*

My dear Child.

Thank you for that sweet note, which came so long ago, and thank you for asking me to come and visit you, and thank you for loving me, long ago, and today, and too for all the sweetness, and all the gentleness, and all the tenderness with which you remember me — your quaint, old fashioned friend.

I wanted very much to write you sooner, and I tried frequently, but till now in vain, and as I write tonight, it is with haste, and fear lest something still detain me. You know my dear Abiah, that the summer has been warm, that we have not a girl, that at this pleasant season, we have much company — that this irresolute body refuses to serve sometimes, and the indignant tenant can only hold it's peace — all this you know, for I have often told you, and yet I say it again, if mayhap it persuade you that I do love you indeed, and have not done neglectfully. Then Susie, our dear friend, has been very ill for several weeks, and every hour possible I have taken away to her, which has made even smaller my "inch or two, of time." Susie is better now, but has been suffering much within the last few weeks, from a Nervous Fever, which has taken her strength very fast. She has had an excellent Nurse, a faithful Physician, and her sister has been unwearied in her watchfulness, and last of all, *God* has been loving and kind, so to reward them all, poor Susie just begins to trudge around a little — went as far as her garden, Saturday, and picked a few flowers, so when I called to see her, Lo a bright boquet, sitting upon the mantel, and Susie in the easy-chair, quite faint from the effort of arranging them — I make my story long, but I knew you loved Susie — Abiah, and I thought her mishaps, quite as well as her brighter fortunes, would interest you.

I think it was in June, that your note reached here, and I did snatch a moment to call upon your friend. Yet I went in the dusk, and it was Saturday evening, so even then, Abiah, you see how cares pursued me — I found her very lovely in what she said to me, and I fancied in her face so, although the gentle dusk would draw her curtain close, and I did'nt see her clearly. We talked the most of you — a theme we surely loved, or we had not discussed it in preference to all. I would love to meet her again — and love to see her longer.

Please give my love to her, for your sake. You asked me to come and see you — I must speak of that. I thank you Abiah, but I dont go from home, unless emergency leads me by the hand, and then I do it obstinately, and draw back if I can. Should I ever leave home, which is improbable, I will with much delight, accept your invitation; till then, my dear Abiah, my warmest thanks are your's, but dont expect me. I'm so old fashioned, Darling, that all your friends would stare. I should have to bring my work bag, and my big spectacles, and I half forgot my grandchildren, my pin-cushion, and Puss – Why think of it seriously, Abiah – *do* you think it my *duty* to leave? Will you write me again? Mother and Vinnie send their love, and here's a kiss from me –

Good Night, from Emily –

Manuscript: HCL (ARS 10). Ink. Dated: Tuesday Evening.
Publication: L (1894) 63–64, in part; L (1931) 55–56, in part.

On August 4, Susan Gilbert went to Geneva. This is ED's last known letter to Abiah, who married the Reverend Samuel W. Strong later in the year. There is a finality to the last paragraph which suggests that this letter terminated the correspondence between them.

167

To Austin Dickinson   *summer 1854*

Dear Austin.

Your letter came – I have just come from Sue's – I suppose you did'nt expect to hear from me today, as you saw Sue yesterday. I sat with her some time tonight. She is better and gaining – seemed quite like herself tonight – talked a good deal; and laughed.

Several had been in to see her this afternoon – Mr Dwight – Abbie Wood and Emeline – I guess Mr Dwight knows you have gone – he called to inquire for her yesterday, and went in to see her today – You had better come *hum* and shoot him. Such liberties towards "a man," when a man is gone away, are not to be tolerated! I gave your note to Mrs Cutler – She told me to tell you from her, that Sue had eaten chicken broth *twice* today, and a chicken leg – She designs eating a wing tomorrow – and Mrs Cutler wished me to tell you that she thought she would soon be off. I tell you just as she told me – dont know whether it's to be understood literally or figuratively – cant tell – you must act according to your best judgment. I think it's rather a serious thing to be an affianced being – I dont want to frighten you –

still, when I think it over, it seems no trifling matter. They all allude to you as to a missing Saint, from whose serener presence suddenly called to remove, and as none of them speak of you, or of your noble acts, without plentiful tears, I have considerable work to arrange my emotions. Mrs. Cutler sends word also, that the package came today, safely. As she did not allude to the contents – I naturally conclude that it contained a Bear – derive much satisfaction from contemplating my shrewdness – Hope "Self and wife" will always be so "uniform" – hope I give no offense – Had a letter from father yesterday – well and in excellent spirits. Today has been very fine – Little Pat is in rotary motion. I will attend to the Horse – am going to spend tomorrow forenoon with Sue – Must'nt write any more – Come as soon as your business is over – glad you took care of the Newman's – Dont forget the guano – What did you think of Joe Howard's wife?

Vinnie will write you a note, if she concludes her exercises in the morning. Love from all.

Good night – Emily.

P.S – For *home* read *hum*. For Mrs C – Miss Williams –

MANUSCRIPT: HCL (L 12). Ink (except for the postscript, which is in pencil). Dated: Tuesday night.

PUBLICATION: FF 195, in part.

The Reverend Edward S. Dwight was installed in the First Church, July 19. Austin was graduated from the Law School on July 19, but did not stay to receive his diploma because his mother wished him to take her to the semicentennial celebration of Monson Academy, held July 17–18. (Edward Dickinson did not return from Washington until August 7.) Austin then went back to Cambridge, packed up, and returned permanently to Amherst. This letter must have been written either on July 25 or August 1.

168

To Henry V. Emmons   *8 August 1854*

Friend –

Will *your* friend be in town this evening?

If so, cant you steal her away a little while from the Exercises, and bring her down to me?

Our guests will all be out, and I'd so love to see her that asking it, I write –

Your friend,
Emily –

Manuscript: HCL (E 8). Pencil. Dated: Tuesday morning.
Publication: NEQ XVI (1943) 374.
The 1854 commencement exercises at Amherst College were held on Thursday, August 10, and Emmons was to graduate. ED wanted to meet Susan Phelps of Hadley, to whom he had become engaged.

169

To Henry V. Emmons   *August 1854*

My heart is full of joy, Friend – Were not my parlor full, I'd bid you come this morning, but the hour must be *stiller* in which we speak of *her*. Yet must I see you, and I will love most dearly, if quite convenient to you, to ride a little while this afternoon – Do not come if it's not so, and please tell little Pat when you will like to go, if you still find it possible – Of her I cannot write, yet do I thank the Father who's given her to you, and wait impatiently to spe.ık with you – Please not regard the ride, unless it be most convenient –

My hand trembles –

Truly and warmly,
Emily –

Manuscript: HCL (E 14). Pencil.
Publication: NEQ XVI (1943) 374.
ED met Susan Phelps sometime before Emmons left Amherst during the week after commencement. This note seems to have been written the morning after the meeting.

170

To John L. Graves   *15 August 1854*

Dear John –

Are you very happy? Why did'nt you tell me so before you went away? And why too, did'nt I ask you that pleasant evening long, when we sat and talked together?

[301]

l have wanted to ask you many times, and I thought you would tell me, but someone would come in, and something else would happen and put me all to flight — but tonight, John, so still is it, and the moon so mild, I'm sure that you would tell me, were you sitting here. You know what I mean, dont you, and if you are so happy, I kneel and thank God for it, before I go to sleep.

Then you and your former College friend are reconciled again — he told me all about it, and tears of happiness came shining in my eyes. Forgiving one another as Jesus — us.

I have hoped for this very often, John, when you were fast asleep, and my eyes will shut much sooner, now all is peace. I loved to have you both my friends, and friends to one another, and it grieved me very often that you were enemies — now all is safe. It is lonely without you John — we miss you very much, and I'm thinking we'll miss you more when a year from now comes, and the crickets sing.

Quite sad it is when friends go, and sad when all are gone, to sit by pensive window, and recollect them, but I would not forget them — Please not forget us John, in your long vacation — We'll often think of you, and wish that we could see you. Mary is with us yet. Eliza went yesterday morning. I miss her thoughtful eyes, and did not Mary's merry ones linger with us still, the day would be too long; but Mary strokes the sunshine and coaxes it along, and drives the shadows home — much like a "honie bee" she seems, among more antique insects! She wants me to give you her compliments, and say to you beside, that she thanks you sincerely for the "social capacity,["] which she forgot to do, there were so many in. Good night, and gentle dreams, John — my pen is very bad. I write not any more. Vinnie sends her love.

Mine if you will to Hattie, and for your mother too. Had you been here tonight, John, I should have talked with you — You are not, and I write — I "wish you a merry Christmas," and a vacation as good as summer days are long —

Affy,
Emilie —

MANUSCRIPT: HCL (G 3). Ink. Dated: Tuesday Evening.
PUBLICATION: *Home* 399–400.
Since there is no other allusion to the misunderstanding and recon-

ciliation between John Graves and his friend, the natural inference that Henry Emmons was the friend cannot be verified (but see letter no. 160). The identity of "Mary" is also uncertain. She and Eliza Coleman seem to have been among the Dickinson commencement guests of whom ED had written in her letter to Emmons of August 8. A year earlier there had been some correspondence between Lavinia and Austin about inviting a Mary Nichols to visit them (*Home* 307). Another Boston girl, Mary Lyman, may have been the one (see nos. 71 and 87). "Hattie" was John Graves's younger sister. He had gone home for the summer vacation before starting his senior year at Amherst.

171

To Henry V. Emmons   *18 August 1854*

I find it Friend – I read it – I stop to thank you for it, just as the world is still – I thank you for them all – the pearl, and then the onyx, and then the emerald stone.

My crown, indeed! I do not fear the king, attired in this grandeur.

Please send me gems again – I have a flower. It looks like them, and for it's bright resemblances, receive it.

A pleasant journey to you, both in the pathway home, and in the longer way – *Then* "golden morning's open flowings, *shall* sway the trees to murmurous bowings, in metric chant of blessed poems" –

Have I convinced you Friend?

Pleasantly,
Emily.

MANUSCRIPT: HCL (E 8). Pencil. Dated: Friday Evening.

PUBLICATION: *NEQ* XVI (1943) 371.

Before leaving Amherst, Emmons sent a farewell gift to ED, probably a book of poems. An interpretation is offered by Aurelia G. Scott in *NEQ* XVI (December 1943) 627–628, in which the writer points out that the initial letters of pearl, onyx, and emerald spell "Poe." The lines at the end form the conclusion of an essay by Emmons published in the *Amherst Collegiate Magazine* for July 1854, entitled "The Words of Rock Rimmon": "And I arose and looked forth upon the broad plain with a strange earnestness thrilling in my heart.

> The golden morning's open flowings,
> Did sway the trees in murmurous bowings,
> In metric chant of blessed poems."

[303]

172

To Susan Gilbert (Dickinson)   *late August 1854*

Susie –

I have been very busy since you went away, but that is'nt the reason I've not written to you, and we've had a great deal of company too, but *that* is not the reason – I was foolish eno' to be vexed at a little thing, and I hope God will forgive me, as he'll have to many times, if he lives long enough.

Thro' Austin, I've known of you, and nobody in this world except Vinnie and Austin, know that in all the while, I have not heard from you. Many have asked me for you, and I have answered promptly that you had reached there safely, and were better every day, and Susie, do you think, H. Hinsdale came to our house several days ago; came just to ask for you, and went away supposing I'd heard from you quite often. Not that I told her so, but spoke of you so naturally, in such a daily way, she never guessed the fact that I'd not written to you, nor had you thus to me.

Never think of it, Susie – never mention it – I trust your truth for that, but when you meet, and I meet – we'll try and forgive each other. There has not been a day, Child, that I've not thought of you, nor have I shut my eyes upon a summer night, without your sweet remembrance, and tho' full much of sorrow has gathered at your name, that ought but peace was 'tween us, yet I remembered on, and bye and bye the day came. I do not miss you Susie – of course I do not miss you – I only sit and stare at nothing from my window, and know that all is gone – Dont *feel* it – no – any more than the stone feels, that it is very cold, or the block, that it is silent, where once 'twas warm and green, and birds danced in it's branches.

I rise, because the sun shines, and sleep has done with me, and I brush my hair, and dress me, and wonder what I am and who has made me so, and then I wash the dishes, and anon, wash them again, and then 'tis afternoon, and Ladies call, and evening, and some members of another sex come in to spend the hour, and then that day is done. And, prithee, what is Life? There was much that was sweet Commencement week – much too that was dusty, but my bee gathered many drops of the sweetest and purest honey –

I had many talks with Emmons, which I will not forget, and a charming farewell ride, before he went away – he stayed more than a week after Commencement was done, and came to see me often – He brought his Hadley friend to pass the day with me, and we passed it very sweetly – *Her* name is Susie too, and that endeared me to her.

I shall miss Emmons very much. Father and mother were gone last week, upon a little journey – and we rested somewhat, like most ungodly children – John came down twice from Sunderland, to pass a day with us. Susie, I wished for you – Tell that little Sister of your's, I would have welcomed her – She understands the orgies! When Mr Pan Prankin takes his leave, I trust to hear from her – *Until* then, "Mr Bugby understands it perfectly." It's of no use to write to you – Far better bring dew in my thimble to quench the endless fire – My love for those I love – not many – not very many, but dont I love them so? – and Vinnie's love and Mother's for Martha and for you. Write if you love, to

Emilie –

Pat "still lives." I am going to meeting now – Meet me at the Academy, and we will sit together – Mrs Timothy Smith and Mrs Noble Goodale take turns sitting by me now – Mrs Goodale got me the last time.

MANUSCRIPT: HCL (L 21). Ink. Dated: Sabbath Evening.

PUBLICATION: *LL* 49, in part, and altered (the final sentence is from a letter to Mrs. Holland, no. 318).

Susan Gilbert, after spending some weeks with relatives in Geneva and Aurora, New York, joined her brothers in Grand Haven, Michigan, where she remained several months. For Pat, see letter no. 165, and Appendix 2.

173

To Susan Gilbert (Dickinson)   *about 1854*

Sue – you can go or stay – There is but one alternative – We differ often lately, and this must be the last.

You need not fear to leave me lest I should be alone, for I often part with things I fancy I have loved, – sometimes to the grave, and sometimes to an oblivion rather bitterer that death – thus my heart bleeds so frequently that I shant mind the hemorrhage, and I only add an agony to several previous ones, and at the end of day remark — a bubble burst!

Such incidents would grieve me when I was but a child, and perhaps I could have wept when little feet hard by mine, stood still in the coffin, but eyes grow dry sometimes, and hearts get crisp and cinder, and had as lief burn.

Sue — I have lived by this. It is the lingering emblem of the Heaven I once dreamed, and though if this is taken, I shall remain alone, and though in that last day, the Jesus Christ you love, remark he does not know me — there is a darker spirit will not disown it's child.

Few have been given me, and if I love them so, that for *idolatry*, they are removed from me — I simply murmur *gone*, and the billow dies away into the boundless blue, and no one knows but me, that one went down today. We have walked very pleasantly — Perhaps this is the point at which our paths diverge — then pass on singing Sue, and up the distant hill I journey on.

> I have a Bird in spring
> Which for myself doth sing —
> The spring decoys.
> And as the summer nears —
> And as the Rose appears,
> Robin is gone.
>
> Yet do I not repine
> Knowing that Bird of mine
> Though flown —
> Learneth beyond the sea
> Melody new for me
> And will return.
>
> Fast in a safer hand
> Held in a truer Land
> Are mine —
> And though they now depart,
> Tell I my doubting heart
> They're thine.

In a serener Bright,
In a more golden light
I see
Each little doubt and fear,
Each little discord here
Removed.

Then will I not repine,
Knowing that Bird of mine
Though flown
Shall in a distant tree
Bright melody for me
Return.

E –

MANUSCRIPT: HCL (L 17). Ink. Dated: Tuesday morning.
PUBLICATION: The letter is unpublished. The poem is in *FF* 181–182;
Poems (1955) 7–8.

There is nothing in other letters to indicate a rift between the girls at
this time. The draft of a letter (HCL-Dickinson collection) from Austin
to Susan, 23 September 1851, alludes to some differences between the girls
about which he refuses to take sides, but this letter is in the handwriting of
1854. It is placed here to follow the emotional tone of the letter to Susan
of late August, though the disagreement on spiritual matters that seems to
lie behind it may have no connection with the feeling of neglect shown
in the earlier one.

174

To Mrs. J. G. Holland   *15 September 1854*

Thank you, dear Mrs. Holland — Vinnie and I will come, if you
would you like to have us. We should have written before, but mother
has not been well, and we hardly knew whether we could leave her,
but she is better now, and I write quite late this evening, that if you
still desire it, Vinnie and I will come. Then, dear Mrs. Holland, if
agreeable to you, we will take the Amherst train on Tuesday morning,
for Springfield, and be with you at noon.

The cars leave here at nine o'clock, and I think reach Springfield at twelve. I can think just how we dined with you a year ago from now, and it makes my heart beat faster to think perhaps we'll see you so little while from now.

To live a thousand years would not make me forget the day and night we spent there, and while I write the words, I don't believe I'm coming, so sweet it seems to me. I hope we shall not tire you; with all your other cares, we fear we should not come, but you *will* not let us trouble you, will you, dear Mrs. Holland?

Father and mother ask a very warm remembrance to yourself and Dr. Holland.

We were happy the grapes and figs seemed acceptable to you, and wished there were many more. I am very sorry to hear that "Kate" has such excellent lungs. With all your other cares, it must be quite a trial to you.

It is also a source of pleasure to me that Annie goes to sleep, on account of the "interregnum" it must afford to you.

Three days and we are there — happy — very happy! Tomorrow I will sew, but I shall think of you, and Sunday sing and pray — yet I shall not forget you, and Monday's very near, and here's to me on Tuesday! Good-night, dear Mrs. Holland — I see I'm getting wild — you will forgive me all, and not *forget* me all, though? Vinnie is fast asleep, or her love would be here — though she is, it is. Once more, if it is fair, we will come on Tuesday, and you love to have us, but if not convenient, please surely tell us so.

Affectionately,

Emilie.

MANUSCRIPT: missing.

PUBLICATION: L (1894) 155–157; LL 184–185; L (1931) 155–156; LH 42–44, dated (presumably by ED): Friday Evening.

The occasion for the visit may have been the flower show that was held in Springfield on Tuesday, 19 September 1854. The *Springfield Republican* for Wednesday of that week reported that an unusual number of visitors had come to town to attend the show.

175

To Dr. and Mrs. J. G. Holland   *about 26 November 1854*

Dear Friends,

I thought I would write again. I write you many letters with pens which are not seen. Do you receive them?

I think of you all today, and dreamed of you last night.

When father rapped on my door to wake me this morning, I was walking with you in the most wonderful garden, and helping you pick — roses, and though we gathered with all our might, the basket was never full. And so all day I pray that I may walk with you, and gather roses again, and as night draws on, it pleases me, and I count impatiently the hours 'tween me and the darkness, and the dream of you and the roses, and the basket never full.

God grant the basket fill not, till, with hands purer and whiter, we gather flowers of gold in baskets made of pearl; higher — higher! It seems long since we heard from you — long, since how little Annie was, or any one of you — so long since Cattle Show, when Dr. Holland was with us. Oh, it always seems a long while from our seeing you, and even when at your house, the nights seemed much more long than they're wont to do, because separated from you. I want so much to know if the friends are all well in that dear cot in Springfield — and if well whether happy, and happy — *how* happy, and why, and what bestows the joy? And then those other questions, asked again and again, whose answers are so sweet, do they love — remember us — wish sometimes we were there? Ah, friends — dear friends — perhaps my queries tire you, but I so long to know.

The minister to-day, not our own minister, preached about death and judgment, and what would become of those, meaning Austin and me, who behaved improperly — and somehow the sermon scared me, and father and Vinnie looked very solemn as if the whole was true, and I would not for worlds have them know that it troubled me, but I longed to come to you, and tell you all about it, and learn how to be better. He preached such an awful sermon though, that I didn't much think I should ever see you again until the Judgment Day, and then you would not speak to me, according to his story. The subject of perdition seemed to please him, somehow. It seems very solemn to me. I'll tell you all about it, when I see you again.

I wonder what you are doing today—if you have been to meeting? Today has been a fair day, very still and blue. Tonight the crimson children are playing in the west, and tomorrow will be colder. How sweet if I could see you, and talk of all these things! Please write us very soon. The days with you last September seem a great way off, and to meet you again, delightful. I'm sure it won't be long before we sit together.

Then will I not repine, knowing that bird of mine, though flown — learneth beyond the sea, melody new for me, and will return.

Affectionately,

Emily.

MANUSCRIPT: missing.

PUBLICATION: L (1894) 160–162; L (1931) 157–159; LH 37–38, dated (presumably by ED): Sabbath Afternoon.

The letter is placed here because the phrasing of the reference to the weather exactly parallels that in the letter which follows, written to Susan Gilbert on November 27; and because the conclusion echoes lines from the poem sent to Susan in September (letter no. 173).

176

To Susan Gilbert (Dickinson)   *27 November–3 December 1854*

Susie—it is a little thing to say how lone it is—anyone can do it, but to wear the loneness next your heart for weeks, when you sleep, and when you wake, ever missing something, *this*, all cannot say, and it baffles me. I would paint a portrait which would bring the tears, had I canvass for it, and the scene should be—*solitude*, and the figures— solitude—and the lights and shades, each a solitude. I could fill a chamber with landscapes so lone, men should pause and weep there; then haste grateful home, for a loved one left. Today has been a fair day, very still and blue. Tonight, the crimson children are playing in the West, and tomorrow will be colder. In all I number you. I want to think of you each hour in the day. What you are saying—doing— I want to walk with you, as seeing yet unseen. You say you walk and sew alone. *I* walk and sew alone. I dont see much of Vinnie—she's mostly dusting stairs!

We go out very little — once in a month or two, we both set sail in silks — touch at the principal points, and then put into port again — Vinnie cruises about some to transact the commerce, but coming to anchor, is most that I can do. Mr and Mrs Dwight are a sunlight to me, which no night can shade, and I still perform weekly journeys there, much to Austin's dudgeon, and my sister's rage.

I have heard it said "persecution kindles" — think it kindled me! They are sweet and loving, and one thing, dear Susie, always ask for you. Sunday Afternoon. I left you a long while Susie, that is, in pen and ink — my heart kept on. I was called down from you to entertain some company — went with a sorry grace, I fear, and trust I acted with one. There is a tall – pale snow storm stalking through the fields, and bowing here, at my window — shant let the fellow in!

I went to church all day in second dress, and boots. We had such precious sermons from Mr Dwight. One about unbelief, and another Esau. Sermons on unbelief ever did attract me. Thanksgiving was observed throughout the state last week! Believe we had a Turkey, and two kinds of Pie. Otherwise, no change. Father went Thanksgiving night. Austin goes tomorrow, unless kept by storm. He will see you, Darling! What I cannot do. Oh *could* I! We did not attend the Thanksgiving "Soiree" — owing to our sadness at just parting with father. Your sister will give particulars. Abby is much better — rode horseback every day until the snow came, and goes down street now just like other girls – Abby seems more gentle, more affectionate, than she has.

Eme Kellogg wonders she does not hear from you. I gave your message to her, and bring you back the same. Eme is still with Henry, tho' no outward bond has as yet encircled them. Edward Hitchcock and baby, and Mary, spent Thanksgiving here. I called upon Mary — she appears very sweetly, and the baby is quite becoming to her. They all adore the baby. Mary inquired for you with a good deal of warmth, and wanted to send her love when I wrote. Susie — had that been you — well — well! I must stop, *Sister*. Things *have* wagged, dear Susie, and they're wagging still. "Little Children, love one another." Not all of life to live, is it, nor all of death to die.

Susie — we all love you — Mother — Vinnie — me. *Dearly!* Your Sister Harriet is our most intimate friend. The last night of the term, John sent his love to you. I have not heard from Mat for months.

"They say that absence conquers." It has vanquished me. Mother and Vinnie send their love. Austin must carry his.

MANUSCRIPT: HCL (L 9). Ink. Dated: Monday Evening.
PUBLICATION: FF 211–213, in part.

The letter, begun on Monday, November 27, was concluded on the following Sunday. Austin and Susan were expecting to be married in the autumn of 1855. For some time Austin had been planning a trip to Chicago, to size up his prospects for establishing a good law practice there. He left Amherst on December 4, and returned early in January, after a visit to the Gilberts in Grand Haven, Michigan. Edward Dickinson returned to Washington on November 30 for the second session of the Thirty-third Congress, which convened about December first.

The conclusion of the next to the last paragraph is a paraphrase of the two lines concluding the second stanza of James Montgomery's hymn, beginning: "O where shall rest be found:"

> The world can never give
> The bliss for which we sigh;
> 'Tis not the *whole* of life to live;
> Nor *all* of death to die.

V

LETTERS

177–186

[1855–1857]

"To live, and die, and mount
again in triumphant body . . .
is no schoolboy's theme!"

The substantial exchange of letters between Austin and Emily Dickinson came abruptly to an end when he returned to Amherst from law school and settled into the practice of law there for the rest of his life. Her correspondence with Susan Gilbert necessarily altered its character after Susan's marriage to Austin in July 1856.

The most important event in these years for the family occurred when, after Deacon David Mack died in September 1854, the Dickinson homestead on Main Street came onto the market. Mack had purchased it in 1833, and Edward Dickinson bought it back in April 1855. The family moved into it in November. The other event in that year of particular significance to Emily was her trip to Washington and her return stopover in Philadelphia, where probably she met the Reverend Charles Wadsworth, though the import of the meeting came later.

The few surviving letters of 1855 and 1856 merely hint at the changes taking place within her. No poem or letter can certainly be placed in the year 1857, and one trivial event only can be associated with it. In October 1856 she had won second prize at the Cattle Show for her rye and indian bread, and the Hampshire and Franklin Express, on 27 August 1857, announced her name as one of the members of the Cattle Show committee for that year who would act as judges of the Rye and Indian Bread display.

Perhaps in a desultory manner she was trying to write poetry. Whatever was happening, the inner forces shaping her destiny are hinted at in her recurrently expressed speculations on the theme of immortality.

177

I am sick today, dear Susie, and have not been to church. There has been a pleasant quiet, in which to think of you, and I have not been sick eno' that I cannot write to you. I love you as dearly, Susie, as when love first began, on the step at the front door, and under the Evergreens, and it breaks my heart sometimes, because I do not hear from you. I wrote you many days ago — I wont say many weeks, because it will look sadder so, and then I cannot write — but Susie, it troubles me.

I miss you, mourn for you, and walk the Streets alone — often at night, beside, I fall asleep in tears, for your dear face, yet not one word comes back to me from that silent West. If it is finished, tell me, and I will raise the lid to my box of Phantoms, and lay one more love in; but if it *lives* and *beats* still, still lives and beats for *me*, then say me *so*, and I will strike the strings to one more strain of happiness before I die. Why Susie — think of it — you are my precious Sister, and will be till you die, and will be still, when Austin and Vinnie and Mat, and you and I are marble — and life has forgotten us!

Vinnie and I are going soon — either this week or next — father has not determined. I'm sure I cannot go, when I think that you are coming, and I would give the whole world if I could stay, instead.

I cant believe you are coming — but when I think of it, and tell myself it's so, a wondrous joy comes over me, and my old fashioned life capers as in a dream. Sue — I take the words of that Sweet Kate Scott, I have never seen — and say "it is too blissful." I never will be "so busy" when you get back to me, as I used to be. I'll get "my spinning done," for Susie, it steals over me once in a little while, that as my fingers fly and I am so busy, a far more wondrous Shuttle shifts the subtler thread, and when *that's* web is spun, *indeed my* spinning will be done. I think with you, dear Susie, and Mat by me again, I shall be still for joy. I shall not fret or murmur — shall not care when the wind blows, shall not observe the storm — "Such, and so precious" are you.

Austin told me about you when he came from the West — though many little things I wanted most to know, he "had not noticed." I asked him how you looked, and what you wore, and how your hair was fixed, and what you said of me — his answers were quite limited — "you looked as you always did — he did'nt know what you wore — never did know what people wore — you said he must tell me *everything*," which by the way dear Child, he has not done to this day, and any portion of which, I would savour with joy, might I but obtain it. Vinnie inquired with promptness "if you wore a Basque" — "it seemed to him," he said, "you *did* have on a *black thing*."

Ah Susie — you must train him — 'twill take full many a lesson in the fashion plate, before he will respect, and speak with proper deference of this majestic garment. I have some new clothes, Susie — presume I shall appear like an embarrassed Peacock, quite unused to its plumes. Dear Susie — you will write to me when I am gone from home —

Affy, Emilie —

I asked Austin if he had any messages — he replied he – had not! The good for nothing fellow! I presume he will fill a fools Cap with protestations to you, as soon as I leave the room! Bats think Foxes have no eyes — Ha Ha!! Mother and Vinnie send much love — they will be delighted to see you. My dearest love to Mat.

MANUSCRIPT: HCL (L 1). Ink. Dated: Sabbath Day.
PUBLICATION: *LL* 33–34, in small part; *FF* 200–202, in part.

After Austin returned from his western trip, both sisters prepared to join their father in Washington. His name is in the *Washington Evening Star*, on January 11, as a recent arrival at Willard's Hotel, but no other members of the family are mentioned. Susan and Martha Gilbert planned to return to Amherst from Michigan early in February. See the note to letter no. 186.

178

To Susan Gilbert (Dickinson)   *Washington, 28 February 1855*

Sweet and soft as summer, Darlings, maple trees in bloom and grass green in the sunny places — hardly seems it possible this is winter still; and it makes the grass spring in this heart of mine and each linnet sing, to think that you have come.

Dear Children — Mattie — Sue — for one look at you, for your gentle voices, I'd exchange it all. The pomp — the court — the etiquette — they are of the earth — will not enter Heaven.

Will you write to me — why hav'nt you before? I feel so tired looking for you, and still you do not come. And you love me, come soon — this is *not* forever, you know, this mortal life of our's. Which had you rather I wrote you — what I am doing here, or who I am loving *there?*

Perhaps I'll tell you both, but the "last shall be first, and the first last." I'm loving you at home — I'm coming every hour to your chamber door. I'm thinking when awake, how sweet if you were with me, and to talk with you as I fall asleep, would be sweeter still.

I think I cannot wait, when I remember you, and that is *always*, Children. I shall love you more for this sacrifice.

Last night I heard from Austin — and I think he fancies we are losing sight of the things at home — Tell him "not so," Children — Austin is mistaken. He says we forget "the Horse, the Cats, and the geraniums" — have not remembered Pat — proposes to sell the farm and move west with mother — to make boquets of my plants, and send them to his friends — to come to Washington in his Dressing gown and mortify me and Vinnie. Should be delighted to see him, even in "dishabille," and will promise to *notice* him whenever he will come. The *cats* I will confess, have not so absorbed my attention as they are apt at home, yet do I still remember them with tender emotion; and as for my sweet flowers, I shall know each leaf and every bud that bursts, while I am from home. Tell Austin, never fear! My thoughts are far from idle, concerning e'en the *trifles* of the world at home, but all is jostle, here — scramble and confusion, and sometimes in writing home I cant stop for detail, much as I would love. Vinnie met the other evening, in the parlor here a certain Mr Saxton, who inquired of her for his Amherst cousins. Vinnie told him joyfully, all she knew of you, and another evening, took me down to him. We walked in the hall a long while, talking of you, my Children, vieing with each other in compliment to those we loved so well. I told him of you both, he seemed very happy to hear so much of you. He left Washington yesterday morning. I have not been well since I came here, and that has excused me from some gaieties, tho' at that, I'm gayer than I was before. Vinnie is asleep this morning — she has been out walking with some ladies here and is very tired. She says much of you — wants so much to see you. Give my love to your sister — Kiss Dwightie for me —

my love for Abbie and Eme, when you see them, and for dear Mr &
Mrs Dwight – Tell Mother and Austin they need'nt flatter themselves
we are forgetting them — they'll find themselves much mistaken before long. We think we shall go to Philadelphia next week, tho'
father has'nt decided. Eliza writes most every day, and seems impatient for us. I dont know how long we shall stay there, nor how long
in New York. Father has not de[ci]ded. Shant you write, when this
gets to you?

Affy – E –

MANUSCRIPT: HCL (L 14). Ink. Dated: Wednesday morning. Envelope addressed: Miss Susan H. Gilbert./Amherst./Mass. Franked: Edw.
Dickinson M.C.

PUBLICATION: FF 202–205, in part.

The sisters stayed in Washington with their father from the middle of
February until early March, and visited the Colemans in Philadelphia on
the way home. Aside from this letter and the one that follows, hitherto
associated with the spring of 1854, the only record of the weeks spent in
Washington is the inscription in Elizabeth Stuart Phelps, *The Last Leaf
from Sunnyside*, given to the girls by Mrs. James Brown, and dated "February 19, 1855, Washington." The book is in the Jones Library, Amherst,
Massachusetts. "J. Brown & Lady" from Alabama are recorded as arrivals at
Willard's Hotel on February 5. Susan and Martha Gilbert arrived at Amherst on February 10. "Little Dwightie" was the youngest child of their
sister Harriet, Mrs. William Cutler, with whom they now lived. For evidence that ED was not in Washington in the spring of 1854, see the note
accompanying letter no. 157. See Appendix 1: Eastman.

179

To Mrs. J. G. Holland   *Philadelphia, 18 March 1855*

Dear Mrs. Holland and Minnie, and Dr. Holland too – I have
stolen away from company to write a note to you; and to say that I
love you still.

I am not at home – I have been away just five weeks today, and
shall not go quite yet back to Massachusetts. Vinnie is with me here,
and we have wandered together into many new ways.

We were three weeks in Washington, while father was there, and have been two in Philadelphia. We have had many pleasant times, and seen much that is fair, and heard much that is wonderful — many sweet ladies and noble gentlemen have taken us by the hand and smiled upon us pleasantly — and the sun shines brighter for our way thus far.

I will not tell you what I saw — the elegance, the grandeur; you will not care to know the value of the diamonds my Lord and Lady wore, but if you haven't been to the sweet Mount Vernon, then I *will* tell you how on one soft spring day we glided down the Potomac in a painted boat, and jumped upon the shore — how hand in hand we stole along up a tangled pathway till we reached the tomb of General George Washington, how we paused beside it, and no one spoke a word, then hand in hand, walked on again, not less wise or sad for that marble story; how we went within the door — raised the latch he lifted when he last went home — thank the Ones in Light that he's since passed in through a brighter wicket! Oh, I could spend a long day, if it did not weary you, telling of Mount Vernon — and I will sometime if we live and meet again, and God grant we shall!

I wonder if you have all forgotten us, we have stayed away so long. I hope you haven't — I tried to write so hard before I went from home, but the moments were so busy, and then they *flew* so. I was sure when days *did* come in which I was less busy, I should seek your forgiveness, and it did not occur to me that you might not forgive me. Am I too late today? Even if you are angry, I shall keep praying you, till from very weariness, you will take me in. It seems to me many a day since we were in Springfield, and Minnie and the *dumb-bells* seem as vague — as vague; and sometimes I wonder if I ever dreamed — then if I'm dreaming now, then if I *always* dreamed, and there is not a world, and not these darling friends, for whom I would not count my life too great a sacrifice. Thank God there is a world, and that the friends we love dwell forever and ever in a house above. I fear I grow incongruous, but to meet my friends does delight me so that I quite forget time and sense and so forth.

Now, my precious friends, if you won't forget me until I get home, and become more sensible, I will write again, and more properly. Why didn't I ask before, if you were well and happy?

Forgetful

Emilie.

Manuscript: missing.

Publication: L (1894) 162–164; LL 190–191; L (1931) 160–161; LH 40–42, dated (presumably by ED): Philadelphia.

Congress adjourned on Sunday, March 4, and Edward Dickinson arrived home presumably on Wednesday. (On Tuesday, March 6, Susan Gilbert wrote her brother Dwight, mentioning Mr. Dickinson and saying: "I suppose he will be home Wednesday." HCL – Dickinson collection). One conjectures that the girls left Washington with their father, who saw them met in Philadelphia, then continued on home. They remained as guests in Philadelphia of Mr. and Mrs. Coleman and their daughter Eliza, an early friend of ED's. The Colemans were members of the Arch Street Presbyterian Church, of which the Reverend Charles Wadsworth was the pastor.

180

To Jane Humphrey   *16 October 1855*

I'm just from the frosts, Jennie, and my cheeks are ruddy and cold – I have many a Bairn that cannot care for itself, so I must needs care *for* it, on such a night as this, and I've shrouded little forms and muffled little faces, till I almost feel maternal, and wear the anxious aspect that careful parents do – but for you I leave them, Darling, dearer than leaves or blossoms, or all my speechless mates, wh' will fade at last –

Jennie – my Jennie Humphrey – I love you well tonight, and for a beam from your brown eyes, I would give a pearl.

How much I would buy, were they to purchase, but Jennie, I am *poor*. Only the loss of friends and the longing for them – that's all, tonight Jennie, and I keep thinking and wishing, and then I think and wish, till for your sakes, who stray from me, *tears* patter as the rain.

How I wish you were mine, as you once were, when I had you in the morning, and when the sun went down, and was sure I should never go to sleep without a moment from you. I try to prize it, Jennie, when the loved are here, try to love *more*, and *faster*, and *dearer*, but when all are gone, seems as had I tried *harder*, they would have stayed with me. Let us love with all our might, Jennie, for who knows where our hearts go, when this world is done?

[320]

Do you love to be in Groton, and are you happy and well, and is Mr Hammond kind to you? I am sure he is, for I like Mr Hammond.

Will you teach always, Jennie, or in a Seminary *smaller*, one day assume the rule?

You did not tell me of *yourself* when you were in Amherst, so how many knights are slain and wounded, and how many now remain, is to me unknown. Keep a list of the conquests, Jennie, this is an *enemy's* Land!

Mr Bliss' *Coronation* takes place tomorrow, at the College church. Charge to the Heathen, by the Pastor! Front seats reserved for Foreign Lands! Jennie – dont let your duty call you "far hence." Distances *here* seem pretty long, but I confess, when it gets to that, that one crosses the Mediterranean, tis even *farther* off, nor can car, nor can carriage take me. Vinnie sends her love, and says "tell Jennie Humphrey I *do* want to see her.["]

No day goes by, little One, but has its thought of you, and its wish to see you. When shall you come again? We shall be in our new house soon; they are papering now, and – Jennie, we have *other* home – "house not made with hands." Which first will we occupy? Jennie – give Mr Hammond a bright smile from me, and tell him it is Autumn – and tell him I have nuts and squirrels, and gold and scarlet trees – and tell him here is the *king*! My love for you, my Child, and will you write me instantly?

Your Emilie Dickinson –

MANUSCRIPT: Rosenbach 1170/17 (5). Ink. Dated: Wednesday Evening. Addressed: Miss Jane Humphrey/care Charles Hammond Esq./ Groton/Mass. Franked: E. Dickinson M C. Postmarked: Amherst Ms. Oct 18. Unpublished.

Jane Humphrey had returned from Ohio, and after a visit in Amherst was teaching at Groton. The Reverend Charles Hammond, who had a statewide reputation as an educator, was at this time principal of Groton Academy. He had earlier been connected with Monson Academy, both as student and teacher, and ED's acquaintance with him was probably made through her Monson family connections. The ordination of Daniel Bliss took place on 17 October. The Dickinson homestead, built in 1813 by Samuel Fowler Dickinson, had been bought in 1833 by Deacon David Mack when S. F. Dickinson had been compelled by financial reverses to sell it. Edward Dickinson and his family continued to live in part of it until the spring of 1840, when he bought a house on North Pleasant Street and moved into it. Shortly after Mack died in September 1854, the house came onto the market and Edward Dickinson purchased it in April 1855. After extensive remodeling, the house was almost ready for occupancy when this letter was written. The move was actually made in November. This is ED's last known letter to Jane Humphrey.

The scripture quotation in the last paragraph is from 2 Corinthians 5.1 (see letters 182, 458, and 866).

181

To Dr. J. G. Holland   *3? November 1855*

I come in flakes, dear Dr. Holland, for verily it snows, and as descending swans, here a pinion and there a pinion, and anon a plume, come the bright inhabitants of the white home.

I know they fall in Springfield; perhaps you see them now — and therefore I look out again, to see if you are looking.

How pleasant it seemed to hear your voice — so said Vinnie and I, as we as individuals, and then collectively, read your brief note. Why didn't you speak to us before? We thought you had forgotten us — we concluded that one of the bright things had gone forever more. That is a sober feeling, and it mustn't come too often in such a world as this. A violet came up next day, and blossomed in our garden, and were it not for these same flakes, I would go in the dark and get it, so to send to you. Thank Him who is in Heaven, Katie Holland lives! Kiss her on every cheek for me — I really can't remember how many the bairn has — and give my warmest recollection to Mrs. Holland and Minnie, whom to love, this Saturday night, is no trifling thing, I'm very happy that you are happy — and that you cheat the angels of another one.

I would the many households clad in dark attire had succeeded so. You must all be happy and strong and well. I love to have the lamps shine on your evening table. I love to have the sun shine on your daily walks.

The "new house!" God bless it! You will leave the "maiden and married life of Mary Powell" behind.

Love and remember
Emilie.

MANUSCRIPT: missing.
PUBLICATION: L (1894) 164-165; LL 193; L (1931) 161-162; LH
44-45, dated (presumably by ED): Saturday Eve.
On 17 October 1855 Dr. Holland inserted an advertisement in the
Springfield Republican offering his present house for sale. This letter
answers one from him which evidently comments on his new house. Little
Kate, the Hollands's second child, has just recovered from a serious illness.
(Mrs. Holland, in writing to Mrs. Todd in 1893, when the latter was preparing the letters for publication [AB 193], stated that Kate's illness was
in the summer and autumn of 1854, but since ED's letter brings the two
items of news together, it is apparent that Mrs. Holland miscalculated the
date.) Ann Manning's *The Maiden and Married Life of Mary Powell*
(1852) is described by the publishers as "a nicely drawn and more poetical
version" of the story of John Milton's first wife.

182

To Mrs. J. G. Holland   *about 20 January 1856*

Your voice is sweet, dear Mrs. Holland — I wish I heard it oftener.
One of the mortal musics Jupiter denies, and when indeed its
gentle measures fall upon my ear, I stop the birds to listen. Perhaps
you think I *have* no bird, and this is rhetoric — pray, Mr. Whately,
what is *that* upon the cherry-tree? Church is done, and the winds
blow, and Vinnie is in that pallid land the simple call "sleep." They
will be wiser by and by, we shall all be wiser! While I sit in the snows,
the summer day on which you came and the bees and the south wind,
seem fabulous as *Heaven* seems to a sinful world — and I keep remembering it till it assumes a *spectral* air, and nods and winks at me, and
then all of you turn to phantoms and vanish slow away. We cannot
talk and laugh more, in the parlor where we met, but we learned to
love for aye, there, so it is just as well.
We shall sit in a parlor "not made with hands" unless we are very
careful!
I cannot tell you how we moved. I had rather not remember. I
believe my "effects" were brought in a bandbox, and the "deathless
me," on foot, not many moments after. I took at the time a memorandum of my several senses, and also of my hat and coat, and my best

shoes — but it was lost in the *mêlée*, and I am out with lanterns, looking for myself.

Such wits as I reserved, are so badly shattered that repair is useless — and still I can't help laughing at my own catastrophe. I supposed we were going to make a "transit," as heavenly bodies did — but we came budget by budget, as our fellows do, till we fulfilled the pantomime contained in the word "moved." It is a kind of *gone-to-Kansas* feeling, and if I sat in a long wagon, with my family tied behind, I should suppose without doubt I was a party of emigrants!

They say that "home is where the heart is." I think it is where the *house* is, and the adjacent buildings.

But, my dear Mrs. Holland, I have another story, and lay my laughter all away, so that I can sigh. Mother has been an invalid since we came *home*, and Vinnie and I "regulated," and Vinnie and I "got settled," and still we keep our father's house, and mother lies upon the lounge, or sits in her easy chair. I don't know what her sickness is, for I am but a simple child, and frightened at myself. I often wish I was a grass, or a toddling daisy, whom all these problems of the dust might not terrify — and should my own machinery get slightly out of gear, *please*, kind ladies and gentlemen, some one stop the wheel, — for I know that with belts and bands of gold, I shall whizz triumphant on the new stream! Love for you — love for Dr. Holland — thanks for his exquisite hymn — tears for your sister in sable, and kisses for Minnie and the bairns.

From your mad

Emilie.

MANUSCRIPT: missing.

PUBLICATION: *L* (1894) 166–168; *LL* 198, in part; *L* (1931) 162–164; *LH* 46–47, dated (presumably by ED): Sabbath Day.

Mrs. Dickinson's illness was a condition that lasted for several years and caused the family much anxiety. Later in 1856 she spent some time at a water cure establishment in Northampton. Dr. Holland's "exquisite hymn" may have been the poem "Things New and Old," published in the *Springfield Republican*, 1 January 1856. Mrs. Holland's sister Sarah lost her husband Otis Knight, January 12. The quotation in the third paragraph is from 2 Corinthians 5. 1: ". . . we have a building of God, an house not made with hands . . ." (see also letters no. 180, 458, and 866).

183

"I cannot make him dead!
His fair sunshiny head
Is ever bounding round my study chair –
Yet, when my eyes, now dim
With tears, I turn to him –
The vision vanishes – he is not there!

I walk my parlor floor
And, through the open door,
I hear a footfall on the chamber stair –
I'm stepping toward the hall
To give the boy a call –
And then bethink me
That – he is not there –

I thread the crowded street –
A satchelled lad I meet,
With the same beaming eyes, and colored hair –
And, as he's running by, –
Follow him with my eye –
Scarcely believing that – he is not there!

I know his face is hid
Under the coffin lid,
Closed are his eyes; cold is his forehead;
My hand that marble felt –
O'er it in prayer I knelt,
Yet my heart whispers that, he is not there!

I cannot *make* him dead –
When passing by the bed
So long watched over with parental care –
My spirit and my eye
Seek it inquiringly,
Before the tho't comes that, he is not there!

When, at the cool, gray break
Of day, from sleep I wake
With my first breathing of the morning air
My soul goes up, with joy,
To him who gave my boy, –
Then comes the sad tho't, that he is not there!

When at the day's calm close,
Before we seek repose –
I'm with his mother, offering up our prayer –
Whate'er I may be saying,
I am, in spirit, praying
For our boy's spirit, tho', he is not there!

Not there? – Where, then, is he?
The form I used to see
Was but the *raiment* that he used to wear;
The grave – that now doth press
Upon that cast-off dress –
Is but his wardrobe locked, *he* is not there!

He lives! – In all the past
He lives; nor to the last,
Of seeing him again will I despair;
In dreams I see him now –
And, on his angel brow,
I see it written – "thou shalt see me *there!*"

Yes, we all live to God! –
Father, thy chastening rod
So help us, thine afflicted ones to bear,
That, in the spirit land –
Meeting at thy right hand –
'Twill be our heaven to find that – he is *there!*"

Dear Mary —

I send the verses of which I spoke one day — I think them very
sweet – I'm sure that you will love them – They make me think beside, of a Little Girl at *your* house, who stole away one morning, and

tho' I cannot find her, I'm sure that she "is there." My love for your mother and Jennie – Love too for you

from Emilie –

MANUSCRIPT: HCL (L 35). Ink.
PUBLICATION: (letter only) *Mount Holyoke Alumnae Quarterly* XXIX (February 1946) 130.

The manuscript is dated in an unknown hand, at the bottom of the last page: April, 1853. On 19 April 1853 Mary Warner's younger sister, Anna Charlotte Warner, died (see letter no. 118). But the handwriting of the letter is that of 1856, not 1853, and the message presumably was sent on the third anniversary of the occasion. The poem, by John Pierpont, was popular in the early forties when it appeared, in several variants, in a number of newspapers and gift books. ED's version is closest to that in *The Sacred Rosary* . . . , compiled by N. P. Willis, New York, 1844.

184

To John L. Graves   *late April 1856*

It is Sunday – now – John – and all have gone to church – the wagons have done passing, and I have come out in the new grass to listen to the anthems.

Three or four Hens have followed me, and we sit side by side – and while they crow and whisper, I'll tell you what I see today, and what I would that you saw –

You remember the crumbling wall that divides us from Mr Sweetser – and the crumbling elms and evergreens – and *other* crumbling things – that spring, and fade, and cast their bloom within a simple twelvemonth – well – *they* are *here*, and skies on me fairer far than Italy, in blue eye look down – up – see! – away – a league from here, on the way to Heaven! And here are Robins – just got home – and giddy Crows – and Jays – and will you trust me – as I live, here's a *bumblebee* – not such as *summer* brings – John – earnest, manly bees, but a kind of a Cockney, dressed in jaunty clothes. Much that is gay – have I to show, if you were with me, John, upon this April grass – then there are *sadder* features – here and there, *wings* half gone to dust, that fluttered so, last year – a mouldering plume, an empty house, in which a bird resided. Where last year's flies, their errand ran, and last year's *crickets fell*! We, too, are flying – fading, John – and the song "here lies," soon upon lips that love us now – will have hummed and ended.

To live, and die, and mount again in triumphant body, and *next* time, try the upper air – is no schoolboy's theme!

It is a jolly thought to think that we can be Eternal – when air and earth are *full* of lives that are gone – and done – and a conceited thing indeed, this promised Resurrection! *Congratulate* me – John – Lad – and "here's a health to *you*" – that we have each a *pair* of lives, and need not chary be, of the one "that *now* is" –

Ha – ha – if any can afford – 'tis *us* a roundelay!

Thank you for your letter, John – Glad I was, to get it – and gladder had I got them *both*, and glad indeed to see – if in your heart, *another* lies, bound one day to me – Mid your momentous cares, pleasant to know that "Lang Syne" has it's own place – that nook and cranny still retain their accustomed guest. And when busier cares, and dustier days, and cobwebs, less unfrequent – shut what *was* away, still, as a ballad hummed, and lost, remember early friend, and drop a tear, if a *troubadour* that strain may chance to sing.

I am glad you have a school to teach – and happy that it is pleasant – amused at the *Clerical Civility* – of your new friends – and shall feel – I know, delight and pride, always, when you succeed. I play the old, odd tunes yet, which used to flit about your head after honest hours – and wake dear Sue, and madden me, with their grief and fun — How far from us, that spring seems – and those triumphant days – Our April got to Heaven *first* – Grant we may meet her there – at the "right hand of the Father." Remember, tho' you rove – John – and those who do *not* ramble will remember you. Susie's, and Mattie's compliments, and Vinnie's just here, and write again if you will –

MANUSCRIPT: HCL (G 4). Ink.
PUBLICATION: *Home* 401–402.

John Graves had graduated in the previous August and was now serving as principal of Orford Academy, Orford, New Hampshire. He had recently become engaged to Fanny Britton, daughter of one of the founders of the school. The allusion to "our April" is probably in recollection of the time, two years before, when John stayed with Emily and Susan Gilbert at the Dickinson house, while the family was in Washington (see letter no. 157).

185

To Mrs. J. G. Holland   *early August 1856?*

Don't tell, dear Mrs. Holland, but wicked as I am, I read my Bible sometimes, and in it as I read today, I found a verse like this, where friends should "go no more out"; and there were "no tears," and I wished as I sat down to-night that we were *there* — not *here* — and that wonderful world had commenced, which makes such promises, and rather than to write you, I were by your side, and the "hundred and forty and four thousand" were chatting pleasantly, yet not disturbing us. And I'm half tempted to take my seat in that Paradise of which the good man writes, and begin forever and ever *now*, so wondrous does it seem. My only sketch, profile, of Heaven is a large, blue sky, bluer and larger than the *biggest* I have seen in June, and in it are my friends — all of them — every one of them — those who are with me now, and those who were "parted" as we walked, and "snatched up to Heaven."

If roses had not faded, and frosts had never come, and one had not fallen here and there whom I could not waken, there were no need of other Heaven than the one below — and if God had been here this summer, and seen the things that *I* have seen — I guess that He would think His Paradise superfluous. Don't tell Him, for the world, though, for after all He's said about it, I should like to see what He *was* building for us, with no hammer, and no stone, and no journeyman either. Dear Mrs. Holland, I love, to-night — love you and Dr. Holland, and "time and sense" — and fading things, and things that do *not* fade.

I'm so glad you are not a blossom, for those in my garden fade, and then a "reaper whose name is Death" has come to get a few to help him make a bouquet for himself, so I'm glad you are not a rose — and I'm glad you are not a bee, for where they go when summer's done, only the thyme knows, and even were you a robin, when the west winds came, you would coolly wink at me, and away, some morning!

As "little Mrs. Holland," then, I think I love you most, and trust that tiny lady will dwell below while we dwell, and when with many a wonder we seek the new Land, *her* wistful face, *with* ours, shall look the last upon the hills, and first upon — well, *Home!*

Pardon my sanity, Mrs. Holland, in a world *in*sane, and love me if you will, for I had rather *be* loved than to be called a king in earth, or a lord in Heaven.

Thank you for your sweet note — the clergy are very well. Will bring such fragments from them as shall seem me good. I kiss my paper here for you and Dr. Holland — would it were cheeks instead.

Dearly,

Emilie.

P.S. The bobolinks have gone.

MANUSCRIPT: missing.

PUBLICATION: L (1894) 169–170; LL 199–200; L (1931) 164–165; LH 48–50, dated (presumably by ED): Sabbath Night.

Since the manuscript is missing, and the contents do not indicate the time of writing, the date given by Mrs. Todd — 1856 — has been retained. The departure of the bobolinks sets the season as early August. Several phrases in the first paragraph are taken from Revelation, where they are found in 3.12; 21.4; and 14.3. The final sentence in the paragraph is suggested by Luke 24.51. The quoted phrase in the third paragraph is the opening line of Longfellow's "The Reaper and the Flowers."

186

To John L. Graves   *about 1856*

Ah John – *Gone?*

Then I lift the lid to my box of Phantoms, and lay another in, unto the Resurrection – Then will I gather in *Paradise*, the blossoms fallen here, and on the shores of the sea of Light, seek my missing sands.

Your Coz —

Emilie.

MANUSCRIPT: HCL (G 10). Ink. Addressed on the fold: Mr John L. Graves – Present. Unpublished.

The date is conjectured from the handwriting. This letter, delivered by hand, was perhaps sent during the summer vacation when Graves visited Amherst at commencement time in August. The thought of the first sentence, almost identically expressed, is in letter no. 177, written in January 1855. Perhaps this letter was written earlier, though if so the circumstances have not been identified.

VI

LETTERS

187–245

[1858–1861]

"Much has occurred . . . so much —
that I stagger as I write, in
its sharp remembrance."

The number of letters surviving in each of the years that follow is materially larger than it was in the years just preceding. Of special importance is the year 1858, for sometime then Emily Dickinson became seriously interested in writing poetry, and began to fashion her packets — the slim manuscript volumes that she continued to assemble for another decade or so. It is also the year when she began her correspondence with Samuel Bowles and his wife, an association that became intimate for all members of the Dickinson family.

There is no certainty when she first wrote the Reverend Charles Wadsworth, but he paid a call upon her early in 1860. Whether he or another is the one she addresses as "Dear Master" in the draft of the letter with which this group opens, may never be surely known. At present one conjectures no other whom she might thus have designated.

In 1861 the first child of Austin and Susan Dickinson was born, an event that engrossed Sue's attention. The continued exchange of notes with Sue thereafter is warm but never urgent.

This too is the period when she began to correspond with her younger cousins, Louise and Frances Norcross. At a domestic level it continued until her death, with an intimacy she shared with no others except Mrs. Holland.

It is, finally, the period when she was beginning to think of herself as one who might write for posterity. The letter exchange with Sue about the "Alabaster" poem, which occurred in the middle or late summer of 1861, seems to have been her first effort at consultation about her way of poetry. Her next and last takes place in April 1862, when she initiated a correspondence with T. W. Higginson. The years 1858 to 1861 are a period when her forces were gathering. The flood of her talent is rising.

To recipient unknown   *about 1858*

Dear Master

I am ill, but grieving more that you are ill, I make my stronger hand work long eno' to tell you. I thought perhaps you were in Heaven, and when you spoke again, it seemed quite sweet, and wonderful, and surprised me so – I wish that you were well.

I would that all I love, should be weak no more. The Violets are by my side, the Robin very near, and "Spring" – they say, Who is she – going by the door –

Indeed it is God's house – and these are gates of Heaven, and to and fro, the angels go, with their sweet postillions – I wish that I were great, like Mr. Michael Angelo, and could paint for you. You ask me what my flowers said – then they were disobedient – I gave them messages. They said what the lips in the West, say, when the sun goes down, and so says the Dawn.

Listen again, Master. I did not tell you that today had been the Sabbath Day.

Each Sabbath on the Sea, makes me count the Sabbaths, till we meet on shore – and (will the) whether the hills will look as blue as the sailors say. I cannot talk any more (stay any longer) tonight (now), for this pain denies me.

How strong when weak to recollect, and easy, quite, to love. Will you tell me, please to tell me, soon as you are well.

MANUSCRIPT: AC. Ink.
PUBLICATION: *Home* 431–432.

This draft was left among ED's own papers, and no one knows whether a fair copy was made or sent to the person addressed. That it was meant as a reply to one from him is shown by the allusion to his question. She may have had the Reverend Charles Wadsworth in mind as "Master."

188

To Elizabeth Dickinson (Currier)?   *about 1858*

I send a Violet, for Libby. I should have sent a *stem*, but was overtaken by snow drifts. I regret deeply, not to add a Butterfly, but have lost my *Hat*, which precludes my catching one. Shall send "Little Jennie" as soon as I know where the Owner is. Am much ashamed to have kept it so long.

Emily.

MANUSCRIPT: AC. Ink.

PUBLICATION: L (1894) 422, in part; *Bachelor of Arts*, May 1895, in part; L (1931) 410, in part; NEQ XXVIII (1955) 293 n, in part.

The date is conjectured from the handwriting. A fragment of violet is still affixed to the sheet. Though there is no certainty that ED's aunt Elizabeth Dickinson (but eight years older than ED) was the recipient of this letter, she is the only person ED is known to have called Libbie (see letters no. 897 and 1041).

189

To Mr. and Mrs. Samuel Bowles   *about June 1858*

Dear Friends.

I am sorry you came, because you went away.

Hereafter, I will pick no Rose, lest it fade or prick me.

I would like to have you dwell here. Though it is almost nine o'clock, the skies are gay and yellow, and there's a purple craft or so, in which a friend could sail. Tonight looks like "Jerusalem." I think Jerusalem must be like Sue's Drawing Room, when we are talking and laughing there, and you and Mrs Bowles are by. I hope we may all behave so as to reach Jerusalem. How are your Hearts today? Ours are pretty well. I hope your tour was bright, and gladdened Mrs Bowles. Perhaps the Retrospect will call you back some morning.

You shall find us all at the gate, if you come in a hundred years, just as we stood that day.

If it become of "Jasper," previously, you will not object, so that we lean there still, looking after you.

I rode with Austin this morning.

He showed me mountains that touched the sky, and brooks that sang like Bobolinks. Was he not very kind? I will give them to you, for they are mine and "all things are mine" excepting "Cephas and Apollos," for whom I have no taste.

Vinnie's love brims mine.

Take   Emilie.

MANUSCRIPT: AC. Ink.
PUBLICATION: L (1894) 212–213; LL 245–246; L (1931) 187–188, in part.

The extensive collection of the letters of Samuel Bowles to Austin and Susan Dickinson (HCL) shows that their friendship began to develop about 1858. At that time a letter written in friendly but not intimate terms speaks of Mrs. Bowles's sorrow at the birth of a stillborn child. ED's hope that their trip had "gladdened Mrs. Bowles" suggests that the visit to Amherst had been made for Mrs. Bowles's sake. The time of the year is indicated by the nine o'clock sunset. The concluding biblical allusion is to 1 Corinthians 3.21–22: "Therefore let no man glory in men. For all things are yours."

This is the only letter written jointly to Mr. and Mrs. Bowles.

190

To Joseph A. Sweetser   early summer 1858

Much has occurred, dear Uncle, since my writing you – so much – that I stagger as I write, in its sharp remembrance. Summers of bloom – and months of frost, and days of jingling bells, yet all the while this hand upon our fireside. Today has been so glad without, and yet so grieved within – so jolly, shone the sun – and now the moon comes stealing, and yet it makes none glad. I cannot always see the light – please tell me if it shines.

I hope you are well, these many days, and have much joy.

There is a smiling summer here, which causes birds to sing, and sets the bees in motion.

Strange blooms arise on many stalks, and trees receive their tenants.

I would you saw what I can see, and imbibed this music. The day went down, long time ago, and still a simple choir bear the canto on.

I dont know who it is, that sings, nor *did* I, would I tell!

God gives us many cups. Perhaps you will come to Amherst, before the wassail's done. Our man has mown today, and as he plied his scythe, I thought of *other* mowings, and garners far from here.

I wonder how long we shall wonder; how early we shall *know.*

Your brother kindly brought me a Tulip Tree this morning. A blossom from his tree.

I find them very thoughtful friends, and love them much. It seems very pleasant that other ones will so soon be near.

We formed Aunt Kate's acquaintance, for the first–last spring, and had a few sweet hours, as do new found *girls.*

I meet some octogenarians–but men and women seldomer, and at *longer* intervals–"little children," of whom is the "Kingdom of Heaven." How tiny some will have to grow, to gain admission there! I hardly know what I have said–my words put all their feathers on– and fluttered here and there. Please give my warmest love to my aunts and cousins–and write me, should you please, some summer's evening.

Affy,
Emilie.

MANUSCRIPT: Jones Library. Ink. Dated: Friday night.
PUBLICATION: L (1931) 397–398.

After the Dickinsons moved back to Main Street, the Luke Sweetsers were their closest neighbors. ED here anticipates a visit at the home of the latter of some members of the Joseph Sweetser family. In a letter to Mrs. Joseph Sweetser written many years later (no. 478), ED alludes to her childhood memories of her Aunt Kate, possibly in the period of 1840– 1842, when, as Mrs. Bingham suggests (*Home* 506), the family was probably living in Amherst. The visit of the previous spring, here mentioned, may have been ED's first opportunity as an adult to know her aunt. In "this hand upon our fireside," ED alludes probably to the continued poor health of her mother.

The date is conjectured from the handwriting.

191

To Mrs. Joseph Haven   *early summer 1858*

Dear Mrs Haven –

Have you – or has Mr Haven – in his Library, either "Kloster-heim," or "The Confessions of an Opium Eater," by De-Quincey? I have sent to Northampton, but cannot get them there, and they are

[336]

missing just now, from the College Library. I thank you very much, should you have them, if you will please lend them to me – for tho' the hours are very full, I think that I might snatch here and there a moment, if I had the books.

I hope you are happy this summer day, tho' I know you are lonely. I should love to pass an hour with you, and the little girls, could I leave home, or mother. I do not go out at all, lest father will come and miss me, or miss some little act, which I might forget, should I run away – Mother is much as usual. I know not what to hope of her. Please remember Vinnie and I, for we are perplexed often –

Affy –
Emilie –

MANUSCRIPT: HCL (Haven 1). Ink. Addressed on the fold: Mrs. Haven./Present.

PUBLICATION: *Indiana Quarterly for Bookmen* I (1945) 116; *Home* 403.

The *Hampshire and Franklin Express* announced on 9 June 1858 that Professor Haven had accepted an appointment to the faculty of the Congregational Seminary in Chicago. His absence from Amherst, here implied, may have been on business connected with the change. ED's interest in De Quincey appears here for the first time. De Quincey's only novel, *Klosterheim*, had been written some years before (1832). Like the letter preceding, this refers to the concern felt about Mrs. Dickinson's health.

192

To Mrs. Joseph Haven   *late August 1858*

Good night, dear Mrs Haven! I am glad I did not know you better, since it would then have grieved me more that you went away.

Some summer-afternoon, I thought – we might be acquainted, but summer afternoons to me have had so many wings, and meanwhile, you have flown! Thank you for recollecting me in the sweet moss – which with your memory, I have lain in a little box, unto the Resurrection. I hoped to see your face again – hoped to see Mr Haven, and the little girls.

Though I met you little, I shall miss you all – Your going will redden the maple – and fringe the Gentian sooner, in the soft fields.

[337]

Permit us to keep you in our hearts, although you seem to outward eye, to be travelling from us! That is the sweet prerogative of the left behind.

I know you will come again – if not today – *tomorrow* – if not to-morrow as we count – after the little interval we pass in lifetime here. Then we wont say "Goodbye," since immortality – makes the phrase quite obsolete. Good night is long eno',

I bid it, smiling!

Emilie –

MANUSCRIPT: HCL (Haven 2). Ink. Addressed: Mrs. Haven. A small rosebud which accompanied the letter is still in the envelope.

PUBLICATION: *Indiana Quarterly for Bookmen* I (1945) 116–117; *Home* 403–404.

The Haven family left Amherst for Chicago after the college commencement, 12 August 1858.

193

To Samuel Bowles   *late August 1858?*

Dear Mr Bowles.

I got the little pamphlet. I think you sent it to me, though unfamiliar with your hand – I may mistake.

Thank you if I am right. Thank you, if not, since here I find bright pretext to ask you how you are tonight, and for the health of four more, Elder and Minor "Mary," Sallie and Sam, tenderly to inquire. I hope your cups are full. I hope your vintage is untouched. In such a porcelain life, one likes to be *sure* that all is well, lest one stumble upon one's hopes in a pile of broken crockery.

My friends are my "estate." Forgive me then the avarice to hoard them! They tell me those were poor early, have different views of gold. I dont know how that is. God is not so wary as we, else he would give us no friends, lest we forget him! The Charms of the Heaven in the bush are superceded I fear, by the Heaven in the hand, occasionally. Summer stopped since you were here. Nobody noticed her – that is, no men and women. Doubtless, the fields are rent by petite anguish, and "mourners go about" the Woods. But this is not for us. Business enough indeed, our stately Resurrection! A special Courtesy, I judge, from what the Clergy say! To the "natural man," Bumblebees would seem an improvement, and a spicing of Birds, but far be it from me, to impugn such majestic tastes. Our Pastor says we are a "Worm." How is that reconciled? "Vain – sinful Worm" is possibly of another species.

Do you think we shall "see God"? Think of "Abraham" strolling with him in genial promenade!

The men are mowing the second Hay. The cocks are smaller than the first, and spicier.

I would distill a cup, and bear to all my friends, drinking to her no more astir, by beck, or burn, or moor!

Good night, Mr Bowles! This is what they say who come back in the morning, also the closing paragraph on repealed lips. Confidence in Daybreak modifies Dusk.

Blessings for Mrs Bowles, and kisses for the bairns' lips. We want to see you, Mr Bowles, but spare you the rehearsal of "familiar truths."

Good Night,
Emily.

MANUSCRIPT: AC. Ink. Dated: Amherst.
PUBLICATION: L (1894) 190–192; LL 202–203; L (1931) 182–183.

No information has been found on the nature of the "little pamphlet" that Bowles had sent. At this time there were three young children in the Bowles family: Sarah Augusta (Sallie), born in 1850; Samuel, born in 1851; and Mary (Mamie), born in 1854.

194

To Susan Gilbert Dickinson   *26 September 1858*

I hav'nt any paper, dear, but faith continues firm – Presume if I met with my "deserts," I should receive nothing. Was informed to that effect today by a "dear pastor." What a privilege it is to be so insignificant! Thought of intimating that the "Atonement" was'nt needed for such atomies! I think you went on Friday. Some time is longer than the rest, and some is very short. Omit to classify Friday – Saturday– Sunday! Evenings get longer with the Autumn – that is nothing new!

The Asters are pretty well. "How are the other blossoms?" "Pretty well, I thank you." Vinnie and I are pretty well. Carlo – comfortable – terrifying man and beast, with renewed activity –is cuffed some – hurled from piazza frequently, when Miss Lavinia's "flies" need her action elsewhere.

She has the "patent action," I have long felt!

I attended church early in the day. Prof Warner preached. Subject – "little drops of dew."

Este[*y*] took the stump in the afternoon. Aunt [Catharine] Sweetser's dress would have startled Sheba. Aunt [Lucretia] Bullard was not out – presume she stayed at home for "self examination." Accompanied by father, they visited the grave yard, after services. These are stirring scenes! Austin supped with us. "Appears well." Ah – Dobbin – Dobbin – you little know the chink which your dear face makes. We would'nt mind the sun, dear, if it did'nt *set* – How much you cost – how much Mat costs – I will never sell you for a piece of silver. I'll buy you back with red drops, when you go away. I'll keep you in a casket – I'll bury you in the garden – and keep a bird to watch the spot – perhaps my pillow's safer – Try my bosom last – That's nearest of them all, and I should hear a foot the quickest, should I hear a foot – The thought of the little *brown plumes* makes my eye awry. The pictures in the air have few visitors.

You see they come to their own and their own do not receive them. "Power and honor" are here today, and "dominion and glory"! I shall never tell!

You may tell, when "the seal" is opened; *Mat* may tell when they "fall on their faces" – but I shall be lighting the lamps then in my new house – and I cannot come.

God bless you, if he please! Bless Mr John and Mrs Mat – Bless two or three others! I wish to be there – Shall I come? If I jump, shall you catch me. Hav'nt the conceit to jump! Vinnie is asleep – and must dream her message. Good night, little girls!

Since there are two varieties, we will say it softly – Since there are snowier beds, we'll talk a little every night, before we sleep in these!

Love Emilie –

MANUSCRIPT: HCL (L 3). Ink. Dated: Sunday.
PUBLICATION: LL 28–29, in part.
Late in September Susan Dickinson went to visit her sister Martha Smith at Geneva, New York. The visit in Amherst of the Joseph Sweetser

family, anticipated earlier, occurred in September, and the Dickinson reunion was augmented by the coming of the Reverend and Mrs. Asa Bullard
from Cambridge. ED's dog Carlo (breed unknown), is first mentioned in
letter no. 34. Captain William Dobbin is the faithful friend of Amelia
Sedley in *Vanity Fair*. The allusion in the third paragraph from the end
is to Revelation 7.11: "And all the angels . . . fell before the throne on
their faces, and worshipped God."

195

To Dr. and Mrs. J. G. Holland   *about 6 November 1858*

Dear Hollands,

Good-night! I can't stay any longer in a world of death. Austin is
ill of fever. I buried my garden last week — our man, Dick, lost a little
girl through the scarlet fever. I thought perhaps that *you* were dead,
and not knowing the sexton's address, interrogate the daisies. Ah!
dainty — dainty Death! Ah! democratic Death! Grasping the proudest
zinnia from my purple garden, — then deep to his bosom calling the
serf's child!

Say, is he everywhere? Where shall I hide my things? Who is
alive? The woods are dead. Is Mrs. H. alive? Annie and Katie — are
they below, or received to nowhere?

I shall not tell how short time is, for I was told by lips which sealed
as soon as it was said, and the open revere the shut. You were not here
in summer. *Summer?* My memory flutters — had I — was there a summer? You should have seen the fields go — gay little entomology! Swift
little ornithology! Dancer, and floor, and cadence quite gathered away,
and I, a phantom, to you a phantom, rehearse the story! An orator of
feather unto an audience of fuzz, — and pantomimic plaudits. "Quite
as good as a play," indeed!

Tell Mrs. Holland she is mine. Ask her if *vice versa?* Mine
is but just the thief's request — "Remember me to-day." Such are the
bright chirographies of the "Lamb's Book." Goodnight! My ships are
in! — My window overlooks the wharf! One yacht, and a man-of-war;
two brigs and a schooner! "Down with the topmast! Lay her a' hold,
a' hold!"

Emilie.

[341]

MANUSCRIPT: missing.

PUBLICATION: L (1894) 179–180; LL 307–308; L (1931) 173–174; LH 51–52: dated (presumably by ED): Saturday Eve.

In October 1858, Austin Dickinson was taken ill with typhoid fever. Harriet Matthews, the eight-year-old daughter of Richard Matthews, the Dickinson stableman, died of scarlet fever on November 1. ED uses the same phrase "Mine is but just the thief's request" in a later letter to Higginson (no. 282).

196

To Mrs. Samuel Bowles   *about December 1858*

Dear Mrs Bowles.

Since I have no sweet flower to send you, I enclose my heart; a little one, sunburnt, half broken sometimes, yet close as the spaniel, to it's friends. Your flowers came from Heaven, to which if I should ever go, I will pluck you palms.

My words are far away when I attempt to thank you, so take the silver tear instead, from my full eye. You have often remembered me.

I have little dominion — Are there not wiser than I, who with curious treasure, could requite your gift. Angels fill the hand that loaded

Emily's!

MANUSCRIPT: AC. Ink. Undated.

PUBLICATION: L (1894) 213; LL 246; L (1931) 201.

The date is conjectured from the handwriting. The gift which this letter acknowledges may have been a birthday remembrance. There was hardly another month when ED could have said: "I have no sweet flower to send you."

197

To Susan Gilbert Dickinson   *about 19 December 1858*

One Sister have I in our house,
And one, a hedge away.
There's only one recorded,
But both belong to me.

One came the road that I came –
And wore my last year's gown –
The other, as a bird her nest,
Builded our hearts among.

She did not sing as we did –
It was a different tune –
Herself to her a music
As Bumble bee of June.

Today is far from Childhood –
But up and down the hills
I held her hand the tighter –
Which shortened all the miles –

And still her hum
The years among,
Deceives the Butterfly;
Still in her Eye
The Violets lie
Mouldered this many May.

I spilt the dew –
But took the morn –
I chose this single star
From out the wide night's numbers –
Sue – forevermore!

Emilie –

MANUSCRIPT: HCL (pasted into Martha Dickinson Bianchi's copy of
The Single Hound). Ink.

PUBLICATION: *The Single Hound* 1–2; *Poems* (1955) 17–18.

The date is conjectured from the handwriting. The lines were perhaps
sent as a greeting on Sue's twenty-eighth birthday.

To Susan Gilbert Dickinson   *about 1858*

To my Father –
   to whose untiring efforts in my behalf, I am indebted for my *morn-ing-hours* – viz – 3. AM. to 12. PM. these grateful lines are inscribed by his aff

                                                      Daughter.

> Sleep is supposed to be
> By souls of sanity –
> The shutting of the eye.

> Sleep is the station grand
> Down wh' on either hand –
> The Hosts of Witness stand!

> Morn is supposed to be
> By people of degree –
> The breaking of the Day!

> Morning has not occurred!

> That shall Aurora be
> East of Eternity!
> One with the banner gay,
> One in the red array –
> *That* is the Break of Day!

MANUSCRIPT: HCL (B 127). Ink.
PUBLICATION: FF 226–227; *Poems* (1955) 16–17.
   Since ED sent a copy of this poem with its accompanying note to Susan Dickinson, and preserved another in one of her packets, it is probable that she never intended it for delivery to her father, whose household custom is indicated in a letter to the Hollands (no. 175): ". . . father rapped on my door to wake me this morning. . ."

To Louise Norcross   *about 4 January 1859*

Since it snows this morning, dear Loo, too fast for interruption, put your brown curls in a basket, and come and sit with me. I am sewing for Vinnie, and Vinnie is flying through the flakes to buy herself a little hood. It's quite a fairy morning, and I often lay down my needle, and "build a castle in the air" which seriously impedes the sewing project. What if I pause a little longer, and write a note to you! Who will be the wiser? I have known little of you, since the October morning when our families went out driving, and you and I in the dining-room decided to be distinguished. It's a great thing to be "great," Loo, and you and I might tug for a life, and never accomplish it, but no one can stop our looking on, and you know some cannot sing, but the orchard is full of birds, and we all can listen. What if we learn, ourselves, some day! Who indeed knows? [?] said you had many little cares; I hope they do not fatigue you. I would not like to think of Loo as weary, now and then. Sometimes *I* get tired, and I would rather none I love would understand the word. . . .

Do you still attend Fanny Kemble? "Aaron Burr" and father think her an "animal," but I fear zoölogy has few such instances. I have heard many notedly *bad* readers, and a fine one would be almost a fairy surprise. When will you come again, Loo? For you remember, dear, you are one of the ones from whom I do not run away! I keep an ottoman in my heart exclusively for you. My love for your father and Fanny.

Emily.

MANUSCRIPT: destroyed.

PUBLICATION: *L* (1894) 229–230; *LL* 207–208; *L* (1931) 215–216, dated January, 1859.

A three-day snowstorm commenced on 4 January 1859. The Norcross and Dickinson families had been together during the previous October. Fanny Kemble gave public readings from Shakespeare after her retirement from the stage in 1849. This is perhaps ED's first letter to Louise Norcross, who was but sixteen at the time.

To Mrs. Joseph Haven   *13 February 1859*

Dear Mrs Haven.

Your remembrance surprises me. I hardly feel entitled to it. A most sweet surprise, which can hardly be affirmed of all our surprises. I grieve that I cannot claim it in a larger degree. Perhaps tho', sweeter as it is – *unmerited* remembrance – "Grace" – the saints would call it. Careless girls like me, cannot testify. Thank you for this, and your warm note.

We have hardly recovered laughing from Mr Haven's jolly one. I insist to this day, that I have received internal injuries. Could Mr H. be responsible for an early grave? The Coat is still in the dark, but the mirth to which it has given rise, will gleam when coats and rascals have passed into tradition.

The letters of suspected gentlemen form quite a valuable addition to our family library, and father pursues the search with a mixture of fun and perseverence, which is quite diabolical! I will give you the earliest intelligence of the arrest of our friend, who for the mirth he has afforded, surely merits *triumph*, more than transportation.

Father is in New York, just now, and Vinnie in Boston – while Mother and I for greater celebrity, are remaining at home.

My mother's only sister has had an invalid winter, and Vinnie has gone to enliven the house, and make the days shorter to my sick aunt. I would like more sisters, that the taking out of one, might not leave such stillness. Vinnie has been all, so long, I feel the oddest fright at parting with her for an hour, lest a storm arise, and I go unsheltered.

She talked of you before she went – often said she missed you, would add a couplet of her own, were she but at home. I hope you are well as I write, and that the far city seems to you like home. I do not know your successors. Father has called upon Mr S[eelye] but I am waiting for Vinnie to help me do my courtesies. Mr S. preached in our church last Sabbath upon "predestination," but I do not respect "doctrines," and did not listen to him, so I can neither praise, nor blame. Your house has much of pathos, to those that pass who loved you.

I miss the geranium at the window, and the hand that tended the geranium.

I shall miss the clustering frocks at the door, bye and bye when summer comes, unless myself in a *new* frock, am too far to see. How short, dear Mrs Haven!

A darting fear – a pomp – a tear –
A waking on a morn
to find that what one waked for,
inhales the different dawn.

Receive much love from

Emilie –

MANUSCRIPT: HCL (Haven 3). Ink. Dated: Sabbath Eve.
PUBLICATION: *Indiana Quarterly for Bookmen* I (1945) 117–118; *Home* 404–405. The concluding quatrain is in *Poems* (1955) 71.

The Reverend Julius H. Seelye was elected, 20 August 1858, to the chair in philosophy vacated by Professor Haven. Seelye preached in the First Church on February 6. Vinnie was in Boston with Mrs. Loring Norcross, who died in the following year.

201

To Susan Gilbert Dickinson   *about 1859*

Dear Sue –

I should love dearly to spend the Evening with the girls, but have made calls this afternoon, and accidentally left my mind at Prof Warner's.

Please reserve an Ottoman for my Spirit, which is behind Vinnie's. Love for the Germanians –

Emily.

MANUSCRIPT: HCL (B 69). Pencil.
PUBLICATION: FF 225–226.
The date is conjectured from the handwriting. A note in FF reads: "Declining an invitation to an evening of amateur music." Here "the girls" are represented as "the Germanians" (see letter no. 118).

To Mrs. J. G. Holland   *about 20 February 1859*

Not alone to thank you for your sweet note, is my errand, dear Mrs. Holland, tho' I do indeed, but will you please to help me?

I guess I have done wrong – I don't know certainly, but Austin tells me so, and he is older than I, and knows more of ordinances.

When Vinnie is here – I ask her; if she says I sin, I say, "Father, I have sinned" – If she sanctions me, I am not afraid, but Vinnie is gone now, and to my sweet elder sister, in the younger's absence, something guides my feet.

These are the circumstances. Your friend and neighbor, Mr. Chapman, was in town last week, with Mr. Hyde of Ware, as a business ally.

They called upon us Wednesday evening, and were our guests on the evening following. After most pleasant conversations, we parted for the night – the gentlemen then proposing to return next day. Business did not terminate, and sitting next evening with S[ue], as I often do, some one rang the bell and I ran, as is my custom.

What was my surprise and shame, on hearing Mr. Chapman ask for "Mrs. D!" K[ate] S[cott], a guest of [Sue]'s, was my confederate, and clinging fast like culprit mice, we opened consultation. Since the dead might have heard us scamper, we could not allege that we did not run, besides, it was *untrue*, which to people so scared as we, was a minor consideration, but would have its weight with our seniors. I proposed that we ask forgiveness.

K. was impenitent and demurred. While we were yet deliberating, S[ue] opened the door, announced that we were detected, and invited us in.

Overwhelmed with disgrace, I gasped a brief apology, but the gentlemen simply looked at us with a grave surprise.

After they had retired, Austin said we were very rude, and I crept to my little room, quite chagrined and wretched. Now do you think Mr. Chapman will forgive me? I do not mind Mr. Hyde of Ware, because he does not please me, but Mr. Chapman is my friend, talks of my books with me, and I would not wound him.

I write a little note to him, saying I am sorry, and will he forgive me, and remember it no more? Now will I ask so much of you, that you read it for me, judge if it is said as yourself would say it, were *you* rude instead of me – that if you approve, when you walk again, you will take it for me to Mr. Chapman's office – tell him for me, intercede as my sister should? Then if he forgives me, I shall write you quickly, but if he should not, and we meet the next in Newgate, know that I was a loving felon, sentenced for a door bell.

Emilie.

MANUSCRIPT: missing. The text derives from a transcript (AC) made by Mrs. Todd.

PUBLICATION: *L* (1931) 153–155; *LH* 53–54.

In mid-February Catherine Scott Turner (later Anthon) visited her former schoolmate Susan Dickinson. On Wednesday, February 15 the question of ownership of the meetinghouse in South Amherst came before referees: the Honorable Reuben A. Chapman of Springfield, and William Hyde of Ware. Counsel included, for the new society, Edward Dickinson, and for the old, Ithamar F. Conkey. This letter seems to have been written about Sunday, February 20.

203

To Catherine Scott Turner (Anthon)   *about March 1859*

I never missed a Kate before, – Two Sues – Eliza and a Martha, comprehend my girls.

Sweet at my door this March night another Candidate – Go Home! We don't like Katies here! – Stay! My heart votes for you, and what am I indeed to dispute her ballot – ? – What are your qualifications? Dare you dwell in the *East* where we dwell? Are you afraid of the Sun? – When you hear the new violet sucking her way among the sods, shall you be *resolute?* All *we* are *strangers* – dear – The world is not acquainted with us, because we are not acquainted with her. And Pilgrims! – Do you hesitate? and *Soldiers* oft – some of us victors, but those I do not *see* tonight owing to the smoke. – We are hungry, and thirsty, sometimes – We are barefoot – and cold –

Will you still come? *Then* bright I record you! *Kate* gathered in March!

It is a small bouquet, dear – but what it lacks in size, it gains in fadelessness, – Many can boast a hollyhock, but few can bear a *rose!*

[349]

And should new flower smile at limited associates, pray her remember, were there *many* they were not worn upon the breast – but tilled in the pasture! So I rise, wearing her – so I sleep, holding, – Sleep at last with her fast in my hand and wake bearing my flower. –

Emilie –

MANUSCRIPT: missing. The text is from a transcript (HCL) made by Mrs. Anthon for Susan Dickinson. It is dated: Amherst. Mrs. Anthon made another transcript (AC) for Mrs. Todd. There are slight variations in punctuation.

PUBLICATION: L (1894) 146–147; LL 206; L (1931) 144–145.

Mrs. Anthon dated the letter 1859, and it may have been written after her February visit, referred to in the preceding letter. The persons named in the first paragraph (omitted in all printed versions) are probably Susan Gilbert Dickinson, Susan Phelps (see letter no. 221), Eliza Coleman, and Martha Gilbert Smith.

204

To Mrs. J. G. Holland *2 March 1859*

"Sister."

You did my will. I thank you for it. Let me work for you! What prettier negotiation than of friend for friend? I did not suspect complacency in "Mr Brown of Sheffield"! It is plain that Vinnie is gone – she assays them for me.

Complacency! My Father! in such a world as this, when we must all stand barefoot before thy jasper doors!

Thank you for putting me on trail. I will make quite a fox, in time, unless I die early.

I gather from "Republican" that you are about to doff your weeds for a Bride's Attire. Vive le fireside! Am told that fasting gives to food marvellous Aroma, but by birth a Bachelor, disavow Cuisine.

Meeting is well worth parting. How kind in some to die, adding *impatience* to the rapture of our thought of Heaven!

> As by the dead we love to sit –
> Become so wondrous dear –
> As for the lost we grapple
> Though all the rest are here –

In broken Mathematics
We estimate our prize
Vast, in it's *fading* ratio
To our penurious eyes.

I had rather you lived nearer — I would like to touch you. Pointed attentions from the Angels, to two or three I love, make me sadly jealous.

People with *Wings* at option, look loftily at hands and feet, which induces watchfulness! How gay to love one's friends! How *passing* gay to fancy that they reciprocate the whim, tho' by the Seas divided, tho' by a single Daisy hidden from our eyes! I would not exchange it for all the funds of the Father. Vinnie is yet in Boston. Thank you for recollecting. I am somewhat afraid at night, but the Ghosts have been very attentive, and I have no cause to complain. Of course one cant expect one's furniture to sit still all night, and if the Chairs do prance — and the Lounge polka a little, and the shovel give it's arm to the tongs, one dont mind such things! From fearing them at first, I've grown to quite admire them, and now we understand each other, it is most enlivening! How near, and yet how far we are! The new March winds could bring me, and yet "whole legions of Angels" may lie between our lips!

Emilie

MANUSCRIPT: HCL (H 16). Ink. Dated: Wednesday.
PUBLICATION: *LH* 62–63. The verse is in *Poems* (1955) 71.
This letter acknowledges Mrs. Holland's reply to ED's letter of February 20 (no. 202). On February 28 Dr. Holland returned from a lecture tour. In *David Copperfield*, Brooks (not Brown) of Sheffield designates a person who would remain nameless (see also letters no. 548 and 820). Vinnie was still in Boston (see letter no. 200).

205

To Samuel Bowles   *early April 1859*

Friend,

Sir,

I did not see you. I am very sorry. Shall I keep the Wine till you come again, or send it in by "Dick?" It is now behind the door in the

[351]

Library, also an unclaimed flower. I did not know you were going so soon — Oh my tardy feet!

Will you not come again? Friends are gems – infrequent. Potosi is a care, Sir. I guard it reverently, for I could not afford to be poor now, after affluence. I hope the hearts in Springfield are not so heavy as they were — God bless the hearts in Springfield!

I am happy you have a "Horse." I hope you will get stalwart, and come and see us many years.

I have but two acquaintance, the "Quick and the Dead" — and would like more.

I write you frequently, and am much ashamed.

My voice is not quite loud enough to cross so many fields, which will, if you please, apologize for my pencil. Will you take my love to Mrs Bowles, whom I remember every day.

Emilie

Vinnie halloos from the world of nightcaps, "dont forget her love!"

MANUSCRIPT: AC. Ink and pencil. Undated. Reproduced in facsimile in *Letters* (1931) 188.

PUBLICATION: *L* (1894) 198–199; *LL* 221; *L* (1931) 188–189.

On 8 April 1859 Samuel Bowles wrote Charles Allen: "I had the present of a bottle of wine this week, from a woman, with an affectionate note. We had some good food Fast-day [April 7] and we drank the wine." (George S. Merriam, *Life and Times of Samuel Bowles* 296.)

206

To Louise Norcross   *late April 1859*

Dear Loo,

You did not acknowledge my vegetable; perhaps you are not familiar with it. I was reared in the garden, you know. It was to be eaten with mustard! Bush eighty feet high, just under chamber window — much used at this season when other vegetables are gone. You should snuff the hay if you were here to-day, infantile as yet, homely, as cubs are prone to be, but giving brawny promise of hay-cocks by and by. "Methinks I see you," as school-girls say, perched upon a cock with the "latest work," and confused visions of bumblebees tugging at your hat. Not so far off, cousin, as it used to be, that vision and the hat. It makes me feel so hurried, I run and brush my hair so to be all ready.

I enjoy much with a precious fly, during sister's absence, not one of your blue monsters, but a timid creature, that hops from pane to pane of her white house, so very cheerfully, and hums and thrums, a sort of speck piano. Tell Vinnie I'll kill him the day she comes, for I sha'n't need him any more, and she don't mind flies!

Tell Fanny and papa to come with the sweet-williams.

Tell Vinnie I counted three peony noses, red as Sammie Matthews's, just out of the ground, and get her to make the accompanying face.

"By-Bye."

Emily.

MANUSCRIPT: destroyed.

PUBLICATION: L (1894) 231–232; LL 209–210; L (1931) 216–217, dated 1859.

Sammie Matthews was a son of Dick Matthews, the Dickinson stableman. Vinnie was still with Mrs. Norcross.

207

To Dr. and Mrs. J. G. Holland   *September 1859*

Dear Hollands,

Belong to me! We have no fires yet, and the evenings grow cold. To-morrow, stoves are set. How many barefoot shiver I trust their Father knows who saw not fit to give them shoes.

Vinnie is sick to-night, which gives the world a russet tinge, usually so red. It is only a headache, but when the head aches next to you, it becomes important. When she is well, time leaps. When she is ill, he lags, or stops entirely.

Sisters are brittle things. God was penurious with me, which makes me shrewd with Him.

One is a dainty sum! One bird, one cage, one flight; one song in those far woods, as yet suspected by faith only!

This is September, and you were coming in September. Come! Our parting is too long. There has been frost enough. We must have summer now, and "whole legions" of daisies.

[353]

The gentian is a greedy flower, and overtakes us all. Indeed, this world is short, and I wish, until I tremble, to touch the ones I love before the hills are red — are gray — are white — are "born again"! If we knew how deep the crocus lay, we never should let her go. Still, crocuses stud many mounds whose gardeners till in anguish some tiny, vanished bulb.

We saw you that Saturday afternoon, but heedlessly forgot to ask where you were going, so did not know, and could not write. Vinnie saw Minnie flying by, one afternoon at Palmer. She supposed you were all there on your way from the sea, and untied her fancy! To say that her fancy wheedled her is superfluous.

We talk of you together, then diverge on life, then hide in you again, as a safe fold. Don't leave us long, dear friends! You know we're children still, and children fear the dark.

Are you well at home? Do you work now? Has it altered much since I was there? Are the children women, and the women thinking it will soon be afternoon? We will help each other bear our unique burdens.

Is Minnie with you now? Take her our love, if she is. Do her eyes grieve her now? Tell her she may have half ours.

Mother's favorite sister is sick, and mother will have to bid her good-night. It brings mists to us all; — the aunt whom Vinnie visits, with whom she spent, I fear, her last inland Christmas. Does God take care of those at sea? My aunt is such a timid woman!

Will you write to us? I bring you all their loves — *many*.

They tire me.

Emilie.

MANUSCRIPT: missing.

PUBLICATION: L (1894) 172–174; L (1931) 167–168; LH 57–58.

It was in her letter of February 20 (no. 202) that ED first called Mrs. Holland her "sister." In New England the wild gentian blooms in August, and it here is alluded to as a harbinger of the season's end. On Saturday, 6 August 1859, the Hollands attended an excursion to Amherst of the American Association for the Advancement of Science. Mrs. Dickinson's sister Lavinia Norcross, fatally ill, lived until the following April (see letter no. 217).

208

To Catherine Scott Turner (Anthon)   *1859?*

When Katie walks, this simple pair accompany her side,
When Katie runs unwearied they follow on the road,
When Katie kneels, their loving hands still clasp her pious knee —
Ah! Katie! Smile at Fortune, with *two* so *knit to thee!*

                                                    Emilie.

MANUSCRIPT: missing. The text is from a transcript (HCL) made by
Mrs. Anthon.
PUBLICATION: *L* (1931) 146; *Poems* (1955) 159.
The transcript bears the notation: "Emily knitted a pair of *garters* for
me & *sent them over* with these lines." Kate Turner visited Susan Dickinson some four or five times during the years 1859–1861. Any date for this
note and for the letter following (no. 209) is conjectural, but the tone
suggests that they were written near the beginning of the friendship.

209

To Catherine Scott Turner (Anthon)   *late 1859?*

Katie –

Last year at this time I did not miss you, but positions shifted,
until I hold your black in strong hallowed remembrance, and trust my
colors are to you tints slightly beloved. You cease indeed to talk, which
is a custom prevalent among things parted and torn, but shall I class
this, dear, among elect exceptions, and bear you just as usual unto the
kind Lord? – We dignify our Faith, when we can cross the ocean with
it, though most prefer ships.

How do you do this year? I remember you as fires begin, and evenings open at Austin's, without the Maid in black, Katie, without the
Maid in black. Those were unnatural evenings. – *Bliss* is unnatural –
How many years, I wonder, will sow the moss upon them, before we
bind again, a little altered it may be, elder a little it *will* be, and yet
the same as suns, which shine, between our lives and loss, and violets,
not last years, but having the Mother's eyes. —

Do you find plenty of food at home? Famine is unpleasant. —

It is too late for "Frogs," or which pleases me better, dear – not quite early enough! The pools were full of you for a brief period, but that brief period blew away, leaving me with many stems, and but a few foliage! Gentlemen here have a way of plucking the tops of trees, and putting the fields in their cellars annually, which in point of taste is execrable, and would they please omit, I should have fine vegetation & foliage all the year round, and never a winter month. Insanity to the sane seems so unnecessary – but I am only one, and they are "four and forty," which little affair of numbers leaves me impotent. Aside from this dear Katie, inducements to visit Amherst are as they were. – I am pleasantly located in the deep sea, but love will row you out if her hands are strong, and don't wait till I land, for I'm going ashore on the other side —

Emilie.

MANUSCRIPT: missing.
PUBLICATION: L (1894) 149–150, in part; LL 221–222, in part; L (1931) 147–148, in part: dated "1861 ?."

The text is from the transcript (AC) made by Mrs. Anthon for Mrs. Todd. For the date, see the letter preceding. The phrase "I am pleasantly located in the deep sea" is similar to expressions used in letters written in 1864 and 1865, when ED's eyes were giving her trouble (nos. 294 and 306). But in context here the expression does not imply a physical handicap.

210

To Mrs. J. G. Holland   *December 1859*

God bless you, dear Mrs. Holland! I read it in the paper.

I'm so glad it's a little boy, since now the little sisters have some one to draw them on the sled – and if a grand old lady you should live to be, there's something sweet, they say, in a son's arm.

I pray for the tenants of that holy chamber, the wrestler, and the wrestled for. I pray for distant father's heart, swollen, happy heart!

Savior keep them all!

Emily.

MANUSCRIPT: missing.
PUBLICATION: L (1894) 172; L (1931) 167; LH 59.

Theodore Holland was born, 7 December 1859, and the birth was announced in the *Springfield Republican*. Dr. Holland was away on a lecture tour. Annie Holland was now eight years old; Kate was six.

211

To Mrs. J. G. Holland   *December 1859?*

Will someone lay this little flower on Mrs. Holland's pillow?

Emilie.

MANUSCRIPT: missing.
PUBLICATION: L (1895) 178; L (1931) 171; LH 61.
This note may shortly have followed the preceding letter.

212

To Mrs. Samuel Bowles   *10 December 1859*

Dear Mrs Bowles

You send sweet messages. Remembrance is more sweet than Robins in May orchards.

I love to trust that round bright fires, some, braver than me, take my pilgrim name. How are papa, mama, and the little people?

Traditions of "Memes" eyes, and little Sallie's virtues, and Sam's handsome face, are handed down

It storms in Amherst five days — it snows, and then it rains, and then soft fogs like vails hang on all the houses, and then the days turn Topaz, like a lady's pin.

Thank you for bright boquet, and afterwards Verbena. I made a plant of a little bough of yellow Heliotrope which the boquet bore me, and call it "Mary Bowles." It is many days since the summer day when you came with Mr Bowles, and before another summer day it will be many days. My garden is a little knoll with faces under it, and only the pines sing tunes, now the birds are absent. I cannot walk to the distant friends on nights piercing as these, so I put both hands on the window-pane, and try to think how birds fly, and imitate, and fail, like Mr "Rasselas." I could make a balloon of a Dandelion, but the

[357]

fields are gone, and only "Prof Lowe" remains to weep with me. If I built my house I should like to call you. I talk of all these things with Carlo, and his eyes grow meaning, and his shaggy feet keep a slower pace. Are you safe tonight? I hope you may be glad. I ask God on my knee to send you much prosperity, few winter days, and long suns. I have a childish hope to gather all I love together – and sit down beside, and smile.

Austin and Sue went to Boston Saturday, which makes the Village very large.

I find they are my crowd. Will you come to Amherst? The streets are very cold now, but we will make you warm. But if you never came, perhaps you could write a letter, saying how much you would like to, if it were "God's will." I give Goodnight, and daily love to you and Mr Bowles.

Emilie.

MANUSCRIPT: AC. Ink. Dated: Monday Eve.

PUBLICATION: L (1894) 192–193, in part; LL 203–204, in part; L (1931) 183–194, in part.

The weather reports confirm the date. The New Hampshire balloonist T. S. C. Lowe abandoned his idea of crossing the Atlantic after three months of preparation. The *Springfield Republican* comments on December 9: "'Professor' Lowe boasts that he cleared $4,000 by his Atlantic balloon humbug." On the spelling of "Mamie's" name, see letter no. 235.

213

To Mrs. Samuel Bowles   *after Christmas 1859*

I should like to thank dear Mrs Bowles for the little Book, except my cheek is red with shame because I write so often.

Even the "Lilies of the field" have their dignities.

Why did you bind it in green and gold?

The *immortal* colors.

I take it for an emblem. I never read before what Mr Parker wrote. I heard that he was "poison." Then I like poison very well. Austin stayed from service yesterday afternoon, and I, calling upon him, found him reading my Christmas gift. This – together with the fact that

Sue asked me the other day how to spell "Puseyite," looks very suspicious!

I wish the "faith of the fathers" did'nt wear brogans, and carry blue umbrellas, I give you all "New Year"! I think you kept gay Christmas, from the friend's account, and can only sigh with one not present at "John Gilpin," "and when he next doth ride a race," &c. You picked four berries from my Holly – Grasping Mrs Bowles!

Today is very cold, yet have I much boquet upon the window pane of moss and fern. I call them *Saints'* flowers, because they do not romp as other flowers do, but stand so still and white. The snow is very tall between our house and Austin's, which makes the trees so low that they tumble my hair, when I cross the bridge.

I think there will be no spring this year, the flowers are gone so far. Let us have spring in our heart, and never mind the Orchises! Sue looks like "Madame Roland" in the scarlet cape. I tell her so, and she plays Revolution, which has a fine effect! Please have my love, Mother's, and Vinnie's – Carlo sends a brown kiss, and Pussy, a gray and white one, to each of the Children.

Please, now I write so often, make lamplighter of me, then I shall not have lived in vain.

Dear Mrs Bowles, dear Mr Bowles, dear Sally, Sam, and Meme, now all shut your eyes, while I do benediction!

Lovingly,
Emily.

MANUSCRIPT: AC. Ink. Dated: Amherst.

PUBLICATION: L (1894) 193–195, in part; LL 205–206, in part; L (1931) 184–185, in part.

ED seems to be acknowledging as a Christmas remembrance Theodore Parker's *The Two Christmas Celebrations* (1859), a volume which does not survive. By saying "make lamplighter of me," she means a *spill*, a roll of paper for lighting a lamp.

214

To Susan Gilbert Dickinson   *about 1859*

My "position"!
Cole.
P. S. Lest you misapprehend, the unfortunate insect upon the left is

[359]

Myself, while the Reptile upon the *right* is my more immediate friends, and connections.

As ever,

Cole.

MANUSCRIPT: HCL (B 114). Pencil.
PUBLICATION: *LL*, where it is reproduced in facsimile facing page 156. The date is conjectured from the handwriting.

Thomas Cole (1801–1848) was a well known American painter, and his name is here used to typify talent in sketching. Pasted above the message is a woodcut clipped from *The New England Primer*. The copy was a reprint made for distribution to all Yale graduates at commencement in 1850. It represents the letter "T" in the alphabet: "Young Timothy/Learnt sin to fly," and shows a youth pursued by an upright wolf-like creature with forked tail. To the note is another attached by Mrs. Bianchi: "Sent over the morning after a revel — when my Grandfather with his lantern appeared suddenly to take Emily home the hour nearing indecent midnight."

215

To Louise Norcross   *March 1860*

The little "apple of my eye," is not dearer than Loo; she knows I remember her, – why waste an instant in defence of an absurdity? My birds fly far off, nobody knows where they go to, but you see I know they are coming back, and other people don't, that makes the difference.

I've had a curious winter, very swift, sometimes sober, for I haven't felt well, much, and March amazes me! I didn't think of it, that's all! Your "hay" don't look so dim as it did at one time. I hayed a little for the horse two Sundays ago, and mother thought it was summer, and set one plant out-doors which she brought from the deluge, but it snowed since, and we have fine sleighing, now, on *one* side of the road, and wheeling on the other, a kind of variegated turnpike quite picturesque to see!

You are to have Vinnie, it seems, and I to tear my hair, or engage in any other vocation that seems fitted to me. Well, the earth is round, so if Vinnie rolls your side sometimes, 't isn't strange; I wish I were there too, but the geraniums felt so I couldn't think of leaving them, and one minute carnation pink cried, till I shut her up – see box!

Now, my love, robins, for both of you, and when you and Vinnie sing at sunrise on the apple boughs, just cast your eye to my twig.

Poor Plover.

MANUSCRIPT: destroyed.
PUBLICATION: L (1894) 230–231; LL 208–209; L (1931) 216: where it is dated March 1859.

The letter could not have been written in March 1859, since in that year Vinnie had gone to stay with Mrs. Norcross in February (see letter no. 200). In 1860 Vinnie left home in March, and remained with the Norcross family for some weeks (see letter no. 217). The plover is so named because it was said to appear during the rainy season.

216

To Mrs. Samuel Bowles   *1860?*

Don't cry, dear Mary. Let us do that for you, because you are too tired now. We don't know how dark it is, but if you are at sea, perhaps when we say that we are there, you won't be as afraid.

The waves are very big, but every one that covers you, covers us, too.

Dear Mary, you can't see us, but we are close at your side. May we comfort you?

Lovingly,
Emily.

MANUSCRIPT: missing.
PUBLICATION: L (1894) 198; L (1931) 187.

Three Bowles children were stillborn. This note perhaps was written after the third occasion, prior to the birth of Charles, in December 1861.

217

To Lavinia N. Dickinson   *late April 1860*

Vinnie –

I can't believe it, when your letters come, saying what Aunt Lavinia said "just before she died." Blessed Aunt Lavinia now; all the world goes out, and I see nothing but her room, and angels bearing her into those great countries in the blue sky of which we don't know anything.

Then I sob and cry till I can hardly see my way 'round the house again; and then sit still and wonder if she sees us now, if she sees *me*, who said that she "loved Emily." Oh! Vinnie, it is dark and strange to think of summer afterward! How she loved the summer! The birds keep singing just the same. Oh! The thoughtless birds!

Poor little Loo! Poor Fanny! You must comfort them.

If you were with me, Vinnie, we could talk about her together.

And I thought she would live I wanted her to live so, I thought she could not die! To think how still she lay while I was making the little loaf, and fastening her flowers! Did you get my letter in time to tell her how happy I would be to do what she requested? Mr. Brady is coming to-morrow to bring arbutus for her. Dear little aunt! Will she look down? You must tell me all you can think about her. Did she carry my little bouquet? So many broken-hearted people have got to hear the birds sing, and see all the little flowers grow, just the same as if the sun hadn't stopped shining forever! . . . How I wish I could comfort you! How I wish you could comfort me, who weep at what I did not see and never can believe. I will try and share you a little longer, but it is so long, Vinnie.

We didn't think, that morning when I wept that you left me, and you, for other things, that we should weep more bitterly before we saw each other.

Well, she is safer now than "we know or even think." Tired little . aunt, sleeping ne'er so peaceful! Tuneful little aunt, singing, as we trust, hymns than which the robins have no sweeter ones.

Good-night, broken hearts, Loo, and Fanny, and Uncle Loring. Vinnie, remember

Sister

MANUSCRIPT: missing.
PUBLICATION: *L* (1894) 233–234; *LL* 213–215; *L* (1931) 217–218.
Lavinia stayed on for a short time with her uncle Loring Norcross and the children after her aunt's death on April 17.

218

To Mrs. Horace Ward   *about 1860*

Dear Mrs. Ward.

I hope you are not too ill to taste my Punch, and Jelly.

Please accept my love, with Mother's and Vinnie's, and tell us how you are today, through the little Boy.

Your friend,
E. Dickinson.

MANUSCRIPT: AC. Ink. Unpublished.

The date is conjectured from the handwriting. The outer fold is endorsed in ink by an unidentified hand (Mr. Ward's?): Mr Horace Ward Esq.

To Samuel Bowles   *about 1860*

I cant explain it, Mr Bowles.

> Two swimmers wrestled on the spar
> Until the morning sun,
> When one turned, smiling, to the land –
> Oh God! the other One!
> The stray ships – passing, spied a face
> Upon the waters borne,
> With eyes, in death, still begging, raised,
> And hands – beseeching – thrown!

MANUSCRIPT: AC. Pencil.

PUBLICATION: *Home* 420.

The date is conjectured from the handwriting and from the fact that the same poem is included by ED in one of her packets (HCL) written about this time. The circumstances to which the poem appears to allude have not been identified. But it is clear that about this time she was undergoing a turbulent emotional disturbance (see letters no. 187 and 233). Early in 1862 she in fact made a confidant of Bowles (see letter no. 250).

To Samuel Bowles   *about 1860*

Dear Mr Bowles.

    Thank you.

        "Faith" is a fine invention
        When Gentlemen can *see* –
        But *Microscopes* are prudent
        In an Emergency.

You spoke of the "East." I have thought about it this winter.

Dont you think you and I should be shrewder, to take the *Mountain Road?*

That *Bareheaded life* – under the grass – worries one like a Wasp.

The Rose is for Mary.

                                      Emily.

MANUSCRIPT: AC. Ink.

PUBLICATION: *L* (1894) 200; *L* (1931) 191.

    The date is conjectured from the handwriting, but the import of the message remains obscure.

    In the Bingham collection (AC) among the poems and letters sent to Bowles is the poem beginning "A feather from the Whippowil." On the inside of the folded sheet is this message:

    Enclosed in this was a sprig of white pine, which I have carefully preserved; I have also laid aside for you a letter of thanks from Clara Pease. You may expect to hear from the children by the next bulletin. I hope you are all well. F. H. C.

The handwriting of the poem places it about 1860. "F. H. C." has not been identified, nor is it clear whether "F. H. C." was an intermediary between ED and Bowles, or one of her correspondents. No correspondent with those initials is known, and since the poem is signed "Emily," one suspects it was intended for Bowles.

To Susan Davis Phelps   *May 1860*

    "When thou goest through the Waters, I will go with thee."

                                      Emilie

MANUSCRIPT: Smith College. Ink. Unpublished. On one outer fold
ED wrote: Dear Petite. On the other: Emilie.

Susan Phelps's engagement to Henry V. Emmons was broken on 8 May 1860. The quotation is from Isaiah 43.2: "When thou passeth through the waters, I will be with thee. . ."

222

To Catherine Scott Turner (Anthon)   *summer 1860?*

The prettiest of pleas, dear, but with a Lynx like me quite unavailable, – Finding is slow, facilities for losing so frequent in a world like this, I hold with extreme caution, a prudence so astute may seem unnecessary, but plenty moves those most dear, who have been in want, and Saviour tells us, Kate, "the poor are always with us" – Were you ever poor? I *have* been a Beggar, and rich tonight, as by God's leave I believe I am, The "Lazzaroni's" faces haunt, pursue me still! You do not yet "dislimn," Kate, Distinctly sweet your face stands in its phantom niche – I touch your hand – my cheek your cheek – I stroke your vanished hair, Why did you enter, sister, since you must depart? Had not its heart been torn enough but *you* must send your shred? Oh! our Condor Kate! Come from your crags again! Oh: Dew upon the bloom fall yet again a summer's night. Of such have been the friends which have vanquished faces – sown plant by plant the churchyard plats and occasioned angels. – There is a subject dear – on which we never touch, Ignorance of its pageantries does not deter me – I, too went out to meet the "Dust" early in the morning, I, too in Daisy mounds possess hid treasure – therefore I guard you more – You did not tell me you had once been a "Millionaire." Did my sister think that opulence could be mistaken? – Some trinket will remain – some babbling plate or jewel! – I write you from the summer. The murmuring leaves fill up the chinks thro' which the winter red shone, when Kate was here, and Frank was here – and "Frogs" sincerer than our own splash in their Maker's pools – Its but a little past – dear – and yet how far from here it seems – fled with the snow! So through the snow go many loving feet parted by "Alps" how brief from Vineyards and the Sun! – Parents and Vinnie request love to be given Girl –

Emilie –

Manuscript: missing. The text is from a transcript (HCL) made by Mrs. Anthon for Susan Dickinson. Mrs. Anthon made another transcript (AC) for Mrs. Todd. There are slight variations in punctuation.
Publication: L (1894) 148–149; LL 212–213; L (1931) 145–146.
After Campbell Turner's death in 1857 his widow reverted to her maiden name, and ED seems to have been previously unaware that Kate Scott had been married. Frank Gilbert had been visiting his sister Susan Dickinson on some occasion during the winter here recalled.

223

To Samuel Bowles   *early August 1860*

Dear Mr Bowles.

I am much ashamed. I misbehaved tonight. I would like to sit in the dust. I fear I am your little friend no more, but Mrs Jim Crow.

I am sorry I smiled at women.

Indeed, I revere holy ones, like Mrs Fry and Miss Nightingale. I will never be giddy again. Pray forgive me now: Respect little Bob o' Lincoln again!

My friends are a very few. I can count them on my fingers – and besides, have fingers to spare.

I am gay to see you – because you come so scarcely, else I had been graver.

Good night, God will forgive me – Will you please to *try?*

Emily.

Manuscript: Hooker. Ink. Dated: Sunday night. Addressed: Mr Bowles. Unpublished.
Bowles was in Amherst during the week of August 5 to report commencement festivities.

224

To Susan Gilbert Dickinson   *August 1860*

Dear Sue,

God bless you for the Bread! Now – can you spare it? Shall I send it back? Will you have a Loaf of mine – which is spread? Was silly

eno' to cut six, and have three left. Tell me just as it is, and I'll send home your's, or a Loaf of mine, *spread*, you understand –
Great times –
Love for Fanny.
Wish Pope to Rome – that's all –

Emily.

Esqr in parlor –

MANUSCRIPT: HCL (B 61). Pencil. Unpublished.
The date, conjectured from the handwriting, is confirmed by the details in the note, sent next door. Its breathlessness is explained by ED's attempt to organize tea or dinner for her father's guests. The *Springfield Republican* for Thursday, August 9, reports that Governor and Mrs. Banks were guests of Edward Dickinson during commencement, and the references to *pope* and *esquire* are evidently to the governor. The Norcross girls were both in Amherst for at least part of the festivities (see the letter following).

225

To Louise and Frances Norcross   *mid-September 1860*

Bravo, Loo, the cape is a beauty, and what shall I render unto Fanny, for all her benefits? I will take my books and go into a corner and give thanks! Do you think I am going "upon the boards" that I wish so smart attire? Such are my designs, though. I beg you not to disclose them! May I not secure Loo for drama, and Fanny for comedy? You are a brace of darlings, and it would give me joy to see you both, in any capacity. . . . Will treasure all till I see you. Never fear that I shall forget! In event of my decease, I will still exclaim "Dr. Thompson," and he will reply, "Miss Montague." My little Loo pined for the hay in her last communication. Not to be saucy, dear, we sha'n't have any more before the first of March, Dick having hid it all in the barn in a most malicious manner; but he has not brought the sunset in, so there is still an inducement to my little girls. We have a sky or two, well worth consideration, and trees so fashionable they make us all *passés*.
I often remember you both, last week. I thought that flown mamma

[367]

could not, as was her wont, shield from crowd, and strangers, and was glad Eliza was there. I knew she would guard my children, as she has often guarded me, from publicity, and help to fill the deep place never to be full. Dear cousins, I know you both better than I did, and love you both better, and always I have a chair for you in the smallest parlor in the world, to wit, my heart.

This world is just a little place, just the red in the sky, before the sun rises, so let us keep fast hold of hands, that when the birds begin, none of us be missing.

"Burnham" must think Fanny a scholastic female. I wouldn't be in her place! If she feels delicate about it, she can tell him the books are for a friend in the East Indies.

Won't Fanny give my respects to the "Bell and Everett party" if she passes that organization on her way to school? I hear they wish to make me Lieutenant-Governor's daughter. Were they cats I would pull their tails, but as they are only patriots, I must forego the bliss. . . .

Love to papa.

Emily.

Manuscript: destroyed.
Publication: L (1894) 234–236; LL 215–216; L (1931) 218–219.

The phrase "last week," in the beginning of the second paragraph is figurative, for more than a month had elapsed since commencement. The "Bell and Everett party" (John Bell and Edward Everett, respectively candidates for president and vice president on the short-lived Constitutional-Union party) was formed, September 12. Edward Dickinson declined the nomination for lieutenant governor of the state on their ticket, September 18. He was in Boston for the convention, staying with the Norcrosses, when this letter was written. John Dudley brought his fiancée, Eliza Coleman, to commencement in August, and Eliza had evidently chaperoned the Norcross girls, Louise and Frances, now respectively aged eighteen and thirteen. It is assumed that ED first met John Dudley on this occasion. Dr. Joseph P. Thompson had been a commencement speaker, and ED's comment on him suggests that he may have mistaken her for one of the Montague cousins. The Burnham Antique Book Shop was an established Boston store.

To Susan Gilbert Dickinson   *October 1860*

Dear Sue –

You cant think how much I thank you for the Box – Wont you put the things in *this* one – it is'nt half so pretty, you know, but it's such a bother to tip one's duds out –

Thank Sue, *so* much.

Emily.

MANUSCRIPT: HCL (B 98). Pencil.
PUBLICATION: *FF* 258.
The date is conjectured from the handwriting and confirmed by the fact that Emily and Lavinia went to visit Eliza Coleman at Middletown, Connecticut, October 19. Lyman Coleman lived there briefly after he left Philadelphia in 1858, before settling in Easton, Pennsylvania, in 1861, where he taught at Lafayette College. Eudocia Flynt, Mrs. Coleman's sister-in-law, met the girls en route to Middletown, according to her diary (in the possession of her granddaughter, Mrs. Raymond W. Jones).

To Mrs. J. G. Holland   *1860*

How is your little Byron? Hope he gains his foot without losing his genius. Have heard it ably argued that the poet's genius lay in his foot – as the bee's prong and his song are concomitant. Are you stronger than these? To assault so minute a creature seems to me malign, unworthy of Nature – but the frost is no respecter of persons.

I should be glad to be with you, or to open your letter. Blossoms belong to the bee, if needs be by *habeas corpus*.

Emily.

MANUSCRIPT: missing.
PUBLICATION: *L* (1894) 174–175; *L* (1931) 168; *LH* 63–64.
The Hollands' baby, Theodore, born in 1859, was operated on in 1860 to correct a congenital trouble with the tendons of one foot.

To Louise Norcross   *December 1860?*

Dear Peacock,

    I received your feather with profound emotion. It has already surmounted a work, and crossed the Delaware. Doubtless you are moulting *à la* canary bird – hope you will not suffer from the reduction of plumage these December days. The latitude is quite stiff for a few nights, and gentlemen and ladies who go barefoot in our large cities must find the climate uncomfortable. A land of frosts and zeros is not precisely the land for me; hope you find it congenial. I believe it is several hundred years since I met you and Fanny, yet I am pleased to say, you do not become dim; I think you rather brighten as the hours fly. I should love to see you dearly, girls; perhaps I may, before south winds, but I feel rather confused to-day, and the future looks "higglety-pigglety."

    You seem to take a smiling view of my finery. If you knew how solemn it was to me, you might be induced to curtail your jests. My sphere is doubtless calicoes, nevertheless I thought it meet to sport a little wool. The mirth it has occasioned will deter me from further exhibitions! Won't you tell "the public" that at present I wear a brown dress with a cape if possible browner, and carry a parasol of the same! We have at present one cat, and twenty-four hens, who do nothing so vulgar as lay an egg, which checks the ice-cream tendency.

    I miss the grasshoppers much, but suppose it is all for the best. I should become too much attached to a trotting world.

    My garden is all covered up by snow; picked gilliflower Tuesday, now gilliflowers are asleep. The hills take off their purple frocks, and dress in long white nightgowns.

    There is something fine and something sad in the year's toilet. . . .

    We often talk of you and your father these new winter days. Write, dear, when you feel like it.

                              Lovingly,
                                    Emily.

MANUSCRIPT: destroyed.
PUBLICATION: L (1894) 238–239; LL 224–225; L (1931) 221–222.

The month is December, and the tone of the letter suggests that it was written during the first winter after Mrs. Norcross's death. The cape here referred to is probably the one the girls sent to her (see letter no. 225).

229

To Samuel Bowles   *about February 1861*

Dear friend.

You remember the little "Meeting" – we held for you – last spring? We met again – Saturday – 'Twas May – when we "adjourned" – but then Adjourns – are all – The meetings wore alike – Mr Bowles – The Topic – did not tire us – so we chose no new – We voted to remember you – so long as both should live – including Immortality. To count you as ourselves – except sometimes more tenderly – as now – when you are ill – and we – the haler of the two – and so I bring the Bond – we sign so many times – for you to read, when Chaos comes – or Treason – or Decay – still witnessing for Morning.

We hope – it is a tri-Hope – composed of Vinnie's – Sue's – and mine – that you took no more pain – riding in the sleigh.

We hope our joy to see you – gave of it's own degree – to you – We pray for your new health – the prayer that goes not down – when they shut the church – We offer you our cups – stintless – as to the Bee – the Lily, her new Liquors –

Would you like Summer? Taste of our's –
Spices? Buy, here!
Ill! We have Berries, for the parching!
Weary! Furloughs of Down!
Perplexed! Estates of Violet – Trouble ne'er looked on!
Captive! We bring Reprieve of Roses!
Fainting! Flasks of Air!
Even for Death – a Fairy Medicine –
But, which is it – Sir?

Emily

Manuscript: AC. Ink.
Publication: L (1894) 213–214, in part; LL 247, in part; L (1931) 201–202, in part.

[371]

The date is conjectured from the handwriting, and the occasion sounds as though the girls had had a "Meeting" on Bowles's birthday. In 1861, February 9 occurred on Saturday.

230

To Louise and Frances Norcross   *early March 1861?*

Dear Friends,

Loo's note to Miss Whitney only stopped to dine. It went out with a beautiful name on its face in the evening mail. "Is there nothing else," as the clerk says? So pleased to enact a trifle for my little sister. It is little sisters you are, as dear Fanny says in the hallowed note. Could mamma read it, it would blur her light even in Paradise.

It was pretty to lend us the letters from the new friends. It gets us acquainted. We will preserve them carefully. . . . I regret I am not a scholar in the Friday class. I believe the love of God may be taught not to seem like bears. Happy the reprobates under that loving influence.

I have one new bird and several trees of old ones. A snow slide from the roof, dispelled mother's "sweetbrier." You will of course feel for her, as you were named for him! There are as yet no streets, though the sun is riper, and these small bells have rung so long I think it "tea-time" always.

MANUSCRIPT: destroyed.
PUBLICATION: L (1894) 236; LL 216–217; L (1931) 220, dated 1860–61.
Loo had enclosed a note to be addressed to Maria Whitney.

231

To Susan Gilbert Dickinson   *about April 1861*

Will Susan please lend Emily "Life in the Iron Mills" – and accept Blossom

from Emily –

MANUSCRIPT: HCL (B 133). Pencil.

PUBLICATION: *FF* 227.
Rebecca Harding Davis's "Life in the Iron Mills" appeared in the April 1861 issue of the *Atlantic Monthly*.

232

To Susan Gilbert Dickinson   *about 19 June 1861*

> Is it true, dear Sue?
> Are there *two*?
> I should'nt like to come
> For fear of joggling Him!
> If I could shut him up
> In a Coffee Cup,
> Or tie him to a pin
> Till I got in –
> Or make him fast
> To "Toby's" fist –
> Hist! Whist! I'd come!
>
>   Emily –

MANUSCRIPT: HCL (B 140). Ink.
PUBLICATION: *LL* 53; *Poems* (1955) 156–157.
Edward (Ned) Dickinson, Susan's first child, was born 19 June 1861. Toby was the cat.

233

To recipient unknown   *about 1861*

Master.

If you saw a bullet hit a Bird – and he told you he was'nt shot – you might weep at his courtesy, but you would certainly doubt his word.

One drop more from the gash that stains your Daisy's bosom – then would you *believe*? Thomas' faith in Anatomy, was stronger than his faith in faith. God made me – [Sir] Master – I did'nt be – myself. I dont know how it was done. He built the heart in me – Bye and bye it outgrew me – and like the little mother – with the big child – I got tired holding him. I heard of a thing called "Redemption" – which rested men and women. You remember I asked you for it – you gave me something else. I forgot the Redemption [in the Redeemed – I did'nt tell you for a long time, but I knew you had altered me – I] and was tired – no more – [so dear did this stranger become that were it, or my breath – the Alternative – I had tossed the fellow away with a smile.] I am older – tonight, Master – but the love is the same – so are the moon and the crescent. If it had been God's will that I might breathe where you breathed – and find the place – myself – at night – if I (can) never forget that I am not with you – and that sorrow and frost are nearer than I – if I wish with a might I cannot repress – that mine were the Queen's place – the love of the Plantagenet is my only apology – To come nearer than presbyteries – and nearer than the new Coat – that the Tailor made – the prank of the Heart at play on the Heart – in holy Holiday – is forbidden me – You make me say it over – I fear you laugh – when I do not see – [but] "Chillon" is not funny. Have you the Heart in your breast – Sir – is it set like mine – a little to the left – has it the misgiving – if it wake in the night – perchance – itself to it – a timbrel is it – itself to it a tune?

These things are [reverent] holy, Sir, I touch them [reverently] hallowed, but persons who pray – dare remark [our] "Father"! You say I do not tell you all – Daisy confessed – and denied not.

Vesuvius dont talk – Etna – dont – [Thy] one of them – said a syllable – a thousand years ago, and Pompeii heard it, and hid forever – She could'nt look the world in the face, afterward – I suppose – Bashfull Pompeii! "Tell you of the want" – you know what a leech is, dont you – and [remember that] Daisy's arm is small – and you have felt the horizon hav'nt you – and did the sea – never come so close as to make you dance?

I dont know what you can do for it – thank you – Master – but if I had the Beard on my cheek – like you – and you – had Daisy's petals – and you cared so for me – what would become of you? Could you forget me in fight, or flight – or the foreign land? Could'nt Carlo, and you and I walk in the meadows an hour – and nobody care but the Bobolink – and *his* – a *silver* scruple? I used to think when I died – I could see you – so I died as fast as I could – but the "Corporation" are going Heaven too so [Eternity] wont be sequestered – now [at all] – Say I may wait for you – say I need go with no stranger to the to me –

untried [country] fold – I waited a long time – Master – but I can wait more – wait till my hazel hair is dappled – and you carry the cane – then I can look at my watch – and if the Day is too far declined – we can take the chances [of] for Heaven – What would you do with me if I came "in white?" Have you the little chest to put the Alive – in?

I want to see you more – Sir – than all I wish for in this world – and the wish – altered a little – will be my only one – for the skies.

Could you come to New England – [this summer – could] would you come to Amherst – Would you like to come – Master?

[Would it do harm – yet we both fear God –] Would Daisy disappoint you – no – she would'nt – Sir – it were comfort forever – just to look in your face, while you looked in mine – then I could play in the woods till Dark – till you take me where Sundown cannot find us – and the true keep coming – till the town is full. [Will you tell me if you will?]

I did'nt think to tell you, you did'nt come to me "in white," nor ever told me why,

No Rose, yet felt myself a'bloom,
No Bird – yet rode in Ether.

Manuscript: AC. Ink. Words which ED crossed out are here enclosed in brackets; alternative readings are in parentheses.

Publication: L (1894) 422–423, six sentences only, and dated 1885; L (1931) 411, six sentences only, and dated "early 60's"; Home 422–430, entire, with facsimile in full.

For an earlier "Master" letter, see no. 187. The handwriting is the only clue to the date. This rough draft was left among ED's own papers, and no one knows whether a fair copy was made or sent to the person envisioned as the recipient.

234

To Louise and Frances Norcross　　　　　　　　　　　　　　*1861?*

. . . Send a sundown for Loo, please, and a crocus for Fanny. Shadow has no stem, so they could not pick him.

. . . D—— fed greedily upon *Harper's Magazine* while here. Suppose he is restricted to Martin Luther's works at home. It is a criminal thing to be a boy in a godly village, but maybe he will be forgiven.

. . . The seeing pain one can't relieve makes a demon of one. If angels have the heart beneath their silver jackets, I think such things could make them weep, but Heaven is so cold! It will never look kind to me that God, who causes all, denies such little wishes. It could not hurt His glory, unless it were a lonesome kind. I 'most conclude it is.

. . . Thank you for the daisy. With nature in my ruche I shall not miss the spring. What would become of us, dear, but for love to reprieve our blunders?

. . . I'm afraid that home is almost done, but do not say I fear so. Perhaps God will be better. They're so happy, you know. That makes it doubtful. Heaven hunts round for those that find itself below, and then it snatches.

. . . Think Emily lost her wits – but she found 'em, likely. Don't part with wits long at a time in this neighborhood.

. . . Your letters are all real, just the tangled road children walked before you, some of them to the end, and others but a little way, even as far as the fork in the road. That Mrs. Browning fainted, we need not read *Aurora Leigh* to know, when she lived with her English aunt; and George Sand "must make no noise in her grandmother's bedroom." Poor children! Women, now, queens, now! And one in the Eden of God. I guess they both forget that now, so who knows but we, little stars from the same night, stop twinkling at last? Take heart, little sister, twilight is but the short bridge, and the moon (morn) stands at the end. If we can only get to her! Yet, if she sees us fainting, she will put out her yellow hands. When did the war really begin?

MANUSCRIPT: destroyed.

PUBLICATION: *L* (1894) 236–238; *LL* 217, 223–224; *L* (1931) 220–221.

These seven extracts are placed together in *Letters* and dated: "Spring, 1861." They cannot be from one letter, for the fourth certainly is addressed to but one recipient. The last extract was written after the death of Elizabeth Barrett Browning, 29 June 1861. The Norcross sisters did not show ED's letters to Mrs. Todd; they gave her transcripts of such letters or parts of letters as they chose to select. Frances Norcross was not sure whether ED wrote *moon* or *morn* in the fourth sentence from the end, and entered both.

Aurora Leigh (1856), a romance in blank verse, ED especially liked and often alludes to in her letters. It is Mrs. Browning's vehicle for expressing her views on a variety of subjects, social, literary, and ethical.

To Mrs. Samuel Bowles   *about August 1861*

Mary.

I do not know of you, a long while – I remember you – several times – I wish I knew if you kept me? The Dust like the Mosquito, buzzes round my faith.

We are all human – Mary – until we are divine – and to some of us – that is far off, and to some [of] us – near as the lady, ringing at the door – perhaps that's what alarms – I say I will go myself – I cross the river – and climb the fence – now I am at the gate – Mary – now I am in the hall – now I am looking your heart in the Eye!

Did it wait for me – Did it go with the Company? Cruel Company – who have the stocks – and farms – and creeds – and *it* has just it's heart! I hope you are glad – Mary – no pebble in the Brook – today – no film on noon –

I can think how you look – You cant think how I look – I've got more freckles, since you saw me – playing with the schoolboys – then I pare the "Juneating" to make the pie – and get my fingers "tanned."

Summer went very fast – she got as far as the woman from the Hill – who brings the Blueberry – and that is a long way – I shall have no winter this year – on account of the soldiers – Since I cannot weave Blankets, or Boots – I thought it best to omit the season – Shall present a "Memorial" to God – when the Maples turn –

Can I rely on your "name"?

How is your garden – Mary? Are the Pinks true – and the Sweet Williams faithful? I've got a Geranium like a Sultana – and when the Humming birds come down – Geranium and I shut our eyes – and go far away –

Ask "Meme" – if I shall catch her a Butterfly with a vest like a Turk? I will – if she will build him a House in her "Morning – Glory." Vinnie would send her love, but she put on a white frock, and went to meet tomorrow – a few minutes ago. Mother would send her love – but she is in the "Eave spout," sweeping up a leaf, that blew in, last November. Austin would send his – but he dont live here – now — He married – and went East.

I brought my own – myself, to you and Mr Bowles. Please remember me, because I remember you – Always.

[377]

My River runs to thee –
Blue Sea! Wilt welcome me?
My River waits reply –
Oh Sea – look graciously –
I'll fetch thee Brooks
From spotted nooks –
Say – Sea –

Take *Me!*

MANUSCRIPT: AC. Ink.
PUBLICATION: L (1894) 196–197; LL 219–220; L (1931) 185–186.
Mary Bowles, now seven years old, was called "Mamie" by her family, but ED's spelling is clearly "Meme."

236

To Mary Warner Crowell   *about August 1861*

Dear Mary –

You might not know I remembered you, unless I told you so –

Emily –

MANUSCRIPT: HCL (L 34). Pencil.
PUBLICATION: *Mount Holyoke Alumnae Quarterly* XXIX (1946) 130.
The handwriting is that of 1861. Mary Warner married Edward C. Crowell on 13 August 1861.

237

To Edward S. Dwight   *September 1861*

Will little Ned lay these on Mama's pillow?
Softly – not to wake her!

Emily.

MANUSCRIPT: AC. Ink. Unpublished.
The Reverend Edward S. Dwight resigned his pastorate in the First Church at Amherst during August 1860, because of his wife's illness. She died 11 September 1861 at Gorham, Maine. This note seems to have accompanied flowers sent at the time of her funeral. Edward (Ned) Huntington Dwight was five years old.

238

To Susan Gilbert Dickinson   *summer 1861*

    Safe in their Alabaster Chambers,
    Untouched by morning
    And untouched by noon,
    Sleep the meek members of the Resurrection,
    Rafter of satin
    And Roof of stone.

    Light laughs the breeze
    In her Castle above them,
    Babbles the Bee in a stolid Ear,
    Pipe the Sweet Birds in ignorant cadence, –
    Ah, what sagacity perished here!

[The earlier version, above, ED sent to Sue during the summer of 1861. Sue appears to have objected to the second stanza, for ED sent her the following:]

    Safe in their Alabaster Chambers,
    Untouched by Morning –
    And untouched by Noon –
    Lie the meek members of the Resurrection –
    Rafter of Satin – and Roof of Stone –

    Grand go the Years – in the Crescent – about them –
    Worlds scoop their Arcs –
    And Firmaments – row –
    Diadems – drop – and Doges – surrender –
    Soundless as dots – on a Disc of Snow –

Perhaps this verse would please you better – Sue +

                        Emily –

[The new version elicited an immediate response:]
    I am not suited dear Emily with the second verse – It is remarkable as the chain lightening that blinds us hot nights in the Southern sky

but it does not go with the ghostly shimmer of the first verse as well as the other one – It just occurs to me that the first verse is complete in itself it needs no other, and can't be coupled – Strange things always go alone – as there is only one Gabriel and one Sun – You never made a peer for that verse, and I *guess* you[r] kingdom does'nt hold one – I always go to the fire and get warm after thinking of it, but I never *can* again – The flowers are sweet and bright and look as if they would kiss one – ah, they expect a humming-bird – Thanks for them of course – and not thanks only recognition either – Did it ever occur to you that is all there is here after all – "Lord that I may receive my sight" –

Susan is tired making *bibs* for her bird – her ring-dove – he will paint my cheeks when I am old to pay me –

Sue –

Pony Express

[ED answered thus:]

Is *this frostier?*

Springs – shake the sills –
But – the Echoes – stiffen –
Hoar – is the Window –
And numb – the Door –
Tribes of Eclipse – in Tents of Marble –
Staples of Ages – have buckled – there –

Dear Sue –

Your praise is good – to me – because I *know* it *knows* – and *suppose* – it *means* –

Could I make you and Austin – proud – sometime – a great way off – 'twould give me taller feet –

Here is a crumb – for the "Ring dove" – and a spray for *his Nest,* a little while ago – *just* – "*Sue."*

Emily.

MANUSCRIPTS: HCL (B 74a, 74b, 74c, and 203d). All are ink except 74a.

PUBLICATION: FF 164, in part; *Poems* (1955) 151–155, where the story of the development of the poem is told in full, but with portions of the letters – touching upon the infant Ned – omitted.

239

To Susan Gilbert Dickinson   *about 1861*

Could *I* – then – shut the door –
Lest *my* beseeching face – at last –
Rejected – be – of *Her?*

MANUSCRIPT: HCL (B 125). Pencil.
PUBLICATION: FF 255; *Poems* (1955) 158.
The tension which developed between ED and Sue, when the infant
Ned began to absorb Sue's attention, is hinted at in this note, which is in
the handwriting of about 1861.

To Austin Dickinson   *about 1861*

Austin –

Father said Frank Conkey – touched you –

A Burdock – clawed my Gown –
Not *Burdock's* – blame –
But *mine* –
Who went too near
The Burdock's *Den* –

A *Bog* – affronts my shoe –
What *else* have Bogs – *to do* –
The only Trade they *know* –
The *splashing Men!*
Ah, *pity – then!*

'Tis *Minnows can despise!*
The *Elephant's* – calm eyes
Look *further on!*

Emily –

MANUSCRIPT: AC. Ink.
PUBLICATION: *Poems* (1955) 165–166.
The date is conjectured from the handwriting. There was keen political
rivalry between Edward Dickinson, a "straight" Whig, and Ithamar Francis
Conkey, a "republican" Whig. ED evidently thought that Austin had been
"touched" by Conkey's political thinking.

To Samuel Bowles   *October 1861*

Perhaps you thought I did'nt care – because I stayed out, yesterday, I *did* care, Mr Bowles. I pray for your sweet health – to "Alla" – every morning – but something troubled me – and I knew you needed light – and air – so I did'nt come. Nor have I the conceit that you *noticed* me – but I could'nt bear that you, or Mary, so gentle to me – should think me forgetful – It's little, at the most – we can do for our's, and we must do that – flying – or our things are *flown!* Dear friend, I wish you were well –

It grieves me till I cannot speak, that you are suffering. Wont you come back? Cant I bring you something? My little Balm might be *o'erlooked* by wiser eyes – you know – Have you tried the Breeze that swings the Sign – or the Hoof of the Dandelion? *I* own 'em – Wait for *mine!*

This is all that I have to say – Kinsmen need say nothing – but "Swiveller" may be sure of the

                                           "Marchioness."

Love for Mary.

MANUSCRIPT: AC. Ink.
PUBLICATION: *L* (1894) 202; *LL* 230; *L* (1931) 192–193.

During the autumn of 1861 Bowles became a patient at Dr. Denniston's water-cure in Northampton, and in October he visited the Dickinsons several times. He was suffering from sciatica. Dick Swiveller and the "Marchioness" (the drudge who in the end marries Dick) are characters in Dickens's *The Old Curiosity Shop*. ED's signature to the letter may well be a descriptive term which Bowles had jokingly applied to her when she had refused to see him.

242

To Samuel Bowles   *early December 1861*

Dear Mr Bowles.

It grieves us – that in near Northampton – we have now – no friend – and the old-foreigner-look blurs the Hills – *that* side – It will be bravest news – when our friend is well – tho' "Business" leaves but little place for the sweeter sort.

The hallowing – of pain – makes one afraid to convalesce – because they differ – wide – as *Engines* – and *Madonnas*. We trust no City give our friend – the "Helena" feeling.

The Cages – do not suit the *Swiss* – well as steeper Air.

I think the Father's Birds do not all carol at a time – to prove the *cost* of *Music* – not doubting at the last each Wren shall bear it's "Palm" –

To take the pearl – costs Breath – but then a pearl is not impeached – let it strike the East!

Dear Mr Bowles – We told you we did not learn to pray – but then our freckled bosom bears it's friends – in it's own way – to a simpler sky – and many's the time we leave their pain with the "Virgin Mary."

Jesus! thy Crucifix
Enable thee to guess
The smaller size –

Jesus! thy *second* face
Mind thee – in Paradise –
Of Our's.

Emily.

MANUSCRIPT: Hooker. Ink. Unpublished.

Bowles was not entirely cured of his sciatica when he left Northampton to take Mrs. Bowles to New York to be under a doctor's care before the birth of Charles in mid-December.

243

To Edward S. Dwight   *December 1861*

Dear friend.

We thought for sorrow – perhaps you had rather no one talk – but we had rather go away – when our friend is *glad* – We never like to leave the eye that is full of tears – and if too – it be one that always looked so kind on us – that makes it harder – I suppose your friend – the Stranger – can comfort more than all of us – but that is Dusk – to me – and so I knock tonight – on that far study door – that used to open kindly – but if you'd rather see no one – you need not say "Come in."

Upon these winter nights – I have much recollection of evenings passed with you – and her – at the "parsonage" – and the fire crackles – still – and her cheek softly reddens – as we talk – and laugh – and then I strain my eyes to that low sleep – she takes – and something bars my throat. I presume it is better – where she is – and holier – and safer – but then I like my little friend where I can see it's face, and *that's* so far –

I took her notes – today – I had a tiny pacquet – prompted by gentle gratitudes for trifling favor done – I held them to my lips – I put them in my breast – to see if I could warm them – and then the tears fell so – I feared that they would blot them out – as they were but in pencil – and so I laid them back. These – and the little Tennyson – in which she wrote my name – are all I have of her – yet of so sweet a life all – is memorial – and I – to her remembrance – as to a timid portrait – the *lady* – quite transfigured – now – turn every day – I think it sad to have a friend – it's sure to break the Heart so – and yet – if it had none – the Heart must seek another trade.

I hope that Annie and Ned – are well – Tell them – the lady who loved Mama – could not forget *them* –

Father and Mother talk of you – with frequent affection – and when you shall please – will always be happy to see you.

Mr and Mrs Sweetser – too – bear you in strong remembrance – and many more – I doubt not, whom I do not meet. I hope Mrs Waterman is well – please give her my love, and tell her I will remember her daughter.

Affy,
Emily.

MANUSCRIPT: AC. Ink. Unpublished.
Although this letter speaks of winter nights, it seems to have been written earlier than the one written to Mr. Dwight on 2 January 1862 (no. 246). The Sweetsers here mentioned were probably Mr. and Mrs. Luke Sweetser, near neighbors of the Dickinsons. Mrs. Waterman was the mother of the late Mrs. Dwight. The location of the Tennyson volume is not known.

244

To Mrs. Samuel Bowles   *about 20 December 1861*

Dear Mary –

Can you leave *your* flower long enough – just to look at *mine?*

Which is the prettiest? I shall tell for myself – some day – I *used* to come – to *comfort* you – but *now* – to tell you how glad I am – and how glad we all are – I wish it were a lady – for then – it would be just big enough – to waltz – with Austin's little Boy – but they can play Ball – together – and that will do as well! You must not stay in New York – any more – you must come back – now – and bring the Blanket to Massachusetts – where we can all look. What a responsible shepherd – Four lambs – in it's flock! Shall you be glad to see us – or shall we seem old-fashioned – by the face in the crib?

Tell him – I've got a pussy – for him – with a spotted Gown – and a Dog – with Ringlets –

We have very cold days – since you went away – and I think you hear the wind blow, far as the Brevoort House – it comes from so far – and crawls so – Dont let it blow Baby away – will you call him Robert – for me. He is the bravest man – alive – but *his* Boy – has no mama – *that* makes us all weep – dont it?

Good night – Mary –

                              Emily.

MANUSCRIPT: AC. Ink. It still shows the marks of a once-enclosed flower.

PUBLICATION: L (1894) 195; LL 218; L (1931) 189; in part.

The *Springfield Republican* announced on December 20: "At the Brevoort House, New York, 19th, a son to Samuel Bowles of this city." Elizabeth Barrett Browning died in June 1861.

245

To Louise Norcross   *31 December 1861*

. . . Your letter didn't surprise me, Loo; I brushed away the sleet from eyes familiar with it – looked again to be sure I read it right – and then took up my work hemming strings for mother's gown. I think

I hemmed them faster for knowing you weren't coming, my fingers had nothing else to do. . . . Odd, that I, who say "no" so much, cannot bear it from others. Odd, that I, who run from so many, cannot brook that one turn from me. Come when you will, Loo, the hearts are never shut here. I don't remember "May." Is that the one that stands next April? And is that the month for the river-pink?

Mrs. Adams had news of the death of her boy to-day, from a wound at Annapolis. Telegram signed by Frazer Stearns. You remember him. Another one died in October – from fever caught in the camp. Mrs. Adams herself has not risen from bed since then. "Happy new year" step softly over such doors as these! "Dead! Both her boys! One of them shot by the sea in the East, and one of them shot in the West by the sea." . . . Christ be merciful! Frazer Stearns is just leaving Annapolis. His father has gone to see him to-day. I hope that ruddy face won't be brought home frozen. Poor little widow's boy, riding to-night in the mad wind, back to the village burying-ground where he never dreamed of sleeping! Ah! the dreamless sleep!

Did you get the letter I sent a week from Monday? You did not say, and it makes me anxious, and I sent a scrap for Saturday last, that too? Loo, I wanted you very much, and I put you by with sharper tears than I give to many. Won't you tell me about the chills – what the doctor says? I must not lose you, sweet. Tell me if I could send a tuft to keep the cousin warm, a blanket of a thistle, say, or something!

Much love and Christmas, and sweet year, for you and Fanny and papa.

Emilie.

Dear little Fanny's note received, and shall write her soon.
Meanwhile, we wrap her in our heart to keep her tight and warm.

MANUSCRIPT: destroyed.
PUBLICATION: L (1894) 239–241; LL 225–226, in part; L (1931) 222–224.

Sylvester H. Adams died at Annapolis, 31 December 1861, of typhoid fever. Frazar Stearns was the son of President Stearns of Amherst. He was killed in March of the following year (see letter no. 255).

VII

LETTERS

246–313

[1862–1865]

"*Perhaps you smile at me.*
I could not stop for that –
My Business is Circumference."

The most crucial and — though she could not know it — historically eventful year in Emily Dickinson's life was 1862. She was undergoing an emotional disturbance of such magnitude that she feared for her reason. At the same time she had developed her poetic sensibilities to a degree that impelled her to write Thomas Wentworth Higginson in April to learn what a professional man of letters might have to say about her verses. In no other year did she ever write so much poetry.

There is no direct evidence that the Reverend Charles Wadsworth was the man with whom she fell in love, but the circumstantial evidence is impressive that such was true, and is at no point contradicted by other evidence.

By far the most important correspondence in these years are the letters to Higginson and to Samuel Bowles. She clearly made Bowles a confidant in the matter which touched her heart most closely, and when Higginson had made certain by midsummer 1862 that in his opinion her verses were not for publication, she continued to write him because his interest in her thoughts and her writing was genuine, and his concern somehow gave her the curative she sought. "You were not aware," she wrote him seven years later, "that you saved my Life."

The nature of the eye affliction which required a specialist's attention is not known, but her eyesight was not seriously impaired (she never wore glasses), and during the months she spent in Boston in 1864 and 1865 she continued to write both poems and letters.

The letters of this group are the most moving of all, for they reveal the pathos of unrequited yearning and the assurance of a mature artist who cannot expect fame in her lifetime.

246

To Edward S. Dwight   *2 January 1862*

Dear friend.

I made the mistake – and was just about to recall the note – *mis-
enveloped* to you – and *your's* – to the other friend – which I just knew
– when my "Sister's" face – put this world from mind – nor should I
mention it – except the familiar address – must have surprised your
taste – I have the friend who loves me – and thinks me larger than I
am – and to reduce a Glamour, innocently caused – I sent the little
Verse to *Him*. Your gentle answer – undeserved, I more thank you for.

My little Sister's face – so dear – so unexpected – filled my eyes
with the old rain – and I hid my face in my apron – my only shelter –
now she sleeps – and wondered why a love was given – but just to tear
away – I cared for Her – so long – she spoiled me for a ruder love –
and other women – seem to me bristling – and very loud.

Do you remember telling me that I "should soon forget you both?"
You did not mean to deceive me – but you made the *mistake!* If you
please – I remember *more* – and *not* "less" – as you said. You thought
the portrait "might remind me of my former friend."

I trust she is more my friend – today – when I cannot see her – and
learn it from her own sweet lips.

The World is not the *shape* it was – when I went to your House –
a little tipsy – maybe – that I could have a friend – so near – who found
them at rare distances – as *Mints* – and *precious stones* – but I will not
review a time – that cuts – at every step. You were very thoughtful – to
send me the face – How tenderly I thank you – it's preciousness to
you – will tell. It is exquisitely like her – we all think – and at Austin's
– where it was borne in a little basket – through the storm – last night.

I do not ask if you are "better" – because split lives – never "get
well" – but the love of friends – sometimes helps the Staggering – when
the Heart has on it's great freight.

Dear friend – I read the verse – You must not deny your little
Church – who "called" no pastor – yet – Again – I thank you for the

face – her memory did not need –

> Sufficient troth – that she will rise –
> Deposed – at last – the Grave –
> To that *new* fondness – Justified –
> by Calvaries of love –

Emily.

MANUSCRIPT: AC. Ink. Dated: Amherst. Envelope addressed: Rev Edward S. Dwight./Gorham./Maine. Postmarked: Amherst Ms Jan 3 1862. Unpublished.

ED had reversed the contents of envelopes posted about the same time in December, one to Dwight and one to the (unidentified) friend who "thinks me larger than I am." Dwight replied, enclosing a verse and a photograph of his late wife. This letter, which acknowledges Dwight's, concludes with the final stanza of "There came a Day at Summer's full," adapted to the memory of Mrs. Dwight.

247

To Samuel Bowles *about 11 January 1862*

Dear friend.

Are you willing? I am so far from Land – To offer *you* the cup – it might some Sabbath come *my* turn – Of wine how solemn – full!

Did you get the Doubloons – did you vote upon "Robert"? You said you would come in "Febuary." Only three weeks more to wait at the Gate!

While you are sick – we – are homesick – Do you look out tonight? The Moon rides like a Girl – through a Topaz Town – I dont think we shall ever be merry again – you are ill so long –

When did the Dark happen?

I skipped a page – tonight – because I come so often – now – I might have tired you.

That page is fullest – tho'. Vinnie sends her love. I think Father and Mother care a great deal for you – and hope you may be well. When you tire with pain – to know that eyes would cloud, in Amherst – might that comfort – *some*?

Emily.

We never forget Mary –

Manuscript: AC. Ink.
Publication: L (1894) 199; LL 226; L (1931) 190.
If ED is literal in her time reckoning, she wrote this letter on Saturday, January 11. The Bowleses were still in New York. The opening paragraph suggests that she enclosed a poem, perhaps one intended to reveal something of a personal nature.

248

To recipient unknown   *early 1862?*

Oh, did I offend it – [Did'nt it want me to tell it the truth] Daisy – Daisy – offend it – who bends her smaller life to his (it's) meeker (lower) every day – who only asks – a task – [who] something to do for love of it – some little way she cannot guess to make that master glad –

A love so big it scares her, rushing among her small heart – pushing aside the blood and leaving her faint (all) and white in the gust's arm –

Daisy – who never flinched thro' that awful parting, but held her life so tight he should not see the wound – who would have sheltered him in her childish bosom (Heart) – only it was'nt big eno' for a Guest so large – *this* Daisy – grieve her Lord – and yet it (she) often blundered – Perhaps she grieved (grazed) his taste – perhaps her odd – Backwoodsman [life] ways [troubled] teased his finer nature (sense). Daisy [fea] knows all that – but must she go unpardoned – teach her, preceptor grace – teach her majesty – Slow (Dull) at patrician things – Even the wren upon her nest learns (knows) more than Daisy dares –

Low at the knee that bore her once unto [royal] wordless rest [now] Daisy [stoops a] kneels a culprit – tell her her [offence] fault – Master – if it is [not so] small eno' to cancel with her life, [Daisy] she is satisfied – but punish [do not] dont banish her – shut her in prison, Sir – only pledge that you will forgive – sometime – before the grave, and Daisy will not mind – She will awake in [his] your likeness.

Wonder stings me more than the Bee – who did never sting me – but made gay music with his might wherever I [may] [should] did go – Wonder wastes my pound, you said I had no size to spare –

[391]

You send the water over the Dam in my brown eyes –

I've got a cough as big as a thimble – but I dont care for that – I've got a Tomahawk in my side but that dont hurt me much. [If you] Her master stabs her more –

Wont he come to her – or will he let her seek him, never minding [whatever] so long wandering [out] if to him at last.

Oh how the sailor strains, when his boat is filling – Oh how the dying tug, till the angel comes. Master – open your life wide, and take me in forever, I will never be tired – I will never be noisy when you want to be still. I will be [glad] [as the] your best little girl – nobody else will see me, but you – but that is enough – I shall not want any more – and all that Heaven only will disappoint me – will be because it's not so dear

MANUSCRIPT: AC. Penciled rough draft.

PUBLICATION: *Home* 430–431.

The alternative suggested changes are placed in parentheses; words crossed out, in brackets. Like the earlier "Master" letters (nos. 187 and 233) this draft was among ED's papers at the time of her death. Whether a fair copy was made and sent, or intended to be sent, is not known. Accurate dating is impossible. The letter may have been written earlier, but the characteristics of the handwriting make the present assignment reasonable.

248a

[*Charles Wadsworth to ED*]

My Dear Miss Dickenson

I am distressed beyond measure at your note, received this moment, — I can only imagine the affliction which has befallen, or is now befalling you.

Believe me, be what it may, you have all my sympathy, and my constant, earnest prayers.

I am very, very anxious to learn more definitely of your trial — and though I have no right to intrude upon your sorrow yet I beg you to write me, though it be but a word.

In great haste
Sincerely and most
Affectionately *Yours* ——

MANUSCRIPT: AC. It is unsigned and without date, but is in the handwriting of the Reverend Charles Wadsworth, with an embossed crest "C W."
PUBLICATION: *Home* 369–372, with facsimile reproduction.

This solicitous pastoral letter is placed here because it thus follows the last of the "Master" letters, and because the present assumption is that ED thought of Wadsworth as "Master." Actually the letter may have been written at a quite different time.

249

To Samuel Bowles   *early 1862*

Dear friend.

If I amaze[d] your kindness – My Love is my only apology. To the people of "Chillon" – this – is enoug[h] I have met – no othe[rs.] Would you – ask le[ss] for your *Queen* – M[r] Bowles?

Then – I mistake – [my] scale – To Da[?] 'tis *daily* – to be gran[ted] and not a "Sunday Su[m] [En]closed – is my [d]efence – [F]orgive the Gills that ask for Air – if it is harm – to breathe! To *"thank"* you – [s]hames my thought!

> [Sh]ould you but fail [at] – Sea –
> [In] sight of me –
> [Or] doomed lie –
> [Ne]xt Sun – to die –
> [O]r rap – at Paradise – unheard
> I'd *harass God*
> Until he let [you] in!

                                                                              Emily.

MANUSCRIPT: Hooker. Ink. Outside edges torn away. Unpublished except for the poem, which is in *Poems* (1955) 162, and there dated 1861. There can be no exact date assigned. Here the letter is moved somewhat ahead, since the letter seems to be part of a sequence that ED wrote Bowles between January and early April, when he sailed for Europe.

[393]

250

To Samuel Bowles   *early 1862*

Title divine – is mine!
The Wife – without the Sign!
Acute Degree – conferred on me –
Empress of Calvary!
Royal – all but the Crown!
Betrothed – without the swoon
God sends us Women –
When you – hold – Garnet to Garnet –
Gold – to Gold –
Born – Bridalled – Shrouded –
In a Day –
"My Husband" – women say –
Stroking the Melody –
Is *this* – the way?

Here's – what I had to "tell you" –
You will tell no other? Honor – is it's
own pawn –

MANUSCRIPT: AC. Ink.
PUBLICATION: *Poems* (1955) 758. A variant of the poem, sent to Susan
Dickinson about the same time, was first published in LL 49–50.
    The phrase "Honor is it's own pawn" ED used again, to conclude her
first letter to Higginson, written on 15 April 1862 (no. 260).

To Samuel Bowles   *early 1862*

Dear friend

    If you doubted my Snow – for a moment – you never will – again –
I know –
    Because I could not say it – I fixed it in the Verse – for you to
read – when your thought wavers, for such a foot as mine –

Through the strait pass of suffering –
The Martyrs – even – trod.
Their feet – upon Temptation –
Their faces – upon God –

A stately – shriven – Company –
Convulsion – playing round –
Harmless – as streaks of Meteor –
Upon a Planet's Bond –

Their faith – the everlasting troth –
Their Expectation – fair –
The Needle – to the North Degree –
Wades – so – thro' polar Air!

MANUSCRIPT: AC. Ink.

PUBLICATION: *Poems* (1955) 598. Another copy of the poem only furnished the text first published in 1891.

In *Poems* (1955) the letter is dated 1863. Since this group of notes and poems to Bowles can be dated by handwriting only, no date can be surely assigned. It cannot be said with assurance that this letter follows no. 250, but it certainly is an attempt to make her position clear, a position which the preceding letter makes ambiguous.

252

To Samuel Bowles   *early 1862*

Dear Mr Bowles.

I cant thank you any more – You are thoughtful so many times, you grieve me *always – now*. The old words are *numb* – and there *a'nt* any *new* ones – Brooks – are useless – in *Freshet-time* –

When you come to Amherst, please God it were *Today* – I will tell you about the picture – if I *can*, I will –

"*Speech*" – is a prank of *Parliament* –
"*Tears*" – a trick of the *nerve* –
But the Heart with the heaviest freight on –
Does'nt – always – move –

Emily.

Manuscript: AC. Ink.
Publication: L (1894) 210–211; LL 244; L (1931) 200.
ED's gratitude for Bowles's sympathetic understanding is thus acknowledged.

253

To Mrs. Samuel Bowles   early March 1862

Dear Mary –
    Could you leave "Charlie" – long enough? Have you time for *me?*
I sent Mr Bowles – a little note – last Saturday morning – asking him –
to do an errand for me –
    I forgot he was going to Washington – or I should'nt have troubled him – so late – Now – Mary – I fear he did not get it – and *you*
tried to do the errand for me – and it troubled you – *Did* it? Will you
tell me? Just say with your pencil – "it did'nt tire me – Emily" – and
then – I shall be sure – for with all your care – I would not have taxed
you – for the world –
    You never refused me – Mary – you cherished me – many times –
but I thought it must seem so selfish – to ask the favor of Mr Bowles –
just as he went from Home – only I *forgot* that –
    Tell me – *tonight* – just a word – Mary – with your own hand – so
I shall know I harassed none – and I will be *so* glad –
    Austin told us of Charlie. I send a Rose – for his small hands.
    Put it in – when he goes to sleep – and then he will dream of Emily
– and when you bring him to Amherst – we shall be "old friends."
    Dont love him so well – you know – as to forget us – We shall wish
he was'nt *there* – if you do – I'm afraid – *shant* we?
    I'll remember you – if you like me to – while Mr. Bowles is gone –
and that will stop the lonely – *some* – but I cannot agree to *stop* – when
he gets home from Washington.
    Good night – Mary –
    You wont forget my little note – *tomorrow* – in the mail – It will
be the *first one* – you ever wrote me – in your life – and yet – was I the
little friend – a *long time?* *Was* I – Mary?
                                                            Emily.

[396]

MANUSCRIPT: AC. Ink. Dated: Sunday night.
PUBLICATION: L (1894) 201–202; L (1931) 192.
Samuel Bowles left for Washington about 1 March.

254

To Frances Norcross   March 1862?

Dear Fanny,

I fear you are getting as driven as Vinnie. We consider her standard for superhuman effort erroneously applied. Dear Loo remembers
the basket Vinnie "never got to." But we must blame with lenience.
Poor Vinnie has been very sick, and so have we all, and I feared one
day our little brothers would see us no more, but God was not so hard.
Now health looks so beautiful, the tritest "How do you do" is living
with meaning. No doubt you "heard a bird," but which route did he
take? Hasn't reached here yet. Are you sure it wasn't a "down brakes"?
Best of ears will blunder! Unless he come by the first of April, I shan't
countenance him. We have had fatal weather – thermometer two below zero all day, without a word of apology. Summer was always dear,
but such a kiss as she'll get from me if I ever see her again, will make
her cry, I know. . . .

MANUSCRIPT: destroyed.
PUBLICATION: L (1894) 241–242; LL 228; L (1931) 224.
The text is dated "February 1862" by Mrs. Todd, but ED speaks of
April as if it were the next month, and such cold as they had not expected.

255

To Louise and Frances Norcross   late March 1862

Dear Children,

You have done more for me – 'tis least that I can do, to tell you
of brave Frazer – "killed at Newbern," darlings. His big heart shot
away by a "minie ball."

I had read of those – I didn't think that Frazer would carry one to
Eden with him. Just as he fell, in his soldier's cap, with his sword at

[397]

his side, Frazer rode through Amherst. Classmates to the right of him, and classmates to the left of him, to guard his narrow face! He fell by the side of Professor Clark, his superior officer – lived ten minutes in a soldier's arms, asked twice for water – murmured just, "My God!" and passed! Sanderson, his classmate, made a box of boards in the night, put the brave boy in, covered with a blanket, rowed six miles to reach the boat, – so poor Frazer came. They tell that Colonel Clark cried like a little child when he missed his pet, and could hardly resume his post. They loved each other very much. Nobody here could look on Frazer – not even his father. The doctors would not allow it.

The bed on which he came was enclosed in a large casket shut entirely, and covered from head to foot with the sweetest flowers. He went to sleep from the village church. Crowds came to tell him goodnight, choirs sang to him, pastors told how brave he was – early-soldier heart. And the family bowed their heads, as the reeds the wind shakes.

So our part in Frazer is done, but you must come next summer, and we will mind ourselves of this young crusader – too brave that he could fear to die. We will play his tunes – maybe he can hear them; we will try to comfort his broken-hearted Ella, who, as the clergyman said, "gave him peculiar confidence." . . . Austin is stunned completely. Let us love better, children, it's most that's left to do.

Love from

Emily.

MANUSCRIPT: destroyed.
PUBLICATION: L (1894) 242–244; LL 228–229; L (1931) 224–226.
Lieutenant Frazar A. Stearns, son of President Stearns of Amherst, was killed at Newbern (N. C.), 14 March. The funeral was held in Amherst on 22 March.

256

To Samuel Bowles   *late March 1862*

Dear friend.

Will you be kind to *Austin* – again? And would you be kinder than sometimes – and put the name – on – too – He tells me to tell you

– He could not thank you – Austin is disappointed – He expected to see you – today –

He is sure you wont go to Sea – without first speaking to Him. I presume if Emily and Vinnie knew of his writing – they would entreat Him to ask you – not –

Austin is chilled – by Frazer's murder – He says – his Brain keeps saying over "Frazer is killed" – "Frazer is killed," just as Father told it – to Him. Two or three words of lead – that dropped so deep, they keep weighing –

Tell Austin – how to get over them!

He is very sorry you are not better – He cares for you – when at the Office – and afterwards – too – at Home – and sometimes – wakes at night, with a worry for you – he did'nt finish – quite – by Day – He would not like it – that I betrayed Him – so you'll never tell. And I must betray Sue – too –

Do not think it dishonorable –

I found out – accidentally – that *she* – was trying to find out – if you had a little *Drinking Flask* – to take abroad with you – I would like to serve – Sue – and if you will tell *me* by Monday's mail – whether you have one – and promise me – for *her sake – not to get one* – if you hav'nt – I can fix the *telling her* –

Mary sent beautiful flowers. Did she tell – you?

Austin hopes his errand will not tire you.

MANUSCRIPT: AC. Ink.

PUBLICATION: L (1894) 202–203, in part; LL 230–231, in part; L (1931) 193–194, in part.

This letter, which apparently enclosed another letter for Bowles to forward to somebody, uses Austin's name throughout as a cover.

Bowles was planning to sail for Europe early in April. He evidently replied that he did not have a flask (see letter no. 259).

257

To Samuel Bowles   *late March 1862?*

Dear Mr Bowles.

        Victory comes late,
        And is held low to freezing lips

Too rapt with frost
To mind it!
How sweet it would have tasted!
Just a drop!
Was God so economical?
His table's spread too high
Except we dine on tiptoe!
Crumbs fit such little mouths –
Cherries – suit *Robins* –
The Eagle's golden breakfast – *dazzles them!*
God keep his vow to *"Sparrows,"*
Who of little love – know how to starve!

Emily.

MANUSCRIPT: Hooker. Ink.

PUBLICATION: Poems (1955) 533–534. A variant of the poem was first published in 1891. There is no stanza break.

The dating of the letter is based solely upon handwriting, and in *Poems* (1955) is assigned to the year 1861. It may indeed have been written in either 1861 or 1862. It is possible that the poem is associated with the death of Frazar Stearns. The event was especially shocking to all who knew him. Samuel Bowles wrote to Austin and Susan Dickinson (HCL – Dickinson collection): ". . . and then the news from Newbern took away all the remaining life. I did not care for victory, for anything now." (Newbern was a Union victory.)

258

To Susan Gilbert Dickinson   *early 1862*

Dear Sue,

Your – Riches – taught me – poverty!
Myself, a "Millionaire"
In little – wealths – as Girls can boast –
Till broad as "Buenos Ayre" –
You drifted your Dominions –
A Different – Peru –
And I esteemed – all – poverty –
For Life's Estate – with you!

[400]

Of "Mines" – I little know – myself –
But just the *names* – of *Gems* –
The *Colors* – of the *Commonest* –
And scarce of Diadems –
So much – that did I meet *the Queen* –
Her glory – I should know –
But *this* – must be a *different Wealth* –
To miss it – beggars – so!

I'm sure 'tis *"India"* – all day –
To those who look on you –
Without a stint – without a blame –
Might I – but be the Jew!
I know it is "Golconda" –
Beyond my power to dream –
To have a smile – for mine – each day –
How *better* – than a *Gem*!

At least – it solaces – to know –
That there *exists* – a *Gold* –
Altho' I prove it, just in time –
It's distance – to behold!
It's far – far – Treasure – to surmise –
And estimate – the Pearl –
That slipped – my simple fingers – thro'
While yet a Girl – at School!

Dear Sue –
    You see I remember –

                                        Emily.

MANUSCRIPT: HCL (B 44). Ink.
PUBLICATION: FF 228, with poem omitted; *Poems* (1955) 220–221.
George Frisbie Whicher suggested that this poem might have been
written in memory of Benjamin Franklin Newton, the early friend who
ED said taught her immortality (*This Was a Poet* 92). The handwriting
is certainly that of letters known to be written early in 1862, and Whicher's
conjecture is plausible; the ninth anniversary of Newton's death was
24 March 1862. On the other hand the poem may not be an elegy, but
written about a person living whom ED feels that she has lost, perhaps

Sue herself. Such indeed seems to have been her feeling about Sue at this time (see T. H. Johnson, *Emily Dickinson: An Interpretive Biography* 38–41).

Another poem which ED sent to Sue in 1862 or 1863 is the one beginning "The Love a Child can show – below" (*Poems*, 1955, 520–521). It is headed *"Excuse me – Dollie –"* and is signed "Emily." The occasion that prompted it is not known.

259

To Samuel Bowles   *early April 1862*

Dear friend.

The Hearts in Amherst – ache – tonight – You could not know how hard – They thought they could not wait – last night – until the Engine – sang – a pleasant tune – that time – because that you were coming – The flowers waited – in the Vase – and love got peevish, watching – A Rail Road person, rang, to bring an evening paper – Vinnie tipped Pussy – over – in haste to let you in – and I, for Joy – and Dignity – held tight in my chair – My Hope put out a petal –

You would come – today – but Sue and Vinnie, and I, keep the time, in tears – We dont *believe* it – *now* – "Mr Bowles – not coming"! *Would'nt* you – *tomorrow* – and this be but a *bad Dream – gone by – next morning?*

Please do not take our *spring* – away – since you blot Summer – out! We cannot *count* – our tears – for this – because they drop so fast – and the Black eye – and the Blue eye – and a Brown – I know – hold their lashes full – Part – will go to see you – I cannot tell how many – now – It's too hard – to plan – yet – and Susan's little "Flask" – *poor* Susan – who doted so on putting it in your own hand –

Dear friend – we meant to make *you* – brave – but moaned – before we thought. If we should play 'twas *Austin* – perhaps we could'nt let *him* go – to do Goodnight – to you – If you'll be sure and get well – we'll try to bear it – If we could only care – the less – it would be so much easier – Your letter, troubled my throat. It gave that little scalding, we could not know the reason for, till we grow far up.

I must do my Goodnight, in *crayon* – I *meant* to – in Red. Love for Mary.

Emily.

MANUSCRIPT: AC. Ink.

PUBLICATION: *L* (1894) 203–204, in part; *LL* 231–232, in part; *L* (1931) 194, in part.

Bowles soon recovered enough to visit Amherst on 5 April, before sailing for Europe in the *China* on the ninth.

260

To T. W. Higginson   *15 April 1862*

Mr Higginson,

Are you too deeply occupied to say if my Verse is alive?

The Mind is so near itself – it cannot see, distinctly – and I have none to ask –

Should you think it breathed – and had you the leisure to tell me, I should feel quick gratitude –

If I make the mistake – that you dared to tell me – would give me sincerer honor – toward you –

I enclose my name – asking you, if you please – Sir – to tell me what is true?

That you will not betray me – it is needless to ask – since Honor is it's own pawn –

MANUSCRIPT: BPL (Higg 50). Ink. Envelope addressed: T. W. Higginson./Worcester./Mass. Postmarked: Amherst Ms Apr 15 1862.

PUBLICATION: *AM* LXVIII (October 1891) 444; *L* (1894) 301; *LL* 238; *L* (1931) 272.

In place of a signature, ED enclosed a card (in its own envelope) on which she wrote her name. This first letter to Higginson, which begins a correspondence that lasted until the month of her death, she wrote because she had just read his "Letter to a Young Contributor," the lead article in the *Atlantic Monthly* for April, offering practical advice to beginning writers. She also enclosed four poems: "Safe in their Alabaster Chambers," "The nearest Dream recedes unrealized," "We play at Paste," and "I'll tell you how the Sun rose." When Higginson first published the letter (in the first publication named above), he introduced it by saying: "On April 16, 1862, I took from the post office in Worcester, Mass., where I was then living, the following letter."

To T. W. Higginson   *25 April 1862*

Mr Higginson,

Your kindness claimed earlier gratitude – but I was ill – and write today, from my pillow.

Thank you for the surgery – it was not so painful as I supposed. I bring you others – as you ask – though they might not differ –

While my thought is undressed – I can make the distinction, but when I put them in the Gown – they look alike, and numb.

You asked how old I was? I made no verse – but one or two – until this winter – Sir –

I had a terror – since September – I could tell to none – and so I sing, as the Boy does by the Burying Ground – because I am afraid – You inquire my Books – For Poets – I have Keats – and Mr and Mrs Browning. For Prose – Mr Ruskin – Sir Thomas Browne – and the Revelations. I went to school – but in your manner of the phrase – had no education. When a little Girl, I had a friend, who taught me Immortality – but venturing too near, himself – he never returned – Soon after, my Tutor, died – and for several years, my Lexicon – was my only companion – Then I found one more – but he was not contented I be his scholar – so he left the Land.

You ask of my Companions Hills – Sir – and the Sundown – and a Dog – large as myself, that my Father bought me – They are better than Beings – because they know – but do not tell – and the noise in the Pool, at Noon – excels my Piano. I have a Brother and Sister – My Mother does not care for thought – and Father, too busy with his Briefs – to notice what we do – He buys me many Books – but begs me not to read them – because he fears they joggle the Mind. They are religious – except me – and address an Eclipse, every morning – whom they call their "Father." But I fear my story fatigues you – I would like to learn – Could you tell me how to grow – or is it unconveyed – like Melody – or Witchcraft?

You speak of Mr Whitman – I never read his Book – but was told that he was disgraceful –

I read Miss Prescott's "Circumstance," but it followed me, in the Dark – so I avoided her –

Two Editors of Journals came to my Father's House, this winter –

and asked me for my Mind – and when I asked them "Why," they said I was penurious – and they, would use it for the World –

I could not weigh myself – Myself –

My size felt small – to me – I read your Chapters in the Atlantic – and experienced honor for you – I was sure you would not reject a confiding question –

Is this – Sir – what you asked me to tell you?

Your friend,
E – Dickinson.

MANUSCRIPT: BPL (Higg 51). Ink. Envelope addressed: T. W. Higginson./Worcester./Mass. Postmarked: Amherst Ms Apr 26 1862.

PUBLICATION: *AM* LXVIII (Oct. 1891) 445–446; *L* (1894) 301–303; LL 238–240; *L* (1931) 272–274.

Higginson says in his *Atlantic Monthly* article introducing the letter (cited above) that the enclosed poems were two: "Your riches taught me poverty," and "A bird came down the walk." But the evidence after study of the folds in the letters and poems suggest that he was in error. The enclosures seem to have been: "There came a Day at Summer's full," "Of all the Sounds despatched abroad," and "South Winds jostle them." Harriet Prescott Spofford's "Circumstance" was published in the *Atlantic Monthly* for May 1860. Higginson's "Letter to a Young Contributor" quotes Ruskin and cites Sir Thomas Browne for vigor of style. The article's comment on "what a delicious prolonged perplexity it is to cut and contrive a decent *clothing of words* . . ." may explain ED's phrase "While my thought is undressed." The friend who taught her "Immortality" has generally been thought to be Benjamin Franklin Newton. The two editors who recently had asked her for her mind may have been Bowles and Holland.

Though ED frequently refers to the Brownings, she never again mentions Ruskin, and Keats but twice (see letters no. 1018 and 1034).

262

To Mrs. Samuel Bowles   *spring 1862*

Dear Mary –

When the Best is gone – I know that other things are not of consequence – The Heart wants what it wants – or else it does not care –

You wonder why I write – so – Because I cannot help – I like to have you know some care – so when your life gets faint for it's other life – you can lean on us – We wont break, Mary. We look very small – but the Reed can carry weight.

Not to see what we love, is very terrible – and talking – does'nt ease it – and nothing does – but just itself.

The Eyes and Hair, we chose – are all there are – to us – Is'nt it so – Mary?

I often wonder how the love of Christ, is done – when that – below – holds – so –

I hope the little "Robert" coos away the pain – Perhaps your flowers, help – some –

Vinnie and Sue, are making Hot beds – but then, the Robins plague them so – they dont accomplish much –

The Frogs sing sweet – today – They have such pretty – lazy – times – how nice, to be a Frog! Sue – draws her little Boy – pleasant days – in a Cab – and Carlo – walks behind, accompanied by a Cat – from each establishment –

It looks funny to see so small a man, going out of Austin's House – Mother sends her love to you – She has a sprained foot – and can go, but little, in the House, and not abroad – at all. Dont dishearten – Mary – We'll keep thinking – of you – Kisses for all.

Emily.

Manuscript: AC. Ink.

Publication: L (1894) 204–205, in part; LL 232–233, in part; L (1931) 195, in part.

Samuel Bowles was abroad. ED continued to maintain the fiction that the infant Charles will be (or has been) named Robert. Ned Dickinson, the "small man," was less than a year old. It was not long before this letter was written that ED probably wrote the poem beginning "I'm Nobody," containing the lines "How dreary – to be – Somebody!/How public – like a Frog."

263

To Louise Norcross   *early May 1862*

When you can leave your little children, Loo, you must tell us all you know about dear Myra's going, so sudden, and shocking to us all, we are only bewildered and cannot believe the telegrams. I want so much to see you, and ask you what it means, and why this young life's sacrifice should come so soon, and not far off. I wake in the morning saying "Myra, no more Myra in this world," and the thought of that young face in the dark, makes the whole so sorrowful, I cover my face with the blanket, so the robins' singing cannot get through – I had rather not hear it. Was Myra willing to leave us all? I want so much to know if it was very hard, husband and babies and big life and sweet home by the sea. I should think she would rather have stayed. . . . She came to see us first in May. I remember her frock, and how prettily she fixed her hair, and she and Vinnie took long walks, and got home to tea at sundown; and now remembering is all there is, and no more Myra. I wish 'twas plainer, Loo, the anguish in this world. I wish one could be sure the suffering had a loving side. The thought to look down some day, and see the crooked steps we came, from a safer place, must be a precious thing. . . .

Loo, you are a dear child to go to Uncle Joel, and all will thank you, who love him. We will remember you every day, and the little children, and make a picture to ourself, of the small mamma. . . . Father and Vinnie would have gone immediately to Lynn, but got the telegram too late. Tell Uncle they wanted to. But what can Emily say? Their Father in Heaven remember them and her.

MANUSCRIPT: destroyed.
PUBLICATION: L (1894) 244–245; L (1931) 226.
Lamira, wife of Joel W. Norcross, died on 3 May 1862, at Lynn. Loo is taking care of her uncle's children.

264

To Louise and Frances Norcross   *late May 1862*

My little girls have alarmed me so that notwithstanding the comfort of Austin's assurance that "they will come," I am still hopeless and scared, and regard Commencement as some vast anthropic bear, ordained to eat me up. What made 'em scare 'em so? Didn't they know Cousin Aspen couldn't stand alone? I remember a tree in McLean Street, when you and we were a little girl, whose leaves went topsy-turvy as often as a wind, and showed an ashen side – that's fright, that's Emily. Loo and Fanny were that wind, and the poor leaf, who? Won't they stop a'blowing? . . . Commencement would be a dreary spot without my double flower, that sows itself and just comes up when Emily seeks it most. Austin gives excellent account, I trust not overdrawn. "Health and aspect admirable, and lodgings very fine." Says the rooms were marble, even to the flies. Do they dwell in Carrara? Did they find the garden in the gown? Should have sent a farm, but feared for our button-hole. Hope to hear favorable news on receipt of this. Please give date of coming, so we might prepare our heart.

Emily.

MANUSCRIPT: destroyed.
PUBLICATION: L (1894) 245–246; L (1931) 227.
Louise arrived in Amherst on 10 June. Commencement was held on 10 July.

265

To T. W. Higginson   *7 June 1862*

Dear friend.

Your letter gave no Drunkenness, because I tasted Rum before – Domingo comes but once – yet I have had few pleasures so deep as your opinion, and if I tried to thank you, my tears would block my tongue –

My dying Tutor told me that he would like to live till I had been a poet, but Death was much of Mob as I could master – then – And when far afterward – a sudden light on Orchards, or a new fashion in the wind troubled my attention – I felt a palsy, here – the Verses just relieve –

Your second letter surprised me, and for a moment, swung – I had not supposed it. Your first – gave no dishonor, because the True – are not ashamed – I thanked you for your justice – but could not drop the Bells whose jingling cooled my Tramp – Perhaps the Balm, seemed better, because you bled me, first.

I smile when you suggest that I delay "to publish" – that being foreign to my thought, as Firmament to Fin –

If fame belonged to me, I could not escape her – if she did not, the longest day would pass me on the chase – and the approbation of my Dog, would forsake me – then – My Barefoot-Rank is better –

[408]

You think my gait "spasmodic" – I am in danger – Sir –
You think me "uncontrolled" – I have no Tribunal.

Would you have time to be the "friend" you should think I need? I have a little shape – it would not crowd your Desk – nor make much Racket as the Mouse, that dents your Galleries –

If I might bring you what I do – not so frequent to trouble you – and ask you if I told it clear – 'twould be control, to me –

The Sailor cannot see the North – but knows the Needle can –

The "hand you stretch me in the Dark," I put mine in, and turn away – I have no Saxon, now –

> As if I asked a common Alms,
> And in my wondering hand
> A Stranger pressed a Kingdom,
> And I, bewildered, stand –
> As if I asked the Orient
> Had it for me a Morn –
> And it should lift it's purple Dikes,
> And shatter me with Dawn!

But, will you be my Preceptor, Mr Higginson?

Your friend
E Dickinson –

MANUSCRIPT: BPL (Higg 52). Ink. Envelope addressed: T. W. Higginson./Worcester./Mass. Postmarked: Amherst Ms Jun 7 1862.

PUBLICATION: AM LXVIII (Oct. 1891) 447; L (1894) 303–304; LL 240–241; L (1931) 274–275.

The phrase "I have no Saxon" means "Language fails me": see *Poems* (1955) 197, where in poem no. 276 she offers "English language" as her alternative for "Saxon." She enclosed no poems in this letter.

266

To Samuel Bowles   *early summer 1862*

Dear friend –

You go away – and where you go, we cannot come – but then the Months have names – and each one comes but once a year – and though it seems they never could, they sometimes do – go by.

We hope you are more well, than when you lived in America – and that those Foreign people are kind, and true, to you. We hope you recollect each life you left behind, even our's, the least –

We wish we knew how Amherst looked, in your memory. Smaller than it did, maybe – and yet things swell, by leaving – if big in themselves – We hope you will not alter, but be the same we grieved for, when the "China" sailed. If you should like to hear the news, we did not die – here – We did not change. We have the Guests we did, except yourself – and the Roses hang on the same stems – as before you went. Vinnie trains the Honeysuckle – and the Robins steal the string for Nests – quite, quite as they used to – I have the errand from my heart – I might forget to tell it. Would you please to come Home? The long life's years are scant, and fly away, the Bible says, like a told story – and sparing is a solemn thing, somehow, it seems to me – and I grope fast, with my fingers, for all out of my sight I own – to get it nearer –

I had one letter from Mary – I think she tries to be patient – but you would'nt want her to succeed, would you, Mr Bowles?

It's fragrant news, to know they pine, when we are out of sight. It is most Commencement. The little Cousin from Boston, has come, and the Hearts in Pelham, have an added thrill. We shall miss you, most, dear friend, who annually smiled with us, at the Gravities. I question, if even Dr Vaill, have his wonted applause.

Should anybody where you go, talk of Mrs. Browning, you must hear for us – and if you touch her Grave, put one hand on the Head, for me – her unmentioned Mourner –

Father and Mother, and Vinnie, and Carlo, send their love to you, and warm wish for your health – and I am taking lessons in prayer, so to coax God to keep you safe – Good night – dear friend. You sleep so far, how can I know you hear?

Emily.

MANUSCRIPT: AC. Ink. Envelope addressed (in pencil): Mr Bowles. PUBLICATION: L (1894) 205–207; LL 233–234; L (1931) 195–196.

This letter must have been sent to someone, perhaps Mary Bowles, to be forwarded to Samuel Bowles, still abroad. It was written after the arrival of Louise Norcross in June, and before commencement, in July. Bowles customarily attended the "Gravities," and himself wrote the account annually for the *Republican*.

To Louise and Frances Norcross   *mid-July 1862*

. . . Just a word for my children, before the mails shut. Loo left a tumbler of sweet-peas on the green room bureau. I am going to leave them there till they make pods and sow themselves in the upper drawer, and then I guess they'll blossom about Thanksgiving time. There was a thunder-shower here Saturday at car-time, and Emily was glad her little ones had gone before the hail and rain, lest it frighten them. . . . We wish the visit had just begun instead of ending now; next time we'll leave "the mountains" out, and tell good Dr. Gregg to recommend the orchards. I defrauded Loo of 1 spool of thread; we will "settle," however – and Fanny's ruff is set high in my book of remembrance. They must be good children and recollect, as they agreed, and grow so strong in health that Emily won't know them when they show again. . . . Such a purple morning – even to the morning-glory that climbs the cherry-tree. The cats desire love to Fanny.

                                                              Emily.

MANUSCRIPT: destroyed.
PUBLICATION:L (1894) 246; L (1931) 227–228.
Both the Norcross girls were present for commencement, and left Amherst shortly thereafter.

268

To T. W. Higginson   *July 1862*

Could you believe me – without? I had no portrait, now, but am small, like the Wren, and my Hair is bold, like the Chestnut Bur – and my eyes, like the Sherry in the Glass, that the Guest leaves – Would this do just as well?

It often alarms Father – He says Death might occur, and he has Molds of all the rest – but has no Mold of me, but I noticed the Quick wore off those things, in a few days, and forestall the dishonor – You will think no caprice of me –

You said "Dark." I know the Butterfly – and the Lizard – and the Orchis –

Are not those *your* Countrymen?

I am happy to be your scholar, and will deserve the kindness, I cannot repay.

If you truly consent, I recite, now –

Will you tell me my fault, frankly as to yourself, for I had rather wince, than die. Men do not call the surgeon, to commend – the Bone, but to set it, Sir, and fracture within, is more critical. And for this, Preceptor, I shall bring you – Obedience – the Blossom from my Garden, and every gratitude I know. Perhaps you smile at me. I could not stop for that – My Business is Circumference – An ignorance, not of Customs, but if caught with the Dawn – or the Sunset see me – Myself the only Kangaroo among the Beauty, Sir, if you please, it afflicts me, and I thought that instruction would take it away.

Because you have much business, beside the growth of me – you will appoint, yourself, how often I shall come – without your inconvenience. And if at any time – you regret you received me, or I prove a different fabric to that you supposed – you must banish me –

When I state myself, as the Representative of the Verse – it does not mean – me – but a supposed person. You are true, about the "perfection."

Today, makes Yesterday mean.

You spoke of Pippa Passes – I never heard anybody speak of Pippa Passes – before.

You see my posture is benighted.

To thank you, baffles me. Are you perfectly powerful? Had I a pleasure you had not, I could delight to bring it.

Your Scholar

MANUSCRIPT: BPL (Higg 54), dated by Higginson: July 1862. Ink. Envelope addressed: T. W. Higginson/Princeton/Massachusetts. Postmarked: Jul [?] 1862.

PUBLICATION: AM LXVIII (Oct. 1891) 447–448; L (1894), 305–306; LL 241–243; L (1931) 276–277.

"Pippa Passes," the first of the series in Browning's "Bells and Pomegranates," had been published in 1841. The letter enclosed four poems: "Of Tribulation these are they," "Your Riches taught me poverty," "Some keep the Sabbath going to Church," and "Success is counted sweetest."

To Dr. and Mrs. J. G. Holland   *summer 1862?*

Dear Friends,

I write to you. I receive no letter.

I say "they dignify my trust." I do not disbelieve. I go again. *Cardinals* wouldn't do it. Cockneys wouldn't do it, but I can't *stop* to strut, in a world where bells toll. I hear through visitor in town, that "Mrs. Holland is not strong." The little peacock in me, tells me not to inquire again. Then I remember my tiny friend – how brief she is – how dear she is, and the peacock quite dies away. Now, you need not speak, for perhaps you are weary, and "Herod" requires all your thought, but if you are *well* – let Annie draw me a little picture of an erect flower; if you are *ill*, she can hang the flower a little on one side!

Then, I shall understand, and you need not stop to write me a letter. Perhaps you laugh at me! Perhaps the whole United States are laughing at me too! *I* can't stop for that! *My* business is to love. I found a bird, this morning, down – down – on a little bush at the foot of the garden, and wherefore sing, I said, since nobody *hears?*

One sob in the throat, one flutter of bosom – "*My* business is to *sing*" – and away she rose! How do I know but cherubim, once, themselves, as patient, listened, and applauded her unnoticed hymn?

Emily.

MANUSCRIPT: missing.

PUBLICATION: L (1894) 175–176; L (1931) 169; LH 55–56: dated (presumably by ED): Friday.

This letter is dated by conjecture only. Mrs. Ward, though placing it with a question mark in 1859 (in LH), now feels that 1862 is perhaps more likely. The evidence for the later date is in the phrase "in a world where bells toll" – suggesting the war period, and especially in the sentences: "Perhaps you laugh at me! . . . *I* can't stop for that! *My* business is to love . . . *My* business is to *sing*." The juxtaposition of the sentences closely follows that in the preceding letter to Higginson: "Perhaps you smile at me. I could not stop for that – My Business is Circumference." It was in 1862 that ED indeed felt that her business was to sing.

Bulwer-Lytton's widely popular drama *Richelieu* (1839) might account for ED's opinion of cardinals, and Emerson's *English Traits* (1856) could be the source of her opinion of "cockney conceit." In context, "Herod" seems to personify the persecution of illness. Annie was ten years old in the summer of 1862.

This letter asking to hear from the Hollands, if it belongs here, is the only surviving message to them between 1860 and 1865 (see nos. 227 and 311).

270

To Eudocia C. Flynt   *about 20 July 1862*

Dear Mrs Flint

You and I, did'nt finish talking. Have you room for the sequel, in your Vase?

> All the letters I could write,
> Were not fair as this –
> Syllables of Velvet –
> Sentences of Plush –
> Depths of Ruby, undrained –
> Hid, Lip, for Thee,
> Play it were a Humming Bird
> And sipped just Me –
>
> > Emily.

MANUSCRIPT: YUL. Ink.
PUBLICATION: *Yale University Library Gazette* VI (1931) 43.
Eudocia Flynt's diary (see letter no. 226) records her visit to Amherst at commencement, 10 July, and her receipt of this letter on 21 July: "Had a letter from Emily Dickinson! ! ! !"

271

To T. W. Higginson   *August 1862*

Dear friend –

Are these more orderly? I thank you for the Truth –

I had no Monarch in my life, and cannot rule myself, and when I try to organize – my little Force explodes – and leaves me bare and charred –

[414]

I think you called me "Wayward." Will you help me improve?

I suppose the pride that stops the Breath, in the Core of Woods, is not of Ourself –

You say I confess the little mistake, and omit the large – Because I can see Orthography – but the Ignorance out of sight – is my Preceptor's charge –

Of "shunning Men and Women" – they talk of Hallowed things, aloud – and embarrass my Dog – He and I dont object to them, if they'll exist their side. I think Carl[o] would please you – He is dumb, and brave – I think you would like the Chestnut Tree, I met in my walk. It hit my notice suddenly – and I thought the Skies were in Blossom –

Then there's a noiseless noise in the Orchard – that I let persons hear – You told me in one letter, you could not come to see me, "now," and I made no answer, not because I had none, but did not think myself the price that you should come so far –

I do not ask so large a pleasure, lest you might deny me –

You say "Beyond your knowledge." You would not jest with me, because I believe you – but Preceptor – you cannot mean it? All men say "What" to me, but I thought it a fashion –

When much in the Woods as a little Girl, I was told that the Snake would bite me, that I might pick a poisonous flower, or Goblins kidnap me, but I went along and met no one but Angels, who were far shyer of me, than I could be of them, so I hav'nt that confidence in fraud which many exercise.

I shall observe your precept – though I dont understand it, always.

I marked a line in One Verse – because I met it after I made it – and never consciously touch a paint, mixed by another person –

I do not let go it, because it is mine.

Have you the portrait of Mrs Browning? Persons sent me three – If you had none, will you have mine?

Your Scholar –

MANUSCRIPT: BPL (Higg 55). Ink.

PUBLICATION: AM LXVIII (October 1891) 448–449; L (1894) 307–309; LL 243–244; L (1931) 277–278.

With this letter ED enclosed two poems: "Before I got my Eye put out," and "I cannot dance upon my Toes."

To Samuel Bowles   *about August 1862*

Dear Mr Bowles.

Vinnie is trading with a Tin peddler – buying Water pots for me to sprinkle Geraniums with – when you get Home, next Winter, and Vinnie and Sue, have gone to the War.

Summer a'nt so long as it was, when we stood looking at it, before you went away, and when I finish August, we'll hop the Autumn, very soon – and then 'twill be Yourself. I dont know how many will be glad to see you, because I never saw your whole friends, but I have heard, that in large Cities – noted persons chose you. Though how glad those I know – will be, is easier told.

I tell you, Mr Bowles, it is a Suffering, to have a sea – no care how Blue – between your Soul, and you. The Hills you used to love when you were in Northampton, miss their old lover, could they speak – and the puzzled look – deepens in Carlo's forehead, as Days go by, and you never come.

I've learned to read the Steamer place – in Newspapers – now. It's 'most like shaking hands, with you – or more like your ringing at the door, when Sue says you will call.

We reckon – your coming by the Fruit.

When the Grape gets by – and the Pippin, and the Chestnut – when the Days are a little short by the clock – and a little long by the want – when the sky has new Red Gowns – and a Purple Bonnet – then we say, you will come – I am glad that kind of time, goes by.

It is easier to look behind at a pain, than to see it coming. A Soldier called – a Morning ago, and asked for a Nosegay, to take to Battle. I suppose he thought we kept an Aquarium.

How sweet it must be to one to come Home – whose Home is in so many Houses – and every Heart a "Best Room." I mean you, Mr Bowles.

Sue gave me the paper, to write on – so when the writing tires you – play it is Her, and "Jackey" – and that will rest your eyes – for have not the Clovers, *names*, to the Bees?

                                                              Emily.

MANUSCRIPT: AC. Ink.

PUBLICATION: *L* (1894) 207–208, in part; *LL* 234–235, in part; *L* (1931) 197–198, in part.
The stationery, on which ED comments, is especially lightweight, intended for overseas correspondence. Bowles remained in Europe until November. "Jackey" was the nickname for Ned, used by his parents when he was a baby. ED's identification with issues of the day was slight throughout her life. Her remark about the soldier here is one of her relatively few comments on any aspect of the Civil War.

273

To Louise and Frances Norcross   *1862?*

. . . Uncle told us you were too busy. Fold your little hands – the heart is the only workman we cannot excuse.

. . . Gratitude is not the mention of a tenderness, but its mute appreciation, deeper than we reach – all our LORD demands, who sizes better knows than we. Willing unto death, if only we perceive He die.

MANUSCRIPT: destroyed.
PUBLICATION: *L* (1894) 241; *L* (1931) 224.
The date given by Mrs. Todd, 29 December 1861, was probably supplied by Frances Norcross. "Uncle" refers to the girls' father, Loring Norcross, who died 17 January 1863. The extracts are from a letter (or letters) written before that date.

274

To T. W. Higginson   *6 October 1862*

Did I displease you, Mr Higginson?
But wont you tell me how?

Your friend,
E. Dickinson –

MANUSCRIPT: BPL (Higg 53). Ink. Envelope addressed: T. W. Higginson./Worcester./Mass. Postmarked: Amherst Mass Oct 6 1862.
PUBLICATION: *AM* LXVIII (Oct. 1891) 450; *L* (1931) 290.

In *AM* Higginson introduces the letter with the comment: "Sometimes there would be a long pause, on my part, after which would come a plaintive letter, always terse, like this."

275

To Samuel Bowles   *mid-November 1862*

Dear friend.

Had We the Art like You – to endow so many, by just recovering our Health, 'twould give us tender pride – nor could we keep the news – but carry it to you – who seem to us to own it most.

So few that live – have life – it seems of quick importance – not one of those – escape by Death. And since you gave us Fear – Congratulate us – for Ourselves – you give us safer – Peace.

How extraordinary that Life's large Population contain so few of power to us – and those – a vivid species – who leave no mode – like Tyrian Dye.

Remembering these Minorities – permit our gratitude for you – We ask that you be cautious – for many sakes – excelling Our's. To recapitulate the Stars – were useless as supreme. Yourself is Your's – dear friend – but ceded – is it not – to here and there a minor Life? Do not defraud These – for Gold – may be bought – and Purple – may be bought – but the sale of the Spirit – never did occur.

Do not yet work. No Public so exorbitant of Any – as it's Friend – and we can wait your Health.

Besides – there is an idleness – more Tonic than Toil.

<blockquote>
The loss by Sickness – was it loss –
Or that Etherial Gain –
You earned by measuring the Grave –
Then – measuring the Sun.
</blockquote>

Be sure, dear friend, for Want – you have Estates of Lives.

Emily.

MANUSCRIPT: AC. Ink.
PUBLICATION: *L* (1894) 209–210; *LL* 236–237; *L* (1931) 199.
The letter seems to be a greeting written to Bowles after his return from

[418]

Europe on 17 November 1862. The quatrain at the end of the letter is the concluding stanza of the poem beginning "My first well Day – since many ill."

276

To Samuel Bowles   *late November 1862*

Dear friend

I cannot see you. You will not less believe me. That you return to us alive, is better than a Summer. And more to hear your voice below, than News of any Bird.

Emily.

MANUSCRIPT: AC. Pencil.
PUBLICATION: L (1894) 207; LL 234; L (1931) 197.
Bowles paid a call after his return from Europe, but ED, finding herself unable to see him, sent this brief note downstairs.

277

To Samuel Bowles   *late November 1862*

Dear friend.

I did not need the little Bat – to enforce your memory – for that can stand alone, like the best Brocade – but it was much – that far and ill, you recollected me – Forgive me if I prize the Grace – superior to the Sign. Because I did not see you, Vinnie and Austin, upbraided me – They did not know I gave my part that they might have the more – but then the Prophet had no fame in his immediate Town – My Heart led all the rest – I think that what we *know* – we can endure that others doubt, until their faith be riper. And so, dear friend, who knew me, I make no argument – to you –

Did I not want to see you? Do not the Phebes want to come? Oh They of little faith! I said I was glad that you were alive – Might it bear repeating? Some phrases are too fine to fade – and Light but just confirms them – Few absences could seem so wide as your's has done,

[419]

to us – If 'twas a larger face – or we a smaller Canvas – we need not know – now you have come –

We hope often to see you – Our poverty – entitle us – and friends are nations in themselves – to supersede the Earth –

'Twould please us, were you well – and could your health be had by sacrifice of ours – 'twould be contention for the place – We used to tell each other, when you were from America – how failure in a Battle – were easier – and you here – I will not tell you further –

Perhaps you tire – now – A small weight – is obnoxious – upon a weary Rope – but had you Exile – or Eclipse – or so huge a Danger, as would dissolve all other friends – 'twould please me to remain –

Let others – show this Surry's Grace –
Myself – assist his Cross.

Emily –

MANUSCRIPT: Hooker. Ink. Unpublished.

This letter closely followed the note which precedes it. The allusion to brocade that stands alone was probably suggested by a sentence in George Eliot's *The Mill on the Floss* (chapter 12), recently published (1860), which ED was perhaps now reading: "Mrs. Glegg . . . had inherited from her grandmother . . . a brocaded gown that would stand up empty, like a suit of armour. . ." (see also letter no. 368). Henry Howard, earl of Surrey (1517–1547), the first English writer of blank verse, was accused of high treason, tried before a packed jury, and beheaded.

278

To Louise and Frances Norcross   *late January 1863*

What shall I tell these darlings except that my father and mother are half their father and mother, and my home half theirs, whenever, and for as long as, they will. And sometimes a dearer thought than that creeps into my mind, but it is not for to-night. Wasn't dear papa so tired always after mamma went, and wasn't it almost sweet to think of the two together these new winter nights? The grief is our side, darlings, and the glad is theirs. Vinnie and I sit down to-night, while mother tells what makes us cry, though we know it is well and easy

with uncle and papa, and only our part hurts. Mother tells how gently
he looked on all who looked at him – how he held his bouquet sweet,
as he were a guest in a friend's parlor and must still do honor. The
meek, mild gentleman who thought no harm, but peace toward all.

Vinnie intended to go, but the day was cold, and she wanted to
keep Uncle Loring as she talked with him, always, instead of this
new way. She thought too, for the crowd, she could not see you, children, and she would be another one to give others care. Mother said
Mr. V[aill], yes, dears, even Mr. V[aill], at whom we sometimes
smile, talked about "Lorin' and Laviny" and his friendship towards
them, to your father's guests. We won't smile at him any more now,
will we? Perhaps he'll live to tell some gentleness of us, who made
merry of him.

But never mind that now. When you have strength, tell us how
it is, and what we may do for you, of comfort, or of service. Be sure
you crowd all others out, precious little cousins. Good-night. Let Emily
sing for you because she cannot pray:

> It is not dying hurts us so, –
> 'Tis living hurts us more;
> But dying is a different way,
> A kind, behind the door, –
> The southern custom of the bird
> That soon as frosts are due
> Adopts a better latitude.
> We are the birds that stay,
> The shiverers round farmers' doors,
> For whose reluctant crumb
> We stipulate, till pitying snows
> Persuade our feathers home.

Emily.

MANUSCRIPT: destroyed.
PUBLICATION: *L* (1894) 250–251; *LL* 252–253; *L* (1931) 228–229.

The girls were orphaned by the death of their father, Loring Norcross,
on 17 January 1863. The service was conducted by the Reverend Joseph
Vaill of Palmer.

To Louise and Frances Norcross   *early February 1863*

So many ask for the children that I must make a separate letter to tell them what they say, and leave my kisses till next time.

Eliza wrote last week, faint note in pencil – dressed in blankets, and propped up, having been so sick – and yet too weak to talk much, even with her slate. She said this of you, I give it in her own words, "Make them know I love them," and added, should have written immediately herself, except for weakness.

Mr. Dwight asks for you in the phrase "Of your sweet cousins." He does not yet know papa is asleep – only very weary.

The milliner at the head of the street wipes her eye for Fanny and Loo, and a tear rumples her ribbons. Mr. and Mrs. Sweetser care – Mrs. Sweetser most tenderly.

. . . Even Dick's wife, simple dame, with a kitchen full, and the grave besides, of little ragged ones, wants to know "more about" you, and follows mother to the door, who has called with bundle.

Dick says, in his wise way, he "shall always be interested in them young ladies." One little young lady of his own, you know, is in Paradise. That makes him tenderer-minded.

Be sure you don't doubt about the sparrow.

Poor H[arriet] and Z[ebina Montague], in their genteel antique way express their sympathy, mixing admiring anecdotes of your father and mother's youth, when they, God help them, were not so sere. Besides these others, children, shall we tell them who else cherish, every day the same, the bright day and the black one too – Could it be Emily?

Would it interest the children to know that crocuses come up, in the garden off the dining-room? and a fuchsia, that pussy partook, mistaking it for strawberries. And that we have primroses – like the little pattern sent in last winter's note – and heliotropes by the aprons full, the mountain colored one – and a jessamine bud, you know the little odor like Lubin – and gilliflowers, magenta, and few mignonette and sweet alyssum bountiful, and carnation buds?

Will it please them to know that the ice-house is filled, to make their tumblers cool next Summer – and once in a while a cream?

And that father has built a new road round the pile of trees between our house and Mr. S[weetser]'s, where they can take the soldier's shirt to make, or a sweet poem, and no man find them, but the fly and he such a little man.

Love dears, from us all, and wont you tell us how you are? We seem to hear so little.

Emily —

MANUSCRIPT: destroyed.
PUBLICATION: L (1894) 252–253; LL 263, in part; L (1931) 229–231.
Eliza Coleman Dudley was recovering from an illness. ED seems still to be in communication with the Reverend Edward S. Dwight. On Dick Matthews, see Appendix 2.

Frances Norcross's transcript of the last five paragraphs is in the Bingham collection (AC), and is here reproduced. Brackets supply names of persons who are indicated in the transcript by initials only.

280

To T. W. Higginson   *February 1863*

Dear friend

I did not deem that Planetary forces annulled – but suffered an Exchange of Territory, or World –

I should have liked to see you, before you became improbable. War feels to me an oblique place – Should there be other Summers, would you perhaps come?

I found you were gone, by accident, as I find Systems are, or Seasons of the year, and obtain no cause – but suppose it a treason of Progress – that dissolves as it goes. Carlo – still remained – and I told him –

Best Gains – must have the Losses' Test –
To constitute them – Gains –

My Shaggy Ally assented –

Perhaps Death – gave me awe for friends – striking sharp and early, for I held them since – in a brittle love – of more alarm, than peace. I trust you may pass the limit of War, and though not reared to prayer – when service is had in Church, for Our Arms, I include yourself – I, too, have an "Island" – whose "Rose and Magnolia" are in the Egg, and

[423]

it's "Black Berry" but a spicy prospective, yet as you say, "fascination" is absolute of Clime. I was thinking, today – as I noticed, that the "Supernatural," was only the Natural, disclosed –

> Not "Revelation" – 'tis – that waits,
> But our unfurnished eyes –

But I fear I detain you –

Should you, before this reaches you, experience immortality, who will inform me of the Exchange? Could you, with honor, avoid Death, I entreat you – Sir – It would bereave

Your Gnome –

I trust the "Procession of Flowers" was not a premonition –

MANUSCRIPT: BPL (Higg 56). Ink. Dated: Amherst.

PUBLICATION: *AM* LXVIII (October 1891) 449; *L* (1894) 309–310, in part; *LL* 248–249, in part; *L* (1931) 278–279, entire.

In the letter ED enclosed "The Soul unto itself." Higginson had gone to South Carolina, in command of a Negro regiment, in November 1862. The *Springfield Republican* carried long items about Higginson and his troops in the issues of 1 January and 6 February 1863. Higginson's "Procession of Flowers" appeared in the December 1862, issue of the *Atlantic Monthly*. He could never explain the reason for the signature. One conjectures that perhaps he had earlier commented on the gnomic quality of her verses.

281

To Louise and Frances Norcross   *late May 1863*

I said I should come "in a day." Emily never fails except for a cause; that you know, dear Loo.

The nights turned hot, when Vinnie had gone, and I must keep no window raised for fear of prowling "booger," and I must shut my door for fear front door slide open on me at the "dead of night," and I must keep "gas" burning to light the danger up, so I could distinguish it – these gave me a snarl in the brain which don't unravel yet, and that old nail in my breast pricked me; these, dear, were my cause. Truth is so best of all I wanted you to know. Vinnie will tell of her visit. . . .

About Commencement, children, I can have no doubt, if you

should fail me then, my little life would fail of itself. Could you only lie in your little bed and smile at me, that would be support. Tell the doctor I am inexorable, besides I shall heal you quicker than he. You need the balsam word. And who is to cut the cake, ask Fanny, and chirp to those trustees? Tell me, dears, by the coming mail, that you will not fail me. . . .

Jennie Hitchcock's mother was buried yesterday, so there is one orphan more, and her father is very sick besides. My father and mother went to the service, and mother said while the minister prayed, a hen with her chickens came up, and tried to fly into the window. I suppose the dead lady used to feed them, and they wanted to bid her good-by.

Life is death we're lengthy at, death the hinge to life.

Love from all,

Emily.

MANUSCRIPT: destroyed.
PUBLICATION: L (1894) 246–247; LL 249–250; L (1931) 231.
Professor Edward Hitchcock's wife died on 26 May 1863.

282

To T. W. Higginson   *about 1863*

Dear friend –

You were so generous to me, that if possible I offended you, I could not too deeply apologize.

To doubt my High Behavior, is a new pain – I could be honorable no more – till I asked you about it. I know not what to deem myself – Yesterday "Your Scholar" – but might I be the one you tonight, forgave, 'tis a Better Honor – Mine is but just the Thief's Request –

Please, Sir, Hear

"Barabbas" –

The possibility to pass
Without a Moment's Bell –
Into Conjecture's presence –
Is like a face of steel

[425]

That suddenly looks into our's
With a Metallic Grin –
The Cordiality of Death
Who Drills his welcome – in –

_____

MANUSCRIPT: BPL (Higg 58). Ink. Dated: Amherst.
PUBLICATION: L (1894) 311; LL 266; L (1931) 281.
Higginson dated the letter "1865?," but the handwriting is clearly earlier. The poem with which the letter concludes is the second stanza of "That after Horror – that 'twas *us*." For "the Thief's Request," see letter no. 195.

283

To Samuel Bowles   *about* 1863

The Zeroes – taught us – Phosphorus –
We learned to like the Fire
By playing Glaciers – when a Boy –
And Tinder – guessed – by power
Of Opposite – to balance Odd –
If White – a Red – must be!
Paralysis – our Primer – dumb –
Unto Vitality!

I could'nt let Austin's note go – without a word –

Emily.

MANUSCRIPT: AC. Ink.
PUBLICATION: L (1894) 200; LL 227; L (1931) 191; *Poems* (1955) 532.
The date is conjectured from the handwriting.

284

To Samuel Bowles   *autumn* 1863

Mother never asked a favor of Mr Bowles before – that He accept from Her the little Barrel of Apples –

[426]

"Sweet Apples" – She exhorts me – with an occasional Baldwin –
for Mary, and the squirrels

Emily

MANUSCRIPT: missing. The text reproduces the facsimile published in
Letters (1894). Dated: Saturday.
PUBLICATION: L (1894) 217, with facsimile; LL 255; L (1931) 204.
The date is conjectured from the handwriting.

285

To Louise and Frances Norcross   *7 October 1863*

Dear Children,

Nothing has happened but loneliness, perhaps too daily to relate.
Carlo is consistent, has asked for nothing to eat or drink, since you
went away. Mother thinks him a model dog, and conjectures what
he might have been, had not Vinnie "demoralized" him. Margaret
objects to furnace heat on account of bone decrepitudes, so I dwell in
my bonnet and suffer comfortably. . . .

Miss Kingman called last evening to inspect your garden; I gave
her a lanthorn, and she went out, and thanks you very much. No one
has called so far, but one old lady to look at a house. I directed her to
the cemetery to spare expense of moving.

I got down before father this morning, and spent a few moments
profitably with the South Sea rose. Father detecting me, advised wiser
employment, and read at devotions the chapter of the gentleman with
one talent. I think he thought my conscience would adjust the gender.

Margaret washed to-day, and accused Vinnie of calicoes. I put her
shoe and bonnet in to have them nice when she got home. I found
a milliner's case in Miss N[orcross]'s wardrobe, and have opened business. I have removed a geranium leaf, and supplied a lily in Vinnie's
parlor vase. The sweet-peas are unchanged. Cattle-show is to-morrow.
The coops and committees are passing now. . . . They are picking
the Baldwin apples. Be good children, and mind the vicar. Tell me
precisely how Wakefield looks, since I go not myself.

Emily.

[427]

MANUSCRIPT: destroyed.
PUBLICATION: L (1894) 248–249; LL 250–251; L (1931) 232, dated (presumably by ED): Wednesday.
The Cattle Show in 1863 took place on 8–9 October, but the sisters did not stay for it. ED may mean by "the South Sea rose" that she is reading Melville's *Typee*.

286

To Louise and Frances Norcross mid-October 1863?

. . . I should be wild with joy to see my little lovers. The writing them is not so sweet as their two faces that seem so small way off, and yet have been two weeks from me – two wishful, wandering weeks. Now, I begin to doubt if they ever came.

I bid the stiff "good-night" and the square "good-morning" to the lingering guest, I finish mama's sacque, all but the overcasting – that fatal sacque, you recollect. I pick up tufts of mignonette, and sweet alyssum for winter, dim as winter seems these red and gold, and ribbon days.

I am sure I feel as Noah did, docile, but somewhat sceptic, under the satinet.

No frost at our house yet. Thermometer frost, I mean. Mother had a new tooth Saturday. You know Dr. S[tratton] had promised her one for a long time. "Teething" didn't agree with her, and she kept her bed, Sunday, with a face that would take a premium at any cattle-show in the land. Came to town next morning with slightly reduced features, but no eye on the left side. Doubtless we are "fearfully and wonderfully made," and occasionally grotesquely.

L[ibbie] goes to Sunderland, Wednesday, for a minute or two; leaves here at 6½ – what a fitting hour – and will breakfast the night before; such a smart atmosphere! The trees stand right up straight when they hear her boots, and will bear crockery wares instead of fruit, I fear. She hasn't starched the geraniums yet, but will have ample time, unless she leaves before April. Emily is very mean, and her children in dark mustn't remember what she says about damsel.

Grateful for little notes, and shall ask for longer when my birds locate. Would it were here. Three sisters are prettier than one. . . Tabby is a continual shrine, and her jaunty ribbons put me in mind of fingers far out at sea. Fanny's admonition made me laugh and cry too. In the hugest haste, and the engine waiting.

Emily.

MANUSCRIPT: destroyed. The text derives from *Letters* (1931), and is checked against the surviving part of the transcript (AC), which ends at "and will bear" in the fifth paragraph, made by Frances Norcross. Mrs. Todd dated it: Autumn, 1863.

PUBLICATION: L (1894) 249–250; LL 251–252; L (1931) 232–233.

Two weeks have passed since the visit of the Norcross sisters, who are looking for a place to board. They had been orphaned by the death of their father in January, and did not have the means to keep up their former home. The description of the person identified as "L" applies most aptly to Edward Dickinson's youngest sister Elizabeth (Libbie), who remained throughout her life a somewhat redoubtable figure, described by ED in letter no. 473 as "the only male relative on the female side." She was still unmarried when this letter was written. (See letter no. 331.)

287

To Susan Gilbert Dickinson   *about 1864*

I could not drink it, Sue,
Till you had tasted first –
Though cooler than the Water – was
The Thoughtfulness of Thirst –

Emily.

MANUSCRIPT: HCL (B 139). Pencil. Addressed on the fold: Sue.
PUBLICATION: FF 270; *Poems* (1955) 619.

The date is conjectured from the handwriting. The note may have accompanied a small gift in acknowledgment of some attention from Sue before ED left home for her eye treatment in April. The nature of the eye affliction is not known. She made a trip to Boston on 4 February 1864 to consult Henry W. Williams, M.D., at 15 Arlington Street. He must have prescribed a course of treatments requiring his supervision, for late in April she went back to stay, remaining until 21 November. During this sojourn of nearly seven months she lived with her Norcross cousins in the boarding house of Mrs. Bangs, at 86 Austin Street, Cambridge (see letter no. 293).

To Susan Gilbert Dickinson   *Cambridge, about 1864*

Sweet Sue –

There is no first, or last, in Forever – It is Centre, there, all the time –

To believe – is enough, and the right of supposing –

Take back that "Bee" and "Buttercup" – I have no Field for them, though for the Woman whom I prefer, Here is Festival – Where my Hands are cut, Her fingers will be found inside –

Our beautiful Neighbor "moved" in May – It leaves an Unimportance.

Take the Key to the Lily, now, and I will lock the Rose –

MANUSCRIPT: HCL (B 56). Pencil.
PUBLICATION: *FF* 267.
The date is conjectured from the handwriting. The friend who "moved" in May has not been identified. This note may have been written soon after ED arrived in Cambridge.

289

To Lavinia N. Dickinson   *Cambridge, about May 1864*

Dear Vinnie,

I miss you most, and I want to go Home and take good care of you and make you happy every day.

The Doctor is not willing yet, and He is not willing I should write. He wrote to Father, himself, because He thought it not best for me.

You wont think it strange any more, will you?

Loo and Fanny take sweet care of me, and let me want for nothing, but I am not at Home, and the calls at the Doctor's are painful, and dear Vinnie, I have not looked at the Spring.

Wont you help me be patient?

I cannot write but this, and send a little flower, and hope you wont forget me, because I want to come so much I cannot make it show.

                                                                Emily.

MANUSCRIPT: AC. Pencil.

PUBLICATION: L (1894) 153; L (1931) 150–151; *Home* 434.
The tone of the letter suggests that it was written shortly after ED arrived in Cambridge, but subsequent to the letter preceding.

Three other letters probably written about this time are nos. 1047, 1048, and 1049.

290

To T. W. Higginson   Cambridge, early June 1864

Dear friend,

Are you in danger –

I did not know that you were hurt. Will you tell me more? Mr Hawthorne died.

I was ill since September, and since April, in Boston, for a Physician's care – He does not let me go, yet I work in my Prison, and make Guests for myself –

Carlo did not come, because that he would die, in Jail, and the Mountains, I could not hold now, so I brought but the Gods –

I wish to see you more than before I failed – Will you tell me your health?

I am surprised and anxious, since receiving your note –

The only News I know
Is Bulletins all day
From Immortality.

Can you render my Pencil?

The Physician has taken away my Pen.

I enclose the address from a letter, lest my figures fail – Knowledge of your recovery – would excel my own –

E – Dickinson

MANUSCRIPT: BPL (Higg 57). Pencil. Endorsed by TWH on last (blank) page: Miss Dickinson/86 Austin St/Cambridgeport/Mass.

PUBLICATION: AM LXVIII (October 1891) 450; L (1894) 310–311; LL 262; L (1931) 280.

Higginson had been wounded in July 1863, and left the army in May 1864. From 10 June until 2 September the Higginsons were at Pigeon Cove; in November they settled at Newport, Rhode Island. Hawthorne died on 19 May 1864.

[431]

To Edward (Ned) Dickinson   *Cambridge, 19 June 1864*

My little Uncle must remember me till I come Home a Hundred miles to see his Braided Gown –

Emily knows a Man who drives a Coach like a Thimble, and turns the Wheel all day with his Heel – His name is Bumblebee. Little Ned will see Him before

His Niece.

Manuscript: HCL (B 16). Pencil.
Publication: LL 57–58, in part.
This was written for Ned on his third birthday. The Amherst dressmaker's account (Jones Library) shows a dress made for him at this time.

292

To Susan Gilbert Dickinson   *Cambridge, June 1864*

Thank Susan for the effort, I shall not mind the Gloves – I knew it was the Bell, and not the Noon, that failed – For caution of my Hat, He says, the Doctor wipes my cheeks, so the Old Thimble will do –

I knew it was "November," but then there is a June when Corn is cut, whose option is within. That is why I prefer the Power – for Power is Glory, when it likes, and Dominion, too –

To include, is to be touchless, for Ourself cannot cease – Hawthorne's interruption does not seem as it did – Noon is Morning's Memoir, and I notice

Manuscript: HCL (B 161). Pencil. The ending is missing.
Publication: FF 231, in part.
For another reference to Hawthorne's death, see letter no. 290.

To Lavinia N. Dickinson   *Cambridge, July 1864*

Dear Vinnie

Many write that they do not write because that they have too

[432]

much to say – I, that I have enough. Do you remember the Whippowil that sang one night on the Orchard fence, and then drove to the South, and we never heard of Him afterward?

He will go Home and I shall go Home, perhaps in the same Train.

It is a very sober thing not to have any Vinnie, and to keep my Summer in strange Towns, what I have not told – but I have found friends in the Wilderness.

You know "Elijah" did, and to see the "Ravens" mending my stockings, would break a Heart long hard – Fanny and Loo are solid Gold, Mrs Bangs and her Daughter very kind, and the Doctor enthusiastic about my getting well – I feel no gayness yet. I suppose I had been discouraged so long.

You remember the Prisoner of Chillon did not know Liberty when it came, and asked to go back to Jail.

Clara and Anna came to see me and brought beautiful flowers. Do you know what made them remember me? I was most surprised. Give them my love and gratitude. They told me about the Day at Pelham, You – dressed in Daisies, and Mr McDonald. I could'nt see you Vinnie. I am glad of all the Roses you find, while your Primrose is gone. How kind Mr Copeland grew.

Was Mr Dudley dear –

Emily wants to be well and with Vinnie – If any one alive wants to get well more, I would let Him first.

I am glad it is me, not Vinnie. Long time might seem further to Her. Give my love to Father and Mother, and Austin. Am so glad His Tobacco is well – I asked Father about it.

Tell Margaret I remember Her, and hope Richard is well.

Dear Vinnie, This is the longest letter I wrote since I was sick, but who needed it most, if not my little Sister? I hope she is not very tired, tonight. How I wish I could rest all those who are tired for me – Big Kiss for Fanny.

Emily.

MANUSCRIPT: AC. Pencil.

PUBLICATION: L (1894) 151–152; LL 256–257; L (1931) 148–149; Home 434–435.

Fanny Norcross was in Amherst for commencement, 15 July. ED has received a visit from Clara and Anna Newman, who made their home at this time with Austin and Susan Dickinson. Vinnie frequently visited

Eliza and John Dudley at Middletown, Connecticut. Melvin B. Copeland, a Middletown businessman, was a friend of Vinnie's. On Mrs. Bangs, see the note in letter no. 287. For another allusion to Elijah and the ravens, see letter no. 326.

294

To Susan Gilbert Dickinson   *Cambridge, September 1864*

At Centre of the Sea –

I am glad Mrs – Gertrude lived – I believed she would – Those that are worthy of Life are of Miracle, for Life is Miracle, and Death, as harmless as a Bee, except to those who run –

It would be best to see you – it would be good to see the Grass, and hear the Wind blow the wide way in the Orchard – Are the Apples ripe – Have the Wild Geese crossed – Did you save the seed to the pond Lily?

Love for Mat, and John, and the Foreigner – And kiss little Ned in the seam in the neck, entirely for Me –

The Doctor is very kind –

I find no Enemy – Till the Four o'Clocks strike Five, Loo will last, she says. Do not cease, Sister. Should I turn in my long night I should murmur "Sue" –

Emily.

MANUSCRIPT: HCL (B 179). Pencil.
PUBLICATION: FF 231 and 266–267, excerpts only.
Susan's friend Gertrude Vanderbilt was accidentally wounded by a gun shot on 20 March 1864. A daughter, Susan Gilbert Smith, was born 8 September 1864 to Susan's sister, Martha Gilbert Smith. The phrase "At Centre of the Sea" forms the last line of the first stanza of the poem beginning "I many times thought Peace had come," written about 1863. This letter may or may not be complete.

295

To Lavinia N. Dickinson   *Cambridge, about 1864*

. . . walk all the way, and sleep in the Bushes at night, but the Doctor says I must tell you that I "cannot yet walk alone" – Thank you all for caring about me when I do no good. I will work with all my might, always, as soon as I get well –

Tell Mother to catch no more cold, and lose her cough, so I cannot find it, when I get Home – Tell Margaret I recollect her, and hope her finger is better – You must not miss Gray Pussy, I'll try to fill her place –

MANUSCRIPT: HCL (B 166). Pencil. Addressed: Vinnie. Unpublished.
The beginning of the letter is wanting. The date is conjectured from the handwriting. The last paragraph seems to respond to details transmitted by Vinnie in a recent letter.

296

To Lavinia N. Dickinson   *Cambridge, November 1864*

Does Vinnie think of Sister? Sweet news. Thank Vinnie.

Emily may not be able as she was, but all she can, she will.

Father told me that you were going. I wept for the little Plants, but rejoiced for you.

Had I loved them as well as I did, I could have begged you to stay with them, but they are Foreigners, now, and all, a Foreigner.

I have been sick so long I do not know the Sun.

I hope they may be alive, for Home would be strange except them, now the World is dead.

Anna Norcross lives here, since Saturday, and two new people more, a person and his wife, so I do little but fly, yet always find a nest.

I shall go Home in two weeks. You will get me at Palmer, yourself. Let no one beside come.

Love for Eliza, and Mr Dudley.

                                        Sister.

MANUSCRIPT: AC. Pencil.
PUBLICATION: L (1894) 153; LL 258; L (1931) 151; *Home* 435.
Vinnie is about to visit Eliza and John Dudley at Middletown, Connecticut. The letter was written about 6 November, for ED returned home on the twenty-first.

To Lavinia N. Dickinson   *Cambridge, 13 November 1864*

. . . Her, when I get Home. The Doctor will let me go Monday of Thanksgiving week. He wants to see me Sunday, so I cannot before. Vinnie will go to Palmer for me certainly?

I took the little Sac to wear in walking, under Cloak, to keep away more cold. I did not think to tell before.

Vinnie will forgive me?

Love for the Middletown Pearls. Shall write Eliza after Tuesday, when I go to the Doctor. Thank her for sweet note.

The Drums keep on for the still Man, but Emily must stop.

Love of Fanny and Loo.

Sister.

MANUSCRIPT: AC. Pencil. The beginning is missing.

PUBLICATION: *L* (1894) 153; *LL* 258; *L* (1931) 151; *Home* 435–436.

Internal evidence clearly places this letter in November 1864, about the thirteenth. Thanksgiving was on the twenty-fourth, and ED returned on Monday the twenty-first. Vinnie at the moment is visiting the Dudleys. The "still Man" seems to be Lincoln, who was reelected on 8 November. The *Boston Post* reported on Monday, 14 November: "The Lincoln Clubs of Cambridge had a torchlight procession last evening, and invited Hon. Samuel Hooper, and were addressed by that gentleman." By "Drums" ED evidently refers to the Cambridge celebration. For a similar reference to *drums*, many years later, see letter no. 950.

298

To Louise and Frances Norcross   1864?

. . . Sorrow seems more general than it did, and not the estate of a few persons, since the war began; and if the anguish of others helped one with one's own, now would be many medicines.

'Tis dangerous to value, for only the precious can alarm. I noticed that Robert Browning had made another poem, and was astonished – till I remembered that I, myself, in my smaller way, sang off charnel steps. Every day life feels mightier, and what we have the power to be, more stupendous.

MANUSCRIPT: destroyed.
PUBLICATION: L (1894) 243–244; LL 229–230; L (1931) 225–226.
This extract is not datable beyond the fact that the opening statement places it later in the War years. Browning's *Dramatis Personae* was published in 1864.

299

To Samuel Bowles   about 1864

Mr Bowles.

Keep the Yorkshire Girls, if you please, with the faith of their friend, and your's.

E.

MANUSCRIPT: AC. Pencil.
PUBLICATION: L (1931) 203.
It will be apparent from the next letter that Bowles returned ED's copy of the Brontë sisters' poems. See the letter written to ED by Thomas Niles, 31 March 1883 (no. 813b), where he too returns a copy of "Currer, Ellis & Acton Bells Poems." It may have been the same copy that she offered Bowles. If the copy survives, it has not been located.

300

To Samuel Bowles   about 1864

Dear friend.

How hard to thank you – but the large Heart requites itself. Please to need me – I wanted to ask you to receive *Mr* Browning – from me – but you denied my Bronte – so I did not dare – Is it too late – now? I should like so much, to remind you – how kind you had been to *me*.

You could choose – as you did before – if it would not be obnoxious – except where you "measured by *your* heart," you should measure – *this* time – by *mine*. I wonder which would be biggest!

Austin told – Saturday morning – that you were not so well. 'Twas Sundown – all day – Saturday – and Sunday – such a long Bridge – no news of you – could cross! Teach us to miss you *less* – because the fear to miss you *more* – haunts us – all the time. We did'nt *care* so much –

once – I wish it was *then – now* – but you kept tightening – so – it cant be *stirred – today* – You did'nt *mean* to be worse – did you? Was'nt it a *mistake?* Wont you decide soon – to be the strong man we first knew? 'Twould *lighten* things – so much – and yet *that* man – was not so dear – I guess you'd better *not.*

We pray for you – every night – a homely shrine – our knee – but Madonna looks at the Heart – first. Dear friend – dont discourage!

Affy, Emily.

MANUSCRIPT: AC. Ink.
PUBLICATION: *L* (1894) 215–216; *LL* 254; *L* (1931) 203–204.
For another reference to Browning, whose *Dramatis Personae* was published in 1864, see letter no. 298.

301

To Louise Norcross   *early 1865?*

Dear Loo,

This is my letter – an ill and peevish thing, but when my eyes get well I'll send you thoughts like daisies, and sentences could hold the bees . . .

MANUSCRIPT: destroyed.
PUBLICATION: *L* (1894) 256; *LL* 265; *L* (1931) 236.
The tone suggests that this letter may have been written about the first of the year.

302

To Louise Norcross   *early 1865*

All that my eyes will let me shall be said for Loo, dear little solid gold girl. I am glad to the foot of my heart that you will go to Middletown. It will make you warm. Touches "from home," tell Gungl, are better than "sounds."

You persuade me to speak of my eyes, which I shunned doing, because I wanted you to rest. I could not bear a single sigh should tarnish your vacation, but, lest through me one bird delay a change of latitude, I will tell you, dear.

The eyes are as with you, sometimes easy, sometimes sad. I think they are not worse, nor do I think them better than when I came home. The snow-light offends them, and the house is bright; notwithstanding, they hope some. For the first few weeks I did nothing but comfort my plants, till now their small green cheeks are covered with smiles. I chop the chicken centres when we have roast fowl, frequent now, for the hens contend and the Cain is slain. . . . Then I make the yellow to the pies, and bang the spice for cake, and knit the soles to the stockings I knit the bodies to last June. They say I am a "help." Partly because it is true, I suppose, and the rest applause. Mother and Margaret are so kind, father as gentle as he knows how, and Vinnie good to me, but "cannot see why I don't get well." This makes me think I am long sick, and this takes the ache to my eyes. I shall try to stay with them a few weeks more before going to Boston, though what it would be to see you and have the doctor's care – that cannot be told. You will not wait for me. Go to Middletown now. I wish I were there, myself, to start your little feet "lest they seem to come short of it." I have so much to tell I can tell nothing, except a sand of love. When I dare I shall ask if I may go, but that will not be now.

Give my love to my lamp and spoon, and the small Lantana. Kindest remembrance for all the house, and write next from Middletown. Go, little girl, to Middletown. Life is so fast it will run away, notwithstanding our sweetest *whoa.*

Already they love you. Be but the maid you are to me, and they will love you more.

Carry your heart and your curls, and nothing more but your fingers. Mr. D[udley] will ask for these every candle-light. How I miss ten robins that never flew from the rosewood nest!

MANUSCRIPT: destroyed.
PUBLICATION: L (1894) 255–256; LL 264–265; L (1931) 235–236.
Among the selections in the bound volume of ED's music (HCL) is *Sounds from Home,* a set of waltzes by the Hungarian composer Josef Gung'l (1810–1889). ED's eyes continued to trouble her, and early in 1865 she made plans to return to Boston for a second series of treatments by Dr. Williams. This letter appears to answer one from Louise Norcross inquiring whether she will have time to visit the Dudleys before expecting ED, who plans to begin the treatments about the first of April.

[439]

To Susan Gilbert Dickinson   *early 1865?*

> Thank Sue, but not tonight.
> Further Nights.

                                          Emily.

MANUSCRIPT: HCL (B 31). Pencil.
PUBLICATION: LL 62.
The handwriting is that of about 1865. The note may have been written between February and April, in which latter month she returned to Boston for further eye treatment.

To Louise Norcross   *March 1865*

. . . I am glad my little girl is at peace. Peace is a deep place. Some, too faint to push, are assisted by angels.

I have more to say to you all than March has to the maples, but then I cannot write in bed. I read a few words since I came home – John Talbot's parting with his son, and Margaret's with Suffolk. I read them in the garret, and the rafters wept.

Remember me to your company, their Bedouin guest.

Every day in the desert, Ishmael counts his tents. New heart makes new health, dear.

Happiness is haleness. I dreamed last night I heard bees fight for pond-lily stamens, and waked with a fly in my room.

Shall you be strong enough to lift me by the first of April? I won't be half as heavy as I was before. I will be good and chase my spools.

I shall think of my little Eve going away from Eden. Bring me a jacinth for every finger, and an onyx shoe.

                                          Emily.

MANUSCRIPT: destroyed.
PUBLICATION: L (1894) 253–254; LL 264; L (1931) 234.
Louise is with the Dudleys. ED has been reading scenes from 1 Henry VI.

To Susan Gilbert Dickinson   *March 1865*

Dear Sue –

    Unable are the Loved – to die –
    For Love is immortality –
    Nay – it is Deity –

                                Emily.

MANUSCRIPT: HCL (B 18). Pencil.
PUBLICATION: FF 263.
The date, conjectured from the handwriting, is confirmed by the circumstances. Susan's sister, Harriet Gilbert Cutler, died, 18 March 1865.

To Susan Gilbert Dickinson   *about March 1865*

    You must let me go first, Sue, because I live in the Sea always and know the Road.
    I would have drowned twice to save you sinking, dear, If I could only have covered your Eyes so you would'nt have seen the Water.

MANUSCRIPT: HCL (B 162). Pencil.
PUBLICATION: LL 100, in part; FF 270.
This is in the handwriting of the note preceding, and may have been written about the same time. The tropes involving water are especially predominant in messages written during the period that ED was under treatment for her eyes. See, for instance, letters no. 294 and 466.

To Louise Norcross   *March 1865*

Dear Sister,

    Brother has visited, and the night is falling, so I must close with a little hymn.
    I had hoped to express more. Love more I never can, sweet D[udleys] or yourself.

This was in the white of the year,
That was in the green.
Drifts were as difficult then to think,
As daisies now to be seen.
Looking back is best that is left,
Or if it be before,
Retrospection is prospect's half,
Sometimes almost more.

             Emily.

MANUSCRIPT: destroyed.
PUBLICATION: *L* (1894) 254; *LL* 265–266; *L* (1931) 234.

This letter was written shortly before ED returned to Cambridge, evidently while Louise was still with the Dudleys.

308

To Lavinia N. Dickinson   *Cambridge, mid-May 1865*

Dear Vinnie

The Hood is far under way and the Girls think it a Beauty. I am so glad to make it for you, who made so much for me.

I hope the Chimneys are done and the Hemlocks set, and the Two Teeth filled, in the Front yard — How astonishing it will be to me.

I hope Mother is better, and will be careful of her Eye.

The Doctor says it must heal while warm Weather lasts, or it will be more troublesome.

How is Margarets lameness? Tell her the Girl's name, here, is Margaret, which makes me quite at Home.

The Pink Lily you gave Loo, has had five flowers since I came, and has more Buds. The Girls think it my influence.

Is Sue still improving? Give her love from us all, and how much we talk of her.

Loo wishes she knew Father's view of Jeff Davis' capture — thinks no one but He, can do it justice.

She wishes to send a Photograph of the Arrest to Austin, including the Skirt and Spurs, but fears he will think her trifling with him. I advised her not to be rash. How glad I should be to see you all, but it wont be long, Vinnie—You will be willing, wont you, for a little while.

It has rained, and been very hot, and Mosquitoes as in August. I hope the flowers are well. The Tea Rose I gave Aunt Lavinia has a flower, now.

Much love for both Houses, from the Girls and me. Is the Lettuce ripe.

Shall you go to Springfield? Persons wear no Bonnets here. Fanny has a Blade of Straw, with Handle of Ribbon.

Aff, Emily.

MANUSCRIPT: AC. Pencil.

PUBLICATION: L (1894) 152–153, in part; LL 257–258, in part; L (1931) 149–150, in part; Home 436–437, entire.

Jefferson Davis was captured on 10 May 1865.

309

To Lavinia N. Dickinson   *Cambridge, May 1865*

. . . Town Meeting –

Do not get tired, Vinnie, or troubled about things – all I can do, leave till I come –

I have more to say than I can, but Loo goes now to the Office – Am happy to hear of Hemlocks – Love for All and dont work too hard, picking up after Chimneys – The Grass will cover it all up, and I can sweep, next Fall – The Girls were never dearer or kinder and say much of you and Mother, and ask many questions of Sue – I will write again after seeing the Doctor –

Aff, Emily –

MANUSCRIPT: HCL (B 167). Pencil. Unpublished.

This letter, the first part of which is wanting, seems to follow the preceding, and answers one from Lavinia saying that the hemlock trees have been planted. There was a special town meeting, called on 15 May 1865, to discuss plans for establishing the Agricultural College at Amherst.

To Susan Gilbert Dickinson   *about 1865*

Are you sure we are making the most of it?

Emily –

MANUSCRIPT: HCL (B 1). Pencil.
PUBLICATION: LL 57.

The date is conjectured from the handwriting. ED returned from
Cambridge in October. The exuberance of the tone suggests that it was
dispatched to Sue after her return, rather than before her departure for
Cambridge in April.

To Mrs. J. G. Holland   *early November 1865*

Dear Sister,

Father called to say that our steelyard was fraudulent, exceeding
by an ounce the rates of honest men. He had been selling oats. I cannot stop smiling, though it is hours since, that even our steelyard will
not tell the truth.

Besides wiping the dishes for Margaret, I wash them now, while
she becomes Mrs. Lawler, vicarious papa to four previous babes. Must
she not be an adequate bride?

I winced at her loss, because I was in the habit of her, and even a
new rolling-pin has an embarrassing element, but to all except anguish,
the mind soon adjusts.

It is also November. The noons are more laconic and the sundowns
sterner, and Gibraltar lights make the village foreign. November always seemed to me the Norway of the year. [Susan] is still with the
sister who put her child in an ice nest last Monday forenoon. The
redoubtable God! I notice where Death has been introduced, he frequently calls, making it desirable to forestall his advances.

It is hard to be told by the papers that a friend is failing, not even
know where the water lies. Incidentally, only, that he comes to land.
Is there no voice for these? Where is Love today?

Tell the dear Doctor we mention him with a foreign accent, party already to transactions spacious and untold. Nor have we omitted to breathe shorter for our little sister. Sharper than dying is the death for the dying's sake.

News of these would comfort, when convenient or possible.

Emily.

MANUSCRIPT: missing.
PUBLICATION: L (1894) 176–177; L (1931) 169–170; LH 69–70.

Letters written to Mrs. Holland in the three-year interval since the last (no. 269) do not survive, but the tone of this one certainly suggests that there had been no hiatus in their correspondence. Margaret O'Brien (sometimes O'Bryan) married Stephen Lawler on 18 October; it was her first marriage and his second (see Appendix 2). Martha Gilbert Smith's two-year-old daughter died on 3 November; an infant son had died in 1861.

The word *failing* in the fifth paragraph is probably a misprint for *sailing*. Samuel Bowles sailed from San Francisco on 28 October, and the *Republican* announced his return but did not name the port for which he was bound. (A photograph of Bowles made at this time is mentioned in letter no. 962.) The remark about Dr. Holland probably alludes to the fact that his *Life of Abraham Lincoln* (1865) was at the moment being translated into German, an item of news which one supposes Mrs. Holland had passed on to ED; the volume was issued in Springfield from the same press that published the version in English. Mrs. Holland must also have commented on the fact that a friend was dying, evidently a person unknown to ED.

312

To Susan Gilbert Dickinson   *early December 1865*

Sister,

We both are Women, and there is a Will of God – Could the Dying confide Death, there would be no Dead – Wedlock is shyer than Death. Thank you for Tenderness –

I find it is the only food that the Will takes, nor that from general fingers – I am glad you go – It does not remove you – I seek you first in Amherst, then turn my thoughts without a Whip – so well they follow you –

An Hour is a Sea
Between a few, and me –
With them would Harbor be –

MANUSCRIPT: HCL (B 78). Pencil.
PUBLICATION: AM CXV (1915) 37, in part; LL 49, in part; FF 236, in part.

ED's friend Susan Phelps died, 2 December 1865. Susan Dickinson was still with her sister Martha Smith, in Geneva, New York.

313

To Mrs. J. G. Holland   *late 1865?*

Dear Sister,

It was incredibly sweet that Austin had seen you, and had stood in the dear house which had lost its friend. To see one who had seen you was a strange assurance. It helped dispel the fear that you departed too, for nothwithstanding the loved notes and the lovely gift, there lurked a dread that you had gone or would seek to go. "Where the treasure is," there is the prospective.

Austin spoke very warmly and strongly of you, and we all felt firmer, and drew a vocal portrait of Kate at Vinnie's request, so vivid that we saw her. . . .

MANUSCRIPT: missing.
PUBLICATION: L (1894) 177; L (1931) 171; LH 72.

The conclusion has been deleted. The date, at best conjectural, is that assigned in *Letters*, and followed in *LH*. The poem beginning "Not all die early, dying young" is not a part of the letter, though in *Letters* it seems to conclude it, and is so printed in *LH*.

The friend whom the Hollands lost has not been identified. The quotation is from Matthew 6.21 (also Luke 12.34).

VIII

LETTERS

314–337

[1866–1869]

" *A Letter always feels to me*
like immortality because it is
the mind alone without corporeal friend. "

[1866–1869]

The total number of known letters for the four years that conclude the decade of the sixties is the smallest by far that Emily Dickinson is known to have written during her mature years. The reason probably is not that some letters of this period are irrecoverable. Psychologically she was dormant. The great poetic drive was suddenly at an end, and though she would continue to write poems, she would never again match the fecundity of the years just concluded.

Such a change must have been for her, in both her conscious and unconscious relations, a taxing experience which reflected itself in the pace of her living. The year 1867, for instance, remains almost totally blank. But one letter can assuredly be placed within it. A handful of poems are conjecturally so assigned simply because there is no reason to think that the year ceased to exist for her.

The eye affliction is never alluded to again, and seems not to have troubled her capacity to read and write with comfort. Her few correspondents at this time are the familiar ones, principally Colonel Higginson and Mrs. Holland. On the whole, this group suggests that she is trying to restore her strength and build up a new reserve.

To T. W. Higginson   *late January 1866*

Carlo died –
E. Dickinson
Would you instruct me now?

MANUSCRIPT: BPL (Higg 64). Ink. Dated: Amherst. Envelope addressed: Col. T. W. Higginson/Newport/Rhode Island. Postmarked: Hadley Ms Jan 27.
PUBLICATION: *AM* LXVIII (October 1891) 450; *L* (1931) 281.

This brief note, in which was enclosed the poem "Further in Summer than the Birds," attempts to reestablish a correspondence that had lapsed for eighteen months. ED's dog Carlo had been a favorite companion, and she never got another. (See letter no. 34.)

To Mrs. J. G. Holland   *early March 1866*

. . . the Sere.

Febuary passed like a Skate and I know March. Here is the "light" the Stranger said "was not on land or sea." Myself could arrest it but we'll not chagrin Him. Ned has been ill for a Week, maturing all our faces. He rides his Rocking-Horse today, though looking apparitional.

His Mama just called, leaving a Cashmere print.

Cousin Peter told me the Doctor would address Commencement. Trusting it insure you both for Papa's Fete, I endowed Peter.

We do not always know the source of the smile that flows to us. Ned tells that the Clock purrs and the Kitten ticks. He inherits his Uncle Emily's ardor for the lie.

My flowers are near and foreign, and I have but to cross the floor to stand in the Spice Isles.

The Wind blows gay today and the Jays bark like Blue Terriers.

I tell you what I see. The Landscape of the Spirit requires a lung, but no Tongue. I hold you few I love, till my heart is red as Febuary and purple as March.

Hand for the Doctor.

Emily.

MANUSCRIPT: HCL (H 20). Pencil. The opening of the letter is missing.

PUBLICATION: L (1894) 168–169, in part; L (1931) 170–171, in part; LH 73, in part.

ED's cousin Perez Cowan was a senior in Amherst College. "The light that never was, on sea or land" is from William Wordsworth's *Elegiac Stanzas*. ED has placed a "1" over *sea* and a "2" over *land*. The same line is quoted in letter no. 394.

316

To T. W. Higginson   *early 1866*

Dear friend.

Whom my Dog understood could not elude others.

I should be glad to see you, but think it an apparitional pleasure – not to be fulfilled. I am uncertain of Boston.

I had promised to visit my Physician for a few days in May, but Father objects because he is in the habit of me.

Is it more far to Amherst?

You would find a minute Host but a spacious Welcome –

Lest you meet my Snake and suppose I deceive it was robbed of me – defeated too of the third line by the punctuation. The third and fourth were one – I had told you I did not print – I feared you might think me ostensible. If I still entreat you to teach me, are you much displeased?

I will be patient – constant, never reject your knife and should my my [sic] slowness goad you, you knew before myself that

> Except the smaller size
> No lives are round –
> These – hurry to a sphere
> And show and end –

The larger – slower grow
And later hang –
The Summers of Hesperides
Are long.

Dickinson

MANUSCRIPT: BPL (Higg 59). Ink. Dated: Amherst. Envelope addressed: Col. T. W. Higginson/Newport/Rhode Island.

PUBLICATION: AM LXVIII (October 1891) 451; in part; L (1894) 312, in part; LL 268–269, in part; L 281–282, entire, with facsimile reproduction of part, facing page 282. There is no stanza break in this version.

ED enclosed one poem in the letter: "A Death blow is a Life blow to some," together with a clipping of "The Snake" from the 17 February issue of the *Springfield Weekly Republican*. This replies to a letter from Higginson which expressed a desire to see her, and evidently called her "elusive." In the opening sentence it is to herself that she refers as "Whom." Her poem "A narrow Fellow in the Grass" appeared in both the *Daily* and the *Weekly Republican* during the week of the seventeenth (a Saturday). The full account of the publication is in *Poems* (1955) 713–714. But see also the correction noted by John L. Spicer in *Boston Public Library Quarterly* VIII (July 1956) 135–143.

317

To Catherine Scott Turner (Anthon) *spring 1866?*

Thank you Katie, it *was* relief, you had'nt spoke so long, I got a bad whim –

Please don't leave Emily again, it gnarls her character! You say winter was long. We thought so, too, but it went by – Call nothing long, Katie, that stops! I read about your fire, in the "Midnight Cry" – Vinnie's favourite journal – "Katie is doubtless in *ashes*," I thought, I'm much obliged to God for not burning you up. Sue's little boy rides by with a long stick in his hand, beating imaginary beasts. – He is fond of Hens and other Songsters, and visits a colt in our barn demi-daily: The decease of a cat connected with the estate solemnized us Friday. – "Tabby" is still on "praying ground." and catches dandelions mistaking them for *Topaz* mice, – *Will* folks get rested, Katie? – You spoke of "Heaven" you know. "I" will take *so many beds*. Theres

[451]

you & me & Vinnie & the "other house." & the *Israelites* & those *Hittite* folks, it *does* appear confused to me! – Come & have tea with us again Katie! *How* it rained that night! We must take many a tea together in a Northeast storm o' Saturday nights, before Da Vinci's Supper!

So tired, Katie, so good night Speak, will it more to

Emily——

MANUSCRIPT: missing. The text is from a transcript (HCL) made by Mrs. Anthon. Unpublished.

The date is conjectural. The description of Ned would fit a boy of four. The last words of the letter are uncertain, and may have been misread by Mrs. Anthon.

318

To Mrs. J. G. Holland   *early May 1866*

Dear Sister,

After you went, a low wind warbled through the house like a spacious bird, making it high but lonely. When you had gone the love came. I supposed it would. The supper of the heart is when the guest has gone.

Shame is so intrinsic in a strong affection we must all experience Adam's reticence. I suppose the street that the lover travels is thenceforth divine, incapable of turnpike aims.

That you be with me annuls fear and I await Commencement with merry resignation. Smaller than David you clothe me with extreme Goliath.

Friday I tasted life. It was a vast morsel. A circus passed the house – still I feel the red in my mind though the drums are out.

The book you mention, I have not met. Thank you for tenderness.

The lawn is full of south and the odors tangle, and I hear today for the first the river in the tree.

You mentioned spring's delaying – I blamed her for the opposite. I would eat evanescence slowly.

Vinnie is deeply afflicted in the death of her dappled cat, though I convince her it is immortal which assists her some. Mother resumes lettuce, involving my transgression — suggestive of yourself, however, which endears disgrace.

"House" is being "cleaned." I prefer pestilence. That is more classic and less fell.

Yours was my first arbutus. It was a rosy boast.

I will send you the first witch hazel.

A woman died last week, young and in hope but a little while – at the end of our garden. I thought since of the power of death, not upon affection, but its mortal signal. It is to us the Nile.

You refer to the unpermitted delight to be with those we love. I suppose that to be the license not granted of God.

> Count not that far that can be had,
> Though sunset lie between –
> Nor that adjacent, that beside,
> Is further than the sun.

Love for your embodiment of it.

Emily.

MANUSCRIPT: missing.
PUBLICATION: L (1894) 171–172; L (1931) 165–166; LH 74–75.
Laura Dickey, daughter of L. M. Hills, died at her parents' home on 1 May. The Hills's property adjoined the Dickinsons' on the east. A circus was in town on the third.

319

To T. W. Higginson   *9 June 1866*

Dear friend

Please to thank the Lady. She is very gentle to care.

I must omit Boston. Father prefers so. He likes me to travel with him but objects that I visit.

Might I entrust you, as my Guest to the Amherst Inn? When I have seen you, to improve will be better pleasure because I shall know which are the mistakes.

Your opinion gives me a serious feeling. I would like to be what you deem me.

Thank you, I wish for Carlo.

> Time is a test of trouble
> But not a remedy –
> If such it prove, it prove too
> There was no malady.

Still I have the Hill, my Gibraltar remnant.

Nature, seems it to myself, plays without a friend.

You mention Immortality.

That is the Flood subject. I was told that the Bank was the safest place for a Finless Mind. I explore but little since my mute Confederate, yet the "infinite Beauty" – of which you speak comes too near to seek.

To escape enchantment, one must always flee.

Paradise is of the option.

Whosoever will Own in Eden notwithstanding Adam and Repeal.

Dickinson.

MANUSCRIPT: BPL (Higg 60). Ink. Dated: Amherst. Envelope addressed: Col. T. W. Higginson/Newport/Rhode Island. Postmarked: Hadley Ms Jun 9.

PUBLICATION: L (1931) 282–283.

Higginson has again urged her to come to Boston, and this is her second refusal. It is her first invitation that he visit Amherst. In the letter she enclosed four poems: "Blazing in Gold," "Ample make this Bed," "To undertake is to achieve," and "As imperceptibly as Grief."

320

To Susan Gilbert Dickinson *about August 1866*

Sister

Ned is safe – Just "serenaded" Hannah, and is running off with a Corn Leaf "tail," looking back for cheers, Grandma "hoped" characteristically "he would be a very good Boy."

"Not very dood" he said, sweet defiant child! Obtuse ambition of Grandmamas! I kissed my hand to the early train but forgot to open the Blind, partly explaining your negligence.

Nothing is heard from Worcester though Father demanded a telegram, and the Dudleys delay for weather, so Susan shall see Hugh –

It rains in the Kitchen, and Vinnie trades Blackberries with a Tawny Girl – Guess I wont go out. My Jungle fronts on Wall St – Was the Sea cordial? Kiss him for Thoreau –

Do not fear for Home –

Be a bold Susan –

Clara sold the tobacco, and is good to Ned –

Dreamed of your meeting Tennyson in Ticknor and Fields –

Where the Treasure is, there the Brain is also –

Love for Boy –

Emily

MANUSCRIPT: HCL (B 59 and B 147). Pencil.

PUBLICATION: *AM* CXV (1915) 40, in part; *FF* 256, in part.

The date is conjectured from the handwriting. Evidently Susan and Austin were vacationing at the seashore, perhaps in Swampscott, where they sometimes went. Ned was now five. Edward Dickinson's brother William lived in Worcester. John and Eliza Dudley were expected for a visit. "Hugh" has not been identified.

Clara Newman, now twenty, was at this time living with Austin and Susan; the tobacco she has sold presumably was a crop which she herself had raised. The reference to Thoreau is one which Sue would be expected to understand. His *Cape Cod* had been published in 1865, and perhaps Sue and ED had been discussing it. Ticknor and Fields was a well known Boston publishing firm. (See Prose Fragment 7.)

321

To Mrs. J. G. Holland   *late November 1866?*

Sister,

A mutual plum is not a plum. I was too respectful to take the pulp and do not like a stone.

Send no union letters. The soul must go by Death alone, so, it must by life, if it is a soul.

If a committee – no matter.

I saw the sunrise on the Alps since I saw you. Travel why to Nature, when she dwells with us? Those who lift their hats shall see her, as devout do God.

I trust you are merry and sound. The chances are all against the dear, when we are not with them, though paws of principalities cannot affront if we are by.

Dr. Vaill called here Monday on his way to your house to get the Doctor to preach for him. Shall search *The Republican* for a brief of the sermon. Today is very homely and awkward as the homely are who have not mental beauty.

> The sky is low, the clouds are mean,
> A travelling flake of snow
> Across a barn or through a rut
> Debates if it will go.
>
> A narrow wind complains all day
> How someone treated him;
> Nature, like us, is sometimes caught
> Without her diadem.

MANUSCRIPT: missing.
PUBLICATION: L (1894) 180–181; L (1931) 174; LH 76–77.
The Reverend Joseph Vaill was pastor of a church in Palmer from 1854 until 1867. The first snow on the Pelham Hills in 1866 fell on 22 November. A separate draft of the poem here incorporated has been dated about 1866: *Poems* (1955) 760–761.

322

To Louise Norcross   1866?

. . . Oh, Loo, why were the children sent too faint to stand alone? . . . Every hour is anxious now, and heaven protect the lamb who shared her fleece with a timider, even Emily.

MANUSCRIPT: destroyed.
PUBLICATION: L (1894) 256; LL 267; L (1931) 236, where these extracts are dated 1866.
The nature of the anxiety has not been explained.

To T. W. Higginson   *mid-July 1867*

> Bringing still my "plea for Culture,"
> Would it teach me now?

MANUSCRIPT: BPL (Higg 63). Ink. Dated: Amherst. Envelope addressed: Col. T. W. Higginson/Newport/Rhode Island. Postmarked: Middletown Ct Jul 16.

PUBLICATION: L (1931) 284.

This brief note enclosed one poem: "The Luxury to apprehend." The postmark suggests that this letter was mailed by some member of the Dickinson family who was visiting the Dudleys in Middletown. No detail whatever, except what this letter reveals, is known about ED during the year 1867, but the probability is that she was not the visitor. Since the Dudleys left Middletown in June 1868, and since Higginson's essay "A Plea for Culture" had appeared in the January 1867, issue of the *Atlantic Monthly*, this letter almost certainly was written in 1867. It attempts to renew a correspondence with Higginson that apparently had lapsed after ED's second refusal, in the summer of 1866, to visit Boston (see letter no. 319). It is the only letter known which with reasonable certainty may be assigned to this year.

To Susan Gilbert Dickinson   *about April 1868*

Going is less, Sister, long gone from you, yet We who take all with us, leave not much behind – Busy missing you – I have not tasted Spring – Should there be other Aprils, We will perhaps dine –

                                                        Emily –

MANUSCRIPT: HCL (B 135). Pencil. Addressed: Sue –

PUBLICATION: AM CXV (1915) 37, in part; LL 57, in part; FF 237, in part.

The handwriting is that of about 1868. The letter may be incomplete.

325

To Susan Gilbert Dickinson   *about 1868*

Susan's Idolator keeps a Shrine for Susan.

MANUSCRIPT: HCL (B 71). Pencil.
PUBLICATION: FF 247.
The date is conjectured from the handwriting.

326

To Mrs. Luke Sweetser   *about 1868*

Dear Mrs Sweetser
My Breakfast surpassed Elijah's, though served by Robins instead
of Ravens.   Affy
                                                          Emily.

MANUSCRIPT: Rosenbach 1170/18 (5). Pencil. Folded and addressed:
Mrs Sweetser. Unpublished.
The letter is dated by handwriting, which is that of about 1868. The
Sweetsers were near neighbors. Had the letter been sent to some other
member of the Sweetser family, ED would have headed it "Mrs. Howard"
("Mrs. Nellie"), or "Aunt Katie." The allusion is to 1 Kings 17. 6: "And
the ravens brought [Elijah] bread . . ."

327

To Susan Gilbert Dickinson   *about 1868*

Dear Sue –

Just say one word,
"Emily has not grieved me"
Sign your name to that and I will wait for the rest.

MANUSCRIPT: HCL (B 80). Pencil. Addressed on the fold: Sue.
PUBLICATION: FF 264.
The date is conjectured from the handwriting. Perhaps ED had refused
some request.

To Susan Gilbert Dickinson   *about 1868*

That my sweet Sister remind me to thank her for *herself* is valuablest.

Emily.

MANUSCRIPT: HCL (B 97). Pencil. Unpublished.
The date is conjectured from the handwriting.

To Louise and Frances Norcross   *late 1868?*

Dear Children,

The little notes shall go as fast as steam can take them.

Our hearts already went. Would we could mail our faces for your dear encouragement.

Remember

The longest day that God appoints
Will finish with the sun.
Anguish can travel to its stake,
And then it must return.

I am in bed to-day – a curious place for me, and cannot write as well as if I was firmer, but love as well, and long more. Tell us all the load. Amherst's little basket is never so full but it holds more. That's a basket's cause. Not a flake assaults my birds but it freezes me. Comfort, little creatures – whatever befall us, this world is but this world. Think of that great courageous place we have never seen!

Write at once, please. I am so full of grief and surprise and physical weakness. I cannot speak until I know.

Lovingly,
Emily.

MANUSCRIPT: destroyed.
PUBLICATION: L (1894) 257; LL 269; L (1931) 236–237.
Mrs. Todd dated the letter 1868, presumably because the Norcross sisters assigned that date, though they could recall no trouble at that time.

To T. W. Higginson   *June 1869*

Dear friend

A Letter always feels to me like immortality because it is the mind alone 'without corporeal friend. Indebted in our talk to attitude and accent, there seems a spectral power in thought that walks alone – I would like to thank you for your great kindness but never try to lift the words which I cannot hold.

Should you come to Amherst, I might then succeed, though Gratitude is the timid wealth of those who have nothing. I am sure that you speak the truth, because the noble do, but your letters always surprise me. My life has been too simple and stern to embarrass any.

"Seen of Angels" scarcely my responsibility

It is difficult not to be fictitious in so fair a place, but test's severe repairs are permitted all.

When a little Girl I remember hearing that remarkable passage and preferring the "Power," not knowing at the time that "Kingdom" and "Glory" were included.

You noticed my dwelling alone – To an Emigrant, Country is idle except it be his own. You speak kindly of seeing me. Could it please your convenience to come so far as Amherst I should be very glad, but I do not cross my Father's ground to any House or town.

Of our greatest acts we are ignorant –

You were not aware that you saved my Life. To thank you in person has been since then one of my few requests. The child that asks my flower "Will you," he says – "Will you" – and so to ask for what I want I know no other way.

You will excuse each that I say, because no other taught me?

Dickinson

MANUSCRIPT: BPL (Higg 61). Ink. Dated by Higginson: June 1869.
PUBLICATION: *AM* LXVIII (October 1891) 451–452, in part; *L* (1894) 313–314, in part; *LL* 270, in part; *L* (1931) 283–284, entire.

ED echoes her opening sentence in a letter to James Clark written in 1882 (no. 788). This is ED's third refusal to go to Boston, and her second invitation to Higginson to come to Amherst, and it answers the letter which follows (HCL), written by Higginson and dated: May 11. 1869. ED's conviction that Higginson was the friend who saved her life must have been very deep, for she uses the same phrase in a letter written to him ten years later (see no. 621).

The woman Higginson mentions at the end of his first paragraph is Helen Hunt (Jackson). In 1890 Higginson wrote Mrs. Todd (AB 82): "H.H. did not know of her poems till I showed them to her (about 1866) and was very little in Amherst after that. But she remembered her at school."

330a

From T. W. Higginson

Sometimes I take out your letters & verses, dear friend, and when I feel their strange power, it is not strange that I find it hard to write & that long months pass. I have the greatest desire to see you, always feeling that perhaps if I could once take you by the hand I might be something to you; but till then you only enshroud yourself in this fiery mist & I cannot reach you, but only rejoice in the rare sparkles of light. Every year I think that I will contrive somehow to go to Amherst & see you: but that is hard, for I often am obliged to go away for lecturing, &c & rarely can go for pleasure. I would gladly go to Boston, at any practicable time, to meet you. I am always the same toward you, & never relax my interest in what you send to me. I should like to hear from you very often, but feel always timid lest what I *write* should be badly aimed & miss that fine edge of thought which you bear. It would be so easy, I fear, to miss you. Still, you see, I try. I think if I could once see you & know that you are real, I might fare better. It brought you nearer e[ven] to know that you had an actual [?] uncle, though I can hardly fancy [any?] two beings less alike than yo[u] [&?] him. But I have not seen him [for] several years, though I have seen [a lady] who once knew you, but could [not] tell me much.

It is hard [for me] to understand how you can live s[o alo]ne, with thoughts of such a [quali]ty coming up in you & even the companionship of your dog withdrawn. Yet it isolates one anywhere to think beyond a certain point or have such luminous flashes as come to you – so perhaps the place does not make much difference.

You must come down to Boston sometimes? All ladies do. I wonder if it would be possible to lure you [to] the meetings on the 3^d Monday of every month at Mrs. [Sa]rgent's 13 Chestnut St. at 10 am – when somebody reads [a] paper & others talk or listen. Next Monday Mr. Emerson [rea]ds & then at 3½ P.M. there is a meeting of the Woman's [Cl]ub at 3 Tremont Place, where I read a paper on the [Gre]ek goddesses. That would be a good time for you to come [alth]ough I should still rather have you come on some [da]y when I shall not be so much taken up – for my object is to see you, more than to entertain you. I shall be in Boston also during anniversary week, June 25 * & 28, – or will the Musical Festival in June tempt you down. You see I am in earnest. Or don't you need sea air in summer. Write & tell me something in prose or verse, & I will be less fastidious in future & willing to write clumsy things, rather than none.

Ever your friend
[signature cut out]

* There is an extra meeting at Mrs. Sargent's that day & Mr. Weiss reads an essay. I have a right to invite you & you can merely ring & walk in.

331

To Louise and Frances Norcross   *summer 1869?*

. . . J—— is coming to put away her black hair on the children's pillow. I hoped she'd come while you were here, to help me with the starch, but Satan's ways are not as our ways. I'm straightening all the property, and making things erect and smart, and tomorrow, at twilight, her little heel boots will thump into Amherst. It being summer season she will omit the sleigh-bell gown, and that's a palliative. Vinnie is all disgust, and I shall have to smirk for two to make the manners even.

MANUSCRIPT: destroyed.
PUBLICATION: L (1894) 270; L (1931) 247.

Louise Norcross was in Amherst during the spring of 1869. The person described may be ED's aunt Elizabeth (Libbie). "J" could easily have been a misreading for "L." (See letters no. 286 and 473.)

To Perez Cowan   *October 1869*

These Indian-Summer Days with their peculiar Peace remind me
of those stillest things that no one can disturb and knowing you are
not at Home and have a sister less I liked to try to help you. You might
not need assistance?

You speak with so much trust of that which only trust can prove,
it makes me feel away, as if my English mates spoke sudden in Italian.

It grieves me that you speak of Death with so much expectation.
I know there is no pang like that for those we love, nor any leisure
like the one they leave so closed behind them, but Dying is a wild
Night and a new Road.

I suppose we are all thinking of Immortality, at times so stimu-
latedly that we cannot sleep. Secrets are interesting, but they are also
solemn – and speculate with all our might, we cannot ascertain.

I trust as Days go on your sister is more Peace than Pang – though
to learn to spare is a sharp acquirement. The subject hurts me so that
I will put it down, because it hurts you.

We bruise each other less in talking than in writing, for then a
quiet accent helps words themselves too hard.

Do you remember Peter, what the Physician said to Macbeth?
"That sort must heal itself."

I am glad you are working. Others are anodyne. You remembered
Clara.

The Wedding was small, but lovely, and the sisters have gone. I
give you a look of her flowers as Sue and Austin arranged them.

Tell us more of yourself, when you have time and please.

                                                        Emily.

MANUSCRIPT: NYPL (Berg Collection). Ink.
PUBLICATION: *Libbie Auction Catalogue* (of the Edward Abbott collection), 25, 26 February 1909, 6 pp.; *NEQ* 163:25 (1932), 441, in part.

Cowan was ordained 8 April 1869, and was still unmarried. Clara Newman married Sidney Turner, 14 October 1869. For the quotation from
Macbeth, see letters no. 669 and 986.

To Susan Gilbert Dickinson   *autumn 1869*

To take away our Sue leaves but a lower World, her firmamental quality our more familiar Sky.

It is not Nature – dear, but those that stand for Nature.

The Bird would be a soundless thing without Expositor. Come Home and see your Weather. The Hills are full of Shawls, and I am going every Day to buy myself a Sash.

Grandma moans for Neddie, and Austin's face is soft as Mist when he hears his name. Tell "Dexter" I miss his little team.

I humbly try to fill your place at the Minister's, so faint a competition, it only makes them smile.

Mattie is stern and lovely – literary, they tell me – a graduate of Mother Goose and otherwise ambitious.

We have a new man whose name is Tim.

Father calls him "Timothy" and the Barn sounds like the Bible.

Vinnie is still on her "Coast Survey" and I am so hurried with Parents that I run all Day with my tongue abroad, like a Summer Dog.

Tell Mattie for me glad little Girl is safe, and congratulate minor little Girl on her priceless Mama. Susan's

Emily.

Manuscript: HCL (B 185). Ink.

Publication: FF 239–240, in part.

Vinnie was in Boston during the autumn of 1869. With Ned, now eight, Susan was visiting her sister Martha Smith at Geneva, New York. Martha Dickinson, the first Mattie mentioned, was then three years old. Elizabeth Throop Smith, the "minor little Girl," was an infant. The minister is J. L. Jenkins. On "Timothy," see Appendix 2.

To Susan Gilbert Dickinson   *about 1869*

The things of which we want the proof are those we knew before –

Manuscript: HCL (B 20). Pencil.

Publication: LL 62.

This and the two following notes, all written to Susan Dickinson, are in the handwriting of about 1869.

To Susan Gilbert Dickinson   *about 1869*

Dont do such things, dear Sue – The "Arabian Nights" unfit the heart for it's Arithmetic –

                             Emily –

MANUSCRIPT: HCL (B 70). Pencil. Addressed: Sue.
PUBLICATION: *LL* 62.

To Susan Gilbert Dickinson   *about 1869*

             Rare to the Rare –

             Her Sovreign People
             Nature knows as well
             And is as fond of signifying
             As if fallible –

                     Emily –

MANUSCRIPT: Smith College. Pencil.
PUBLICATION: *Daily Hampshire Gazette*, 18 December 1952; *Poems* (1955) 800.

To Louise Norcross   *late 1869*

Vinnie was "gone" indeed and is due to-day, and before the tumult that even the best bring we will take hold of hands. It was sweet and antique as birds to hear Loo's voice, worth the lying awake from five o'clock summer mornings to hear. I rejoice that my wren can rise and touch the sky again. We all have moments with the dust, but the dew is given. Do you wish you heard "A[ustin] talk"? Then I would you did, for then you would be here always, a sweet premium. Would you like to "step in the kitchen"? Then you shall by faith, which is the first sight. Mr. C[hurch] is not in the tree, because the rooks won't let him, but I ate a pear as pink as a plum that he made last spring, when he was ogling you. Mother has on the petticoat you so gallantly gathered while he sighed and grafted.

Tabby is eating a stone dinner from a stone plate, . . . Tim is washing Dick's feet, and talking to him now and then in an intimate way. Poor fellow, how he warmed when I gave him your message! The red reached clear to his beard, he was so gratified; and Maggie stood as still for hers as a puss for patting. The hearts of these poor people lie so unconcealed you bare them with a smile.

Thank you for recollecting my weakness. I am not so well as to forget I was ever ill, but better and working. I suppose we must all "ail till evening."

Read Mr. Lowell's *Winter*. One does not often meet anything so perfect.

In many little corners how much of Loo I have.

Maggie "dragged" the garden for this bud for you. You have heard of the "last rose of summer." This is that rose's son.

Into the little port you cannot sail unwelcome at any hour of day or night. Love for Fanny, and stay close to

Emily

MANUSCRIPT: destroyed.
PUBLICATION: L (1894) 258; L (1931) 237–238.
This letter, written with the casual intimacy which characterizes those addressed to the Norcross girls, draws to an unusual extent upon the literary and domestic associations which the girls will understand. At the household level ED speaks about the horse Dick, about Tim (Scannell?), Maggie Maher, and Horace Church (see Appendix 2 for identification of the persons named). The phrase "ail till evening" recalls Browning's *Sordello* (see letter 477). Thomas Moore's "The Last Rose of Summer," set to music, was in any volume of familiar songs. The *Atlantic Almanac* (profusely illustrated and edited, with literary selections, by Oliver Wendell Holmes and Donald Grant Mitchell) in its issue for 1870 carried two prose essays that would have special appeal for ED: one by Higginson, titled "Swimming"; and one by James Russell Lowell, "A Good Word for Winter." It is this latter essay, almost certainly, which she here warmly recommends to Louise Norcross.

IX

LETTERS

338–431

[1870–1874]

"I find ecstasy in living –
the mere sense of living
is joy enough."

[1870–1874]

With the year 1870 the number of surviving letters markedly increases, and the fact is that events at this time helped to stimulate the flow of correspondence with the two friends to whom Emily Dickinson then was writing her most interesting letters. In May 1870 the Holland family returned from a two-year sojourn in Europe. In August Higginson paid his first and long hoped-for visit. After eight years of baffling correspondence, he found the meeting so stimulating that he recorded it fully in his diary and in letters to his wife and sister.

Important events in the lives of other friends called for attention, and the first letter in the group was written in response to the news of the death of a son of her favorite aunt.

But in 1870 she was in her fortieth year, and thus the important events in the lives of those in her own generation were usually leading to fulfillment. The death of her cousin Henry Sweetser did not touch her closely, for she scarcely knew him. The death of her father, in 1874, was the first major encroachment upon the routines of duty and love which she now made her total concern.

To Mrs. Joseph A. Sweetser   *late February 1870*

My sweet Aunt Katie.

When I am most grieved I had rather no one would speak to me, so I stayed from you, but I thought by today, perhaps you would like to see me, if I came quite soft and brought no noisy words. But when I am most sorry, I can say nothing so I will only kiss you and go far away. Who could ache for you like your little Niece – who knows how deep the Heart is and how much it holds?

I know we shall certainly see what we loved the most. It is sweet to think they are safe by Death and that that is all we have to pass to obtain their face.

There are no Dead, dear Katie, the Grave is but our moan for them.

> Were it to be the last
> How infinite would be
> What we did not suspect was marked
> Our final interview.

Henry had been a prisoner. How he had coveted Liberty probably his Redeemer knew – and as we keep surprise for those most precious to us, brought him his Ransom in his sleep.

Emily.

MANUSCRIPT: Rosenbach 1170/18 (27). Ink. Unpublished.

The Sweetser's eldest son, Henry Edwards, a young journalist of thirty-three, died on 17 February, after a long illness. He had collaborated with his cousin Charles Sweetser in founding the periodical *The Round Table*. The quatrain is in *Poems* (1955) 812.

339

To Louise and Frances Norcross   *early spring 1870*

Dear Children,

I think the bluebirds do their work exactly like me. They dart around just so, with little dodging feet, and look so agitated. I really feel for them, they seem to be so tried.

The mud is very deep – up to the wagons' stomachs – arbutus making pink clothes, and everything alive.

Even the hens are touched with the things of Bourbon, and make republicans like me feel strangely out of scene.

Mother went rambling, and came in with a burdock on her shawl, so we know that the snow has perished from the earth. Noah would have liked mother.

I am glad you are with Eliza. It is next to shade to know that those we love are cool on a parched day.

Bring my love to —— and Mr. ——. You will not need a hod. C[lara] writes often, full of joy and liberty. I guess it is a case of peace. . . .

Pussy has a daughter in the shavings barrel.

Father steps like Cromwell when he gets the kindlings.

Mrs. S[weetser] gets bigger, and rolls down the lane to church like a reverend marble. Did you know little Mrs. Holland was in Berlin for her eyes? . . .

Did you know about Mrs. J——? She fledged her antique wings. 'Tis said that "nothing in her life became her like the leaving it."

> Great Streets of Silence led away
> To Neighborhoods of Pause –
> Here was no Notice – no Dissent,
> No Universe – no Laws –
>
> By Clocks – 'twas Morning, and for Night
> The Bells at Distance called –
> But Epoch had no basis here,
> For Period exhaled.

Emily.

MANUSCRIPT: destroyed. The text of *Letters* (1931), where the letter but not the poem is published, is followed here. The poem follows the AC autograph, as published in *Poems* (1955) 810.

PUBLICATION: *L* (1894) 259–260; *LL* 271–272, in part; *L* (1931) 238–239. In all three the poem is omitted, but in both editions of *L* it is indicated as being part of the letter.

In the early spring of 1870 the Norcross sisters went to Milwaukee to be with their cousin Eliza Dudley, now an invalid. The Hollands returned from their trip to Europe in May. The person identified as C[lara] is probably Clara Newman Turner, who married Sidney Turner of Norwich, Connecticut, 14 October 1869. Mrs. Luke Sweetser was a rotund lady whose interest in fashions was locally recognized. (See letter no. 389.) The paraphrase in the last sentence is from *Macbeth*, I, iv, 7–8: "Nothing in his life/Became him like the leaving it. . ."

340

To Louise Norcross   *May 1870?*

This little sheet of paper has lain for several years in my Shakespeare, and though it is blotted and antiquated is endeared by its resting-place.

I always think of you peculiarly in May, as it is the peculiar anniversary of your loving kindness to me, though you have always been dear cousins, and blessed me all you could.

I cooked the peaches as you told me, and they swelled to beautiful fleshy halves and tasted quite magic. The beans we fricasseed and they made a savory cream in cooking that "Aunt Emily" liked to sip. She was always fonder of julep food than of more substantial. Your remembrance of her is very sweetly touching.

Maggie is ironing, and a cotton and linen and ruffle heat makes the pussy's cheeks red. It is lonely without the birds to-day, for it rains badly, and the little poets have no umbrellas. . . .

. . . Fly from Emily's window for Loo. Botanical name unknown.

MANUSCRIPT: destroyed.
PUBLICATION: *L* (1894) 260–261; *LL* 272, in part; *L* (1931) 239, and dated: May 1870.

In *Letters* (1894) and later, the final sentences are separated as above from the main text. They may or may not be a part of this letter. It is stated that they enclosed a pressed insect. ED is thinking of May as the anniversary month when she stayed in Cambridge, in 1864 and 1865, with the Norcrosses.

To Samuel Bowles   *June 1870?*

He is alive, this morning –
He is alive – and awake –
Birds are resuming for Him –
Blossoms – dress for His Sake.
Bees – to their Loaves of Honey
Add an Amber Crumb
Him – to regale – Me – Only –
Motion, and am dumb.

                                        Emily.

MANUSCRIPT: *HCL* (263). Pencil. Addressed on the fold: Mr Bowles –
PUBLICATION: *Poems* (1955) 811.

In June 1870 Mr. and Mrs. Bowles were overnight guests of the Dickinsons. It might have been on that occasion that the poem was written, but since it remained among her own papers it was probably never delivered.

To T. W. Higginson   *16 August 1870*

Dear friend

I will be at Home and glad.

I think you said the 15th. The incredible never surprises us because it is the incredible.

                                        E. Dickinson

MANUSCRIPT: BPL (Higg 62). Ink. Envelope addressed: Mr Higginson.

PUBLICATION: *L* (1894) 314; *LL* 275; *L* (1931) 284.

This note was delivered evidently by hand at the Amherst House, in response to one Higginson sent ED on his arrival, asking if he might call. She had expected him on the previous day, Monday. The following letter (BPL) Higginson wrote his wife that evening, dating it: Amherst/Tuesday 10 P.M.:

I shan't sit up tonight to write you all about E.D. dearest but if you had read Mrs. Stoddard's novels you could understand a house where each member runs his or her own selves. Yet I only saw her.

A large county lawyer's house, brown brick, with great trees & a garden — I sent up my card. A parlor dark & cool & stiffish, a few books & engravings & an open piano — Malbone & O D [Out Door] Papers among other books.

A step like a pattering child's in entry & in glided a little plain woman with two smooth bands of reddish hair & a face a little like Belle Dove's; not plainer — with no good feature — in a very plain & exquisitely clean white pique & a blue net worsted shawl. She came to me with two day lilies which she put in a sort of childlike way into my hand & said "These are my introduction" in a soft frightened breathless childlike voice — & added under her breath Forgive me if I am frightened; I never see strangers & hardly know what I say — but she talked soon & thenceforward continuously — & deferentially — sometimes stopping to ask me to talk instead of her — but readily recommencing. Manner between Angie Tilton & Mr. Alcott — but thoroughly ingenuous & simple which they are not & saying many things which you would have thought foolish & I wise — & some things you wd. hv. liked. I add a few over the page.

This is a lovely place, at least the view Hills everywhere, hardly mountains. I saw Dr. Stearns the Pres't of College — but the janitor cd. not be found to show me into the building I may try again tomorrow. I called on Mrs. Banfield & saw her five children – She looks much like H. H. *when ill* & was very cordial & friendly. Goodnight darling I am very sleepy & do good to write you this much. Thine am I

I got here at 2 & leave at 9. E.D. dreamed all night of *you* (not me) & next day got my letter proposing to come here!! She only knew of you through a mention in my notice of Charlotte Hawes.

"Women talk: men are silent: that is why I dread women.

"My father only reads on Sunday – he reads *lonely* & *rigorous* books."

"If I read a book [and] it makes my whole body so cold no fire ever

[473]

can warm me I know *that* is poetry. If I feel physically as if the top of my head were taken off, I know *that* is poetry. These are the only way I know it. Is there any other way."

"How do most people live without any thoughts. There are many people in the world (you must have noticed them in the street) How do they live. How do they get strength to put on their clothes in the morning"

"When I lost the use of my Eyes it was a comfort to think there were so few real *books* that I could easily find some one to read me all of them"

"Truth is such a *rare* thing it is delightful to tell it."

"I find ecstasy in living — the mere sense of living is joy enough"

I asked if she never felt want of employment, never going off the place & never seeing any visitor "I never thought of conceiving that I could ever have the slightest approach to such a want in all future time" (& added) "I feel that I have not expressed myself strongly enough."

She makes all the bread for her father only likes hers & says "& people must have puddings" this *very* dreamily, as if they were comets — so she makes them.

[That evening Higginson made this entry in his diary (HCL):]

To Amherst, arrived there at 2 Saw Prest Stearns, Mrs. Banfield & Miss Dickinson (twice) a remarkable experience, quite equalling my expectation. A pleasant country town, unspeakably quiet in the summer aftn.

[Next day he wrote his wife again, enclosing further notes (BPL), on ED. He dated the letter: Wednesday noon]:

342b

I am stopping for dinner at White River Junction, dearest, & in a few hours shall be at Littleton thence to go to Bethlehem. This morning at 9 I left Amherst & sent you a letter last night. I shall mail this at L. putting with it another sheet about E.D. that is in my valise.

She said to me at parting "Gratitude is the only secret that cannot reveal itself."

I talked with Prest Stearns of Amherst about her — & found him a very pleasant companion in the cars. Before leaving today, I got in to the Museums & enjoyed them much; saw a meteoric stone almost as long as my arm & weighing 436 lbs! a big slice of some other planet. It fell in Colorado. The collection of bird tracks of extinct birds in stone is very wonderful & unique & other good things. I saw Mr. Dickinson this morning a little — thin dry & speechless — I saw what her life has been. Dr. S. says her sister is proud of her.

I wd. have stolen a *totty* meteor, dear but they were under glass.

Mrs. Bullard I have just met in this train with spouse & son — I shall ride up with her.

Some pretty glimpses of mts. but all is dry and burnt I never saw the river at Brattleboro so low.

Did I say I staid at Sargents in Boston & she still hopes for Newport.

This picture of Mrs Browning's tomb is from E.D. "Timothy Titcomb" [Dr. Holland] gave it to her.

I think I will mail this here as I hv. found time to write so much. I miss you little woman & wish you were here but you'd hate travelling.

Ever

E D again

"Could you tell me what home is"

"I never had a mother. I suppose a mother is one to whom you hurry when you are troubled."

"I never knew how to tell time by the clock till I was 15. My father thought he had taught me but I did not understand & I was afraid to say I did not & afraid to ask any one else lest he should know."

Her father was not severe I should think but remote. He did not wish them to read anything but the Bible. One day her brother brought home Kavanagh hid it under the piano cover & made signs to her & they read it: her father at last found it & was displeased. Perhaps it was before this that a student of his was amazed that they had never heard of Mrs. [Lydia Maria] Child & used to bring them books & hide in a bush by the door. They were then little things in short dresses with their feet on the rungs of the chair. After the first book she thought in ecstasy "This then is a book! And there are more of them!"

"Is it oblivion or absorption when things pass from our minds?"

Major Hunt interested her more than any man she ever saw. She remembered two things he said — that her great dog "understood gravi-

[475]

tation" & when he said he should come again "in a year. If I say a shorter time it will be longer."

When I said I would come again *some time* she said "Say in a long time, that will be nearer. Some time is nothing."

After long disuse of her eyes she read Shakespeare & thought why is any other book needed.

I never was with any one who drained my nerve power so much. Without touching her, she drew from me. I am glad not to live near her. She often thought me *tired* & seemed very thoughtful of others.

[The postscript of a letter Higginson wrote his sisters (HCL) on Sunday, 21 August, adds:]

Of course I hv. enjoyed my trip very very much. In Amherst I had a nice aftn & evng with my singular poetic correspondent & the remarkable cabinets of the College.

[Recalling the interview twenty years later, Higginson wrote in the *Atlantic Monthly* LXVIII (October 1891) 453:]

The impression undoubtedly made on me was that of an excess of tension, and of an abnormal life. Perhaps in time I could have got beyond that somewhat overstrained relation which not my will, but her needs, had forced upon us. Certainly I should have been most glad to bring it down to the level of simple truth and every-day comradeship; but it was not altogether easy. She was much too enigmatical a being for me to solve in an hour's interview, and an instinct told me that the slightest attempt at direct cross-examination would make her withdraw into her shell; I could only sit still and watch, as one does in the woods; I must name my bird without a gun, as recomm_nded by Emerson.

343

To Louise and Frances Norcross   *late summer 1870?*

. . . Mother drives with Tim to carry pears to settlers. Sugar pears with hips like hams, and the flesh of bonbons. Vinnie fastens flowers from the frosts. . . .

Lifetime is for two, never for committee.

I saw your Mrs. H——. She looks a little tart, but Vinnie says makes excellent pies after one gets acquainted.

MANUSCRIPT: destroyed.
PUBLICATION: L (1894) 263; LL 274; L (1931) 241, where it is dated 1870.
Tim, the stableman, came to the Dickinsons in 1868.

344

To Louise and Frances Norcross   *1870?*

Dear Children,

When I think of your little faces I feel as the band does before it makes its first shout . . .

                                                                Emily.

MANUSCRIPT: destroyed.
PUBLICATION: L (1894) 262; LL 274; L (1931) 241, where it is dated 1870.

345

To Susan Gilbert Dickinson   *1870?*

My Turks will feel at Home in her familiar East—

                                                                Emily—

MANUSCRIPT: HCL (B 5). Pencil.
PUBLICATION: FF 241, with the note:" . . . sent with Sweet Sultans."
This and the following five messages sent to Susan Dickinson can be dated only by handwriting. They seem to have been written about the same time.

346

To Susan Gilbert Dickinson   *about 1870*

To see you unfits for staler meetings.
I dare not risk an intemperate moment before a Banquet of Bran.

MANUSCRIPT: HCL (B 10). Pencil. Addressed: Sue.
PUBLICATION: LL 65.

To Susan Gilbert Dickinson   *about 1870*

Oh Matchless Earth – We underrate the chance to dwell in Thee

MANUSCRIPT: HCL (B 49). Pencil.
PUBLICATION: *FF* 238.

348

To Susan Gilbert Dickinson   *about 1870*

We meet no Stranger but Ourself.

MANUSCRIPT: HCL (B 57). Pencil.
PUBLICATION: *FF* 259.

349

To Susan Gilbert Dickinson   *about 1870*
Were not Day of itself memorable, dear Sue's remembrance would
make it so

Emily.

MANUSCRIPT: HCL (B 8). Pencil.
PUBLICATION: *FF* 241.

350

To Susan Gilbert Dickinson   *about 1870*

Best Witchcraft is Geometry
To a Magician's eye –

Emily –

MANUSCRIPT: HCL (B 23). Pencil.
PUBLICATION: *Poems* (1955) 810.
These are the first two lines only of a quatrain which, in another ver-
sion written at the same time (HCL), reads:

Best Witchcraft is Geometry
To the magician's mind –
His ordinary acts are feats
To thinking of mankind.

351

To Mrs. J. G. Holland   *about 1870*

Our little Note was written several days ago, but delayed for Vinnie. Perhaps it's circumstances cease. Tears do not outgrow, however, so I venture sending.

Landscapes reverence the Frost, though it's gripe be past.

MANUSCRIPT: HCL (H 25). Pencil.
PUBLICATION: *LH* 86.
The circumstances here referred to have not been identified. The date is conjectured from the handwriting.

352

To T. W. Higginson   *26 September 1870*

Enough is so vast a sweetness I suppose it never occurs – only pathetic counterfeits – Fabulous to me as the men of the Revelations who "shall not hunger any more." Even the Possible has it's insoluble particle.

After you went I took Macbeth and turned to "Birnam Wood." Came twice "to Dunsinane" – I thought and went about my work.

I remember your coming as serious sweetness placed now with the Unreal –

Trust adjusts her "Peradventure" –
Phantoms entered "and not you."

The Vein cannot thank the Artery – but her solemn indebtedness to him, even the stolidest admit and so of me who try, whose effort leaves no sound.

You ask great questions accidentally. To answer them would be events. I trust that you are safe.

I ask you to forgive me for all the ignorance I had.

I find no nomination sweet as your low opinion.

Speak, if but to blame your obedient child. You told me of Mrs Lowell's Poems.

Would you tell me where I could find them or are they not for sight?

An article of your's, too, perhaps the only one you wrote that I never knew. It was about a "Latch."

Are you willing to tell me? If I ask too much, you could please refuse — Shortness to live has made me bold.

Abroad is close tonight and I have but to lift my Hands to touch the "Hights of Abraham."

Dickinson

MANUSCRIPT: BPL (Higg 65). Ink. Endorsed by TWH: R[eceived] Sept 27, 1870 (after my visit). Envelope addressed: Mr. Higginson.

PUBLICATION: *AM* LXVIII (October 1891) 453–454; *L* (1894) 315–316, in part; *LL* 276–277, in part; *L* (1931) 288–289.

Relative to the second paragraph: Higginson did in fact make a second call on ED in December 1873. Maria White Lowell's poems were posthumously issued in 1855. Higginson's article about a "Latch" could have been either of two, both on the subject of women's rights: "The Door Unlatched," in *The Woman's Journal*, 15 January 1870 (reprinted on the same day in the *Springfield Republican*); or "The Gate Unlatched," in *The Woman's Journal*, 9 July 1870. "The Hights of Abraham" may be intended to refer to Mount Moriah, but ED's evident fascination with the drama of the Wolfe-Montcalm conflict ("Wolfe demanded during dying") suggests that she has in mind the citadel above Quebec. The quotation is from Revelation 7.16: "They shall hunger no more. . ."

353

To T. W. Higginson   *about October 1870*

> The Riddle that we guess
> We speedily despise –
> Not anything is stale so long
> As Yesterday's Surprise –

The Risks of Immortality are perhaps its' charm – A secure Delight suffers in enchantment –

The larger Haunted House it seems, of maturer Childhood – distant, an alarm – entered intimate at last as a neighbor's Cottage –
> The Spirit said unto the Dust
> Old Friend, thou knewest me
> And Time went out to tell the news
> Unto Eternity –

Those of that renown personally precious, harrow like a Sunset, proved but not obtained –

Tennyson knew this, "Ah Christ – if it be possible" and even in Our Lord's ["]that they be with me where I am," I taste interrogation.
> Experiment escorts us last –
> His pungent company
> Will not allow an Axiom
> An Opportunity –

You speak of "tameless tastes" – A Beggar came last week – I gave him Food and Fire and as he went, "Where do you go,"
"In all the directions" –
That was what you meant
> Too happy Time dissolves itself
> And leaves no remnant by –
> 'Tis Anguish not a Feather hath
> Or too much weight to fly –

I was much refreshed by your strong Letter –
Thank you for Greatness – I will have deserved it in a longer time!
I thought I spoke to you of the shadow –
It affects me –
This was still another –
I saw it's notice in the Papers just before you came – Is there a magazinine called the "Woman's Journal"? I think it was said to be in that – a Gate, or Door, or Latch –
Someone called me suddenly, and I never found it –
You told me Mrs Lowell was Mr Lowell's "inspiration" What is inspiration?
You place the truth in opposite – because the fear is mine, dear friend, and the power your's –
> 'Tis Glory's far sufficiency   far sufficiency] overtakelessness
> that make's our trying poor –   trying] running

[481]

With the Kingdom of Heaven on his knee, could Mr Emerson hesitate?

"Suffer little Children" –

Could you not come without the Lecture, if the project failed?

MANUSCRIPT: AC. Pencil.
PUBLICATION:*NEQ* XXVIII (1955) 297-298.
This is the rough draft of a letter which perhaps was never sent, since no fair copy of it is among the Higginson papers.

ED here expresses in a series of quatrains a condensation of the thoughts that followed her conversation with Higginson in August. The letter replies to one from him, received since her last was written, in which he evidently suggested that the essay of his she might have in mind was "A Shadow" (*Atlantic Monthly*, July 1870). She here makes clear that she had read "A Shadow."

354

To Mrs. J. G. Holland   *early October 1870*

I guess I wont send that note now, for the mind is such a new place, last night feels obsolete.

Perhaps you thought dear Sister, I wanted to elope with you and feared a vicious Father.

It was not quite that.

The Papers thought the Doctor was mostly in New York. Who then would read for you? Mr Chapman, doubtless, or Mr Buckingham! The Doctor's sweet reply makes me infamous.

Life is the finest secret.

So long as that remains, we must all whisper.

With that sublime exception I had no clandestineness.

It was lovely to see you and I hope it may happen again. These beloved accidents must become more frequent.

We are by September and yet my flowers are bold as June. Amherst has gone to Eden.

To shut our eyes is Travel.

The Seasons understand this.

How lonesome to be an Article! I mean – to have no soul.

An Apple fell in the night and a Wagon stopped.
I suppose the Wagon ate the Apple and resumed it's way.
How fine it is to talk.
What Miracles the News is!
Not Bismark but ourselves.

> The Life we have is very great.
> The Life that we shall see
> Surpasses it, we know, because
> It is Infinity.
> But when all Space has been beheld
> And all Dominion shown
> The smallest Human Heart's extent
> Reduces it to none.

Love for the Doctor, and the Girls.
Ted might not acknowledge me.

Emily.

MANUSCRIPT: HCL (H 24). Ink.
PUBLICATION: LH 84–86.
The Hollands had returned to Springfield in the spring of 1870, and
visited in Amherst during the summer. A new enterprise kept Dr. Holland
much in New York during October, when the first issue of the magazine
he edited, *Scribner's Monthly*, was being prepared for the press. In the
person of Bismark, ED alludes to the principal news of the day, the Franco-
Prussian war.

355

To Perez Cowan   *late October 1870*

Dear Peter

It is indeed sweet news.

I am proud of your happiness. To Peter and Peter's, let me give
both Hands. Delight has no Competitor, so it is always most.

"Maggie" is a warm name. I shall like to take it. Home is the
definition of God.

Emily.

MANUSCRIPT: Huntington Memorial Library, Oneonta, N. Y. Ink.

PUBLICATION: *L* (1894) 332; *LL* 275, in part; *L* (1931) 322.
Perez Cowan, at this time pastor of a Presbyterian church in Rogersville, Tennessee, married Margaret Rhea of Blountville, Tennessee, on 26 October 1870.

356

To Susan Gilbert Dickinson   *19 December 1870*

> Lest any doubt that we are glad that they were born Today
> Whose having lived is held by us in noble Holiday
> Without the date, like Consciousness or Immortality –
>
>   Emily –

MANUSCRIPT: HCL (B 33). Pencil.
PUBLICATION: *FF* 225, with note: "To Sue with flowers on her birthday"; *Poems* (1955) 809.
The handwriting suggests 1870, the year in which Sue celebrated her fortieth birthday.

357

To Louise and Frances Norcross   *December 1870?*

Untiring Little Sisters,

What will I ever do for you, yet have done the most, for love is that one perfect labor nought can supersede. I suppose the pain is still there, for pain that is worthy does not go so soon. The small can crush the great, however, only temporarily. In a few days we examine, muster our forces, and cast it away. Put it out of your hearts, children. Faith is too fair to taint it so. There are those in the morgue that bewitch us with sweetness, but that which is dead must go with the ground. There is a verse in the Bible that says there are those who shall not see death. I suppose them to be the faithful. Love will not expire. There was never the instant when it was lifeless in the world, though the quicker deceit dies, the better for the truth, who is indeed our dear friend.

I am sure you will gain, even from this wormwood. The martyrs may not choose their food.

God made no act without a cause,
Nor heart without an aim,
Our inference is premature,
Our premises to blame.
. . . Sweetest of Christmas to you both, and a better year.

Emily.

MANUSCRIPT: destroyed.
PUBLICATION: L (1894) 262; LL 273–274; L (1931) 240–241.
Although containing Christmas greetings, this letter is chiefly concerned with the emotional difficulties of the sisters, who seem to have found complications in personal relations while living in the home of the Reverend John Dudley in Milwaukee.

358

To Edward (Ned) Dickinson   *about 1 January 1871*

Lacking New-Year, without little Ned.

MANUSCRIPT: HCL (B 105). Pencil. Unpublished.
The date is conjectured from the handwriting. The note may have accompanied some small gift, sent at a time when Ned was confined by an illness.

359

To Mrs. J. G. Holland   *early January 1871*

I have a fear I did not thank you for the thoughtful Candy.
Could you conscientiously dispel it by saying that I did?
Generous little Sister!
I will protect the Thimble till it reaches Home —
Even the Thimble has it's Nest!
The Parting I tried to smuggle resulted in quite a Mob at last!
The Fence is the only Sanctuary. That no one invades because no one suspects it.
Why the Thief ingredient accompanies all Sweetness Darwin does not tell us.
Each expiring Secret leaves an Heir, distracting still.

[485]

Our unfinished interview like the Cloth of Dreams, cheapens other fabrics.

That Possession fairest lies that is least possest.

Transport's mighty price is no more than he is worth –
Would we sell him for it? That is all his Test.

Dont affront the Eyes –

Little Despots govern worst.

Vinnie leaves me Monday – Spare me your remembrance while I buffet Life and Time without –

Emily.

MANUSCRIPT: HCL (H 26). Ink.
PUBLICATION: LH 87.

Early in January Vinnie went to New York to visit the Hills. Mrs. Holland had evidently, on a recent call, forgotten her thimble, which she has asked ED to forward. The expression "Mob at last" implies that ED and Mrs. Holland had tried to converse privately when they parted after Mrs. Holland's call, but had been interrupted. The place probably was the little back hall connected with the kitchen, which had come to be known as the "Northwest Passage" (see FF 25).

360

To Louise Norcross   *spring 1871*

The will is always near, dear, though the feet vary. The terror of the winter has made a little creature of me, who thought myself so bold.

Father was very sick. I presumed he would die, and the sight of his lonesome face all day was harder than personal trouble. He is growing better, though physically reluctantly. I hope I am mistaken, but I think his physical life don't want to live any longer. You know he never played, and the straightest engine has its leaning hour. Vinnie was not here. Now we will turn the corner. All this while I was with you all, much of every hour, wishing we were near enough to assist each other. Would you have felt more at home, to know we were both in extremity? That would be my only regret that I had not told you.

As regards the "pine" and the "jay," it is a long tryst, but I think they are able. I have spoken with them.

Of the "thorn," dear, give it to me, for I am strongest. Never carry what I can carry, for though I think I bend, something straightens me. Go to the "wine-press," dear, and come back and say has the number altered. I descry but one. What I would, I cannot say in so small a place.

Interview is acres, while the broadest letter feels a bandaged place. . . .

Tell Fanny we hold her tight. Tell Loo love is oldest and takes care of us, though just now in a piercing place.

Emily.

MANUSCRIPT: destroyed.

PUBLICATION: L (1894) 263–264; LL 274–275; L (1931) 241–242.

Vinnie was in New York visiting the Hills. Samuel Bowles wrote his son, 24 March 1871 (MS: Bowles): "The elder Dickinson has been quite feeble all winter, a sort of breaking-down with dyspepsia — & it shames him that he is hardly to be recognized in his old character." Louise Norcross has evidently written ED about the distressing condition of Eliza Dudley, with whom she is now staying. Eliza died three months later.

361

To Mrs. Henry Hills   *spring 1871*

Dear friend.

To be remembered is next to being loved, and to be loved is Heaven, and is this quite Earth? I have never found it so. Most affectionately thanking you for the care of Vinnie and the delight you have given all in delighting her, especially acknowledging the sweetness done myself, I am the trifling Neighbor, praying you Tonight as always, to come back and dwell. To "Little Emily's" Mama, could name be more familiar than that of a remoter, though scarcely vaster

Emily.

MANUSCRIPT: Brown. Ink. Unpublished.

Vinnie had just returned from a visit to the Hills in New York. Emily Hills was born 12 September 1870.

To Louise Norcross   *mid-July 1871*

I like to thank you, dear, for the annual candy. Though you make no answer, I have no letter from the dead, yet daily love them more. No part of mind is permanent. This startles the happy, but it assists the sad.

This is a mighty morning. I trust that Loo is with it, on hill or pond or wheel. Too few the mornings be, too scant the nights. No lodging can be had for the delights that come to earth to stay, but no apartment find and ride away. Fanny was brave and dear, and helped as much by counsel as by actual team. Whether we missed Loo we will let her guess; riddles are healthful food.

Eliza was not with us, but it was owing to the trains. We know she meant to come.

Oh! Cruel Paradise! We have a chime of bells given for brave Frazer. You'll stop and hear them, won't you?

"We conquered, but Bozzaris fell." That sentence always chokes me.

                                                                 Emily.

MANUSCRIPT: destroyed.
PUBLICATION: L (1894) 265–266; LL 279–280; L (1931) 243–244.

The bells given in memory of Frazar Stearns were hung on July fourth; commencement took place, 13 July. The Norcross girls were always guests of the Dickinsons, when they could attend commencement, as Fanny did this year. Loo, being unable, had nevertheless sent a box of candy, her "annual" gift, which this letter acknowledges. Eliza Coleman Dudley had died on 3 June; Loo was still in Milwaukee. "Marco Bozzaris," by Fitz-Greene Halleck, was a widely popular ballad, first published in 1825. The line reads: "They conquered — but Bozzaris fell."

To Mrs. Lucius Boltwood   *late July 1871*

To thank my dear Mrs Boltwood would be impossible. That is a paltry debt — we are able to pay.

It is sweet to be under obligation to my School Mate's Mother.

I thought the flowers might please him, though he made like Birds, the exchange of Latitudes.

It is proud to believe that his Privilege so far surpasses Ours.

Let me congratulate his Mother.

Tenderly,
Emily

MANUSCRIPT: missing.

PUBLICATION: *Amherst Graduates Magazine*, XXVI (1937) 305; Allen: *Around a Village Green*, pp. 54-55.

Charles Upham Boltwood died, 23 July 1871, aged 34; both George and Henry Boltwood had graduated from Amherst Academy in ED's class in 1847. Charles had been in the Academy, in a much lower class.

364

To Susan Gilbert Dickinson   *September 1871*

To miss you, Sue, is power.

The stimulus of Loss makes most Possession mean.

To live lasts always, but to love is firmer than to live. No Heart that broke but further went than Immortality.

The Trees keep House for you all Day and the Grass looks chastened.

A silent Hen frequents the place with superstitious Chickens – and still Forenoons a Rooster knocks at your outer Door.

To look that way is Romance. The Novel "out," pathetic worth attaches to the Shelf.

Nothing has gone but Summer, or no one that you knew.

The Forests are at Home – the Mountains intimate at Night and arrogant at Noon, and lonesome Fluency abroad, like suspending Music.

> Of so divine a Loss
> We enter but the Gain,
> Indemnity for Loneliness
> That such a Bliss has been.

Tell Neddie that we miss him and cherish "Captain Jinks." Tell Mattie that "Tim's["] Dog calls Vinnie's Pussy names and I don't dis-

[489]

courage him. She must come Home and chase them both and that will make it square.

For Big Mattie and John, of course a strong remembrance.

I trust that you are warm. I keep your faithful place. Whatever throng the Lock is firm upon your Diamond Door.

Emily.

MANUSCRIPT: HCL (B 184). Ink.
PUBLICATION: FF 233–234, in part.
Sue was visiting her sister Martha Smith, in Geneva, New York. "Captain Jinks," associated with the horse marines in popular song, was ED's nickname for Ned (see also letter no. 397).

365

To Susan Gilbert Dickinson   *about 1871*

Trust is better than Contract, for one is still, but the other moves.

Emily.

MANUSCRIPT: HCL (B 107). Pencil.
PUBLICATION: FF 254.
The date of this and the following brief note to Susan Dickinson is conjectured from the handwriting to be about 1871.

366

To Susan Gilbert Dickinson   *about 1871*

Has All – a codicil?

Emily.

MANUSCRIPT: HCL (B 182). Pencil. Addressed: Sue.
PUBLICATION: LL 62.
The occasions or situations which prompted these notes are not known.

367

To Louise and Frances Norcross   *early October 1871*

We have the little note and are in part relieved, but have been too alarmed and grieved to hush immediately. The heart keeps sobbing in its sleep. It is the speck that makes the cloud that wrecks the vessel, children, yet no one fears a speck. I hope what is not lost is saved. Were any angel present, I feel it could not be allowed. So grateful that our little girls are not on fire too. Amherst would have quenched them. Thank you for comforting innocent blamed creatures. We are trying, too. The mayor of Milwaukee cuts and you and Loo sew, don't you? The *New York Times* said so. Sorrow is the "funds" never quite spent, always a little left to be loaned kindly. We have a new cow. I wish I could give Wisconsin a little pail of milk. Dick's Maggie is wilting. Awkward little flower, but transplanting makes it fair. How are the long days that made the fresh afraid?

Brother Emily.

MANUSCRIPT: destroyed.
PUBLICATION: *L* (1894) 264–265; *L* (1931) 242.
The great Chicago fire was on 8–9 October 1871, but there were forest fires in Wisconsin that month at exactly the same time, less publicized but involving much greater loss of life. On Maggie Kelley, see letters no. 372 and 375.

368

To T. W. Higginson   *November 1871*

I did not read Mr Miller because I could not care about him –
Transport is not urged –
Mrs Hunt's Poems are stronger than any written by Women since Mrs – Browning, with the exception of Mrs Lewes – but truth like Ancestor's Brocades can stand alone – You speak of "Men and Women." That is a broad Book – "Bells and Pomegranates" I never saw but have Mrs Browning's endorsement. While Shakespeare remains Literature is firm –
An Insect cannot run away with Achilles' Head. Thank you for having written the "Atlantic Essays." They are a fine Joy – though to possess the ingredient for Congratulation renders congratulation superfluous.
Dear friend, I trust you as you ask – If I exceed permission, excuse the bleak simplicity that knew no tutor but the North. Would you but guide

Dickinson

[491]

Manuscript: BPL (Higg 74). Ink. Envelope addressed: Mr Higginson.
Publication: L (1894) 320, garbled; LL 293–294, garbled; L (1931) 295.

Four poems are enclosed: "When I hoped I feared," "The Days that we car spare," "Step lightly on this narrow spot," and "Remembrance has a Rear and Front." Joaquin Miller's *Songs of the Sierras* appeared in 1871. Helen Hunt's *Verses* had appeared the year before. Browning is referred to by *Men and Women* (1855) and *Bells and Pomegranates* (1846). Higginson's *Atlantic Essays* was issued in September 1871.

For a note on "Ancestor's Brocades," see letter no. 277.

369

To Mrs. J. G. Holland   *late November 1871*

Dear Sister.

Bereavement to yourself your faith makes secondary. We who cannot hear your voice are chastened indeed —

"Whom he loveth, he punisheth," is a doubtful solace finding tart response in the lower Mind.

I shall cherish the Stripes though I regret that your latest Act must have been a Judicial one. It comforts the Criminal little to know that the Law expires with him.

Beg the Oculist to commute your Sentence that you may also commute mine. Doubtless he has no friend and to curtail Communion is all that remains to him.

This transitive malice will doubtless retire – offering you anew to us and ourselves to you.

I am pleased the Gingerbread triumphed.

Let me know your circumstance through some minor Creature, abler in Machinery if unknown to Love.

Steam has his Commissioner, tho' his substitute is not yet disclosed of God.

Emily.

Manuscript: HCL (H 27). Ink.
Publication: LH 88–89.
A friend of both Bowles and Holland, Albert D. Briggs of Springfield,

was appointed one of the Massachusetts railroad commissioners on 22 November. The quotation is from Hebrews 12.6: ". . . whom the Lord loveth he chasteneth. . ." This letter implies that ED had sent Mrs. Holland her recipe for gingerbread, doubtless the same as that which she supplied Susan Dickinson, who added it to her manuscript cookbook. It follows below.

369a

  1 Quart Flour,
½ Cup Butter,
½ Cup Cream,
  1 Table Spoon Ginger,
  1 Tea Spoon Soda,
  1 Salt

Make up with Molasses –

MANUSCRIPT: HCL (B 164). Pencil.
PUBLICATION: FF 230, in part.
The handwriting is the same as that of the preceding letter.

370

To Mrs. J. G. Holland   *about 1872*

That so trifling a Creature grieve any I could hardly suppose – though with Love all things are possible.

Thanking you tenderly as a child for a sweet favor I can never go. This will not retard my place in Affection will it?

I shall still be mentioned when the children come?

Some must seem a Traitor, not because it is, but it's Truth belie it.

Andre had not died had he lived Today.

Only Love can wound –

Only Love assist the Wound.

Worthier let us be of this Ample Creature.

If my Crescent fail you, try me in the Moon –

This will make no difference in the daily dearness?

You will keep the same Face and myself no other Heart, with the slight repairs Thought and Nature make –

In adequate Music there is a Major and a Minor –

Should there not also be a Private?

Good Night – I am going to sleep if the Rat permit me – I hear him singing now to the Tune of a Nut.

I could wish to know, be it by a Trifle, that you name me still.

Emily.

MANUSCRIPT: HCL (H 28). Ink.
PUBLICATION: *LH* 89–90.

Evidently Mrs. Holland asked ED to pay a visit to Springfield. The date is conjectured from the handwriting.

371

To T. W. Higginson   *mid-March* 1872

Dear friend –

I am sorry your Brother is dead.

I fear he was dear to you.

I should be glad to know you were painlessly grieved –

> Of Heaven above the firmest proof
> We fundamental know –
> Except for it's marauding Hand
> It had been Heaven below –

Dickinson

MANUSCRIPT: BPL (Higg 75). Ink.
PUBLICATION: *L* (1894) 321; *LL* 300; *L* (1931) 296.

Higginson's brother Dr. Francis John Higginson died on 9 March 1872; the notice of his death in the *Springfield Republican* speaks of him as "one of the pioneers in the anti-slavery cause." Higginson has dated the letter "1875," clearly an error as the handwriting reveals. He was probably placing the date later, from memory. His sister Susan Louisa died 27 August 1875.

To *Louise and Frances Norcross*   *early May 1872*

Dear Children,

We received the news of your loving kindness through Uncle Joel last evening, and Vinnie is negotiating with neighbor Gray, who goes to a wedding in Boston next week, for the procuring of the nest. Vinnie's views of expressage do not abate with time. The crocuses are with us and several other colored friends. Cousin H[arriet] broke her hip, and is in a polite bed, surrounded by mint juleps. I think she will hate to leave it as badly as *Marian Erle* did. Vinnie says there is a tree in Mr. Sweetser's woods that shivers. I am afraid it is cold. I am going to make it a little coat. I must make several, because it is tall as the barn, and put them on as the circus men stand on each other's shoulders. . . . There is to be a "show" next week, and little Maggie's bed is to be moved to the door so she can see the tents. Folding her own like the Arabs gives her no apprehension. While I write, dear children, the colors Eliza loved quiver on the pastures, and day goes gay to the northwest, innocent as she.

                                                                  Emily.

MANUSCRIPT: destroyed.

PUBLICATION: L (1894) 269; LL 280–281; L (1931) 246–247.

Harriet Montague broke her hip 28 March 1872. The circus was in town on 14 May. Maggie Kelley lived until July. (See letter no. 375.) "Marian Erle" is a character in Mrs. Browning's *Aurora Leigh*.

To *Edward (Ned) Dickinson*   *mid-May 1872?*

Neddie never would believe that Emily was at his Circus, unless she left a fee —

MANUSCRIPT: HCL (L 52). Pencil. Envelope addressed: Neddie. Unpublished. The impression of a coin still shows in the note. Ned may have had his circus soon after the visiting circus had been in Amherst, 14 May.

To Louise Norcross   *1872?*

Thank you dear for the passage. How long to live the truth is.
> A word is dead, when it is said
> Some say —
> I say it just begins to live
> That day.

MANUSCRIPT: destroyed. The text is from *AB* 284.
PUBLICATION: *L* (1894) 269; *LL* 281; *L* (1931) 247; *AB* 284, where
the word "dear" is restored. In *Letters* the text is dated 1872.

To Louise and Frances Norcross   *27 July 1872*

Little Irish Maggie went to sleep this morning at six o'clock, just
the time grandpa rises, and will rest in the grass at Northampton tomorrow. She has had a hard sickness, but her awkward little life is
saved and gallant now. Our Maggie is helping her mother put her
in the cradle. . . .

Month after this – after that is October, isn't it? That isn't much
long. Joy to enfold our little girls in so close a future. That was a
lovely letter of Fanny's. It put the cat to playing and the kettle to
purring, and two or three birds in plush teams reined nearer to the
window. . . . You will miss the nasturtiums, but you will meet the
chestnuts. You also will miss the south wind, but I will save the
west. . . .

Of course we shall have a telegram that you have left for Ne-
braska. . . .

                                                                    Emily.

MANUSCRIPT: destroyed.
PUBLICATION: *L* (1894) 269–270; *L* (1931) 247.
Margaret Kelley, aged 17, daughter of James and Ellen Kelley, died,
27 July 1872.

To Mrs. Henry Hills   *1872?*

Will Mrs Hills please break an Ounce Isinglass in a Quart of fresh Milk, placing in boiling Water till quite dissolved, adding afterward four table spoons Chocolate shavings and two of Sugar, boiling together fifteen minutes and straining before turning into molds.

Let me thank my sweet neighbor for her thoughtfulness.

Dickinson

MANUSCRIPT: missing. The text is from a transcript made by George Frisbie Whicher of the autograph when it was still in the possession of Mrs. Hills's daughter, Mrs. Susan H. Skillings. He thought it might have been written in 1872. It is in ink, on paper watermarked 1862. Unpublished.

This is a recipe for chocolate dessert.

377

To Mrs. J. G. Holland   *late August 1872*

To have lost an Enemy is an Event with all of us – almost more memorable perhaps than to find a friend. This severe success befalls our little Sister – and though the Tears insist at first, as in all good fortune, Gratitude grieves best.

Fortified by Love, a few have prevailed.

"Even so, Father, for so it seemed faithful in thy Sight."

We are proud of her safety – Ashamed of our dismay for her who knew no consternation.

It is the Meek that Valor wear too mighty for the Bold.

We should be glad to know of her present Lifetime, it's project, though a little changed – so precious to us all.

Be secure of this, that whatever waver – her Gibraltar's Heart is firm.

Emily.

MANUSCRIPT: HCL (H 29). Ink.
PUBLICATION: *LH* 91.

Mrs. Holland's eye disease became acute, and necessitated an operation for the removal of one eye. ED perhaps wrote this letter on reading the report of the operation in the *Springfield Republican* for 29 August 1872. The Hollands were now in New York. The scripture quotation, from Matthew 11. 26, is evidently from memory, for ED substitutes *faithful* for *good*.

378

To Susan Gilbert Dickinson   autumn 1872

My Sue,

   Loo and Fanny will come tonight, but need that make a difference? Space is as the Presence –

> A narrow Fellow in the Grass
> Occasionally rides –
> You may have met him? Did you not
> His notice instant is –
>
> The Grass divides as with a Comb –
> A spotted shaft is seen,
> And then it closes at your Feet
> And opens farther on –
>
> He likes a Boggy Acre –
> A Floor too cool for Corn –
> But when a Boy and Barefoot
> I more than once at Noon
>
> Have passed I thought a Whip Lash
> Unbraiding in the Sun
> When stooping to secure it
> It wrinkled and was gone –
>
> Several of Nature's People
> I know and they know me
> I feel for them a transport
> Of Cordiality

But never met this Fellow
Attended or alone
Without a tighter Breathing
And Zero at the Bone.

Emily –

MANUSCRIPT: HCL (B 193). Ink.
PUBLICATION: FF 231–232, letter only; *Poems* (1955) 712–713, entire.
The Norcross sisters returned from Milwaukee in the autumn, 1872.
Sue appears to have asked for a copy of "The Snake." (See letter no. 316.)

379

To Louise Norcross *late 1872*

. . . How short it takes to go, dear, but afterward to come so many weary years – and yet 'tis done as cool as a general trifle. Affection is like bread, unnoticed till we starve, and then we dream of it, and sing of it, and paint it, when every urchin in the street has more than he can eat. We turn not older with years, but newer every day.

Of all these things we tried to talk, but the time refused us. Longing, it may be, is the gift no other gift supplies. Do you remember what you said the night you came to me? I secure that sentence. If I should see your face no more it will be your portrait, and if I should, more vivid than your mortal face. We must be careful what we say. No bird resumes its egg.

A word left careless on a page
May consecrate an eye,
When folded in perpetual seam
The wrinkled author lie.

Emily.

MANUSCRIPT: destroyed.
PUBLICATION: L (1894) 276–277; LL 288; L (1931) 252.
A worksheet draft of the poem (AC) can be dated about 1872. ED seems to have in mind the visit of the previous autumn.

To Louise Norcross   *late 1872*

An ill heart, like a body, has its more comfortable days, and then its days of pain, its long relapse, when rallying requires more effort than to dissolve life, and death looks choiceless.

Of Miss P—— I know but this, dear. She wrote me in October, requesting me to aid the world by my chirrup more. Perhaps she stated it as my duty, I don't distinctly remember, and always burn such letters, so I cannot obtain it now. I replied declining. She did not write to me again – she might have been offended, or perhaps is extricating humanity from some hopeless ditch. . . .

MANUSCRIPT: destroyed. The text is from L (1894).
PUBLICATION: L (1894) 267; LL 281, garbled; L (1931) 244–245.
The "ill heart" seems to have been Loo's; she had been very upset by John Dudley's marriage, 23 October, to Marion V. Churchill. The Miss P may be Elizabeth Stuart Phelps. Though only twenty-eight at the time, she was already well known through *Gates Ajar* (1868), an impassioned plea for a wider life for women. She was an editor of *The Woman's Journal*, and Higginson knew her.

To T. W. Higginson   *late 1872*

To live is so startling, it leaves but little room for other occupations though Friends are if possible an event more fair.

I am happy you have the Travel you so long desire and chastened – that my Master met neither accident nor Death.

> Our own Possessions though our own
> 'Tis well to hoard anew
> Remembering the dimensions
> Of Possibility.

I often saw your name in illustrious mention and envied an occasion so abstinent to me. Thank you for having been to Amherst. Could you come again that would be far better – though the finest wish is the futile one.

When I saw you last, it was Mighty Summer — Now the Grass is Glass and the Meadow Stucco, and "Still Waters" in the Pool where the Frog drinks.

These Behaviors of the Year hurt almost like Music — shifting when it ease us most. Thank you for the "Lesson."

I will study it though hitherto
<blockquote>
Menagerie to me
My Neighbor be.
</blockquote>

Your Scholar

MANUSCRIPT: BPL (Higg 67). Ink.

PUBLICATION: L (1894) 316–317; LL 277; L (1931) 290.

Higginson sailed for Europe in late April, 1872, and returned early in July. His name appeared frequently in the *Springfield Republican* during that time. His penciled date on the letter "1871?" was obviously added later. ED enclosed three poems: "To disappear enhances," "He preached upon Breadth," and "The Sea said 'Come' to the Brook."

382

To Louise and Frances Norcross   *winter 1873?*

. . . I know I love my friends — I feel it far in here where neither blue nor black eye goes, and fingers cannot reach. I know 'tis love for them that sets the blister in my throat, many a time a day, when winds go sweeter than their wont, or a different cloud puts my brain from home.

<blockquote>
I can not see my soul, but know 'tis there —
Nor ever saw his house, nor furniture —
Who has invited me with him to dwell;
But a confiding guest, consult as well,
What raiment honor him the most,
That I be adequately dressed —
For he insures to none
Lest men specifical adorn —
Procuring him perpetual drest
By dating it a sudden feast.
</blockquote>

— Love for the glad if you know them, for the sad if they know you.

Manuscript: destroyed.
Publication: L (1894) 272; LL 283; L (1931) 248–249.
In *Letters* this is dated "Winter, 1873." Frances Norcross's transcript of the poem and final sentence is in the Bingham collection (AC), and is here reproduced. The dash preceding the final sentence may have been Miss Norcross's way of indicating an omission. She seems also to have omitted the beginning of the letter.

383

To Susan Gilbert Dickinson   *early 1873?*

Dear Sue –

I would have liked to be beautiful and tidy when you came –

You will excuse me, wont you, I felt so sick. How it would please me if you would come once more, when I was palatable.

Emily

Manuscript: HCL (B 153). Ink.
Publication: FF 267.
The handwriting places the letter about this time.

384

To Susan Gilbert Dickinson   *early 1873?*

Sue makes sick Days so sweet, we almost hate our health.

Emily –

Manuscript: HCL (B 122). Pencil.
Publication: FF 238, with facsimile reproduction.
The handwriting and the tone of the messages suggest that this and the preceding one go together.

385

To Frances Norcross   *early 1873*

. . . I was sick, little sister, and write you the first that I am able. The loveliest sermon I ever heard was the disappointment of

Jesus in Judas. It was told like a mortal story of intimate young men. I suppose no surprise we can ever have will be so sick as that. The last "I never knew you" may resemble it. I would your hearts could have rested from the first severity before you received this other one, but "not as I will." I suppose the wild flowers encourage themselves in the dim woods, and the bird that is bruised limps to his house in silence, but we have human natures, and these are different. It is lovely that Mrs. W—— did not disappoint you; not that I thought it possible, but you were so much grieved. . . . A finite life, little sister, is that peculiar garment that were it optional with us we might decline to wear. Tender words to Loo, not most, I trust, in need of them.

Lovingly,

Emily.

MANUSCRIPT: destroyed.
PUBLICATION: L (1894) 276; LL 287–288; L (1931) 251–252.

Though dated 1874 in *Letters*, this letter, with its reference to Louise, may be part of the sequence following letters no. 380 and 382. Mrs. W has not been identified.

386

To Perez Cowan   *about February 1873*

It is long since I knew of you, Peter, and much may have happened to both, but that is the rarest Book which opened at whatever page, equally enchants us. I hope that you have Power and as much of Peace as in our deep existence may be possible. To multiply the Harbors does not reduce the Sea.

We learn thro' Cousins Montague that you have lost your Sister through that sweeter Loss which we call Gain.

I am glad she is glad.

Her early pain had seemed to me peculiarly cruel.

Tell her how tenderly we are pleased.

Recall me too to your other Sisters, who tho' they may have mislaid me I can always find and include me to your sweet Wife. We are daily reminded of you by the Clergyman, Mr Jenkins, whom you strongly resemble.

Thank you for the Paper –

It is Home-like to know where you are.

We can almost hear you announce the Text, when the Air is clear and how social if you should preach us a note some Sunday in Recess.

Emily.

MANUSCRIPT: Morgan Library. Ink.

PUBLICATION: L (1894) 333; LL 278; L (1931) 322–323.

The Amherst Student for February 1873 notes that Cowan is editor of *The Record*, a monthly religious paper published at Knoxville, Tennessee. The handwriting confirms the date.

387

To Louise and Frances Norcross   *March 1873?*

. . . I open my window, and it fills the chamber with white dirt. I think God must be dusting; and the wind blows so I expect to read in *The Republican* "Cautionary signals for Amherst," or, "No ships ventured out from Phœnix Row." . . . Life is so rotatory that the wilderness falls to each, sometime. It is safe to remember that. . . .

MANUSCRIPT: destroyed.

PUBLICATION: L (1894) 272; LL 283; L (1931) 249.

The text is dated "March 1873" in *Letters*.

388

To Louise and Frances Norcross   *April 1873?*

Sisters,

I hear robins a great way off, and wagons a great way off, and rivers a great way off, and all appear to be hurrying somewhere undisclosed to me. Remoteness is the founder of sweetness; could we see all we hope, or hear the whole we fear told tranquil, like another tale, there would be madness near. Each of us gives or takes heaven in corporeal person, for each of us has the skill of life. I am pleased by your sweet acquaintance. It is not recorded of any rose that it failed of its bee, though obtained in specific instances through scarlet experience. The career of flowers differs from ours only in inaudibleness. I feel more reverence as I grow for these mute creatures whose suspense or transport may surpass my own. Pussy remembered the judgment, and remained with Vinnie. Maggie preferred her home to "Miggles" and "Oakhurst," so with a few spring touches, nature remains unchanged.

> The most triumphant bird
> I ever knew or met,
> Embarked upon a twig to-day, –
> And till dominion set
> I perish to behold
> So competent a sight –
> And sang for nothing scrutable
> But impudent delight.
> Retired and resumed
> His transitive estate;
> To what delicious accident
> Does finest glory fit!

Emily.

Manuscript: destroyed.
Publication: L (1894) 277–278; LL 289–290; L (1931) 253.

The poem included here was also sent to Mrs. Holland in the early summer of 1873 (see letter no. 391). Though Mrs. Todd dated the letter "Spring, 1874," it may have been written in 1873. Maggie Maher's brother, who had gone as a miner to California in the sixties, had urged Maggie to join him, but she had family cares in Amherst and did not go (see Jay Leyda, "Miss Emily's Maggie," *New World Writing*, May 1953, page 263). Bret Harte's *The Luck of Roaring Camp and Other Sketches* (1870) contained "Miggles" and "The Outcasts of Poker Flat," in which latter story the chief character is the gambler John Oakhurst. It is clearly with a sense of relief that ED concludes her letter, knowing that the faithful Maggie will not have to be replaced.

389

To Louise and Frances Norcross   *late April 1873*

. . . There is that which is called an "awakening" in the church, and I know of no choicer ecstasy than to see Mrs. [Sweetser] roll out in crape every morning, I suppose to intimidate antichrist; at least it would have that effect on me. It reminds me of Don Quixote demanding the surrender of the wind-mill, and of Sir Stephen Toplift, and of Sir Alexander Cockburn.

Spring is a happiness so beautiful, so unique, so unexpected, that I don't know what to do with my heart. I dare not take it, I dare not leave it – what do you advise?

Life is a spell so exquisite that everything conspires to break it.

"What do I think of *Middlemarch?*" What do I think of glory – except that in a few instances this "mortal has already put on immortality."

George Eliot is one. The mysteries of human nature surpass the "mysteries of redemption," for the infinite we only suppose, while we see the finite. . . . I launch Vinnie on Wednesday; it will require the combined efforts of Maggie, Providence and myself, for whatever advances Vinnie makes in nature and art, she has not reduced departure to a science. . . .

                                        Your loving
                                                Emily.

MANUSCRIPT: destroyed.
PUBLICATION: L (1894) 279; L (1931) 254.

There were evangelical meetings in Amherst during the week of 22 April 1873. A card (HCL) written and signed by Edward Dickinson is dated 1 May, and says: "I hereby give myself to God." Vinnie made her visit, here spoken about, to the Hollands, now living in New York; she probably left Amherst in May. For an earlier description of Mrs. Luke Sweetser, written in similar vein, see letter no. 339. Sir Alexander Cockburn (1802–1880), the lord chief justice of England from 1859 until his death, is here alluded to as the epitome of awesome sedateness. Sir Stephen Toplift has not been identified. Since no person of that name is known, he presumably is a somewhat modish character from fiction, familiar to ED and the Norcrosses. The quotation used to characterize *Middlemarch* is adapted from 1 Corinthians 15.53: ". . . and this mortal must put on immortality." The final quotation may be ED's attempt to recall Matthew 13.11: "Because it is given unto you to know the mysteries of the kingdom of heaven, but to them it is not given."

To Frances Norcross   *late May 1873*

Thank you, dear, for the love. I am progressing timidly. Experiment has a stimulus which withers its fear.

> This is the place they hoped before,
> Where I am hoping now.
> The seed of disappointment grew
> Within a capsule gay,
> Too distant to arrest the feet
> That walk this plank of balm –
> Before them lies escapeless sea –
> The way is closed they came.

Since you so gently ask, I have had but one serious adventure – getting a nail in my foot, but Maggie pulled it out. It only kept me awake one night, and the birds insisted on sitting up, so it became an occasion instead of a misfortune. There was a circus, too, and I watched it away at half-past three that morning. They said "hoy, hoy" to their horses.

Glad you heard Rubinstein. Grieved Loo could not hear him. He makes me think of polar nights Captain Hall could tell! Going from ice to ice! What an exchange of awe!

I am troubled for Loo's eye. Poor little girl! Can I help her? She has so many times saved me. Do take her to Arlington Street. Xerxes must go now and see to her worlds. You shall "taste," dear.

Lovingly.

Manuscript: destroyed.
Publication: L (1894) 270–271; LL 282; L (1931) 248.

The Arctic explorer Captain Charles F. Hall died in Greenland in 1871. The rescue of his party was reported in the papers, 10–15 May 1873. The circus came to Amherst this year on 20 May. Anton Rubinstein had played in Boston during April.

To Mrs. J. G. Holland   *early summer 1873*

I was thinking of thanking you for the kindness to Vinnie.

She has no Father and Mother but me and I have no Parents but her.

She has been very happy and returns with her Sentiments at rest. Enclosed please find my gratitude.

You remember the imperceptible has no external Face.

Vinnie says you are most illustrious and dwell in Paradise. I have never believed the latter to be a superhuman site.

Eden, always eligible, is peculiarly so this noon. It would please you to see how intimate the Meadows are with the Sun. Besides —

> The most triumphant Bird I ever knew or met
> Embarked upon a twig today
> And till Dominion set
> I famish to behold so eminent a sight
> And sang for nothing scrutable
> But intimate Delight.
> Retired, and resumed his transitive Estate –
> To what delicious Accident
> Does finest Glory fit!

While the Clergyman tells Father and Vinnie that "this Corruptible shall put on Incorruption" – it has already done so and they go defrauded.

Emily –

MANUSCRIPT: Holland. Ink.
PUBLICATION: *LH* 92–93.
Written after Vinnie's return from her visit. The poem had been sent to the Norcrosses earlier. (See letter no. 388.) The scripture quotation is from 1 Corinthians 15.42.

392

To Susan Gilbert Dickinson   *August 1873*

Sister

Our parting was somewhat interspersed and I cannot conclude which went. I shall be cautious not to so as to miss no one.

Vinnie drank your Coffee and has looked a little like you since, which is nearly a comfort.

Austin has had two calls and is very tired – One from Professor Tyler, and the other from Father. I am afraid they will call here.

Bun has run away –

Disaffection – doubtless – as to the Supplies. Ned is a better Quarter Master than his vagrant Papa.

The little Turkey is lonely and the Chickens bring him to call. His foreign Neck in familiar Grass is quaint as a Dromedary. I suppose the Wind has chastened the Bows on Mattie's impudent Hat and the Sea presumed as far as he dare on her stratified Stockings.

If her Basket wont hold the Boulders she picks, I will send a Bin.

Ned is much lamented and his Circus Airs in the Rowen will be doubly sweet.

Bela Dickinson's son is the only Basso remaining. It rains every pleasant Day now and Dickens' Maggie's Lawn will be green as a Courtier's.

Love for your Brother and Sister – please – and the dear Lords.

Nature gives her love –

Twilight touches Amherst with his yellow Glove.

Miss me sometimes, dear – Not on most occasions, but the Seldoms of the Mind.

Emily.

MANUSCRIPT: HCL (B 150). Ink.
PUBLICATION: LL 63, ending only; FF 234–235, in part.

The date is conjectured from the handwriting. Susan took the children to Swampscott in the summer of 1873, where they visited as guests of one of her brothers.

393

To Susan Gilbert Dickinson   *summer 1873*

Part to whom Sue is precious gave her a note Wednesday, but as Father omitted the "Ocean House" presume it is still groping in the Swampscott Mail –

We remind her we love her – Unimportant fact, though Dante did'nt think so, nor Swift, nor Mirabeau.

Could Pathos compete with that simple statement
"Not that we loved him but that he loved us"?

Emily –

Manuscript: HCL (B 95). Pencil.
Publication: AM CXV (1915) 37, in part; FF 235, in part.
This letter may shortly have followed the preceding. The hyperbole
of the second paragraph alludes to the great loves of Dante, Swift, and
Mirabeau – respectively Beatrice, Stella, and Sophie de Ruffey. The quotation is from 1 John 4.10: ". . . not that we loved God, but that he
loved us."

394

To Louise and Frances Norcross   *September 1873*

Little Sisters,

I wish you were with me, not precisely here, but in those sweet
mansions the mind likes to suppose. Do they exist or nay? We believe
they may, but do they, how know we? "The light that never was on
sea or land" might just as soon be had for the knocking.

Fanny's rustic note was as sweet as fern; Loo's token also tenderly
estimated. Maggie and I are fighting which shall give Loo the "plant,"
though it is quite a pleasant war. . . . Austin went this morning, after
a happy egg and toast provided by Maggie, whom he promised to
leave his sole heir.

The "pussum" is found. "Two dollars reward" would return John
Franklin. . . .

Love for Aunt Olivia. Tell her I think to instruct flowers will be
her labor in heaven. . . .

Nearly October, sisters! No one can keep a sumach and keep a
secret too. That was my "pipe" Fanny found in the woods.

Affectionately,
Modoc.

Manuscript: destroyed.
Publication: L (1894) 261; LL 272–273; L (1931) 239–240.
The Modoc Indians in Oregon at this time were resisting the efforts of
the government to place them on a reservation. The Arctic explorer Sir

John Franklin was lost in 1847. Mrs. Alfred Norcross was "Aunt Olivia." The quoted line in the first paragraph is from Wordsworth's *Elegiac Stanzas* (see letter no. 315).

395

To Mrs. J. G. Holland   *about September 1873*

Owning but little Stock in the "Gold of Ophir" I am not subject to large Reverses – though may not the small prove irreparable? I have lost a Sister. Her name was not Austin and it was not Vinnie. She was scant of stature though expansive spirited and last seen in November – Not the November heretofore, but Heretofore's Father.

Trite is that Affliction which is sanctified. "I have chosen whom I have chosen."

Possibly she perished?

Extinction is eligible.

Science will not trust us with another World.

Guess I and the Bible will move to some old fashioned spot where we'll feel at Home.

Emily.

MANUSCRIPT: HCL (H 31). Ink.
PUBLICATION: LH 94.

The opening sentence alludes probably to the panic of 1873, when half the railroads in the country were in receivership. The depression began in September (see letter no. 401).

396

To T. W. Higginson   *about 1873*

Could you teach me now?

Will you instruct me then no more?

MANUSCRIPT: BPL (Higg 92a and 90). Respectively pencil and ink.
PUBLICATION: L (1931) 291.

These are two separate notes, the first a card, the second a sheet of stationery. They seem to have been written about the same time, and with one three poems were evidently enclosed: "Not any higher stands the Grave," "Longing is like the Seed," and "Dominion lasts until obtained." It is possible that the poems went with the first, that she had no response from Higginson, so wrote the second.

397

To Susan Gilbert Dickinson   *autumn 1873*

Without the annual parting I thought to shun the Loneliness that parting ratifies. How artfully in vain!

Your Coffee cooled untouched except by random Fly.

A one armed Man conveyed the flowers. Not all my modest schemes have so perverse a close.

My love to "Captain Jenks" who forbore to call.

If not too uncongenial to the Divine Will, a kiss also for Mattie. "God is a jealous God."

I miss the Turkey's quaint face – once my grave Familiar, also the former Chickens, now forgotten Hens. "Pussum" cries I hear, but it is too select a grief to accept solace. Tell Mattie Tabby caught a Rat and it ran away. Grandpa caught it and it stayed.

He is the best Mouser.

The Rabbit winks at me all Day, but if I wink back, he shuffles a Clover.

What Rowen he leaves, Horace will pick for the Cow.

This is the final Weather. The transport that is not postponed is is [sic] stopping with us all.

But Subjects hinder talk.

Silence is all we dread.
There's Ransom in a Voice –
But Silence is Infinity.
Himself have not a face.

Love for John and Mattie.

Sister.

Manuscript: HCL (B 123). Ink.
Publication: FF 232–233.
Sue took the children with her on her annual autumn visit to her sister

[512]

Martha Smith at Geneva, New York. For "Captain Jenks" ("Jinks"), see letter no. 364. The sixth paragraph is a paraphrase of "I thy God am a jealous God," which appears in Exodus 20.5, and elsewhere.

398

To Edward (Ned) Dickinson   *autumn 1873*

Ned – Bird –

It was good to hear you. Not a voice in the Woods is so dear as your's.

Papa is living with me.

He is a gentle Passenger.

It will be an excellent Day when you and Mattie come. The Robins have all gone but a few infirm ones and the Cricket and I keep House for the Frost. He is very tidy.

You must excuse "the Lake." I dont think he meant to be "rough."

You and I should get tired of bowing all Day, in a Silver Pen.

I am pleased with your "Store." If you sell your Goods at Isaiah's price, I will take them all. Hope Mama is refreshed and refreshing Aunt Mattie. Did you know Mama was a precious Inn, where the Fair stopped?

I have borrowed a little Honey for Aunt Mattie's Cold of a religious Bee, who can be relied on. Sometime, when you are intimate, you can let her know.

I am saving a Miller for Mattie.

It laid six eggs on the Window Sill and I thought it was getting tired, so I killed it for her.

Good Night, Little Brother. I would love to stay.

Vinnie and Grandma and Grandpa and Maggie give their love.

Pussy, her striped Respects.

Ned's most little Aunt.

Emily.

MANUSCRIPT: HCL (B 121). Ink.

PUBLICATION: LL 58, in part; FF 236, in part.

This letter follows the letter preceding. The allusion to Isaiah may be to chapter 55, where great blessings are offered freely to those who wish to receive them.

To Mrs. J. G. Holland   *autumn 1873*

Little Sister.

I miss your childlike Voice –

I miss your Heroism.

I feel that I lose combinedly a Soldier and a Bird.

I trust that you experience a trifling destitution.

Thank you for having been.

These timid Elixirs are obtained too seldom.

Thank you for every Patience. You won the love of all, even a sweet remark from Austin, in itself an achievement.

I am glad "the Jessamine lived."

To live is Endowment. It puts me in mind of that singular Verse in the Revelations – "Every several Gate was of one Pearl."

Little Sister – Good Night – I am sure you went.

Parting is one of the exactions of a Mortal Life. It is bleak – like Dying, but occurs more times.

To escape the former, some invite the last. The Giant in the Human Heart was never met outside.

The Sun came out when you were gone.

I chid him for delay –

He said we had not needed him. Oh prying Sun!

Love for Doctor.

Emily.

MANUSCRIPT: HCL (H 32). Ink.
PUBLICATION: LH 95.
Mrs. Holland had visited in Amherst during the autumn.

400

To Louise and Frances Norcross   *1873?*

. . . I think of your little parlor as the poets once thought of Windermere, – peace, sunshine, and books.

There is no frigate like a book
To take us lands away,
Nor any coursers like a page
Of prancing poetry.
This traverse may the poorest take,
Without oppress of toll;
How frugal is the chariot
That bears the human soul!

MANUSCRIPT: destroyed.

PUBLICATION: L (1894) 273; L (1931) 249, where it is dated "Autumn, 1873."

Windermere, the largest lake in England (in the Lake District), has had literary association since the time of Wordsworth.

401

To Louise and Frances Norcross   *November 1873*

Dear Berkeleys,

I should feel it my duty to lay my "net" on the national altar, would it appease finance, but as Jay Cooke can't wear it, I suppose it won't. I believe he opened the scare. M[attie] says D[id] pulled her hair, and D[id] says M[attie] pulled her hair, but the issue at court will be, which pulled the preliminary hair. I am not yet "thrown out of employment," nor ever receiving "wages" find them materially "reduced," though when bread may be a "tradition" Mr. C[hurch] alone knows. I am deeply indebted to Fanny, also to her sweet sister *Mrs. Ladislaw*; add the funds to the funds, please. Keep the cap till I send – I could not insult my country by incurring expressage now. . . . Buff sings like a nankeen bumble-bee, and a bird's nest on the syringa is just in a line with the conservatory fence, so I have fitted a geranium to it and the effect is deceitful.

I see by the paper that father spends the winter with you. Will you be glad to see him? . . . Tell Loo when I was a baby father used to take me to mill for my health. I was then in consumption! While he obtained the "grist," the horse looked round at me, as if to say "'eye hath not seen or ear heard the things that' I would do to you if I weren't tied!" That is the way I feel toward her. . . .

[515]

Maggie will write soon, says it was Mount Holyoke, and not sweet-brier she gave you! Thanks for the little "news." Did get Fanny's note and thank it. Have thousands of things to say as also ten thousands, but must abate now.

Lovingly,

Emily.

MANUSCRIPT: destroyed.

PUBLICATION: L (1894) 274–275; LL 286, in small part; L (1931) 250.

The Norcross sisters lived in Boston at the Hotel Berkeley from February 1873 until April 1874. Edward Dickinson was elected a representative to the Massachusetts legislature on 5 November. Jay Cooke (1821–1905), a Philadelphia banker, was principal financial agent for the Federal Government during the Civil War. His house suspended business, 18 September 1873, having overextended credit in building the Northern Pacific Railroad, and thus precipitated one of the worst financial panics in United States history. Middlemarch, by George Eliot, had recently been published (1872), and all had evidently been reading it. Loo is here identified with the heroine, the unhappy Dorothea Casaubon, who in the end marries Will Ladislaw. "Did" was the nickname of Martha Dickinson's friend Sally Jenkins. The Dickinson's gardener, Horace Church, was regarded as a village "tradition" (see letter no. 692). The scripture paraphrase is from I Corinthians 2.9.

402

To F. B. Sanborn *about 1873*

Thank you, Mr Sanborn. I am glad there are Books.

They are better than Heaven for that is unavoidable while one may miss these.

Had I a trait you would accept I should be most proud, though he has had his Future who has found Shakespeare –

E – Dickinson

MANUSCRIPT: Barrett. Ink. Unpublished.

This is the only letter ED is known to have written Franklin Benjamin Sanborn, whose editorial association with the *Springfield Republican* would account for the acquaintance, however slight. She may have written him to inquire about some new book in which she was interested. As correspondent for the paper, Sanborn wrote one column dealing with literary topics, another dealing with national politics.

The last sentence may be an allusion to her own writing.

To Martha Dickinson   *30 November 1873?*

Dear Mattie,

I am glad it is your Birthday –
It is this little Bouquet's Birthday too –
It's Father is a very old Man by the name of Nature, whom you never saw –
I am going away to live in a Tippet that a South Down built me, so I cant say any more –
Be sure to live in vain and never mingle with the mouse – like Papa's Tongs –

Aunt Emily –

MANUSCRIPT: HCL (B 15). Pencil.
PUBLICATION: *AM* CXV (1915) 37, in part; *LL* 58, in part.
Mattie was born, 30 November 1866.

To Mrs. Hanson L. Read   *28 December 1873*

Vinnie says your martyrs were fond of flowers.
Would these profane their vase?

Emily.

MANUSCRIPT: missing. The text is from *L* (1931).
PUBLICATION: *L* (1894) 375; *L* (1931) 365.
The two Read sons, in their late teens, were drowned, 26 December 1873, while skating on Adams Pond.

To T. W. Higginson   *January 1874*

Thank you, dear friend, for my "New Year;" but did you not confer it? Had your scholar permission to fashion your's, it were perhaps too fair. I always ran Home to Awe when a child, if anything befell me.

He was an awful Mother, but I liked him better than none. There remained this shelter after you left me the other Day.

Of your flitting Coming it is fair to think.

Like the Bee's Coupe – vanishing in Music.

Would you with the Bee return, what a Firm of Noon!

Death obtains the Rose, but the News of Dying goes no further than the Breeze. The Ear is the last Face.

We hear after we see.

Which to tell you first is still my Dismay.

Meeting a Bird this Morning, I begun to flee. He saw it and sung.

> Presuming on that lone result
> His infinite Disdain
> But vanquished him with my Defeat –
> 'Twas Victory was slain.

I shall read the Book.

Thank you for telling me.

"Field Lilies" are Cleopatra's "Posies."

I was re-reading "Oldport."

Largest last, like Nature.

Was it you that came?

> A Wind that woke a lone Delight
> Like Separation's Swell –
> Restored in Arctic confidence
> To the Invisible.

> Your Scholar –

MANUSCRIPT: BPL (Higg 84). Ink.

PUBLICATION: L (1894) 325–326, in part; LL 304–305, in part; L (1931) 306–307, entire. One prose passage is printed as verse.

Higginson's volume of sketches, *Oldport Days*, had been published in 1873. With this letter ED enclosed one poem: "Because that you are going." On 3 December 1873 Higginson had been invited to lecture at Amherst. While there, he called on ED for the second (and last) time, though the occasion was not significant enough for him to make record of the fact in his diary (HCL). After his return to Newport he wrote a letter (HCL) to his sisters on 9 December:

> . . . the boys are numerous & hearty & better taken care of physically than at Harvard – all being *obliged* to exercise in gymnasium. I saw my eccentric poetess Miss Emily Dickinson who *never* goes out-

[518]

side her father's grounds & sees only me & a few others. She says, "there is always one thing to be grateful for — that one is one's self & not somebody else" but [my wife] Mary thinks this is singularly out of place in E.D.'s case. She (E.D.) glided in, in white, bearing a Daphne odora for me, & said under her breath "How long are you going to stay." I'm afraid Mary's other remark "Oh why do the insane so cling to you?" still holds. I will read you some of her poems when you come.

Apparently it was Higginson, however, who picked up the correspondence, for ED's letter above is a reply to one (HCL) which he wrote to her, dated Newport, Rhode Island, 31 December 1873. One gathers from it that ED had recently sent or given him a copy of her poem beginning "The Wind begun to rock and Grass," a copy, now lost, which Higginson told Mrs. Todd in May 1891 that he had in his possession (AB 129). Since ED clearly had not written Higginson after his call, one conjectures that she presented the poem to him during his visit, and that the acknowledgment is made in the following letter.

405a

Dear friend

This note shall go as a New Year's gift & assure you that you are not forgotten. I am glad to remember my visit to Amherst, & especially the time spent with you. It seemed to give you some happiness, and I hope it did; — certainly I enjoyed being with you. Each time we seem to come together as old & tried friends; and I certainly feel that I have known you long & well, through the beautiful thoughts and words you have sent me. I hope you will not cease to trust me and turn to me; and I will try to speak the truth to you, and with love.

Today is perfectly beautiful, all snow & azure — our snow is apt to be dingy, but today the Amherst hills can hardly be whiter. Such days ought to give us strength to go by all the storms & eclipses unmoved. Your poem about the storm is fine — it gives the sudden transitions. While there is anything so sudden in the world as lightning, no event among men can seem anything but slow.

I wish you could see some field lilies, yellow & scarlet, painted in water colors that are just sent to us for Christmas. These are not your favorite colors, & perhaps I love the azure & gold myself — but perhaps we should learn to love & cultivate these ruddy hues of life. Do you remember Mrs. Julia Howe's poem "I stake my life upon the red."

Pray read the enlarged edition of Verses by H.H. — the new poems are so beautiful. She is in Colorado this winter, & enjoys the out-door climate.

I always am glad to hear from you, and hope that your New Year may be very happy.

Your friend
T. W. Higginson

406

To Mrs. Edward Tuckerman   *January 1874?*

Dear Friend,

I fear my congratulation, like repentance according to Calvin, is too late to be plausible, but might there not be an exception, were the delight or the penitence found to be durable?

Emily.

MANUSCRIPT: missing.
PUBLICATION: *L* (1894) 379–380; *LL* 286; *L* (1931) 370.

Dated in *Letters*: January, 1874. Mrs. Tuckerman is known to have supplied the dates in letters to her from ED. The occasion that prompted this letter has not been identified.

407

To Susan Gilbert Dickinson   *about 1874*

Dear Sue —

It is sweet you are better —

I am greedy to see you. Your Note was like the Wind. The Bible chooses that you know to define the Spirit.

> A Wind that rose though not a Leaf
> In any Forest stirred,
> But with itself did cold engage
> Beyond the realm of Bird.
>
> A Wind that woke a lone Delight
> Like Separation's Swell —

Manuscript: HCL (B 190). Ink.
Publication: FF 256–257.
The third and final page of the letter, extant when it was published in 1932, is now missing. As printed, the lines read:

> Restored in Arctic confidence
> To the invisible.

The same quatrain (the second stanza) is in the letter to Higginson (no. 405) written in January. The letters appear to have been written about the same time.

408

To Mrs. Joseph A. Sweetser   *late January 1874*

Saying nothing, My Aunt Katie, sometimes says the Most.

> Death's Waylaying not the sharpest
> Of the thefts of Time –
> There Marauds a sorer Robber,
> Silence – is his name –
> No Assault, nor any Menace
> Doth betoken him.
> But from Life's consummate Cluster –
> He supplants the Balm.

                                                                    Emily.

Manuscript: missing. The text is from a transcript of the autograph made when it was on exhibit at the Jones Library in 1935.
Publication: Kate Dickinson Sweetser, *Great American Girls* (1931) 135; *Poems* (1955) 899.
Joseph Sweetser walked out of his New York apartment on the evening of 21 January 1874, and was never subsequently traced. Many papers carried the account. The *Springfield Republican* noted it on 29 January.

409

To Louise and Frances Norcross   *late February 1874*

Dear Children,

Father is ill at home. I think it is the "Legislature" reacting on an otherwise obliging constitution. Maggie is ill at Tom's – a combination of cold and superstition of fever — of which her enemy is ill – and longing for the promised land, of which there is no surplus. "Apollyon" and the "Devil" fade in martial lustre beside Lavinia and myself. "As thy day is so shall thy" stem "be." We can all of us sympathize with the man who wanted the roan horse to ride to execution, because he said 'twas a nimble hue, and 'twould be over sooner. . . .

Dear Loo, shall I enclose the slips, or delay till father? Vinnie advises the latter. I usually prefer formers, latters seeming to me like Dickens's hero's dead mamma, "too some weeks off" to risk. Do you remember the "sometimes" of childhood, which invariably never occurred? . . .

Be pleased you have no cat to detain from justice. Ours have taken meats, and the wife of the "general court" is trying to lay them out, but as she has but two wheels and they have four, I would accept their chances. Kitties eat kindlings now. Vinnie thinks they are "cribbers." I wish I could make you as long a call as De Quincey made North, but that morning cannot be advanced.

Emily.

MANUSCRIPT: destroyed.

PUBLICATION: L (1894) 275–276; LL 286–287; L (1931) 250–251, dated: 1874.

Edward Dickinson's notation on an almanac for 1874 (AC) indicates that he was at home in late February and early March of this year. De Quincey's call on Christopher North is related by North's daughter, Mary Wilson Gordon, *Memoir of John Wilson* (Christopher North), 1862, 327:

> I remember his [De Quincey's] coming to Gloucester Place one stormy night. He remained hour after hour, in vain expectation that the waters would assuage and the hurly-burly cease. There was nothing for it but that our visitor should remain all night. The Professor [Wilson] ordered a room to be prepared for him, and they found each other such good company that this accidental detention was prolonged, without further difficulty, for the greater part of *a year*.

ED's interest in De Quincey, who died in 1859, began evidently in 1858 (see letter no. 191). The scripture paraphrase is from Deuteronomy 33. 25: ". . . as thy days, so shall thy strength be."

To Louise and Frances Norcross   *early March 1874*

Thank you, own little girls, for the sweet remembrance – sweet specifically. Be sure it was pondered with loving thoughts not unmixed with palates.

But love, like literature, is "its exceeding great reward." . . . I am glad you heard "Little Em'ly." I would go far to hear her, except I have lost the run of the roads. . . . Infinite March is here, and I "hered" a bluebird. Of course I am standing on my head!

> Go slow, my soul, to feed thyself
> Upon his rare approach.
> Go rapid, lest competing death
> Prevail upon the coach.
> Go timid, should his testing eye
> Determine thee amiss,
> Go boldly, for thou paidst the price,
> Redemption for a kiss.

Tabby is singing *Old Hundred*, which, by the way, is her maiden name. Would they address and mail the note to their friend J——W——?

Tidings of a book.

Emily.

MANUSCRIPT: missing.
PUBLICATION: *L* (1894) 265; *LL* 278–279; *L* (1931) 243.
The play "Little Em'ly," based on *David Copperfield*, was at the Boston Museum for six weeks from 5 January to 16 February 1874. The identity of J. W. is not known.

To Mrs. Jonathan L. Jenkins   *March 1874*

Dear friend

I am picking you a flower for remembering Sumner – He was his Country's – She – is Time's –

When Continents expire
The Giants they discarded – are
Promoted to Endure –

Emily –

MANUSCRIPT: HCL (L 43). Ink.
PUBLICATION: FN 124.
Charles Sumner died, 11 March 1874.

412

To Mrs. J. G. Holland   *May 1874*

Little Sister.

I hope you are safe and distinguished. Is the latter the former?
Experience makes me no reply.

Nature begins to work and I am assisting her a little, when I can
be spared.

It is pleasant to work for so noble a Person.

Vinnie and "Pat" are abetting the Farm in Papa's absence. A
Triumph of Schemes, if not of Executions. Pat is as abnegating as a
Dromedary and I fear will find his Lot as unique.

When you were here – there were Flowers and there are Flowers
now, but those were the Nosegays of Twilight and these – are the
Nosegays of Dawn –

It is plain that some one has been asleep!

Suffer Rip – Van Winkle!

Vinnie says Maggie is "Cleaning House." I should not have suspected it, but the Bible directs that the "Left Hand" circumvent the
Right!

We are to have another "Circus," and again the Procession from
Algiers will pass the Chamber-Window.

The Minor Toys of the Year are alike, but the Major – are different.

But the dimensions of each subject admonish me to leave it.

Love, though, for your own. When a Child and fleeing from Sacra-

[524]

ment I could hear the Clergyman saying "All who loved the Lord
Jesus Christ – were asked to remain –"
My flight kept time to the Words.

Emily.

MANUSCRIPT: HCL (H 33). Ink.
PUBLICATION: LH 97.
In 1874 Maginley's Circus came to town on 23 May. For an expression
similar to that in the next to last paragraph, see letter no. 926.

413

To T. W. Higginson *late May 1874*

I thought that being a Poem one's self precluded the writing
Poems, but perceive the Mistake. It seemed like going Home, to see
your beautiful thought once more, now so long forbade it – Is it Intel-
lect that the Patriot means when he speaks of his "Native Land"?
I should have feared to "quote" to you what you "most valued."
You have experienced sanctity.
It is to me untried.

> Of Life to own –
> From Life to draw –
> But never touch the Reservoir –

You kindly ask for my Blossoms and Books — I have read but a
little recently — Existence has overpowered Books. Today, I slew a
Mushroom —

> I felt as if the Grass was pleased
> To have it intermit.
> This Surreptitious Scion
> Of Summer's circumspect.

The broadest words are so narrow we can easily cross them – but
there is water deeper than those which has no Bridge. My Brother
and Sisters would love to see you. Twice, you have gone – Master –
Would you but once come —

MANUSCRIPT: BPL (Higg 88). Ink.
PUBLICATION: L (1931) 304–305.
Higginson's poem "Decoration," appropriate to Memorial Day, appeared
in the June issue of *Scribner's Monthly*.

To Louise and Frances Norcross   summer 1874

You might not remember me, dears. I cannot recall myself. I thought I was strongly built, but this stronger has undermined me.

We were eating our supper the fifteenth of June, and Austin came in. He had a despatch in his hand, and I saw by his face we were all lost, though I didn't know how. He said that father was very sick, and he and Vinnie must go. The train had already gone. While horses were dressing, news came he was dead.

Father does not live with us now – he lives in a new house. Though it was built in an hour it is better than this. He hasn't any garden because he moved after gardens were made, so we take him the best flowers, and if we only knew he knew, perhaps we could stop crying. . . . The grass begins after Pat has stopped it.

I cannot write any more, dears. Though it is many nights, my mind never comes home. Thank you each for the love, though I could not notice it. Almost the last tune that he heard was, "Rest from thy loved employ."

Emily.

MANUSCRIPT: destroyed.
PUBLICATION: L (1894) 280; LL 290–291; L (1931) 255.
Edward Dickinson died on 16 (not 15) June. ED concludes her letter by recalling the James Montgomery hymn (which she had evidently played for her father):

> Servant of God, well done!
> Rest from thy loved employ.
> The battle fought, the victory won,
> Enter thy Master's joy!

To Samuel Bowles   late June 1874

I should think you would have few Letters for your own are so noble that they make men afraid – and sweet as your Approbation is – it is had in fear – lest your depth convict us.

You compel us each to remember that when Water ceases to rise –
it has commenced falling. That is the law of Flood. The last Day that
I saw you was the newest and oldest of my life.

Resurrection can come but once – first – to the same House. Thank
you for leading us by it.

Come always, dear friend, but refrain from going. You spoke of
not liking to be forgotten. Could you, tho' you would? Treason never
knew you.

Emily.

MANUSCRIPT: AC. Ink.
PUBLICATION: L (1894) 220; LL 271; L (1931) 206.

The Bowleses had been with the Dickinson family at the time of the
funeral of Edward Dickinson. Bowles sailed for Europe in mid-July.

416

To Mrs. James S. Cooper   *June 1874*

Though a stranger, I am unwilling not to thank you personally
for the delicate attention to my Family.

For the comprehension of Suffering One must ones Self have
Suffered.

E. Dickinson

MANUSCRIPT: Sheldon. Ink.
PUBLICATION: L (1894) 391; L (1931) 380.

This and the note that follows are messages written to neighbors after
Edward Dickinson's death.

417

To Mrs. Henry Hills   *summer 1874*

Dear friend,

I believe that the sweetest thanks are inaudible. They occur in the
Heart and no other knows them. But as two or three awkward Tears
supersede Orations, I will say no more.

Flowers are not quite earthly. They are like the Saints. We should

doubtless feel more at Home with them than with the Saints of God.
Were the "Great Crowd of Witnesses" chiefly Roses and Pansies, there would be less to apprehend, though let me not presume upon Jehovah's Program.

Thank Mr. Hills for the lovely message.

Please tell the Children the Acorns sell me Saucers still for the little Pies, but I have lent my only Wing to a lame Robin, so cannot freight them. Children's Hearts are large.

I shall not need an Intercessor.

Vinnie gives her love, and will write.

Emily

MANUSCRIPT: missing. The text has the same provenance as that of letter no. 376. The paper is watermarked 1871. Unpublished.

418

To T. W. Higginson   *July 1874*

The last Afternoon that my Father lived, though with no premonition – I preferred to be with him, and invented an absence for Mother, Vinnie being asleep. He seemed peculiarly pleased as I oftenest stayed with myself, and remarked as the Afternoon withdrew, he "would like it to not end."

His pleasure almost embarrassed me and my Brother coming – I suggested they walk. Next morning I woke him for the train – and saw him no more.

His Heart was pure and terrible and I think no other like it exists.

I am glad there is Immortality – but would have tested it myself – before entrusting him.

Mr Bowles was with us – With that exception I saw none. I have wished for you, since my Father died, and had you an Hour unengrossed, it would be almost priceless. Thank you for each kindness.

My Brother and Sister thank you for remembering them.

Your beautiful Hymn, was it not prophetic? It has assisted that Pause of Space which I call "Father" –

MANUSCRIPT: BPL (Higg 68). Ink. Endorsed by TWH: July 1874 Her father's death.

[528]

PUBLICATION: *AM* LXVIII (October 1891) 455, in part; *L* (1894) 317–318; *LL* 291–292; *L* (1931) 291–292.
In her final paragraph ED again alludes to Higginson's poem "Decoration" (see letter no. 413).

419

To Mrs. James S. Cooper   *late summer 1874*

Dear friend –

It was my first impulse to take them to my Father – whom I cannot resist the grief to expect.

Thank you.

Vinnie's Sister —

MANUSCRIPT: AC. Pencil.
PUBLICATION: *L* (1894) 391; *LL* 295; *L* (1931) 381.

420

To Samuel Bowles   *about October 1874*

Dear friend.

The Paper wanders so I cannot write my name on it, so I give you Father's Portrait instead.

> As Summer into Autumn slips
> And yet we sooner say
> "The Summer" then "the Autumn," lest
> We turn the sun away,
>
> And almost count it an Affront
> The presence to concede
> Of one however lovely, not
> The one that we have loved –
>
> So we evade the charge of Years
> On one attempting shy
> The Circumvention of the Shaft
> Of Life's Declivity.

Emily.

MANUSCRIPT: AC. Ink.
PUBLICATION: L (1894) 222; LL 285; L (1931) 208; Poems (1955) 929–930.
The date is conjectured from the handwriting. Bowles called on the Dickinsons on 4 October 1874, and the tone of the letter suggests that it was written shortly thereafter.

421

To Emily Fowler Ford   *about 1874*

Should it be possible for me to speak of My Father before I behold him, I shall try to do so to you, whom he always remembered —

Emily –

MANUSCRIPT: AC. Ink.
PUBLICATION: L (1894) 392; LL 296; L (1931) 381.
This message probably acknowledges a note of condolence from Emily Ford, written after the death of Edward Dickinson.

422

To Mrs. Jonathan L. Jenkins   *1874*

The Absence of the big Brother is a Temptation to shield the little Sister, were she not of herself a sufficing one –

Emily.

MANUSCRIPT: HCL (L 42). Ink.
PUBLICATION: FN 83, somewhat altered.
Mr. Jenkins made a carriage trip to the White Mountains early in September 1874.

423

To Mr. and Mrs. Jonathan L. Jenkins   *about 1874*

For my Mr. and Mrs Clergyman, with confiding love –

MANUSCRIPT: HCL (L 45). Pencil.
PUBLICATION: FN 85.
The date is conjectured from the handwriting.

To Mrs. William A. Stearns   *autumn 1874?*

Will the dear ones who eased the grieved days spurn the fading orchard?

Emily.

MANUSCRIPT: missing.
PUBLICATION: *L* (1894) 376; *L* (1931) 366.
The note probably was sent with fruit. The date is that given in *Letters.*

To Clara Newman Turner   *December 1874*
I am sure you must have remembered that Father had "Become as Little Children," or you would never have dared send him a Christmas gift, for you know how he frowned upon Santa Claus – and all such prowling gentlemen –

MANUSCRIPT: missing.
PUBLICATION: *L* (1894) 372; *LL* 294; *L* (1931) 362.
The text is from a transcript (AC) given to Mrs. Todd by Mrs. Turner, who states in her reminiscences (HCL) that the letter was sent to her in thanks for a Christmas wreath for Edward Dickinson's grave. The quotation is from Matthew 18.3.

To Mrs. Hanson L. Read   *26 December 1874?*
My dear Mrs. Read,
We have often thought of you today, and almost spoken with you, but thought you might like to be alone – if one can be alone with so thronged a Heaven.

E. Dickinson.

MANUSCRIPT: missing.
PUBLICATION: *L* (1894) 375–376; *LL* 377; *L* (1931) 366.
This was probably sent on the anniversary of the death of the two boys by drowning (see letter no. 404).

To Susan Gilbert Dickinson   *about 1874*

Trifles – like Life – and the Sun, we Acknowledge in Church, but the Love that demeans them, having no Confederate, dies without a Term.

                                  Emily.

MANUSCRIPT: HCL (B 99). Ink.
PUBLICATION: FF 247.
This and the following four messages sent to Sue can be dated only by handwriting, and they appear to have been written about 1874.

To Susan Gilbert Dickinson   *about 1874*

Never mind dear.
Trial as a Stimulus far exceeds Wine though it would hardly be prohibited as a Beverage.

                                  Emily.

MANUSCRIPT: HCL (B 38). Ink.
PUBLICATION: LL 87.

To Susan Gilbert Dickinson   *about 1874*

To lose what we never owned might seem an eccentric Bereavement but Presumption has it's Affliction as actually as Claim –

                                  Emily.

MANUSCRIPT: HCL (B 6). Pencil.
PUBLICATION: LL 62.

To Susan Gilbert Dickinson   *about 1874*

   "Egypt – thou knew'st" –

MANUSCRIPT: HCL (B 25). Pencil.
PUBLICATION: FF 237
Antony and Cleopatra, III, xi, 56–61 (Antony):
              Egypt, thou knew'st too well,
     My heart was to thy rudder tied by the strings,
     And thou shouldst tow me after. O'er my spirit
     Thy full supremacy thou knew'st, and that
     Thy beck might from the bidding of the gods
     Command me.

To Susan Gilbert Dickinson   *about 1874*

   May I do nothing for my dear Sue?

                                                   Emily –

MANUSCRIPT: HCL (L 26). Pencil. Unpublished.

Thomas Wentworth Higginson

Helen Hunt Jackson

The Reverend Jonathan L. Jenkins

Samuel Bowles

Samuel Bowles — with friends in California

X

LETTERS

432–626

[1875–1879]

"Nature is a Haunted House –
but Art – a House that tries to be haunted."

[1875–1879]

During the final decade of her life Emily Dickinson's withdrawal from outside association became nearly absolute. She chose now communication through the medium of letters, and more than half of all that survive were written in the brief span of years that remain. She wrote few poems after 1874, but among them are some of her finest genre sketches of movement and color observed from the world of nature, for this world had become an awesome reality into which she projected her imagination with an artist's mature skill.

The birth of her nephew Gilbert in 1875 was an event which increased in importance, for it brought members of the two houses closer together as the boy grew. He was not destined to survive his ninth year. The death of Samuel Bowles from sheer exhaustion, in 1878, closed a chapter in her life, for he had been the friend whom she had always treated with affectionate deference, as a much-loved elder brother.

Two events now occurred of far reaching consequence. She came to know Helen Hunt Jackson, and her love for Judge Otis Lord became important. Helen Jackson by this time was acclaimed the leading woman poet in America and had become a most successful writer of stories. She had learned about Emily Dickinson's poetry through Colonel Higginson, and she was the only qualified contemporary who believed Dickinson to be an authentic poet. That opinion was of no small moment to the woman who now and then is signing her letters "Dickinson."

Judge Lord had been a lifelong friend of Edward Dickinson. He and his wife had been frequent overnight guests in the Dickinson house and thus Emily had always known him. His wife died in 1877. The attachment between the Judge and Emily became intimate soon thereafter. Marriage may have been contemplated; the nature and degree of her affection is patent in the letters that she wrote him.

Though the outer manifestations of what is commonly called an active life are now absent, the inner never abate, as the letters, particularly those to Mrs. Holland and to Colonel Higginson, make amply clear.

To Mrs. J. G. Holland   *late January 1875*

Sister.

This austere Afternoon is more becoming to a Patriot than to one whose Friend is it's sole Land.

No event of Wind or Bird breaks the Spell of Steel.

Nature squanders Rigor – now – where she squandered Love.

Chastening – it may be – the Lass that she receiveth.

My House is a House of Snow – true – sadly – of few.

Mother is asleep in the Library – Vinnie – in the Dining Room – Father – in the Masked Bed – in the Marl House.

> How soft his Prison is —
> How sweet those sullen Bars —
> No Despot – but the King of Down
> Invented that Repose!

When I think of his firm Light – quenched so causelessly, it fritters the worth of much that shines. "Dust unto the Dust" indeed – but the final clause of that marvelous sentence – who has rendered it?

"I say unto you," Father would read at Prayers, with a militant Accent that would startle one.

Forgive me if I linger on the first Mystery of the House.

It's specific Mystery – each Heart had before – but within this World. Father's was the first Act distinctly of the Spirit.

Austin's Family went to Geneva, and Austin lived with us four weeks. It seemed peculiar – pathetic – and Antediluvian. We missed him while he was with us and missed him when he was gone.

All is so very curious.

Thank you for that "New Year" – the first with a fracture. I trust it is whole and hale – to you.

"Kingsley" rejoins "Argemone" —

Thank you for the Affection. It helps me up the Stairs at Night, where as I passed my Father's Door – I used to think was safety. The Hand that plucked the Clover – I seek, and am

Emily.

MANUSCRIPT: HCL (H 34). Ink.
PUBLICATION: *LH* 102–103.
Mrs. Holland had plucked a spray of clover from Edward Dickinson's grave, which ED never visited, and gave it to her. Argemone is the heroine of Kingsley's first novel, *Yeast.* Kingsley died, 23 January 1875.

433

To Mrs. Edward Tuckerman   *March 1875?*

Dear Friend,

   It was so long my custom to seek you with the birds, they would scarcely feel at home should I do otherwise, though as home itself is far from home since my father died, why should custom tire?

                                                                                    Emily.

MANUSCRIPT: missing.
PUBLICATION: (1894) 380; *LL* 296; *L* (1931) 370.
The date "March, 1875," given by Mrs. Todd, was supplied by Mrs. Tuckerman.

434

To Mrs. William A. Stearns   *after Easter 1875?*

   It is possible, dear friend, that the rising of the one we lost would have engrossed me to the exclusion of Christ's – but for your lovely admonition.

   Sabbath morning was peculiarly dear to my father, and his unsuspecting last earthly day with his family was that heavenly one.

   Vinnie and I were talking of you as we went to sleep Saturday night, which makes your beautiful gift of to-day almost apparitional.

   Please believe how sweetly I thank you.

                                                                                    Emily.

MANUSCRIPT: missing.
PUBLICATION: *L* (1894) 376; *LL* 299–300; *L* (1931) 366.
Easter in 1875, the probable year this was written, was 28 March. The note is a response to an Easter greeting.

To Mrs. William A. Stearns   *early spring 1875?*

Dear Friend,

That a pansy is transitive, is its only pang.

This, precluding that, is indeed divine.

Bringing you handfuls in prospective, thank you for the love. Many an angel, with its needle, toils beneath the snow.

With tenderness for your mate,

Emily.

MANUSCRIPT: missing.
PUBLICATION: L (1894) 377; LL 297; L (1931) 367.
The date assigned by Mrs. Todd is 1875.

To Louise and Frances Norcross   *mid-April 1875*

I have only a buttercup to offer for the centennial, as an "embattled farmer" has but little time.

Begging you not to smile at my limited meadows, I am modestly

Yours.

MANUSCRIPT: destroyed.
PUBLICATION: L (1894) 281; LL 298; L (1931) 255–256.
The unveiling of "The Minute Man" monument at Concord, where the Norcross girls now lived, took place on 19 April 1875. Inscribed on the base of the statue are the lines from Emerson's "Concord Hymn" (1837), the poem which Emerson read for the occasion: "Here once the embattled farmers stood/And fired the shot heard round the world."

To Mrs. Edward Tuckerman   *mid-April 1875*

I send you inland buttercups as out-door flowers are still at sea.

Emily.

MANUSCRIPT: missing.
PUBLICATION: L (1894) 380; LL 296; L (1931) 370.
It is dated by Mrs. Todd: May 1875. But see the preceding letter to the
Norcrosses.

438

To Samuel Bowles   *about 1875*

Dear friend.

It was so delicious to see you — a Peach before the time, it makes all
seasons possible and Zones – a caprice.

We who arraign the "Arabian Nights" for their under statement,
escape the stale sagacity of supposing them sham.

We miss your vivid Face and the besetting Accents, you bring from
your Numidian Haunts.

Your coming welds anew that strange Trinket of Life, which each
of us wear and none of us own, and the phosphorescence of your's
startles us for it's permanence. Please rest the Life so many own, for
Gems abscond –

In your own beautiful words, for the Voice is the Palace of all of
us, "Near, but remote,"

Emily.

If we die, will you come for us, as you do for Father?
"Not born" yourself, "to die," you must reverse us all.

———

MANUSCRIPT: AC. Ink.
PUBLICATION: L (1894) 221–222; LL 284–285; L (1931) 207: – the
body of the letter and the signature. The postscript is printed as a separate
message: L (1894) 222–223; LL 285; L (1931) 208.

The date, conjectured from the handwriting, is almost certainly 1875.
It was Bowles's custom to be present at commencement exercises in August.
The first sentence together with the postscript suggest that perhaps this
year he came during the spring, his first visit since he was present with the
family at the time of Edward Dickinson's funeral in June 1874.

Letters (1894) and subsequent editions print the following as a separate
letter.

If we die, will you come for us, as you do for father? "Not born,"
yourself "to die," you must reverse us all.

Last to adhere
When summers swerve away –
Elegy of
Integrity.

To remember our own Mr. Bowles is all we can do.
With grief it is done, so warmly and long, it can never be new.

Emily.

It is not dated, but is placed as one sent to Bowles, presumably in his last illness. The "letter" is in fact a montage of three separate items. The first two sentences conclude this letter. The stanza (AC) is on a separate sheet. The last two sentences constitute the letter sent to Mrs. Bowles after the death of her husband (no. 532). The provenance of the verse is almost certainly Bingham 99–7, described in *Poems* (1955), 964, as written on a sheet of note paper and folded as if enclosed in an envelope. The lines may in fact have been enclosed with letter no. 532, or sent to Mrs. Bowles about the same time, for they are in the handwriting of about 1878. At the time *Poems* was published, the "letter" was thought to be lost; thus the concluding version of the lines as printed in *Poems*, deriving from the montage, is a duplication of the version (Bingham 99–7) already described.

439

To Mrs. J. G. Holland   *about 1875*

Sister –

I have the little Book and am twice triumphant – Once for itself, and once for Those who enabled me –

The embarrassment of the Psalmist who knew not what to render his friend – is peculiarly mine – Though he has canceled his consternations, while my own remain –

Thank you with all my strength – and Doctor as yourself – And again yourself for the sweet note.

Nature assigns the Sun –
That – is Astronomy –
Nature cannot enact a Friend –
That – is Astrology.

Emily.

MANUSCRIPT: HCL (H 35). Pencil.
PUBLICATION: LH 104.

The date is conjectured from the handwriting. The book may have been Dr. Holland's novel *Sevenoaks*, published in 1875, but it is not at present among the Dickinson books. The scripture reference is to Psalms 116.12: "What shall I render unto the Lord for all his benefits toward me?"

440

To T. W. Higginson   *mid-June 1875*

Dear friend –

Mother was paralyzed Tuesday, a year from the evening Father died. I thought perhaps you would care –

Your Scholar.

MANUSCRIPT: BPL (Higg 71). Pencil.
PUBLICATION: *AM* LXVIII (October 1891) 455; *L* (1894) 319; *LL* 293; *L* (1931) 293.
This note was evidently written during the week of the fifteenth.

441

To T. W. Higginson   *July 1875*

Dear friend.

Mother was very ill, but is now easier, and the Doctor thinks that in more Days she may partly improve. She was ignorant at the time and her Hand and Foot left her, and when she asks me the name of her sickness – I deceive for the first time. She asks for my Father, constantly, and thinks it rude he does not come – begging me not to retire at night, lest no one receive him. I am pleased that what grieves ourself so much – can no more grieve him. To have been immortal transcends to become so. Thank you for being sorry.

I thought it value to hear your voice, though at so great distance – Home is so far from Home, since my Father died.

The courtesy to my Brother and Sisters I gave and replace, and think those safe who see your Face.

Your Scholar.

[542]

MANUSCRIPT: BPL (Higg 72). Ink.
PUBLICATION: L (1931) 293–294.
This letter responds to a note of sympathy from Higginson, written after he had received the preceding note.

442

To Louise and Frances Norcross   summer 1875

Dear Children,

I decided to give you one more package of lemon drops, as they only come once a year. It is fair that the bonbons should change hands, you have so often fed me. This is the very weather that I lived with you those amazing years that I had a father. W[illie] D[ickinson']s wife came in last week for a day and a night, saying her heart drove her. I am glad that you loved Miss Whitney on knowing her nearer. Charlotte Brontë said "Life is so constructed that the event does not, cannot, match the expectation."

The birds that father rescued are trifling in his trees. How flippant are the saved! They were even frolicking at his grave, when Vinnie went there yesterday. Nature must be too young to feel, or many years too old.

Now children, when you are cutting the loaf, a crumb, peradventure a crust, of love for the sparrows' table. . . .

MANUSCRIPT: destroyed.
PUBLICATION: L (1894) 281; LL 298; L (1931) 256.
The date Mrs. Todd assigned is retained; the tone of the letter suggests that it was written in the year following her father's death. For a note relating to the Brontë quotation, see letter no. 459.

443

To Susan Gilbert Dickinson   early August 1875

Emily and all that she has are at Sue's service, if of any comfort to Baby –

Will send Maggie, if you will accept her –

Sister –

MANUSCRIPT: HCL (B 42). Pencil.
PUBLICATION: *FF* 244.
Susan's third child, Thomas Gilbert Dickinson, was born 1 August 1875.

444

To Helen Hunt Jackson   *late October 1875*

Have I a word but Joy?
E. Dickinson.
Who fleeing from the Spring
The Spring avenging fling
To Dooms of Balm —

MANUSCRIPT: HCL (L 51). Ink.
PUBLICATION: *Poems* (1955) 924.
On the last blank page a note in Helen Jackson's hand reads: "This is *mine*, remember, You must send it back to me, or else you will be a robber." (Helen Jackson returned the letter to ED, who kept it, for an explanation of the three lines of verse). The letter was written when ED learned of the marriage of Helen Hunt to William S. Jackson, 22 October 1875. The earliest evidence of a correspondence between them is an envelope (AC), never sent, addressed in the handwriting of about 1868 to Mrs. Helen Hunt. That summer she was in Amherst. Another envelope never sent (AC) is addressed, about 1872, to Bethlehem, New Hampshire, where Mrs. Hunt then summered.

After Mrs. Jackson returned the letter above, ED must have written her again, as the following letter (HCL) from Helen Jackson, dated Colorado Springs, 20 March 1876, indicates:

444a

But you did not send it back, though you wrote that you would. Was this an accident, or a late withdrawal of your consent? Remember that it is mine — not yours — and be honest.

Thank you for not being angry with my impudent request for interpretations.

I do wish I knew just what "dooms" you meant, though!

A very clever man — one of the cleverest I ever met — a Mr. Dudley of Milwaukee, spent a day with us last week, and we talked about you. So threads cross, even on the outermost edges of the web.

[544]

I hope some day, somewhere I shall find you in a spot where we can know each other. I wish very much that you would write to me now and then, when it did not bore you. I have a little manuscript volume with a few of your verses in it — and I read them very often — You are a great poet — and it is a wrong to the day you live in, that you will not sing aloud. When you are what men call dead, you will be sorry you were so stingy.

Yours truly
Helen Jackson.

445

To Mrs. James S. Cooper   *about 1875*

My family of Apparitions is select, though dim.

———

MANUSCRIPT: AC. Pencil.
PUBLICATION: *L* (1894) 394; *LL* 323; *L* (1931) 383.
This note, in the handwriting of about 1875, was probably sent with flowers.

446

To recipient unknown   *about 1875*

Sweet is it as Life, with it's enhancing Shadow of Death.

> A Bee his burnished Carriage
> Drove boldly to a Rose —
> Combinedly alighting —
> Himself — his Carriage was —
> The Rose received his visit
> With frank tranquility
> Withholding not a Crescent
> To his Cupidity —
> Their Moment consummated —
> Remained for him — to flee —
> Remained for her — of rapture
> But the humility.

[545]

MANUSCRIPT: AC. Ink.
PUBLICATION: *BM* 70, poem only; *Poems* (1955) 925–926, entire; *NEQ* XXVIII (1955) 311, entire.
The date is conjectured from the handwriting.

447

To Susan Gilbert Dickinson   *about 1875*

Only Woman in the World, Accept a Julep –

MANUSCRIPT: HCL (B 76). Pencil.
PUBLICATION: *FF* 246.
This and the following brief message to Sue are datable only by hand-writing; both seem to have been written about 1875.

448

To Susan Gilbert Dickinson   *about 1875*

"For Brutus, as you know, was Caesar's Angel" –

MANUSCRIPT: HCL (B 34). Pencil.
PUBLICATION: *FF* 245.
The private association of this quotation from Julius Caesar (III, ii, 183) is not known, but may have reference to a local situation wherein some member of the family, in ED's opinion, was "betrayed" by a friend.

449

To T. W. Higginson   *January 1876*

That it is true, Master, is the Power of all you write.

Could it cease to be Romance, it would be Revelation, which is the Seed – of Romance –

I had read "Childhood," with compunction that thought so fair – fall on foreign eyes –

I had also read fervent notices of itself and of you. There is nothing sweeter than Honor, but Love, which is it's sacred price.

I hope most you are happy, and that none closest to you, have received sorrow –

Could "Liquid Hills" be steep?

The last Books that my Father brought me I have felt unwilling to open, and had reserved them for you, because he had twice seen you. They are Theodore Parker, by Frothingham, and George Eliot's Poems. If you have them, please tell me – If not, you will not forbid mine?

Mr. Bowles lent me flowers twice, for my Father's Grave.

> To his simplicity
> To die – was little Fate –
> If Duty live – contented
> But her Confederate –

Your Scholar

MANUSCRIPT: BPL (Higg 83). Ink.
PUBLICATION: L (1931) 304.
In this letter ED enclosed five poems: "The last of Summer is delight," "The Heart is the Capital of the Mind," "The Mind lives on the Heart," "The Rat is the concisest Tenant," and " 'Faithful to the end' Amended." Higginson's "Childhood Fancies" appeared in the January 1876 issue of *Scribner's Monthly*. Frothingham's *Theodore Parker* and George Eliot's *The Legend of Jubal and Other Poems* were both published in 1874. Higginson appears to have had one of the two she offered, probably the Frothingham, as the next letter indicates.

450

To T. W. Higginson   *February 1876*

There is so much that is tenderly profane in even the sacredest Human Life – that perhaps it is instinct and not design, that dissuades us from it.

> The Treason of an accent
> Might Ecstasy transfer –
> Of her effacing Fathom
> Is no Recoverer –

It makes me happy to send you the Book. Thank you for accepting

[547]

it, and please not to own "Daniel Deronda" till I bring it, when it is done. You ask me if I see any one – Judge Lord was with me a week in October and I talked with Father's Clergyman once, and once with Mr Bowles. Little – wayfaring acts – comprise my "pursuits" – and a few moments at night, for Books – after the rest sleep. Candor – my Preceptor – is the only wile. Did you not teach me that yourself, in the "Prelude" to "Malbone"? You once told me of "printing but a few Poems." I hoped it implied you possessed more ——

Would you show me – one? You asked me if I liked the cold – but it is warm now. A mellow Rain is falling.

It wont be ripe till April – How luscious is the dripping of February eaves! It makes our thinking Pink –

It antedates the Robin – Bereaving in prospective that Febuary leaves ——

Thank you for speaking kindly.

I often go Home in thought to you.

Your Scholar –

Manuscript: BPL (Higg 81). Ink.
Publication: L (1931) 297–298.

Daniel Deronda began running serially in the March issue of *Harper's Monthly*, and this letter may well have been written after ED had seen an announcement of its impending publication (in book form later in the year), but before she had read the first installment (see letters no. 456 and 457). "Father's Clergyman" was the pastor of the First Church, the Reverend Jonathan L. Jenkins (see letter no. 464). The expression "Candor is the only wile" is ED's succinct rephrasing of the following thought, in Higginson's "Prelude" to his novel *Malbone: An Oldport Romance* (1869): "One learns, in growing older, that no fiction can be so strange nor appear so improbable as would the simple truth. . ."

451

To T. W. Higginson   *February 1876*

Did you not receive the Letter – or Book? Dear friend, I am alarmed —

Manuscript: BPL (Higg 89). Ink.
Publication: L (1931) 305.

To T. W. Higginson   *February–March 1876*

Could you pardon the elderly Gentleman, who entrusted the circumstances to you, that were designed for him?

MANUSCRIPT: BPL (Higg 70). Ink.
PUBLICATION: L (1931) 293.

Apparently Higginson had written that some mistake had been made,
which ED in the following letter tries to explain. The "elderly Gentleman"
was Luke Sweetser, now in his mid-seventies, who at this time often addressed and mailed her letters and parcels. There is still extant a note
written in a very shaky hand (AC) – on the back of which ED wrote the
rough draft of "Bees are Black, with Gilt Surcingles" (1877): "You don't
know [how] much I have missed these opportunities of service of late.
I shall not believe you are displeased with me until you tell me so. Yours
L. Sweetser." It was some such mistake as this which made ED turn such
pleasant services over to George Montague, who thenceforth often addressed her letters.

To T. W. Higginson   *February–March 1876*

Dear friend –

If you would be willing I should tell you how the mistake was –
perhaps you could forgive it. An elderly friend addresses the notes to
my few friends, and if I send them a Book – folds and mails it for me –

I had asked his permission to fold the Poems — but in sending them
to him omitted his name on the note you received – then he thought it
for you –

When I knew it, I wrote you – It distressed me extremely – but I
hope when I tell you how it is, you will less abhor it – will you not?

Your Scholar –

Fear – like Dying, dilates trust, or enforces it —

MANUSCRIPT: BPL (Higg 96). Pencil.
PUBLICATION: L (1931) 298.

This letter explains the mystery of the missing volume of George Eliot
poems, which presumably Higginson had told her that he had received.

454

To Eugenia Hall   *early 1876?*

My little benefactor,
  The flowers are very sweet, and I am surprised and charmed.
  I raise only robins on my farm and a blossom is quite a guest.
                                       Affectionately
                                          Coz Emily

MANUSCRIPT: missing. The text is a transcript made by George Frisbie
Whicher (HCL), whose notebook states that it was a two-page note, in
ink, with an envelope addressed to Eugenia.
PUBLICATION: *The Collector,* October 1948, in part.
This seems to be the first letter to Genie, who was about twelve.

455

To Eugenia Hall   *early 1876*

Dear "Genie."
  The lovely flower you sent me, is like a little Vase of Spice and
fills the Hall with Cinnamon —
  You must have skillful Hands – to make such sweet Carnations.
Perhaps your Doll taught you.
  I know that Dolls are sometimes wise. Robins are my Dolls.
  I am glad you love the Blossoms so well.
  I hope you love Birds too.

  It is economical. It saves going to Heaven.
                                       Lovingly,
                                          Coz. Emily.

MANUSCRIPT: Loveman. Ink. Envelope addressed: "Genie."
PUBLICATION: L (1894) 427; L (1931) 415–416.
The handwriting belongs to this period, and the letter may follow the
preceding.

To Susan Gilbert Dickinson   *about March 1876*

Thank you, dear, for the "Eliot" –
She is the Lane to the Indes, Columbus was looking for.

Emily –

MANUSCRIPT: HCL (L 25). Ink.
PUBLICATION: *AM* CXV (1915) 40; *FF* 237, with facsimile.
This note to Sue should be read in connection wtih two letters to Higginson, nos. 450 and 457.

To T. W. Higginson   *spring 1876*

But two had mentioned the "Spring" to me – yourself and the Revelations. "I – Jesus – have sent mine Angel."

I inferred your touch in the Papers on Lowell and Emerson – It is delicate that each Mind is itself, like a distinct Bird –

I was lonely there was an "Or" in that beautiful "I would go to Amherst," though grieved for it's cause. I wish your friend had my strength for I dont care for roving – She perhaps might, though to remain with you is Journey – To abstain from "Daniel Deronda" is hard – you are very kind to be willing. I would have liked to wait, but "Sue" smuggled it under my Pillow, and to wake so near it overpowered me – I am glad "Immortality" pleased you. I believed it would. I suppose even God himself could not withhold that now – When I think of my Father's lonely Life and his lonelier Death, there is this redress –

Take all away –
The only thing worth larceny
Is left – the Immortality –

My earliest friend wrote me the week before he died "If I live, I will go to Amherst – if I die, I certainly will."

Is your House deeper off?

Your Scholar

MANUSCRIPT: BPL (Higg 78). Ink.

PUBLICATION: *AM* LXVIII (October 1891) 455, in part; *L* (1894) 323, in part; *LL* 302, in part; *L* (1931) 301, in part.

This and the following letters to Higginson and his wife (nos. 458–460) were all written about the same time in the spring of 1876. The order of their arrangement here is conjectured from their contents.

ED correctly guessed that Higginson wrote the unsigned review of Lowell s *Among My Books: Second Series* for the March 1876 issue of *Scribner's Monthly.* (It is so identified in Mary Thacher Higginson, *Thomas Wentworth Higginson* . . . , Boston, 1914, 413). The review of Emerson's *Letters and Social Aims* in the April issue, likewise unsigned, may be Higginson's but has not been so identified. The "friend" referred to in the third paragraph is Mrs. Higginson, whose illness was increasing. Higginson's reply to the letter ED wrote to him in February (no. 450) told her that he would be glad to refrain from reading *Daniel Deronda* until he had received the copy she wished to send him. It was published late in the year, after being completed serially in the October issue of *Scribner's Monthly.* The second volume of the presentation set, containing Higginson's signature, is now among the books from his library at HCL. The comment on "Immortality" might apply to the poem " 'Faithful to the end' Amended" (see letter no. 449). "My earliest friend" in all probability was B. F. Newton (see the postscript to letter no. 110). The quotation in the first paragraph is from Revelation 22.16.

458

To T. W. Higginson   *spring 1876*

Dear friend.

Your thought is so serious and captivating, that it leaves one stronger and weaker too, the Fine of Delight.

Of it's Bliss to yourself, we are ignorant, though you first teach us "that which is born of the Spirit is Spirit" –

It is still as distinct as Paradise – the opening your first Book –

It was Mansions – Nations – Kinsmen – too – to me –

I sued the News – yet feared – the News
That such a Realm could be –
"The House not made with Hands" it was –
Thrown open wide to me –

I had long heard of an Orchis before I found one, when a child,

but the first clutch of the stem is as vivid now, as the Bog that bore it –
so truthful is transport – Though inaudible to you, I have long thanked
you.

Silence' oblation to the Ear supersedes sound –
Sweetest of Renowns to remain

Your Scholar —

Is your friend better?
And yourself, well?

MANUSCRIPT: BPL (Higg 82).
PUBLICATION: L (1931) 303.
Higginson's first book was *Outdoor Papers* (1863), containing "April
Days," "My Outdoor Study," "Water Lilies," "The Life of Birds," and
"The Procession of Flowers." The quotation in the second sentence is from
John 3.6 (see letter no. 558). The lines quoted in the poem are from 2
Corinthians 5.1 (see letters no. 180, 182 and 866).

459

To T. W. Higginson   *spring 1876*

I am glad to have been of joy to your friend, even incidentally,
and greedy for the supplement of so sweet a privilege. I hope that you
had a happy trip, and became refreshed. Labor might fatigue, though
it is Action's rest.

The things we thought that we should do
We other things have done
But those peculiar industries
Have never been begun –

The Lands we thought that we should seek
When large enough to run
By Speculation ceded
To Speculation's Son –

The Heaven, in which we hoped to pause
When Discipline was done
Untenable to Logic
But possibly the one –

I am glad you remember the "Meadow Grass."
That forestalls fiction.

I was always told that conjecture surpassed Discovery, but it must
have been spoken in caricature, for it is not true –

> The long sigh of the Frog
> Upon a Summer's Day
> Enacts intoxication
> Upon the Passer by.
>
> But his receding Swell
> Substantiates a Peace
> That makes the Ear inordinate
> For corporal release –
>
> Would you but guide
> Your scholar

MANUSCRIPT: BPL (Higg 85). Ink.
PUBLICATION: L (1931) 296, in part.
Higginson's trips in 1876, according to his diary (HCL), were short
ones to fill speaking engagements.

In this letter ED says that conjecture (anticipation, expectation) does
not match or surpass discovery (the event). But see letter no. 442, where
she seems to imply the opposite.

459A

To T. W. Higginson   *1876*

Nature is a Haunted House – but Art – a House that tries to be
haunted.

MANUSCRIPT: BPL (Higg 42). Ink.
PUBLICATION: L (1931) 295.
This may have been sent as a separate message or it may have accom-
panied the preceding letter, for it has the same folds.

460

To Mrs. T. W. Higginson   *spring 1876*
Dear friend,

I have your lovely Gift, and am happy and chastened. May I cherish it twice, for itself, and for you?

The tie to one we do not know, is slightly miraculous, but not humbled by test, if we are simple and sacred. Thank you for recollecting me. I have now no Father, and scarcely a Mother, for her Will followed my Father, and only an idle Heart is left, listless for his sake.

I am sorry your Hand harms you – is it easier now? Mr Higginson told me you loved the Buds – You should own my own, but the Orchard is too jocund to fold and the Robins would rob the mail.

Who knocks not, yet does not intrude, is Nature.

Please to thank Mr Higginson for the delightful note – I shall thank him myself – soon – Please tell him the "Madonnas" I see, are those that pass the House to their work, carrying Saviors with them –

———

MANUSCRIPT: BPL (Higg 94). Pencil. Envelope addressed: Mrs. Higginson.

PUBLICATION: L (1931) 299–300.

This is probably ED's first letter to Mary Channing Higginson. It would seem that Higginson had recently written that his wife was about to send some token, for the opening of letter no. 459 implies as much. It may have been a representation of the madonna and child.

461

To Mrs. William A. Stearns   *spring 1876?*

Dear Friends,

Might these be among the fabrics which the Bible designates as beyond rubies?

Certainly they are more accessible to the fingers of your thief

Emily.

MANUSCRIPT: missing.

PUBLICATION: L (1894) 377; LL 309; L (1931) 367.

Presumably sent with flowers. Mrs. Todd dates it: Spring, 1876.

To Mrs. James S. Cooper   *about 1876*

Dear friend,

I congratulate you.

Disaster endears beyond Fortune –

                                                        E. Dickinson –

MANUSCRIPT: Goodell Library. Ink.

PUBLICATION: L (1894) 393; L (1931) 382.

The date is conjectured from the handwriting. During the year 1876 some ten fires broke out in Amherst, several of them thought to have been of incendiary origin. There are no fire records for that year, but one of them may have been in the Cooper house. The letter does not sound as though the damage had been serious.

463

To Mrs. William A. Stearns   *about 8 June 1876*

Love's stricken "why"
Is all that love can speak –
Built of but just a syllable
The hugest hearts that break.

                                                        Emily.

MANUSCRIPT: missing.

PUBLICATION: L (1894) 377; LL 309; L (1931) 368: *Poems* (1955) 945.

President Stearns died, 8 June 1876.

464

To Jonathan L. Jenkins   *about 1876*

It will make Today more homelike, that he who first made Heaven homelike to Father, is with his Children.

                                                        Emily.

MANUSCRIPT: Howe. Ink. Addressed on the fold: Mr Jenkins.
PUBLICATION: *FN* 109.
The date is conjectured from the handwriting. Perhaps the note was written on the anniversary of her father's death, 16 June. Jenkins had officiated at Edward Dickinson's funeral. The note was perhaps sent to him at a family gathering at Austin's, which ED did not attend.

465

To Samuel Bowles   *about 1876*

Of your exquisite Act there can be no Acknowledgment but the Ignominy that Grace gives.

Emily.

MANUSCRIPT: AC. Pencil.
PUBLICATION: *L* (1894) 221; *LL* 284; *L* (1931) 207.
The date is conjectured from the handwriting. Perhaps this note thanks Bowles for flowers sent on the second anniversary of her father's death, 16 June 1874.

466

To Samuel Bowles   *about 1876*

We part with the River at the Flood through a timid custom, though with the same Waters we have often played.

Emily.

MANUSCRIPT: AC. Pencil.
PUBLICATION: *L* (1894) 210; *LL* 267; *L* (1931) 205.
The handwriting of this message, like that of the message preceding, is almost certainly about 1876, but the occasion which prompted it has not been identified. Perhaps both were written with her father in mind.

467

To Susan Gilbert Dickinson   *about 1876*

The Ignominy to receive – is eased by the reflection that interchange of infamies – is either's antidote.

Emily.

MANUSCRIPT: HCL (B 96). Pencil.
PUBLICATION: FF 242.
Dated by handwriting only, this note is placed here because the phrasing somewhat echoes that in letter no. 465.

468

To Mrs. James S. Cooper   *4 July 1876?*

The Founders of Honey have no Names —

MANUSCRIPT: AC. Ink. Addressed on the fold: Mrs. Cooper.
PUBLICATION: L (1894) 394; LL 323; L (1931) 383.
The note probably accompanied flowers. The date is conjectured from the handwriting and from the fact that the centennial of the founding of the town of Amherst was celebrated on 4 July 1876 (see letter no. 509).

469

To Mrs. James S. Cooper   *about 1876*

Vinnie suggests these little Friends.
    Would they be too groveling? And I add a Face from my Garden. Though you met it before, it might not be charmless.
                                                                    E. Dickinson.

MANUSCRIPT: AC. Ink.
PUBLICATION: L (1894) 394; LL 323; L (1931) 383.
This note, also in the handwriting of about 1876, evidently accompanied flowers from Vinnie's garden and from ED's.

470

To T. W. Higginson   *August 1876*

Dear friend,
    I hope Mrs Higginson is no more ill. I am glad if I did not disturb her. Loneliness for my own Father made me think of her.
    Always begins by degrees.

I almost inferred from your accent you might come to Amherst. I would like to make no mistake in a presumption so precious – but a Pen has so many inflections and a Voice but one, will you think it obtuse, if I ask if I quite understood you?

> Of their peculiar light
> I keep one ray
> To clarify the Sight
> To seek them by –

Your Scholar –

MANUSCRIPT: BPL (Higg 97). Pencil.
PUBLICATION: L (1931) 298.
Mary Channing Higginson's father, Dr. Walter Channing, died 27 July 1876. ED evidently has written to her.

471

To Louise and Frances Norcross   *August 1876*

Dear Cousins,

Mr. S[weetser] had spoken with pleasure of you, before you spoke of him. Good times are always mutual; that is what makes good times. I am glad it cheered you.

We have had no rain for six weeks except one thunder shower, and that so terrible that we locked the doors, and the clock stopped – which made it like Judgment day. The heat is very great, and the grass so still that the flies speck it. I fear Loo will despair. The notices of the "fall trade" in the hurrying dailies, have a whiff of coolness.

Vinnie has a new pussy the color of Branwell Brontë's hair. She thinks it a little "lower than the angels," and I concur with her. You remember my ideal cat has always a huge rat in its mouth, just going out of sight – though going out of sight in itself has a peculiar charm. It is true that the unknown is the largest need of the intellect, though for it, no one thinks to thank God. . . . Mother is worn with the heat, but otherwise not altering. I dream about father every night, always a different dream, and forget what I am doing daytimes, wondering where he is. Without any body, I keep thinking. What kind can that be?

Dr. Stearns died homelike, asked Eliza for a saucer of strawberries, which she brought him, but he had no hands. "In such an hour as ye think not" means something when you try it.

Lovingly,

Emily.

MANUSCRIPT: destroyed.

PUBLICATION: L (1894) 282; LL 298–299; L (1931) 256–257.

The reference to advertisements of the "fall trade" in the newspapers places this letter in August. According to the Amherst weather records, the summer of 1876 was unusually hot and dry. President Stearns had died in June (see letter no. 463). Evidently the Norcrosses were as familiar as ED with Elizabeth Gaskell's remarkable and highly controversial *The Life of Charlotte Brontë*, first published in 1857, and reissued several times thereafter. Branwell Brontë was the black sheep of the family, and ED's connection of the color of his hair with the color of a new cat of Vinnie's is appropriately explained by a sentence in Mrs. Gaskell's *Life* (chapter VII): "Branwell was rather a handsome boy, with 'tawny' hair, to use Miss Brontë's phrase for a more obnoxious color."

The scripture quotation is from Matthew 24.44: "Therefore be ye also ready: for in such an hour as ye think not the Son of man cometh."

472

To Mrs. T. W. Higginson   *late summer 1876*

Dear friend.

The "Happiness" without a cause, is the best Happiness, for Glee intuitive and lasting is the gift of God.

I fear we have all sorrow, though of different forms – but with Life so very sweet at the Crisp, what must it be unfrozen!

I hope you may sometime be so strong as to smile at now –

That is our Hope's criterion, for things that are – are ephemeral, but those to come – long – and besides,

The Flake the Wind exasperate
More eloquently lie
Than if escorted to it's Down
By Arm of Chivalry.

I would love to know your "Ferns and Grasses" and touch your

"Books and Pictures" – but it is of Realms unratified that Magic is made.

I bring you a Fern from my own Forest – where I play every Day.

You perhaps sleep as I write, for it is now late, and I give you Good Night with fictitious lips, for to me you have no Face.

"We thank thee Oh Father" for these strange Minds, that enamor us against thee.

MANUSCRIPT: BPL (Higg 66). Ink. Envelope addressed: Mrs. Higginson.
PUBLICATION: L (1931) 289.
The enclosed polypody is still in the letter.

473

To Mrs. J. G. Holland   *August 1876*

Loved and Little Sister,

Vinnie brought in a sweet pea today, which had a pod on the "off" side. Startled by the omen, I hasten to you.

An unexpected impediment to my reply to your dear last, was a call from my Aunt Elizabeth – "the only male relative on the female side," and though many days since, its flavor of court-martial still sets my spirit tingling.

With what dismay I read of those columns of kindred in the Bible – the Jacobites and the Jebusites and the Hittites and the Jacqueminots!

I am sure you are better, for no rheumatism in its senses would stay after the thermometer struck ninety!

We are revelling in a gorgeous drought.

The grass is painted brown, and how nature would look in other than the standard colors, we can all infer. . . I bade [Sue] call on you, but Vinnie said you were "the other side the globe," yet Vinnie thinks Vermont is in Asia, so I don't intend to be disheartened by trifles.

Vinnie has a new pussy that catches a mouse an hour. We call her the "minute hand." . . .

MANUSCRIPT: missing.

[561]

PUBLICATION: L (1894) 182–183; LL 317–318; L (1931) 175–176; LH 108.

The Hollands were summering at Alexandria Bay, in the Thousand Islands region of the Saint Lawrence. Sue presumably was visiting her sister at Geneva, New York. Aunt Elizabeth was Mrs. Augustus Currier.

474

To Mrs. E. S. Snell and family   *September 1876*

I had a father once.

MANUSCRIPT: missing.
PUBLICATION: L (1894) 378; LL 310; L (1931) 368.
Professor Ebenezer Snell died, 18 September 1876. This note probably accompanied flowers for his funeral.

475

To Mrs. J. G. Holland   *autumn 1876*

I once more come, with my little Load — Is it too heavy, Sister?

You remember from whom I quoted, when you brought me the Clover?

"I find your Benefits no Burden, Jane."

Had I only a Postal, with your Smile, I should sleep safer.

Emily —

MANUSCRIPT: HCL (H 36). Pencil. Addressed on fold: Mrs. Holland.
PUBLICATION: LH 106.
The letter contained an enclosure, and the request is worded as though the "burden" were not new. It was understood by the Holland family that ED made a practice of asking Mrs. Holland to address and forward letters to the Reverend Charles Wadsworth. The quotation is from *Jane Eyre*, chapter 15.

476

To T. W. Higginson   *October 1876*

Dear friend —

Are you willing to tell me what is right? Mrs. Jackson — of Colorado

— was with me a few moments this week, and wished me to write for this – I told her I was unwilling, and she asked me why? – I said I was incapable and she seemed not to believe me and asked me not to decide for a few Days – meantime, she would write me – She was so sweetly noble, I would regret to estrange her, and if you would be willing to give me a note saying you disapproved it, and thought me unfit, she would believe you – I am sorry to flee so often to my safest friend, but hope he permits me –

———

MANUSCRIPT: BPL (Higg 76). Pencil.
PUBLICATION: *AM* LXVIII (October 1891) 451; *L* (1894) 321–322; *LL* 301; *L* (1931) 299.
To explain this letter it is necessary to go back to the summer. ED during this year was in correspondence with Mrs. Jackson, and received from her a letter (HCL), dated: Princeton, Mass/Aug. 20./1876:

476a

My dear Miss Dickinson,

How could you possibly have offended me? I am sorry that such an idea should have suggested itself to you.

I have often and often thought of sending you a line, but there are only sixty minutes to an hour. There are not half enough.

I enclose to you a circular which may interest you. When the volume of Verse is published in this series, I shall contribute to it: and I want to persuade you to. Surely, in the shelter of such *double* anonymousness as that will be, you need not shrink. I want to see some of your verses in print. Unless you forbid me, I will send some that I have. May I? – It will be some time before this volume appears. There ought to be three or four volumes of stories first, I suppose. –

My husband is here with me: and we are enjoying this lovely N. England country, very much: but we shall be here only a few days longer, having that great "chore" of the Exposition to do.

The address
    Care of Messrs Roberts Bros. Boston
will always find me, wherever I am: – and I am always glad to get a line from you.

Thank you for writing in such plain letters! Will you not send me some verses?

Truly your friend
Helen Jackson

P.S. If you ever see Dr. Cate, pray give my love to him; — mine & Mr. Jacksons also.

It seems to answer a letter from ED inquiring why Mrs. Jackson had not written. The first of the poems in Helen Jackson's possession were probably copies she had made of those sent to Colonel Higginson. The enclosed circular dealt with the "No Name Series" of books soon to be issued by Roberts Brothers of Boston, under the editorship of Thomas Niles. They were to be anonymous, each, according to the circular, to be written by "a great unknown." The first was Helen Hunt Jackson's *Mercy Philbrick's Choice*, published in September. ED evidently withheld reply, and Mrs. Jackson visited Amherst on 10 October and paid a call. ED's letter to Higginson written shortly thereafter drew this response from him (HCL), dated: Newport, R. I./Oct. 22. 1876:

476b

My dear friend

My wife wishes to thank you very much for your note & sweet little rosebuds. We are quite busy, as we are just going to housekeeping, which pleases us very much; we have a nice American woman who is to keep house for us, & we both prefer it. (For six years we have been boarding.) When you come to Newport, my wife says, you must come & see us.

Now as to your letter of inquiry; It is always hard to judge for another of the bent of inclination or range of talent; but I should not have thought of advising you to write stories, as it would not seem to me to be in your line. Perhaps Mrs. Jackson thought that the change & variety might be good for you: but if you really feel a strong unwillingness to attempt it, I don't think she would mean to urge you. The celebrated prison-reformer, Mrs. Fry, made it one of her rules that we must follow, not force, Providence; & there is never any good in forcing it.

If you like to do it, I should be glad to be remembered to your brother & sister, and to your sister-in-law.

Ever your friend

T. W. Higginson

PS My wife thought you might like to have this photograph of me, unless you have it; as it is in some respects the best I have ever had taken, though the expression is not altogether true.

Higginson misunderstood, thinking the circular spoke of stories only. The following letter (HCL) Helen Jackson wrote from Ashfield shortly after her call [part has been cut away]:

476c

My dear friend,

I [keep] my promise so [promptly] that I am w[riting] you before bre[akfast, but] it is simply a [post]script to my [call the other] day; which re[ally I] found as mu[ch too] short as you [may] possibly have [felt it.]

I am ver[y sorry if] I have seemed [neglectful] and I hope [to hear from] you again. [I feel] as if I ha[d been] very imperti[nent that] day [in] speaking to you [as] I did, — accusing you of living away from the sunlight — and [telling] you that you [looke]d ill, which is a [mor]tal price of ill[ness] at all times, but re[al]ly you look[ed] so [wh]ite and [mo]th-like[!] Your [hand] felt [l]ike such a wisp in mine that you frigh[tened] me. I felt [li]ke a [gr]eat ox [tal]king to a wh[ite] moth, and beg[ging] it to come and [eat] grass with me [to] see if it could not turn itself into beef! How stupid. —

This morning I have read over again the last verses you sent me: I find them more clear than I thought they were. Part of the dimness must have been in me. Yet I have others which I like better. I like your simplest and [most direct] lines best [*page cut away*]

You say you find great pleasure in reading my verses. Let somebody somewhere whom you do not know have the same pleasure in reading yours: [*strip cut away*]

Goodbye. Whenever you like to send me a word, I shall always be

[565]

glad to hear: and for all the verses you send me, I shall thank you. — [Roberts Bros. Boston] is the address which will always find me wherever I am.

Most truly yours

Helen Jackson

477

To T. W. Higginson *late October 1876*

Dear friend.

Except your coming, I know no Gift so great – and in one extent, it exceeds that, – it is permanent.

Your Face is more joyful, when you speak – and I miss an almost arrogant look that at times haunts you – but with that exception, it is so real I could think it you.

Thank you with delight – and please to thank your friend for the lovely suggestion.

I hope she has no suffering now –

Was it Browning's Flower, that "Ailed till Evening"? I shall think of your "Keeping House" at Night, when I close the shutter – but to be Mrs — Higginson's Guest, is the Boon of Birds. Judge Lord was with us a few days since – and told me the Joy we most revere – we profane in taking.

I wish that was wrong. Mrs Jackson has written. It was not stories she asked of me. But may I tell her just the same that you dont prefer it? Thank you, if I may, for it almost seems sordid to refuse from myself again.

My Brother and Sister speak of you – and covet your remembrance – and perhaps you will not reject my own, to Mrs Higginson?

Summer laid her supple Glove
In it's sylvan Drawer –
Wheresoe'er, or was she –
The demand of Awe?

Your Scholar.

MANUSCRIPT: BPL (Higg 77). Ink.
PUBLICATION: L (1894) 322–323; LL 301–302; L (1931) 300.

[566]

This replies to his letter of 22 October, and thanks him for the photograph. The quotation (also in letter 337) is from *Sordello*, II, 290–295:

A plant they have, yielding a three-leaved bell
Which whitens at the heart ere noon, and ails
Till evening; evening gives it to her gales
To clear away with such forgotten things
As are an eyesore to the morn: this brings
Him to their mind, and bears his very name.

478

To Mrs. Joseph A. Sweetser   *late October 1876?*

Cousin T[imothy] and Cousin O[livia Norcross] little thought when they were paying their antiquated respects to Aunt Katie that they were defrauding Emily of that last moment – but they needed it most – new moments will grow.

When I found it beyond my power to see you, I designed to write you, immediately, but the Lords came as you went, and Judge Lord was my father's closest friend, so I shared my moments with them till they left us last Monday; then seeing directly after, the death of your loved Dr. A——, I felt you might like to be alone – though Death is perhaps an intimate friend, not an enemy. Beloved Shakespeare says, "He that is robbed and smiles, steals something from the thief." . . .

Maggie said you asked should you "eat the flower." Please consult the bees – they are the only authority on Etruscan matters. Vinnie said the sherry I sent you was brandy – a vital misapprehension. Please also forgive it. I did not intend to be so base to the aunt who showed me the first mignonette, and listened with me to the great wheel, from Uncle Underwood's "study," and won me in "divers other ways" too lovely to mention. Of all this we will talk when you come again.

Meanwhile accept your
Trifling Niece.

MANUSCRIPT: missing.
PUBLICATION: L (1894) 411; L (1931) 401.
The date of the letter is conjectural. It belongs here if the visit from the Lords is the same visit as that mentioned in the preceding letter to Higginson. Mrs. Todd placed it with letters written in 1884, but it seems

to have been sent while Mrs. Lord was living. She died in 1877, and until her death the Lords were always guests in the Dickinson home when they visited Amherst. After that time Judge Lord, with his nieces, stopped at the Amherst House. The quotation is from *Othello* (I, iii, 208): "The robb'd that smiles steals something from the thief."

479

To Louise and Frances Norcross   *November 1876?*

. . . Oh that beloved witch-hazel which would not reach me till part of the stems were a gentle brown, though one loved stalk as hearty as if just placed in the mail by the woods. It looked like tinsel fringe combined with staider fringes, witch and witching too, to my joyful mind.

I never had seen it but once before, and it haunted me like childhood's Indian pipe, or ecstatic puff-balls, or that mysterious apple that sometimes comes on river-pinks; and is there not a dim suggestion of a dandelion, if her hair were ravelled and she grew on a twig instead of a tube, – though this is timidly submitted. For taking Nature's hand to lead her to me, I am softly grateful – was she willing to come? Though her reluctances are sweeter than other ones' avowals.

> Trusty as the stars
> Who quit their shining working
> Prompt as when I lit them
> In Genesis' new house,
> Durable as dawn
> Whose antiquated blossom
> Makes a world's suspense
> Perish and rejoice.

Love for the cousin sisters, and the lovely alien. . . .

Lovingly,

Emily.

MANUSCRIPT: destroyed.
PUBLICATION: L (1894) 283; LL 310; L (1931) 257–258.
Mrs. Todd dated the letter: November, 1876.

To Susan Gilbert Dickinson   *late 1876*

Sue – this is the last flower –

       To wane without disparagement
       In a dissembling hue
       That will not let the Eye decide
       If it abide or no
is Sunset's – perhaps – only.

                                     Emily

MANUSCRIPT: HCL (B 54). Ink.
PUBLICATION: *FF* 265.
The date is conjectured from the handwriting, from the apparent time of year the flower was sent, and from the fact that the identical lines are incorporated in a letter to Higginson written in January 1877 (no. 486). A variant of the quatrain is in a letter to Dr. Holland (no. 544).

To Mrs. T. W. Higginson   *Christmas 1876*

Dear friend.

I wish you were strong like me.

I am bringing a little Granite Book you can lean upon. I hope you may not prohibit me. I have not asked Mr – Higginson's leave.

I am sorry you need Health, but rejoice you do not Affection – That can be growing while you rest, for the Heart is the "seed" of which we read that "the Birds of Heaven lodge in it's Branches." With Christmas' permission and affection for Mr – Higginson, I am whom you infer –

———

MANUSCRIPT: BPL (Higg 80). Ink. Envelope addressed: Mrs. Higginson./Newport/Rhode Island.
PUBLICATION: *L* (1931) 305.
The book is Emerson's *Representative Men* (new edition, J. R. Osgood, 1876). It is in HCL, and is inscribed by ED: "To M C H from Emily Dickinson Christmas, 1876." Higginson wrote his sister Anna on 28 De-

cember (HCL): "Last night the Warings had their novel wedding festival of a dozen people . . . The Woolseys were bright as usual & wrote some funny things for different guests — one imaginary letter to me from my partially cracked poetess at Amherst, who writes to me & signs "Your scholar.' (N.B. She writes to Mary now & sent her Emerson's 'Representative Men' as 'a little granite book, for you to lean on!') . . ." The quotation from Matthew 13.32 reads: ". . . so that the birds of the air come and lodge in the branches thereof."

482

To the Jenkins children   *about 1876*

Happy Did and Mac!

   We can offer you nothing so charming as your own Hearts, which we would seek to possess, had we the requisite Wiles —

MANUSCRIPT: Howe. Pencil.
PUBLICATION: *L* (1894) 370; *LL* 280; *FN* 60; *L* (1931) 361.
The date is conjectured from the handwriting.

483

To Mrs. Jonathan L. Jenkins   *about 1876*

   Whose tenderness to my own Sister, constrains me to cherish her's.
                                                             Emily.

MANUSCRIPT: HCL (L 41). Ink.
PUBLICATION: *FN* 85.
   The note may have accompanied flowers sent to Mrs. Jenkins on some occasion when a sister was visiting her. The handwriting places it about this time. During 1877, and perhaps before, Lavinia suffered a "singular illness" (see letter no. 525) for which evidently the ministrations of a sympathetic pastor's wife were more effective than those of a physician. The note was certainly written before the Jenkinses left Amherst in May 1877.

To Susan Gilbert Dickinson   *about 1876*

"Doth forget that ever he heard the name of Death."

MANUSCRIPT: HCL (B 168). Ink.
PUBLICATION: FF 255.
The date is conjectured from the handwriting. Though the occasion that prompted this note is not known, the quotation from *Coriolanus* (III, i, 256–258) leads one to conjecture that the message followed an angry outbreak of feeling on the part of someone.

His heart's his mouth:
What his breast forges, that his tongue must vent;
And, being angry, does forget that ever
He heard the name of death.

The lines are spoken by Menenius Agrippa, Coriolanus's friend, in defense of Coriolanus. The context strongly suggests that ED wrote this as a tender note of apology for one whose heart was frequently her mouth, perhaps for Lavinia.

To Mrs. Jonathan L. Jenkins   *about 1877*

Dear friend.

Were the Velocity of Affection as perceptible as it's Sanctity, Day and Night would be more Affecting.

Emily.

MANUSCRIPT: HCL (L 44). Ink. Addressed: Mrs Jenkins.
PUBLICATION: FN 116.
The handwriting is of this period. The same sentence is incorporated in the following letter to Higginson.

To T. W. Higginson   *early January 1877*

Is the Year too elderly for your acceptance of Lowell, as a slight symbol of a Scholar's Affection? I designed "Harold" to accompany Emerson, but Tennyson declines – like Browning – once so rare!

To wane without disparagement
In a dissembling hue
That will not let the eye decide
If it abide or no
is sunset's, perhaps – only. Please remember me with thoughtfulness
to Mrs – Higginson, to whom I shall soon write. Were the velocity of
Affection as perceptible as it's sanctity, Day and Night would be more
affecting.

My Brother has been very ill for three months, of Malarial Fever –
which he took at the Centennial and we have feared he would die.

I thought your approbation Fame – and it's withdrawal Infamy. I
hope I in no way thought wrong of Mrs Jackson's wish – Did I – could
you excuse it.

MANUSCRIPT: BPL (Higg 87). Ink.
PUBLICATION: L (1931) 302.

ED perhaps refers to Lowell's *Three Memorial Poems* (1877) and
Tennyson's *Harold, a Drama* (1876). Austin attended the Philadelphia
Centennial in the middle of October.

487

To Mrs. J. G. Holland   *early 1877*

Dear Sister.

I have felt so sweet an impatience to write you, that I thought it
perhaps inordinate, and to be disciplined, like other unruly wishful-
ness – but however you stem Nature, she at last succeeds.

Your Letters have the peculiar worth that attaches to all prowess,
as each is an achievement for your delicate Eyes. I almost fear you
urge them too far, though to lag is stale to a rapid Spirit –

I hope you may live till I am asleep in my personal Grave, not but
Earth is Heaven, but I would not like to outlive the smile on your
guileless Face. Doctor's "Child Wife" – indeed – if not Mr Copperfield's.

This is a stern Winter, and in my Pearl Jail, I think of Sun and
Summer as visages unknown.

The Sermon you failed to hear, I can lend you – though Legerdemain is unconveyed – and "Corn in the Ear," Audacity, these inclement Days.

I was much impressed by your sweetness to Austin. He seems the "Child of the Regiment" since he was so sick, and every tenderness to him is caress to us.

Congratulate the Doctor on his growing Fame.

"Stratford on Avon" – accept us all!

With love for your sweet Descendants – and the wish for yourself, I am

Emily –

MANUSCRIPT: HCL (H 38). Ink.
PUBLICATION: *LH* 110.

The Hollands were probably in Philadelphia for the Centennial Exposition when Dr. Wadsworth preached "God's Culture" on 30 November. It was printed shortly thereafter. A chapter in Higginson's *Army Life in a Black Regiment* (1870) is titled: "The Baby of the Regiment."

488

To T. W. Higginson   *early 1877*

Dear friend.

Thank you for permission to write Mrs Higginson. I hope I have not fatigued her – also for thinking of my Brother, who is slowly better, and rides for an hour, kind Days. I am glad if I did as you would like. The degradation to displease you, I hope I may never incur.

Often, when troubled by entreaty, that paragraph of your's has saved me – "Such being the Majesty of the Art you presume to practice, you can at least take time before dishonoring it," and Enobarbus said "Leave that which leaves itself."

I shall look with joy for the "Little Book," because it is your's, though I seek you in vain in the Magazines, where you once wrote –

I recently found two Papers of your's that were unknown to me, and wondered anew at your withdrawing Thought so sought by others. When Flowers annually died and I was a child, I used to read Dr Hitckcock's Book on the Flowers of North America. This comforted their Absence – assuring me they lived.

Your Scholar –

[573]

MANUSCRIPT: BPL (Higg 79). Ink.
PUBLICATION: L (1894) 324–325; LL 303–304; L (1931) 302–303.
The first quotation is from Higginson's April 1862 essay in the *Atlantic Monthly*, which first impelled her to write him (see letter no. 260). The second quotation are lines spoken by Antony, not Enobarbus, in *Antony and Cleopatra* III, xi, 17–20:

> Pray you, look not sad,
> Nor make replies of loathness; take the hint
> Which my despair proclaims. Let that be left
> Which leaves itself

The "Little Book" was Higginson's *A Book of American Explorers* (Young Folks Series), published about 1 April 1877. ED may have had in mind Edward Hitchcock's *Catalogue of Plants Growing . . . in the Vicinity of Amherst* (1829). Austin's recovery was slow (see letter no. 486).

489

To Samuel Bowles   *about 1877*

Dear friend,

You have the most triumphant Face out of Paradise – probably because you are there constantly, instead of ultimately –

> Ourselves – we do inter – with sweet derision
> The Channel of the Dust – who once achieves –
> Invalidates the Balm of that Religion
> That doubts – as fervently as it believes.

                                                                      Emily.

MANUSCRIPT: AC. Pencil.
PUBLICATION: L (1894) 220; LL 271; L (1931) 206–207.
The date is conjectured from the handwriting. A photograph of Bowles taken about this time – he was just past fifty – is reproduced in this volume. This letter may acknowledge receipt of a copy of it.

490

To Mrs. J. G. Holland   *early 1877*

Austin will come tomorrow.

"Tomorrow" – whose location
The Wise deceives
Though it's hallucination
Is last that leaves –
Tomorrow – thou Retriever
Of every tare –
Of Alibi art thou
Or ownest where?

Emily.

MANUSCRIPT: HCL (H 39). Ink. Dated: Saturday Night.
PUBLICATION: *LH* 111.
The date of this letter is determined by the two which follow, and confirmed by the handwriting. Evidently the Hollands had extended a casual invitation to Austin to visit them when he was next in New York. One infers from the next letter that the attempt by ED to reply for him, in this metaphoric language, he felt to be somewhat egregious, but accepted the incident as trivial.

491

To Mrs. J. G. Holland   *early 1877*

Will my little Sister excuse me?
"Douglass, Douglass, tender and true" who never swindled me! I am ashamed and sorry. I meant hypothetic tomorrows – though are there any other?
I deserve to be punished. I am – in regret.
Austin said he should write you, and that Sue w'd too – but he is overcharged with care, and Sue with scintillation, and I fear they have not –
Austin was pleased and surprised, that you wished for him, and still hopes he may go, but not now – but "Beyond," as the Vane says – You remember Little Nell's Grandfather leaned on his Cane on the Knoll that contained her, with "She will come tomorrow." That was the kind of Tomorrow I meant –
I hope I have not tired "Sweetest Eyes were ever seen," for whose beloved Acts, both revealed and covert, I am each Day more fondly, their Possessor's Own —

MANUSCRIPT: HCL (H 40). Pencil.
PUBLICATION: *LH* 112.

This replies to a query from Mrs. Holland, written after she had received the foregoing letter, asking why Austin had not arrived. The tension between the two Amherst households is made explicit in the fourth
paragraph (see letters no. 484 and 736). The popular "Douglas" poem,
set to music, was written by Dinah Maria Craik (Miss Mulock). The
final quotation is from Mrs. Browning's "Catarina to Camoens" (see also
letter no. 801).

492

To Mrs. J. G. Holland   *about March 1877*

Sister.

The vitality of your syllables compensates for their infrequency.
There is not so much Life as *talk* of Life, as a general thing. Had we
the first intimation of the Definition of Life, the calmest of us would
be Lunatics!

Austin described his call in his own way, which was of course
inimitable.

I hope those young Men have the supports of the Gospel, though
that is a dim Elixir, in cases like their's.

Austin said he was much ashamed of Mattie – and she was much
ashamed of him, she imparted to us. They are a weird couple.

I am glad if you love your Clergyman, though the error to love
our's has cost us severely.

God seems much more friendly through a hearty Lens.

There is a Dove in the Street and I own beautiful Mud – so I know
Summer is coming. I was always attached to Mud, because of what it
typifies – also, perhaps, a Child's tie to primeval Pies.

Vinnie put on fresh Cheeks three times, for the Doctor – but I
thought I should have time to change mine, after he came –

As it proved, I did.

I hope you are both safe and in sweet health, and that at some
stage of my swift career, I shall again meet you.

Were but our own immortal Mortals, as with us as Nature, we
should demand few Alms.

Emily.

[576]

MANUSCRIPT: HCL (H 41). Ink.
PUBLICATION: LH 113–114.
Dr. Holland took a vacation in Northampton for the week of 6 February. Evidently Austin and Mattie (now ten years old) called on him there. Jenkins preached his farewell sermon in the First Church on 11 February.

493

To Edward (Ned) Dickinson   *March 1877*

Dear Ned –

I send you a Portrait of the Parish, and the first Sugar – Dont bite the Parish, by mistake, though you may be tempted –

> A Field of Stubble, lying sere
> Beneath the second Sun –
> It's Toils to Brindled People thrust –
> It's Triumphs – to the Bin –
> Accosted by a timid Bird
> Irresolute of Alms –
> Is often seen – but seldom felt,
> On our New England Farms –

I rejoice you are better –
Grandma's fervent love –

                                                        Emily.

MANUSCRIPT: HCL (B 85). Pencil. Addressed on the fold: Ned.
PUBLICATION: FF 257.
In mid-February 1877, Ned, now fifteen, was the victim of a seizure which greatly alarmed his family. He recovered shortly, but the attacks became recurrent.

494

To Mrs. William A. Stearns   *early 1877?*

Dear Friend,

The little package of nectar mother opened herself, though her hands are frail as a child's.

She could not believe them real till I had hidden one in her mouth, which somewhat convinced her. She asks me to thank you tenderly. The love of her friends is the only remnant of her grieved life, and she clings to it timidly.

I hope you are quite well, and am sure we sometimes think of each other, endeared by that most hallowed thorn, a mutual loss.

With sweet remembrance for your niece, of whom my sister speaks,

Emily.

MANUSCRIPT: missing.
PUBLICATION: L (1894) 378; L (1931) 368.
Mrs. Todd says this was written in thanks for strawberries sent to Mrs. Dickinson perhaps in March 1877.

495

To Mrs. Jonathan L. Jenkins   *1 April 1877*

May the Love that occasioned the first "Easter," shelter a few this bereaved Day.

MANUSCRIPT: HCL (L 40). Ink.
PUBLICATION: L (1894) 374; FN 118; L (1931) 364.
Easter in 1877 was on 1 April. Mrs. Jenkins' father died at Lowell on 18 March.

496

To Sally Jenkins   *about 1877?*

Will the sweet child who sent me the butterflies, herself a member of the same ethereal nation, accept a rustic kiss, flavored, we trust, with clover?

MANUSCRIPT: missing.
PUBLICATION: L (1894) 371; FN 64–65; L (1931) 361.
An empty envelope (HCL–L 48) survives, addressed in pencil: Katie "Did,"/from/Katie did'nt –. If the above letter was sent in this envelope – and it was about this time that ED was writing notes to the Jenkins children – the letter belongs here. Sally's nickname was "Did."

To the Jenkins children 1877?

Dear Brother and Sister,

I take you with me to my sleep, but if I do not find it for tenderness for [you], believe me at your side.

Emily.

MANUSCRIPT: missing. The text is from an unpublished letter (HCL) written by MacGregor Jenkins to Martha Dickinson Bianchi in 1930. It follows the transcript verbatim except for a semicolon which Jenkins placed after the salutation – a form of punctuation which ED never so used.

Any date is conjectural, but clearly the note was written after the acquaintance with the children had been warmly established. In 1877 MacGregor was eight and his sister about eleven.

To Mrs. T. W. Higginson *early spring 1877*

Dear friend.

I cannot let the Grass come without remembering you, and half resent my rapid Feet, when they are not your's – The power to fly is sweet, though one defer the flying, as Liberty is Joy, though never used.

I give you half my Birds – upon the sweet condition that you will bring them back – yourself, and dwell a Day with me, and Bliss without a price, I earned myself of Nature –

> Of whose electric Adjunct
> Not anything is known –
> Though it's unique Momentum
> Inebriate our own.

Forgive me if I come too much – the time to live is frugal – and good as is a better earth, it will not quite be this.

How could I find the way to you and Mr Higginson without a Vane, or any Road?

They might not need me – yet they might –
I'll let my Heart be just in sight –
A smile so small as mine might be
Precisely their necessity —

MANUSCRIPT: BPL (Higg 90). Ink.
PUBLICATION: L (1931) 307–308.
ED knew that Mary Channing Higginson, who died the following
September, was seriously ill. The date is conjectured from the handwriting.
For a discussion of the two quatrains, see *Poems* (1955) 958–960. See also
letter no. 499.

499

To the Jenkins family   *spring 1877*

Dear friends,

I send you this little Antidote to the love of others – Whenever you
feel yourselves enticed, cling to it's Admonition –

Emily –

MANUSCRIPT: HCL (L 46). Pencil.
PUBLICATION: FN 126.
This was probably sent to the Jenkinses before they left Amherst for
Pittsfield in May. It evidently enclosed a poem, almost certainly the follow-
ing (HCL), said by MacGregor Jenkins (in *FN*) to have been sent to his
mother at the time of departure.

They might not need me – yet they might.
I'll let my Heart be just in sight –
A smile so small as mine might be
Precisely their necessity –

500

To Mrs. Henry Hills   *about 1877*

"Give us this Day our daily Bread," omits a fragrant Adjunct –

———

MANUSCRIPT: Jones Library. Ink. Unpublished.
The date is conjectured from the handwriting. The note may have
accompanied a gift from the Dickinson kitchen.

To Mrs. Jonathan L. Jenkins   *late May 1877*

Dear friend,

It was pathetic to see your Voice instead of hearing it, for it has grown sweetly familiar in the House, as a Bird's. Father left us in June – you leave us in May. I am glad there will be no April till another year. Austin brought the note and waited like a hungry Boy for his crumb of words. Be sure to speak his name next time, he looks so solitary.

He told me that he could not sleep Friday night or Saturday night, and so rose and read lethargic Books to stupefy himself.

Sorrow is unsafe when it is real sorrow. I am glad so many are counterfeits – guileless because they believe themselves.

Kiss Diddie and Mac for us, precious Refugees, with love for our Brother whom with you we follow in the peculiar distance, "even unto the end."

Perhaps it is "the end" now. I think the Bell thought so because it bade us all goodbye when you stood in the Door.

You concealed that you heard it. Thank you.

                                Emily.

MANUSCRIPT: missing.

PUBLICATION: L (1894) 374, in part; FN 134–135, in part; L (1931) 364–365, in part.

The *Amherst Record* for Wednesday 18 April 1877, announced that Jenkins preached his first sermon in the First Church at Pittsfield on the previous Sunday. This letter, with its clear reference to the growing breach between Austin and Susan, evidently acknowledges a call that Mrs. Jenkins made shortly before the family left Amherst in May. The scripture quotation is from Matthew 28.20.

To Mrs. J. G. Holland   *late May 1877*

Dear friend.

I hesitate where you are, but decide to indite my Letter to my Sister in "Alexandria Bay," as the Irishman does to his "Mother in Dublin."

You have been magnanimous – and I requite you with nothing –
the Sum that Benefactors love.

The Days are very hot and the Weeds pant like the centre of
Summer. They say the Corn likes it. I thought there were others besides the Corn. How deeply I was deluded! Vinnie rocks her Garden
and moans that God wont help her –

I suppose he is too busy, getting "angry with the Wicked – every
Day."

He loves too homogeneously for Vinnie's special Mind.

Would you believe that our sacred Neighbors, the Mr and Mrs
Sweetser, were so enamored of "Nicholas Minturn," that they borrow
our Number before it is cold? But Youth, like Indian Summer, comes
twice a Year –

Vinnie says I must go – or the Mail will leave me.

The etiquette of the admonition is questionable – though of it's
imperativeness there is no doubt.

I must just show you a Bee, that is eating a Lilac at the Window.
There – there – he is gone! How glad his family will be to see him!

> Bees are Black, with Gilt Surcingles –
> Buccaneers of Buzz.
> Ride abroad in ostentation
> And subsist on Fuzz.
>
> Fuzz ordained – not Fuzz contingent –
> Marrows of the Hill.
> Jugs – a Universe's fracture
> Could not jar or spill.

Emily.

MANUSCRIPT: HCL (H 42). Ink.
PUBLICATION: LH 115–116.

Holland's last novel *Nicholas Minturn* appeared serially in *Scribner's*
Monthly during 1876–1877. The reference to lilacs fixes the date. The
scripture quotation is from Psalm 7.11.

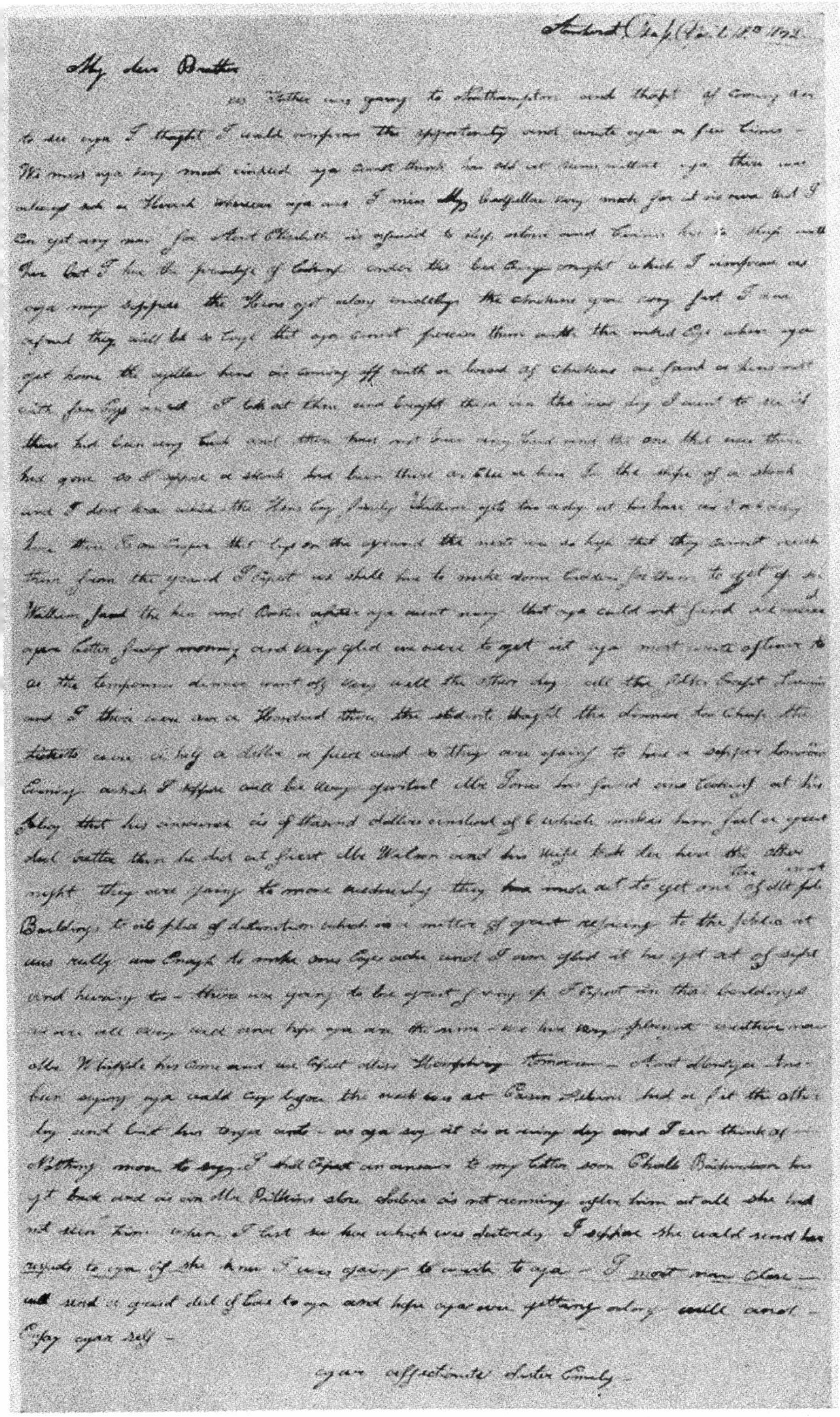

Amherst Mass April 18th 1842

My dear Brother

As Father was going to Northampton and thought of coming on to see you I thought I would improve the opportunity and write you a few lines — We miss you very much indeed you cannot think how odd it seems without you there was always such a Hurrah wherever you was I miss My bedfellow very much for it is rare that I can get any now for Aunt Elisabeth is afraid to sleep alone and Lavinia has to sleep with her but I have the privilege of looking under the bed every night which I improve as you may suppose the Hens get along nicely the chickens grow very fast I am afraid they will be so large that you cannot perceive them with the naked Eye when you get home the yellow hen is coming off with a brood of chickens we found a hens nest with four Eggs in it I took out them and brought them in the next day I went to see if there had been any laid and there had not been any laid and the one that was there had gone so I suppose a skunk had been there or else a hen In the shape of a skunk and I dont know which the Hens lay finely William gets two a day at his house and I am very [illegible] there [illegible] the Eggs on the ground the snow is so high that they cannot reach them from the ground I expect we shall have to make some ladders for them to get up on William found the hen and Rooster after you went away that you could not find we received your letter friday morning and very glad we were to get it you must write oftener to us the temperance dinner went off very well the other day all the [illegible] except Lavinia and I there were over a Hundred there the students thought the dinner too cheap the tickets were a half a dollar a piece and so they are going to have a supper tomorrow Evening which I suppose will be very genteel Mr Jones has found [illegible] at his Policy that his insurance is a thousand dollars instead of 6 which makes him feel a great deal better than he did at first Mr Wilson and his Wife took tea here the other night they are going to move wednesday they have made out to get one of the [illegible] Buildings to its place of destination which is a matter of great rejoicing to the public it was really enough to make ones Eyes ache and I am glad it has got out of sight and hearing too — there are going to be great fixing up I expect in these buildings — we are all very well and hope you are the same — we have very pleasant weather now Mr Whipple has come and we expect Miss Humphrey tomorrow — Aunt Montague has been saying you would come before the week was out Parson Adams had a fit the other day and [illegible] — as you say it is a rainy day and I can think of Nothing more to say I shall expect an answer to my letter soon Charles Richardson has got back and is in Mr Pitkins store Sabra is not running after him at all she had not seen him when I last saw her which was Saturday I suppose she would send her regards to you if she knew I was going to write to you — I must now close — all send a great deal of love to you and hope you are getting along well and Enjoy your self —

your affectionate Sister Emily

Letter 1

Letter 232

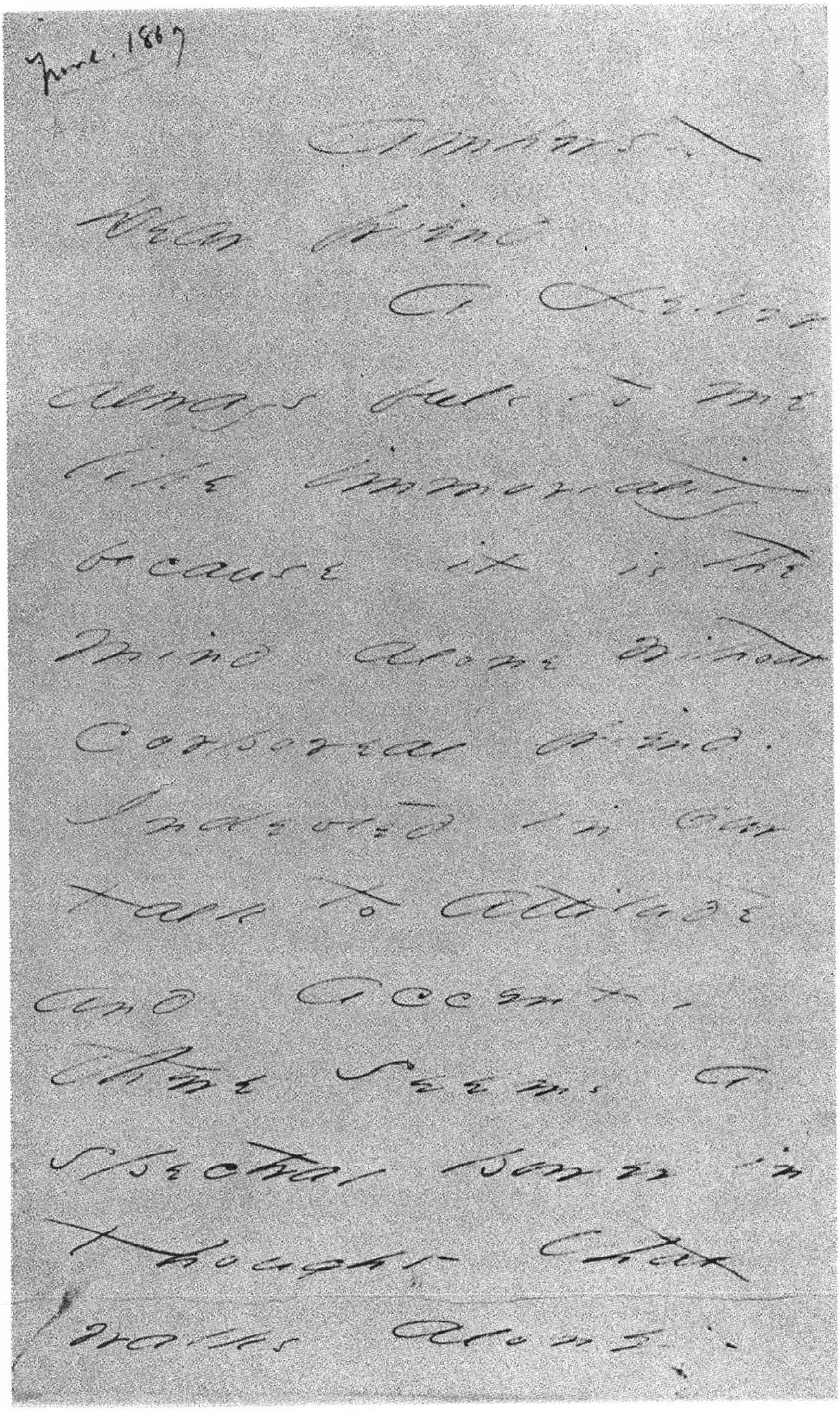

June. 1869

Dear friend

A Letter
always feels to me
like immortality
because it is the
mind alone without
corporeal friend.
Indebted in our
talk to attitude
and accent.
There seems a
spectral power in
thought that
walks alone.

Letter 330

To T. W. Higginson   *June 1877*

Dear friend.

I find you with Dusk – for Day is tired, and lays her antediluvian cheek to the Hill like a child.

Nature confides now –

I hope you are joyful frequently, these beloved Days. And the health of your friend bolder.

I remember her with my Blossoms and wish they were her's.

> Whose Pink career may have a close
> Portentous as our own, who knows?
> To imitate these Neighbors fleet
> In awe and innocence, were meet.

Summer is so kind I had hoped you might come. Since my Father's dying, everything sacred enlarged so – it was dim to own – When a few years old – I was taken to a Funeral which I now know was of peculiar distress, and the Clergyman asked "Is the Arm of the Lord shortened that it cannot save?"

He italicized the "cannot." I mistook the accent for a doubt of Immortality and not daring to ask, it besets me still, though we know that the mind of the Heart must live if it's clerical part do not. Would you explain it to me?

I was told you were once a Clergyman. It comforts an instinct if another have felt it too. I was rereading your "Decoration." You may have forgotten it.

> Lay this Laurel on the One
> Too intrinsic for Renown –
> Laurel – vail your deathless tree –
> Him you chasten, that is He!

Please recall me to Mrs — Higginson —

                    Your scholar.

MANUSCRIPT: BPL (Higg 69). Ink.
PUBLICATION: L (1894) 318–319; LL 292–293; L (1931) 292–293.
On Higginson's "Decoration," see notes to letters no. 413 and 418. For the full story, with Higginson's poem quoted, see *Poems* (1955) 960–962.

To Mrs. James S. Cooper   *about 1877*

Dear friend.
  You thought of it.
  Now dear, how delicate!
        With peculiar love,
                        Your Stranger

MANUSCRIPT: YUL. Ink.
PUBLICATION: L (1894) 392; L (1931) 381.
Mrs. Cooper perhaps had remembered the anniversary of Edward Dickinson's death, 16 June; the date is conjectured from the handwriting. The signature may suggest that ED had not communicated with Mrs. Cooper since the previous-summer (see letter no. 469).

To Samuel Bowles   *about 1877*

                        Wednesday.
Dear Mr. Bowles' Note, of itself a Blossom, came only Tonight.
I am glad it lingered, for each was all the Heart could hold.
                        Emily.

MANUSCRIPT: AC. Pencil.
PUBLICATION: L (1894) 221; LL 284; L (1931) 207.
The date is conjectured from the handwriting. The message acknowledges receipt of flowers sent perhaps, as Bowles tried annually to remember to do, during the week of the anniversary of her father's death. The flowers had arrived before his note. In 1877 the anniversary date, 16 June, fell on Saturday.

To Mrs. Jonathan L. Jenkins   *20 June 1877*

  You deserved a Tiding – before – dear –
  Your little punctualities are generous and precious.
  Vinnie rode last Twilight – with Austin and the Baby, but the

latter cried for the Moon, which saddened their Trip. He is an ardent Jockey, for so old a man, and his piercing cries of "Go Cadgie," when they leave him behind, rend the neighborhood.

There is circus here, and Farmers' Commencement, and Boys and Girls from Tripoli, and Governors and swords, parade the Summer Streets. They lean upon the Fence that guards the quiet Church Ground, and jar the Grass, now warm and soft as a Tropic Nest.

Many people call, and wish for you with tears, and Vinnie beats her wings like a maddened Bird, whose Home has been invaded.

So much has been Sorrow, that to fall asleep in Tennyson's Verse, seems almost a Pillow. "To where beyond these voices there is peace." I hope you are each safe. It is homeless without you, and we think of others possessing you with the throe of Othello.

Mother gives her love — Maggie pleads her own. Austin smiles when you mention him. He told me that one of the fine Nights – the Tenants of your House sat in the Door together, and he remarked to Sue – "Those are [not] for whom I built that Parsonage."

Daisies and Ferns are with us, and he whose Meadow they magnify, is always linked with you.

Emily.

Manuscript: Sister Mary James. Ink.

Publication: L (1894) 374–375, in part; L (1931) 365, in part; FN 129–130, entire.

On 20 June, Van Amburgh's Menagerie exhibited in Amherst, and the Agricultural College held its commencement. The quotation from Tennyson, in the third from the last paragraph, is the concluding line of "Guinevere" in *The Idylls of the King*.

Among ED's prose fragments (AC – pencil) is a draft of the comment about Gilbert:

> He is an ardent Jockey for so old a man and his
> piercing cries of go cadgie when they leave him
> behind – rend the neighborhood –

On the verso is the sentence:

> I feel Barefoot all over as the Boys say –

Both fragments are published in *NEQ* XXVIII (1955) 300.

To Mrs. Julius H. Seelye   *late June 1877*

My dear Mrs Seelye —

Let me congratulate not you, but Ourselves.

E. Dickinson.

MANUSCRIPT: Colby College. Ink.
PUBLICATION: *Colby Library Quarterly* (June 1946) 240.
Seelye was inaugurated as president of Amherst College on 27 June 1877.

508

To Mrs. Julius H. Seelye   *about 1877*

Dead friend —

I requite the celestial suggestion with Blossoms resembling it, and ask with your own timidity, "Will they intrude"?

E. Dickinson.

MANUSCRIPT: Colby College. Ink.
PUBLICATION: *Colby Library Quarterly* (June 1946) 240.
The date is conjectured from the handwriting. Mrs. Seelye may have answered the foregoing note by sending flowers, which ED here acknowledges in kind.

509

To Mrs. James S. Cooper   *about 1877*

"My Country, 'tis of thee," has always meant the Woods — to me —
"Sweet Land of Liberty," I trust is your own —

MANUSCRIPT: AC. Ink.
PUBLICATION: L (1894) 393; L (1931) 382.
The date is conjectured from the handwriting. This note, like a similar one written in 1876 (no. 468), may have been sent on the Fourth of July.

To Mrs. James S. Cooper   *about 1877*

How strange that Nature does not knock, and yet does not intrude!

MANUSCRIPT: Clark. Ink.
PUBLICATION: L (1894) 395; LL 334; L (1931) 384.
The handwriting is the only clue to the date. The note probably accompanied flowers.

To Edward (Ned) Dickinson   *July 1877*

Dear Ned –
You know I never liked you in those Yellow Jackets.

Emily.

MANUSCRIPT: HCL (B 83). Pencil.
PUBLICATION: AM CXV (1915) 37; LL 60.
An item in the *Springfield Republican*, 19 July 1877, reported that Ned had been stung by a hornet on the day preceding.

To Mrs. T. W. Higginson   *summer 1877*

Dear friend
I send you a flower from my garden – Though it die in reaching you, you will know it lived, when it left my hand –
Hamlet wavered for all of us –

———

MANUSCRIPT: BPL (Higg 91). Ink. Envelope addressed: Mrs Higginson.
PUBLICATION: L (1931) 305.
The flower was a cape jasmine (see letter no. 513).

To T. W. Higginson   *August 1877*

Dear friend –

The flower was Jasmin. I am glad if it pleased your friend. It is next dearest to Daphne – except Wild flowers – those are dearer – I have a friend in Dresden, who thinks the love of the Field a misplaced affection – and says he will send me a Meadow that is better than Summer's. If he does, I will send it to you.

I have read nothing of Tourguenéff's, but thank you for telling me – and will seek him immediately. I hoped you might show me something of your's – one of the "few Verses" – the "scarcely any," you called them. Could you be willing now? Reprove me if I longed too bold – but I wished nothing so much –

You asked me if I wrote now?

I have no other Playmate –

I send you a Gale, and an Epitaph – and a Word to a Friend, and a Blue Bird, for Mrs Higginson. Excuse them if they are untrue –

Since you cease to teach me, how could I improve?

Your Pupil.

MANUSCRIPT: BPL (Higg 73). Ink.

PUBLICATION: L (1894) 320, in part; LL 293–294, in part; L (1931) 294–295, entire.

The poems, in the order ED names them, were: "It sounded as if the Streets were running," "She laid her docile Crescent down," "I have no Life but this," and "After all Birds have been investigated and laid aside." Higginson had evidently mentioned in the letter to which this replies that he was writing an article on Turgenev (1818–1883); his diary (HCL) records that he sent it to the *Atlantic Monthly* on 7 August, but it was never published. The Dresden friend has not been identified.

To Martha Gilbert Smith   *summer 1877*

Dear Mattie –

I remember you were peculiarly interested in this little flower – As it never blossoms except in Winter, I think it became on your account.

I have talked with your little Girl, whose persistent resemblance to you is sweet to those who love you –

Love for yourself, Mattie, and tenderness for Sue –

Emily,

MANUSCRIPT: HCL (L 27). Pencil.
PUBLICATION: FF 251.
Mattie and her nine-year-old daughter Elizabeth were visiting Sue. The flower is blooming out of season.

515

To Samuel Bowles   *about 1877*

Dear friend.

Vinnie accidentally mentioned that you hesitated between the "Theophilus" and the "Junius."

Would you confer so sweet a favor as to accept that too, when you come again?

I went to the Room as soon as you left, to confirm your presence – recalling the Psalmist's sonnet to God, beginning

> I have no Life but this –
> To lead it here –
> Nor any Death – but lest
> Dispelled from there –
> Nor tie to Earths to come –
> Nor Action new
> Except through this extent
> The love of you.

.It is strange that the most intangible thing is the most adhesive.

Your "Rascal."

I washed the Adjective.

MANUSCRIPT: AC. Ink.
PUBLICATION: L (1894) 219–220; LL 267; L (1931) 205–206.
Gertrude M. Graves wrote "A Cousin's Memories of Emily Dickinson," *Boston Sunday Globe*, 12 January 1930, telling how Bowles once called upstairs to ED: "Emily, you wretch! No more of this nonsense! I've traveled

[589]

all the way from Springfield to see you. Come down at once." She is said to have complied and never have been more witty. The conclusion to this letter suggests that Bowles had said "You damned rascal."

516

To T. W. Higginson   *September 1877*

With sorrow that the Joy is past, to make you happy first, distrustful of it's Duplicate in a hastening World.

Your scholar.

MANUSCRIPT: BPL (Higg 25). Ink.
PUBLICATION: *L* (1931) 293.
ED probably first learned about the death, 2 September 1877, of Mary Channing Higginson from a newspaper report. The formality of the note may have impelled ED to write the letter that follows soon after.

517

To T. W. Higginson   *September 1877*

Dear friend.

If I could help you?

Perhaps she does not go so far
As you who stay – suppose –
Perhaps comes closer, for the lapse
Of her corporeal clothes –

Did she know she was leaving you? The Wilderness is new – to you. Master, let me lead you.

———

MANUSCRIPT: BPL (Higg 93). Ink.
PUBLICATION: *L* (1931) 308.
A variant of the quatrain is in letter no. 518. Higginson's reply to this and the letter preceding elicited a response (see no. 519).

To Harriet and Martha Dickinson   *about 1877?*

Dear friends

You are very kind to have wished for me, and I think it sweet, but accustomed to all through Father, they remind me too deeply of him for Peace. You, too, have been lessened. Let us remember together.

> Perhaps they do not go so far
> As we who stay, suppose
> Perhaps come closer, for the lapse
> Of their corporeal clothes.
>
> It may be, know so certainly
> How short we have to fear,
> That comprehension antedates,
> And estimates us there.

Emily.

MANUSCRIPT: Laramore. Ink. Unpublished.

The former owner of the manuscript, Mr. Wallace H. Keep, thought that it had been sent to his aunts in the fall of 1876. The date 1877 is conjectured because a worksheet draft of the poem (AC) is in the handwriting of that year, and because a variant of the first stanza is incorporated in letter no. 517, sent to Higginson in September 1877. Harriet Dickinson was present at a Dickinson family reunion in 1883 (see letter no. 861), and the tone of this letter suggests that she and her sister may have been present at a similar gathering earlier; if so, "they" refers to relatives. The father of Harriet and Martha Dickinson, the Reverend Baxter Dickinson, had died in Brooklyn, 7 December 1875.

519

To T. W. Higginson   *September 1877*

Dear friend.

We must be less than Death, to be lessened by it – for nothing is irrevocable but ourselves. I am glad you are better. I had feared to follow you, lest you would rather be lonely, which is the will of sorrow – but the Papers had spoken of you with affectionate deference, and to know you were deeply remembered, might not too intrude. To be human is more than to be divine, for when Christ was divine, he was uncontented till he had been human.

I remember nothing so strong as to see you –

I hope you may come –

Thank you for telling me of your friend.

I had wanted to know –

She reminded me of Thermopylae – Did she suffer – except to leave you? That was perhaps the sum of Death – For the Hand I was never permitted to take, I enclose my own, and am tenderly

Her's –

Shall I keep the Paragraph, or is it too sacred?

MANUSCRIPT: BPL (Higg 86). Ink.

PUBLICATION: L (1894) 326, in part; LL 305, in part; L (1931) 308, entire.

Higginson had replied to the query in ED's last letter to him, evidently enclosing an obituary notice, perhaps from the *Boston Evening Traveller* for 6 September, since a copy of the notice is in his notebook of 1877.

ED associated *Thermopylae* with uncomplaining bravery in the face of certain death (see letter no. 906). See also Prose Fragment 35.

520

To Jonathan L. Jenkins   *September 1877*

Dear Mr and Mrs Pastor.

Mrs Holland pleased us and grieved us, by telling us your Triumphs.

We want you to conquer, but we want you to conquer here –

"Marathon" is me. Is there nothing but Glow – in the new Horizon?

You see we keep a jealous Heart – That is Love's Alloy –

Vinnie is full of Wrath, and vicious as Saul – toward the Holy Ghost, in whatever form. I heard her declaiming the other night, to a Foe that called – and sent Maggie to part them – Vinnie lives on the hope that you will return – Is it quite fictitious?

You are gone too long –

The Red Leaves take the Green Leaves place, and the Landscape yields. We go to sleep with the Peach in our Hands and wake with the Stone, but the Stone is the pledge of Summers to come –

Love for each of you, always, and if there are Lands longer than "Always," Love also for those –

These are Sticks of Rowen for your Stove.

It was chopped by Bees, and Butterflies piled it, Saturday Afternoons.

Emily.

MANUSCRIPT: HCL (L 37). Ink.

PUBLICATION: *L* (1894) 372–373; *L* (1931) 363; *FN* 137.

The Hollands, returning from Alexandria Bay at the end of August, stopped first in Pittsfield, then in Amherst. The letter enclosed a few stalks of hay tied with a white ribbon.

521

To Mrs. J. G. Holland   *September 1877*

I miss my little Sanctuary and her redeeming ways. A Savior in a Nut, is sweeter to the grasp than ponderous Prospectives.

Come again, and go not – which when a faithful invitation, is the sweetest known!

Mother pines for you, and says you were "so social." Mother misses power to ramble to her Neighbors – and the stale inflation of the minor News.

I wish the Sky and she had been better friends, for that is "sociability" that is fine and deathless.

How precious Thought and Speech are! "A present so divine," was in a Hymn they used to sing when I went to Church.

Vinnie talks of you –

Your cheerful view of Woe remodeled her's, I think – and Maggie deems you a Mistress most to be desired.

You see each looks at you through her specific Vista.

There is not yet Frost, and Vinnie's Garden from the Door looks like a Pond, with Sunset on it.

Bathing in that heals her.

How simple is Bethesda!

Love to your World – or Worlds.

[593]

Manuscript: HCL (H 43). Ink.

Publication: LH 117.

This letter probably was written soon after the preceding. No hymn in collections ED was likely to know contains the phrase "A present (or presence) so divine." Perhaps she was trying to recall lines from the last stanza of Watts's "When I survey the wondrous cross:"

> Were the whole realm of nature mine,
> That were a present far too small;
> Love so amazing, so divine,
> Demands my soul, my life, my all.

522

To T. W. Higginson   *early autumn 1877*

Dear friend,

I think of you so wholly that I cannot resist to write again, to ask if you are safe?

Danger is not at first, for then we are unconscious, but in the after – slower – Days –

Do not try to be saved – but let Redemption find you – as it certainly will – Love is it's own rescue, for we – at our supremest, are but it's trembling Emblems –

Your scholar —

Manuscript: BPL (Higg 103). Pencil.

Publication: AM LXVIII (October, 1891) 450; L (1894) 326–327; LL 305–306; L (1931) 308–309.

Higginson's annotation on the letter reads: "(Newport) Sept 1877 Written to me after a bereavement."

523

To Richard H. Mather   *November 1877*

Dear friend,

The few words of Lowell's seemed true to me – I hope you have felt like reading them – That the Divine has been human is at first an unheeded solace, but it shelters without our consent – To have lived is a Bliss so powerful – we must die – to adjust it – but when you have strength to remember that Dying dispels nothing which was firm before, you have avenged sorrow –

E. Dickinson.

MANUSCRIPT: Mather. Pencil.
PUBLICATION: *Scribner's Magazine* XCV (April 1934) 290.
On the outer fold Mather wrote: "Miss E. Dickinson/Nov. 9th 1877."
His first wife, Elizabeth Carmichael Mather, died, 28 October 1877. Evidently she had sent some lines by Lowell to him at the time of Mrs. Mather's death.

524

To Maria Whitney   *December 1877?*

Vinnie and her sister thank Miss Whitney for the delicate kindness, and remember her with peculiar love these acuter days. . . .
I fear we think too lightly of the gift of mortality, which, too gigantic to comprehend, certainly cannot be estimated.

E. Dickinson.

MANUSCRIPT: missing.
PUBLICATION: L (1894) 336; L (1931) 325.
The date is conjectural. This is the earliest known letter to Maria Whitney, and the formal signature implies that the acquaintance, initiated presumably either by the Bowleses or by Austin and Sue, began not long before the "acuter days" of the severe illness of Samuel Bowles, in early December. At that time Miss Whitney was making trips from Northampton to Springfield two or three times a week. Perhaps she had delivered some message from Bowles.

525

To Mrs. J. G. Holland   *December 1877*

I always feel that the Minutest Effort of the dear Eyes, demands a peculiarly immediate reply – and internally it receives it, but time to say we are sorry, is sometimes withheld –
Wrenched from my usual Route by Vinnie's singular illness – and

Mother's additional despair – I have felt like a troubled Top, that spun without reprieve. Vinnie's relief is slow – She has borne more than she could, as you and I know more of, than her Physician does –

Torture for worthless sakes is equally Torture –

I shall try superhumanly to save her, and believe I shall, but she has been too lacerated to revive immediately.

Mrs Lord – so often with us – has fled – as you know – Dear Mr Bowles is hesitating – God help him decide on the Mortal Side!

This is Night – now – but we are not dreaming. Hold fast to your Home, for the Darling's stealthy momentum makes each moment – Fear –

I enclose a Note, which if you would lift as far as Philadelphia, if it did not tire your Arms – would please me so much.

Would the Doctor be willing to address it? Ask him, with my love.

Maggie remembers you with fondness – and Mother gives her love – Vinnie longs for you.

Is not the distinction of Affection, almost Realm enough?

Emily.

MANUSCRIPT: HCL (H 44). Ink.

PUBLICATION: LH 118–119.

Mrs. Holland's eyesight was seriously impaired after her operation in 1872 (see letter no. 377), and many letters from ED allude to it in this manner. Vinnie's illness may also be inferred from letter no. 483. Mrs. Otis P. Lord died on 10 December. The letter enclosed for Dr. Holland to address and forward to Philadelphia was presumably intended for Charles Wadsworth.

526

To Edward (Ned) Dickinson   *Christmas 1877*

Santa Claus' Bridge blew off, obliging him to be frugal –
Otherwise, he is your boundless Aunt.

———

MANUSCRIPT: HCL (B 87). Ink.

PUBLICATION: FF 250.

The Northampton bridge had blown away, 14 June. The note in FF says the reference is to the Sunderland bridge, of which the Dickinsons were stockholders.

To Mrs. George Cutler   *about 1877*

Blossoms are so peculiarly consecrated – that there is no Language sufficiently sanctifying to indorse them, but if a delighted Gratitude is not too undevout, Mrs Cutler . . .

MANUSCRIPT: Jones Library. Ink. Unpublished. The conclusion is missing, for the page is torn.

George Cutler and his brother William were prosperous Amherst merchants (see Appendix 1).

To Mrs. Edward Tuckerman   *about 1877*

Dear friend.

Accept my timid happiness. No Joy can be in vain, but adds to some bright total, whose Dwelling is unknown –

The immortality of Flowers must enrich our own, and we certainly should resent a Redemption that excluded them –

Was not the "Breath of fragrance" designed for your cheek solely?

The fear that it was – crimsons my own – though to divide it's Heaven is Heaven's highest Half.

E. Dickinson –

MANUSCRIPT: AC. Ink. This note probably enclosed a poem.

PUBLICATION: L (1894) 381; L (1931) 371.

Mrs. Tuckerman has sent ED half a bouquet that had been sent to her. A first rough pencil draft of part of the letter survives (AC):

> Accept my timid happiness – no Joy can be in
> vain but adds to some bright (sweet) [?]
> whose dwelling

To Mrs. James S. Cooper   *about 1877*

Dear friend.

Maggie was taking you a flower as you were going out.

Please accept the design, and bewail the flower, that sank of chagrin last evening.

E. Dickinson.

MANUSCRIPT: HCL (B 170). Ink. Addressed on the fold: Mrs. Cooper.
PUBLICATION: L (1894) 394; LL 323; L (1931) 383.

A note in the Dickinson collection at Amherst College, signed "A. I. C." (Abigail Ingersoll Cooper), reads:

> It may be that the flower faded from conscious failure
> in its mission — but the remembrance of the gentle
> kindly thought which suggested the gift, will abide with
> me in perpetual freshness —

The note was preserved because ED used the back of it to set down in rough draft the poem "It was a quiet seeming Day."

530

To Susan Gilbert Dickinson   *about 1877*

> But Susan is a Stranger yet —
> The Ones who cite her most
> Have never scaled her Haunted House
> Nor compromised her Ghost —
>
> To pity those who know her not
> Is helped by the regret
> That those who know her know her less
> The nearer her they get —
>
>   Emily —

MANUSCRIPT: HCL (B 62). Pencil.
PUBLICATION: FF 260; Poems (1955) 971.

This and the following letter-poem for Susan Dickinson, written about the same time, are dated by handwriting only.

531

To Susan Gilbert Dickinson   *about 1877*

> To own a Susan of my own
> Is of itself a Bliss —
> Whatever Realm I forfeit, Lord,
> Continue me in this!

[598]

Manuscript: HCL (B 4). Ink.
Publication: FF 243; *Poems* (1955) 972.

532

To Mrs. Samuel Bowles   *about 16 January 1878*

To remember our own Mr Bowles is all we can do.
With grief it is done, so warmly and long, it can never be new.

Emily.

Manuscript: AC. Pencil.
Publication: L (1894) 223; LL 286; L (1931) 208.
These "broken words" (see letter no. 536) were probably written on
the day that Samuel Bowles died, 16 January 1878. Mrs. Bowles answered
the note soon after, eliciting ED's reply in the letter referred to above. On
this letter, see the note to letter no. 438.

533

To T. W. Higginson   *19 January 1878*

Dear friend,

I felt it shelter to speak to you.
My Brother and Sister are with Mr Bowles, who is buried this
afternoon.
The last song that I heard – that was since the Birds – was "He
leadeth me – he leadeth me – yea, though I walk." Then the voices
stooped – the arch was so low –

———

Manuscript: BPL (Higg 105). Pencil.
Publication: AM LXVIII (October 1891) 455; L (1894) 327; LL
306; L (1931) 309.
On 11 February 1877 Nora Green sang the Twenty-Third Psalm in
church for Mr. Jenkins's farewell sermon. Lavinia heard her. ED was so
impressed by the account that she asked to hear it. With her brother and

sister, Miss Green sang it in the Dickinson drawingroom while ED and Lavinia listened upstairs. ED came down and greeted them afterward: as reported by Clara Bellinger Green, *Bookman* LX (November 1924) 291.

534

To Susan Gilbert Dickinson   *January 1878*

Sister spoke of Springfield – The beginning of "Always" is more dreadful than the close – for that is sustained by flickering identity – His nature was Future –
He had not yet lived –
David's route was simple – "I shall go to him" –

Emily –

MANUSCRIPT: HCL (B 82). Pencil.
PUBLICATION: *FF* 254.
This note was written to Sue upon her return from the funeral of Samuel Bowles. After the death of David's son, David said (2 Samuel 12.23): "But now he is dead, wherefore should I fast? can I bring him back again? I shall go to him, but he shall not return to me."

535

To Mrs Henry Hills   *January 1878*

Dear Mr and Mrs Hills,

It is a little more than three years since you tried to help us bid Father Good-Night, which was so impossible that it has never become less so –

Now we have given our Mr Bowles – to the deep Stranger –

To seek to be nobler for their sakes, is all that remains – and our only Plot for discovering them –

I want to thank you for the kindness, so very sweet and large – and ask if you are well – and hope you may remain. Heaven is so presuming that we must hide our Gems.

I am glad you care so much for Austin – He will need you more – and trust you may include us all in your fond number.

Nor do we forget the lovely assault between the two Years, and Trust each fair and noble thing may befall you both –

Emily.

Manuscript: Skillings. Unpublished.
Enclosed in the same envelope is a letter from Lavinia, dated: January 23. Both are letters of thanks for Christmas remembrances. In the same envelope is a penciled note which may or may not have been sent at the same time:

535A

"Was it from Heaven, or of Men?"

Lovingly,
Emily.

536

To Mrs. Samuel Bowles *early 1878*

I hasten to you, Mary, because no moment must be lost when a heart is breaking, for though it broke so long, each time is newer than the last, if it broke truly. To be willing that I should speak to you was so generous, dear.

Sorrow almost resents love, it is so inflamed.

I am glad if the broken words helped you. I had not hoped so much, I felt so faint in uttering them, thinking of your great pain. Love makes us "heavenly" without our trying in the least. 'Tis easier than a Saviour – it does not stay on high and call us to its distance; its low "Come unto me" begins in every place. It makes but one mistake, it tells us it is "rest" – perhaps its toil is rest, but what we have not known we shall know again, that divine "again" for which we are all breathless.

I am glad you "work." Work is a bleak redeemer, but it does redeem; it tires the flesh so that can't tease the spirit.

Dear "Mr. Sam" is very near, these midwinter days. When purples come on Pelham, in the afternoon we say "Mr. Bowles's colors." I spoke to him once of his Gem chapter, and the beautiful eyes rose till they were out of reach of mine, in some hallowed fathom.

Not that he goes – we love him more
Who led us while he stayed.
Beyond earth's trafficking frontier,
For what he moved, he made.

Mother is timid and feeble, but we keep her with us. She thanks
you for remembering her, and never forgets you. . . . Your sweet
"and left me all alone," consecrates your lips.

Emily.

MANUSCRIPT: missing.
PUBLICATION: L (1894) 223–224; LL 314–315; L (1931) 209–210.
See the note to letter no. 532. Mr. Bowles's "Gem chapter" may have
been Revelation 21, of which ED herself was particularly fond.

537

To Maria Whitney   *early 1878*

Dear friend,

I have thought of you often since the darkness, – though we cannot assist another's night. I have hoped you were saved. That he has
received Immortality who so often conferred it, invests it with a more
sudden charm. . . .

I hope you have the power of hope, and that every bliss we know
or guess hourly befalls you.

E. Dickinson.

MANUSCRIPT: missing.
PUBLICATION: L (1894) 336; L (1931) 325.
ED knew that Bowles's death was poignantly felt by Maria Whitney.
This and the three following extracts, dated by Mrs. Todd "1878," evi-
dently were written about the same time. See Prose Fragment 37.

538

To Maria Whitney   *early 1878?*

. . . To relieve the irreparable degrades it.
Brabantio's resignation is the only one – "I here do give thee that

with all my heart, which, but thou hast already, with all my heart I
would keep from thee."

Emily.

MANUSCRIPT: missing.
PUBLICATION: L (1894) 336; LL 311; L (1931) 325.
The death of Bowles probably stimulated a correspondence between
ED and Maria Whitney. The quotation from *Othello* (I, iii, 193–195) is,
in fact, verbatim. (See letter no. 622.)

539

To Maria Whitney *early 1878?*

. . . The crucifix requires no glove.

MANUSCRIPT: missing.
PUBLICATION: L (1894) 337; LL 312; L (1931) 326.

540

To Maria Whitney *early 1878?*

Intrusiveness of flowers is brooked by even troubled hearts.
They enter and then knock – then chide their ruthless sweetness,
and then remain forgiven.
May these molest as fondly!

Emily.

MANUSCRIPT: missing.
PUBLICATION: L (1894) 338; LL 312; L (1931) 327.
Mrs. Todd placed this letter among those that she dated 1878.

541

To Susan Gilbert Dickinson *about 1878*

Where we owe but a little, we pay.
Where we owe so much it defies Money, we are blandly insolvent.

[603]

Adulation is inexpensive except to him who accepts it.
It has cost him – Himself.

Emily –

MANUSCRIPT: HCL (B 93). Ink.
PUBLICATION: LL 62, in part; FF 241, in part.
The handwriting confirms the inference that this note was written after
the death of Samuel Bowles.

542

To Mrs. J. G. Holland   *early 1878*

Your sweet Face alighted in the Rain, with it's Smile unharmed –
All was there but Breath, and even that seemed optional – it was so
confiding. Thank you for coming Home –
"Home – sweet Home" – Austin's Baby sings – "there is no place
like Home – 'tis too – over to Aunt Vinnie's."
Thank you for Dr Gray's Opinion – that is peace – to us. I am
sorry your Doctor is not well. I fear he has "improved" too many "shining Hours."
Give my love to him, and tell him the "Bee" is a reckless Guide.
Dear Mr Bowles found out too late, that Vitality costs itself.
How mournful without him! I often heard the Students sing –
delicious Summer nights, "I've seen around me fall – like Leaves in
wintry weather" – This was what they meant –
You kindly ask for Mother's health.
It is tranquil, though trifling. She reads a little – sleeps much –
chats – perhaps – most of all – about nothing momentous, but things
vital to her – and reminds one of Hawthorne's blameless Ship – that
forgot the Port –
Vinnie is better – though sober – Maggie – invulnerable, and loyal
to you – Ned has brought his Hens to live in our Hen House, which
adds to our little Group.
Three is a scant Assembly, but Love makes "One to carry –" as
the Children say –
That is all of my Learning that I recall.

Tenderly,

Emily.

MANUSCRIPT: HCL (H 45). Ink.
PUBLICATION: *LH* 121–122.
The letter acknowledges a photograph ED had received from Mrs. Holland. Dr. Holland spoke at Bowles's funeral; he was not well at the time this letter was written. "Hawthorne's blameless Ship" refers not to a story by Hawthorne, but to a Salem legend of a ship that haunted the port but never came to land.

543

To Mrs. James S. Cooper   *early 1878*

The Keeper of Golden Flowers need have no fear of the "Silver Bill."

An Indies in the Hand, at all times fortifying, is peculiarly so – perhaps – today. Midas was a Rogue –

———

MANUSCRIPT: AC. Ink.
PUBLICATION: *L* (1894) 393; *LL* 323; *L* (1931) 382.
Congress passed the silver bill in February. (Similar bills had been passed in 1873 and 1875, but the writing fits this year.)

544

To Dr. J. G. Holland   *early 1878*

Dear Doctor,

We rejoice in your repaired health, though it grieves us that repairs should be necessary in a Structure so able – yet when we recall that the "Soul's poor Cottage, battered and dismayed, lets in new light through chinks that time has made," your predicament becomes one of con-gratulation.

You seem to have reared Fames as rapidly as Houses, and we trust, of more lasting ingredient, though the Abode without a Nail, has its consternations.

We hope that you are happy so far as Peace is possible, to Mortal and immortal Life – for those ways "Madness lies."

"About" *which* "Ranks the Sunbeams play," is a touching question.

But I intrude on Sunset, and Father and Mr Bowles.

These held their Wick above the West —
Till when the Red declined —
Or how the Amber aided it —
Defied to be defined —

Then waned without disparagement
In a disembling Hue
That would not let the Eye decide
Did it abide or no —

Emily.

MANUSCRIPT: HCL (H 46). Ink.
PUBLICATION: LH 122–123.
The line quoted from Edmund Waller reads: "The soul's dark cottage, batter'd and decayed." ED has marginally entered *decayed*. For the same quoted lines, see letter no. 888. The opening lines of a Reginald Heber poem are: "I see them on their winding way,/Above their ranks the moonbeams play." The phrase quoted in the third paragraph is from *King Lear* III, iv, 21.

545

To Mrs. Edward Tuckerman   *about March 1878?*

Vinnie says the dear friend would like the rule. We have no statutes here, but each does as it will, which is the sweetest jurisprudence.

With it, I enclose Love's "remainder biscuit," somewhat scorched perhaps in baking, but "Love's oven is warm." Forgive the base proportions.

The fairer ones were borne away. The canna was a privilege, the little box a bliss, and the blossoms so real that a fly waylaid them, but I lured him away.

Again receive the love which comes without aspect, and without herald goes.

Emily.

MANUSCRIPT: missing.
PUBLICATION: L (1894) 380–381; LL 297; L (1931) 370–371.
A letter of 1 March from Fannie Norcross to Vinnie (photostat in AC)

says: "Now I will give you the caramel rule." The phrase "remainder biscuit" is from *As You Like It*, II, vii, 39–40: "Which is as dry as the remainder biscuit/After a voyage;" (see also letter no. 882).

546

To T. W. Higginson   *March 1878*

Dear friend,

The Hope of seeing you was so sweet and serious — that seeing this — by the Papers, I fear it has failed. I hope I in no way spoke less reverently than I felt – of a Pleasure so priceless –

Your Pupil –

MANUSCRIPT: BPL (Higg 100). Pencil.
PUBLICATION: L (1931) 310.
On 11 March the *Springfield Republican* mentions that Higginson had spent a fortnight in South Carolina.

547

To Mrs. J. G. Holland   *about March 1878*

Dear Sister.

I take Mrs Browning's little Basket to bring the note to you – and when you find it is not her, you will be disappointed, but there is many a discipline before we obtain Heaven – Your little Note protected, as it always does, and the "Whips of Time" felt a long way off.

Your little Trip still lingers, for is not all petite you do – you are such a Linnet?

Vinnie was much elated by your rogueries. She thinks you are stealthy as Talleyrand –

We learn of you in the Papers and of your new House, of which it is said there will be a Portrait – "so I shall see it in just three Days," though I would rather see it's vital inhabitants.

I gave your words to Ned – who bowed and seemed much raised —

Baby does all the errands now – and I enclose a Circular, setting forth his wants.

[607]

To see the little Missionary starting with his Basket, would warm the chillest Heart.

I know you will do what I ask you, and so I only thank you, and make no outer remarks.

Lovingly,

Emily.

MANUSCRIPT: HCL (H 47). Ink.
PUBLICATION: LH 124–125.

The "Portrait" was an article in the *Springfield Republican* of some length, in the 24 July issue, describing the Hollands' new house in the Thousand Islands. The last sentence evidently asks Mrs. Holland to forward an enclosure, probably a letter intended for Dr. Wadsworth. "Whips of Time" paraphrases Hamlet's "whips and scorns of time" (III, i, 70). The second quotation paraphrases the opening line of Browning's "In Three Days": "So, I shall see her in three days." Mrs. Ward conjectures that "Mrs Browning's little Basket" means that ED folded the letter in a circular notice or the wrapping from a copy of Elizabeth Barrett Browning's *Earlier Poems*, first published in the United States in March 1878.

548

To Edward (Ned) Dickinson   *spring 1878*

But were'nt you a little premature in laying aside your "Cutter"?

MANUSCRIPT: HCL (B 84). Pencil. Addressed: Ned. Unpublished.

This and the following note to Ned seem to have been written about the same time, this one after a spring snowstorm. The date is conjectured from the handwriting.

549

To Edward (Ned) Dickinson   *spring 1878*

Omit to return Box –
Omit to know you received Box –

"Brooks of Sheffield."

MANUSCRIPT: HCL (B 39). Pencil.

PUBLICATION: *AM* CXV (1915) 39; *LL* 61.
Mrs. Bianchi says the box contained the year's first maple sugar. The character Brooks of Sheffield, in *David Copperfield*, designated one who remained nameless (see also letters no. 204 and 820).

550

To Mrs. J. Howard Sweetser   *spring 1878*

Sweet Mrs Nellie comes with the Robins.

Would she remain with the Robins April would need no Codicil, but Mrs Nellie has Wings –

Hours – have Wings –

Riches – have Wings –

Wings are a mournful perquisite –

A Society for the Suppression of Wings would protect us all.

                                                                      Emily.

MANUSCRIPT: Rosenbach 1170/18 (24). Pencil. Addressed on the fold: Mrs Nellie.

PUBLICATION: *L* (1894) 407; *L* (1931) 397; in part and altered, for it was reconstructed from memory.

The date, conjectured from the handwriting, is confirmed by the recollection of a daughter (Todd papers. AC) that the occasion was a visit in Amherst five years before the Sweetsers inherited the Amherst home of Mr. Sweetser's parents.

551

To Mrs. J. G. Holland   *spring 1878*

I thought that "Birnam Wood" had "come to Dunsinane." Where did you pick arbutus? In Broadway, I suppose. They say that God is everywhere, and yet we always think of Him as somewhat of a recluse. . . It is hard not to hear again that vital "Sam is coming" — though if grief is a test of a priceless life, he is compensated. He was not ambitious for redemption — that was why it is his. "To him that hath, shall be given." Were it not for the eyes, we would know of you oftener. Have they no remorse for their selfishness? "This tabernacle" is a blissful trial, but the bliss predominates.

I suppose you will play in the water at Alexandria Bay, as the baby does at the tub in the drive. . . Speak to us when your eyes can spare you, and "keep us, at home, or by the way," as the clergyman says, when he folds the church till another Sabbath.

Emily.

MANUSCRIPT: missing.
PUBLICATION: L (1894) 181–182; L (1931) 174–175; LH 125–126.
It had been Bowles's custom to make a call on his Amherst friends about blossom time.

552

To Mrs. Thomas P. Field   *about 1878*

Expulsion from Eden grows indistinct in the presence of flowers so blissful, and with no disrespect to Genesis, Paradise remains.

Beaconsfield says "the time has now come when it must be decided forever, who possesses the great gates to India."

I think it must be my neighbor.

With delicate gratitude,

E. Dickinson.

MANUSCRIPT: missing.
PUBLICATION: L (1894) 421; LL 365; L (1931) 409–410.
The note was written to acknowledge a gift of flowers. The Fields were recent arrivals in Amherst. Following the Russo-Turkish war, Great Britain negotiated for occupation of Cyprus, and moved Indian troops to Malta.

553

To T. W. Higginson   *early June 1878*

Dear friend.

When you wrote you would come in November, it would please me it were November then – but the time has moved – You went with the coming of the Birds – they will go with your coming – but to see you is so much sweeter than Birds, I could excuse the spring.

With the bloom of the flower your friend loved, I have wished for her, but God cannot discontinue himself.

Mr Bowles was not willing to die.

When you have lost a friend, Master, you remember you could not begin again, because there was no World. I have thought of you often since the Darkness – though we cannot assist another's Night –

I have hoped you were saved –

That those have immortality with whom we talked about it, makes it no more mighty – but perhaps more sudden –

> How brittle are the Piers
> On which our Faith doth tread –
> No Bridge below doth totter so –
> Yet none hath such a Crowd.
>
> It is as old as God –
> Indeed – 'twas built by him –
> He sent his Son to test the Plank,
> And he pronounced it firm.

I hope you have been well. I hope your rambles have been sweet and your reveries spacious – To have seen Stratford on Avon – and the Dresden Madonna, must be almost Peace –

And perhaps you have spoken with George Eliot. Will you "tell me about it"? Will you come in November, and will November come – or is this the Hope that opens and shuts, like the eye of the Wax Doll?

Your Scholar –

MANUSCRIPT: BPL (Higg 106). Ink.

PUBLICATION: L (1894) 327–328; LL 306–307; L (1931) 309–310.

Higginson sailed for Europe during the spring, and had evidently written ED that he expected to return in November. He was in fact home by late October. This letter must have been sent to some address abroad. Its conclusion is a variant of that in the letter which follows.

A variant of the fourth paragraph is among the prose fragments (AC – pencil):

> If ever you lost a friend – Master – You remember you could not begin again because there was no world –
> A breathless Death is not so cold as a Death that breathes

The fragment is published in NEQ XVIII (1955) 298. For another finished draft of the conclusion of the second paragraph, see Prose Fragment 34.

To Susan Gilbert Dickinson   *mid-June 1878*

Susan knows she is a Siren – and that at a word from her, Emily would forfeit Righteousness – Please excuse the grossness of this morning – I was for a moment disarmed – This is the World that opens and shuts, like the Eye of the Wax Doll –

MANUSCRIPT: HCL (B 11). Pencil.
PUBLICATION: LL 62, in part.
The year is conjectured from the handwriting, and the month is inferred from the context. In mid-May, 1878, Sue spent a month visiting in the Midwest. She appears to have paid an unexpected morning call on her return. The same conclusion is used in the letter preceding, to Higginson.

To Mrs. J. G. Holland   *June 1878*

I thought it was you, little Chocolate Sister – but Vinnie demurred – and Vinnie decides. I said "let me thank her conditionally" – "No" – said Vinnie – "'twould be remorse – provided it were not her –" and so we guessed and sighed and nibbled and propounded – and felt how base we were – until the Doctor's note.

The Bonbons were delightful, but better than Bonbons was the love – for that is the basis of Bonbons. And in all the confusion to think of us – Loyal little Sister – the Bird going South – is not so mindful of the Birds behind. To never forget you – is all we can –

That is how faint a Stipend –

The Doctor's Pun was happy – How lovely are the wiles of Words!

We thought you cherished Bryant, and spoke of you immediately when we heard his fate – if Immortality *be* Fate.

Dear friends – we cannot believe for each other. I suppose there are depths in every Consciousness, from which we cannot rescue ourselves – to which none can go with us – which represent to us Mortally – the Adventure of Death –

How unspeakably sweet and solemn – that whatever await us of Doom or Home, we are mentally permanent.

"It is finished" can never be said of us.

I am glad of your bright Home —

I hope you are well – you did not tell me – Thank you peculiarly sweetly – With grief for the eyes only, happy for your happiness,

Emily.

MANUSCRIPT: HCL (H 49). Ink.
PUBLICATION: LH 127.

William Cullen Bryant, one of Dr. Holland's close literary friends, died, 12 June. The Hollands were spending the first summer in their new house at Alexandria Bay.

556

To Mrs. Edward Tuckerman   *June 1878*

Is it that words are suddenly small or that we are suddenly large, that they cease to suffice us, to thank a friend?

Perhaps it is chiefly both.

———

MANUSCRIPT: AC. Pencil.
PUBLICATION: L (1894) 381; LL 313; L (1931) 371.

The date is that supplied Mrs. Todd by Mrs. Tuckerman, and is confirmed by the handwriting.

557

To Mrs. Henry Hills   *summer 1878*

Dear friend,

Your memory of others, among your almost superhuman cares, is so astonishing that I cannot refrain from surprise and love.

How near this suffering Summer are the divine words "There is a World elsewhere."

E —

MANUSCRIPT: Jones Library. Pencil. Envelope addressed: Mrs Henry Hills. Unpublished.

Henry Hills failed in business during the summer of 1878, and the announcement was made on 11 July. Austin took over the business to save his friend from ruin. No passage in scripture exactly matches ED's quotation. Perhaps she had in mind Romans 8.18: "For I reckon that the sufferings of this present time are not worthy to be compared with the glory which shall be revealed in us."

558

To Mrs. Edward Tuckermann   *July 1878*

Would it be prudent to subject an apparitional interview to a grosser test? The Bible portentously says "that which is Spirit is Spirit."

> Go not too near a House of Rose –
> The depredation of a Breeze
> Or inundation of a Dew
> Alarm it's walls away –
> Nor try to tie the Butterfly,
> Nor climb the Bars of Ecstasy,
> In insecurity to lie
> Is Joy's insuring quality.
>
> E. Dickinson –

MANUSCRIPT: AC. Pencil.
PUBLICATION: L (1894) 382; LL 313; L (1931) 371–372, where it is dated "July, 1878," on Mrs. Tuckerman's authority.
The quotation is from John 3.6; "That which is born of the flesh is flesh; and that which is born of the Spirit is spirit." (See letter no. 458.)

559

To Otis P. Lord   *about 1878*

[*fair copy – first two pages only extant*]
My lovely Salem smiles at me. I seek his Face so often – but I have done with guises.
I confess that I love him – I rejoice that I love him – I thank the maker of Heaven and Earth – that gave him me to love – the exultation

floods me. I cannot find my channel – the Creek turns Sea – at thought of thee –

Will you punish me? "Involuntary Bankruptcy," how could that be Crime?

Incarcerate me in yourself – rosy penalty – threading with you this lovely maze, which is not Life or Death – though it has the intangibleness of one, and the flush of the other – waking for your sake on Day made magical with you before I went

[*rough draft of fair copy above*]

My lovely Salem smiles at me I seek his Face so often – but I am past disguises (have dropped –) (have done with guises –)

I confess that I love him – I rejoice that I love him – I thank the maker of Heaven and Earth that gave him me to love – the exultation floods me – I can not find my channel – The Creek turned Sea at thoughts of thee – will you punish it – [turn I] involuntary Bankruptcy as the Debtors say. Could that be a Crime – How could that be crime – Incarcerate me in yourself – that will punish me – Threading with you this lovely maze which is not Life or Death tho it has the intangibleness of one and the flush of the other waking for your sake on Day made magical with [before] you before I went to sleep – What pretty phrase – we went to sleep as if it were a country – let us make it one – we could (will) make it one, my native Land – my Darling come oh *be* a patriot now – Love is a patriot now Gave her life for its (its) country Has it meaning now – Oh nation of the soul thou hast thy freedom now

MANUSCRIPTS: AC. Both are in pencil.

PUBLICATION: *Revelation* 78–81, with facsimile.

The rough draft is on a discarded envelope addressed in Lord's hand: Miss Vinnie Dickinson,/Amherst/By Mr Cooper's Kindness. (James I. Cooper was Austin Dickinson's law partner.)

The letters, and drafts and fragments of letters, to Lord were found among ED's papers after her death, and given to Mrs. Todd by Austin Dickinson (*Revelation* 1–2). It would appear that ED and Lord in time came to make a practice of writing each other weekly – or intending to do so. The intimacy of the relationship continued until his death in 1884. This letter and the four that follow are in the handwriting of about 1878. They are here grouped, since no specific time of the year is indicated in the letters.

[615]

To Otis P. Lord   *about 1878*

Ned and I were talking about God and Ned said "Aunt Emily –
does Judge Lord belong to the Church"?

"I think not, Ned, technically."

"Why, I thought he was one of those Boston Fellers who thought
it the respectable thing to do." "I think he does nothing ostensible –
Ned." "Well – my Father says if there were another Judge in the
Commonwealth like him, the practice of Law would amount to something." I told him I thought it probable – though recalling that I had
never tried any case in your presence but my own, and that, with your
sweet assistance – I was murmurless.

I wanted to fondle the Boy for the fervent words – but made the
distinction. Dont you know you have taken my will away and I "know
not where" you "have laid" it? Should I have curbed you sooner?
"Spare the 'Nay' and spoil the child"?

Oh, my too beloved, save me from the idolatry which would crush
us both –

"And very Sea – Mark of my utmost Sail" –

MANUSCRIPT: AC. Pencil. It is a fair copy.
PUBLICATION: *Revelation* 77–82.

To Otis P. Lord   *about 1878*

To beg for the Letter when it is written, is bankrupt enough, but
to beg for it when it is'nt, and the dear Donor is sauntering, mindless
of it's worth, *that* is bankrupter.

Sweet One – to make the bright week noxious, that was once so
gay, have you quite the warrant? Also, my Naughty one, too seraphic
Naughty, who can sentence you? Certainly not my enamored Heart.
Now my blissful Sophist, you that can make "Dont" "Do" – though
forget that I told you so, [*part of two pages cut out*]

Perhaps, please, you are sinful? Though of power to make Perdition divine, who can punish you?

Manuscript: AC. Pencil. Fair copy.
Publication: *Revelation* 82.

562

To Otis P. Lord   *about 1878*

Dont you know you are happiest while I withhold and not confer – dont you know that "No" is the wildest word we consign to Language?
You do, for you know all things – [*top of sheet cut off*] . . . to lie so near your longing – to touch it as I passed, for I am but a restive sleeper and often should journey from your Arms through the happy night, but you will lift me back, wont you, for only there I ask to be – I say, if I felt the longing nearer – than in our dear past, perhaps I could not resist to bless it, but must, because it would be right
The "Stile" is God's – My Sweet One – for your great sake – not mine – I will not let you cross – but it is all your's, and when it is right I will lift the Bars, and lay you in the Moss – You showed me the word.
I hope it has no different guise when my fingers make it. It is Anguish I long conceal from you to let you leave me, hungry, but you ask the divine Crust and that would doom the Bread.
That unfrequented Flower
Embellish thee – (deserving be) [*sheet cut off*]
I was reading a little Book – because it broke my Heart I want it to break your's – Will you think that fair? I often have read it, but not before since loving you – I find that makes a difference – it makes a difference with all. Even the whistle of a Boy passing late at Night, or the Low [?] of a Bird – [*sheet cut away*] Satan" – but then what I have not heard is the sweet majority – the Bible says very roguishly, that the "wayfaring Man, though a Fool – need not err therein"; need the "wayfaring" Woman? Ask your throbbing Scripture.
It may surprise you I speak of God – I know him but a little, but Cupid taught Jehovah to many an untutored Mind – Witchcraft is wiser than we –

Manuscript: AC. Pencil.
Publication: *Revelation* 83, with the first page reproduced in facsimile.

[617]

In the next to last paragraph ED recalls Isaiah 35.8: "And an highway shall be there, and a way, and it shall be called The way of holiness . . . the wayfaring men, though fools, shall not err therein."

563

To Otis P. Lord   *about 1878*

Tuesday is a deeply depressing Day – it is not far enough from your dear note for the embryo of another to form, and yet what flights of Distance – and so I perish softly and spurn the Birds (spring) and spurn the Sun – with pathetic (dejected) malice – but when the Sun begins to turn the corner Thursday night – everything refreshes – the soft uplifting grows till by the time it is Sunday night, all my Life (Cheek) is Fever with nearness to your blissful words – (rippling words)

MANUSCRIPT: AC. Pencil. Jotted on a discarded scrap of letter.
PUBLICATION:*Revelation* 94, with facsimile reproduction.
It is written on a scrap of letter from Maggie Maher.

564

To Jonathan L. Jenkins   *August 1878*

There would have been no smile on Amherst's Face, had she believed her Clergyman's sweet wife to be suffering, but the Paper spoke so obligingly, we thought it an accident that endeared – rather than endangered – That Sorrow dare to touch the Loved is a mournful insult – we are all avenging it all the time, though as Lowell quotes from the Stranger "Live – live even to be unkind" –
It is hard to think of our "little Friend" as a Sufferer – we – peculiarly know how hard, through our suffering Mother – but the tiniest ones are the mightiest – The Wren will prevail –
Mother asked me last Sabbath "why Father did'nt come from Church," and ["] if Mr Jenkins preached"?
I told her he did and that Father had lingered to speak with him –

[618]

It was touching that harm should suggest "Amherst." "Bruised for our iniquities" I had almost feared – Amherst – tell her – suggests her – each of you – my Shepherd, and will – while will remains –

Emily.

MANUSCRIPT: HCL (L 38). Pencil.
PUBLICATION: L (1894) 373, in part; L (1931) 363–364, in part; FN 125, entire.

The *Springfield Republican* reported on Friday, 16 August, that on the previous day Mrs. Jenkins had been thrown from a carriage by a shying horse. Though intended as a note of condolence for Mrs. Jenkins, the letter is written to Mr. Jenkins. The quotation of Lowell's is from *Among My Books* (1870). In his essay on Dryden, Lowell quotes from Dryden's tragedy *Aurengzebe*: "Live still! oh live! live even to be unkind!" ED's reference to "stranger" evidently means someone outside the United States; in letter no. 315, Wordsworth is so designated. The scripture allusion is from Isaiah 53.5: "But he was wounded for our transgressions, he was bruised for our iniquities . . ."

565

To Mrs. Edward Tuckerman   *August 1878*

To see is perhaps never quite the sorcery that it is to surmise, though the obligation to enchantment is always binding –

It is sweet to recall that we need not retrench, as Magic is our most frugal Meal.

I fear you have much happiness because you spend so much. Would adding to it – take it away or is that a penurious question?

To cherish you is intuitive –

As we take nature, without permission, let us covet you –

———

MANUSCRIPT: AC. Pencil.
PUBLICATION: L (1894) 382; LL 314; L (1931) 372.

Mrs. Tuckerman told Mrs. Todd that she received the note in August.

To Mrs. J. Howard Sweetser   *about 1878*

Dear friend,

I fear you think your sweetness "fell among Thorns –" I have hoped for a moment in which to thank you, since your Parents returned – but have not obtained it, and must come with my Pencil – now – which will you forgive?

The Grapes were big and fresh, tasting like Emerald Dew – I know you picked them yourself!

How spacious must be the Heart that can include so many, and make no error of Love toward one – Thank you, dear, with Affection – and recall me to those closest to you – with sincerity –

Your beautiful Boy and Girls are part of the Summer's Picture, which is not yet mottled by the Snow. That no Flake of it fall on you or them – is a wish that would almost be a Prayer, were Emily not a Pagan —

MANUSCRIPT: Rosenbach 1170/18 (23). Pencil. Unpublished.

Of the three children, Nettie and Howard were respectively the ages of Mattie and Ned Dickinson. The quotation is from Matthew 13.7.

To Mrs. Samuel Bowles   *late summer 1878*

Had you never spoken to any, dear, they would not upbraid you, but think of you more softly, as one who had suffered too much to speak. To forget you would be impossible, had we never seen you; for you were his for whom we moan while consciousness remains. As he was himself Eden, he is with Eden, for we cannot become what we were not.

I felt it sweet that you needed me — though but a simple shelter I will always last. I hope your boys and girls assist his dreadful absence, for sorrow does not stand so still on their flying hearts.

How fondly we hope they look like him – that his beautiful face may be abroad.

Was not his countenance on earth graphic as a spirit's? The time will be long till you see him, dear, but it will be short, for have we not each our heart to dress – heavenly as his?

He is without doubt with my father. Thank you for thinking of him, and the sweet, last respect you so faithfully paid him.

Mother is growing better, though she cannot stand, and has not the power to raise her head for a glass of water. She thanks you for being sorry, and speaks of you with love. . . . Your timid "for his sake," recalls the sheltering passage, "for his sake who loved us, and gave himself to die for us."

Emily.

MANUSCRIPT: missing.
PUBLICATION: L (1894) 224-225; LL 315-316; L (1931) 210.

Mrs. Dickinson fell and broke her hip in June. No passage in scripture exactly matches that which ED attempts to recall. Perhaps she had in mind Galatians 2.20: "I live by the faith of the Son of God, who loved me, and gave himself for me."

568

To recipient unknown   *about 1878*

Were the Statement "We shall not all sleep, but we shall all be changed," made in earthly Manuscript, were his Residence in the Universe, we should pursue the Writer till he explained it to us.

It is strange that the Astounding subjects are the only ones we pass unmoved.

Emily.

MANUSCRIPT: AC. Pencil.
PUBLICATION: NEQ XXVIII (1955) 312.

The date is conjectured from the handwriting. This fair copy, bearing every mark of completion, may or may not have left ED's desk. Presumably it came into Mrs. Todd's possession in the 1890's. The scripture quotation is from 1 Corinthians 15.51.

569

To Mrs. James S. Cooper   *about 1878*

Dear friend.

Mother thanks you through me, as she does not use her Hand for writing. I hope the vicariousness may not impair the fervor. Mother is very fond of Flowers and of Recollection, that sweetest Flower. Please accept her happiness, and our's, for causing her's –

E. Dickinson.

MANUSCRIPT: AC. Ink.
PUBLICATION: L (1894) 393; L (1931) 382–383.
The date is conjectured from the handwriting. Probably Mrs. Cooper had sent flowers to Mrs. Dickinson sometime during the summer, after Mrs. Dickinson was confined to her bed, in June, with a broken hip.

570

To Edward (Ned) Dickinson   *about 1878*

Ned, with indignation.
Emily.

MANUSCRIPT: HCL (B 14). Pencil. Addressed on the fold: Ned.
PUBLICATION: FF 250.
Presumably the note accompanied some token of "indignation," though none has been identified. The date of this note and the following, also to Ned, is conjectured as about 1878 from the handwriting. There may or may not be a connection between them.

571

To Edward (Ned) Dickinson   *about 1878*

Dear Ned,

You know that Pie you stole – well, this is that Pie's Brother –

Mother told me when I was a Boy, that I must "turn over a new Leaf" – I call that the Foliage Admonition –

Shall I commend it to you?

MANUSCRIPT: HCL (B 117). Pencil. The signature has been torn away.
PUBLICATION: AM CXV (1915) 37; LL 58.
If this note bears a relation to that above, it probably followed it. See also letter no. 580.

To Mrs. William A. Stearns   *1878?*

Dear friends,

The seraphic shame generosity causes is perhaps its most heavenly result.

To make even Heaven more heavenly, is within the aim of us all.

I was much touched by the little fence dividing the devotions, though devotion should always wear a fence, to preempt its claim.

Why the full heart is speechless, is one of the great wherefores.

Emily, with love.

MANUSCRIPT: missing.
PUBLICATION: L (1894) 378–379; LL 314; L (1931) 368–369.
Mrs. Todd dated this note 1878. The circumstances that prompted it have not been identified.

To Maria Whitney   *late 1878*

Dear friend,

I had within a few days a lovely hour with Mr and Mrs Jackson of Colorado, who told me that love of Mr Bowles and longing for some trace of him, led them to his house, and to seek his wife. They found her, they said, a stricken woman, though not so ruthless as they feared. That of ties remaining, she spoke with peculiar love of a Miss Whitney of Northampton, whom she would soon visit, and almost thought of accompanying them as far as yourself.

To know that long fidelity in ungracious soil was not wholly squandered, might be sweet to you.

I hope that you are well, and in full receipt of the Great Spirit whose leaving life was leaving you.

Faithfully

MANUSCRIPT: missing.
PUBLICATION: L (1931) 327. The present text derives from a transcript (AC) made by Mrs. Todd when she saw the letter.
The Jacksons had been in Amherst for a few days, leaving there on

24 October. It is significant that ED received not only Mrs. Jackson but her husband, a total stranger. Such an act for ED this late in her life was unprecedented (see letters no 573c and 574). The second paragraph makes clear ED's awareness that Maria Whitney's devotion to Samuel Bowles had not always been appreciated.

ED's letters to Helen Jackson written during 1878 are missing, but the contents of them can be inferred from those Mrs. Jackson wrote ED (HCL). The first, dated Colorado Springs, 29 April 1878, asks for a poem to be included in a volume of the No Name series. The full story of Mrs. Jackson's effort to get it is told in *Poems* (1955) xxx–xxxiii, and begins with the following letter (unpublished), which returns a photograph of Gilbert.

573a

My dear friend,

My face was not "averted" in the least. It was only that I did not speak: and of my not speaking, I ought to be very much ashamed, and should be, if I had not got past being ashamed of my delinquencies in the matter of letter writing. But I assure you I have never forgotten that you kindly wrote one day, asking if all were well with me: and I have all along meant to write and say "yes," if no more.

All last summer and autumn I was very busy, in altering over and fitting up our cottage. I think to alter one house is equal to building ten! and to do any such work in Colorado is ten times harder than to do it any where else in the world. But now it is all done, and we are "settled" — (odd word that and does a good deal of double duty in the language) — I can hardly recollect the fatigues and discomforts which went before. It is a very picturesque and cozy little house, and I enjoy it unspeakably. I should like to see all my Eastern friends in it.

Would it be of any use to ask you once more for one or two of your poems, to come out in the volume of "no name" poetry which is to be published before long by Roberts Bros.? If you will give me permission I will copy them — sending them in my own handwriting — and promise never to tell any one, not even the publishers, whose the poems are. Could you not bear this much of publicity? only you and I would recognize the poems. I wish very much you would do this—and I think you would have much amusement in seeing to whom the critics, those shrewd guessers would ascribe your verses.

I am hoping to come East with Mr. Jackson, before next winter: but we have no fixed plan—and may not get off. It is a long way to come.

I wish you would give my love to Doctor Cate—I was about to say "when you see him," but you never see anybody! Perhaps however you have improved. I send back the little baby face to tell you that I had not "averted" my face—only the habit of speaking. It is an earnest and good little face: your brother's child I presume.—Will you ask Mrs. Dickinson some day, if she still hears from Jane Goodenow—I would like very much to know where and how she is. Goodbye—

Always cordially yours—
Helen Jackson

On her October visit Mrs. Jackson pursued her effort to secure a poem. From Hartford, Connecticut, where she and Mr. Jackson were sojourning at the home of Charles Dudley Warner, she wrote on 25 October, the day following her Amherst visit, the following note, pressing her request.

573b

My dear Friend—

Here comes the line I promised to send—we had a fine noon on Mt. Holyoke yesterday—and took the 5 o clk train to Springfield—; but there, Mr. Jackson found a telegram from New York which compelled him to go on without stopping here—and so I came alone to Mr. Warners, which was a disappointment.

Now—will you send me the poem? No—will you let me send the "Success"—which I know by heart—to Roberts Bros for the Masque of Poets? If you will, it will give me a great pleasure. I ask it as a personal favor to myself—Can you refuse the only thing I perhaps shall ever ask at your hands?

Yours ever
Helen Jackson

ED must have granted permission, for Mrs. Jackson wrote the following letter, dated Colorado Springs, 8 December 1878:

[625]

My dear friend,

I suppose by this time you have seen the Masque of Poets. I hope you have not regretted giving me that choice bit of verse for it. I was pleased to see that it had in a manner, a special place, being chosen to end the first part of the volume, — on the whole, the volume is a disappointment to me. Still I think it has much interest for all literary people. I confess myself quite unable to conjecture the authorship of most of the poems.

Colorado is as lovely as ever: — our mountains are white with snow now, but there is no snow in the town: at noon one can have windows open, if the fires blaze well on the hearths. What would you think of that in N. England.

I am very glad that I saw you this autumn: also that you saw my husband and liked him, as I perceived that you did –

Thank you once more for the verses.

Yours always
Helen Jackson

The story of the publishing of "Success" comes to an end with the following letter (HCL), written to ED by Thomas Niles, the publisher of Roberts Brothers. It is dated 15 January 1879, and was a reply to one from ED, written to thank him for a copy of *A Masque of Poets*.

573d

Dear Miss Dickinson

You were entitled to a copy of "A Masque of Poets" without thanks, for your valuable contribution which for want of a known sponsor Mr Emerson has generally had to father.

I wanted to send you a proof of your poem, wh. as you have doubtless perceived was slightly changed in phraseology

Yrs very truly
T. Niles

Typical of the reviews of *A Masque of Poets* which attributed "Success" to Emerson is that which appeared in the influential *Literary World*, 10

December 1878 (IX, 118): "If anything in the volume was contributed by Emerson, we should consider these lines upon 'Success' most probably his." And the comment is followed with a quotation of the whole poem.

574

To T. W. Higginson   *early November 1878*

Dear friend,

It was joyful that you came – I saw the Steamer's name – though saddened to me by Mother's illness – who broke her Hip in June – soon after I wrote you and was since helpless – It was thought for many weeks she must die, but she has grown easier, though not of power to lift her Head for a Glass of Water.–

I missed yourself and Mr Bowles, and without a Father, seemed even vaster than before. To see you would be almost Hope – I had a sweet Forenoon with Mrs Jackson recently, who brought her Husband to me for the first time – I hope that you are strong and refreshed by Travel and ask for you not Peace, for that would be treason to those that sleep, but confiding Patience – To hope with the Imagination is inevitable, but to remember – with it is the most consecrated ecstasy of the Will –

Your Scholar –

MANUSCRIPT: BPL (Higg 98). Pencil.
PUBLICATION: L (1931) 310–311.
Higginson returned from his trip to Europe in October.

575

To T. W. Higginson   *December 1878*

Dear friend,

I heard you had found the Lane to the Indies, Columbus was looking for –

There is no one so happy her Master is happy as his grateful Pupil. The most noble congratulation it ever befell me to offer – is that you are yourself.

Till it has loved – no man or woman can become itself – Of our first Creation we are unconscious –

> We knew not that we were to live –
> Nor when – we are to die –
> Our ignorance – our Cuirass is –
> We wear Mortality
> As lightly as an Option Gown
> Till asked to take it off –
> By his intrusion, God is known –
> It is the same with Life –

MANUSCRIPT: BPL (Higg 99). Pencil.
PUBLICATION: L (1931) 312.
The *Springfield Republican* on 1 December 1878 carried the announcement of Higginson's engagement to Mary Potter Thacher of Newton.

576

To Mrs. Henry Hills   *Christmas 1878*

With sweet Christmas for the "little Brethren and Sisters of the mystic tie" –

Emily.

MANUSCRIPT: missing. The text has the same provenance as that of letter no. 376.
PUBLICATION: L (1894) 397; L (1931) 386.

577

To Martha Gilbert Smith   *late December 1878*

Mattie –

A faithful "I am sorry" will sometimes save the Heart – when every other Savior fails – I want to take hold of your Hand and tell you that Love lasts – though it grows unknown – in some dreadful instants –

We are eternal – dear, which seems so worthless, now – but will be by and by, all we can remember – because it owns our own and must give them back –

The Noble cannot go from Home – and your friend was noble –
When you have seen him, dear, as you certainly will – these mo-
ments will change –
I am glad of your little Girl – She will be a Balm – and remember
the Boy and Girl that are with their Father –
What an anticipation!
Smile – for their sake, dear, to whom you have added a "Father in
Heaven" –
To me the word grew fond since I gave my own –

Lovingly,

Emily –

MANUSCRIPT: HCL (L 31). Pencil. Envelope addressed: Mrs. J. W.
Smith-/Geneva-/New York.
PUBLICATION: *FF* 253, in part.
John Williams Smith died, 2 December 1878. An infant son, Frank,
had died, 14 June 1861; and a daughter Susan, on 3 November 1865.

578

To Mrs. A. B. H. Davis   *late 1878?*

Dear friends,

We are snatching our jewels from the frost, and ask you to help
us wear them, as also the trinkets more rotund, which serve a baser
need.

Emily.

MANUSCRIPT: missing.
PUBLICATION: *L* (1894) 397; *L* (1931) 386.
Mrs. Todd placed the letter among those written about 1878, with the
note: "On sending flowers and apples to Mrs. Davis and her daughter."

579

To Mrs. William H. Dickinson   *late 1878*

The sweet anniversary was not unheeded – nor that dear later Day
which you and Willie have kept with us – Death has only to touch a

trifle to make it portentous (stupendous) – though a Past that is [sweet is] true has a calmed Pang – I am sure it will grieve you that Prof Lewes has died – for the Light of your home with Willie – will [teach] show you how dark (dim) – [where] it goes out – The dying of an ideal is more dreadful than that of a Person because it includes besides the decease of a Pageant which [except] to [ourself never existed] – trust – guess – to us only existed Willie and his glasses are a pathetic Fiction (picture –) [John Anderson indeed is near] if they dont prevent his seeing his friends – I can tolerate them Memory's sweet eyes – I could not be balked by – I gave your message to mother which seemed to cheer her very much she grows dependent on dear words as the sick (sad) do I was sorry I could not write before and hope you will not think wrongly of it

I give my love which is most (newest –) new venerable times – and am fondly Willies and yours –

> warmly
> [newest –]
> venerable times –

MANUSCRIPT: AC. Penciled rough draft.
PUBLICATION: NEQ XXVIII (1955) 300–301.
Words crossed out are in brackets; alternative suggestions in parentheses.
The philosopher and critic George Henry Lewes, lifelong companion of George Eliot, died, 28 November 1878.

580

To Susan Gilbert Dickinson   *about 1878*
The Solaces of Theft are first – Theft – second – Superiority to Detection –

Emily.

MANUSCRIPT: HCL (B 9). Pencil. Addressed on fold: Susan.
PUBLICATION: AM CXV (1915) 39; LL 61.
This and the following seven messages sent to Susan Dickinson are in the handwriting of about 1878. The circumstances connected with them are not known, though it is possible that this letter may refer to Ned (see letter no. 571).

[630]

To Susan Gilbert Dickinson   *about 1878*

I must wait a few Days before seeing you – You are too momentous. But remember it is idolatry, not indifference.

Emily.

MANUSCRIPT: HCL (B 181). Pencil. Envelope addressed: Susan.
PUBLICATION: LL 57.

582

To Susan Gilbert Dickinson   *about 1878*

I can defeat the rest, but you defeat me, Susan –

MANUSCRIPT: HCL (B 129). Pencil. Addressed on fold: Mrs. Dickinson.
PUBLICATION: FF 269.

583

To Susan Gilbert Dickinson   *about 1878*

Susan –

Whoever blesses, you always bless – the last – and often made the
Heaven of Heavens – a sterile stimulus.

Cherish Power – dear –

Remember that stands in the Bible between the Kingdom and the
Glory, because it is wilder than either of them.

Emily.

MANUSCRIPT: HCL (B 37). Pencil.
PUBLICATION: LL 62, in part.

584

To Susan Gilbert Dickinson   *about 1878*

Sue – to be lovely as you is a touching Contest, though like the
Siege of Eden, impracticable – Eden never capitulates –

Emily –

Manuscript: HCL (B 50). Pencil.
Publication: *FF* 264, with facsimile reproduction.

585

To Susan Gilbert Dickinson   *about 1878*

Susan – I dreamed of you, last night, and send a Carnation to indorse it –

> Sister of Ophir –
> Ah Peru –
> Subtle the Sum
> That purchase you –

Manuscript: HCL (B 32). Pencil.
Publication: *LL* 79; *FF* 243.

586

To Susan Gilbert Dickinson   *about 1878*

Susan –

The sweetest acts both exact and defy, gratitude, so silence is all the honor there is – but to those who can estimate silence, it is sweetly enough –

In a Life that stopped guessing, you and I should not feel at home –

Manuscript: HCL (B 55): Pencil. Lower part of sheet torn away.
Publication: *LL* 62; *FF* 255.

587

To Susan Gilbert Dickinson   *about 1878*

To the faithful Absence is condensed presence.
To others – but there *are* no others –

Manuscript:YUL. Pencil.
Publication: *AM* CXV (1915) 37; *LL* 57.

[632]

To Mrs. Edward Tuckerman   *January 1879*

Your coming is a symptom of Summer – The Symptom excels the malady.

Manuscript: AC. Pencil.
Publication: *L* (1894) 383; *L* (1931) 372.
The handwriting is of this period. On Mrs. Tuckerman's authority Mrs. Todd dated it January 1879. Perhaps Mrs. Tuckerman had made a New Year's call.

To Mrs. J. G. Holland   *early January 1879*

The lovely little Bronzes in the Lace House – came just as I had written you –
The deference to my predilection pleased and smote me too.
I am glad you are not hung – like the "Mollie Maguires," tho' doubtless heinous as themselves – in a sweet way –
Austin's Baby says when surprised by statements – "There's – *sumthn* – else – there's – *Bumbul* – Beese."
God's little Blond Blessing – we have long deemed you, and hope his so called "Will" – will not compel him to revoke you.
The "rectification of his Frontier," costs the Earth too much –
Vinnie and I watch Mother, which makes the Days too short – till we wear the same Heart – Day and Night, and wash our Hand with our Tongue as the Pussy does – I shall not write again for a few moments, which will defray your cares – Vinnie wants to write, but was it "Atlas'" fault the World was on his Shoulders?
Mother and Sister give their love, and let my own preponderate –

Emily.

Manuscript: HCL (H 50). Pencil
Publication: *LH* 128–129.
Members of the "Mollie Maguires," a secret organization of Irish miners in Pennsylvania, were hanged for various outrages on four occasions between June 1877 and 14 January 1879. This letter, thanking Mrs.

Holland for her annual Christmas gift of a box of chocolates, may have been written in mid-January. The "rectification of his Frontier" was a phrase used by Beaconsfield in a speech on Lord Mayor's Day, November 1878, and refers to India's northwest frontier.

590

To Samuel Bowles the younger   *January 1879*

Coveting the power to send your Father a Flower – ignorant, hallowed be his name, of his route of Down – reverence for sorrow, if not profanation, may we also offer you?

MANUSCRIPT: Bowles. Pencil. Unpublished.
This seems to have been written on the first anniversary of the elder Bowles's death, 16 January.

591

To Maria Whitney   *early 1879?*

Dear Friend,
    Your touching suggestion . . . is a tender permission. . . .
    We cannot believe for each other – thought is too sacred a despot, but I hope that God, in whatever form, is true to our friend. . . . Consciousness is the only home of which we *now* know. That sunny adverb had been enough, were it not foreclosed.
    When not inconvenient to your heart, please remember us, and let us help you carry it, if you grow tired. Though we are each unknown to ourself and each other, 'tis not what well conferred it, the dying soldier asks, it is only the water.

Emily

MANUSCRIPT: missing.
PUBLICATION: L (1894) 339; LL 319–320; L (1931) 328–329.
Mrs. Todd dated the letter 1879. Quite possibly it was written at about the same time as the letter preceding. Mrs. Todd says in a footnote that following the letter is the poem beginning "We knew not that we were to live" (see letter no. 575).

To Mrs. Jonathan L. Jenkins   *late January 1879*

Would you feel more at Home with a Flower from Home, in your Hand, dear?

Manuscript: HCL (L 39). Pencil.
Publication: L (1894) 364; L (1931) 364; FN 123.
Probably this note was sent on the occasion of the birth of Austin Dickinson Jenkins, 19 January 1879.

593

To T. W. Higginson   *February 1879*

Dear friend,

To congratulate the Redeemed is perhaps superfluous for Redemption leaves nothing for Earth to add – It is very sweet and serious to suppose you at Home, and reverence I cannot express is all that remains – I have read of Home in the Revelations —— "Neither thirst any more" –

You speak very sweetly of the Stranger –

I trust the Phantom Love that enrolls the "Sparrow" – enfolds her softer than a Child –

The name of the "little Book she wrote," I do not quite decipher – "– and Prairie"? Should you perhaps tell me, I think I could see her Face in that – I am sorry not to have seen your "Hawthorne," but have known little of Literature since my Father died – that and the passing of Mr Bowles, and Mother's hopeless illness, overwhelmed my Moments, though your Pages and Shakespeare's, like Ophir – remain –

To see you seems improbable, but the Clergyman says I shall see my Father –

The subterranean stays –

Manuscript: HCL – the first two pages; and BPL (Higg 117) – the last two pages. Pencil.
Publication: AM CXXXIX (June 1927) 800; L (1931) 312–313. Higginson's marriage to Mary Potter Thacher took place during the first week in February, 1879. The book she had written and to which he had

alluded was a small collection of discursive essays, *Seashore and Prairie,* published in 1877. Higginson's *Short Studies of American Authors,* which contains a brief estimate of Hawthorne, Higginson sent to ED as soon as it was published, but it had not yet been written (see letter no. 622). He had published two earlier essays on Hawthorne: "An Evening with Mrs. Hawthorne," *Atlantic Monthly,* XXVIII (October 1871), 432–433; and "Hawthorne's Last Bequest," *Scribner's Monthly,* V (November 1872), 100–105. He had evidently alluded to one of these, probably to the second, since it deals more directly with Hawthorne. The quotation in the first paragraph is from Revelation 7.16: "They shall hunger no more, neither thirst any more. . .'"

594

To Mrs. Henry Hills   *1879?*

Our gentle Neighbor must have known that we did not know she was ill, or we should immediately have enquired for her.

Emily and Sister.

MANUSCRIPT: missing. The text of this letter and of the four that follow, written to Mrs. Hills presumably between the first of the year and Easter, have the same provenance as that of letter no. 376. Mrs. Todd dated this one "January 1879?."
PUBLICATION: L (1894) 397; L (1931) 386.

595

To Mrs. Henry Hills   *1879?*

"Come unto me." Beloved Commandment. The Darling obeyed.

MANUSCRIPT: missing.
PUBLICATION: L (1894) 398; L (1931) 387.
An infant, Samuel, died, 23 February, 1879.

596

To Mrs. Henry Hills   *1879?*

The power to console is not within corporeal reach – though its' attempt, is precious.

[636]

To die before it feared to die, may have been a boon —

MANUSCRIPT: missing. Addressed on the fold: Mrs Henry Hills.
PUBLICATION: L (1894) 398; LL 322; L (1931) 387.
This note perhaps soon followed the preceding.

597

To Mrs. Henry Hills   *1879?*

Dear friend,

The only Balmless Wound is the departed Human Life we had learned to need.

For that, even Immortality is a slow solace. All other Peace has many Roots and will spring again.

With cheer from one who knows.

MANUSCRIPT: missing.
PUBLICATION: L (1894) 398; LL 322; L (1931) 387.

598

To Mrs. Henry Hills   *1879?*

Dear friend,

The Gift was sadly exquisite. Were the actual "Cross" so divinely adorned, we should covet it.

Thank you for the sacred "flowers" — typical, both of them.

Gethsemene and Cana are still a traveled route.

Emily.

MANUSCRIPT: missing.
PUBLICATION: L (1894) 399; L (1931) 387-388.
Easter in 1879 fell on 13 April. This note evidently acknowledges an Easter gift.

599

To Mrs. Henry Hills   *about 1879*

Sweet Mrs Hills.

We think of you and know you think of us.
To come – from Heaven – is casual – but to return – eternal.
        Emily.

MANUSCRIPT: Jones Library. Pencil. Envelope addressed: Mrs Henry Hills. Unpublished. The date is conjectured from the handwriting.

This may also have been an Easter note, perhaps sent just before the preceding, and accompanying flowers for Mrs. Hills, appropriate to the season and to the memory of the child Samuel.

600

To Otis P. Lord   *about 1879*

. . . You spoke of "Hope" surpassing "Home" – I thought that Hope *was* Home – a misapprehension of Architecture – but then if I knew . . .

MANUSCRIPT: AC. Pencil.
PUBLICATION: *Revelation* 88.
It is a fragment seemingly clipped from a letter or draft of a letter.

601

To Helen Hunt Jackson   *about mid-April 1879*

     Spurn the temerity –
     Rashness of Calvary –
     Gay were Gethsemene
     Knew we of Thee –

MANUSCRIPT: HCL (Higginson). Pencil.
PUBLICATION: *AM* CXXXIX (June 1927) 801; *L* (1931) 318; *Poems* (1955) 992.

[638]

This may have been an Easter greeting and a reminder to Mrs. Jackson that ED has not recently heard from her. At the bottom of the sheet Mrs. Jackson wrote: "Wonderful twelve words! – H. J.," and evidently sent the message to Higginson, for it now rests among his papers. Mrs. Jackson wrote the following letter (HCL) to ED, dated Colorado Springs, 12 May 1879:

601a

My dear friend,

I know your "Blue bird" by heart – and that is more than I do of any of my own verses. –

I also want your permission to send it to Col. Higginson to read. These two things are my testimonial to its merit.

We have blue birds here – I might have had the sense to write something about one myself, but I never did: and now I never can. For which I am inclined to envy, and perhaps hate you.

"The man I live with" (I suppose you recollect designating my husband by that curiously direct phrase) is in New York, – and I am living alone, – which I should find very insupportable except that I am building on a bath room, & otherwise setting my house to rights. To be busy is the best help I know of, for all sorts of discomforts. –

What should you think of trying your hand on the oriole? He will be along presently

Yours ever –

Helen Jackson

P.S. Write & tell me if I may pass the Blue Bird along to the Col? –

602

To Helen Hunt Jackson   *1879*

Dear friend,

To the Oriole you suggested I add a Humming Bird and hope they are not untrue –

A Route of Evanescence
With a revolving Wheel
A Resonance of Emerald
A Rush of Cochineal
And every Blossom on the Bush
Adjusts it's tumbled Head –
The Mail from Tunis, probably,
An easy Morning's Ride.

PUBLICATION: AC. Pencil.
PUBLICATION: *Poems* (1955) 1011.
The "Blue bird" which Mrs. Jackson knew was probably "Before you thought of Spring." The poem ED wrote on the oriole begins: "One of the ones that Midas touched."

603

To Edward (Ned) Dickinson   *about 1879*

Ned –

Belshazzar had a Letter –
He never had but one –
Belshazzar's Correspondent
Concluded and begun
In that immortal Copy
The Conscience of us all
Can read without it's Glasses
On Revelation's Wall –

———

Suggested by our Neighbor –

Emily –

MANUSCRIPT: HCL (B 196). Pencil.
PUBLICATION: *Poems* (1955) 1008–1009.
This and the following two notes, sent to Ned, were written about 1879. The above may refer to the Lothrop case, settled in April 1879. The case is outlined in *Poems* (1955) 1006.

604

To Edward (Ned) Dickinson   *about 1879*

    Ned –

        Time's wily Chargers will not wait
        At any Gate but Woe's –
        But there – so gloat to hesitate
        They will not stir for blows –

Dick –

Jim –

MANUSCRIPT: HCL (B 45). Pencil.

PUBLICATION: FF 251; *Poems* (1955) 1008.

Mrs. Bianchi's note in *FF* says the lines were sent after Ned's horses Dick and Jim had run away with him. The verses, however, would seem more appropriate to an occasion when Ned inadvertently found himself in a funeral procession from which he could not extricate himself by whipping up the horses.

605

To Edward (Ned) Dickinson   *about 1879*

Dear Ned –

    Dennis was happy yesterday, and it made him graceful – I saw him waltzing with the Cow – and suspected his status, but he afterward started for your House in a frame that was unmistakable –

    You told me he had'nt tasted Liquor since his Wife's decease – then she must have been living at six o'clock last Evening –

    I fear for the rectitude of the Barn –

    Love for the Police –

MANUSCRIPT: HCL (B 130). Pencil.

PUBLICATION: LL 55, in part; *New World Writing* (Third Mentor Selection) May 1953, 260, entire except for the last line.

Dennis Scannell was a gardener and handyman. His wife had died in September 1876. See letter no. 616 and Appendix 2.

606

To Mrs. James S. Cooper   *about 1879*

Dear friend,

It distressed us that you were pained –

Are you easier now?

You have sheltered our tears too often – that your's should fall unsolaced –

Give us half the Thorn – then it will tear you less – To divulge itself is Sorrow's Right – never – its presumption.

Faithfully,
E. Dickinson

MANUSCRIPT: AC. Pencil.

PUBLICATION: L (1894) 396–397; LL 335, in part; L (1931) 385.

This and the following two notes, sent to Mrs. Cooper, are in the handwriting of about 1879.

607

To Mrs. James S. Cooper   *about 1879*

Is sickness pathos or infamy?

While you forget to decide, please confirm this trifle.

MANUSCRIPT: missing. The text derives from a transcript probably made by Mrs. Frederick Tuckerman, in the possession of Mr. Orton Clark.

PUBLICATION: L (1894) 394; LL 324; L (1931) 383.

608

To Mrs. James S. Cooper   *about 1879*

"Give me thine Heart" is too peremptory a Courtship for Earth, however irresistible in Heaven —

MANUSCRIPT: AC. Pencil.

PUBLICATION: L (1894) 395; LL 334; L (1931) 384.

The quotation is from Proverbs 23.26: "My son, give me thine heart, and let thine eyes observe my ways."

To Mrs. Samuel Bowles   1879?

How lovely to remember! How tenderly they told of you! Sweet toil for smitten hands to console the smitten!

Labors as endeared may engross our lost. Buds of other days quivered in remembrance. Hearts of other days lent their solemn charm.

Life of flowers lain in flowers – what a home of dew! And the bough of ivy; was it as you said? Shall I plant it softly?

There were little feet, white as alabaster.

Dare I chill them with the soil?

Nature is our eldest mother, she will do no harm.

Let the phantom love that enrolls the sparrow shield you softer than a child.

MANUSCRIPT: missing.

PUBLICATION: *L* (1894) 225–226; *LL* 316–317; *L* (1931) 211.

Mrs. Todd dated the letter 1879. It may be a message to thank Mrs. Bowles for flowers and a cutting of ivy which had some association with Samuel Bowles. The last sentence echoes one in letter no. 593.

To Louise and Frances Norcross   *early July 1879*

Dear Cousins,

Did you know there had been a fire here, and that but for a whim of the wind Austin and Vinnie and Emily would have all been homeless? But perhaps you saw *The Republican.*

We were waked by the ticking of the bells, – the bells tick in Amherst for a fire, to tell the firemen.

I sprang to the window, and each side of the curtain saw that awful sun. The moon was shining high at the time, and the birds singing like trumpets.

Vinnie came soft as a moccasin, "Don't be afraid, Emily, it is only the fourth of July."

I did not tell that I saw it, for I thought if she felt it best to deceive, it must be that it was.

She took hold of my hand and led me into mother's room. Mother had not waked, and Maggie was sitting by her. Vinnie left us a moment, and I whispered to Maggie, and asked her what it was.

"Only Stebbins's barn, Emily;" but I knew that the right and left of the village was on the arm of Stebbins's barn. I could hear buildings falling, and oil exploding, and people walking and talking gayly, and cannon soft as velvet from parishes that did not know that we were burning up.

And so much lighter than day was it, that I saw a caterpillar measure a leaf far down in the orchard; and Vinnie kept saying bravely, "It's only the fourth of July."

It seemed like a theatre, or a night in London, or perhaps like chaos. The innocent dew falling "as if it thought no evil," . . . and sweet frogs prattling in the pools as if there were no earth.

At seven people came to tell us that the fire was stopped, stopped by throwing sound houses in as one fills a well.

Mother never waked, and we were all grateful; we knew she would never buy needle and thread at Mr. Cutler's store, and if it were Pompeii nobody could tell her.

The post-office is in the old meeting-house where Loo and I went early to avoid the crowd, and – fell asleep with the bumble-bees and the Lord God of Elijah.

Vinnie's "only the fourth of July" I shall always remember. I think she will tell us so when we die, to keep us from being afraid.

Footlights cannot improve the grave, only immortality.

Forgive me the personality; but I knew, I thought, our peril was yours.

Love for you each.

Emily.

MANUSCRIPT: destroyed.
PUBLICATION: L (1894) 284–285; LL 320–321; L (1931) 258–259.
The fire that started in the early morning of 4 July 1879 gutted the business center of Amherst.

611

To Mrs. Edward Tuckerman   *September 1879*

Should dear Mrs Tuckerman have no Pears like mine, I should never cease to be harrowed –

Should she, that also would be dismay –

I incur the peril –

Emily.

MANUSCRIPT: AAS. Pencil. Endorsed by Mrs. Tuckerman: September 1879.
PUBLICATION: L (1894) 383; L (1931) 372–373.

612

To Mrs. William A. Stearns   1879?

Dear Friends,

I hope no bolder lover brought you the first pond lilies. The water is deeper than the land. The swimmer never stagnates.

I shall bring you a handful of lotus next, but do not tell the Nile. He is a jealous brook.

Emily.

MANUSCRIPT: missing.
PUBLICATION: L (1894) 379; LL 297; L (1931) 369.
This and the following note sent to Mrs Stearns, Mrs. Todd thought might have been written in 1879.

613

To Mrs. William A. Stearns   1879?

"A little flower, a faded flower, the gift of one who cared for me." Please usurp the pronoun.

Emily.

MANUSCRIPT: missing.
PUBLICATION: L (1894) 379; LL 297; L (1931) 369.

614

To Mrs. Henry Hills   1879?

Vocal is but one form of remembrance, dear friend. The cherishing that is speechless, is equally warm.

MANUSCRIPT: missing. The text has the same provenance as that of letter no. 376.
PUBLICATION: *L* (1894) 400; *L* (1931) 389.

615

To Mrs. Henry Hills   *1879?*

"Babes in the Wood." [*outside*]
Berries [*inside*]

MANUSCRIPT: missing. The text has the same provenance as that of letter no. 376. Unpublished. The date of this note and the one that precedes it is very uncertain.

616

To Mrs. John Dole   *about 1879*

Dear friend,

Had I known of Vinnie's inquiry, I should have dispelled it –

Dennis' constancy *here* – is impregnable, but obloquy out of sight is one of Vinnie's spectres – I dont remember meeting "the Lines," though they fall like Tennyson – The Parents of Beauty are seldom known – I hope you may fast grow stronger – and only recall the Sickness, as a bad Dream – Night's capacity varies, but Morning, is inevitable –

E. Dickinson –

MANUSCRIPT: Jones Library. Pencil. Unpublished.
The date is conjectured from the handwriting. The reference to Dennis Scannell may be explained in letter no. 605.

617

To Forrest F. Emerson   *1879?*

Though tendered by a stranger, the fruit will be forgiven.
Valor in the dark is my Maker's code.

E. Dickinson.

[646]

MANUSCRIPT: missing.
PUBLICATION: L (1894) 403; LL 333; L (1931) 392.
Emerson was installed as pastor of the First Church in June 1879. Mrs. Todd placed it early among the notes to Emerson. The signature is formal, yet ED thanks him for a gift of fruit and hints that a call will be appreciated. The gift may have been for Mrs. Dickinson, now bedridden, who may have expressed the wish to have her pastor call.

618

To Forrest F. Emerson   1879?

Mother congratulates Mr. Emerson on the discovery of the "philosopher's stone." She will never divulge it. It lay just where she thought it did — in making others happy.

E. Dickinson.

MANUSCRIPT: missing.
PUBLICATION: L (1894) 403; L (1931) 393.
The tone of this note suggests that it was written shortly after that above. Emerson has done something which Mrs. Dickinson appreciates and ED acknowledges; quite possibly he paid a call.

619

To Mrs. J. G. Holland   *October 1879*

Little Sister,

I was glad you wrote — I was just about addressing the Coroner of Alexandria — You spared me the melancholy research —

Are you pretty well — have you been happy —

Are your Eyes safe?

A thousand questions rise to my lips, and as suddenly ebb — for how little I know of you recently — An awkward loneliness smites me — I fear I must ask with Mr Wentworth, "Where are our moral foundations?"

Should you ask what had happened here, I should say nothing perceptible. Sweet latent events — too shy to confide —

[647]

It will vivify us to your remembrance to tell you that Austin and Sue have just returned from Belchertown Cattle Show –

Austin brought me a Balloon and Vinnie a Watermelon and each of his family a Whip – Wasn't it primitive?

When they drove away in the dust this morning, I told them they looked like Mr and Mrs "Pendexter," turning their backs upon Longfellow's Parish –

Brave Vinnie is well – Mother does not yet stand alone and fears she never shall walk, but I tell her we all shall fly so soon, not to let it grieve her, and what indeed is Earth but a Nest, from whose rim we are all falling?

One day last Summer I laughed once like "Little Mrs Holland," Vinnie said I did – how much it pleased us all –

I ask you to ask your Doctor will he be so kind as to write the name of my Philadelphia friend on the Note within, and your little Hand will take it to him –

You were so long so faithful, Earth would not seem homelike without your little sunny Acts –

Love for you each –

Emily.

MANUSCRIPT: HCL (H 51). Pencil.
PUBLICATION: LH 129–130.
The Belchertown Cattle Show took place on 9 October 1879. Mr. Wentworth is a character in Henry James's *The Europeans*, serialized at this time in *Scribner's Monthly*. Mr. Pendexter is a character in Longfellow's *Kavanagh*.

620

To Perez Cowan   *November 1879*

Will it comfort my grieved cousin to know that Emily and Vinnie are among the ones this moment thinking of him with peculiar tenderness, and is his sweet wife too faint to remember to Whom her loved one is consigned?

"Come unto me" could not alarm those minute feet – how sweet to remember.

If you feel able, write a few words; if you do not – remember forgetting is a guile unknown to your faithful cousin

Emily.

MANUSCRIPT: missing.
PUBLICATION: L (1894) 334; L (1931) 323.
Cowan's daughter Margaret died, 8 November 1879.

621

To T. W. Higginson   *about 1879*

Must I lose the Friend that saved my Life, without inquiring why?
Affection gropes through Drifts of Awe – for his Tropic Door –
That every Bliss we know or guess – hourly befall him – is his scholar's
prayer ——

MANUSCRIPT: BPL (Higg 104). Pencil.
PUBLICATION: L (1894) 327; LL 306; L (1931) 309.
The handwriting is that of 1879. The two datable letters written during the year are in February and December (nos. 593 and 622). This one evidently was written to remind Higginson that a reply to her February letter was overdue. For the reference to him as the friend who had saved her life, see the letter she wrote him ten years earlier (no. 330). For a similar concluding sentence, see letter no. 537.

622

To T. W. Higginson   *December 1879*

Dear friend,

Brabantio's Gift was not more fair than your's, though I trust without his pathetic inscription – "Which but thou hast already, with all my Heart I would keep from thee" – Of Poe, I know too little to think – Hawthorne appalls, entices –

Mrs Jackson soars to your estimate lawfully as a Bird, but of Howells and James, one hesitates – Your relentless Music dooms as it redeems –

Remorse for the brevity of a Book is a rare emotion, though fair as Lowell's "Sweet Despair" in the Slipper Hymn –

[649]

One thing of it we borrow
And promise to return –
The Booty and the Sorrow
It's Sweetness to have known –
One thing of it we covet –
The power to forget –
The Anguish of the Avarice
Defrays the Dross of it –

Had I tried before reading your Gift, to thank you, it had perhaps been possible, but I waited and now it disables my Lips –

Magic, as it electrifies, also makes decrepit – Thank you for thinking of me –

Your Scholar –

MANUSCRIPT: BPL (Higg 109). Pencil.
PUBLICATION: L (1894) 329; LL 318–319; L (1931) 313.
Higginson's *Short Studies of American Authors*, advertised as a holiday book, was published shortly before Christmas, priced at fifty cents. It contained brief critical sketches of Hawthorne, Poe, Thoreau, Howells, Helen Hunt Jackson, and Henry James. The lines from *Othello*, I, iii, 194–195, are also in letter no. 538. The allusion to Lowell's "Sweet Despair" in his "Slipper Hymn" must surely have mystified Higginson as it perhaps was intended to do. Yet it clearly refers to the sixth and the last stanzas of Lowell's *After the Burial*:

To the spirit its splendid conjectures,
To the flesh its sweet despair,
Its tears o'er the thin-worn locket
With its anguish of deathless hair!

That little shoe in the corner,
So worn and wrinkled and brown,
With its emptiness confutes you,
And argues your wisdom down.

To Mrs. Henry Hills   *after Christmas 1879*

Dear friend,

I think Heaven will not be as good as earth, unless it bring with it that sweet power to remember, which is the Staple of Heaven – here. How can we thank each other, when omnipotent?

You, who endear our mortal Christmas, will perhaps assure us.

E.

MANUSCRIPT: missing. The text has the same provenance as that of letter no. 376.

PUBLICATION: *L* (1894) 399; *L* (1931) 388, dated: Christmas, 1879.

Mrs. Hills annually sent Christmas remembrances. The fervor of the acknowledgment may suggest the pleasure which Mrs. Dickinson now took in such events.

To Susan Gilbert Dickinson   *about 1879*

So sorry for Sister's hardships – "Make me thy wrack when I come back, but spare me when I gang."

Emily –

MANUSCRIPT: HCL (B 169). Pencil.

PUBLICATION: *FF* 240.

This and the following two notes, sent to Susan Dickinson, are in the handwriting of about 1879.

To Susan Gilbert Dickinson   *about 1879*

Emily is sorry for Susan's Day –

To be singular under plural circumstances, is a becoming heroism –

Opinion is a flitting thing,
But Truth, outlasts the Sun –
If then we cannot own them both –
Possess the oldest one –

Emily –

MANUSCRIPT: HCL (B 26). Pencil. Addressed: Susan.
PUBLICATION: LL 62, prose part only.

626

To Susan Gilbert Dickinson   *about 1879*

Mrs Delmonico's things were very nice – Art has a "Palate," as well
as an Easel –

Susan breaks many Commandments, but *one* she obeys – "Whatsoever ye do, do it unto the Glory" –

Susan will be saved –

Thank her –

Emily –

MANUSCRIPT: HCL (B 48). Pencil.
PUBLICATION: FF 243.

Many notes written at this time suggest that ED is acknowledging
thoughtful attentions which friends and members of the family are trying
to show Mrs. Dickinson. Delmonico's was a fashionable New York restau-
rant. The quotation draws on 1 Corinthians 10.31: "Whether therefore ye
eat, or drink, or whatsoever ye do, do all to the glory of God."

XI

LETTERS

627–878

[1880–1883]

" *I hesitate which word to take,*
as I can take but few and each
must be the chiefest . . ."

The letters which comprise this group show an increased nervous tension brought on in part by the frictions between the two houses — particularly between Vinnie and Sue, and in part by the death of friends. Dr. Holland's death in 1881 was not the personal loss that Bowles's death had been; it chiefly touched her through her deep affection for Mrs. Holland, who in these years seems to have been her staunchest comforter and most steady correspondent. The extent of her correspondence with Lord can never be known, since presumably the bulk of it has been long destroyed, but its nature is clear from the surviving fragments.

Charles Wadsworth's death in April 1882 concluded one of the meaningful associations of her life, and served to open a new correspondence. James Clark had been a lifelong friend of Wadsworth's, and the spate of letters she now wrote James Clark (and later his brother Charles) are almost solely testimonials to the departed friend. Her mother survived into November of that year, and the letters of this period are clear evidence that the demands made on Emily by a helpless invalid strengthened the bond between mother and daughter.

The most shattering experience proved to be, not the death of an adult friend, but that of her eight-year-old nephew Gilbert, in the autumn of 1883. With his departure went a certain inner light. She still groped for words with which to form poems, now chiefly elegies, but hardly more than fragments were produced. There are, however, noble utterances in the letters.

627

To Mrs. Edward Tuckerman   *early 1880*

I send you only a Humming Bird.
Will you let me add a few Jasmin in a few Days?

A Route of Evanescence
With a revolving Wheel –
A Resonance of Emerald –
A Rush of Cochineal –
And every Blossom on the Bush
Adjusts it's tumbled Head –
The mail from Tunis, probably,
An easy Morning's Ride –

Emily.

MANUSCRIPT: AC. Pencil.
PUBLICATION: *Poems* (1955) 1010–1011.
The conjecture that this may have been set as a New Year's greeting
is supported by the fact that a similar greeting was sent in 1881, and that
thereafter some sort of New Year's exchange seems to have been annual.
ED raised jasmine in her conservatory.

628

To Mrs. Edward Tuckerman   *January 1880*

Dear friend,

Your sweetness intimidates –
Had it been a Mastiff that guarded Eden, we should have feared
him less than we do the Angel –
I read your little Letter – it had like Bliss – the minute length. It
were dearer had you protracted it, but the Sparrow must not propound
his Crumb –

We shall find the Cube of the Rainbow.
Of that, there is no doubt.
But the Arc of a Lover's conjecture
Eludes the finding out.

Confidingly,
Emily –

MANUSCRIPT: AC. Pencil. The envelope is addressed by George Montague, and postmarked 5 January.
PUBLICATION: L (1894) 383; LL 340, poem only; L (1931) 373.
The year is conjectured from the handwriting. The message may acknowledge a New Year's greeting, or a note of appreciation for the "Humming Bird."

629

To Mrs. Lucius Boltwood   *March 1880?*

The Spring of which dear Mrs Boltwood speaks, is not so brave as herself, and should bring her of right, it's first flower.

Though a Pie is far from a flower, Mr Howells implies in his "Undiscovered Country," that "our relation to Pie" will unfold in proportion to finer relations.

With sweet thoughts from us all, and thanks for the charming Butter, and the gallant notes,

Very faithfully,
Emily

MANUSCRIPT: missing. The text is from a transcript in the Jones Library, made when the autograph was on loan exhibit in 1929.
PUBLICATION: Amherst Graduates' Magazine XXVI (1937) 297–307; Adèle Allen: *Around a Village Green*, pp. 54–55.
A note from Vinnie to Mrs. Boltwood, dated 8 March 1880, expresses sympathy for an accident to her son, who had been thrown from a carriage. This note may have been written then. Howells's *Undiscovered Country* was published serially in *Scribner's Monthly*, beginning in January. This note, accompanying a pie, acknowledges the gift of butter.

630

To T. W. Higginson   *March 1880*

I was sorry for what the Paper told me – I hoped it was not true –

> The Face in evanescence lain
> Is more distinct than our's –
> And our's surrendered for it's sake
> As Capsules are for Flower's –
> Or is it the confiding sheen
> Dissenting to be won
> Descending to enamor us
> Of Detriment divine?

MANUSCRIPT: BPL (Higg 113). Pencil.
PUBLICATION: L (1931) 318.
Higginson's infant daughter Louisa died, 15 March 1880; the *Springfield Republican* announced the death on 21 March.

631

To Mrs. Henry Hills   *March 1880*

Dear friend,

The heavenly flowers were brought to my room. I had lain awake with the Gale and overslept this morning. That you may wake in Eden, as you enabled me to do, is my happy wish.

Emily.

MANUSCRIPT: missing. The text of this letter and the one that follows, both written to Mrs. Hills, have the same provenance as that of letter no. 376. Addressed: Mrs Hills.
PUBLICATION: L (1894) 399–400; L (1931) 388.
The note that follows makes apparent that this is written in appreciation of flowers sent on Easter Sunday, 28 March 1880.

632

To Mrs. Henry Hills   *March 1880*

Without the hope of requiting the Sabbath Morning Blossoms, still sweetly remembered, please allow me to try.

E –

MANUSCRIPT: as above.
PUBLICATION: *L* (1894) 400; *L* (1931) 388.

633

To Mrs. Forrest F. Emerson   *1880?*

Any gift but spring seems a counterfeit, but the birds are such sweet neighbors they rebuke us all.

E. Dickinson.

MANUSCRIPT: missing.
PUBLICATION: *L* (1894) 404; *L* (1931) 393.
This and the two following notes, written to the Rev. Forrest Emerson and his wife, may have been sent about 1880.

634

To Mrs. Forrest F. Emerson   *1880?*

Mother was much touched by dear Mrs. Emerson's thoughtfulness, and thanks her exceedingly sweetly. She also asks a remembrance to Mr. Emerson, whom she trusts is well.

Earnestly,
E. Dickinson.

MANUSCRIPT: missing.
PUBLICATION: *L* (1894) 404; *L* (1931) 393.

635

To Forrest F. Emerson   *1880?*

Should Mr. Emerson ever become ill and idle, mother hopes his clergyman will be as delicately thoughtful of him as he has been of her.

Gratefully,

E. Dickinson.

MANUSCRIPT: missing.
PUBLICATION: *L* (1894) 404; *L* (1931) 393.

636

To Susan Gilbert Dickinson   *spring 1880*

That Susan lives – is a Universe which neither going nor coming could displace –

—

MANUSCRIPT: HCL (B 141). Pencil.
PUBLICATION: FF 247.
During the spring of 1880 Susan, feeling nervously exhausted, left town for a rest. This note perhaps accompanied some token sent at the time of Sue's departure or return.

637

To Mrs. Edward Tuckerman   *about 1880*

Will the little Hands that have brought me so much tenderness, the sweet Hands, in which a Bird would love to lie, the Fingers that knew no estrangement except the Gulf of Down – will such enfold a Daphne?

Almost I trust they will, yet trust is such a shelving word – Part of our treasures are denied us – part of them provisoed, like Bequests available far hence – part of them we partake?

Which, dear, are divinest?

Emily –

MANUSCRIPT: AC. Pencil.
PUBLICATION: L (1894) 384–385; L (1931) 374.
The date is conjectured from the handwriting.

638

To Mrs. Henry D. Fearing   *24 April 1880*

Dear friend,

We hope you are not too much fatigued with the alarm of last Night, and rejoice that your beautiful Home was unharmed –

The regret my Father would offer, please accept from his Children.

E. Dickinson.

MANUSCRIPT: Jones Library. Pencil. Unpublished.
Fearing's hat factory was destroyed by fire, 23 April 1880.

639

To Mrs. Henry Hills   *late April 1880*

We are ignorant of the dear friends, and eager to know how they are, and assure them that we are near them in these grieved hours.

Emily and Vinnie.

MANUSCRIPT: missing. The text of this letter has the same provenance as that of letter no. 376.
PUBLICATION: L (1894) 399; L (1931) 388.
The fire that destroyed the Fearing factory also destroyed Mr. Hills's.

640

To Mrs. Henry Hills   *late April 1880*

Are the little flowers too near the hue of the last week's fright to delight the Neighbor of whom we thought so tenderly?

Emily and Vinnie.

MANUSCRIPT: Unpublished. Same provenance as above.

641

To T. W. Higginson   *spring 1880*

Dear friend –

Most of our Moments are Moments of Preface – "Seven Weeks" is a long Life – if it is all lived –

The little Memoir was very touching. I am sorry she was not willing to stay –

The flight of such a fraction takes all our Numbers Home –

"Room for one more" was a plea for Heaven –
I misunderstood – Heaven must be a lone exchange for such a parentage –
These sudden intimacies with Immortality, are expanse – not Peace – as Lightning at our feet, instills a foreign Landscape. Thank you for the Portrait – it is beautiful, but intimidating – I shall pick "May flowers" more furtively, and feel new awe of "Moonlight."
The route of your little Fugitive must be a tender wonder – and yet

A Dimple in the Tomb
Makes that ferocious Room
A Home –

Your Scholar –

MANUSCRIPT: Hallowell. Pencil.
PUBLICATION: AM CXXXIX (1927) 800; L (1931) 315.
Higginson sent ED a "memoir" of the baby that died in March. In 1879 Mary Thacher Higginson published *Room for One More*, a story for children.

642

To Edward (Ned) Dickinson   *mid-May 1880*

Phoebus – "I'll take the Reins."

Phaeton.

MANUSCRIPT: HCL (B 86). Pencil. Unpublished. Addressed: Ned.
Amherst Record, 12 May: "W. A. Dickinson has just purchased a fine young stepper to take the place of his old family carriage horse, and shows plenty of style as well as life."

643

To Maria Whitney   *about June 1880*

Dear friend –

I am constantly more astonished that the Body contains the Spirit – Except for overmastering work it could not be borne –
I shall miss saying to Vinnie when we hear the Northhampton

[661]

Bell – as in subtle states of the West we do – "Miss Whitney is going to Church" – though must not everywhere be Church to Hearts that have or have had – a Friend?

> Could that sweet Darkness where they dwell
> Be once disclosed to us
> The clamor for their loveliness
> Would burst the Loneliness –

I trust you may have the dearest summer possible to Loss –

One sweet sweet more – One liquid more – of that Arabian presence!

You spoke very sweetly to both of us and your sewing and recollecting is a haunting picture – a sweet spectral protection – Your name is taken as tenderly as the names of our Birds, or the Flower, for some mysterious cause, sundered from it's Dew – Hoarded Mr Samuel – not one bleat of his Lamb – but is known to us –

In a brief memoir of Parepa, in which she was likened to a Rose – "thornless until she died," some bereaved one added – to miss him is his only stab, but that – he never gave.

A word from you would be sacred.

Emily.

MANUSCRIPT: missing. The text is from a transcript made of the autograph when it was offered for sale by Zeitlin in 1936.

PUBLICATION: L (1894) 337, in part; LL 311, in part; L (1931) 326, in part.

Maria Whitney made known her intention to resign as Teacher of French and German at Smith College in May 1880. Many of ED's letters to her after the death of Samuel Bowles mention him. Madame Parepa-Rosa (1836–1874), wife of the impressario Carl Rosa, was an English soprano singer of oratorio and opera. She first sang in the United States in 1866.

644

To Mrs. Samuel Bowles   *June 1880?*

Dear Mary,

The last April that father lived, lived I mean below, there were several snow-storms, and the birds were so frightened and cold they sat by the kitchen door. Father went to the barn in his slippers and came back with a breakfast of grain for each, and hid himself while he scattered it, lest it embarrass them. Ignorant of the name or fate of their benefactor, their descendants are singing this afternoon.

As I glanced at your lovely gift, his April returned. I am powerless toward your tenderness.

Thanks of other days seem abject and dim, yet antiquest altars are the fragrantest. The past has been very near this week, but not so near as the future – both of them pleading, the latter priceless.

David's grieved decision haunted me when a little girl. I hope he has found Absalom.

Immortality as a guest is sacred, but when it becomes as with you and with us, a member of the family, the tie is more vivid. . . .

If affection can reinforce, you, dear, shall not fall.

Emily.

MANUSCRIPT: missing.
PUBLICATION: *L* (1894) 226; *LL* 322–323; *L* (1931) 211–212.

Mrs. Todd dated this letter April 1880. Possibly it was occasioned by Mrs. Bowles's annual remembrance on the anniversary of Edward Dickinson's death.

645

To Otis P. Lord   *about 1880*

[I never heard you call anything beautiful before. It remained with me curiously –] There is a fashion in delight as other things.

Still (stern) as the Profile of a Tree against a winter sky (sunset sky –) (evening –)

[I kissed the little blank – you made it on the second page you may have forgotten –] I will not wash my arm – the one you gave the scarf to – it is brown as an Almond – 'twill take your touch away –

[I try to think when I wake in the night what the chapter would be for the chapter would be in the night would'nt it – but I cannot decide –]

It is strange that I miss you at night so much when I was never with you – but the punctual love invokes you soon as my eyes are shut – and I wake warm with the want sleep had almost filled – I dreamed

[663]

last week that you had died – and one had carved a statue of you and I was asked to unvail it – and I said what I had not done in Life I would not in death when your loved eyes could not forgive – [The length of the hour was beautiful. The length of the heavenly hour how sweetly you counted it. The numerals of Eden do not oppress the student long] for Eden ebbs away to diviner Edens. [Therefore Love is so speechless – Seems to withold Darling]
I never seemed toward you
Lest I had been too frank was often my fear –
How could I long to give who never saw your natures Face –

This has been a beautiful Day – dear – given solely to you – carried in my thin hand to your distant hope [offer] offered softly and added – The haste of early summer is gone and a foreboding leisure is stealing over [natures] bustling things –

But why did you distrust your little Simon Peter yesterday – you said you did'nt but she knew you did – What did Nestor say you begun to tell me – To rest (cling) with you swept all day –

I sometimes [have] almost feared Language was done between us – [if you grew] too dear, except for breath, then words flowed softly in like [some] a shining secret, the Lode of which the miner dreams

I wonder we ever leave the Improbable – it is so fair a Home, and perhaps we dont –
What is half so improbable . . .

MANUSCRIPT: AC. Pencil.
PUBLICATION: *Revelation* 87–91.
These fragment rough drafts are in the handwriting of about 1880. Words crossed out are here placed in brackets; alternative suggestions are in parentheses.

646

To Mrs. Jonathan L. Jenkins *about 1880*

Hope they are with each other – Never saw a little Boy going Home to Thanksgiving, so happy as Austin, when he passed the Door –

Emily.

MANUSCRIPT: Sister Mary James. Pencil.
PUBLICATION: *FN* 112.
Austin had gone to visit Mr. Jenkins, who was his close friend.

647

To Mrs. James S. Cooper   *about 1880*

Please accept the Progeny of the Pinks you so kindly brought Mother in Winter, with the hope that "Wisdom is justified of her Children" —

MANUSCRIPT: AC. Pencil.
PUBLICATION: *L* (1894) 395; *L* (1931) 384.
The handwriting is that of about 1880. The quotation is from Matthew 11.19.

648

To Mrs. James S. Cooper   *about 1880?*

Dear Friend,

So valiant is the intimacy between Nature and her children, she addresses them as "comrades in arms."

E. Dickinson.

MANUSCRIPT: missing.
PUBLICATION: *L* (1894) 395; *LL* 334; *L* (1931) 384.
The date is unknown. Mrs. Todd places it among letters written about 1880.

649

To Mrs. Lucius Boltwood   *1880?*

Will dear Mrs Boltwood taste a little loaf of "Federal Cake" and a few Wild Roses, which are not so aboriginal as I could wish?

Affly
Emily.

[665]

MANUSCRIPT: missing.

PUBLICATION: *Amherst Graduates' Magazine* XXVI (1937) 305; Allen: *Around a Village Green*, pp. 54–55.

This message may have been sent about June 1880, shortly before the Boltwoods left Amherst.

650

To Mrs. J. G. Holland   *July 1880*

Dear friend,

While Little Boys are commemorating the advent of their Country, I have a Letter from "Aunt Glegg" saying "Summer is nearly gone," so I thought I would pick a few Seeds this Afternoon and bid you Good bye as you would be off for Winter. I think Persons dont talk about "Summer stopping" this time o' year, unless they are inclement themselves.

I wish you would speak to the Thermometer about it – I dont like to take the responsibility.

Perhaps you never received a Note I sent you or you would have answered the little question was in it?

It was not about the "promised Messiah –"

The Weather is like Africa and the Flowers like Asia and the Numidian Heart of your "Little Friend" neither slow nor chill –

> The Road to Paradise is plain,
> And holds scarce one.
> Not that it is not firm
> But we presume
> A Dimpled Road
> Is more preferred.
> The Belles of Paradise are few –
> Not me – nor you –
> But unsuspected things –
> Mines have no Wings.

[666]

July 15th

You see I have been delayed – but we will begin where we left off –

Austin and I were talking the other Night about the Extension of Consciousness, after Death and Mother told Vinnie, afterward, she thought it was "very improper."

She forgets that we are past "Correction in Righteousness –"

I dont know what she would think if she knew that Austin told me confidentially "there was no such person as Elijah."

I suppose Doctor is catching Trout and Convalescence and wish I could meet them both at Breakfast – and bid my very little Sister a most sweet Good Night –

Manuscript: HCL (H 52). Pencil.
Publication: LH 131–132.

ED dated the letter "July 4th" but put it aside and finished it on "July 15th." Aunt Glegg, a character in George Eliot's *The Mill on the Floss*, cast a shadow over members of the family, whether she was present or absent; ED undoubtedly has in mind her Aunt Elizabeth Currier. The scripture allusion is to 2 Timothy 3.16: "All scripture is given . . . for correction, for instruction in righteousness."

651

To Samuel Bowles the younger   *early August 1880*

Dear friend,

Our friend your Father was so beautifully and intimately recalled Today that it seemed impossible he had experienced the secret of Death – A servant who had been with us a long time and had often opened the Door for him, asked me how to spell "Genius," yesterday – I told her and she said no more – Today, she asked me what "Genius" meant? I told her none had known –

She said she read in a Catholic Paper that Mr Bowles was "the Genius of Hampshire," and thought it might be that past Gentleman – His look could not be extinguished to any who had seen him, for "Because I live, ye shall live also," was his physiognomy –

I congratulate you upon his immortality, which is a constant stimulus to my Household – and upon your noble perpetuation of his cherished "Republican."

Please remember me tenderly to your Mother –

With honor,

Emily Dickinson –

MANUSCRIPT: Bowles. Pencil.

PUBLICATION: L (1894) 349; LL 342–343; L (1931) 337.

ED got Maggie Maher to address the envelope, probably because Maggie had called attention to the tribute to Bowles: Saml Bowles Esq/ Republican/Springfield/Mass. Postmarked: Amherst Mass Aug 2.

652

To Susan Gilbert Dickinson   *about 1880*

Great Hungers feed themselves, but little Hungers ail in vain.

MANUSCRIPT: HCL (B 36). Pencil.

PUBLICATION: LL 87.

The date, conjectured from the handwriting, is certainly not earlier than 1880, and may be somewhat later.

653

To T. W. Higginson   *August 1880*

Dear friend,

I was touchingly reminded of your little Louisa this Morning by an Indian Woman with gay Baskets and a dazzling Baby, at the Kitchen Door – Her little Boy "once died," she said, Death to her dispelling him – I asked her what the Baby liked, and she said "to step." The Prairie before the Door was gay with Flowers of Hay, and I led her in – She argued with the Birds – she leaned on Clover Walls and they fell, and dropped her – With jargon sweeter than a Bell, she grappled Buttercups – and they sank together, the Buttercups the heaviest – What sweetest use of Days!

[668]

'Twas noting some such Scene made Vaughn humbly say "My Days that are at best but dim and hoary" –

I think it was Vaughn –

It reminded me too of "Little Annie," of whom you feared to make the mistake in saying "Shoulder Arms" to the "Colored Regiment" – but which was the Child of Fiction, the Child of Fiction or of Fact, and is "Come unto me" for Father or Child, when the Child precedes?

MANUSCRIPT: HCL (Higginson). Pencil.

PUBLICATION: AM LXVIII (October 1891) 455–456, in part; L (1894) 330–331, in part; LL 325, in part; AM CXXXIX (June 1927) 801, entire; L (1931) 316–317, entire.

The *Amherst Record* for 18 August 1880 notes: "The poor Indian has arrived and a party of some such nationality is in camp at East Street." "Little Annie" was "The Baby of the Regiment" in Higginson's *Army Life in a Black Regiment* (1870). The quotation from Henry Vaughan is from the third stanza of "They are all gone into the world of light," and reads: "My days, which are at best but dull and hoary."

654

To Martha Gilbert Smith   *August 1880*

It was like my Mattie to send the Peaches, pink as the Heart they indorse –

I wish I had something as sumptuous to enclose to her –

I have, but it is anonymous –

I love to hear you are growing better – I hope you may be a hale Mattie before you go away – vast as Vinnie and I, who tower like Acorns – Thank you from each, delightedly – If the transitive be but the minor, we shall need a large accession of strength, for the major sweetness –

Lovingly,
Emily –

MANUSCRIPT: HCL (L 30). Pencil.

PUBLICATION: FF 252–253.

Mattie was visiting her sister Sue in Amherst. Her husband had died in December 1878.

To Martha Gilbert Smith   *late summer 1880*

Dear Mattie –

"Sultans" in Tippets is rather a perversion of Hemispheres, but then we are such a vivacious Climate – The Shah in Mittens will doubtless ensue – I bring you my first Jasmin, minute and alone, but to me incomparably precious –

"Several" is a Mob, but a "two or three in my name" a confiding multitude –

Lovingly,
Emily –

MANUSCRIPT: HCL (L 28). Pencil.

PUBLICATION: FF 252.

The date is conjectured from the handwriting. This note probably follows the preceding, for the reference in the first sentence is to sweet sultans, one of ED's garden flowers, surviving after a cold snap. The scripture allusion is to Matthew 18.20: "For where two or three are gathered together in my name, there am I in the midst of them."

To Louise Norcross   *early September 1880*

What is it that instructs a hand lightly created, to impel shapes to eyes at a distance, which for them have the whole area of life or of death? Yet not a pencil in the street but has this awful power, though nobody arrests it. An earnest letter is or should be life-warrant or death-warrant, for what is each instant but a gun, harmless because "unloaded," but that touched "goes off"?

Men are picking up the apples to-day, and the pretty boarders are leaving the trees, birds and ants and bees. I have heard a chipper say "dee" six times in disapprobation. How should we like to have our privileges wheeled away in a barrel? . . .

The Essex visit was lovely. Mr. L[ord] remained a week. Mrs. —— re-decided to come with her son Elizabeth. Aunt Lucretia [Bullard] shouldered arms. I think they lie in my memory, a muffin and a bomb. Now they are all gone, and the crickets are pleased. Their bombazine reproof still falls upon the twilight, and checks the softer uproars of the departing day.

Earnest love to Fanny. This is but a fragment, but wholes are not below.

Emily.

MANUSCRIPT: destroyed.

PUBLICATION: *L* (1894) 292; *L* (1931) 264–265.

Louise Norcross had visited in Amherst in mid-August, at the same time Martha Smith was there. On 1 September the *Amherst Record* notes: "Quite a large gathering of the descendants of the late Samuel F. Dickinson, including sisters and families, cousins and friends of the late Hon. Edward Dickinson, have been for more than a week guests of our new 'Amherst House' . . . Judge Lord of Salem, with a party have been guests at the hotel for several days." "The Essex visit" refers to the Lord group; Salem is the county seat of Essex County.

657

To Mrs. Henry Hills 1880?

With a sweet September for Mrs. Henry.

MANUSCRIPT: missing. The text of this letter and the two that follow, sent to Mrs. Hills, have the same provenance as that of letter no. 376. They may have been written about 1880. All three are unpublished, and manuscripts are missing.

658

To Mrs. Henry Hills 1880?

Dear friends,

Neither in Heaven nor Earth, have I seen such Beauty. Superb as Aurora, celestial as Snow.

With grateful delight.

E. Dickinson.

659

To Mrs. Henry Hills 1880?

With a Neighbor's love.

To Susan Gilbert Dickinson   *about* 1880

Susan is a vast and sweet Sister, and Emily hopes to deserve her, but not now –

Thanks for the profligate little Box that lacked only Cigars –

MANUSCRIPT: HCL (B 7). Pencil.
PUBLICATION: FF 241.

This perhaps was written during ED's illness, which was intermittent and protracted, in the autumn of 1880. The four notes that follow, all written to Sue, are in the same handwriting. (See letters no. 672 and 673.)

To Susan Gilbert Dickinson   *about* 1880

"Thank you" ebbs between us, but the Basis of thank you, is sterling and fond –

                                                              Emily.

MANUSCRIPT: HCL (B 43). Pencil. Addressed on the fold: Susan.
PUBLICATION: FF 260.

To Susan Gilbert Dickinson   *about* 1880

Susan –

I would have come out of Eden to open the Door for you if I had known you were there – You must knock with a Trumpet as Gabriel does, whose Hands are small as yours – I knew he knocked and went away – I did'nt dream that you did –

                                                              Emily –

MANUSCRIPT: HCL (B 63). Pencil.
PUBLICATION: LL 65.

To Susan Gilbert Dickinson   *about 1880*

A Spell cannot be tattered, and mended like a Coat —

                             Emily.

MANUSCRIPT: HCL (B 35). Pencil.
PUBLICATION: *LL* 62.

664

To Susan Gilbert Dickinson   *about 1880*

Memoirs of Little Boys that live —
"Were'nt you chasing Pussy," said Vinnie to Gilbert?
"No — she was chasing herself" —
"But was'nt she running pretty fast"? "Well, some slow and some
fast" said the beguiling Villain — Pussy's Nemesis quailed —
Talk of "hoary Reprobates"!
Your Urchin is more antique in wiles than the Egyptian Sphinx —
Have you noticed Granville's Letter to Lowell?
"Her Majesty" has contemplated you, and reserves her decision!

                             Emily —

MANUSCRIPT: HCL (B 72). Pencil.
PUBLICATION: *AM* CXV (1915) 37–38; *LL* 58.
Lowell went as minister to England in 1880, the year that Granville
took over the Foreign Office.

665

To Mrs. Elizabeth Carmichael   *about 1880?*

. . . I fear Vinnie gave my message as John Alden did the one
from Miles Standish, which resulted delightfully for John, but not as
well for his friend.
Had you seen the delighted crowd that gathered round the box —
did you ever see a crowd of three? — you would have felt requited.
Your presenting smile was alone wanting.

"Dear Mrs. Carmichael," said one; "The one that never forgets," said another; and a tear or two in the eyes of the third, and the reception was over. Can you guess which the third was?

The candy was enchanting, and is closeted in a deep pail, pending Vinnie's division, and the little box, like Heaven and mice, far too high to find.

Failure be my witness that I have sought them faithfully.

We often think of your evening circle – Mr. Skeel presiding at the piano, and Mrs. Skeel and yourself taking mutual lessons.

I am studying music now with the jays, and find them charming artists.

Vinnie and Gilbert have pretty battles on the pussy question, and you are needed for umpire, oftener than you think.

"Weren't you chasing pussy?" said Vinnie to Gilbert. "No, she was chasing herself."

"But wasn't she running pretty fast?" said pussy's Nemesis. "Well, some slow and some fast," said the beguiling villain.

With the little kiss he gave me last, and a pair of my own, and love for Mr. and Mrs. Skeel.

Warmly,
Emily.

Manuscript: missing.
Publication: L (1894) 418–419; L (1931) 407–408.

Mrs. Todd dated the letter "1882?." Because the story about Gilbert repeats the account in the letter to Sue, above, one surmises that the two letters were written about the same time. The allusion in the first sentence is to Longfellow's "The Courtship of Miles Standish."

Among the penciled jottings (AC) dating from about this time is the following recipe for coconut cake, which ED evidently obtained from Mrs. Carmichael. It is published in *Home* 115.

1 pound sugar –
½ – Butter –
½ – Flour –
6 eggs –
1 grated Cocoa Nut –

Mrs. Carmichael's –

To Louise and Frances Norcross   *about September 1880*

I have only a moment, exiles, but you shall have the largest half. Mother's dear little wants so engross the time, – to read to her, to fan her, to tell her health will come tomorrow, to explain to her *why* the grasshopper is a burden, because he is not so new a grasshopper as he was, – this is so ensuing, I hardly have said "Good-morning, mother," when I hear myself saying "Mother, good-night."

MANUSCRIPT: destroyed.
PUBLICATION: L (1894) 294; L (1931) 266.
This letter was written on the day preceding that on which ED wrote the following letter to Mrs. Holland. The scripture allusion to the grasshopper is from Ecclesiastes 12.5.

667

To Mrs. J. G. Holland   *about September 1880*

Dear Sister –

The responsibility of Pathos is almost more than the responsibility of Care. Mother will never walk. She still makes her little Voyages from her Bed to her Chair in a Strong Man's Arms – probably that will be all.

Her poor Patience loses it's way and we lead it back – I was telling her Nieces yesterday, who wrote to ask for her, that to read to her – to fan her – to tell her "Health would come Tomorrow," and make the Counterfeit look real – to explain *why* "the Grasshopper is a Burden" – because it is not as new a Grasshopper as it was – this is so ensuing, that I hardly have said, "Good Morning, Mother," when I hear myself saying "Mother, – Good Night –"

Time is short and full, like an outgrown Frock –

You are very kind to give me leave to ask "the question" again, but on renewed self examination I find I have not the temerity –

I thought of your Garden in the Rocks those unfeeling Nights – perhaps it had "Watchers" as Vinnie's did –

I hope the Doctor is improving – in his health – I mean – his other perfections precluding the suggestion, and that my little Sister is in sweet robustness –

Vinnie is far more hurried than Presidential Candidates – I trust in more distinguished ways, for *they* have only the care of the Union, but Vinnie the Universe –

With her love and mine,

Emily –

MANUSCRIPT: HCL (H 53). Pencil.
PUBLICATION: *LH* 133.

This letter was written in response to one from Mrs. Holland which evidently invited ED to repeat the question now lost (see letter no. 650). It had also described her flowerbeds at Bonniecastle in the Thousand Islands after the first September frosts. The political campaigns of a presidential election year, ED's letter notes, are gathering momentum.

668

To Mrs. Joseph A. Sweetser   *autumn 1880*

Aunt Katie and the Sultans have left the Garden now, and parting with my own, recalls their sweet companionship –

Mine were not I think as exuberant as in other Years – Perhaps the Pelham Water shocked their stately tastes – but cherished avariciously, because less numerous. I trust your Garden was willing to die – I do not think that mine was – it perished with beautiful reluctance, like an evening star –

I hope you were well since we knew of you, and as happy as Sorrow would allow –

There are Sweets of Pathos, when Sweets of Mirth have passed away –

Mother has had a weary Cold, and suffers much from Neuralgia, since the changing Airs, though I trust is no feebler than when you were here –

She has her little pleasures as the patient have – the voices of Friends – and devotion of Home.

The "Ravens" must "cry," to be ministered to – she – need only sigh.

Vinnie knows no shadow – brave – faithful – punctual – and courageous Maggie not yet caught in the snares of Patrick – Perhaps it is quite the Home it was when you last beheld it –

I hope your Few are safe, and your Flowers encouraging –

News of your Sultans and yourself, would be equally lovely, when you feel inclined. Blossoms have their Leisures –

Lovingly,
Emily –

MANUSCRIPT: Jones Library. Pencil.

PUBLICATION: L (1894) 407–408; L (1931) 398–399.

Water was first brought by pipes from Pelham in June 1880. The allusion to ravens is from Psalms 147.9: "He giveth to the beast his food, and to the young ravens which cry."

669

To Louise and Frances Norcross   *1880?*

. . . Did the "stars differ" from each other in anything but "glory," there would be often envy.

The competitions of the sky
Corrodeless ply.

. . . We asked Vinnie to say in the rear of one of her mental products that we had neuralgia, but evidently her theme or her time did not admit of trifles. . . . I forget no part of that sweet, smarting visit, nor even the nettle that stung my rose.

When Macbeth asked the physician what could be done for his wife, he made the mighty answer, "That sort must heal itself;" but, sister, that was guilt, and love, you know, is God, who certainly "gave the love to reward the love," even were there no Browning.

. . . The slips of the last rose of summer repose in kindred soil with waning bees for mates. How softly summer shuts, without the creaking of a door, abroad for evermore.

. . . Vinnie has also added a pilgrim kitten to her flock, which besides being jet black, is, I think, a lineal descendant of the "beautiful hearse horse" recommended to Austin.

MANUSCRIPT: destroyed.

PUBLICATION: L (1894) 285–286; LL 326–327; L (1931) 259–260.

Mrs. Todd placed these extracts together, among letters thought to have been written about 1880. It is not clear whether they are from one letter or from four. The same quotation from *Macbeth* (V, iii, 45–46), is in letters no. 332 and 986; the lines are: "Therein the patient/Must minister to himself." The scripture quotation is from 1 Corinthians 15.41: "There is one glory of the sun, and another glory of the moon, and another glory of the stars: for one star differeth from another star in glory." The line quoted from Browning recalls stanza 4 of "Evelyn Hope":

> No, indeed! for God above
> Is great to grant, as mighty to make,
> And creates the love to reward the love;
> I claim you still for my own love's sake!

670

To Louise and Frances Norcross   *autumn 1880*

. . . God is rather stern with his "little ones." "A cup of cold water in my name" is a shivering legacy February mornings.

. . . Maggie's brother is killed in the mine, and Maggie wants to die, but Death goes far around to those that want to see him. If the little cousins would give her a note – she does not know I ask it – I think it would help her begin, that bleeding beginning that every mourner knows.

MANUSCRIPT: destroyed.
PUBLICATION: L (1894) 287; LL 327–328; L (1931) 260.

Maggie's brother died in September 1880. The "cup of water" quotation is from Matthew 10.42: "And whosoever shall give to drink unto one of these little ones a cup of cold water in the name of a disciple, verily I say unto you, he shall in no wise lose his reward."

671

To Perez Cowan   *October 1880*

Dear Cousin –

The sweet Book found me on my Pillow, where I was detained or I should have thanked you immediately –

The little Creature must have been priceless – Your's, and not your's, how hallowed –

It may have been she came to show you Immortality – Her startling little flight would imply she did –

May I remind you what Paul said, or do you think of nothing else, these October Nights, without her Crib to visit? The little Furniture of Loss has Lips of Dirks to stab us – I hope Heaven is warm – There are so many Barefoot ones – I hope it is near – the little Tourist was so small – I hope it is not so unlike Earth that we shall miss the peculiar form – the Mold of the Bird –

"And with what Body do they come?" –
Then they *do* come – Rejoice!
What Door – What Hour – Run – run – My Soul!
Illuminate the House!

"Body"! Then real – a Face – and Eyes –
To know that it is them! –
Paul knew the Man that knew the News –
He passed through Bethlehem –

With love for you and your sweet wife, "whom seeing not, we" trust.

Cousin Emily –

MANUSCRIPT: HCL. Pencil.
PUBLICATION: L (1894) 334–335; LL 325–326; L (1931) 324.
Cowan's daughter Margaret had died, 8 November 1879. This letter thanks him for a memorial. A notation on a blank page of the letter, entered probably by Cowan, reads: "Oct 11. 1880 After receiving copy of 'The Lamb Folded.'" The first quotation is from 1 Corinthians 15.35: "But some man will say, How are the dead raised up? and with what body do they come?" The final sentence paraphrases the opening of 1 Peter 1.8: "Whom not having seen, ye love. . ." (see also letter no. 747).

672

To Mrs. James S. Cooper   *October 1880*

Dear friend,

Is not the sweet resentment of friends that we are not strong, more inspiriting even than the strength itself?

E Dickinson –

MANUSCRIPT: AC. Pencil.
PUBLICATION: L (1894) 397; L (1931) 386.
ED's illness during the autumn of 1880 was protracted, as several notes written during this period indicate.

673

To Mrs. Edward Tuckerman   *late 1880*

Thank you sweet friend, I am quite better –
Were I not, your dainty redemption would save me –
With love and a happy flower –

Emily –

MANUSCRIPT: AC. Pencil.
PUBLICATION: L (1894) 385; L (1931) 374.
Mrs. Tuckerman dated this letter November 1880.

674

To T. W. Higginson   *November 1880*

Dear friend,

You were once so kind as to say you would advise me – Could I ask it now –

I have promised three Hymns to a charity, but without your approval could not give them –

They are short and I could write them quite plainly, and if you felt it convenient to tell me if they were faithful, I should be very grateful, though if public cares too far fatigue you, please deny

Your Scholar –

MANUSCRIPT: BPL (Higg 110). Pencil.
PUBLICATION: L (1894) 330; LL 324; L (1931) 315–316.
The Annual Sale of the Mission Circle, for the support of children in India and other Far Eastern countries, was held in the First Church, 30

November. The "public cares" refers to the election of Higginson, 4 November, to the Massachusetts legislature.

675

To T. W. Higginson   *November 1880*

Dear friend,

I am tenderly happy that you are happy – Thank you for the Whisper –

If I dared to give the Madonna my love –

The thoughtfulness I may not accept is among my Balms – Grateful for the kindness, I enclose those you allow, adding a fourth, lest one of them you might think profane –

They are Christ's Birthday – Cupid's Sermon – A Humming-Bird – and My Country's Wardrobe –

Reprove them as your own –

To punish them would please me, because the fine conviction I had so true a friend –

Your Scholar –

MANUSCRIPT: Porter. Pencil.
PUBLICATION: *AM* CXXXIX (June 1927) 800; *L* (1931) 314.
The poems enclosed, in the order ED names them, were: "The Savior must have been," "Dare you see a Soul at the White Heat," "A Route of Evanescence," and "My country need not change her gown."

676

To T. W. Higginson   *November 1880*

Dear friend,

Thank you for the advice – I shall implicitly follow it –

The one who asked me for the Lines, I had never seen –

He spoke of "a Charity" – I refused but did not inquire – He again earnestly urged, on the ground that in that way I might "aid unfortunate Children" – The name of "Child" was a snare to me and I hesitated – Choosing my most rudimentary, and without criterion, I inquired of you – You can scarcely estimate the opinion to one utterly guideless –

Again thank you –

Your Scholar –

MANUSCRIPT: BPL (Higg 111). Pencil.
PUBLICATION: AM LXVIII (October 1891) 451; L (1894) 330; LL 324–325; L (1931) 316.
This letter concludes the correspondence with Higginson relative to the selection of poems to be donated to the Mission Circle. One infers that Higginson advised her to offer one or more. Of the persons in Amherst who might have urged ED to contribute poems, the one who most nearly fits the description is Joseph K. Chickering, professor of English in Amherst College. ED in fact never saw him, then or later, though he was especially thoughtful at the time of Mrs. Dickinson's death in 1882. He unsuccessfully tried, more than once, to call on ED. (See letters no. 786 and 798.)

677

To Mrs. Edward Tuckerman   *early December 1880*

Dear friend,

I thought of you, although I never saw your friend.

> Brother of Ophir
> Bright Adieu,
> Honor, the shortest route
> To you –

Emily –

MANUSCRIPT: AC. Pencil.
PUBLICATION: L (1894) 385; LL 332; L (1931) 375.
Mrs. Tuckerman said that this note was sent after the death of Professor Elihu Root, 3 December 1880, aged thirty-five. Root was an unusually promising mathematician.

To Mrs. J. G. Holland   *early December 1880*

Yes, Little Sister – we "thought of you" and had not quite finished, but shall resume at intervals, while you live, and we –

I trust the "Hand" has "ceased from troubling" – it has saved too many to be assailed by an "envious sliver –"

Had we known the Doctor was falling, we had been much alarmed, though Grace – perhaps – is the only hight from which falling is fatal –

Each of us wish the Doctor were stronger – three importunities, tell him, to recover immediately.

The Snow is so white and sudden it seems almost like a Change of Heart – though I dont mean a "Conversion" – I mean a Revolution.

We had a timid Thanksgiving together – Mother did'nt cry much, which pleased us very much – but the Sweet of the Day was in sending a Crumb to a poor fluttering Life, a few Boughs from our own, which will soon pass from our privilege –

The dying of your Kinsman Root, has bereaved the Village – He was exceedingly cherished by both Townsmen and Scholars – and thirteen Cars of Comrades take him Home next Tuesday.

The career of a Taper, I infer, though I never met him –

Austin is much won by his dying – he only knew him technically, till Election Day – when a few moments of sudden honor disclosed his farther Nature – There was great effort to save him, but the "Life saving Service" was impotent –

I trust we are grateful for the Life that sees – and steps – and touches, if it is only the thrilling preface to supremer things – Very lovely in Little Sister to transfer the particulars – Am not unmindful of the Dew or it's fervent circuit –

Fondly,

Emily.

MANUSCRIPT: HCL (H 54). Pencil.
PUBLICATION: *LH* 134–135.
Elihu Root, who died 3 December, was related to Dr. Holland. This letter was written probably on 5 December.

679

To Susan Gilbert Dickinson   *about 1880*

Birthday of but a single pang
That there are less to come –
Afflictive is the Adjective
But affluent the doom –

Emily.

MANUSCRIPT: HCL (B 155). Pencil.
PUBLICATION: AM CXV (1915) 41; *Poems* (1955) 1028.
This was probably sent to Sue as a greeting on her fiftieth birthday,
19 December.

680

To Susan Gilbert Dickinson   *about 1880*

Thank Susan for the lovely Supper, and "thy Son – Our" Nephew,
for bringing it.

Emily.

MANUSCRIPT: HCL (B 92). Pencil. Unpublished.
The date is conjectured from the handwriting.

681

To Mrs. Henry Hills   *late 1880*

The little Annual Creatures solicit your regard.

MANUSCRIPT: missing. The text has the same provenance as that of
letter no. 376.
PUBLICATION: L (1894) 400; L (1931) 389.
Mrs. Todd's note reads: "With Christmas delicacies."

682

To Sally Jenkins   *late December 1880*

Dear "Did" –

Atmospherically it was the most beautiful Christmas on record –

[684]

The Hens came to the Door with Santa Claus, and the Pussies washed themselves in the open Air without chilling their Tongues – and Santa Claus himself – sweet old Gentleman, was even gallanter than usual – Visitors from the Chimney were a new dismay, but all of them brought their Hands so full, and behaved so sweetly – only a Churl could have turned them away – And then the ones at the Barn, were so happy – Maggie gave her Hens a Check for Potatoes, and each of the Cats a Gilt Edged Bone – and the Horses had both new Blankets from Boston – Do you remember Dark Eyed Mr – Dickinson, who used to shake your Hand when it was so little it had hardly a Stem – He too had a beautiful Gift of Roses – from a friend away –

It was a lovely Christmas –

Please give my love to your Father and Mother – and the "Lantern" Brother, and the Lad unknown – But what made you remember me? Tell me, with a kiss, or is it a secret?

Emily –

Manuscript: HCL (L 36). Pencil.
Publication: L (1894) 371, in part; LL 295, in part; FN 63, in part; L (1931) 362, in part.
The "Lad unknown" is Austin Dickinson Jenkins, born in January 1879. Sally ("Did") was about fourteen; her brother Mac (MacGregor), eleven.

683

To Mrs. J. G. Holland   *28 December 1880*

Was it the Brother –

Was it the Sister –

Was it the Two One – that conflicting Numeral? Not in this instance conflicting – Oh No. Cupid forbid!

The Honey reached us yesterday –

Honey not born of Bee – but Constancy – which is "far better –" I can scarcely tell you the sweetness it woke, nor the sweetness it stilled –

Grieving for "George Eliot" – grieved for Dr Smith, our Family Savior, living Fingers that are left, have a strange warmth –

It is deep to live to experience "And there was no more Sea" – the Fathom though is a daily one and traversed by the simplest Child – I hope you are both hopeful –

My Two give you their love, and my part of one, her docile respects —

I trust Doctor is stronger.

"As thy Day so shall thy Strength be" is an elastic ratio.

Please "consider" me — An antique request, though in behalf of Lilies –

Lovingly,

Emily.

MANUSCRIPT: HCL (H 55). Pencil. Dated: Tuesday.
PUBLICATION: *LH* 136–137.

Dr. David P. Smith, a lecturer at the Yale Medical School, was an esteemed citizen of Springfield, and his death on Sunday, 26 December, was poignantly noted throughout the Connecticut Valley. He had been a consultant physician for the Dickinsons for some years.

This brief letter is freighted with scripture quotation, allusion, and paraphrase. The first quotation has in mind Philippians 1.23: "For I am in a strait betwixt two, having a desire to depart, and to be with Christ: which is far better." The second quotes the conclusion of Revelation 21.1: "And I saw a new heaven and a new earth: for the first heaven and the first earth were passed away; and there was no more sea." From Deuteronomy 33.25, comes the line: ". . . and, as thy days, so shall thy strength be." The conclusion of the letter alludes to Matthew 6.28: "Consider the lilies of the field. . ."

684

To Mrs. Edward Tuckerman   *1 January 1881*

Saturday –

My Bird – Who is "Today"?
"Yesterday" was a Year ago, and yet,

The stem of a departed Flower
Has still a silent rank.

[686]

The Bearer from an Emerald Court
Of a Despatch of Pink.

Thank you for the lovely Love.

Emily –

MANUSCRIPT: AAS. Pencil.
PUBLICATION: L (1894) 386; LL 333; L (1931) 375.
This acknowledges Mrs. Tuckerman's annual New Year's greeting. In
1881 the day fell on Saturday.

685

To Mrs. J. G. Holland   *early January 1881*

Sister Golconda must look very burnished in her Christmas Gifts,
and the bashful Gem that the Scripture enjoins, "a meek and lowly
Spirit," must be quite obscured – but one must clad demurely to please
the Scripture's taste, a very plain Old Gentleman, with few Expenses
out –

Your sweet light-hearted manner informed me more than statements, that the Doctor was better – the inferential Knowledge – the
distinctest one, and I congratulate you – and not omit ourselves –

How sweet the "Life that now is," and how rugged to leave it –
and ruggeder to stay behind when our Dear go –

A Little Boy ran away from Amherst a few Days ago, and when
asked where he was going, replied, "Vermont or Asia." Many of us
go farther. My pathetic Crusoe –

Vinnie had four Pussies for Christmas Gifts – and two from her
Maker, previous, making six, in toto, and finding Assassins for them,
is my stealthy Aim – Mother, we think unchanged – Vinnie's ideal
"Irons" in the ideal "Fire" and me, prancing between – a Gymnastic
Destiny –

Vails of Kamtchatka dim the Rose – in my Puritan Garden, and
as a farther stimulus, I had an Eclipse of the Sun a few Mornings ago,
but every Crape is charmed –

I knew a Bird that would sing as firm in the centre of Dissolution,
as in it's Father's nest –

[687]

Phenix, or the Robin?
While I leave you to guess, I will take Mother her Tea –
Emily.

MANUSCRIPT: HCL (H 56). Pencil.
PUBLICATION: LH 137–138.
Dr. Holland had given his wife a pair of diamond earrings for Christmas. The *Amherst Record* for 29 December reports the disappearance of Jerry Scanlan (Scannell), aged fourteen. A few days later he turned up in Springfield. The new year opened with a few days of intense cold. There had been a partial eclipse of the sun on 31 December.
The "lowly Spirit" alludes to Matthew 11.29.

686

To Mrs. Henry D. Fearing   *about January 1881*

Nectar in January is as unexpected as charming. Will Mrs Fearing accept the thanks which are a faint requital, with the Affection of each?
E. Dickinson.

MANUSCRIPT: Jones Library. Pencil. Unpublished.
The date is conjectured from the handwriting.

687

To Mrs. J. G. Holland   *early 1881*

A Letter was lying warm in my Pocket for my Little Sister, when her Letter came, but had delayed a Night for Vinnie, as is the melancholy case in many instances – I feel so punctual hearted I think I cannot wait, but an appeal from Vinnie, and I will sit in Love's Back Seat, and let the Horses walk –

I am glad that the dear Doctor has the Angel Wife, and not the Bride of Socrates to frown at tired Strength and make the weakness lonely – and *Prudence* is a tedious one, and needs beguiling – too – "Give me Liberty or give me Death" has a willful meaning – but never mind the "Liberty" for a few wise Days, then Doctor can "go Barefoot," and rollick with the best of us –

[688]

You always seemed to me like David and Goliath, and if Goliath is not as strong, David is needed more, but David is competent — in his – her – small – pathetic Hands, there is strength for both – The latent Sinew of the Love is faithful when 'tis called, and let it lurk till then –

I ask Mother "what message" she sends – She says, "Tell them I wish I could take them both in my Arms and carry them –"

I never before have heard her speak so – those were the very words –

Will you let me take hold of your Hand to lead this little Note to the Mail?

Keeping you and the Doctor in beloved thought – you know who I am –

MANUSCRIPT: HCL (H 57). Pencil.
PUBLICATION: *LH* 139–140.
The letter enclosed a note to be forwarded, presumably to Dr. Wadsworth.

688

To Susan Gilbert Dickinson   *early 1881*

Thank you, Sue – I was glad to read it –

Perhaps she who Experienced Eternity in Time, may receive Time's omitted Gift as part of the Bounty of Eternity –

Emily –

MANUSCRIPT: HCL (B 142). Pencil. Addressed: Susan.
PUBLICATION: *FF* 254.
This may acknowledge some critical notice Susan had sent ED about George Eliot, who died, 26 December 1880 (see letter no. 710).

689

To Mrs. J. G. Holland   *early spring 1881*

Dear Sister,

Spring, and not a Blue Bird, but I have seen a Crow – "in his own Body on the Tree," almost as prima facie –

They love such outlawed Trees –

[689]

An Antiquated Tree
Is cherished of the Crow
Because that Junior Foliage is desrespectful now
To venerable Birds
Whose Corporation Coat
Would decorate Oblivion's
Remotest Consulate.

Could you condone the profanity?
We have had two Hurricanes since the "Ides of March," and one of them came near enough to untie My Apron – a boldness please resent –

Mother is lying changeless on her changeless Bed, hoping a little, and fearing much – Vinnie in Bliss' Catalogue, prospecting for Summer –

You and I can content ourselves with only "Bliss" itself. What a parsimony! Maggie, good and noisy, the North Wind of the Family, but Sweets without a Salt would at last cloy –

The Neighborhood are much amused by the "Fair Barbarian" and Emily's Scribner is perused by all the Boys and Girls.

Even the Cynic Austin confessed himself amused –

I hope the Little Sister's Eyes have refrained from sighing – and very often carry them to the "Throne" of Tenderness – the only God I know – and if I take her too, it does'nt break My Basket, though Fondness' untold Load does tire rugged Baskets some –

I hope that nothing makes you afraid. Give my Heart to each, and my slim Circumference to her who often shared it –

Lovingly,

Emily.

MANUSCRIPT: HCL (H 59). Pencil.
PUBLICATION: LH 141–142.
The quotation in the first sentence is from 1 Peter 2.24, where it is used in a very different context: "Who his own self bare our sins in his own body on the tree, that we, being dead to sins, should live unto righteousness: by whose stripes ye were healed." Frances Hodgson Burnett's *The Fair Barbarian* was published serially in *Scribner's Monthly* during the first quarter of 1881.

To Louise and Frances Norcross   *early spring 1881*

The divine deposit came safely in the little bank. We have heard of the "deeds of the spirit," but are his acts gamboge and pink? A morning call from Gabriel is always a surprise. Were we more fresh from Eden we were expecting him – but Genesis is a "far journey." Thank you for the loveliness.

We have had two hurricanes within as many hours, one of which came near enough to untie my apron – but this moment the sun shines, Maggie's hens are warbling, and a man of anonymous wits is making a garden in the lane to set out slips of bluebird. The moon grows from the seed. . . Vinnie's pussy slept in grass Wednesday – a Sicilian symptom – the sails are set for summer, East India Wharf. Sage and saucy ones talk of an equinoctial, and are trying the chimneys, but I am "short of hearing," as the deaf say. Blessed are they that play, for theirs is the kingdom of heaven. Love like a rose from each one, and Maggie's a Burgundy one she ardently asks.

Emily.

MANUSCRIPT: destroyed.
PUBLICATION: L (1894) 287–288; LL 328; L (1931) 261.
The date of this letter is made certain by the identical phrasing used about two hurricanes which, she says, untied her apron. The note thanks the cousins for a gift of bulbs. The letter following tells them that the bulbs have been planted.

To Louise and Frances Norcross   *mid-April 1881*

The dear ones will excuse – they knew there was a cause. Emily was sick, and Vinnie's middle name [Norcross] restrained her loving pen.

These are my first words since I left my pillow – that will make them faithful, although so long withheld. We had another fire – it was in Phoenix Row, Monday a week ago, at two in the night. The horses were harnessed to move the office – Austin's office, I mean. After a night of terror, we went to sleep for a few moments, and I could not rise. The others bore it better. The brook from Pelham saved the town. The wind was blowing so, it carried the burning shingles as far as Tom's piazza. We are weak and grateful. The fire-bells are oftener now, almost, than the church-bells. Thoreau would wonder which did the most harm.

The little gifts came sweetly. The bulbs are in the sod – the seeds in homes of paper till the sun calls them. It is snowing now. . . . "Fine sleighing we have this summer," says Austin with a scoff. The box of dainty ones – I don't know what they were, buttons of spice for coats of honey – pleased the weary mother. Thank you each for all.

The beautiful words for which Loo asked were that genius is the ignition of affection – not intellect, as is supposed, – the exaltation of devotion, and in proportion to our capacity for that, is our experience of genius. Precisely as they were uttered I cannot give them, they were in a letter that I do not find, but the suggestion was this.

It is startling to think that the lips, which are keepers of thoughts so magical, yet at any moment are subject to the seclusion of death.

. . . I must leave you, dear, to come perhaps again, –

We never know we go – when we are going
We jest and shut the door –
Fate following behind us bolts it
And we accost no more.

I give you my parting love.

Emily.

MANUSCRIPT: destroyed.
PUBLICATION: L (1894) 289–290; LL 329–330; L (1931) 262–263.

The fire occurred on Monday, 4 April 1881. Mrs. Todd left a space between the paragraph concluding with "the seclusion of death," and the section following. The ending does not seem to be a part of this letter, since it addresses but one person.

692

To Mrs. J. G. Holland   *spring 1881*

Dear Sister.

We are making a few simple repairs, what Dickens would call

qualifications and aspects – and looking in Vinnie's Basket for the Lightning Rod, which she had mislaid, "What *would* Mrs Holland think" said Vinnie?

"I would inquire," I said.

I can always rely on your little Laugh, which is what the Essayist calls "the immortal Peewee."

Did you know that Father's "Horace" had died – the "Cap'n Cuttle" of Amherst? He had lived with us always, though was not congenial – so his loss is a pang to Tradition, rather than Affection – I am sure you remember him – He is the one who spoke patronizingly of the Years, of Trees he sowed in "26," or Frosts he met in "20," and was so legendary that it seems like the death of the College Tower, our first Antiquity – I remember he was at one time disinclined to gather the Winter Vegetables till they had frozen, and when Father demurred, he replied "Squire, ef the Frost is the Lord's Will, I dont popose to stan in the way of it." I hope a nearer inspection of that "Will" has left him with as ardent a bias in it's favor.

Vinnie is under terrific headway, but finds time to remember you with vivid affection – and Mother is unchanged, though my new gratitude every morning, that she is still with us, convinces me of her frailty.

Vinnie is eager to see the Face of George Eliot which the Doctor promised, and I wince in prospective, lest it be no more sweet. God chooses repellant settings, dont he, for his best Gems?

All you will say of yourselves is dear to Emily and Vinnie, and is'nt to say it soon – prudent – in so short a Life?

MANUSCRIPT: HCL (H 60). Pencil.

PUBLICATION: LH 143–144.

Horace Church, gardener and sexton of the First Church, died, 7 April 1881. Higginson's essay "The Life of Birds," published in the *Atlantic Monthly*, September, 1862, has the sentence: "And penetrating to some yet lonelier place, we find it consecrated to that life-long sorrow . . . which is made immortal in the plaintive cadence of the Peewee-Flycatcher." Cap'n Cuttle is a character in *Dombey and Son*. The picture of George Eliot which Dr. Holland had promised may have been the one used as a frontispiece in the first issue of the *Century Magazine*, November 1881, which Holland was preparing for the press.

To Louise and Frances Norcross 1881?

My dear little cousins,

I bring you a robin who is eating a remnant oat on the sill of the barn. The horse was not as hungry as usual, leaving an ample meal for his dulcet friend. . . .

Maggie was charmed with her donkeys, and has long been talking of writing, but has not quite culminated. They stand on the dining-room side-board, by the side of an orange, and a *Springfield Republican*. It will please you to know that the clover in the bill of the brown one is fresh as at first, notwithstanding the time, though the only "pastures" I know gifted with that duration, are far off as the psalms.

Mr. C—— called with a twilight of you. It reminded me of a supper I took, with the pictures on Dresden china. Vinnie asked him "what he had for supper," and he said he "could easier describe the nectar of the gods." . . . We read in a tremendous Book about "an enemy," and armed a confidential fort to scatter him away. The time has passed, and years have come, and yet not any "Satan." I think he must be making war upon some other nation.

Emily.

MANUSCRIPT: destroyed.
PUBLICATION:L (1894) 288–289; LL 328–329; L (1931) 261–262.
Mrs. Todd dated the letter 1881.

To Mrs. William F. Stearns *May 1881*

Dear friend,

I hope you may know with what unspeakable tenderness we think of you and your dear child.

Were it any kingdom but the "Kingdom of Heaven," how distant! But my heart breaks – I can say no more.

E. D.

MANUSCRIPT: missing.
PUBLICATION: L (1894) 406; L (1931) 396.
Mrs. Stearns's son William ("Willie") died of tuberculosis at Colorado Springs, 12 May 1881.

695

To Otis P. Lord   *1881?*

[*scrap 1*]

My little devices to live till Monday would woo (win) your sad attention – (fill your eyes with Dew) – Full of work and plots and little hap-
pinesses the thought of you protracts (derides) them all and makes
them sham and cold.

> How fleet – how indiscreet an one –
> how always wrong is Love –
> The joyful little Deity
> We are not scourged to serve –

[*scrap 2*]

My little devices to live till Monday would darken all your glee – for
you have a good deal of glee (many a glee) in your nature's corners
the most lurking – and never to be trusted as Brown said of sleep – without ones prayers –

MANUSCRIPTS: AC. Pencil. Fragment drafts.
PUBLICATION: *Revelation* 94.
The date is conjectured from the handwriting.

696

To Louise Norcross   *1881?*

Dear Loo,

    Thank you, with love, for the kindness; it would be very sweet to
claim if we needed it, but we are quite strong, and mother well as
usual, and Vinnie spectacular as Disraeli and sincere as Gladstone, –
was only sighing in fun. When she sighs in earnest, Emily's throne
will tremble, and she will need both Loo and Fanny; but Vinnie "still
prevails." When one or all of us are lain on "*Marian Erle's* dim pallet,"
so cool that she deplored to live because that she must leave it, Loo and
the ferns, and Fanny and her fan shall supplement the angels, if they
have not already joined them.

> Lovingly,
>
> Emily.

MANUSCRIPT: destroyed.
PUBLICATION: L (1894) 292–293; L (1931) 265.
Mrs. Todd placed the letter with others written in 1881. The quotation is from Mrs. Browning's *Aurora Leigh.*

697

To Mrs. Richard H. Mather   *about 1881*

Permit me to duplicate the presumption —

E. Dickinson.

MANUSCRIPT: Mather. Pencil. Unpublished.
The date is conjectured from the handwriting. Professor Mather's first wife died in 1877. He married again in March 1881. ED never saw the second Mrs. Mather, but they were near neighbors and from time to time exchanged tokens of friendship, such as flowers or an oven delicacy. This note may have initiated the exchange, for it implies that Mrs. Mather had "presumed" to send a small gift which ED acknowledges in kind. Mrs. Mather may have sent flowers at the time of ED's illness in April.

698

To Mrs. Henry Hills   *about 1881*

Tropics, and Dairies, and Fairies! Thank the "Arabian Nights."

Emily.

MANUSCRIPT: missing. The text has the same provenance as that of letter no. 376.
PUBLICATION: L (1894) 400; L (1931) 389.

699

To Mrs. Henry Hills   *about 1881*

With a kiss and a flower, one of which will endure. I am whom you infer —

MANUSCRIPT: missing. The text has the same provenance as that of letter no. 376.
PUBLICATION: L (1894) 401; LL 335; L (1931) 389.

700

To Mr. and Mrs. George Montague   1881?

Dear Cousin,

Thank you for the delightful cake, and the heart adjacent.

Emily.

MANUSCRIPT: missing.
PUBLICATION: L (1894) 405; L (1931) 395.
This and the five letters which follow, all written to the George Montagues, are grouped by Mrs. Todd and dated: 1881? They are similarly grouped here, for they probably were written during this period of years when George Montague was addressing ED's letters for her, and wrapping and mailing her parcels. A note from him is preserved among ED's papers (AC) because she used the back of it to set down a draft of "How happy is the little stone." It reads:

> Cousin Emily will please forgive me, — I have made a blemish and a mistake on *two* of her envelopes, & have substituted two of mine, which I am sorry to say, are not quite so nice. If they will do, I shall be glad.
>
> Cousin G.

701

To Mr. and Mrs. George Montague   1881?

Delicate as bread of flowers. How sweetly we thank you!

MANUSCRIPT: missing.
PUBLICATION: L (1894) 405; L (1931) 395.

702

To George Montague   1881?

To have "been faithful in a few things" was the delicate compliment paid one by God. Could I not commend a rarer candidate for his approval in my loyal Cousin?

MANUSCRIPT: missing.
PUBLICATION: L (1894) 406; LL 334; L (1931) 395.

703

To Mr. and Mrs. George Montague   *1881?*

Which will I thank – the perpetrator, the propagator, or the almoner of the delightful bread – or may I compromise and thank them all?

I for the first time appreciate the exultation of the robin toward a crumb, though he must be a seductive robin, with whom I would share my own.

With the hope to requite the loveliness is a future way,

Gratefully,

Emily.

MANUSCRIPT: missing.
PUBLICATION: L (1894) 406; L (1931) 396.

704

To Mr. and Mrs. George Montague   *1881?*

We trust the dear friend is convalescing.
These loveliest of days are certainly with that design.

Emily.

MANUSCRIPT: missing.
PUBLICATION: L (1894) 405; L (1931) 395.

705

To George Montague   *1881?*

Dear Cousin,

The "Golden Rule" is so lovely, it needs no police to enforce it.

Cousin.

MANUSCRIPT: missing.
PUBLICATION: L (1894) 406; LL 333; L (1931) 395.

706

To Mrs. James S. Cooper   about 1881

Dear friend,

The thoughtfulness was picturesque and the glimpse delightful –
The Residence of Vinnie's friends could but be fair, to me.

And will you in exchange, accept a View of *my* House, which
Nature painted White, without consulting me – but Nature is "old-
fashioned," perhaps a Puritan –

E – Dickinson –

MANUSCRIPT: AC. Pencil.
PUBLICATION: L (1894) 396; L (1931) 385.

The Coopers moved to a new house about June 1879. ED evidently
enclosed a poem with the letter. One conjectures it may have been her
"Snow," as she titled a copy that she sent Thomas Niles in March 1882,
beginning "It sifts from Leaden Sieves."

707

To Susan Gilbert Dickinson   about 1881

Susan –

To thank one for Sweetness, is possible, but for Spaciousness, out
of sight –

The Competition of Phantoms is inviolate –

Emily.

MANUSCRIPT: HCL (B 138). Pencil.
PUBLICATION: FF 237.

This and the two following notes to Susan are all in the handwriting
of about 1881.

[699]

To Susan Gilbert Dickinson   *about 1881*

"Boast not" myself "of Tomorrow" for I "knowest not what a" Noon "may bring forth" —

MANUSCRIPT: YUL. Pencil.
PUBLICATION: *LL* 62.
This paraphrases Proverbs 27.1: "Boast not thyself of tomorrow; for thou knowest not what a day may bring forth."

To Susan Gilbert Dickinson   *about 1881*

Balm for Susan's Voice – Could sooner spare the Nightingale's –
                               Emily.

MANUSCRIPT: HCL (B 116). Pencil.
PUBLICATION: *FF* 230.

To Louise and Frances Norcross   *about 1881?*

. . . The look of the words [stating the death of George Eliot] as they lay in the print I shall never forget. Not their face in the casket could have had the eternity to me. Now, *my* George Eliot. The gift of belief which her greatness denied her, I trust she receives in the child-hood of the kingdom of heaven. As childhood is earth's confiding time, perhaps having no childhood, she lost her way to the early trust, and no later came. Amazing human heart, a syllable can make to quake like jostled tree, what infinite for thee? . . .

MANUSCRIPT: destroyed.
PUBLICATION: *L* (1894) 286–287; *LL* 327; *L* (1931) 260.
ED poignantly felt the death of George Eliot (see letter no. 688). Because the last sentence is identical with one in a letter to Dr. Holland, written in the summer of 1881 (no. 715), one conjectures that the two letters were written about the same time.

To Gilbert Dickinson   *about 1881*

Gilbert asked a little Plant of Aunt Emily, once, to carry to his
Teacher – but Aunt Emily was asleep – so Maggie gave him one instead – Aunt Emily waked up now, and brought this little Plant all the
way from her Crib for Gilbert to carry to his Teacher – Good Night –
Aunt Emily's asleep again –

MANUSCRIPT: HCL (L 49). Pencil. Unpublished.

To Gilbert Dickinson   *about 1881*

For Gilbert to carry to his Teacher –

    The Bumble Bee's Religion –

    His little Hearse like Figure
    Unto itself a Dirge
    To a delusive Lilac
    The vanity divulge
    Of Industry and Morals
    And every righteous thing
    For the divine Perdition
    Of Idleness and Spring –

"All Liars shall have their part" –
Jonathan Edwards –
"And let him that is athirst come" –
Jesus –

MANUSCRIPT: HCL (B 177). Pencil. Addressed: Gilbert.
PUBLICATION: AM CXV (1915) 38–39; LL 60; Poems (1955) 1050.
It is said to have been accompanied by a dead bee.

To George Montague   *early July 1881*
Will Cousin George be so kind as to address and mail the enclosed
to
Dr Holland
Alexandria Bay
New York,
and thank Cousin Sarah and himself for the kindness of last night and
this morning.
                                                              Cousin.

MANUSCRIPT: missing. Unpublished.
The text derives from a transcript (AC) made by Mrs. Todd in the
1890's, when she was preparing the *Letters* (1894). An envelope is dated:
"July 1 or 2, 1881." Montague's function as ED's mailing assistant is explained in the note to letter no. 700.
There is a possible sequence in this and the two letters following. The
note here enclosed for Dr. Holland may have been the question in the
note to Sue that follows.

714

To Susan Gilbert Dickinson   *about 1881*

Doctor –
How did you snare Howells?
                                                              Emily –
"Emily –
Case of Bribery – Money did it –
                              Holland –["]

MANUSCRIPT: HCL (B 17). Pencil.
PUBLICATION: LL 83, altered.
The date is conjectured from the handwriting. During the summer of
1881 William D. Howells's novel *A Fearful Responsibility* was appearing
in installment in Holland's *Scribner's Monthly*. ED's note to Dr. Holland
probably elicited the reply here quoted to Sue. The letter following, to Dr.
Holland, seems to answer it.

To Dr. J. G. Holland   *about 1881*

Dear Doctor,

Your small Note was as merry as Honey, and enthralled us all –
I sent it over to Sue, who took Ned's Arm and came across – and we
talked of Mr Samuel and you, and vital times when you two bore the
Republican, and came as near sighing – all of us – as would be often
wise – I should say next door – Sue said she was homesick for those
"better Days," hallowed be their name.

Amazing Human Heart – a syllable can make to quake like jostled
Tree – what Infinite – for thee!

I wish you were rugged, and rejoice you are gay, and am re-con-
vinced by your arch note that Unless we become as Rogues, we cannot
enter the Kingdom of Heaven –

Emily.

MANUSCRIPT: HCL (H 58). Pencil.
PUBLICATION: *LH* 140–141.

This was evidently written shortly after ED received the "small Note,"
a copy of which she sent over to Sue. There is a hint toward the end of the
first paragraph, which ED knew would be clear to the Hollands, that the
stresses at the house next door have not abated.

716

To George Montague   *early August 1881*

Could I perhaps have the address of Mrs. Samuel Bowles, Springfield, and Judge Lord

Crawford House
White Mountains,

and will Cousin, if walking today, please call, as I have a trifle for
Cousin Sarah, which I fear to entrust to what Gilbert calls the "Cloudy
Man"?

MANUSCRIPT: missing. Unpublished.

The text (AC) has the same provenance as letter no. 713. It is dated
"August 4, 1881." The letter enclosed to be addressed to Judge Lord is

not identifiable. That for Mrs. Bowles is missing, but elicited a reply to which no. 724 is an answer. The "Cloudy Man" is the "new Black Man" of letter no. 721.

717

To MacGregor Jenkins   *about August 1881*

Dear Boys –

Please never grow up, which is "far better" – Please never "improve" — you are perfect now.

Emily.

MANUSCRIPT: HCL. Pencil.
PUBLICATION: *L* (1894) 370; *LL* 280; *FN* 53; *L* (1931) 361.
The date, conjectured from the handwriting, is confirmed by a report in the *Amherst Record* for 5 August 1881: "Rev. J. L. Jenkins and family are stopping in town, the guests of W. A. Dickinson." MacGregor was twelve years old. This note was evidently sent at that time, as was the following note to Sally Jenkins, aged fifteen.

718

To Sally Jenkins   *about August 1881*

"Little Women –"

Which shall it be, Geranium or Juleps?

The Butterfly upon the Sky
That does'nt know it's Name
And has'nt any tax to pay
And has'nt any Home
Is just as high as you and I,
And higher, I believe,
So soar away and never sigh
And that's the way to grieve —

MANUSCRIPT: Squires. Pencil. Addressed on fold: Sallie and Mattie —
PUBLICATION: *L* (1894) 370; *LL* 280; *FN* 57–58; *L* (1931) 361.

Mrs. Grant Squires (Sally Jenkins) presented an envelope to HCL addressed: "Did" and Mattie. She thought it had contained this note. She wrote on the verso of the envelope (and it now contains the card): "Emily Dickinson's calling card — used when she called on Mrs. Adams Allen in Amherst — and given me by Adele Allen —"

719

To Jonathan L. Jenkins and family   *about 1881*

Dear friends,

    You have our sympathy. When an old friend like the Decalogue, turns his back on us, who then can we trust?

                                     Emily.

MANUSCRIPT: HCL (L 47). Pencil.
PUBLICATION: FN 98–99.
ED pasted this unidentified clipping onto the letter:

> John Jenkins, hailing from Philadelphia, was arrested at Baltimore yesterday on charge of passing counterfeit half and quarter-dollar pieces, and 200 pieces of counterfeit coin were found on his person. It is suspected that he is employed by a gang of counterfeiters.

720

To recipient unknown   *about 1881*

    "Let me go for the day breaketh."

MANUSCRIPT: AC. Pencil. Unpublished.

    This autograph did not leave ED's desk, for she used the verso to jot the draft of the poem " 'Secrets' is a daily word." The words are those of the angel wrestling with Jacob (Genesis 32.26): "And he said, Let me go, for the day breaketh. And he said, I will not let thee go, except thou bless me." (See letters no. 1035 and 1042.)

To Mrs. J. G. Holland   *August 1881*

Dear Sister.

I think everything will get ripe today so it can be Autumn tomorrow if it would like, for such heat was never present and I think of your Forest and Sea as a far off Sherbet.

We have an artificial Sea, and to see the Birds follow the Hose for a Crumb of Water is a touching Sight. They wont take it if I hand it to them – they run and shriek as if they were being assassinated, but oh, to steal it, that is bliss – I cant say that their views are not current.

When I look in the Morning Paper to see how the President is, I know you are looking too, and for once in the Day I am sure where you are, which is very friendly.

The Pilgrim's Empire seems to stoop – I hope it will not fall –

We have a new Black Man and are looking for a Philanthropist to direct him, because every time he presents himself, I run, and when the Head of the Nation shies, it confuses the Foot –

When you read in the "Massachusetts items" that he has eaten us up, a memorial merriment will invest these preliminaries.

Who wrote Mr Howells' story? Certainly he did not. Shakespeare was never accused of writing Bacon's works, though to have been suspected of writing his, was the most beautiful stigma of Bacon's Life – Higher, is the doom of the High.

Doctor's betrothal to "Blanco" I trust you bear unmurmuringly. Mother and Vinnie wept – I read it to both at their request –

Thank you for surviving the duplicity – Thank you for not stopping being anxious about us. Not to outgrow Suspense, is beloved indeed.

                                                            Emily.

MANUSCRIPT: HCL (H 61). Pencil.
PUBLICATION: LH 145–146.
President Garfield, shot on 2 July, lingered through the summer and died, 19 September. On Howells's *A Fearful Responsibility*, which ED was finding not to her taste, see letter no. 714. The August issue of *Scribner's Monthly*, in which the Howells novel was concluded, also contained a poem by Holland: "To My Dog Blanco."

To Susan Gilbert Dickinson   *late summer 1881*

It was like a breath from Gibraltar to hear your voice again, Sue –
Your impregnable syllables need no prop, to stand –
The Loaf for Ned, I will send Wednesday evening, unless he
prefer before – If he would, let him whisper to me –

Emily –

MANUSCRIPT: HCL (B 89). Pencil. Addressed on the fold: Susan.
PUBLICATION: LL 79, in part; FF 241, in part.
The date is conjectured from the handwriting. One surmises that Sue
had returned from summer vacation, and that Ned, who was just entering
Amherst College, had asked for the bread for some special occasion.

To Mrs. J. G. Holland   *late summer 1881*

Dear Sister,

What must you have thought that no one wrote? My Will did
write immediately, but friends who were boarding at the Hotel claimed
evey moment that Duty could give till this Moment's Mail –
Thank you for apprizing us of the sweet Disaster in your family,
which I trust you will meet as you meet all, with sunny heroism – and
present our beatific congratulations to Annie. The impulse to write
her myself, is strong as gravitation, but I know how busy the Heart
is when it is very busy, and think it unkind to disturb her – Cupid
still drives the Pink Coupe he did when we were Children, though I
fear his affecting toils are not what Mrs Micawber would call "re-
munerative –" I rejoice that Annie is happy –
To flee from the "Family Tree" is an innovation, but Birds are
predatory – I am glad that you feel so sweetly toward the invading
powers –
If the "Ark of the Lord" must be "taken," one has a choice in the
Foe.
Your picture of Doctor was very ensnaring, but I remembered my
rectitudes – though Vinnie, even at this distance, is captivated by the
Dog –

Fascination is portable.

Today is parched and handsome, though the Grass is the color of Statesmen's Shoes, and only the Butterfly rises to the situation –

His little Body glistens with crispness – an ell of rapture to an inch of Wing –

I hope my little Sister is well, and her Best better, and be sure we are glad of the Happiness and each give it our love –

Emily.

MANUSCRIPT: HCL (H). Pencil.
PUBLICATION: *LH* 147–148.

Mrs. Holland had evidently sent a photograph of Dr. Holland with his dog Blanco. The announcement of the engagement of Annie Holland to John Howe of Troy, New York, was made during the summer. The story of the capture of the Ark of the Covenant by the Philistines is in 1 Samuel 4.

724

To Mrs. Samuel Bowles　　　　　　　　　　　　　*6 September 1881*

Dear Mary,

I give you only a word this mysterious morning in which we must light the lamps to see each other's faces, thanking you for the trust too confiding for speech.

You spoke of enclosing the face of your child. As it was not there, forgive me if I tell you, lest even the copy of sweetness abscond; and may I trust you received the flower the mail promised to take you, my foot being incompetent?

The timid mistake about being "forgotten," shall I caress or reprove? Mr. Samuel's "sparrow" does not "fall" without the fervent "notice."

"Would you see us, would Vinnie?" Oh, my doubting Mary! Were you and your brave son in my father's house, it would require more prowess than mine to resist seeing you.

Shall I still hope for the picture? And please address to my full name, as the little note was detained and opened, the name being so frequent in town, though not an Emily but myself.

[708]

Vinnie says "give her my love, and tell her I would delight to see her;" and mother combines.

There should be no tear on your cheek, dear, had my hand the access to brush it away.

Emily.

MANUSCRIPT: missing.
PUBLICATION: L (1894) 227; LL 331; L (1931) 212, where it is dated "Tuesday."

The phenomenon which ED records, known as "yellow day," occurred on Tuesday, 6 September 1881. The allusion to the sparrow recalls one of Hamlet's final remarks (*Hamlet*, V, ii, 229–233): ". . . there's a special providence in the fall of a sparrow. . . The readiness is all. . . ."

725

To Mrs. Edward Tuckerman   *6 September 1881*

To find my sweet friend is more difficult than to bless her, though I trust both are slightly possible this dearest Afternoon –

Emily.

MANUSCRIPT: Esty. Pencil.
PUBLICATION: L (1894) 386; L (1931) 375.

Frederick Tuckerman, a nephew who lived with the Tuckermans, married Alice Girdler Cooper, 6 September 1881. The Rev. J. L. Jenkins came from Pittsfield to perform the ceremony.

726

To Mrs. Samuel Bowles   *September 1881*

Dear Mary,

To have been the mother of the beautiful face, is of itself fame, and the look of Arabia in the eyes is like Mr. Samuel. "Mr. Samuel" is his memorial name. "Speak, that we may see thee," and Gabriel no more ideal than his swift eclipse. Thank you for the beauty, which I reluctantly return and feel like committing a "startling fraud" in that sweet direction. If her heart is as magical as her face, she will wreck many a spirit, but the sea is ordained.

Austin looked at her long and earnestly.

"Yes, it is Sam's child." His Cashmere confederate. It is best, dear, you have so much to do. Action is redemption.

"And again a little while and ye shall not see me," Jesus confesses is temporary.

Thank you indeed.

Emily.

MANUSCRIPT: missing.

PUBLICATION: L (1894) 227–228; LL 332; L (1931) 212–213.

The letter acknowledges receipt of the photograph mentioned in letter no. 724. The final quotation recalls John 16.16: "A little while, and ye shall not see me: and again, a little while, and ye shall see me, because I go to the Father."

727

To Louise and Frances Norcross   *24 September 1881*

Dear Ones,

If I linger, this will not reach you before Sunday; if I do not, I must write you much less than I would love. "Do unto others as ye would that they should do unto you." I would rather they would do unto me *so*.

After infinite wanderings the little note has reached us. It was mailed the twelfth – we received it the twenty-third. The address "Misses Dickinson" misled the rustic eyes – the postmaster knows Vinnie, also by faith who Emily is, because his little girl was hurt, and Emily sent her juleps – but he failed of the intellectual grasp to combine the names. So after sending it to all the *Mrs.* Dickinsons he could discover, he consigned it to us, with the request that we would speedily return it if not ours, that he might renew his research. Almost any one under the circumstances would have doubted if it were theirs, or indeed if they were themself – but to us it was clear. Next time, dears, direct Vinnie, or Emily, and perhaps Mr. [Jameson]'s astuteness may be adequate. I enclose the battered remains for your Sabbath perusal, and tell you we think of you tenderly, which I trust you often believe.

Maggie is making a flying visit to cattle-show, on her very robust

wings – for Maggie is getting corpulent. Vinnie is picking a few seeds
– for if a pod "die, shall he not live again"; and with the shutting mail
I go to read to mother about the President. When we think of the
lone effort to live, and its bleak reward, the mind turns to the myth
"for His mercy endureth forever," with confiding revulsion. Still, when
Professor Fisk died on Mount Zion, Dr. Humphrey prayed "to whom
shall we turn but thee"? "I have finished," said Paul, "the faith." We
rejoice that he did not say discarded it.

The little postman has come – Thomas's "second oldest," and I
close with reluctant and hurrying love.

Emily.

MANUSCRIPT: destroyed.

PUBLICATION: L (1894) 290–291; L (1931) 263–264, where it is dated:
"Saturday," presumably the date given by ED.

The Cattle Show in 1881 took place on Saturday, 24 September. Garfield died, 19 September. The postmaster was John Jameson. Thomas Kelley
was Maggie Maher's brother-in-law. For a note on Professor Fiske, which
will explain the allusion here, see letter no. 1042. Most of the scriptural
quotations are too well known to need identification. The last one, from
2 Timothy 4.7, may have been purposely altered: "I have fought a good
fight, I have finished my course, I have kept the faith."

728

To T. W. Higginson   *autumn 1881*

Dear friend,

I am very glad of the Little Life, and hope it may make no farther
flight than it's Father's Arms – Home and Roam in one – I know but
little of Little Ones, but love them very softly –

They seem to me like a Plush Nation or a Race of Down –

If she will accept a vicarious kiss, please confide it to her — Does
she coo with "discraytion"? I am very grateful for the delight to you
and Mrs Higginson – I had thought of your Future with soft fear –
I am glad it has come –

"Go traveling with us"!
Her travels daily be
By routes of ecstasy
To Evening's Sea —

Your Scholar —

MANUSCRIPT: HCL (Higginson). Pencil.
PUBLICATION: *AM* CXXXIX (June 1927) 800; *L* (1931) 313–314.

Margaret Waldo Higginson was born, 25 July 1881. The "discraytion" is quoted back to Higginson from his article "Carlyle's Laugh" in the October issue of *Atlantic Monthly*.

729

To Mrs. J. G. Holland   *October 1881*

We read the words but know them not. We are too frightened with sorrow. If that dear, tired one must sleep, could we not see him first?

Heaven is but a little way to one who gave it, here. "Inasmuch," to him, how tenderly fulfilled!

Our hearts have flown to you before — our breaking voices follow. How can we wait to take you all in our sheltering arms?

Could there be new tenderness, it would be for you, but the heart is full — another throb would split it — nor would we dare to speak to those whom such a grief removes, but we have somewhere heard "A little child shall lead them."

Emily.

MANUSCRIPT: missing.
PUBLICATION: *L* (1894) 183; *L* (1931) 176; *LH* 149.

Dr. Holland died of a heart attack, 12 October 1881. This letter was written immediately upon receipt of the telegram which notified the Dickinsons of his death. This and the three letters that follow were written to Mrs. Holland in quick succession before the end of the month.

730

To Mrs. J. G. Holland   *October 1881*

Panting to help the dear ones and yet not knowing how, lest any voice bereave them but that loved voice that will not come, if I can rest them, here is down — or rescue, here is power.

One who only said "I am sorry" helped me the most when father ceased — it was too soon for language.

Fearing to tell mother, some one disclosed it unknown to us. Weeping bitterly, we tried to console her. She only replied "I loved him so."

Had he a tenderer eulogy?

Emily.

MANUSCRIPT: missing.
PUBLICATION: L (1894) 184; L (1931) 177; LH 149.

731

To Mrs. J. G. Holland   *October 1881*

After a while, dear, you will remember that there is a heaven — but you can't now. Jesus will excuse it. He will remember his shorn lamb.

The lost one was on such childlike terms with the Father in Heaven. He has passed from confiding to comprehending — perhaps but a step.

The *safety* of a beloved lost is the first anguish. With you, that is peace.

I shall never forget the Doctor's prayer, my first morning with you — so simple, so believing. *That* God must be a friend — *that* was a different God — and I almost felt warmer myself, in the midst of a tie so sunshiny.

I am yearning to know if he knew he was fleeing — if he spoke to you. Dare I ask if he suffered? Some one will tell me a very little, when they have the strength. . . Cling tight to the hearts that will not let you fall.

Emily.

.MANUSCRIPT: missing.
PUBLICATION: L (1894) 183–184; L (1931) 176–177; LH 150.

To Mrs. J. G. Holland   *October 1881*

. . . I know you will live for our sake, dear, you would not be willing to for your own. That is the duty which saves. While we are trying for others, power of life comes back, very faint at first, like the new bird, but by and by its has wings.

How sweetly you have comforted me — the toil to comfort you, I hoped never would come. A sorrow on your sunny face is too dark a miracle — but how sweet that he rose in the morning — accompanied by dawn. How lovely that he spoke with you, that memorial time! How gentle that he left the pang he had not time to feel! Bequest of darkness, yet of light, since unborne by him. "Where thou goest, *we* will go" — how mutual, how intimate! No solitude receives him, but neighborhood and friend.

Relieved forever of the loss of those that must have fled, but for his sweet haste. Knowing he could not spare *them*, he hurried like a boy from that unhappened sorrow. Death has mislaid his sting — the grave forgot his victory. Because the flake fell not on him, we will accept the drift, and wade where he is lain.

Do you remember the clover leaf? The little hand that plucked it will keep tight hold of mine.

Please give her love to Annie, and Kate, who also gave a father.

Emily.

MANUSCRIPT: missing.
PUBLICATION: L (1894) 184–185; L (1931) 177–178; LH 150–151.

To Mrs. J. G. Holland   *late 1881*

Dear Sister.

The Things that never can come back, are several –
Childhood – some forms of Hope – the Dead –
Though Joys – like Men – may sometimes make a Journey –
And still abide –
We do not mourn for Traveler, or Sailor,

Their Routes are fair –
But think enlarged of all that they will tell us
Returning here –
"Here!" There are typic "Heres" –
Foretold Locations –
The Spirit does not stand –
Himself – at whatsoever Fathom
His Native Land –

Emily, in love —

MANUSCRIPT: HCL (H 70). Pencil.
PUBLICATION: LH 157; *Poems* (1955) 1045–1046.
This letter-poem, in the handwriting of late 1881, seems to be part of the series of notes that ED sent Mrs. Holland during the month in which Dr. Holland died. There is no stanza break.

734

To Louise and Frances Norcross   *October 1881*

Did the little sisters know that Dr. Holland had died – the dark man with the doll-wife, whom they used to see at "Uncle Edward's" before "Uncle Edward" went too?

Do they know any of the circumstances?

Did they know that the weary life in the second story had mourned to hear from them, and whether they were "comfortable"? "Comfortable" seems to comprise the whole to those whose days are weak. "Happiness" is for birds and other foreign nations, in their faint esteem.

Mother heard Fanny telling Vinnie about her graham bread. She would like to taste it. Will Fanny please write Emily how, and not too inconvenient? Every particular, for Emily is dull, and she will pay in gratitude, which, though not canned like quinces, is fragrantest of all we know.

Tell us just how and where they are, and if October sunshine is thoughtful of their heads.

Emily.

MANUSCRIPT: destroyed.
PUBLICATION: L (1894) 293; L (1931) 265–266.
It is Mrs. Dickinson who is referred to in the third paragraph.

To T. W. Higginson   *about 1881*

Dear friend,

Thank you for the consent I am eager to verify—

It grieves me that anything disturb you—the dearer sorrow of which you spoke, or less lovely care—Both fears, I hope may pass away—We dwell as when you saw us—the mighty dying of my Father made no external change—Mother and Sister are with me, and my Brother and pseudo Sister, in the nearest House—When Father lived I remained with him because he would miss me—Now, Mother is helpless—a holier demand—

I do not go away, but the Grounds are ample—almost travel—to me, and the few that I knew—came—since my Father died—

I should rejoice to see you, and had earnestly asked you to my Home with your sweet friend, but for a Cowardice of Strangers I cannot resist, and my Mother's illness. I trust the Life of which you spoke is in no peril, and every unconferred Bliss tenderly in store—It is solemn to remember that Vastness—is but the Shadow of the Brain which casts it—

> All things swept sole away
> This—is immensity—

Your Scholar—

MANUSCRIPT: BPL (Higg 108). Pencil.
PUBLICATION: L (1931) 311.

The date is conjectured from the handwriting, and from the fact that Mrs. Dickinson is still living. What consent ED had asked has not been identified. For a similar reference to Susan Dickinson, see letter no. 491.

To Mabel Loomis Todd   *autumn 1881*

The parting of those that never met, shall it be delusion, or rather, an unfolding snare whose fruitage is later?

MANUSCRIPT: AC. Pencil.
PUBLICATION: L (1931) 418.

The Todds arrived early in September at Amherst, where Todd began his teaching of astronomy. Later in the autumn Mabel Todd returned to Washington to visit her parents.

737

To Frances Norcross   *about November 1881*

. . . Thank you, dear, for the quickness which is the blossom of request, and for the definiteness – for a new rule is a chance. The bread resulted charmingly, and such pretty little proportions, quaint as a druggist's formula – "I do remember an apothecary." Mother and Vinnie think it the nicest they have ever known, and Maggie so extols it.

Mr. Lathrop's poem was piteously sweet.

To know of your homes is comforting. I trust they are both peace. Home is the riddle of the wise – the booty of the dove. God bless the sunshine in Loo's room, and could he find a sweeter task than to "temper the wind" to her curls? . . .

Tell us when you are happy, but be sure and tell us when you are sad, for Emily's heart is the edifice where the "wicked cease from troubling."

MANUSCRIPT: destroyed.
PUBLICATION: L (1894) 294; L (1931) 266.
Fanny replied to letter no. 734, and this letter acknowledges the receipt of Fanny's recipe for graham bread. The first quotation is from *Romeo and Juliet*, V, i, 37. The conclusion of the letter recalls Job 3.17: "There the wicked cease from troubling; and there the weary be at rest." George Parsons Lathrop (1851–1898), journalist and miscellaneous author, was a son-in-law of Hawthorne. He was an associate editor of the *Atlantic Monthly* (1875–1877), and edited *A Masque of Poets* (1878). (See letter no. 573c.) The reference is to a poem written after the death of his small son in 1881, titled "The Child's Wish Granted."

To Mrs. J. G. Holland   *late November 1881*

Sister.

I wanted to read the dear Articles slowly – one by one – and alone –
as under the circumstances each one of them seemed an interview with
the Departed – but that was unpermitted – so I snatched a Line at a
time – taking it with me as I worked, and then returning for another –

Each is true – and more – and so warmly lifelike, it almost gives a
diffidence, like admiration of a friend in his tender presence.

I have rarely seen so sincere a modesty on a mature Cheek as on
Dr Holland's – and one almost feels an intrusiveness in proclaiming
him, lest it profane his simplicity.

It was nearly Morning, last Night, when I went to my Room from
the loved perusal, and when I laid it in the Drawer, the Telegram of
the Heavenly Flight was close beside without design.

It shall always remain there – nearest us – in the Room to the East
Father loved the most, and where I bade the Doctor Good Night, that
November Morning — He put one Hand on Vinnie's Head and the
other on mine, and his Heart on your's, as we both knew, and said
that the Sunshine and the Scene he should always remember.

> No Autumn's intercepting Chill
> Appalls that Tropic Breast –
> But African Exuberance
> And Asiatic Rest.

Poor "Little Child Wife"!

                                        Lovingly,

                                                    Emily.

MANUSCRIPT: HCL (H 67). Pencil.
PUBLICATION: *LH* 153–154.

ED has received a copy of the December *Century and Scribner's*, a
memorial number for Josiah Gilbert Holland.

To Mrs. Edward Tuckerman   *8 November 1881*

The Dandelion's pallid Tube
Astonishes the Grass,
And Winter instantly becomes
An infinite Alas –
The Tube uplifts a signal Bud
And then a shouting Flower, –
The Proclamation of the Suns
That sepulture is o'er.

Vinnie told me, dear friend, you were speaking of Mr Root –
Emily –

MANUSCRIPT: AAS. Pencil.
PUBLICATION: L (1894) 386; L (1931) 376.
Presumably on the authority of Mrs. Tuckerman, Mrs. Todd dates the note 8 November 1881, and says that it was accompanied by a pressed dandelion tied with a scarlet ribbon. Root died, 3 December 1880 (see letter no. 677).
Among the scraps that were in Mrs. Todds possession (AC – pencil), and that date from about this time, is the following:

Ferocious as a Bee without a wing
The Prince of Honey and the Prince of Sting
So plain a flower presents her Disk to thee

On the verso is written: Prof Tuckerman. The lines may or may not have been a trial draft of a brief note, similar to the above, intended for Mrs. Tuckerman.

To Mrs. J. G. Holland   *December 1881*

Sweet Sister,

We were much relieved to know that the dear event had occurred without overwhelming any loved one, and perhaps it is sweeter and safer so. I feared much for the parting to you to whom parting has come so thickly in the last few days. I knew all would be beautiful, and rejoice it was so.

Few daughters have the Immortality of a Father for a bridal gift. Could there be one more costly!

As we never have ceased to think of you, we will more tenderly, now. Confide our happiness to Annie, in her happiness.

We hope the unknown Balm may ease the Balm withdrawn. You and Katie, the little Sisters, lose her yet obtain her, for each new width of love largens all the rest.

Mother and Vinnie think and speak. Vinnie hopes to write. Would that Mother could – but her poor hand is idle.

Shall I return to you your last and sweetest word — "But I love you all"

Emily.

MANUSCRIPT: missing.

PUBLICATION: Mrs. Todd first published this letter, probably following a transcript furnished by Mrs. Holland, in the *Kappa Alpha Theta*, VI, no. 3 (April 1892), 117–118. When she included it in *L* (1894) 185–186, and *L* (1931) 178, she regularized punctuation, capitals, and paragraphs, restoring the last thirteen words of the first sentence, omitted in the 1892 publication. The present text follows that of 1892, but retains the first sentence entire. (The text in *LH* 155 derives from *L* 1931.)

This letter acknowledges Mrs. Holland's account of Annie's marriage, 7 December 1881, to John Howe (see letter no. 723).

741

To Mrs. Edward Tuckerman   *late 1881*

Dear friend,

Vinnie asked me if I had any Message for you, and while I was picking it, you ran away.

> Not seeing, still we know –
> Not knowing, guess –
> Not guessing, smile and hide
> And half caress –

And quake - and turn away,
Seraphic fear -
Is Eden's innuendo
"If you dare"?

Emily.

MANUSCRIPT: Esty. Pencil.
PUBLICATION: L (1894) 387; LL 334; L (1931) 376.
Mrs. Todd dated the letter December 1881.

742

To Mrs. J. G. Holland   *before Christmas 1881*

Dare we wish the brave sister a sweet Christmas, who remembered us punctually in sorrow as in peace?

The broken heart is broadest. Had it come all the way in your little hand, it could not have reached us perfecter, though had it, we should have clutched the hand and forget the rest.

Fearing the day had associations of anguish to you, I was just writing when your token came. Then, humbled with wonder at your self-forgetting, I delayed till now. Reminded again of gigantic Emily Brontë, of whom her Charlotte said "Full of ruth for others, on herself she had no mercy." The hearts that never lean, must fall. To moan is justified.

To thank you for remembering under the piercing circumstances were a profanation.

God bless the hearts that suppose they are beating and are not, and enfold in His infinite tenderness those that do not know they are beating and are.

Shall we wish a triumphant Christmas to the brother withdrawn? Certainly he possesses it.

How much of Source escapes with thee —
How chief thy sessions be —
For thou hast borne a universe
Entirely away.

With wondering love,

Emily.

MANUSCRIPT: missing.
PUBLICATION: L (1894) 186–187; L (1931) 178–179; LH 156–157.
The quotation from Charlotte Brontë is from her "Biographical Notice" used as an introduction to the 1850 edition of *Wuthering Heights*. For a note touching on previous publication, see letter no. 747.

743

To Mrs. J. G. Holland   *about 1881*

Forgive the fervent Ingrate, if *this* time I am right, who had last week a bewitching Box and replied elsewhere, "Elsewhere" replying this Morning that "it is'nt him," though he "would it were," and "will keep the gratitude till the first Delight he may dare to send."

Reexamining points strongly at you –

It was Rose-colored Butterflies, threaded on a Stem – with Antlers of Green, and three Branches of Golden Rod, though not like the Field's – Do you identify?

Dare not thank you until I know, lest I miss again –

Jacob versus Esau, was a trifle in Litigation, compared to the Skirmish in my Mind –

                                                                                    Emily.

MANUSCRIPT: Hart. Pencil. Unpublished.
The handwriting is about 1881. The circumstances may have been as follows: Sometime during the year ED received a box of candy for which she thanked Judge Lord, who replied that he was not the donor. If ED had received the annual Christmas box from Mrs. Holland before Christmas, she quite naturally would not have expected another package from her after Christmas.

744

To Susan Gilbert Dickinson?   *about 1881*

> How happy is the little Stone
> That rambles in the Road alone –
> And does'nt care about careers
> And Exegencies never fears –
> Whose Coat of elemental Brown

A passing Universe put on
And independent as the Sun
Associates or glows alone –
Fulfilling absolute Decree
In casual simplicity –

Heaven the Balm of a surly Technicality!

MANUSCRIPT: Godchaux. Pencil.
PUBLICATION: The poem was first published in 1891; this copy is in
Poems (1955) 1042–1043. There is no stanza break.

The recipient of this message is unknown, but the provenance of the
autograph suggests that it was sent to Sue. The handwriting is that of late
1881 or early 1882. ED's worksheet draft seems to date from 1881; the
copy to Higginson is perhaps late 1882.

745

To Mrs. Edward Tuckerman   *January 1882*

Dear friend,

The Gray Afternoon – the sweet knock, and the ebbing voice of
the Boys are a pictorial Memory – and then the Little Bins and the
Purple Kernels – 'twas like the Larder of a Doll –
To the inditing Heart we wish no sigh had come –

> Sweet Pirate of the Heart,
> Not Pirate of the Sea,
> What wrecketh thee?
> Some Spice's Mutiny –
> Some Attar's perfidy?
> Confide in me.

Emily.

MANUSCRIPT: AC. Pencil.
PUBLICATION: L (1894) 387; L (1931) 377.

The date, given Mrs. Todd by Mrs. Tuckerman, is confirmed by the
handwriting. This note of thanks acknowledges a New Year's gift and a
note, delivered for Mrs. Tuckerman perhaps by her young nephews, the
Esty boys.

To Mrs. Joseph A. Sweetser   *January 1882*

It was the unanimous opinion of the Household that Aunt Katie never wrote so lovely a Letter and that it should be immediately replied to by each member of the Family, from the Geraniums down to the Pussies, but unforeseen malignities prevented – Vinnie lost her Sultans too – it was "Guiteau" Year – Presidents and Sultans were alike doomed –

One might possibly come up, having sown itself – if it should, you shall share – it is an Eastern Creature and does not like this Soil. I think it's first Exuberance was purely accidental – Last was a fatal season — An "Envious Worm" attacked them — then in early Autumn we had Midwinter Frost – "When God is with us, who shall be against us," but when he is against us, other allies are useless –

We were much amused at your "Gardener."

You portrayed his Treason so wittily it was more effective than Loyalty. He knew that Flowers had no Tongues –

We trust you are safe this Norwegian Weather, and "desire your Prayers" for another Snow Storm, just over our Heads, the Snows already repealing the Fences.

With love for your Health, and the promise of Sultans and Viziers too, if the Monarchs come–

                                                        Emily –

MANUSCRIPT: Rosenbach 1170/18 (3). Pencil.
PUBLICATION: L (1894) 408–409; L (1931) 399–400.
Charles Guiteau assassinated President Garfield. The "Envious Worm" recalls *Romeo and Juliet*, I, i, 157: "As is the bud bit with an envious worm." The scripture quotation is from Romans 8.31.

To Mrs. J. G. Holland   *about 1882*

            "Whom seeing not, we" clasp –

                                                        Emily.

MANUSCRIPT: AC. Pencil.

PUBLICATION: *L* (1894) 187; *L* (1931) 179; *LH* 157.
This note to some member of the Holland family was originally published (1894) in such a way as to appear to be attached to letter no. 742, and later printings so rendered it. Actually it is a separate note. In September 1884 Kate Holland Van Wagenen called at the Dickinson home (see letter no. 936), and possibly this note was delivered to her at that time. But the handwriting seems to be earlier, and was perhaps sent to Mrs. Holland in the spring of 1882. The quotation paraphrases the opening of 1 Peter 1.8: "Whom not having seen, ye love. . ." (see also letter no. 671).

748

To Mabel Louise Todd?   *about 1882*

The little sentences I began and never finished – the little wells I dug and never filled –

MANUSCRIPT: AC. Pencil.
PUBLICATION: *L* (1931) 421.
This scrap, measuring about two by six inches, was among Mrs. Todd's papers, but it is unlikely that ED sent it as a message for it is in her hastily jotted handwriting which she used for first drafts, never for fair copies. Mrs. Todd says that it was sent with a flower or a poem. This rough-draft handwriting was almost illegible at times, and Mrs. Todd transcribed it: "The title sentences I began and never finished — the little wells I dug and verses filled."

749

To Thomas Niles   *late April 1882*

Thank you, Mr. Niles,
I am very grateful for the Mistake.
I should think it irreparable deprivation to know no farther of her here, with the impregnable chances – The kind but incredible opinion of "H. H." and yourself I would like to deserve – Would you accept a Pebble I think I gave to her, though I am not sure.

With thanks,
E. Dickinson.

MANUSCRIPT: AC. Pencil.
PUBLICATION: L (1894) 417; LL 377; L (1931) 406.
She enclosed a copy of"How happy is the little Stone." The two letters which follow, written by Niles to ED earlier in the month, explain this one. ED had initiated the correspondence early in April to inquire evidently when Cross's life of George Eliot and Lowell's life of Hawthorne would be published. Niles answered her inquiry with the following letter (HCL), dated 13 April 1882 (the signature has been cut away).

749a

Miss Dickinson

The very latest London Athenaeum, Apl 1st., says "it is rumored that Mr Cross has abandoned the idea of writing a biography of George Eliot"
We gather from Mr Lowell's publishers that they have not yet rec^d the M.S.S. of Lowell's Hawthorne and do not know when the work will be ready

Yrs tru[ly]
[T. Niles]

She acknowledged the letter. On 24 April he wrote again to give her further information. (HCL)

749b

Miss Dickinson

I have rec^d yours & I want to say that the last London Athenaeum contradicts the rumor in its previous issue and asserts by authority that ["] Mr Cross has not abandoned the idea of writing a biography of George Eliot"
"H. H." once old me that she wished you could be induced to publish a volume of poems. I should not want to say how highly she praised them, but to such an extent that I wish also that you could.

Yrs truly
T. Niles

To Otis P. Lord   30 *April 1882*

His little "Playthings" were very sick all the Week that closed, and
except the sweet Papa assured them, they could not believe – it had one
grace however, it kept the faint Mama from sleep, so she could dream
of Papa awake – an innocence of fondness.

To write you, not knowing where you are, is an unfinished pleasure – Sweeter of course than not writing, because it has a wandering
Aim, of which you are the goal – but far from joyful like yourself, and
moments we have known – I have a strong surmise that moments we
have *not* known are tenderest to you. Of their afflicting Sweetness, you
only are the judge, but the moments we had, were very good – they were
quite contenting.

Very sweet to know from Morn to Morn what you thought and
said – the Republican told us – though that Felons could see you and
we could not, seemed a wondering fraud. I feared for your sweet Lungs
in the crowded Air, the Paper spoke of "Throngs" – We were much
amused at the Juror's "cough" you thought not pulmonary, and when
you were waiting at your Hotel for the Kidder Verdict, and the Jury
decided to go to sleep, I thought them the loveliest Jury I had ever met.
I trust you are "at Home," though my Heart spurns the suggestion, hoping all – absence – but itself.

I am told it is only a pair of Sundays since you went from me. I
feel it many years. Today is April's last – it has been an April of meaning to me. I have been in your Bosom. My Philadelphia [Charles Wads-
worth] has passed from Earth, and the Ralph Waldo Emerson – whose
name my Father's Law Student taught me, has touched the secret
Spring. Which Earth are we in?

Heaven, a Sunday or two ago – but that also has ceased –

Momentousness is ripening. I hope that all is firm. Could we yield
each other to the impregnable chances till we had met once more?

Monday –

Your's of a Yesterday is with me. I am cruelly grieved about the
"Cold." I feared it, but entreated it to wrong some other one. Must it
of all the Lives have come to trouble your's? Be gentle with it – Coax
it – Dont drive it or 'twill stay – I'm glad you are "at Home." Please
think it with a codicil. My own were homeless if you were. Was my

sweet "Phil" "proud"? What Hour? Could you tell me? A momentary gleam of him between Morning . . .

. . . Door either, after you have entered, nor any Window, except in the Chimney, and if Folks knock at the Grass, the Grass can let them in. I almost wish it would, sometimes – with reverence I say it. That was a big – sweet Story – the number of times that "Little Phil" read his Letter, and the not so many, that Papa read his, but I am prepared for falsehood.

On subjects of which we know nothing, or should I say *Beings* – is "Phil" a "Being" or a "Theme," we both believe, and disbelieve a hundred times an Hour, which keeps Believing nimble.

But how can "Phil" have one opinion and Papa another – I thought the Rascals were inseparable – "but there again," as Mr New Bedford Eliot used to say, "I may be mistaken."

Papa has still many Closets that Love has never ransacked. I do – do want you tenderly. The Air is soft as Italy, but when it touches me, I spurn it with a Sigh, because it is not you. The Wanderers came last Night – Austin says they are brown as Berries and as noisy as Chipmunks, and feels his solitude much invaded, as far as I can learn. These dislocations of privacy among the *Privateers* amuse me very much, but "the Heart knoweth its own" Whim – and in Heaven they neither woo nor are given in wooing – what an imperfect place!

Mrs Dr Stearns called to know if we didnt think it very shocking for [Benjamin F.] Butler to "liken himself to his Redeemer," but we thought Darwin had thrown "the Redeemer" away. Please excuse the wandering writing. Sleeplessness makes my Pencil stumble. Affection clogs it – too. Our Life together was long forgiveness on your part toward me. The trespass of my rustic Love upon your Realms of Ermine, only a Sovreign could forgive – I never knelt to other – The Spirit never twice alike, but every time another – that other more divine. Oh, had I found it sooner! Yet Tenderness has not a Date – it comes – and overwhelms.

The time before it was – was naught, so why establish it? And all the time to come it is, which abrogates the time.

MANUSCRIPT: AC. Pencil. One page or more in the middle is missing; it is impossible to know whether pages are missing at the beginning and end. The letter is not a rough draft but a fair copy. It is dated: Sunday

(and half way through): Monday. It was written on 30 April and 1 May.
PUBLICATION: *Revelation* 85–87.

Judge Lord presided at a murder trial which opened at Springfield, 25 April; on April 29 Dwight Kidder was convicted of manslaughter in the death of his half-brother Charles, and sentenced to prison for twenty years. The *Republican* reported the case in detail. In his own letter of 30 April, written from Salem, Lord evidently had mentioned a slight indisposition. On 1 May, the day ED concluded her letter, Lord was seriously stricken and lapsed into unconsciousness. On 3 May the *Republican* said that little hope was held for his recovery, but by 8 May he was reported past the crisis.

This letter was written two weeks after Lord had sojourned in Amherst for a few days in mid-April, before going to Springfield. Charles Wadsworth died 1 April; Emerson on 27 April.

751

To Abbie C. Farley   *8 May 1882*

Monday –

Dear Abby –

This was all the Letter we had this Morning – Was it not enough? Oh no – a tiding every Hour would not be enough – I hoped to hear nothing yesterday unless it were through you –

The last we knew was Hope, and that would last till Monday, but Austin brought a Morning Paper as soon as I was down – "I hope there'll be something of Mr Lord – I'll look it over here," he said – "Couldn't I find it quicker," I inquired timidly – Searching and finding nothing he handed the Paper to me – I found nothing, also – and felt relieved and disturbed too – Then I knew I should hear Monday, but Morning brought me nothing but just this little general Note to a listening World – Were our sweet Salem safe, it would be "May" indeed – I shall never forget "May Day."

All our flowers were draped –

Is he able to speak or to hear voices or to say "Come in," when his Amherst knocks?

Fill his Hand with Love as sweet as Orchard Blossoms, which he will share with each of you – I know his boundless ways –

As it was too much sorrow, so it is almost too much joy –
Lovingly,
Emily.

MANUSCRIPT: HCL. Pencil.
PUBLICATION: *Revelation* 62.
ED pasted at the top of the first page of the letter a clipping from the *Springfield Republican* for Monday, 8 May, reading: "Judge Lord has passed the crisis at Salem, and there is hope that he will soon be about again."

Among the rough drafts in the Bingham collection (AC) is the poem beginning "The Pile of Years is not so high." It is written on the verso of a discarded sheet of stationery, in the handwriting of about this time, that starts and ends thus:

Dear Abby,
I am [gri]eved for Mary

Abbie Farley's cousin, another niece of the Judge, also lived with him.

752

To Otis P. Lord   *14 May 1882*

To remind you of my own rapture at your return, and of the loved steps, retraced almost from the "Undiscovered Country," I enclose the Note I was fast writing, when the fear that your Life had ceased, came, fresh, yet dim, like the horrid Monsters fled from in a Dream.

Happy with my Letter, without a film of fear, Vinnie came in from a word with Austin, passing to the Train. "Emily, did you see anything in the Paper that concerned us"? "Why no, Vinnie, what"? "Mr Lord is very sick." I grasped at a passing Chair. My sight slipped and I thought I was freezing. While my last smile was ending, I heard the Doorbell ring and a strange voice said "I thought first of you." Meanwhile, Tom [Kelley] had come, and I ran to his Blue Jacket and let my Heart break there – that was the warmest place. "He will be better. Dont cry Miss Emily. I could not see you cry."

Then Vinnie came out and said "Prof. Chickering thought we would like to telegraph." He "would do it for us."

"Would I write a Telegram"? I asked the Wires how you did, and attached my name.

The Professor took it, and Abby's brave – refreshing reply I shall remember

MANUSCRIPT: AC. Pencil. Dated: Sunday. The letter, which seems to be incomplete, is a fair copy.
PUBLICATION: *Revelation* 87.
ED received an immediate reply from Abbie Farley, and wrote this letter on the Sunday following.

The nature of the next letter, from Washington Gladden, dated Springfield, 27 May 1882 (HCL – unpublished), suggests that when ED made the inquiry which his reply answers, she did so having in mind the death of Wadsworth and the serious illness of Lord.

752a

My friend:

"Is immortality true?" I believe that it is true – the only reality – almost; a thousand times truer than mortality, which is but a semblance after all. I believe that virtue is deathless; that God who is the source of virtue, gave to her "the glory of going on, and not to die"; that the human soul, with which virtue is incorporate, cannot perish. I believe in the life everlasting, because Jesus Christ taught it. Say what you will about him, no one can deny that he knew the human soul, its nature, its laws, its destinies, better than any other being who ever trod this earth; and he testifies, and his testimony is more clear, more definite, more positive on this than on any other subject, that there is life beyond the grave.

"In my Father's house are many mansions: if it were not so I would have told you."

Absolute demonstration there can be none of this truth; but a thousand lines of evidence converge toward it; and I believe it. It is all I can say. God forbid that I should flatter one who is dying with any illusive hope; but this hope is not illusive. May God's spirit gently lead this hope into the heart of your friend, and make it at home there, so that in the last days it shall be an anchor to the soul, sure and steadfast –

Your friend
Washington Gladden

[731]

To Edward (Ned) Dickinson   *about 1882*

"Sanctuary Privileges" for Ned, as he is unable to attend.

> The Bible is an antique Volume –
> Written by faded Men
> At the suggestion of Holy Spectres –
> Subjects – Bethlehem –
> Eden – the ancient Homestead –
> Satan – the Brigadier –
> Judas – the Great Defaulter –
> David – the Troubadour –
> Sin – a distinguished Precipice
> Others must resist –
> Boys that "believe" are very lonesome –
> Other Boys are "lost" –
> Had but the Tale a warbling Teller –
> All the Boys would come –
> Orpheus' Sermon captivated –
> It did not condemn –
>   Emily.

MANUSCRIPT: HCL (B 165). Pencil.
PUBLICATION: LL 91–92; *Poems* (1955) 1065–1066.
This may have been written on an occasion when Ned, ill, was home from college.

To Gilbert Dickinson   *about 1882*

Poor Little Gentleman, and so revered –

MANUSCRIPT: HCL (B 104). Pencil.
PUBLICATION: FF 258, where it is said to have been sent to Gilbert after an attack of croup.

To Susan Gilbert Dickinson   *about 1882*

I send My Own, two answers – Not one of them so spotless nor so
strong as her's – Sinew and Snow in one –
Thank her for all the promise – I shall perhaps need it –
Thank her dear power for having come, an Avalanche of Sun!
                                                                Emily –
MANUSCRIPT: HCL (B 188). Pencil.
PUBLICATION: *FF* 265–266.
This and the three following notes, written to Sue about 1882, are
dated by handwriting only.

To Susan Gilbert Dickinson   *about 1882*

A fresh Morning of Life with it's impregnable chances, and the
Dew, for you –
                                                                Emily.

MANUSCRIPT: HCL (B 194). Pencil.
PUBLICATION: *AM* CXV (1915) 36; *LL* 57.
ED used the same phrase "impregnable chances" in two letters written
late in April, nos. 749 and 750.

To Susan Gilbert Dickinson   *about 1882*

Dear Sue –
With the exception of Shakespeare, you have told me of more
knowledge than any one living – To say that sincerely is strange praise.

MANUSCRIPT: missing. The text derives from a photostat reproduction
(HCL B 2).
PUBLICATION: *LL* 64; *FF* 176 (facsimile reproduction).
The strain between the two houses about this time had perhaps a tem-
porary fission. (See her reference to Sue in letter no. 735.) Mrs. Bingham

quotes a conversation between her mother Mrs. Todd and Susan Dickin-son that took place in the fall of 1881, when the Todds first arrived in Amherst. Lavinia had asked Mrs. Todd to call. "Sue said at that, 'You will not allow your husband to go there, I hope! . . . I went in there one day, and in the drawing room I found Emily reclining in the arms of a man.' " (*Revelation* 59). It is probable that Sue's resentment concerning the attachment of Emily to Judge Lord was made clear to Emily, and may account for this note of "strange praise."

758

To Susan Gilbert Dickinson   *about 1882*

A "Pear" to the Wise is sufficient –

> Follow wise Orion
> Till you waste your Eye –
> Dazzlingly decamping
> He is just as high –

Emily.

MANUSCRIPT: HCL (B 60). Pencil. Addressed: Susan.
PUBLICATION: FF 245.

759

To Mary Ingersoll Cooper   *about 1882*

Dear friend,

In a World too full of Beauty for Peace, I have met nothing more beautiful.

E. Dickinson –

MANUSCRIPT: AC. Pencil. The back of the autograph is endorsed: "Letter from Emily Dickinson to Miss Mary Ingersoll Cooper."
PUBLICATION: L (1894) 396; L (1931) 385 – where it is placed among letters to Mrs. James S. Cooper. Mary was one of Mrs. Cooper's daughters.

To Mrs. Henry Hills   *about 1882*

Only a pond Lily that I tilled myself —

MANUSCRIPT: missing. The text has the same provenance as that of
letter no. 376.
PUBLICATION: L (1894) 401; LL 335; L (1931) 389.
Mrs. Todd dated the letter 1882.

To Samuel Bowles the younger   *about 1882*

Dear friend,

My Mother and Sister hoped to see you, and I, to have heard the
voice in the House, that recalls the strange Music of your Father's —
A little Bin of Blossoms, I designed for your Breakfast, also went astray.
I hope you are in strength, and that the Passengers of Peace exalt, not
rend your Memory — Heaven may give them rank, it could not give
them grandeur, for that they carried with themselves —

With fresh remembrance,

E. Dickinson.

MANUSCRIPT: Bowles. Pencil.
PUBLICATION: L (1894) 348; LL 344; L (1931) 336.
Samuel Bowles had died in 1878; his brother Benjamin, two years before. Bowles the younger came to Amherst on Saturday, 15 July, for a week-
end visit at the Austin Dickinsons. This letter may have been sent across
to him at that time.

To Eudocia C. Flynt   *about 1882*

Would it too deeply inconvenience Mrs Flynt, to tell me Dates of
the Bridal and Death of our dear Eliza Coleman, for Prof Crowell,
who is preparing a Biography of the Graduates of the College and

their Homes, and earnestly asks it? Thanking you for the kindness I
am sure you will give, I enclose the address.

E. E. Dickinson.

MANUSCRIPT: YUL. Pencil.
PUBLICATION: *Yale University Library Gazette* VI (1931) 43.
Eliza's husband, John Dudley, was a member of the class of 1844. The
Biographical Record of Amherst College, for the years 1821–1871, was
published in 1883, edited by Professor W. L. Montague, with the assistance
of Professor E. P. Crowell and Mr. W. S. Biscoe.

763

To Eudocia C. Flynt *about* 1882

With the sweetest of thanks for the prompt and earnest reply, and
the proffer of any service within my tender power,

I am

Eliza's Playmate –

Prof Crowell entrusts his thanks –

MANUSCRIPT: Jones Library. Pencil. Unpublished.

764

To Mrs. Richard H. Mather *about* 1882

Dear friend,

It is "Weeks off" as little Dombey said, since you sent me the lovely
flowers, but Memory is the Sherry Flower not allowed to wilt –

I hope you may never be ill – Should you, I trust some Hand as
fair may refresh your faintness –

E – Dickinson –

MANUSCRIPT: AC. Pencil. Unpublished.
The date is conjectured from the handwriting. This is the second letter
known to have been written to Mrs. Mather. It may in fact follow soon
after the first (no. 697), but the handwriting suggests it may have been
written as much as a year later.

To T. W. Higginson   *summer 1882*

Dear friend,

Please excuse the trespass of sorrow –

My closest earthly friend died in April – I since saw by the Papers you were very ill – I hope you recover – A friend in Boston, a few weeks since, sent at my request a trifle to your Child.

Yesterday he was here –

A little inscription to the Child, I desired enclosed, he says he erred concerning, but did not tell me how – To ask, I thought not noble –

Whatever mistake there may have been, I hope you kindly excused –

I often think of the Little One. Your tradition is still cherished as one of the departures of Light. To be worthy of what we lose is the supreme Aim –

> Your Scholar –

MANUSCRIPT: Dodd. Unpublished. This autograph is rare among letters written after 1880, in that it is in ink.

During the early summer of 1882 Higginson was for some time confined to his house by illness. For a similar allusion to Wadsworth, see letter no. 807.

To James D. Clark   *August 1882*

Dear friend,

Please excuse the trespass of gratitude. My Sister thinks you will accept a few words in recognition of your great kindness.

In a intimacy of many years with the beloved Clergyman, I have never before spoken with one [met one] who knew him, and his Life was so shy and his tastes so unknown, that grief for him seems almost unshared.

He was my Shepherd from "Little Girl"hood and I cannot conjecture a world without him, so noble was he always – so fathomless – so gentle.

I saw him two years since for the last time, though how unsuspected!

He rang one summer evening to my glad surprise – "Why did you not tell me you were coming, so I could have it to hope for," I said – "Because I did not know it myself. I stepped from my Pulpit to the Train," was his quiet reply. He once remarked in talking "I am liable at any time to die," but I thought it no omen. He spoke on a previous visit of calling upon you, or perhaps remaining a brief time at your Home in Northampton.

I hope you may tell me all you feel able of that last interview, for he spoke with warmth of you as his friend, and please believe that your kindness is cherished.

The Sermons will be a sorrowful Treasure. I trust your health is stronger for the Summer Days, and with tender thanks, ask your kind excuse.

E. Dickinson.

MANUSCRIPT: AC. Pencil. Envelope addressed by Lavinia Dickinson: James D. Clark/361 Degraw St./Brooklyn/L.I. Postmarked: Brat & Palmer Jct Aug 22. (ED wrote, then crossed out, the words in brackets.)

PUBLICATION: L (1931) 344.

The correspondence with Clark, which begins with this letter, was initiated by Clark. ED here writes to thank him for sending her sermons by Dr. Wadsworth. The identity of the opening words in this letter and in the preceding one written to Higginson, which also mentions Wadsworth, suggests that they were written at the same time.

James Clark had retired to Northampton, his boyhood home, in 1875. He was seriously ill when he wrote to ED, and was in Brooklyn for medical treatment, living with his brother Charles.

767

To T. W. Higginson   *summer 1882*

Dear friend,

Perhaps "Baby" will pin her Apron or her Shoe with this? It was sent to me a few Moments since, but I never wear Jewels – How I would love to see her!

Come show thy Durham Breast to her who loves thee best –

[738]

Delicious Robin –
And if it be not me, at least within my Tree
Do thy Avowing –
I am glad you are better, and if to cherish the Cherubim be not too
intrepid, desire my love to Baby's Mama – I am glad you are with
the "Elms" – That is a gracious place –

> How happy is the little Stone
> That rambles in the Road alone,
> And does'nt care about Careers
> And Exigencies never fears –
> Whose Coat of elemental Brown
> A passing Universe put on,
> And independent as the Sun
> Associates or glows alone,
> Fulfilling absolute Decree
> In casual simplicity –
>
> Obtaining but our own Extent
> In whatsoever Realm –
> 'Twas Christ's own personal Expanse
> That bore him from the Tomb –

Your Scholar –

MANUSCRIPT: HCL (Higginson). Pencil.
PUBLICATION: *AM* CXXXIX (June 1927) 801; *L* (1931) 317.
Apparently Higginson had replied to her letter commenting on his ill-
ness.

768

To Susan Gilbert Dickinson   *mid-September* 1882

Had "Arabi" only read Longfellow, he'd have never been caught –
Khedive.
"Shall fold their Tents like the Arabs, and as silently steal away" –

MANUSCRIPT: HCL (B 12). Pencil.
PUBLICATION: FF 242.
The quotation from Longfellow's "The Day is Done" is used as a way

of commenting on current news. The rebel Egyptian Ahmed Arabi Pasha, was defeated at Tel-el-Kebir, 13 September 1882, and this note presumably was written shortly after the papers reported his capture.

769

To Mabel Loomis Todd   *late September 1882*

Dear Friend,

That without suspecting it you should send me the preferred flower of life, seems almost supernatural, and the sweet glee that I felt at meeting it, I could confide to none. I still cherish the clutch with which I bore it from the ground when a wondering Child, an unearthly booty, and maturity only enhances mystery, never decreases it. To duplicate the Vision is almost more amazing, for God's unique capacity is too surprising to surprise.

I know not how to thank you. We do not thank the Rainbow, although it's Trophy is a snare.

To give delight is hallowed – perhaps the toil of Angels, whose avocations are concealed –

I trust that you are well, and the quaint little Girl with the deep Eyes, every day more fathomless.

With joy,

E. Dickinson.

MANUSCRIPT: AC. Pencil. Envelope addressed (by George Montague): Mrs. Todd/#1413 College Hill Terrace/Washington/D. C. Postmarked: Brat. & Palmer Jct. Sep 30.

PUBLICATION: *L* (1894) 430–431; *L* (1931) 419–420.

Mrs. Todd was in Washington at the time, and sent a panel of Indian pipes, which she had painted. On 2 October she recorded receipt of this letter.

770

To Mabel Loomis Todd   *October 1882*

Dear friend,

I cannot make an Indian Pipe but please accept a Humming Bird.

[740]

A Route of Evanescence
With a revolving Wheel –
A Resonance of Emerald –
A Rush of Cochineal –
And every Blossom on the Bush
Adjusts it's tumbled Head –
The mail from Tunis probably,
An easy Morning's Ride –

E. Dickinson.

MANUSCRIPT: AC. Pencil.
PUBLICATION: L (1894) 431; L (1931) 420.
This note followed shortly.

771

To Margaret Maher   *October 1882*

The missing Maggie is much mourned, and I am going out for "black" to the nearest store.

All are very naughty, and I am naughtiest of all.

The pussies dine on sherry now, and humming-bird cutlets.

The invalid hen took dinner with me, but a hen like Dr. T[aylor]'s horse soon drove her away. I am very busy picking up stems and stamens as the hollyhocks leave their clothes around.

What shall I send my weary Maggie? Pillows or fresh brooks?

Her grieved Mistress.

MANUSCRIPT: missing.
PUBLICATION: L (1894) 402–403; L (1931) 391.
Maggie, ill with typhoid fever during October 1882, was nursed at the Kelley house (Jameson papers. LC). Dr. Israel H. Taylor lived near the Dickinsons. Part of a note from Maggie, written perhaps in response to this one, is among the Dickinson papers (AC), because on the back of one page ED set down in rough draft the poem (1883): "He ate and drank the precious Words." It reads:

Sometimes I think I dont be sick at all and the next
time I am sick again give my love to Mother and tell
her I miss her and will sone be home to her how is the
colds I hope ye are better

[741]

To Mrs. William F. Stearns   *October 1882*

Dear friend,

Affection wants you to know it is here. Demand it to the utmost.

Tenderly,

E. Dickinson.

MANUSCRIPT: missing.
PUBLICATION: L (1894) 407; LL 335; L (1931) 396.
Mrs. Stearns's daughter Ethel died, 15 October.

773

To James D. Clark   *1882*

Dear friend,

Perhaps Affection has always one question more which it forgot to ask.

I thought it possible you might tell me if our lost one had Brother or Sister.

I knew he once had a Mother, for when he first came to see me, there was Black with his Hat. "Some one has died" I said. "Yes" — he said, "his Mother."

"Did you love her," I asked. He replied with his deep "Yes." I felt too that perhaps you, or the one you confidingly call "Our Charlie," might know if his Children were near him at last, or if they grieved to lose that most sacred Life. Do you know do they resemble him? I hoped that "Willie" might, to whom he clung so tenderly. How irreparable should there be no perpetuation of a nature so treasured! [Wh] Please forgive the requests which I hope have not wearied you, except as bereavement always wearies.

The sharing a sorrow never lessens, but when a Balm departs, the Plants that nearest grew have a grieved significance and you cherished my friend. My Sister gives her love to you. We hope you are more strong.

E. Dickinson.

MANUSCRIPT: AC. Pencil. (ED wrote, then crossed out, the letters in brackets.)
PUBLICATION: L (1931) 345.
Wadsworth's mother died, 1 October 1859.

774

To Susan Gilbert Dickinson   *October 1882*

Excuse Emily and her Atoms – The "North Star" is of small fabric, but it denotes much –

MANUSCRIPT: HCL (B 103). Pencil. Rose petals enclosed are still with the note.
PUBLICATION: FF 260.
ED sent this note on the eve of the departure of Susan and Mattie, 19 October, to attend the marriage of Frank Gilbert's daughter Belle at Grand Rapids, Michigan. They returned three weeks later. Two drafts of the note are also extant (AC). A rough draft is on the verso of the draft of the poem "Cosmopolites without a plea:"

> Sister
>   Excuse me for disturbing Susan with fragilities on
>   the eve of her departure – the North Star is but of a
>   small fabric yet it achieves (implies) much

A more finished draft appears among several poem fragments on an envelope addressed by Otis P. Lord to "Misses Emily and Vinnie Dickinson":

> Excuse Emily and her Atoms
> The North Star is of small fabric
> but it implies (denotes) much besides

775

To Mrs. J. G. Holland   *October 1882*

Dear Sister.

You knew we would come as soon as we knew – The little Group at the Springfield Table has indeed diminished –

Doctor – Mother – Brother. I am glad I have seen your noble Brother, for now I can miss him from Affection rather than report.

Like my Father he went to Boston to die. All who die in Boston are endeared to me — 'Twas his Isle of flight.

I was just writing you in congratulatory gladness, when the dark words came. I hope it is not too much for your dear — Over burdened Spirit. October could not pass you by.

It sometimes seems as if special Months gave and took away —

August has brought the most to me — April — robbed me most — in incessant instances —

Your Brother bore a strong resemblance to a Childhood's friend who long since died, and whose look I never have seen repeated.

It is almost involuntary with me to send my Note to that Home in the Grass where your many lie —

Could I visit the Beds of my own who sleep, as reprovelessly, even Night were sweet —

With tender thought of Kate in her joyful Hour,

Emily.

MANUSCRIPT: HCL (H 71). Pencil.
PUBLICATION: *LH* 163–164.
Mrs. Holland's brother, Charles O. Chapin of Springfield, died, 28 October, in the State House at Boston while serving as a member of the Massachusetts Prison Commission. Kate Holland became engaged to Bleecker Van Wagenen in late September. Judge Lord was an annual August visitor in Amherst; Wadsworth died in April.

776

To James D. Clark   late 1882

Dear friend,

I would like to delay the timid pleasure of thanking you, that it might not be so soon expended, but Gratitude is not willing.

It is almost an apparitional joy to hear him cherished now, for I never knew one who knew him.

The Griefs of which you speak were unknown to me, though I knew him a "Man of sorrow," and once when he seemed almost overpowered by a spasm of gloom, I said "You are troubled." Shivering as he spoke, "My Life is full of dark secrets," he said. He never spoke of himself, and encroachment I know would have slain him. He never spoke of his Home, but of a Child – "Willie," whom, forgive me the arrogance, he told me was like me – though I, not knowing "Willie," was benighted still. I am glad you loved him and please to thank your Brother for prizing him so much. He was a Dusk Gem, born of troubled Waters, astray in any Crest below. Heaven might give him Peace, it could not give him Grandeur, for that he carried with himself to whatever scene –

> Obtaining but his own extent
> In whatsoever Realm –
> 'Twas Christ's own personal Expanse
> That bore him from the Tomb.

Thank you for the Face – which I fear it fatigued you too much to seek – and for the monition, tho' to disclose a grief of his I could not surmise –

Your sweet attempt to repair the irreparable, I must also remember.

I do not yet fathom that he has died – and hope I may not till he assists me in another World – "Hallowed be it's Name"! But I fear I fatigue you. I would be glad to see you, and talk with you more boundlessly – I hope your Health may return. I have not been able to thank you.

E. Dickinson.

MANUSCRIPT: AC. Pencil.
PUBLICATION: L (1894) 353, in part; LL 353–354, in part; L (1931) 345–346, entire.
Clark had sent ED a photograph of Wadsworth.

777

To Maria Whitney   14 November 1882
                                                            Tuesday
Sweet friend,
Our Mother ceased –
While we bear her dear form through the Wilderness, I am sure you are with us.
                                                            Emily.

MANUSCRIPT: Princeton University Library. Pencil.
PUBLICATION: *L* (1894) 340; *LL* 344; *L* (1931) 329.
This was written on the day Mrs. Dickinson died.

778

To Mrs. Henry Hills   *November 1882*

The last Gift on which my fleeing Mother looked, was Mrs. Hills'
little Bird. I trust this Morning, a Bird herself, she requires no Symbol.

MANUSCRIPT: missing. Unpublished. The text has the same provenance
as that of letter no. 376.

779

To Mrs. J. G. Holland   *November 1882*

The dear Mother that could not walk, has *flown*. It never occurred
to us that though she had not Limbs, she had *Wings* – and she soared
from us unexpectedly as a summoned Bird – She had a few weeks
since a violent cold, though so had we all, but our's recovered apparently, her's seemed more reluctant – but her trusted Physician was with
her, who returned her to us so many times when she thought to go,
and he felt no alarm – After her cough ceased she suffered much from
neuralgic pain, which as nearly as we can know, committed the last
wrong – She seemed entirely better the last Day of her Life and took
Lemonade – Beef Tea and Custard with a pretty ravenousness that
delighted us. After a restless Night, complaining of great weariness,
she was lifted earlier than usual from her Bed to her Chair, when a
few quick breaths and a "Dont leave me, Vinnie" and her sweet being
closed – That the one we have cherished so softly so long, should be
in that great Eternity without our simple Counsels, seems frightened
and foreign, but we hope that Our Sparrow has ceased to fall, though
at first we believe nothing –
    Thank you for the Love – I was sure whenever I lost my own I
should find your Hand –
    The Clover you brought me from Father's Grave, Spring will sow
on Mother's – and she carried Violets in her Hand to encourage her.

[746]

Remember me to your Annie and Kate. Tell them I envy them their Mother. "Mother"! What a Name!

Emily.

MANUSCRIPT: HCL (H 72). Pencil.
PUBLICATION: LH 165.
The second paragraph suggests that this is a reply to a letter of condolence from Mrs. Holland.

780

To Otis P. Lord   *November 1882?*

The celestial Vacation of writing you after an interminable Term of *four Days*, I can scarcely express. My Head was so sick when I woke this Morning that I feared I could'nt meet Tom, though how did I know that the dear necessity at that particular moment existed? And *more* afraid, that should it, I could'nt respond tonight, and a Night is *so* long, and it snowing too, another barrier to Hearts that overleap themselves. Emily "Jumbo"! Sweetest name, but I know a sweeter – Emily Jumbo Lord. Have I your approval?

Tim's suspicions however will be allayed, for I have thinner Paper, which can elude the very elect, if it undertake.

MANUSCRIPT: AC. Pencil. On the reverse of this draft is letter no. 800.
PUBLICATION: Revelation 88.
The dating is conjectural. The handwriting is that of late 1882. It snowed during the week of Mrs. Dickinson's death.

781

To Emily Fowler Ford   *about November 1882*

Dear friend,

The little Book will be subtly cherished –

All we secure of Beauty is it's Evanescences – Thank you for recalling us.

Earnestly,
Emily.

MANUSCRIPT: AC. Pencil.
PUBLICATION: L (1894) 405; L (1931) 395.
Emily Ford presented an inscribed copy of her poems, *My Recreations* (1872), to Austin and Susan Dickinson, 19 November 1882. She may have written a note of sympathy after Mrs. Dickinson's death.

782

To Mrs. J. Howard Sweetser   *November 1882*

Dear Nellie,

I cannot resist your sweet appeal, though the departure of our Mother is so bleak a surprise, we are both benumbed – for the Doctor assured us she was recovering and only the night before she died, she was happy and hungry and ate a little Supper I made her with such enthusiasm, I laughed with delight, and told her she was as hungry as Dick.

Wondering with sorrow, how we could spare our lost Neighbors, our first Neighbor, our Mother, quietly stole away.

So unobtrusive was it, so utterly unexpected, that she almost died with Vinnie alone before one could be called. Amid these foreign Days the thought of you is homelike, for you were peculiarly gentle to her for whom service has ceased.

The last Token but one, on which her dear Eyes looked, was the Grapes from you. The very last, a little Bird, from thoughtful Mrs Hills.

Grapes and Birds, how typic, for was she not on her sweet way to a frostless Land?

Plundered of her dear face, we scarcely know each other, and feel as if wrestling with a Dream, waking would dispel.

Thank you for every sweetness to her and to us and please to thank your Husband for the lovely desire to honor her for the last time, and Alice and Nettie too, for many a little Banquet she was indebted to them. Thank them with a Kiss.

I hope you are stronger than you were, and that all is safe in your unspeakable Home.

Oh, Vision of Language!

Emily.

[748]

MANUSCRIPT: Rosenbach 1170/18 (4). Pencil. Unpublished.
Alice and Nettie were the Sweetser daughters.

783

To Mrs. Henry Hills   *November 1882*

Dear friends,

Even the simplest solace, with a loved aim, has a heavenly quality.

Emily.

MANUSCRIPT: missing. The text has the same provenance as that of
letter no. 376.
PUBLICATION: L (1894) 401; LL 335; L (1931) 390.
The dating is conjectural but probable.

784

To Joseph K. Chickering   *November 1882*

Dear friend,

I do not know the depth of my indebtedness. Sorrow, benighted
with Fathoms, cannot find it's Mind.

Thank you for assisting us. We were timidly grateful.

E. Dickinson.

MANUSCRIPT: AC. Pencil. Envelope addressed: Mr Chickering.
PUBLICATION: L (1894) 414; LL 341; L (1931) 403.
Professor Chickering had been especially helpful at the time of Mrs.
Dickinson's death.

785

To Louise and Frances Norcross   *late November 1882*

Dear cousins,

I hoped to write you before, but mother's dying almost stunned my
spirit.

I have answered a few inquiries of love, but written little intuitively. She was scarcely the aunt you knew. The great mission of pain had been ratified – cultivated to tenderness by persistent sorrow, so that a larger mother died than had she died before. There was no earthly parting. She slipped from our fingers like a flake gathered by the wind, and is now part of the drift called "the infinite."

We don't know where she is, though so many tell us.

I believe we shall in some manner be cherished by our Maker – that the One who gave us this remarkable earth has the power still farther to surprise that which He has caused. Beyond that all is silence. . . .

Mother was very beautiful when she had died. Seraphs are solemn artists. The illumination that comes but once paused upon her features, and it seemed like hiding a picture to lay her in the grave; but the grass that received my father will suffice his guest, the one he asked at the altar to visit him all his life.

I cannot tell how Eternity seems. It sweeps around me like a sea. . . . Thank you for remembering me. Remembrance – mighty word.

"Thou gavest it to me from the foundation of the world."

Lovingly,

Emily.

MANUSCRIPT: destroyed.
PUBLICATION: L (1894) 295–296; LL 344–345; L (1931) 267.

The scripture quotation appears to have in mind John 17.24: "Father, I will that they also, whom thou hast given me, be with me where I am; that they behold my glory, which thou hast given me: for thou lovedst me before the foundation of the world." (See also letter no. 50.)

786

To Joseph K. Chickering *late 1882*

Dear friend,

Thank you for being willing to see me, but may I defer so rare a pleasure till you come again? Grief is a sable introduction, but a vital one, and I deem that I knew you long since through your shielding thought.

I hope you may have an electrical absence, as Life never loses it's startlingness, however assailed – "seen of Angels" only, an enthralling Aim.

Thank you for the kindness, the fervor of a stranger the latest forgot.

E. Dickinson.

MANUSCRIPT: AC. Pencil. Envelope addressed: Mr Chickering.
PUBLICATION: L (1894) 414; LL 341; L (1931) 403–404.
Evidently Chickering, before departing for his Christmas vacation, asked if he might call, and received this reply.

787

To Martha Dickinson   *late 1882*

That's the Little Girl I always meant to be, but was'nt – The very Hat I always meant to wear, but did'nt and the attitude toward the Universe, so precisely my own, that I feel very much, as if I were returning Elisha's Horses, or the Vision of John at Patmos –

Emily –

MANUSCRIPT: missing. The text is from the facsimile reproduction in FF.
PUBLICATION: FF 250, with facsimile reproduction.
The photograph (HCL) which prompted this note is endorsed on the back: "Mattie Dickinson, 19 November 1882."

788

To James D. Clark   *late 1882*

Dear friend,

It pains us very much that you have been more ill. We hope you may not be suffering now. Thank you for speaking so earnestly when our Mother died – We have spoken daily of writing you, but have felt unable. The great attempt to save her Life had it been successful, would have been fatigueless, but failing, strength forsook us.

No Verse in the Bible has frightened me so much from a Child as "from him that hath not, shall be taken even that he hath." Was it because it's dark menace deepened our own Door? You speak as if you still missed your Mother. I wish we might speak with you. As we bore her dear form through the Wilderness, Light seemed to have stopped.

Her dying feels to me like many kinds of Cold – at times electric, at times benumbing – then a trackless waste, Love has never trod.

The Letter from the skies, which accompanied your's, was indeed a Boon – A Letter always seemed to me like Immortality, for is it not the Mind alone, without corporeal friend?

I hope you may tell us that you are better.

Thank you for much kindness. The friend Anguish reveals is the slowest to forget.

E. Dickinson.

MANUSCRIPT: AC. Pencil.

PUBLICATION: L (1894) 353–354, with facsimile reproduction of the last page; LL 354; L (1931) 347.

This replies to a letter of condolence written by Clark in November, which evidently enclosed something written by Wadsworth. The sentence comparing a letter to immortality ED had used in almost identical phrase in 1869, in a letter to Higginson (see no. 330). The quotation is from Mark 4.25.

789

To Mary Ingersoll Cooper   *late 1882*

Dear friend –

Thank you for the very sweet Message which you sent me in November, though I did not reply till Today –

The Biography of the Blossom might perhaps endear it –

It was sent to me by your Mother, after the Village Fire – and "Mother," to me, is so sacred a Name, I take even that of the "Seraphim" with less hallowed significance –

E – Dickinson –
with love –

MANUSCRIPT: AC. Pencil. Unpublished.

This note probably acknowledges a message of condolence sent after Mrs. Dickinson's death. It evidently accompanied a flower from a plant given to ED by Mrs. James Cooper. The fire referred to probably was the one which destroyed the business center in 1879 (see letter no 610).

To Otis P. Lord   *3 December 1882*

What if you are writing! Oh, for the power to look, yet were I there, I would not, except you invited me – reverence for each other being the sweet aim. I have written you, Dear, so many Notes since receiving one, it seems like writing a Note to the Sky – yearning and replyless – but Prayer has not an answer and yet how many pray! While others go to Church, I go to mine, for are not you my Church, and have we not a Hymn that no one knows but us?

I hope your "Thanksgiving" was not too lonely, though if it were *a little*, Affection must not be displeased.

Sue [? *name altered*] sent me a lovely Banquet of Fruit, which I sent to a dying Irish Girl in our neighborhood – That was my Thanksgiving. Those that die seem near me because I lose my own.

Not *all* my own, thank God, a darling "own" remains – more darling than I name.

The Month in which our Mother died, closed it's Drama Thursday, and I cannot conjecture a form of space without her timid face. Speaking to you as I feel, Dear, without that Dress of Spirit must be worn for most, Courage is quite changed.

Your Sorrow was in Winter – one of our's in June and the other, November, and my Clergyman passed from Earth in spring, but sorrow brings it's own chill. Seasons do not warm it. You said with loved timidity in asking me to your dear Home, you would "try not to make it unpleasant." So delicate a diffidence, how beautiful to see! I do not think a Girl extant has so divine a modesty.

You even call me to your Breast with apology! Of what must my poor Heart be made?

That the one for whom Modesty is felt, himself should feel it sweetest and ask his own with such a grace, is beloved reproach. The tender Priest of Hope need not allure his Offering – 'tis on his Altar ere he asks. I hope you wear your Furs today. Those and the love of me, will keep you sweetly warm, though the Day is bitter. The love I feel for you, I mean, your own for me a treasure I still keep . . .

MANUSCRIPT: AC. Pencil. Dated: Sunday. This incomplete fair copy, like all the letters and fragments to Lord, was among ED's papers. Whether it was never sent, or is a duplicate, remains a question.

PUBLICATION: *Revelation* 88–89.

791

To Otis P. Lord   *about* 1882

[*scrap 1*]

I know you [are] acutely weary, yet cannot refrain from taxing you

[*scrap 2*]

from taxing you with an added smile – and a pang in it. Was it to him the Thief cried "Lord remember me when thou comest into thy Kingdom," and is it to us that he replies, "This Day thou shalt be with me in Paradise"?

The Propounder of Paradise must indeed possess it – Antony's remark [*scrap 3*] to a friend, "since Cleopatra died" is said to be the saddest ever lain in Language – That engulfing "*Since*" –

MANUSCRIPT: AC. Pencil. Dated by handwriting only.

PUBLICATION: *Revelation* 84.

792

To Mrs. J. G. Holland   *mid-December* 1882

Dear Sister,

I have thought of you with confiding Love, but to speak seemed taken from me – Blow has followed blow, till the wondering terror of the Mind clutches what is left, helpless of an accent –

You have spared so much and so patiently, it seems as if some seraphic Armor must have shielded you –

Mother has now been gone five Weeks. We should have thought it a long Visit, were she coming back – Now the "Forever" thought almost shortens it, as we are nearer rejoining her than her own return – We were never intimate Mother and Children while she was our Mother – but Mines in the same Ground meet by tunneling and when she became our Child, the Affection came – When we were Children and she journeyed, she always brought us something. Now, would she bring us but herself, what an only Gift – Memory is a strange Bell – Jubilee, and Knell.

I hope your Home with the new Children is a Place of Peace, and believe it to be from Austin's Story – The Port of Peace has many Coves, though the main entrance cease – I hope the large sons are docile to their little Mother, whose commands are Balm – I had written to Kate, but ere mailing the Note that great difference came, and to find it would be to open a Past that is safer closed –

Austin told of his Call with much warmth, and I trust the Sun is still shining there, though it is since Night.

I trust the new Home may remain untouched – Is God Love's Adversary?

Emily.

MANUSCRIPT: HCL (H 73). Pencil.
PUBLICATION: LH 166–167.
Mrs. Holland had recently made her home with the Van Wagenens. Her "large sons" were Theodore Holland and Bleecker Van Wagenen.

793

To Susan Gilbert Dickinson   *before Christmas 1882*

Please excuse Santa Claus for calling so early, but Gentlemen 1882 years old are a little fearful of the Evening Air –

Sister –

MANUSCRIPT: HCL (B 27). Pencil. Addressed on the fold: Susan.
PUBLICATION: LL 57.
The note probably accompanied gifts to be opened on Christmas day.

794

To Mrs. J. G. Holland   *after Christmas 1882*

Sweet Sister.

The lovely recollection – the thought of those that cannot "taste" – of one to whose faint Bed all Boons were brought before revealed, made the sweet Package mighty – It came so long it knows the way and almost comes itself, like Nature's faithful Blossoms whom no one summons but themselves, Magics of Constancy –

The Fiction of "Santa Claus" always reminds me of the reply to my early question of "Who made the Bible" — "Holy Men moved by the Holy Ghost," and though I have now ceased my investigations, the Solution is insufficient –

Santa Claus, though *illustrates* – Revelation

But a Book is only the Heart's Portrait – every Page a Pulse –

Thank you for the protecting words – The petit Shepherd would find us but a startled Flock, not an unloving one –

Remember me to your Possessions, in whom I have a tender claim, and take sweet care of the small Life, fervor has made great – deathless as Emerson's "Squirrel" –

Vinnie gives her love and will write, if a Lady goes away who is calling here – Maggie prized your remembrance – Austin seldom calls – I am glad you were glad to see him – He visits rarely as Gabriel –

Lovingly,

Emily –

MANUSCRIPT: HCL (H 74). Pencil.

PUBLICATION: LH 168.

The quotation from scripture recalls 2 Peter 1.21: ". . . but holy men of God spake as they were moved by the Holy Ghost." Emerson's "Squirrel" probably alludes to his "Fable," beginning: "The mountain and the squirrel/ Had a quarrel."

795

To Mrs. Edward Tuckerman   *early January 1883*

The presence in Life of so sweet an one is of itself Fortune – a covert wealth of spirit I shall not disclose –

I have taken all the naughty Boys and Vinnie the Navy –

What lovely conceits!

Then the little Smyrna in the Dish – how tiny – how affecting – though the Heart in the rear *not* tiny – Oh no – vast as the Sea –

To caress it's Billows is our liquid aim –

Emily,

With love –

MANUSCRIPT: AC. Pencil.
PUBLICATION: L (1894) 388; L (1931) 377.
The note thanks Mrs. Tuckerman for her annual New Year's gift.

796

To Mrs. J. Howard Sweetser   *early January 1883*

Dear Nellie,

The Christmas Sweetness comes – sweeter for the straying, as the Bible joyously says of it's Truant, "This was lost and is found."

Thank you for the Symbol – it is belovedly beautiful, though may I deem it less than the inditing Heart?

As friends who take "the Light" at Night, look back with "Happy Dreams," and come no more till Morning, their Night a tender Fiction, "He giveth *our* Beloved Sleep," but does he add a Dream, and one more beggary of Love, is it sometimes of us?

Thank you.

                                                     Emily.

MANUSCRIPT: Rosenbach 1170/18 (6). Pencil. Unpublished.
The first quotation recalls Luke 15.24: ". . . he was lost and is found"; the last, Psalms 127.2: ". . . for so he giveth his beloved sleep."

797

To Mrs. Henry Hills   *January 1883?*

Dear friend,

We often say "how beautiful"! But when we mean it, we can mean no more – a Dream personified –

                                             E——

MANUSCRIPT: missing. The text has the same provenance as that of letter no. 376.
PUBLICATION: L (1894) 401; L (1931) 390.
Mrs. Hills annually sent a Christmas remembrance, and this may acknowledge one for 1882.

To Joseph K. Chickering   *early 1883*

Dear friend —

I had hoped to see you, but have no grace to talk, and my own Words so chill and burn me, that the temperature of other Minds is too new an Awe —

> We shun it ere it comes,
> Afraid of Joy,
> Then sue it to delay
> And lest it fly,
> Beguile it more and more —
> May not this be
> Old Suitor Heaven,
> Like our dismay at thee?

Earnestly,
E. Dickinson.

MANUSCRIPT: AC. Pencil.
PUBLICATION: L (1894) 414–415; LL 342; L (1931) 404.
Professor Chickering tried again to see ED after Christmas vacation, but she sent this note (see letter no. 786).

To Susan Gilbert Dickinson   *early 1883?*

Will Susan lend Emily a little more Alchimy in exchange for a Hyacinth in prospective, and excuse Sister's predilection to a Cold?
The little Vial I still have, labeled "Mere – Sol, Hahn" —
Thanking, always,

Emily —

MANUSCRIPT: HCL (B 29). Pencil. Addressed: Susan –
PUBLICATION: FF 246, in part.
The handwriting is about 1883. The note evidently accompanied a hyacinth still in bud, which ED was sending from her conservatory.

To Alfred Norcross?   *early 1883?*

. . . home. She is rested and pleased Thank you for coming here and please to tell my Cousins how beautiful she was – We hope you are having a lovely Winter and think of [you] with new peace in the warmth (Home) of your Daughter – Accept our love for them and a kiss for the little Grand Boy –

Vinnie received the paper – and (was much interested) thanks you very much (It was very interesting –) How it would interest Mother each of us exclaimed – I know you will remember her with never ceasing love – She never seemed elderly to us – and we think of her in a sweet prime we can scarcely express –

Vinnie gives her love –

Mother's Brother
Good night

MANUSCRIPT: AC. Penciled rough draft, written on the reverse of letter no. 780.

PUBLICATION: *NEQ* XXVIII (1955) 302.

This surviving part of the draft of a letter was probably written to Mrs. Dickinson's younger brother Alfred, whose first grandchild, a girl, was born in December 1882. The first grandchild of Joel Norcross, another brother, was a boy, born in December 1883. The reference to "little Grand Boy" obviously would apply better to Joel, but the tone of the letter suggests that it was written while the memory of Mrs. Dickinson's death and her funeral were still fresh.

801

To Mrs. J. G. Holland   *early 1883*

Dear friend,

We were very sorrowful for the illness of the Gentleman with the long Name, and it must have been a bleak Holiday for your loved Kate – Would it be chivalrous to say, we rejoice it was "Bleeker"? And for Katrina's Eyes, Camoens is sorry –

We hope "Mr-Bridegroom" is better, as Gilbert calls those sacred ones, and that the Eyes relent – May it not be the glazed Light which the Snows make, for with us they are falling always now, and the last is faithful for three Days, an inclement constancy –

Could I thank you for all the sweetness at once, it would deprive me of the joy of thanking you again, which I so much covet – Of the Christmas Munificence two Acorns remain – Those I shall save for Seed, and I know they will bloom by another Christmas – Mother's Christmas Gift of another Life is just as stupendous to us now, as the Morning it came – All other Surprise is at last monotonous, but the Death of the Loved is all moments – *now* – Love has but one Date – "The first of April" "Today, Yesterday, and Forever" –

"*Can* Trouble dwell with April Days?"

"Of Love that never found it's earthly close,
what sequel?"

Both in the same Book – in the same Hymn – Excuse your Mourning

Emily –

MANUSCRIPT: HCL (H 75). Pencil.
PUBLICATION: *LH* 170.

Early in 1883 Bleecker Van Wagenen, who had gone South on a business trip, was taken ill, and was nursed by his wife. For the reference to Camoens, see letter no. 491. Both quoted lines are by Tennyson: the first from *In Memoriam* (no. 83), the second from *Love and Duty*. Wadsworth had died on the first of April 1882.

802

To Mrs. J. G. Holland   *early 1883*

Dear Sister.

Thank you for the glimpse – The Faces are delightful –
Had I imagined Annie's friend, he looks as I believed.
The other two surprised me – Ted's, by the boyishness –
I looked for an Octogenarian flavor in a Graduate – and perhaps Austin's assurance that he wore the Supreme Court Judge's Coat, aided the delusion. The Eyes are the Father's – though why so stealthy – but the Mother's Mouth – Where to flatter is truth, what respite for flattery? The other Face is deep and sweet, a lovely Face to sit by in Life's Mysterious Boat –

I hope the missing Health is rapidly returning – and grieve that
any faintness should waste your second Home –

It acclimates our thought of you to see your Noble Sons –

If the Spirits are fair as the Faces "Nothing is here for Tears –"

May I present your Portrait to your Sons in Law?

> To see her is a Picture –
> To hear her is a Tune –
> To know her an Intemperance
> As innocent as June —
> To know her not – Affliction –
> To own her for a Friend
> A warmth as near as if the Sun
> Were shining in your Hand.

Emily.

MANUSCRIPT: HCL (H 75). Pencil.
PUBLICATION: *LH* 171–172.

Mrs. Holland had sent photographs of her son Theodore, and her two
sons-in-law. Ted, graduated from Yale in June 1882, was attending Columbia Law School. "Nothing is here for tears," relating to Samson's death, is
from Milton's *Samson Agonistes* (line 1721).

803

To Forrest F. Emerson   *early 1883?*

A Blossom perhaps is an introduction, to whom – none can
infer——

MANUSCRIPT: Lane. Pencil.
PUBLICATION: *L* (1894) 403; *LL* 333; *L* (1931) 392.

Emerson, who had been pastor of the First Church since 1879, was dismissed, 21 February 1883. The handwriting is of this period.

804

To James D. Clark   *late February 1883*

Dear friend,

To thank you is impossible, because your Gifts are from the Sky,
more precious than the Birds, because more disembodied. I can only

express my rejoiced surprise by the phrase in the Scripture "And I saw the Heavens opened." I am speechlessly grateful for a friend who also was my friend's, and can scarcely conceal my eagerness for that warbling Silence. The Page to which I opened, showed me first these Words. "I have had a Letter from another World."

Fathoms are sudden Neighbors.

Ignorant till your Note, that our President's dying had defrauded you, we are grieved anew, and hasten to offer you our sorrow.

We shall make Mrs Chadbourne's acquaintance in flowers, after a few Days. "Displeasure" would be a morose word toward a friend so earnest and we only fear when you delay, that you feel more ill. Allow us to hear the Birds for you, should they indeed come.

E. D.

MANUSCRIPT: AC. Pencil.

PUBLICATION: L (1894) 356, in part; LL 355–356, in part; L (1931) 348–349, entire.

Wadsworth's last volume of sermons, proofread by himself, with preface dated March 1882, was posthumously published. This letter acknowledges a copy of them or of a printed memorial of Wadsworth, which Clark had sent. Professor Paul A. Chadbourne of Williams College became president of Massachusetts Agricultural College in 1866. He was a Williams classmate (1848) of Clark's. Ill health forced his resignation in 1867, but he was again elected in 1882. He died, 23 February 1883. The scripture quotation is from Revelation 19.11.

805

To Mrs. J. G. Holland   *3 March 1883*

Were not the Faces too lovely, I should say the remembrance were lovelier, but a perilous Chivalry being involved, I regard the limitude –

Annie looks the pathetic Squirrel that she always was and Kate a questioning Dove –

Her question however is answered now – Please tell her from me –

> The Clock strikes one that just struck two –
> Some schism in the Sum –
> A Vagabond from Genesis
> Has wrecked the Pendulum –

The instant acquiescence was delightfully hearty – the suddenness of a tenderness making it more sweet –

Thank the Suggester and the Enacter, and once more, please, a little news of the ill Linnet –

We trust Mr-Van Wagner retakes his fleeing Health – Should suggest a Policeman, and that Kate found Flowers and wonder in the Sweet Land.

March is three Days with me, but his Face is so unbecoming still, I dont show him to Strangers –

With love for each, and a shy smile at the new Brethren,

Emily –

MANUSCRIPT: HCL (H77). Pencil.
PUBLICATION: LH 172–173.

Perhaps it was Kate Van Wagenen herself who suggested sending photographs of the Holland daughters which ED here acknowledges. Mrs. Holland was becoming subject to rheumatic attacks. ED later sent a variant of the same four lines of verse to Samuel Bowles the younger (see letter no. 902). It is because Kate is married, the poem implies, that her question is answered.

806

To Mrs. J. G. Holland   *March 1883*

Dear friends.

The "Birds" preceded the *Reprimand*, which modified it's chastening –

By some divine contingency that strayed to Austin's Box, which deferred it's rancor till fortified by Birds, we had grown impervious –

Orthography always baffled me, and to "Ns" I had an especial aversion, as they always seemed unfinished *M's*. Will dear Mrs "Van Wagenen" excuse me for taking her portentous name in vain?

I can best express my contrition in the words of the Prayer of a Clergyman I heard when a Child – "Oh thou who sittest upon the Apex of the Cherubim, look down upon this, thine unworthy Terrapin"!

The dear Birds and their Donor will accept our love for the untiring Sweetness – To never forget to be gracious is Remembrance' most touching Ornament –

The Health that omits to mention itself, we trust is so culpable only because it is better, and hope that Annie's Walk on the Water was a pedestrian success –

With memory for each, what sweeter Shelter than the Hearts of such a hallowed Household!

Emily –

MANUSCRIPT: HCL (H 78). Pencil.
PUBLICATION: LH 174–175.

Two items had been received since the preceding letter. The "Birds" evidently was the picture of the Holland girls, showing them with their heads tilted together which, ED having sent back, was returned to her as a gift, not a loan. The other was a letter which brought to her attention the correct spelling of Van Wagenen. Annie and her husband John Howe were about to sail for Europe. A portion of the first draft of this letter also survives (AC):

> The Birds preceded the reprimand, which modified its chastening – by some divine contingency that strayed to Austin's Box (and till fortified by Birds we) which deferred its rancor till flanked by the Birds we had grown impervious – Orthography always baffled me, and to (for) Ns I had a peculiar aversion, they seeming to me imperfect M's – Will Dear Mrs Van Wagenen excuse me for taking her portentous name in vain – I heard a Clergyman

807

To James D. Clark *mid-March 1883*

Dear friend,

In these few Weeks of ignorance of you, we trust that you are growing stronger, and drawing near that sweet Physician, an approaching spring – for the ear of the Heart hears Blue Birds already – those enthralling Signals – I could scarcely have believed, the Morning you called with Mr Brownell that I should eventually speak with you, and you only, with the exception of my Sister, of my dearest earthly friend, though the great confidences of Life are first disclosed by their departure – and I feel that I ceaselessly ought to thank you, were it not indelicate. Our Household is scarcely larger than your's – Vinnie and I, and two Servants, composing our simple Realm, though my Brother is with us so often each Day, we almost forget that he ever passed to a wedded Home. I wish I could show you the Hyacinths that embarrass us by their loveliness, though to cower before a flower is perhaps unwise – but Beauty is often timidity – perhaps oftener – pain.

A soft "Where is she" is all that is left of our loved Mother, and thank you for all you told us of your's. Please remember me to the Brother who loved my lost friend.

Faithfully,
E. Dickinson.

MANUSCRIPT: AC. Pencil. Envelope addressed by Lavinia: James D. Clark/361 Degraw St/Brooklyn L.I. Postmarked: Mar 16.

PUBLICATION: L (1894), 354–356, in part; LL 355, in part; L (1931) 347–348, entire, with facsimile reproduction of two pages.

Brownell had been a partner of Clark's in a private school for boys, "Clark and Brownell," which they founded in New York City in 1858. For a similar allusion to her friendship with Wadsworth, see letter no. 765, to Higginson.

808

To Mrs. J. G. Holland   *March 1883*

We wont fatigue the Fairy Scribe with a farther Letter, but only ask that question small, ever to us so great, how is the Mama? We hope the March Winds may not find her in her dear Retreat, for their ferocious ways would certainly appall her –

We trust the lovely Invalid is growing every Day, not in Grace but Vigor, the latter Foliage needed more –

I have seen one Bird and part of another – probably the last, for Gibraltar's Feathers would be dismayed by this savage Air – beautiful, too, ensnaring – as Spring always is.

"Though he slay me, yet will I trust him" –

Commending the Birds of which I spoke, to your Hearts and Crumbs,

Lovingly,

Emily –

Forever honored be the Tree
Whose Apple Winterworn
Enticed to Breakfast from the Sky
Two Gabriels Yestermorn.

They registered in Nature's Book
As Robins – Sire and Son –
But Angels have that modest way
To screen them from Renown.

MANUSCRIPT: HCL (H 79). Pencil.
PUBLICATION: LH 176.
The allusion in the second paragraph is to 2 Peter 3.18: "But grow in grace, and in the knowledge of our Lord and Savior Jesus Christ." The quotation is from Job 13.15.

809

To recipient unknown   *about March 1883*

Dear friend,

I dream of your little Girl three successive Nights – I hope nothing affronts her –

To see her is a Picture –
To hear her is a Tune –
To know her, a disparagement of every other Boon –
To know her not, Affliction –
To own her for a Friend
A warmth as near as if the Sun
Were shining in your Hand –

Lest she miss her "Squirrels," I send her little Playmates I met in Yesterday's Storm – the lovely first that came –

Forever honored be the Tree
Whose Apple winter-worn –
Enticed to Breakfast from the sky
Two Gabriels Yester Morn.

They registered in Nature's Book
As Robins, Sire and Son –
But Angels have that modest way
To screen them from renown –

MANUSCRIPT: AC. Penciled rough draft.
PUBLICATION: *NEQ* XXVIII (1955) 308.
Variants of both poems were sent to Mrs. Holland at this time (see letters no. 802 and 808).

810

To Mrs. Jonathan L. Jenkins   *date unknown*

I omitted the snow on the roof, distrusting the premonition.

Emily.

MANUSCRIPT: missing.
PUBLICATION: *FN* 129.
This and the two following messages, sent to Mrs. Jenkins or to some member of the Jenkins family, cannot be dated. They are placed here because the year 1883 was the last in which ED is known to have corresponded with the Jenkinses. This note is said to have been sent with a sketch of Amherst covered with snow.

811

To Mrs. Jonathan L. Jenkins   *date unknown*

Area – no test of depth.

———

MANUSCRIPT: missing.
PUBLICATION: FN 113.

812

To Mrs. Jonathan L. Jenkins   *date unknown*

Nature's buff message – left for you in Amherst. She had not time to call. You see her father and my father were brothers.

Emily.

MANUSCRIPT: missing.
PUBLICATION: *FN* 120–121.
The note is said to have been sent with pussy willows.

813

To Thomas Niles   *mid-March 1883*

Dear friend.

I bring you a chill Gift – My Cricket and the Snow. A base return indeed, for the delightful Book, which I infer from you, but an earnest one.

With thanks,

E. Dickinson.

MANUSCRIPT: AC. Pencil.
PUBLICATION: *L* (1894) 416; *LL* 341; *L* (1931) 406.
This letter was written in response to the letter following, from Thomas Niles, dated 13 March 1883. His letter was soon followed by a copy of Mathilde Blind's *Life of George Eliot*, published by Roberts Brothers on 17 March. The poems ED enclosed were "Further in Summer than the Birds" (incorporated in the letter preceding the signature), and "It sifts from Leaden Sieves" (separately enclosed). This letter exchange was probably initiated by ED in a letter (now missing) to Niles inquiring – as she had done a year before – whether Cross's *Life* of George Eliot was in progress.

813a

Dear Miss Dickinson

I do not hear anything about the Life of George Eliot by Mr Cross – at least only rumors that he is at work upon it.

We shall publish on Saturday a life of her by Mathilde Blind wh. will be worth your reading.

I shall be glad at any time to answer your inquiries

Very truly
T. Niles

As a further mark of her appreciation, ED sent Niles her own copy of the Brontë sisters' poems (see letter no. 299), which on 31 March Niles acknowledged thus (all Niles's letters to ED are at HCL in the Dickinson collection, and are unpublished).

813b

My dear Miss Dickinson

I received the copy of "Currer, Ellis & Acton Bells Poems." I already have a copy of a later Ed. which contains all of these and additional poems by Ellis & Acton.

Surely you did not mean to present me with your copy — if you did, I thank you heartily, but in doing so I must add that I would not for the world rob you of this very rare book, of which this is such a nice copy.

If I may presume to say so, I will take instead a M.S. collection of your poems, that is, if you want to give them to the world through the medium of a publisher

Very truly yours
T. Niles

I return the precious little volume by mail.

ED made no response to this request for a manuscript collection of her poems; instead, she sent him a copy of "No Brigadier throughout the Year," for which he seems to have thanked her, remarking that he liked it better than the first two she had sent. The following letter to Niles answers such a letter from him (now lost).

814

To Thomas Niles   *April 1883*

Dear friend –

Thank you for the kindness.

I am glad if the Bird seemed true to you.

Please efface the others and receive these three, which are more like him – a Thunderstorm – a Humming Bird, and a Country Burial. The Life of Marian Evans had much I never knew – a Doom of Fruit without the Bloom, like the Niger Fig.

Her Losses make our Gains ashamed –
She bore Life's empty Pack
As gallantly as if the East
Were swinging at her Back.
Life's empty Pack is heaviest,
As every Porter knows –
In vain to punish Honey –
It only sweeter grows.

———

MANUSCRIPT: AC. Pencil.
PUBLICATION: L (1894) 417–418; LL 377; L (1931) 406–407.
In the letter she enclosed "The Wind begun to rock the Grass," "A Route of Evanescence," and "Ample make this Bed." Niles acknowledged the letter in one dated 23 April 1883:

814a

My dear Miss Dickinson
    I must apologize for neglecting to reply to yours enclosing some specimens of your poetry. You will excuse me, will you not, when I say that sickness & death compelled me to thrust other things one side for the time.
    I am very much obliged to you for the three poems which I have read & reread with great pleasure, but which I have not consumed. I shall keep them unless you order me to do otherwise – in that case I shall as in duty bound obey
                                                        Yrs very truly
                                                            T. Niles

815

To Maria Whitney   *spring 1883*

Dear Friend,
    The guilt of having sent the note had so much oppressed me that I hardly dared to read the reply, and delayed my heart almost to its

stifling, sure you would never receive us again. To come unto our own and our own fail to receive us, is a sere response.

I hope you may forgive us.

All is faint indeed without our vanished mother, who achieved in sweetness what she lost in strength, though grief of wonder at her fate made the winter short, and each night I reach finds my lungs more breathless, seeking what it means.

> To the bright east she flies
> Brothers of Paradise
> Remit her home,
> Without a change of wings,
> Or Love's convenient things,
> Enticed to come.
>
> Fashioning what she is,
> Fathoming what she was,
> We deem we dream –
> And that dissolves the days
> Through which existence strays
> Homeless at home.

The sunshine almost speaks, this morning, redoubling the division, and Paul's remark grows graphic, "the *weight* of glory."

I am glad you have an hour for books, those enthralling friends, the immortalities, perhaps, each may pre-receive. "And I saw the Heavens opened."

I hope that nothing pains you except the pang of life, sweeter to bear than to omit.

> With love and wonder,
> Emily.

MANUSCRIPT: missing.

PUBLICATION: L (1894) 340–341; LL 349–350; L (1931) 329–330.

Sometime during the early spring Maria Whitney had called at the Dickinson house, and ED had sent word to her saying that she could not receive her. This letter replies to the letter that Maria Whitney subsequently wrote. The first quotation is from 2 Corinthians 4.17: "For our light affliction, which is but for a moment, worketh for us a far more exceeding and eternal weight of glory." The second is from Revelation 19.11.

To Helen Hunt Jackson   *early April 1883*

To be remembered what? Worthy to be forgot, is their renown –

MANUSCRIPT: Jackson. Pencil. The envelope, postmarked 10 April
1883, is addressed by George Montague.
PUBLICATION: *Poems* (1955) 1074.
Enclosed were pressed flowers, said to be bluebells. It was written perhaps in an attempt to pick up a correspondence that seems to have lapsed
since 1879 (see letter no. 602). A variant of this letter constitutes the final
lines of poem no. 1500 (*Poems*, 1955, 1073–1074).

817

To Charles H. Clark   *mid-April 1883*
Dear friend,

Would it be possible you would excuse me if I once more inquire
for the health of the Brother whom Association has made sacred?

With the trust that your own is impairless and that fear for your
Brother has not too much depressed you, please accept the solicitude
of myself, and my Sister.

E. Dickinson.

MANUSCRIPT: AC. Pencil. Envelope addressed by George Montague.
Dated by C. H. Clark, 18 April 1883.
PUBLICATION: *L* (1894) 357; *L* (1931) 349.
James Clark, who died early in June, was confined to his bed on 1 April.
This letter opens as though ED, having received no answer to her last letter
to James Clark, had already made inquiry of Charles about his brother's
condition.

818

To Charles H. Clark   *mid-April 1883*
Dear friend,

The sorrowful tidings of your Note almost dissuade reply, lest

I for one moment take you from your Brother's Bedside. I have delayed
to tell my Sister till I hear again, fearing to newly grieve her, and
hoping an encouraging word by another Mail.

Please be sure we are with you in sorrowing thought, and take
your Brother's Hand for me, if it is still with you. Perhaps the one
has called him, of whom we have so often talked, during this grieved
year –

With sympathy,
E. Dickinson.

MANUSCRIPT: AC. Pencil. Envelope addressed by ED, helped by clip-
pings from a Clark letter.
PUBLICATION: L (1894) 357; L (1931) 349–350.
Clark dated this 22 April 1883 – the date on which he received it.

819

To T. W. Higginson   *late April 1883*

Dear friend,

May I ask the delight in advance, of sending you the "Life of Mrs
Cross" by her Husband, which the Papers promise for publication? I
feared some other Pupil might usurp my privilege. Emblem is im-
measurable – that is why it is better than Fulfillment, which can be
drained –

MANUSCRIPT: BPL (Higg 114). Pencil.
PUBLICATION: L (1894) 331; LL 366–367; L (1931) 318.
The publication of Cross's book was announced on 21 April.

820

To Mrs. J. G. Holland   *spring 1883*

It was sweet to touch the familar Hand that so long had led us –
"Though thou walk through the Valley of the Shadow of Death, I
will be with thee," you have taught us was no Exaggeration – How
many times we have each crossed it, would either of us dare to count,
but we must bring no Twilight to one who lost her Dawn –

It is very dear you are better – You have had much struggle – That is the deepest illness –

The Birds are very bold this Morning, and sing without a Crumb. "Meat that we know not of," perhaps, slily handed them – I used to spell the one by that name *"Fee Bee"* when a Child, and have seen no need to improve! Should I spell all the things as they sounded to me, and say all the facts as I saw them, it would send consternation among more than the *"Fee Bees"*!

Vinnie picked the Sub rosas, and handed them to me, in your wily Note.

Kisses for "Brooks of Sheffield" – Am glad Annie is well, and that Kate is sacred – Tell her with my love, "I give my Angels charge." For the sweet Founder of the Fold, the bereft Madonna, more love than "we can ask or think" —

Emily.

MANUSCRIPT: HCL (H 80). Pencil.
PUBLICATION: *LH* 177.
This letter acknowledges one written by Mrs. Holland herself, which said that her daughter Kate was expecting a baby. For "Brooks of Sheffield," see letters no. 204 and 549. The first quotation is from Psalms 23.4; the second from John 4.32. The last two are respectively from Psalms 91.11; and Ephesians 3.20.

821

To Charles H. Clark   *early May 1883*

Dear friend,

The Temptation to inquire every Morning for your sufferer is almost irresistible, but our own Invalid taught us that a Sick Room is at times too sacred a place for a Friend's knock, timid as that is.

I trust this sweet May Morning is not without it's peace to your Brother and you, though the richest peace is of Sorrow. With constant and fervent anxiousness, and the hope of an early Word, please be sure we share your suspense.

E. Dickinson.

MANUSCRIPT: AC. Pencil. Envelope addressed by Lavinia.
PUBLICATION: *L* (1894) 357–358; *L* (1931) 350.
Dated by Charles Clark: May 1/83.

To Mrs. J. G. Holland   *early May 1883*

Sister –

I received a Card a few Days since, saying that "as soon as the Weather permitted," you would not be there. Has the Weather yet made those Advances? Not knowing where the Dear Ones are, I must cherish them heterogeniously till farther notice –

Loving the Blest without Abode, this too can be learned –

I wish the dear Eyes would so far relent as to let you read "Emily Bronte" – more electric far than anything since "Jane Eyre."

Napoleon of the Cross! Try and read a few lines at a time – and then a few more later – It is so so strange a Strength, I must have you possess it – Our Cousin, Willie Dickinson, is dying at Saratoga, and the stricken Letters of his Wife reach us every Mail –

We have written to Willie not to be homesick because his Mother and our Father would'nt have stayed so long if it were not a lovely place – How deep this Lifetime is – One guess at the Waters, and we are plunged beneath!

I send to your New York Home, hoping if you have fled, the Note may pursue you through some of Love's Deputies, and am Emily, with Vinnie's affection, and Maggie's "respects."

MANUSCRIPT: HCL (H 81). Pencil.
PUBLICATION: LH 178–179.
A. Mary F. Robinson's life of Emily Brontë was published in Roberts Brothers' Famous Women Series, 15 April 1883. William Hawley Dickinson died, 15 May.

To Mrs. J. Howard Sweetser   *early May 1883*

Dear Nellie.

I have long been a Lunatic on Bulbs, though screened by my friends, as Lunacy on any theme is better undivulged, but Emerson's intimacy with his "Bee" only immortalized him –

They came in happy safety, and rest in their subterranean Home—

"Remembrance faithful to her trust, brings" us "in beauty from the Dust," their divine prospective – Smitten by the sweetness, I only can take those wasted words "Thank you," on my lips.

We shall tenderly think of you in the foreign Home.

Were affection dependent on location, this would be an anonymous World.

The Apple Trees lend Vinnie Blossoms which she lends to me, and I pay no interest, their rosy Bank in need of none, and the Woods lend Austin Trilliums, shared in the same way – If you will lift your little Hands I will surely fill them, though not agree to let them go, but to that, your Lovers would not consent –

Your great Neighbor the Ocean, will see you oftener than I, and I am jealous already of his Morning calls –

Alice's call is still remembered – and a glance from Nettie in Hyacinth time.

Emily, with love –

MANUSCRIPT: *Rosenbach* 1170/18 (7). Pencil. Unpublished.

The letter acknowledges a gift of bulbs. The Sweetsers have moved, or are about to move, to a new home by the sea.

824

To Maria Whitney   *May 1883?*

Dear Friend,

Is not an absent friend as mysterious as a bulb in the ground, and is not a bulb the most captivating floral form? Must it not have enthralled the Bible, if we may infer from its selection? "The lily of the field!"

I never pass one without being chagrined for Solomon, and so in love with "the lily" anew, that were I sure no one saw me, I might make those advances of which in after life I should repent.

The apple-blossoms were slightly disheartened, yesterday, by a snow-storm, but the birds encouraged them all that they could – and how fortunate that the little ones had come to cheer their damask brethren!

You spoke of coming "with the apple-blossoms" – which occasioned our solicitude.

The ravenousness of fondness is best disclosed by children. . . . Is there not a sweet wolf within us that demands its food?

I can easily imagine your fondness for the little life so mysteriously committed to your care. The bird that asks our crumb has a plaintive distinction. I rejoice that it was possible for you to be with it, for I think the early spiritual influences about a child are more hallowing than we know. The angel begins in the morning in every human life. How small the furniture of bliss! How scant the heavenly fabric!

> No ladder needs the bird but skies
> To situate its wings,
> Not any leader's grim baton
> Arraigns it as it sings.
> The implements of bliss are few –
> As Jesus says of *Him*,
> "Come unto me" the moiety
> That wafts the cherubim.

Emily.

MANUSCRIPT: missing.
PUBLICATION: *L* (1894) 341–342; *LL* 350–351; *L* (1931) 330–331.
Maria Whitney took special interest in the Children's Aid Society. The letter is dated by Mrs. Todd: May, 1883?

825

To Charles H. Clark   *mid-May 1883*

Dear friend,

We have much fear, both for your own strength and the health of your Brother, having heard nothing since we last asked, many days ago.

Will you not when possible, give us but a syllable – even a cheering accent, if no more be true? We think of you and your Sufferer, with intense anxiety, wishing some act or word of our's might be hope or help. The Humming Birds and Orioles fly by me as I write, and I long to guide their enchanted feet to your Brother's chamber.

Excuse me for knocking.

Please also excuse me for staying so long – Spring is a strange Land when our friends are ill.

With my Sister's tenderest alarm, as also my own,

E. Dickinson.

MANUSCRIPT: AC. Pencil. Envelope addressed by George Montague, with corrections by ED.
PUBLICATION: L (1894) 358; L (1931) 350–351.
Dated by Charles Clark: "May 21/83."

826

To Charles H. Clark   *early June 1883*

I had, dear friend, the deep hope that I might see your Brother before he passed from Life, or rather Life we know, and can scarcely express the pang I feel at it's last denial.

His rare and hallowed kindness had strangely endeared him, and I cannot be comforted not to thank him before he went so far. I never had met your Brother but once.

An unforgotten once. To have seen him but once more, would have been almost like an interview with my "Heavenly Father," whom he loved and knew. I hope he was able to speak with you in his closing moment. One accent of courage as he took his flight would assist your Heart. I am eager to know all you may tell me of those final Days. We asked for him every Morning, in Heart, but feared to disturb you by inquiry aloud. I hope you are not too far exausted from your "loved employ."

To know of you, when possible, would console us much, and every circumstance of him we had hoped to see. My Sister gives her love with mine.

Though Strangers, please accept us for the two great sakes.

E. D.

MANUSCRIPT: AC. Pencil. Envelope addressed by Lavinia.
PUBLICATION: L (1894) 359; L (1931) 351.
James D. Clark died, 2 June 1883. Charles Clark dated this letter, 6 June.

Judge Otis P. Lord

Edward (Ned) Dickinson

Gilbert Dickinson

Martha Dickinson

Ned Dickinson and friend

Cast of "The Fair Barbarian"

To Charles H. Clark   *mid-June 1883*

Dear Friend,

Thank you for the paper. I felt it almost a bliss of sorrow that the name so long in Heaven on earth, should be on earth in Heaven.

Do you know if either of his sons have his mysterious face or his momentous nature?

The stars are not hereditary. I hope your brother and himself resumed the tie above, so dear to each below. Your bond to your brother reminds me of mine to my sister – early, earnest, indissoluble. Without her life were fear, and Paradise a cowardice, except for her inciting voice.

Should you have any picture of your brother, I should rejoice to see it at some convenient hour – and though we cannot know the last, would you sometime tell me as near the last as your grieved voice is able? . . .

Are you certain there is another life? When overwhelmed to know, I fear that few are sure.

My sister gives her grief with mine. Had we known in time, your brother would have borne our flowers in his mute hand. With tears,

E. Dickinson.

MANUSCRIPT: missing.
PUBLICATION: L (1894) 359–360; L (1931) 351–352.
This acknowledges a paper which mentioned Wadsworth. Mrs. Todd's date, 16 June 1883, was probably supplied by Clark.

To Mrs. Joseph A. Sweetser   *about 1883*

Dear Aunt –

I have found and give it in love, but reluctant to entrust anything so sacred to my Father as my Grandfather's Bible to a public Messenger, will wait till Mr. Howard comes, whom Mrs Nellie tells us is due this week – Thank you for loving my Father and Mother – I hope they are with the Source of Love – You did not tell me of your Health – I trust because confirmed – Thank you too for sorrow, the one you truly knew – with Vinnie's affection, in haste and fondness,

Emily –

MANUSCRIPT: Rosenbach 1170/18 (2). Pencil.
PUBLICATION: L (1894) 413; L (1931) 403.
Aunt Katie had asked for the Bible which had belonged to her father, Samuel Fowler Dickinson.

829

To Edward (Ned) Dickinson   *19 June 1883*

Stay with us one more Birthday, Ned –
"Yesterday, Today, and Forever," then we will let you go.

Aunt Emily.

MANUSCRIPT: HCL (B 120). Pencil.
PUBLICATION: FF 255.
Ned's birthday was on 19 June. During the summer of 1883 Ned suffered from acute rheumatic fever. The quotation is from Hebrews 13.8: "Jesus Christ the same yesterday, and today, and forever."

830

To Maria Whitney   *late June 1883*

Dear Friend,

You are like God. We pray to Him, and He answers "No." Then we pray to Him to rescind the "no," and He don't answer at all, yet "Seek and ye shall find" is the boon of faith.

You failed to keep your appointment with the apple-blossoms – the japonica, even, bore an apple to elicit you, but that must be a silver bell which calls the human heart.

I still hope that you live, and in lands of consciousness.

It is Commencement now. Pathos is very busy.

The past is not a package one can lay away. I see my father's eyes, and those of Mr. Bowles – those isolated comets. If the future is mighty as the past, what may vista be?

With my foot in a sling from a vicious sprain, and reminded of you almost to tears by the week and its witness, I send this sombre word.

The vane defines the wind.

Where we thought you were, Austin says you are not. How strange to change one's sky, unless one's star go with it, but yours has left an astral wake.

Vinnie gives her hand.

Always with love,

Emily.

MANUSCRIPT: missing.
PUBLICATION: *L* (1894) 342–343; *LL* 351–352; *L* (1931) 331–332.
Commencement took place on 27 June.

831

To Mabel Loomis Todd   *summer 1883*

Will Brother and Sister's dear friend accept my tardy devotion? I have been unable to seek my flowers, having harmed my foot.

Please accept them now, with the retarded fervor quickened by delay.

E. D.

MANUSCRIPT: AC. Pencil.
PUBLICATION: *L* (1931) 419.

832

To Mrs. Edward Tuckerman   *summer 1883*

Sweet Foot, that comes when we call it!
I can go but a Step a Century now –
How slow the Wind – how slow the Sea – how late their Feathers be!

Lovingly,
Emily.

MANUSCRIPT: AC. Pencil.
PUBLICATION: *L* (1894) 388; *L* (1931) 377–378; *Poems* (1955), 1083.

[781]

To Mrs. J. G. Holland   *summer 1883?*

The immediate and accurate loveliness deserved an immediate reply, but I have been hoping all the Days to hear from my poor friend, who I fear has taken fright anew, and gone to Dr Agnew. She has been much in our family, assisting in many crises, and was it not crisis all the time, in our hurrying Home? The support of a Mother, an almost imbecile Husband and two very sweet little Girls, hangs upon her Needle, so her sight is not luxury, but necessity –

Father valued her much, often befriending her, and I love to fulfill the kindness only Death suspends –

Forgive the personality. It seemed inevitable, and thank you again for the full sweetness, to which as to a Reservoir the smaller Waters go. What a beautiful Word "Waters" is! When I slept in the Pond and ate Seraphs for Breakfast, I thought I should know all about it now, but "Now" comes, and I dont –

I hear you are feasting on Army Worms, Canker Worms, and Cut Worms, and envy you your Salad –

We had a gallant Rain last Night, the first for many Days, and the Road is full of little Mirrors, at which the Grass adorns itself, when Nobody is seeing – reminding me of an instance similar, "Turn thou mine Eyes away from beholding Vanity!"

Love of us each –

Emily.

MANUSCRIPT: HCL (H 89). Pencil.
PUBLICATION: *LH* 191–192.

Dr. Agnew was Mrs. Holland's oculist. The seamstress has not been identified.

To Mrs. J. Howard Sweetser   *summer 1883*

Thank Nellie for coming Home – Infinite power of Home, that lurks in that slight figure!

Emily.

MANUSCRIPT: Rosenbach 1170/18 (10). Pencil. Unpublished.
This and the following six letters, all written to Mrs. Sweetser, are in the handwriting of 1883. They are notes sent to her during the summer sojourn of the Sweetsers in Amherst.

835

To Mrs. J. Howard Sweetser   *summer 1883*

Dear Nellie

Your sweet beneficence of Bulbs I return as Flowers, with a bit of the swarthy Cake baked only in Domingo.

Lovingly,
Emily.

MANUSCRIPT: Rosenbach 1170/18 (12). Pencil. Unpublished.
The gift of bulbs had been acknowledged in the spring (letter no. 823). This note accompanied a bouquet of flowers grown from the bulbs, together with the following recipe.

835a

Black Cake –

    2 pounds Flour –
    2 Sugar –
    2 Butter –
    19 Eggs –
    5 pounds Raisins –
    1½ Currants –
    1½ Citron –
    ½ pint Brandy –
    ½ — Molasses –
    2 Nutmegs –
    5 teaspoons
            Cloves – Mace – Cinnamon –
    2 teaspoons Soda –

Beat Butter and Sugar together –

Add Eggs without beating – and beat the mixture again –
Bake 2½ or three hours, in Cake pans, or 5 to 6 hours in
Milk pan, if full –

MANUSCRIPT: HCL. Pencil. Unpublished.

836

To Mrs. J. Howard Sweetser   *summer 1883*

Sweet friend,

Why is it Nobleness makes us ashamed –
Because it is so seldom or so hallowed? The Pitcher shall be an
emblem –

"Rebecca."

MANUSCRIPT: Rosenbach 1170/18 (1). Pencil. Unpublished.
The story of Rebecca at the well is told in Genesis, chapter 24.

837

To Mrs. J. Howard Sweetser   *summer 1883*

Dear Nellie,

I saw Thomas dressing the Horses and thought them just this
color, so if they hav'nt "taken Tea," would they resent this?

Emily.

MANUSCRIPT: Rosenbach 1170/18 (13). Pencil. Unpublished.

838

To Mrs. J. Howard Sweetser   *summer 1883*

Dear Nellie,

To have woven Wine so delightfully, one must almost have been
a Drunkard one's-self – but that is the stealthy franchise of the de-
murest Lips. Drunkards of Summer are quite as frequent as Drunk-

ards of Wine, and the Bee that comes Home sober is the Butt of the Clover.

Emily.

MANUSCRIPT: Rosenbach 1170/18 (16). Pencil. Unpublished.

839

To Mrs. J. Howard Sweetser   *summer 1883*

My first Jasmin,

with love.

MANUSCRIPT: Rosenbach 1170/18 (21). Pencil. Unpublished.

840

To Mrs. J. Howard Sweetser   *summer 1883*

Sweet Nellie,

Blossoms, and Cakes, and Memory! "Choose ye which ye will serve"! *I* serve the Memory.

> Blossoms will run away,
> Cakes reign but a Day,
> But Memory like Melody
> Is pink Eternally.

Emily.

MANUSCRIPT: Rosenbach 1170/18 (15). Pencil.
PUBLICATION: G. F. Whicher, *This Was a Poet* (1938), 144.
The quotation is from Joshua 24.15: ". . . chose you this day whom ye will serve. . ."

841

To Mrs. Richard H. Mather   *about 1883*

Dear friend –

We shared the molten Rubies with Austin, who pronounced them

dazzling, and desire if not presumptuous to know if you dine every
day on Gems? The graphic Cardinal flowers still glow on undimmed –
Thank you –

E – Dickinson –

MANUSCRIPT: AC. Pencil. Unpublished.

842

To Otis P. Lord   *about 1883*

The withdrawal of the Fuel of Rapture does not withdraw the
Rapture itself.
Like Powder in a Drawer, we pass it with a Prayer, it's Thunders
only dormant.

MANUSCRIPT: AC. Pencil. Fragment fair copy.
PUBLICATION: *Revelation* 84–85.
The date of this, and the fragment following, is conjectured from the
handwriting.

843

To Otis P. Lord   *about 1883*

I feel like wasting my Cheek on your Hand tonight – Will you accept
(approve) the squander – Lay up Treasures immediately – that's the
best Anodyne for moth and Rust and the thief whom the Bible knew
enough of Banking to suspect would break in and steal
Night is my favorite Day – I love silence so – I dont mean halt (stop)
of sound – but ones that talk of nought all day mistaking it for [racy?]
– Forgive you

MANUSCRIPT: AC. Pencil. Fragment rough draft on paper strip.
PUBLICATION: *Revelation* 90.

To Sally Jenkins   *about 1883*

Dear Sally –

Do you allow any Roses to compete with your own? Unfortunately, those are stemless –

Emily –

MANUSCRIPT: Squires. Pencil. Addressed on the fold: Sally.
PUBLICATION: *FN* 67.
The note was probably sent to Sally when she was visiting Martha Dickinson.

To Martha Dickinson   *about 1883*

Dear Girls,

I hope you are having superb times, and am sure you are, for I hear your voices, mad and sweet – as a Mob of Bobolinks.

I send you my love – which is always new for Rascals like you, and ask instead a little apartment in your Pink Hearts – call it Endor's Closet –

If ever the World should frown on you – he is old you know – give him a Kiss, and that will disarm him – if it dont – tell him from me,

> Who has not found the heaven – below –
> Will fail of it above –
> For Angels rent the House next our's,
> Wherever we remove –

Lovingly,
Emily –

MANUSCRIPT: Morgan Library. Pencil. Unpublished.
It is impossible to be sure whether this letter was sent next door on an occasion when Sally Jenkins, Mattie's friend now living in Pittsfield, was visiting her, or whether it was sent to Pittsfield at a time Mattie was visiting Sally. The fold of the letter bears no address, which customarily it would do if it had been sent next door. To ED the sound of the voices could come from either place. No envelope survives. The story of the witch of Endor is in 1 Samuel 28.

To Mrs. Henry Hills about 1883

We are much grieved for the sufferings of the Little One, which are so artlessly undeserved, and beg her Mama to assure her of our tender sympathy. The odor of the flower might please her, as these little Beings are only "on a furlough" from Paradise.

With love for the Mama, and sorrow for her weariness.

Emily.

MANUSCRIPT: missing. The text has the same provenance as that of letter no. 376. This and the two following letters to Mrs. Hills, were thought by George F. Whicher on the basis of handwriting to have been written about 1883.

PUBLICATION: *L* (1894) 398; *L* (1931) 387.

847

To Mrs. Henry Hills about 1883

With untold thanks, and the little Dish, founded while she was here, too late to overtake her, too small for her to sip, but her large Heart will excuse.

Emily
with love.

MANUSCRIPT: missing. The text has the same provenance as that of letter no. 376.

PUBLICATION: *L* (1894) 400; *L* (1931) 389.

848

To Mrs. Henry Hills about 1883

Persian Hues for my dark eyed neighbor.

MANUSCRIPT: missing. The text has the same provenance as that of letter no. 376.

PUBLICATION: *L* (1894) 401; *L* (1931) 390.

It is said to have been sent with red lilies.

To Mrs. Henry Hills   *about 1883*

Sometime when our dear Mrs Hills has an unoccupied moment tho
aware [we know] that her innumerable company of Angels leave her
very few of what are called so, will she, please, tell Vinnie's sister how
to make a little loaf of Cake like one she sent in April which is still
a remembrance of nectar.

It was what Austin calls Loaf Cake and the Almanac calls raised
Cake — Then Vinnie spied a Loaf of Bread at our lost neighbors, which
enthralled her – steamed Bran Brown Bread she thought it, from the
same Hand – and lovelier the same Heart – could I know the secret
of that Though I desire crumbs for but a few Robins, they [must be
supreme] desire supreme ones – Feel no haste dear friend – [only]
some propitious sometime and [add to things of sweetness] teach us
how to thank you too [for] (a more thoughtful sacred) act –
the shaggy bloom dear friend and the Druidic odors still make us
think of you. remind us still of you — Forgive the white intrusion
'Twas natures and not mine (Forgive the white intrusion Twas natures
& not mine)
I hope you may not go – That you are near is sinew. With reverential
remembrance

MANUSCRIPT: AC. Penciled rough draft.
PUBLICATION: *NEQ* XXVIII (1955) 302–303.
Words crossed out are placed in brackets. Alternative suggestions not
crossed out are in parentheses. No fair copy of this draft is known to survive.

To Mrs. James C. Greenough   *about 1883*

Lest any Bee should boast —

MANUSCRIPT: AC. Pencil.
PUBLICATION: L (1894) 428; L (1931) 416.
The date is conjectured from the handwriting. Mr. Greenough became
president of the Massachusetts Agricultural College in 1883. This note may
have accompanied flowers sent to the Greenoughs soon after their arrival in
Amherst. For a similarly phrased message to Susan Dickinson, see letter
no. 852.

To Edward (Ned) Dickinson   *about 1883*

We have all heard of the Boy whose Constitution required stolen fruit, though his Father's Orchard was loaded –

There was something in the unlawfulness that give it a saving flavor –

MANUSCRIPT: HCL (B 64). Pencil.
PUBLICATION: FF 248.
The date is conjectured from the handwriting.

To Susan Gilbert Dickinson   *about 1883*

"Lest any" Hen "should boast –"

MANUSCRIPT: HCL (B 47). Pencil.
PUBLICATION: FF 246.
This may have accompanied a gift of eggs, or of a roasting fowl. The paraphrase is from Ephesians 2.9: "For by grace are ye saved through faith. . . Not of works, lest any man should boast."

This note and the six which follow, all sent to Susan, are in the handwriting of about 1883.

To Susan Gilbert Dickinson   *about 1883*

How inspiriting to the clandestine Mind those words of Scripture, "We thank thee that thou hast hid these things" –

> Candor – my tepid friend –
> Come not to play with me –
> The Myrrhs, and Mochas, of the Mind
> Are it's iniquity –
>
> Emily –

MANUSCRIPT: HCL (B 119). Pencil.

PUBLICATION: *AM* CXV (1915) 39; *LL* 61, where it is attached to letter no. 580.

In her quotation ED has in mind Matthew 11.25: "At that time Jesus answered and said, I thank thee, O Father, Lord of heaven and earth, because thou hast hid these things from the wise and prudent, and hast revealed them unto babes."

854

To Susan Gilbert Dickinson   *about 1883*

Will my great Sister accept the minutae of Devotion, with timidity that it is no more?
Susan's Calls are like Antony's Supper —
"And pays his Heart for what his Eyes eat, only –"

                                                          Emily –

MANUSCRIPT: HCL (B 24). Pencil. Addressed: Susan.
PUBLICATION: *FF* 242–243, altered.

The quotation is from *Antony and Cleopatra*, II, ii, 225–226 (Enobarbus): "And for his ordinary, pays his heart,/For what his eyes eat only." (See also letter no. 1026 and Prose Fragment 56.)

855

To Susan Gilbert Dickinson   *about 1883*

To be Susan is Imagination,
To have been Susan, a Dream —
What depths of Domingo in that torrid Spirit!

                                                          Emily –

MANUSCRIPT: HCL (B 51). Pencil.
PUBLICATION: *FF* 237.

856

To Susan Gilbert Dickinson   *about 1883*

Dear Sue –

Your little mental gallantries are sweet as Chivalry, which is to me

a shining Word though I dont know its meaning – I sometimes remember we are to die, and hasten toward the Heart which how could
I woo in a rendezvous where there is no Face?

Emily –

MANUSCRIPT: HCL (B 77). Pencil.
PUBLICATION: LL 79, in part.

857

To Susan Gilbert Dickinson   *about 1883*

Mama and Sister might like a flower to help them welcome Ned –

Emily.

MANUSCRIPT: HCL (B 21). Pencil. Unpublished.

858

To Susan Gilbert Dickinson   *about 1883*

Dear Susan,

An untimely knock necessitating my flight from the Kettle, the
Berries were overdone – I almost fear to send them, though hope they
may have a worthless worth to those for whom they were –

Emily –

MANUSCRIPT: HCL (B 146). Pencil.
PUBLICATION: FF 246.

859

To Charles H. Clark   *July 1883*

Dear friend –

While I thank you immediately for the invaluable Gift, I cannot
express the bereavement that I am no more to behold it.

Believing that we are to have no Face in a farther Life, makes the
Look of a Friend a Boon almost too precious. The resemblance is faith-

ful – the scholarly gentleness – the noble modesty – the absence of every Dross, quite there – What a consoling Prize to you, his Mate through years of Anguish so much sharper to see, because endured so willingly – Chastening would seem unneeded by so supreme a Spirit.

I feel great grief for you – I hope his Memory may help you, so recently a Life. I wish I might say one liquid word to make your sorrow less. Is not the devotion that you gave him, an acute Balm? Had you not been with him, how solitary the Will of God!

Thank you for every word of his pure career – I hope it is nearer us than we are aware.

Will you not still tell us of yourself and your Home – from which this patient Guest has flown?

I am glad he lies near us. And thank you for the tidings of our other Fugitive, whom to know was Life – I can scarcely tell you how deeply I cherish your thoughtfulness. To still know of the Dead is a great permission, and you have almost enabled that. With the ceaseless sympathy of myself and my sister, and the trust that our sufferer rests –

E. Dickinson.

MANUSCRIPT: AC. Pencil. Envelope addressed by George Montague, with corrections by ED. Dated by Clark, 9 July 1883.

PUBLICATION: L (1894) 360–361; LL 359–360; L (1931) 352–353.

This acknowledges receipt of the photograph of James Clark which she had requested in her last letter (no. 827). He was buried at Northampton.

860

To Maria Whitney   *summer 1883*

Dear Friend,

Your sweet self-reprehension makes us look within, which is so wild a place we are soon dismayed, but the seed sown in the lake bears the liquid flower, and so of all your words.

I am glad you accept rest.

Too many disdain it. I am glad you go to the Adirondacks.

To me the name is homelike, for one of my lost went every year with an Indian guide, before the woods were broken. Had you been here it would be sweet, but that, like the peach, is later. With a tomorrow in its cupboard, who would be "an hungered"?

Thank you for thinking of Dick. He is now the horse of association.

Men are picking the grass from father's meadow to lay it away for winter, and it takes them a long time. They bring three horses of their own, but Dick, ever gallant, offers to help, and bears a little machine like a top, which spins the grass away.

It seems very much like a gentleman getting his own supper – for what is his supper winter nights but tumblers of clover?

You speak of "disillusion." That is one of the few subjects on which I am an infidel. Life is so strong a vision, not one of it shall fail.

Not what the stars have done, but what they are to do, is what detains the sky.

We shall watch for the promised words from the Adirondacks, and hope the recess will all be joy. To have been made alive is so chief a thing, all else inevitably adds. Were it not riddled by partings, it were too divine.

I was never certain that mother had died, except while the students were singing. The voices came from another life. . . .

Good-night, dear. Excuse me for staying so long. I love to come to you. To one who creates, or consoles, thought, what an obligation!

                                                                Emily.

MANUSCRIPT: missing.
PUBLICATION: L (1894) 343–344; LL 352–353; L (1931) 332–333.
Maria Whitney went to Long Lake in the Adirondacks in the summer of 1883.

                                        861

To Harriet Austin Dickinson   *mid-August 1883*

Dear friend,

I want to thank you for the tenderness to Vinnie, who has been Soldier and Angel too since our Parents died, and only carries a "drawn Sword" in behalf of Eden – the "Cherubim" her criterion.

I am glad that you have your Mother with you – forgive a pang of covetousness that I have not my own – a sacred place for envy – and you have, I believe, one Sister the most, bereaving me again. Mother – Brother – Sister! "What a Triumvirate"!

But Yesterday, and those three Wealths were actually mine! With sorrowing gluttony I look away from your's. Thanking you again for the affection for Vinnie,

Her Sister –

MANUSCRIPT: AC. Pencil.
PUBLICATION: *AB* 9.

Harriet Dickinson was present at the Dickinson family reunion at Amherst on 8–9 August 1883. This note was probably written after she and Vinnie had met on the occasion.

With this penciled note, and in precisely similar penciled writing, has long been placed this brief memorandum (AC):

Vinnie out for 10 Minutes –
Wait – please –

The note presumably was delivered to Miss Harriet Dickinson at the Dickinson house, while she was in Amherst during the reunion.

862

To Mrs. Timothy W. Sloan mid-August 1883

Will Mrs Sloan accept these few Blossoms for the Hand of her Daughter, with the sorrow of

Emily, and
Vinnie Dickinson –

MANUSCRIPT: Jones Library. Pencil. Unpublished.

This note was sent on the occasion of the death of Mary Emma Sloan, who died, 16 August 1883, aged seventeen. The Sloans lived on the next street, and were thought of as neighbors.

863

To Annie Jameson 1883?

Dear Annie,

Will it fill your eyes too full of tears when I tell you that Delawares were my sweet lost Mother's favorite grape? Eat the bit of cake in your garden, and let the Robins taste.

With thanks.

MANUSCRIPT: missing. Unpublished. The text derives from a transcript

[795]

in the Jones Library purportedly made "From Goodspeed's letter of September 27, 1932."

Annie Jameson was a playmate of young Gilbert Dickinson. Her gift of grapes is acknowledged by this note and a "bit of cake." The letter was written after Mrs. Dickinson's death but, from the tone, probably before the death of Gilbert in October. Perhaps the acquaintance with Mrs. Jameson began through the children. If so, it explains the formality of the later note to the mother (no. 933) in spite of intervening notes written to Annie and her brother Arthur.

864

To Samuel Bowles the younger   *early autumn 1883*

Dear friend,

There is more than one "Deluge," though but one is recorded, and the duplicate of the "Dove," hallows your own Heart. I had feared that the Angel with the Sword would dissuade you from Eden, but rejoice that it only ushered you. "Every several Gate is of one Pearl."

> Morning is due to all –
> To some – the Night –
> To an imperial few –
> The Auroral Light.

Reverently,
E. Dickinson.

MANUSCRIPT: Bowles. Pencil.
PUBLICATION: L (1931) 338.

ED sent this on learning of the engagement of Bowles to Miss Elizabeth Hoar. He forwarded it to his fiancée with this endorsement on the back fold: "This is from the friend whom I have never seen. It has just come. Please keep it for me again." The scripture quotation attempts to recall Revelation 21.21.

865

To Samuel Bowles the younger?   *about 1883*

To ask of each that gathered Life, Oh, where did it grow, is intuitive.

That you have answered this Prince Question to your own delight, is joy to us all.

> Lad of Athens, faithful be
> To Thyself,
> And Mystery –
> All the rest is Perjury –

Please say with my tenderness to your Mother, I shall soon write her.

E. Dickinson –

MANUSCRIPT: AC. Pencil.
PUBLICATION: *L* (1931) 415.
The recipient of this letter is not known. The handwriting is almost certainly late 1883. No other relationship of son and mother, in ED's associations, suggests itself except that with Bowles. Her signature here is that she used to him. The tone of the message is one she adopted for those about to be married.

866

To Mrs. J. G. Holland   *late September 1883*

Dear One.

No one had told me your Sister had died – I sweetly remember her on my first Visit to you – a tender-timid face, with the appealing look that the ones have, who do not hear entirely –
Perhaps the Brother called her –
"The Kingdom and the Power" may not have filled a Sister's place – For this new solitude to you I am freshly grieved. Would that a few familiar Lips might be left to you, now the best have stopped!
We read with deep affection of the dear Doctor's Emblem – in the Republican – proud that each farthest reach of Love had been ratified – I hope he thinks of us – I am glad you are in the open Air – That is nearest Heaven –
The first Abode "not made with Hands" entices to the second –
I have thought of you with peculiar urgency for the last few days. Can it be there was cause?

[797]

Said a rude but wondering Mind to me, a Carpenter at work here, "I cant tell how it is, but there *are* influences."

Even my Puritan Spirit "gangs" sometimes "aglay—"

Sweetest Love for Kate, and Annie when you see her, and say with "Heathcliff" to little Katrina — "Oh Cathie — Cathie!"

Theodore probably witnessed nothing so "royal" as himself, of which with warm remembrance convince him — Vinnie gives her Heart and Maggie her love, though how do the gifts vary? And I, consign myself to you and find the Nest sufficient — Take faithful care of the dear health and flee no sudden day from your dependent

Emily —

MANUSCRIPT: HCL (H 82). Pencil.
PUBLICATION: *LH* 180–181.

The *Springfield Republican* for 10 July 1883 announced that Holland's burial monument had been erected, with a bas-relief by St. Gaudens. Kathrina Holland Van Wagenen, a first grandchild, was born, 8 August. Mrs. Holland's sister Minnie (Amelia Chapin May) died, 9 September. In *Wuthering Heights* Heathcliff says when he last meets Catherine: "Oh, Cathy! Oh my life! how can I bear it?" Theodore Holland had attended the Canadian industrial fair at Toronto, opened by the retiring governor-general, the Marquis of Lorne, and his wife Princess Louise. The quotation in the fifth paragraph is from 2 Corinthians 5.1 (see also letters no. 180, 182, and 458).

867

To Mrs. J. Howard Sweetser   *early October 1883*

Thank you, Dear, for the loveliness. It is very sweet to know you are near. We are so much grieved for the little Boy —

Emily —

MANUSCRIPT: Pohl. Pencil. Unpublished.

The handwriting is unmistakably late 1883. Very early in October, Gilbert Dickinson was stricken with typhoid fever, and died after a few days' illness, on 5 October. No death during ED's lifetime more deeply shocked and grieved her. This letter was probably written during Gilbert's illness, but before he died.

To Susan Gilbert Dickinson   *early October 1883*

Dear Sue –

The Vision of Immortal Life has been fulfilled –

How simply at the last the Fathom comes! The Passenger and not the Sea, we find surprises us –

Gilbert rejoiced in Secrets –

His Life was panting with them – With what menace of Light he cried "Dont tell, Aunt Emily"! Now my ascended Playmate must instruct *me*. Show us, prattling Preceptor, but the way to thee!

He knew no niggard moment – His Life was full of Boon – The Playthings of the Dervish were not so wild as his –

No crescent was this Creature – He traveled from the Full –

Such soar, but never set –

I see him in the Star, and meet his sweet velocity in everything that flies – His Life was like the Bugle, which winds itself away, his Elegy an echo – his Requiem ecstasy –

Dawn and Meridian in one.

Wherefore would he wait, wronged only of Night, which he left for us –

Without a speculation, our little Ajax spans the whole –

> Pass to thy Rendezvous of Light,
> Pangless except for us –
> Who slowly ford the Mystery
> Which thou hast leaped across!

                                              Emily.

MANUSCRIPT: HCL (B 79). Pencil.
PUBLICATION: *AM* CXV (1915) 42; *LL* 85.

This and the three following letters were written to Sue after Gilbert's death. The poem is also in letter no. 972.

To Susan Gilbert Dickinson   *early October 1883*

Perhaps the dear, grieved Heart would open to a flower, which blesses unrequested, and serves without a Sound.

Emily.

MANUSCRIPT: HCL (L 50). Pencil. Unpublished.

870

To Susan Gilbert Dickinson   *early October 1883*

> Climbing to reach the costly Hearts
> To which he gave the worth,
> He broke them, fearing punishment
> He ran away from Earth –

Emily.

MANUSCRIPT: HCL (385). Pencil.
PUBLICATION: *Poems* (1955) 1079.
See letter no. 893.

871

To Susan Gilbert Dickinson   *early October 1883*

Dear Sue –

A Promise is firmer than a Hope, although it does not hold so much –

Hope never knew Horizon –

Awe is the first Hand that is held to us –

Hopelessness in it's first Film has not leave to last – That would close the Spirit, and no intercession could do that –

Intimacy with Mystery, after great Space, will usurp it's place –

Moving on in the Dark like Loaded Boats at Night, though there is no Course, there is Boundlessness –

Expanse cannot be lost –
Not Joy, but a Decree
Is Deity –
His Scene, Infinity –
Whose rumor's Gate was shut so tight
Before my Beam was sown,
Not even a Prognostic's push
Could make a Dent thereon –

The World that thou hast opened
Shuts for thee,
But not alone,
We all have followed thee –
Escape more slowly
To thy Tracts of Sheen –
The Tent is listening,
But the Troops are gone!

Emily –

MANUSCRIPT: HCL (B 91). Pencil.
PUBLICATION: LL 87, prose only; *Poems* (1955) 1091–1092, poem only.

872

To Charles H. Clark   *mid-October 1883*

Dear friend.

These thoughts disquiet me, and the great friend is gone, who could solace them. Do they disturb you?

The Spirit lasts – but in what mode –
Below, the Body speaks,
But as the Spirit furnishes –
Apart, it never talks –
The Music in the Violin
Does not emerge alone
But Arm in Arm with Touch, yet Touch
Alone – is not a Tune –
The Spirit lurks within the Flesh
Like Tides within the Sea

[801]

That make the Water live, estranged
What would the Either be?
Does that know – now – or does it cease –
That which to this is done,
Resuming at a mutual date
With every future one?
Instinct pursues the Adamant,
Exacting this Reply –
Adversity if it may be, or
Wild Prosperity,
The Rumor's Gate was shut so tight
Before my Mind was sown,
Not even a Prognostic's Push
Could make a Dent thereon –

With the trust you live,

E. Dickinson.

MANUSCRIPT: AC. Pencil. Envelope addressed by Lavinia.

PUBLICATION: L (1894) 363–364; L (1931) 355. According to Clark's notation, the letter was mailed 17 October 1883. The dating, 21 April 1884, in *Letters,* was due to a misreading of Clark's notations.

Though ED does not so intimate, the thoughts expressed are as much conjured by Gilbert's death as by that of Wadsworth, who had died eighteen months earlier.

There is no stanza break in the poem.

873

To Mrs. J. G. Holland   *late 1883*

Sweet Sister.

Was that what I used to call you?

I hardly recollect, all seems so different –

I hesitate which word to take, as I can take but few and each must be the chiefest, but recall that Earth's most graphic transaction is placed within a syllable, nay, even a gaze –

The Physician says I have "Nervous prostration."

Possibly I have – I do not know the Names of Sickness. The Crisis of the sorrow of so many years is all that tires me – As Emily Bronte to her Maker, I write to my Lost "Every Existence would exist in thee –"

The tender consternation for you was much eased by the little Card, which spoke *"better"* as loud as a human Voice –

Please, Sister, to wait –

"Open the Door, open the Door, they are waiting for me," was Gilbert's sweet command in delirium. *Who* were waiting for him, all we possess we would give to know – Anguish at last opened it, and he ran to the little Grave at his Grandparents' feet – All this and more, though *is* there more? More than Love and Death? Then tell me it's name!

Love for the sweet Catharines, Rose and Bud in one, and the Gentleman with the vast Name, and Annie and Ted, and if the softest for yourself, would they ever know, or knowing, covet?

How lovely that you went to "Church"!

May I go with you to the "Church of the first born?"

Emily –

MANUSCRIPT: HCL (H 83). Pencil.
PUBLICATION: *LH* 182–183.

Gilbert's last words are quoted also, somewhat differently, in letter no. 1020.

The quoted line of poetry is from Emily Brontë's "Last Lines" (see also letter no. 940). Higginson read the poem at ED's funeral. The final quotation is from Hebrews 12.23.

874

To Susan Gilbert Dickinson   *late November 1883*

Thank Sister with love, and reserve an Apartment for two Cocks in the Thanksgiving planning –

Mattie is almost with you –

The first section of Darkness is the densest, Dear – After that, Light trembles in –

You asked would I remain?

Irrevocably, Susan – I know no other way –

Ether looks dispersive, but try it with a Lever –

Emily –

MANUSCRIPT: HCL (B 67). Pencil.
PUBLICATION: *FF* 263.

875

To Mrs. Elizabeth Carmichael   *late 1883?*

My consoleless Vinnie convinces me of the misfortune of having known dear Mrs. Carmichael, whom "to name is to praise," for indeed, were we both intelligent mourners, I fear delight would close; but the "fair uncertainty" aids me, which is denied Vinnie.

Of her noble loss it is needless to speak – that is incalculable.

Of her sweet power to us when we were overwhelmed, that, too, shall be mute. She has "borne our grief and carried our sorrow," that is the criterion. . . .

Let me hope she is well to-day, and sheltered by every love she deserves, which were indeed countless.

We congratulate sweet Mrs. Skeel on her beloved booty, and ask a remembrance in her prayer for those of us bereaved.

Lovingly,
Emily.

MANUSCRIPT: missing.
PUBLICATION: *L* (1894) 420–421; *L* (1931) 409.

Mrs. Carmichael, the mother of the first wife of Professor Richard H. Mather, was an especially close friend of Lavinia's. After her daughter's death she left the Mather house, close to the Dickinson's, to live with her sister Mrs. Skeel. The letter perhaps was written after the death of Gilbert. The first quotation attempts to recall lines from Fitz-Greene Halleck's "On the Death of Joseph Rodman Drake": "None knew thee but to love thee,/ Nor named thee but to praise." The scripture quotation recalls Isaiah 53.4.

876

To Kendall Emerson   *Christmas 1883*

Dear Kendall –

Christmas in Bethlehem means most of all, this Year, but Santa Claus still asks the way to Gilbert's little friends – Is Heaven an unfamiliar Road?

Come sometime with your Sled and tell Gilbert's

Aunt Emily.

MANUSCRIPT: AC. Pencil.

PUBLICATION: *Amherst Alumni News* IV (July 1951) 14.

ED's special feeling for Gilbert's playmate stemmed from the fact that both children had been playing in the same mud hole when Gilbert contracted the typhoid fever from which he died. She continued annually to remember Kendall with a Christmas note (see letters no. 956 and 1027).

877

To Mrs. Henry Hills   *Christmas 1883*

Santa Claus comes with a Smile and a Tear. Santa Claus has been robbed, not by Burglars but Angels. The Children will pray for Santa Claus?

MANUSCRIPT: missing. Unpublished.
The text has the same provenance as that of letter no. 376.

878

To Annie Jameson?   *Christmas 1883*

Our Santa Claus is draped, this Year, but Gilbert's little Mates are still dear to his Aunt Emily.

MANUSCRIPT: Bennett. Pencil. Unpublished.
The provenance of this autograph remains uncertain, but the probability is that the note was sent with a Christmas remembrance to the young daughter of Mr. and Mrs. John Jameson.

XII

LETTERS

879–1045

[1884–1886]

" . . . *A Letter is a joy of Earth —*
it is denied the Gods."

The elegiac tone of Emily Dickinson's letters, evident after Gilbert's death, becomes insistent after the death of Judge Lord in March 1884. In June she suffered a nervous breakdown and, though she kept up her correspondence, her strength was ebbing and she never fully regained her health. But she continued to read and to correspond about books. Indeed, the long-awaited publication of the first volume of Cross's biography of George Eliot, in 1885, was an event that raised her spirit.

The unexpected passing of Helen Jackson in August 1885, occurred about the time her own final illness was upon her, and after November she was confined for long periods to her room and bed. Yet her pencil was always beside her, and the final messages appropriately were sent to Mrs. Holland, to Colonel Higginson, and to the Norcross cousins.

Perhaps no sentence that she wrote more aptly epitomizes her relationship with people than this, written to James Clark in 1882: "A Letter always seemed to me like Immortality, for is it not the Mind alone, without corporeal friend?" They are the words she had used in writing Higginson in 1869, when for the most part prose rather than poetry had become the mode of her expression.

To Mrs. Elizabeth Carmichael   *early 1884?*

Loved Mrs. Carmichael and Mrs. Skeel,

I heard long since at school that Diogenes went to sea in a tub. Though I did not believe it, it is credible now.

Against the peril of ocean steamers I am sweetly provided, and am sure you had my safety in mind, in your lovely gifts.

I have taken the passengers from the hold – passengers of honey – and the deck of silk is just promenaded by a bold fly, greedy for its sweets. The little tub with the surcingle I shall keep till the birds, filling it then with nectars, in Mrs. Skeel's sweet honor.

Will each of the lovely friends present my thanks to the other, as Vinnie's correspondence with them is too impressive for what dear Dickens calls "the likes of me" to invade.

Their sweet intercession with Santa Claus in my behalf, I shall long remember.

Always,
Emily.

MANUSCRIPT: missing.
PUBLICATION: L (1894) 419–420; L (1931) 408–409, dated "1884?."
The letter acknowledges Christmas remembrances.

To Charles H. Clark   *early January 1884*

Dear friend –

I have been very ill since early October, and unable to thank you for the sacred kindness, but treasured it each Day and hasten with my first steps, and my fullest gratitude. Returning from the dying Child, waiting till he left us, I found it on my Desk, and it seemed an appropriate Message – I never can thank you as I feel –

That would be impossible.

The effort ends in tears.

You seem by some deep Accident, to be the only tie between the Heaven that evanesced, and the Heaven that stays.

I hope the winged Days that bear you to your Brother, are not too destitute of Song, and wish that we might speak with you of him and of yourself, and of the third Member of that sundered Trio. Perhaps another spring would call you to Northampton, and Memory might invite you here.

My Sister asks a warm remembrance, and trusts that you are well. With a deep New Year,

Your friend,
E. Dickinson.

MANUSCRIPT: AC. Pencil. Envelope addressed by Lavinia Dickinson: C. H. Clark/361 Degraw St./Brooklyn/L.I. Postmarked: Jan 4 1884.

PUBLICATION: L (1894) 361–362, in part; LL 360, in part; L (1931) 353, entire.

The "third Member" was probably Wadsworth.

881

To Mrs. J. Howard Sweetser   *about 1884*

Keepsakes for "Suppertime," when all the Bairns come home.

Emily and Vinnie.

MANUSCRIPT: Rosenbach 1170/18 (20). Pencil. Unpublished. Folded and addressed: Nellie – New York –

The handwriting is that of about 1884. Some remembrance was evidently delivered by hand.

882

To Mrs. J. G. Holland   *early 1884*

Sweet Sister.

The contemplation of you as "Grandma" is a touching novelty to which the Mind adjusts itself by reverent degrees.

That nothing in her Life became her like it's last event, it is probable – So the little Engrosser has done her work, and Love's "remainder Biscuit" is henceforth for us –

We will try to bear it as divinely as Othello did, who had he had Love's sweetest slice, would not have charmed the World –

Austin heard Salvini before his Idol died, and the size of that manifestation even the Grave has not foreclosed –

I saw the Jays this Morning, each in a Blue Pelisse, and would have kissed their Lips of Horn, if I could have caught them, but Nature took good care!

I have made a permanent Rainbow by filling a Window with Hyacinths, which Science will be glad to know, and have a Cargo of Carnations, worthy of Ceylon, but Science and Ceylon are Strangers to me, and I would give them both for one look of the gone Eyes, glowing in Paradise – There are too many to count, now, and I measure by Fathoms, Numbers past away –

With longings for the sweet Health and Seraphic Peace of my little Sister,

Her Lover,

Emily.

MANUSCRIPT: HCL (H 84). Pencil.

PUBLICATION: *LH* 183–184.

The expression "remainder biscuit" is from *As You Like It* (see letter no. 545). Salvini's performance of *Othello* Austin probably saw in the winter of 1873–1874, before the death of Salvini's wife, "his Idol," in 1878, but his diary only records the performance he saw 11 April 1883.

883

To Mrs. Edward Tuckerman   *February 1884*

Do "Men gather Grapes of Thorns?" No – but they do of *Roses* – and even the classic Fox hushed his innuendo, as we unclasped the little Box – Sherbets untold, and Recollection more sparkling than Sherbets!

How wondrous is a Friend, the gift of neither Heaven nor Earth, yet coveted of both!

If the "Archangels vail their faces," is not the sacred diffidence on this sweet behalf?

Emily –

MANUSCRIPT: AC. Pencil. Mrs. Tuckerman dated it: February 1884.
PUBLICATION: L (1894) 389; LL 370; L (1931) 378–379.
The first quotation is from Matthew 7.16 (see letter no. 1033). The second reconstructs Isaiah 6.2: "Above it stood the seraphims: each one had six wings; with twain he covered his face, and with twain he covered his feet, and with twain he did fly."

884

To Charles H. Clark   *late February 1884*

Dear friend –

I hoped it might gratify you to meet the little flower which was my final ministry to your Brother, and which even in that faint hour, I trust he recognized, though the thronged Spirit had not access to words.

These are my first out, and their golden trifles are too full of association to remain unshared. With faithful thought of yourself and your Brother, Brothers in bereavement even as myself.

MANUSCRIPT: AC. Pencil. The signature has been clipped from the letter. The envelope is addressed by Lavinia: C. H. Clark/361 Degraw St./ Brooklyn/L.I. Postmarked: Feb 22.
PUBLICATION: L (1894) 362; L (1931) 354.

885

To Mrs. Henry Hills   *February 1884?*

The Snow will guide the Hyacinths to where their Mates are sleeping, in Vinnie's sainted Garden.

"We shall not all sleep, but we shall all be changed."

Paul.

MANUSCRIPT: missing. The text has the same provenance as that of letter no. 376. Unpublished.

The note acknowledges a gift of bulbs. The quotation is from 1 Corinthians 15.51.

886

To Susan Gilbert Dickinson   *February 1884*

Dear Sue –

I was surprised, but Why? Is she not of the lineage of the Spirit? I knew she was beautiful – I knew she was royal, but that she was hallowed, how could I surmise, who had scarcely seen her since her deep Eyes were brought in your Arms to her Grandfather's – Thanksgiving? She is a strange trust – I hope she may be saved – Redemption Mental precedes Redemption Spiritual. The Madonna and Child descend from the Picture – while Creation is kneeling before the Frame – I shall keep the secret.

Emily.

MANUSCRIPT: HCL (B 102). Pencil.
PUBLICATION: LL 54, in part; FF 171, in part.

Although the allusion to the Madonna and child is obscure, the picture referred to has been tentatively identified with a photograph of Martha Dickinson (HCL) by Lovell, Amherst, inscribed on the back: With dearest love of/Your Valentine/February the 14th 1884. Since this letter is to Susan, not to Martha, one infers that Susan lent ED the photograph which Martha gave to her mother. It is probable that ED actually saw little of Martha at this time.

887

To Mrs. James C. Greenough   *early 1884*

Trusting the happy flower will meet you at the Door, where Spring will soon be knocking, we challenge your "Come in."

E. Dickinson.

MANUSCRIPT: AC. Pencil.

[813]

PUBLICATION: L (1894) 428; L (1931) 416.
The date is conjectured from the handwriting. The note suggests that a call from Mrs. Greenough would be welcome.

888

To Mrs. J. G. Holland   *early 1884*

The Organ is moaning – the Bells are bowing, I ask Vinnie what time it is, and she says it is Sunday, so I tell my Pencil to make no noise, and we will go to the House of a Friend "Weeks off," as Dombey said –

Your reunion with Vinnie was amusing and affecting too, and Vinnie still rehearses it to admiring throngs of which Stephen and I are the thrilled components – I think Vinnie has grown since the interview, certainly intellectually, which is the only Bone whose Expanse we woo –

Your flight from the "Sewer" reminded me of the "Mill on the Floss," though "Maggie Tulliver" was missing, and had she been there, her Destiny could not have been packed in the "Bath Tub," though Baby's may be as darkly sweet in the Future running to meet her –

How quickly a House can be deserted, and your infinite inference that the "Soul's poor Cottage" may lose it's Tenant so, was vaster than you thought, and still overtakes me –

How few suggestions germinate!

I shall make Wine Jelly Tonight and send you a Tumbler in the Letter, if the Letter consents, a Fabric sometimes obdurate –

It is warm you are better, and was very cold all the while you were ill –

Baby's flight will embellish History with Gilpin's and Revere's – With love untold,

Your Emily –

MANUSCRIPT: HCL (H 85). Pencil.
PUBLICATION: LH 185–186.
Mrs. Holland had been visiting in Northampton and Vinnie had called on her. Stephen Sullivan was the stableman (see Appendix 2). The Van Wagenens, with whom Mrs. Holland now lived, were driven out of their

[814]

house one night that winter by a clogged sewer which flooded the cellar, and had transported the baby's clothes to a nearby hotel in a small tin bathtub. For the quoted lines in the fourth paragraph, see the note to letter no. 544.

889

To Maria Whitney   *March 1884?*

Dear Friend,

The little package of Ceylon arrived in fragrant safety, and Caliban's "clust'ring filberds" were not so luscious nor so brown.

Honey in March is blissful as inopportune, and to caress the bee a severe temptation, but was not temptation the first zest?

We shall seek to be frugal with our sweet possessions, though their enticingness quite leads us astray, and shall endow Austin, as we often do, after a parched day.

For how much we thank you.

Dear arrears of tenderness we can never repay till the will's great ores are finally sifted; but bullion is better than minted things, for it has no alloy.

Thinking of you with fresher love, as the Bible boyishly says, "New every morning and fresh every evening."

Emily.

MANUSCRIPT: missing.

PUBLICATION: L (1894) 346; L (1931) 334–335. Mrs. Todd dated the letter: "Probably 1884."

It is Caliban speaking to Trinculo who says (*Tempest*, II, ii, 170–171): "I'll bring thee/To clustering filberds." The scripture quotation is from Lamentations 3.22–23: "It is of the Lord's mercies that we are not consumed, because his compassions fail not. They are new every morning: great is thy faithfulness."

890

To Mrs. J. G. Holland   *March 1884*

When I tell my sweet Mrs Holland that I have lost another friend, she will not wonder I do not write, but that I raise my Heart to a drooping syllable – Dear Mr Lord has left us – After a brief unconsciousness, a Sleep that ended with a smile, so his Nieces tell us, he hastened away, "seen," we trust, "of Angels" – "Who knows that secret deep" – "Alas, not I –"

Forgive the Tears that fell for few, but that few too many, for was not each a World?

Your last dear words seemed stronger, and smiling in the feeling that you were to be, this latest sorrow came – I hope your own are with you, and may not be taken – I hope there is no Dart advancing or in store –

> Quite empty, quite at rest,
> The Robin locks her Nest, and tries her Wings.
> She does not know a Route
> But puts her Craft about
> For *rumored* Springs –
> She does not ask for Noon –
> She does not ask for Boon,
> Crumbless and homeless, of but one request –
> The Birds she lost –

Do you remember writing to us you should "write with the Robins?" They are writing *now*, their Desk in every passing Tree, but the Magic of Mates that cannot hear them, makes their Letters dim –

Later –

Vinnie described it all – The going up to take Medicine and forgetting to return – How many times I have taken that very Medicine myself, with lasting benefit! The Jelly and the pink Cheek, the little clutchings at her frame, to make the grace secure, that had too many Wings – Vinnie omitted nothing, and I followed her around, never hearing enough of that mysterious interview, for was it not a lisp from the irrevocable?

> Within that little Hive
> Such Hints of Honey lay
> As made Reality a Dream
> And Dreams, Reality –

Emily

MANUSCRIPT: HCL (H 86). Pencil.
PUBLICATION: *LH* 186–188.

Judge Lord died, 13 March 1884. The quotation "seen of Angels" is from 1 Timothy 3.16. "Who knows that secret deep" may attempt to recall *Paradist Lost*, XII, 575–578: "This having learned, thou hast attained the sum/Of wisdom/. . . All secrets of the deep. . ."

Mrs. Holland had evidently written to ask whether Vinnie had given details of the encounter referred to in letter no. 888, so that here ED adds a postcript assuring Mrs. Holland that Vinnie had indeed omitted no detail.

891

To Louise and Frances Norcross   *late March 1884*

Thank you, dears, for the sympathy. I hardly dare to know that I have lost another friend, but anguish finds it out.

> Each that we lose takes part of us;
> A crescent still abides,
> Which like the moon, some turbid night,
> Is summoned by the tides.

. . . I work to drive the awe away, yet awe impels the work.

I almost picked the crocuses, you told them so sincerely. Spring's first conviction is a wealth beyond its whole experience.

The sweetest way I think of you is when the day is done, and Loo sets the "sunset tree" for the little sisters. Dear Fanny has had many stormy mornings; . . . I hope they have not chilled her feet, nor dampened her heart. I am glad the little visit rested you. Rest and water are most we want.

I know each moment of Miss W[hitney] is a gleam of boundlessness. "Miles and miles away," said Browning, "there's a girl"; but "the colored end of evening smiles" on but few so rare.

Thank you once more for being sorry. Till the first friend dies, we think ecstasy impersonal, but then discover that he was the cup from which we drank it, itself as yet unknown. Sweetest love for each, and a kiss besides for Miss W[hitney]'s cheek, should you again meet her.

Emily.

[817]

MANUSCRIPT: destroyed.

PUBLICATION: L (1894) 296–297; LL 345–346; L (1931) 267–268.

This letter responds to a note of sympathy after the death of Judge Lord. The Norcross sisters were especially fond of Maria Whitney. Fanny Norcross was now working as librarian at the Harvard Divinity School, and commuting daily between Concord and Cambridge. ED tries in this letter to recall lines from Browning's "Love Among the Ruins," which opens with the lines: "Where the quiet-coloured end of evening smiles/ Miles and miles." Stanzas 9 and 10 contain the lines: "And I know, while thus the quiet-coloured eve/Smiles to leave . . . That a girl with eager eyes and yellow hair/Waits me there."

892

To Mrs. Joseph A. Sweetser   *early spring 1884*

Aunt Katie's Rose had many Thorns, but it is still a Rose, and has borne the extremities of a Flower with etherial patience, and every deference to her is so sweetly deserved, we do not call it courtesy, but only recognition. It is sweeter that Noon should be fair than that Morning should, because Noon is the latest, and yet your Morning had it's Dew, you would not exchange.

Thank you for telling us of your triumphs.

"Peace hath her Victories, no less than War."

Thank you for speaking so tenderly of our latest Lost. We had hoped the persuasions of the spring, added to our own, might delay his going, but they came too late. "I met," said he in his last Note, "a Crocus and a Snow Drop in my yesterday's walk," but the sweet Beings outlived him. I thought the Churchyard Tarrytown, when I was a Child, but now I trust 'tis Trans.

In this place of shafts, I hope you may remain unharmed.

I congratulate you upon your Children, and themselves, upon you.

To have had such Daughters is sanctity – to have had such a Mother, divine. To *still* have her, but tears forbid me. My own is in the Grave. "So loved her that he died for her," says the explaining Jesus.

With love,
Your Emily.

[818]

MANUSCRIPT: Rosenbach 1170/18 (26). Pencil.
PUBLICATION: L (1894) 412; L (1931) 402.
The "latest Lost" refers to the death of Judge Lord. The quoted lines of verse are from Milton's sonnet "To the Lord General Cromwell": "Peace hath her victories/No less renowned than War." For some of the phrases used in this letter, see Prose Fragment 49.

893

To T. W. Higginson   *spring 1884*

In memory of your Little Sister
> Who "meddled" with the costly Hearts to which
> she gave the worth and broke them – fearing pun-
> ishment, she ran away from Earth –

MANUSCRIPT: BPL (Higg) 107. Pencil.
PUBLICATION: L (1931) 321.
This letter, sent to Higginson, is a message for his daughter Margaret, not yet three years old. Her infant sister Louisa had died, 15 March 1880 (see letter no. 870). The following letter helps explain this one.

894

To T. W. Higginson   *spring 1884*

Dear friend,

Briefly in Boston, please accept the delayed Valentine for your Little Girl –

It would please me that she take her first Walk in Literature with one so often guided on that great route by her Father –

E   Dickinson –

MANUSCRIPT: Barney. Pencil.
PUBLICATION: AM CXXXIX (June 1927) 801; L (1931) 318.
ED has ordered a book for Margaret, and she asks Higginson to pick it up.

To Mrs. Edward Tuckerman   *1 April 1884*

Be encouraged, sweet friend!

How cruel we did not know! But the Battles of those we love are often unseen – "If thou had'st been here," Mary said, "our Brother had not died –" Hanging my Head and my Heart with it, that you sorrowed alone,

Late, but lovingly,

Emily –

MANUSCRIPT: AC. Pencil.
PUBLICATION: L (1894) 389–390; LL 320; L (1931) 379.

Mrs. Tuckerman dated the letter, 1 April 1884, but the occasion for which it was written has not been identified. The quotation recalls John 11.21: "Then said Martha unto Jesus, Lord, if thou hadst been here, my brother had not died."

896

To Charles H. Clark   *spring 1884*

Never unmindful of your anxiety for your Father, dear friend, I refrained from asking, lest even the moment engrossed by reply might take you from him.

The peril of a Parent is a peculiar pang, and one which my Sister and myself so long experienced. Oh would it were longer, for even fear for them were dearer than their absence, that we cannot resist to offer you our earnest sympathy. I most sincerely trust that the sight is redeemed, so precious to you both, more than vicariously to you — even filially — and that the added fear has not exhausted you beyond the art of spring to cheer.

I have lost since writing you, another cherished friend, a word of whom I enclose – and how to repair my shattered ranks is a besetting pain.

Be sure that my Sister and myself never forget your Brother, nor his bereaved comrade.

[820]

To be certain we were to meet our Lost, would be a Vista of reunion, who of us could bear?

With my own and my Sister's recollection,

Faithfully,
E. Dickinson.

MANUSCRIPT: AC. Pencil. Envelope addressed by Lavinia.

PUBLICATION: L (1894) 362–363, in part; LL 361–362, in part; L
(1931) 354–355, entire.

Clark endorsed the letter: Apl 21/84.

897

To Mrs. Joseph A. Sweetser   *spring 1884*

Dear Aunt,

Thank you for "considering the Lilies."

The Bible must have had us in mind, when it gave that liquid
Commandment. Were all it's advice so enchanting as that, we should
probably heed it. Thank you for promptness, explicitness, sweetness.

Your account of the Lilies was so fresh I could almost pick them,
and the hope to meet them in person, in Autumn, thro' your loving
Hand, is a fragrant Future. I hope you are well as you deserve, which
is a blest circumference, and give my love to each.

Aunt Libbie just looked in on us, and I go to make her a Dish
of Homestead Charlotte Russe.

Always,
Emily.

MANUSCRIPT: Rosenbach 1170/18 (25). Pencil.

PUBLICATION: L (1894) 409–410; L (1931) 400.

This seems to acknowledge a gift of bulbs, perhaps sent at Eastertime.
Easter in 1884 came on 13 April. Aunt Libbie was Mrs. Sweetser's youngest
sister, Mrs. Augustus Currier.

To Daniel Chester French   *April 1884*

Dear Mr. French: –

We learn with delight of the recent acquisition to your fame, and hasten to congratulate you on an honor so reverently won.
Success is dust, but an aim forever touched with dew.
God keep you fundamental!

> Circumference, thou bride
> Of awe, – possessing, thou
> Shalt be possessed by
> Every hallowed knight
> That dares to covet thee.

Yours faithfully,
Emily Dickinson

MANUSCRIPT: missing.
PUBLICATION: *FF* 58, in part; *Poems* (1955) 1112.
The text is from a transcript supplied the editor by French's daughter, Mrs. William Penn Cresson. The John Harvard statue was unveiled in the Harvard Yard in April 1884. ED probably did not know him well, though he had lived as a boy in Amherst; but Susan Dickinson did, and he was a friend of the Norcross cousins.

To Martha Gilbert Smith   *about 1884*

Dear Mattie –

Your "our own" was sweet – Thank you for your constancy –

Icebergs italicize the Sea – they do not intercept it, and "Deep calls to the Deep" in the old way –

To attempt to speak of what has been, would be impossible. Abyss has no Biographer –

Had it, it would not be Abyss – Love for your Little Girl – tho' *is* it now a "Little Girl," Time makes such hallowed strides? The Little Boy was taken –

Ineffable Avarice of Jesus, who reminds a perhaps encroaching Father, "All these are mine."

Emily –

MANUSCRIPT: HCL (L 29). Pencil.
PUBLICATION: FF 252.
This was written while grief for Gilbert's death was still poignant.

900

To Mr. and Mrs. Ebenezer R. Hoar   May 1884

Dear Mr and Mrs Hoar –

I should hardly dare risk the inclemencies of Eden at this perilous Season –

With proud congratulation that the shortest route to India has been supremely found.

Honoringly,
E. Dickinson –

MANUSCRIPT: Bowles. Pencil.
PUBLICATION: L (1931) 338.
Written in answer to an invitation to the wedding of Elizabeth Hoar to Samuel Bowles the younger, 12 June 1884.

901

To Mrs. J. G. Holland   early June 1884

Sweet friend.

I hope you brought your open Fire with you, else your confiding Nose has ere this been nipped –

Three dazzling Winter Nights have wrecked the budding Gardens, and the Bobolinks stand as still in the Meadow as if they had never danced –

I hope your Heart has kept you warm — Should I say your Hearts, for you are yet a Banker –

Death cannot plunder half so fast as Fervor can re-earn –

We had one more, "Memorial Day," to whom to carry Blossoms –

Gilbert had Lilies of the Valley, and Father and Mother, Damson-Hawthorn –

When it shall come my turn, I want a Buttercup – Doubtless the Grass will give me one, for does she not revere the Whims of her flitting Children?

I was with you in all the loneliness, when you took your flight, for every jostling of the Spirit barbs the Loss afresh – even the coming out of the Sun after an Hour's Rain, intensifies their Absence –

Ask some kind Voice to read to you Mark Antony's Oration over his Playmate Caesar –

I never knew a broken Heart to break itself so sweet –

I am glad if Theodore balked the Professors – Most such are Manikins, and a warm blow from a brave Anatomy, hurls them into Wherefores –

MANUSCRIPT: HCL (H 87). Pencil.
PUBLICATION: *LH* 188–189.
Theodore Holland graduated from Columbia Law School in June 1884. The allusion is probably to an oral examination. Mrs. Holland had left New York for her summer home. Amherst weather records indicate that there were freezing temperatures on three successive nights, 29–31 May 1884.

902

To Samuel Bowles the younger   *early June 1884?*

Dear friend,

The Clock strikes One
That just struck Two –
Some Schism in the Sum –
A Sorcerer from Genesis
Has wrecked the Pendulum –

With warmest congratulation,
E. Dickinson.

MANUSCRIPT: Bowles. Pencil. Envelope addressed by ED in ink: Samuel Bowles/Springfield./Mass. Postmark illegible.

PUBLICATION: *L* (1894) 350; *LL* 347; *L* (1931) 338.
This note has generally been assigned to the autumn of 1883, at the time of Bowles's engagement. But ED had sent him one note, perhaps two, at that time (see letters no. 864 and 865). The idea of the poem is more fitting for a wedding than an engagement. The same lines are in the letter to Mrs. Holland (no. 805), written soon after Kate Holland's marriage.

The note may have accompanied a gift for the wedding which took place on 12 June.

903

To Mrs. Frederick Tuckerman   *early June 1884*

Dear friend –

With the trust that the "Madonna and Child" are as safe as sacred, accept this happy flower –

E – Dickinson –

MANUSCRIPT: Clark. Pencil. Unpublished.
Sent to Mrs. Tuckerman at the time of the birth of her daughter Margaret, 6 June 1884.

904

To Mrs. Frederick Tuckerman   *June 1884*

Let me commend to Baby's attention the only Commandment I ever obeyed –
"Consider the Lilies."

E – Dickinson –

MANUSCRIPT: Clark. Pencil.
PUBLICATION: *FF* 58 and 261.
Sent somewhat later than the preceding letter, probably with lilies.

905

To Mrs. James S. Cooper   *about 1884*

How can one be fatherless who has a father's friend within confiding reach?

[825]

MANUSCRIPT: AC. Pencil.
PUBLICATION: L (1894) 392; L (1931) 382.
Mrs. Cooper seems to have remembered the anniversary of Edward Dickinson's death, 16 June, on more than one occasion. Perhaps this acknowledges flowers on the tenth anniversary.

906

To Mabel Loomis Todd   *19 July 1884*

How martial the Apology of Nature! We die, said the Deathless of Thermopylae, in obedience to Law.

> Not Sickness stains the Brave,
> Nor any Dart,
> Nor Doubt of Scene to come,
> But an adjourning Heart –

MANUSCRIPT: AC. Pencil.
PUBLICATION: L (1894) 432; L (1931) 421.
This apostrophe to dying nature was received, according to Mrs. Todd's diary, on 19 July. For its image it draws upon Simonides's epitaph for the Spartans who fell at Thermopylae: "Go tell the Spartans, thou that passeth by/, That here, obedient to the laws, we lie." (See also letter no. 519.)

907

To Louise and Frances Norcross   *early August 1884*

Dear Cousins,

I hope you heard Mr. Sanborn's lecture. My *Republican* was borrowed before I waked, to read till my own dawn, which is rather tardy, for I have been quite sick, and could claim the immortal reprimand, "Mr. Lamb, you come down very late in the morning." Eight Saturday noons ago, I was making a loaf of cake with Maggie, when I saw a great darkness coming and knew no more until late at night. I woke to find Austin and Vinnie and a strange physician bending over me, and supposed I was dying, or had died, all was so kind and hallowed. I had fainted and lain unconscious for the first time in my life. Then I grew very sick and gave the others much alarm, but am now staying. The doctor calls it "revenge of the nerves"; but who but Death had wronged them? Fanny's dear note has lain unanswered for this long season, though its "Good-night, my dear," warmed me to the core. I have all to say, but little strength to say it; so we must talk by degrees. I do want to know about Loo, what pleases her most, book or tune or friend.

I am glad the housekeeping is kinder; it is a prickly art. Maggie is with us still, warm and wild and mighty, and we have a gracious boy at the barn. We remember you always, and one or the other often comes down with a "we dreamed of Fanny and Loo last night"; then that day we think we shall hear from you, for dreams are couriers.

The little boy we laid away never fluctuates, and his dim society is companion still. But it is growing damp and I must go in. Memory's fog is rising.

> The going from a world we know
> To one a wonder still
> Is like the child's adversity
> Whose vista is a hill,
> Behind the hill is sorcery
> And everything unknown,
> But will the secret compensate
> For climbing it alone?

Vinnie's love and Maggie's, and mine is presupposed.

                                        Emily.

MANUSCRIPT: destroyed.
PUBLICATION: L (1894) 297–298; LL 367–368; L (1931) 268–269.
ED's illness occurred Saturday, 14 June, and she was attended by Dr. D. B. N. Fish. Frank Sanborn's lecture, given before the Concord School of Philosophy on Monday, 28 July, was reported in the Tuesday *Springfield Republican*. The "gracious boy at the barn" was Stephen Sullivan (see Appendix 2).

To Susan Gilbert Dickinson   *about 1884*

I felt it no betrayal, Dear – Go to my Mine as to your own, only more unsparingly –

I can scarcely believe that the Wondrous Book is at last to be written, and it seems like a Memoir of the Sun, when the Noon is gone –

You remember his swift way of wringing and flinging away a Theme, and others picking it up and gazing bewildered after him, and the prance that crossed his Eye at such times was unrepeatable –

> Though the Great Waters sleep,
> That they are still the Deep,
> We cannot doubt –
> No Vacillating God
> Ignited this Abode
> To put it out –

I wish I could find the Warrington Words, but during my weeks of faintness, my Treasures were misplaced, and I cannot find them – I think Mr Robinson had been left alone, and felt the opinion while the others were gone –

Remember, Dear, an unfaltering *Yes* is my only reply to your utmost question –

With constancy –
Emily –

MANUSCRIPT: HCL (B 158). Pencil.

PUBLICATION: LL 82, four lines; FF 266, in part.

George S. Merriam, *The Life and Times of Samuel Bowles* (New York, 1885, 2 vols.), is the book referred to. In preparing it, Merriam had asked Susan Dickinson for access to Bowles's letters in her possession (his request is in HCL). William S. Robinson ("Warrington") was the Boston correspondent for the *Springfield Republican*. He died in 1876, several months before Bowles. A collection of his writings, *Pen-Portraits. . .* (Boston, 1877), was issued by his wife. He had become serenely sure of immortality in his last years, and expressed his beliefs, as set forth in the memoirs. ED's letter seems to answer a request, as though Sue knew that ED had the book, or had saved certain clippings over the years. This passage from the book (page 162) very aptly explains ED's remark: "This life is so good, that it seems impossible for it to be wholly interrupted by death."

This and the following six letters written to Susan Dickinson are in the handwriting of 1884.

909

To Susan Gilbert Dickinson   *about 1884*

Dear Sue –

One of the sweetest Messages I ever received, was, "Mrs Dickinson sent you this Cardinal Flower, and told me to tell you she thought of you."

Except for usurping your Copyright – I should regive the Message, but each Voice is it's own –

Emily –

MANUSCRIPT: HCL (B 144). Pencil.
PUBLICATION: *FF* 264.

910

To Susan Gilbert Dickinson   *about 1884*

Wish I had something vital for Susan, but Susan feeds herself – Banquets have no Seed, or Beggars would sow them –

> Declaiming Waters none may dread –
> But Waters that are still
> Are so for that most fatal cause
> In Nature – they are full –

Emily –

MANUSCRIPT: HCL (B 88). Pencil.
PUBLICATION: *FF* 259.

To Susan Gilbert Dickinson   *about 1884*

That any Flower should be so base as to stab my Susan, I believe unwillingly –

"Tasting the Honey and the Sting," should have ceased with Eden –·Choose Flowers that have no Fang, Dear – Pang is the Past of Peace –

                                                                                Sister –

MANUSCRIPT: HCL (B 106). Pencil.
PUBLICATION: FF 249, in part.

To Susan Gilbert Dickinson   *about 1884*

Morning might come by Accident – Sister –
Night comes by Event –
To believe the final line of the Card would foreclose Faith –
Faith is *Doubt.*

                                                                                Sister –

Show me Eternity, and I will show you Memory –
Both in one package lain
And lifted back again –
Be Sue – while I am Emily –
Be next – what you have ever been – Infinity –

MANUSCRIPT: HCL (B 90). Pencil.
PUBLICATION: LL 87.

To Susan Gilbert Dickinson   *about 1884*

No Words ripple like Sister's –
Their Silver genealogy is very sweet to trace –
Amalgams are abundant, but the lone student of the Mines adores Alloyless things –

                                                                                Emily –

MANUSCRIPT: HCL (B 134). Pencil.
PUBLICATION: FF 243.

To Susan Gilbert Dickinson   *about 1884*

Tell the Susan who never forgets to be subtle, every Spark is numbered –

> The farthest Thunder that I heard
> Was nearer than the Sky –
> And rumbles still –
> Though torrid Noons –
> Have lain their Missiles by –

                                                                    Emily –

MANUSCRIPT: HCL (B 108). Pencil.
PUBLICATION: *FF* 265.

To Mrs. J. Howard Sweetser   *about 1884*

Did dear Mrs Nellie think Emily had purloined the Napkin? No – only the Heart of which it was the Exponent, which with roguish love, she will not return —

MANUSCRIPT: Rosenbach 1170/18 (9). Pencil. Unpublished.
This letter and the five that follow, sent to Mrs. Sweetser, are in the handwriting of about 1884, written presumably during the summer while the Sweetsers were sojourning in Amherst. It is entirely possible that some were in fact written a year later, in 1885. This group, together with two notes placed in the autumn, concludes the correspondence with "Mrs. Nellie."

To Mrs. J. Howard Sweetser   *about 1884*

How strange that each tenderness was precisely the tenderness most craved, but Nellie is a Seer –

                                    Lovingly,
                                                            Emily.

MANUSCRIPT: Rosenbach 1170/18 (18). Pencil. Unpublished.

917

To Mrs. J. Howard Sweetser   *about 1884*

I dare not contrast the Summers, Nellie, but I think the Hearts will measure the same, and that is the only girth.

                                                      Emily.

MANUSCRIPT: Rosenbach 1170/18 (19). Pencil. Unpublished.

918

To Mrs. J. Howard Sweetser   *about 1884*

Have I nothing else, Nellie has not? Speak, that she may share it!

                                                      Emily.

MANUSCRIPT: Rosenbach 1170/18 (11). Pencil. Unpublished.

919

To Mrs. J. Howard Sweetser   *about 1884*

Dear Nellie,

You sent me all but the Pond, but the Heavens Today have sent me that, which repairs the omission –

Thanks for the lovely sham – A duplicate of Gabriel could not be more enchanting – and Gabriel has no stem –

Of your lovely Acts I am never mindless. To reprove the Summer that bears you away is instinct and pathos. An Acorn slain with Dew.

                                                    Emily.

MANUSCRIPT: Rosenbach 1170/18 (14). Pencil. Unpublished.

920

To Mrs. J. Howard Sweetser   *about 1884*

Dear Nellie,

I had felt some uncertainty as to my qualification for the final Redemption, but the delightful Melody has entirely fitted me –

[832]

Congratulate your Son on his divine Gift —

Emily —

MANUSCRIPT: Rosenbach 1170/18 (17). Pencil. Unpublished.
The Sweetsers' son, Howard, had evidently come to the Dickinson house to sing. One infers from the last sentence that ED listened but did not see him (see letter no. 951).

921

To Theodore Holland   *summer 1884*

Dear Sir.

Your request to "remain sincerely" mine demands investigation, and if after synopsis of your career all should seem correct, I am tersely your's —

I shall try to wear the unmerited honor with becoming volume —

Commend me to your Kindred, for whom although a Stranger, I entertain esteem —

I approve the Paint — a study of the Soudan, I take it, but the Scripture assures us our Hearts are all Dongola.

E. Dickinson —

"Cousin Vinnie's" smile.

MANUSCRIPT: HCL (H 88). Pencil.
PUBLICATION: *LH* 190–191.
The sketch which ED received must have been intended to amuse, for it is here acknowledged with mock formality. During the summer of 1884 the fate of General Gordon, sent to relieve the British garrison at Khartoum, was in doubt. Gordon's headquarters was in Dongola.

922

To Forrest F. Emerson   *summer 1884?*

Dear Friend,

I step from my pillow to your hand to thank its sacred contents, to hoard, not to partake, for I am still weak.

[833]

The little package has lain by my side, not daring to venture, or Vinnie daring to have me – a hallowed denial I shall not forget.

I fear you may need the papers, and ask you to claim them immediately, would you desire them.

I trust you are sharing this most sweet climate with Mrs. Emerson and yourself, than which remembrance only is more Arabian.

Vinnie brings her love, and her sister what gratitude.

Emily.

MANUSCRIPT: missing.
PUBLICATION: L (1894) 404–405; L (1931) 393–394.

The Emersons had left Amherst in February 1883. Without the autograph, it is impossible to place this letter accurately. Clearly Emerson has sent ED reading matter, perhaps clippings. There were two periods in the last years when she was too sick to read or write. On 7 June 1884 she became acutely ill, confined to her bed for several weeks. From late November 1885 until her death in May 1886 she mustered strength only intermittently. If Emerson's package was clippings about Helen Jackson's death (August 1885), then this letter was written early in 1886. (See letter no. 1018.)

923

To recipient unknown   *about 1884*

With the leave of the Blue Birds, without whose approval we do nothing.

E. Dickinson.

MANUSCRIPT: AC. Pencil.
PUBLICATION: L (1894) 422; L (1931) 410.

The date is conjectured from the handwriting. The message probably was sent with flowers.

924

To Annie Jameson   *about 1884*

Dear Little Annie,

We give her our love, and are each sorry –

E – Dickinson –

MANUSCRIPT: Bennett. Pencil. Unpublished.

The date is conjectured from the handwriting. The provenance of the autograph, as well as the circumstances, are uncertain, but see letter no. 878.

925

To Anna Newman Carleton   *about 1884*

It hardly seems credible that the brave little Boy and the celestial little Girl are Anna's, and yet would we not expect her to be the Mother of Poets and Prophets, were she the Mother of anyone at all, as the Mail so sweetly assures us –

The bestowal of two such Fairies upon a sordid World, is of itself Prowess, and we give our hallowed congratulation to the Madonna Anna –

The picture of the pretty Home is very warm and vivid, and *we* half "touch" it too, unless softly forbidden – not with mortal Fingers, but those more tidy, mental ones, which never leave a blot –

Thanks, Dear, for the beatific Package, a murmur of the Saints, and never hide so long again, from your seeking Cousins –

Emily –

MANUSCRIPT: HCL. Pencil. Unpublished.

The letter, acknowledging a photograph, starts so close to the top of the page that one suspects it is incomplete. Anna and Clara Newman, after their father's death in 1853, came to Amherst to live, for several years, in the home of Austin and Susan Dickinson. Anna was married in 1874.

926

To Clara Newman Turner   *about 1884*

The cordiality of the Sacrament extremely interested me when a Child, and when the Clergyman invited "all who loved the Lord Jesus Christ, to remain," I could scarcely refrain from rising and thanking him for the to me unexpected courtesy, though I now think had it been to all who loved Santa Claus, my transports would have been even more untimely.

Emily –

MANUSCRIPT: HCL. Pencil.
PUBLICATION: *Home* 149–150.
A letter (HCL) from ED's mother to her father, 7 January 1838, says: "I attended Church this morning with Austin and Emily, they staid with me during the communion season."

927

To Mrs. Richard H. Mather   *about 1884*

Dear friend –

Accept this dusk remembrance, and thank you for the Dainty, which sipping just before my sleep, gave me a Sherbet Dream –

With love,
E – Dickinson –

MANUSCRIPT: AC. Pencil. Unpublished.
This and the three following notes, all sent to Mrs. Mather, are in the handwriting of about 1884.

928

To Mrs. Richard H. Mather   *about 1884*

Dear friend –

Accept this spotless Supper from your nearest

Neighbor –

MANUSCRIPT: Mather. Pencil. Unpublished. Perhaps Prose Fragment 25 is a draft of this note.

929

To Mrs. Richard H. Mather   *about 1884*

With the congratulatory trust that "there is no place like Home."

E. Dickinson –

MANUSCRIPT: Mather. Pencil. Unpublished.

To Mrs. Richard H. Mather   *about 1884*

Dear friend,

A reckless Hen devoured the Boon we designed for you, instead of which, please taste the Pears, which are less celestial –

Emily

and Vinnie –

MANUSCRIPT: Mather. Pencil. Unpublished.

931

To Mrs. James S. Cooper   *about 1884*

Dear friend –

I shall deem the little Tumblers forever consecrated by the "Unseemliness" –

With Affection,

E. Dickinson —

MANUSCRIPT: AC. Pencil.
PUBLICATION: L (1894) 395; L (1931) 384.

932

To Mrs. Henry Hills   *1884?*

Dear One,

When Jesus tells us about his Father, we distrust him. When he shows us his Home, we turn away, but when he confides to us that he is "acquainted with Grief," we listen, for that also is an Acquaintance of our own.

With love.

MANUSCRIPT: missing. Unpublished.
The text has the same provenance as that of letter no. 376. It is placed here because this is the last year in which notes are known to have been sent to Mrs. Hills. See Prose Fragment 20.

To Mrs. John Jameson   *date uncertain*

Many and sweet Birthdays to our thoughtful neighbor, whom we have learned to cherish, though ourself unknown —

E. Dickinson.

MANUSCRIPT: missing. The text is from a transcript in the Jones Library, made during the 1930's when the autograph (said to be in ink) was offered for sale.

PUBLICATION: *L* (1894) 401; *L* (1931) 390.

Jameson was postmaster in Amherst from December 1876 until March 1885. The phrasing of this birthday greeting, formal yet cordial, leads one to conjecture that the Jamesons had been Amherst residents for some time. Until the manuscript is located, it can be assigned no exact date.

To Louise and Frances Norcross   *about 1884*

A Tone from the old Bells, perhaps might wake the Children –

> We send the Wave to find the Wave –
> An Errand so divine,
> The Messenger enamored too,
> Forgetting to return,
> We make the wise distinction still,
> Soever made in vain,
> The sagest time to dam the sea is when the sea is gone –

Emily.

with love –

MANUSCRIPT: AC. Pencil.

PUBLICATION: *L* (1894) 277; *LL* 288–289; *L* (1931) 252–253; *Poems* (1955) 1104.

This autograph fair draft never left ED's desk, but ED sent a variant duplicate of it to the Norcross cousins, evidently to remind them that they had not recently written to her. The cousins gave Mrs. Todd a transcript of the actual letter they received, wherein ED had made three substitutions in the poem. For *wise distinction* she wrote *sage decision* (line 5); for *sagest* (line 7) she wrote *only*.

To Samuel Bowles the younger   *about 1884*

Dear friend,

A Tree your Father gave me, bore this priceless flower.
Would you accept it because of him

> Who abdicated Ambush
> And went the way of Dusk,
> And now against his subtle Name
> There stands an Asterisk
> As confident of him as we –
> Impregnable we are –
> The whole of Immortality
> Secreted in a Star.

E. Dickinson.

MANUSCRIPT: Bowles. Pencil.
PUBLICATION: *L* (1894) 348; *LL* 343; *L* (1931) 336.
Said to have been sent with a spray of pressed jasmine.

936

To Mrs. J. G. Holland   *September 1884*

Dear Sister –

To have been in the actual presence of "Dodd, Mead, and Co" is impressive to Vinnie, and she says every day, "I thought we should hear from Mrs-Holland," she being the Chairman of that loved Assembly – Vinnie was charmed with the Stranger – With Kate, she had been always charmed, so the spell was complete – But she found him a dark Man – the Picture depicted him a light – That, she requires explained – Vinnie much regretted that she was'nt in Court Costume, but I told her that high topped Boots would'nt have been expected, which was not the comfort that I could wish –

Autumn is among us, though almost unperceived – and the Cricket sings in the morning, now, a most pathetic conduct –

We have no Fruit this year, the Frost having barreled that in the

Bud – except the "Fruits of the Spirit," but Vinnie prefers Baldwins –

Thank Kate and the Consort, for their beloved visages – the "surprise parties" of Saints are ineffable, and when they bring the assurance of the loved convalescence, they are even more beatific –

Emily –

MANUSCRIPT: HCL (H 90). Pencil.

PUBLICATION: *LH* 193.

Kate and Bleecker Van Wagenen, vacationing at Northampton, drove to Amherst, 17 September. He was a member of the publishing firm of Dodd, Mead and Company. They called at the Dickinson's and were received by Lavinia; ED did not see them. The quotation in the third paragraph is from Galatians 5.22: "But the fruit of the spirit is love. . ."

937

To Helen Hunt Jackson   *September 1884*

Dear friend –

I infer from your Note you have "taken Captivity Captive," and rejoice that that martial Verse has been verified. He who is "slain and smiles, steals something from the" Sword, but you have stolen the Sword itself, which is far better – I hope you may be harmed no more – I shall watch your passage from Crutch to Cane with jealous affection. From there to your Wings is but a stride – as was said of the convalescing Bird,

> And then he lifted up his Throat
> And squandered such a Note –
> A Universe that overheard
> Is stricken by it yet –

I, too, took my summer in a Chair, though from "Nervous prostration," not fracture, but take my Nerve by the Bridle now, and am again abroad – Thank you for the wish –

The Summer has been wide and deep, and a deeper Autumn is but the Gleam concomitant of that waylaying Light –

Pursuing you in your transitions,
In other Motes –
Of other Myths
Your requisition be.
The Prism never held the Hues,
It only heard them play –

Loyally,
E. Dickinson –

MANUSCRIPT: BPL (Higg 112). Pencil.

PUBLICATION: L (1931) 318–319, among the letters to Higginson, but with a footnote: "Though included among the letters to Colonel Higginson, this letter was probably written to 'H. H.'"

Helen Jackson sent this letter to Higginson, who kept it. It is a reply to the letter which follows, from Helen Jackson, dated: Colorado Springs/Sept 5./1884.

937a

My dear friend,

Thanks for your note of sympathy.

It was not quite a "massacre," only a break of one leg: but it was a very bad break – two inches of the big bone smashed in – & the little one snapped: as compound a fracture as is often compounded! –

But I am thankful to say that it has joined & healed – well. I am on crutches now – & am promised to walk with a cane in a few weeks: – a most remarkable success for an old woman past fifty & weighing 170. –

I fell from the top to the bottom of my stairs – & the only wonder was I did not break my neck. – For the first week I wished I had! Since then I have not suffered at all – but have been exceedingly comfortable – ten weeks tomorrow since it happened – the last six I have spent in a wheeled chair on my verandah: – an involuntary "rest cure," for which I dare say, I shall be better all my life. –

I trust you are well – and that life is going pleasantly with you. – What portfolios of verses you must have. –

It is a cruel wrong to your "day & generation" that you will not give them light. – If such a thing should happen as that I should outlive you, I wish you would make me your literary legatee & executor. Surely, after you are what is called "dead," you will be willing that the poor ghosts you have left behind, should be cheered and pleased by your verses, will you not? — You ought to be. — I do not think we have a right to with hold from the world a word or a thought any more than a *deed*, which might help a single soul.

Do you remember Hannah Dorrance? She came to see me the other day! A Mrs. Somebody, from Chicago. I forget her name. She has grandchildren. I felt like Methuselah, when I realized that it was forty years since I had seen her. Her eyes are as black as ever. —

I am always glad to get a word from you —

Truly yours
Helen Jackson.

MANUSCRIPT: HCL (Dickinson collection).

PUBLICATION: The paragraph touching upon the literary executorship is published in the preface to *Poems by Emily Dickinson*, Second Series (1891), edited by Mabel Loomis Todd. Mrs. Todd must have seen the letter when it was in the possession of Lavinia Dickinson.

ED had read of the accident, and had written a note of condolence to which this is the reply. Hannah Dorrance, daughter of Dr. Gardner Dorrance of Amherst, had moved to Attica, New York, after her marriage. Presumably she later moved to Chicago. ED's reply to this letter pointedly ignores the request to be made literary executor.

938

To Susan Gilbert Dickinson   *October 1884*

Twice, when I had Red Flowers out, Gilbert knocked, raised his sweet Hat, and asked if he might touch them —

Yes, and take them too, I said, but Chivalry forbade him — Besides, he gathered Hearts, not Flowers —

> Some Arrows slay but whom they strike —
> But this slew all *but* him —
> Who so appareled his Escape —
> Too trackless for a Tomb —

Emily —

MANUSCRIPT: HCL (B 145). Pencil.
PUBLICATION: FF 258–259.
This letter, in the same handwriting as other letters written at this time,

may have been sent to Sue on the first anniversary of Gilbert's death, 5 October. It survives in part in a fair draft (AC):

Twice when I had Red Flowers out, Gilbert knocked, raised his sweet Hat and asked if he might smell them.

Yes, and pick them too, I said, but Chivalry forbade him.

Tudor was not a Beggar —

Most Arrows slay but whom they strike, [*attached by a pin, on a narrow strip*:] Most Arrows

The verso of this draft is Prose Fragment 49.

939

To Mrs. Samuel E. Mack   *autumn 1884*

Dear Mrs Mack will forgive us — not for not yearning to see her, but for not succeeding!

"While there is Life there is" interview, seems almost inevitable, though in sacred instances it is sometimes not so. We shall never forget you, and your loveliness is a Legend rebateless as the "Babes in the Wood." While you live, you will be dear Mrs Mack, the Angel of Childhood.

I have not been strong for the last year.

The Dyings have been too deep for me, and before I could raise my Heart from one, another has come — and I fear I might not have dared to see you, even could you have come, but fidelity never flickers — it is the one unerring Light.

A word from you would be very dear, but if too much to ask, deny your faithful

Emily.

MANUSCRIPT: Mack. Pencil. Unpublished.

Mrs. Mack, visiting in Amherst after several years' absence, planned to call on ED, but could not go after all.

940

To Mrs. Samuel E. Mack   *autumn 1884*

It was very dear to see Mrs Mack.

A friend is a solemnity and after the great intrusion of Death, each one that remains has a spectral pricelessness besides the mortal worth —

I hope you may live while *we* live, and then with loving selfishness consent that you should go–
Said that marvellous Emily Bronte

> Though Earth and Man were gone
> And Suns and Universes ceased to be
> And thou wert left alone,
> Every Existence would Exist in thee –

Tenderly,

Emily –

MANUSCRIPT: Mack. Pencil. Unpublished.

Mrs. Mack's renewed effort to see ED proved successful. The same Brontë poem, "Last Lines," ED quoted in writing Maria Whitney (see letter no. 948). She is here probably quoting from memory: *ceased* is actually *cease*.

941

To Martha Dickinson   *early October 1884*

What may I do for Mattie, on her way to school?

Asking that of some timid grace I may be the Bearer, say to Mama that I think of her–

Aunt Emily.

MANUSCRIPT: HCL (B 137). Pencil.
PUBLICATION: *FF* 249–250.

This note was sent to Mattie shortly before her departure for Miss Porter's School in Farmington, Connecticut, where she spent one year, 1884–1885. Her mother took her there, 7 October.

942

To Martha Dickinson   *October 1884*

We almost question where we are, without our martial Mattie, Flag and Drum in one, and but for a deceiving Shower just at Ned's departure, should have assured her so in Flowers –

One Bin in the Ancestral Cellar was filled with Jessamine last night, for that enchanting purpose – but Destiny mistook, so they shall go again – "Much is to learn, and much to forget, ere the time be come for" dowering "you –" Browning told me so –

That "Homesickness in the back of the Neck" to which I referred, I fear has transpired, though to have been the missing Hero is it's own reward –

I recall with a pang the lovely Suppers you last Summer brought me, Niece "of my better Days" – endearing you prospectively, as also at the Time – and wish I might respond in some enriching way, now you are far hence –

The Bluebirds are singing cherubically, and all the Colors "we know or think" are prancing in the Trees –

Be true to yourself, Mattie, and "Honor and Immortality" – although the first will do – the last is only inferential, and I shall be prouder of you than I am, which would be unbecoming –

Aunt Emily –
with love –

MANUSCRIPT: HCL (B 174). Pencil.
PUBLICATION: FF xxiv.
This letter Mattie probably received shortly after arriving at school.

943

To Mrs. J. Howard Sweetser   *about 1884*

Are you trying to make me miss you more when you are far hence? You will succeed, Nellie –

Emily.

MANUSCRIPT: Rosenbach 1170/18 (22). Pencil. Unpublished.
This probably acknowledges some small remembrance sent to ED before the Sweetsers left Amherst in the autumn.

To Mr. and Mrs. E. J. Loomis   *autumn 1884*

Dear friends,

The Apostle's inimitable apology for loving whom he saw not, is perhaps monition to us, who are tempted to the same turpitude.

Timidly,

E. Dickinson –

MANUSCRIPT: AC. Pencil.
PUBLICATION: *L* (1931) 424.

In the autumn of 1884 the Loomises visited their daughter Mrs. Todd. This and the two following letters were sent to them at that time. The scripture allusion is to 1 Peter 1.8.

To Mr. and Mrs. E. J. Loomis   *autumn 1884*

It consoles the happy Sorrow of Autumn, to know that plumbless ones are near.

My acquaintance with the Irreparable dates from the Death Bed of a young Flower to which I was deeply attached.

The element of Elegy, like Bugles at a Grave, how solemnly inspiriting!

Ascension has a muffled Route.

E. Dickinson.

MANUSCRIPT: AC. Pencil. Envelope addressed: Mr. and/Mrs Loomis.
PUBLICATION: *L* (1931) 424.

To Mr. and Mrs. E. J. Loomis   *autumn 1884*

Parting with Thee reluctantly,
That we have never met,
A Heart sometimes a Foreigner,
Remembers it forgot –

In all the circumference of Expression, those guileless words of Adam and Eve never were surpassed, "I was afraid and hid Myself."

E. Dickinson –

MANUSCRIPT: AC. Pencil. Envelope addressed: Mr and/Mrs Loomis –
PUBLICATION: L (1931) 424–425.
The note was sent to the Loomises at the time of their departure. In Genesis 3.10, Adam replies to the voice of God: ". . . and I was afraid because I was naked; and I hid myself."

947

To Mrs. James S. Cooper   *about 1884*

She that is "least in the kingdom of Heaven" has the Scripture Warrant for supremacy –

MANUSCRIPT: YUL. Pencil. Unpublished.
Pinned to the top of the note is a strip of paper bearing the words, in ED's hand: Little Margaret. On the verso of Prose Fragment 121 (AC) are the same two words, also in ED's hand. Margaret was Mrs. Cooper's granddaughter (see letter no. 903). See Matthew 11.11.

948

To Maria Whitney   *autumn 1884*

Dear Friend,

Has the journey ceased, or is it still progressing, and has Nature won you away from us, as we feared she would?

Othello is uneasy, but then Othellos always are, they hold such mighty stakes.

Austin brought me the picture of Salvini when he was last in Boston.

The brow is that of Deity – the eyes, those of the lost, but the power lies in the *throat* – pleading, sovereign, savage – the panther and the dove!

Each, how innocent!

I hope you found the mountains cordial – followed your meeting with the lakes with affecting sympathy.

Changelessness is Nature's change.

The plants went into camp last night, their tender armor insufficient for the crafty nights.

That is one of the parting acts of the year, and has an emerald pathos – and Austin hangs bouquets of corn in the piazza's ceiling, also an omen, for Austin believes.

The "golden bowl" breaks soundlessly, but it will not be whole again till another year.

Did you read Emily Brontë's marvellous verse?

> "Though earth and man were gone,
> And suns and universes ceased to be,
> And Thou wert left alone,
> Every existence would exist in Thee."

We are pining to know of you, and Vinnie thinks to see you would be the opening of the burr. . . .

Emily, with love.

MANUSCRIPT: missing.
PUBLICATION: L (1894) 345–346; LL 346–347; L (1931) 333–334.

Austin evidently had brought Salvini's autobiography, published in 1883: *Leaves from the Autobiography of Tommaso Salvini.* Maria Whitney is returning from her summer in the Adirondacks. The same Brontë lines are quoted in the letter to Mrs. Mack (no. 940).

949

To Susan Gilbert Dickinson *about 1884*

Dear Sue –

I never shall see a Rose in the Boat without beholding you, and were you only at the Helm, it would be supreme –

I give you a Pear that was given me – would that it *were* a Pair, but Nature is penurious.

I fear you are very tired, and every Day ask Stephen if you seem weary –

Love for your suffering Brother, whose I am each moment, could

I in any way refresh him and for each in the loved Home – Tell me
any service and my Heart is ready –

Sister –

MANUSCRIPT: HCL (B 124). Pencil.
PUBLICATION: FF 260–261.

Stephen Sullivan was the stableman. Sue's brother Frank (Francis B.
Gilbert) died, 25 May 1885.

950

To Mrs. J. G. Holland   *late autumn 1884*

Dear One.

Upon the presumption that the "Swallows homeward" flew, I
address to their Nest, as formerly – I trust "the Airs were delicate" the
Day they made their flight, and that they still sing Life's portentous
Music – I feared you would steal the Grandchild in the Parents' absence, but then it would be such a happy theft, so joyful to the robbed,
and to the Thief presiding. Could Jurisprudence sigh? I hope the Lass
is hearty, loving and beloved – I know she is Grandmama's Tonic –
but which is the biggest, the Patient or the Medicine? You always
were a Wren, you know, the tenant of a Twig –

The Leaves are flying high away, and the Heart flies with them,
though where that wondrous Firm alight, is not "an open secret –"
What a curious Lie that phrase is! I see it of Politicians – Before I write
to you again, we shall have had a new Czar – Is the Sister a Patriot?

"George Washington was the Father of his Country" – "George
Who?"

That sums all Politics to me – but then I love the Drums, and they
are busy now –

I did not forget the Anniversary you so tenderly marked, but cover
it with Leaves, as it was long since covered with Honor – which is
better than Leaves – To put one's Hand on the sacred figures, is like
touching "the Ark of the Covenant –"

All grows strangely emphatic, and I think if I should see you again,

[849]

I sh'd begin every sentence with "I say unto you –" The Bible dealt with the Centre, not with the Circumference –

Emily,
With love –

MANUSCRIPT: HCL (H 91). Pencil.
PUBLICATION: *LH* 194–195.
Election Day is not far off. The anniversary of Dr. Holland's death was 12 October. Franz Abt's popular "When the swallows homeward fly" is echoed in the first sentence. The swallow metaphor is carried into the second sentence, where Banquo's description of Macbeth's castle is recalled (*Macbeth* I, vi, 9–10): "Where they most breed and haunt, I have observed/The air is delicate." The anniversary covered with leaves echoes line 738 in Elizabeth Barrett Browning's *Aurora Leigh*: "Flies back to cover all that past with leaves."

951

To Mrs. J. Howard Sweetser *late autumn 1884*

Dear Nellie,

I hardly dare tell you how beautiful your Home is, lest it dissuade you from the more mortal Homestead in which you now dwell – Each Tree a Scene from India, and Everglades of Rugs.

Is not "Lead us not into Temptation" an involuntary plea under circumstances so gorgeous? Your little Note dropped in upon us as softly as the flake of Snow that followed it, as spacious and as stainless, a paragraph from Every Where – to which we never go – We miss you more this time, I think, than all the times before –

An enlarged ability for missing is perhaps a part of our better growth, as the strange Membranes of the Tree broaden out of sight.

I hope the Owl remembers me, and the Owl's fair Keeper, indeed the remembrance of each of you, were a gallant boon – I still recall your Son's singing, and when the "Choir invisible" assemble in your Trees, shall reverently compare them – Thank you for all the Acts of Light which beautified a Summer now past to it's reward.

Love for your Exile, when you write her, as for Love's Aborigines – Our Coral Roof, though unbeheld, it's foliage softly adds –

Emily, with Love.

[850]

MANUSCRIPT: Rosenbach 1170/18 (8). Pencil. Unpublished.
The date is conjectured from the handwriting. The Sweetsers had moved into their new home during the previous year (letter no. 823), and ED is describing here their Amherst house. One of the Sweetser children evidently had a pet owl. George Eliot's "The Choir Invisible" is in *The Legend of Jubal and Other Poems* (1874); for a later reference to it, see letter no. 1042. ED speaks here again of Howard Sweetser's singing (see letter no. 920).

952

To Mrs. Joseph A. Sweetser   *November 1884*

Sweet and Gracious Aunt Katie,

The beloved lilies have come, and my heart is so high it overflows, as this was mother's week, Easter in November.

Father rose in June, and a little more than a year since, those fair words were fulfilled, "and a little child shall lead them," — but boundlessness forbids me. . .

It is very wrong that you were ill, and whom shall I accuse? The enemy, "eternal, invisible, and full of glory" — but He declares himself a friend! It is sweet you are better.

More beating that brave heart has to do before the emerald recess.

With sorrow for Emma's accident, and love for all who cherish you, including the roses, your velvet allies,

Tenderly,

Emily.

MANUSCRIPT: missing.
PUBLICATION: L (1894) 410; LL 371; L (1931) 400–401.
Gilbert had died in October of the previous year. Emma was Aunt Katie's daughter. The scripture quotations recall Isaiah 11.6, and 1 Timothy 1.17.

953

To Mr. and Mrs. E. J. Loomis   *19 November 1884*

Dear friends —

The atmospheric acquaintance so recently and delightfully made, is not, I trust, ephemeral, but absolute as Ether, as the delicate emblem just received tenderly implies.

Thank you for the Beauty – Thank you too for Boundlessness – that rarely given, but choicest Gift.

To "know in whom" we "have believed," is Immortality.

> Oh what a Grace is this,
> What Majesties of Peace,
> That having breathed
> The fine – ensuing Right
> Without Diminuet Proceed!

With trust,
E. Dickinson –

MANUSCRIPT: AC. Pencil. Envelope addressed by Lavinia, and letter received in Washington 20 November.

PUBLICATION: L (1931) 425.

This note acknowledges some small gift, and with it is a note from Lavinia. The scripture reference may be to 2 Timothy 1.12: ". . . for I know whom I have believed, and am persuaded that he is able to keep that which I have committed unto him against that day."

954

To Austin Dickinson   *Thanksgiving 1884*

"Resolved,"

That the thanks of this Audience are due to Mr Dickinson for his very interesting and able Turkey –

Samuel Nash –

MANUSCRIPT: HCL (B 30). Pencil. Addressed: Austin –

PUBLICATION: FF 244–245.

Samuel Nash, the first editor of the *Hampshire and Franklin Express*, died in 1861. His name therefore would recall the past.

To Mr. and Mrs. E. J. Loomis   *1 December 1884*

Dear friends –

The etherial Volume is with us – In sweet and rapid evidence the assurance comes.

The Thank you in my heart obstructs the Thank you on my Lips.

How little of our depth we tell, though we confide our shallowness to "every passing Breeze –"

I hope the Ones are well, who bear such loveliness. By their tints ye shall know them.

The Hands I never took, I take anew, still wondering at my privilege.

With love,

E. Dickinson –

MANUSCRIPT: AC. Pencil. Envelope addressed by Lavinia.
PUBLICATION: L (1931) 425–426.

This letter was accompanied by one from Lavinia. Mrs. Todd dated the letter, 1 December 1884, and said it was written to thank the Loomises for a copy of *The Story of Ida.* Written by Francesca Alexander, it was published in 1883, with a preface by Ruskin. It is the personal account of a saintly young girl in Florence, known to the author. The copy in the Dickinson collection (HCL) bears the autograph signature of Susan Dickinson.

956

To Kendall Emerson   *Christmas 1884*

Missing my own Boy, I knock at other Trundle-Beds, and trust the Curls are in –

Little Gilbert's Aunt –

MANUSCRIPT: AC. Pencil.
PUBLICATION: *Amherst Alumni News* IV (July 1951) 14.

This is the second of three Christmas messages ED sent to Kendall in memory of Gilbert (see letter no. 876).

To Arthur Jameson   *Christmas 1884*

Arthur forgot to set a Trap for Santa Claus, but that illustrious Mouse will excuse him, if he will steal the Cakes instead –
And Annie –

E – Dickinson –

MANUSCRIPT: Bennett. Pencil.
PUBLICATION: L (1894) 402; L (1931) 390.
Arthur and Annie were the children of John Jameson.

958

To Mrs. Henry Hills   *Christmas 1884*

When the "Children" for whom the Cakes were founded are "Merchants of Venice" and "Desdemonas," Santa Claus must tell me. I should never guess.

MANUSCRIPT: missing. Unpublished. The text has the same provenance as that of letter no. 376.

959

To Mrs. Frederick Tuckerman   *1 January 1885*

Bringing a New Year to one who never saw one, is roguishly portentous, and if the Basket tips a little, is it the Porter's fault?
Is not that which is called the "Burden of Life," a bewitching weight?

E – Dickinson ――――

MANUSCRIPT: YUL. Pencil. Unpublished.
Margaret was born 6 June 1884 (see letter no. 903).

960

To Mr. and Mrs. E. J. Loomis   *2 January 1885*

Dear friends –
I thought as I saw the exultant Face and the uplifted Letter,

Take all away from me, but leave me Ecstasy,
And I am richer then than all my Fellow Men –
Ill it becometh me to dwell so wealthily
When at my very Door are those possessing more,
In abject poverty –

And what *is* Ecstasy but Affection and what is Affection but the Germ of the little Note?

A Letter is a joy of Earth –
It is denied the Gods –

Emily,
with Love.

MANUSCRIPT: AC. Pencil. Envelope addressed by ED. Postmarked: Amherst 2 Jan.
PUBLICATION: L (1931) 426.
The letter, written to thank the Loomises for a Christmas card, was accompanied by a note from Lavinia. The first poem is also in letters no. 976 and 1014; the second, in letter no. 963.

961

To Martha Dickinson   *early 1885*

Mattie will take this piece of Cake to School instead of the other, and a Crumb, for her Cousin –

MANUSCRIPT: HCL (B 109). Pencil. Unpublished.
Mattie was returning to school. The cousin was Isabel Cutler, a daughter of Susan Dickinson's sister Harriet (see letter no. 988).

962

To Louise and Frances Norcross   *14 January 1885*

Had we less to say to those we love, perhaps we should say it oftener, but the attempt comes, then the inundation, then it is all over, as is said of the dead.

Vinnie dreamed about Fanny last night, and designing for days to write dear Loo, – dear, both of you, – indeed with the astounding nearness which a dream brings, I must speak this morning. I do hope you are well, and that the last enchanting days have refreshed your spirits, and I hope the poor little girl is better, and the sorrow at least adjourned.

Loo asked "what books" we were wooing now – watching like a vulture for Walter Cross's life of his wife. A friend sent me *Called Back*. It is a haunting story, and as loved Mr. Bowles used to say, "greatly impressive to me." Do you remember the little picture with his deep face in the centre, and Governor Bross on one side, and Colfax on the other? The third of the group died yesterday, so somewhere they are again together.

Moving to Cambridge seems to me like moving to Westminster Abbey, as hallowed and as unbelieved, or moving to Ephesus with Paul for a next-door neighbor.

Holmes's *Life of Emerson* is sweetly commended, but you, I know, have tasted that. . . . But the whistle calls me – I have not begun – so with a moan, and a kiss, and a promise of more, and love from Vinnie and Maggie, and the half-blown carnation, and the western sky, I stop.

That we are permanent temporarily, it is warm to know, though we know no more.

Emily.

MANUSCRIPT: destroyed.
PUBLICATION: L (1894) 298–299; LL 368–369; L (1931) 269–270.

The death of Schuyler Colfax, on 13 January 1885, fixes the date of this letter. The photograph to which ED refers (HCL – Dickinson collection) was one taken in San Francisco in 1865. The three others (not two) in the group were Bowles's companions on the trip: Colfax, then Speaker of the House of Representatives (and later Vice President); William Bross, Lieutenant Governor of Illinois; and Albert D. Richardson, Civil War correspondent and staff member of the *New York Tribune*.

The Norcross sisters moved to Cambridge during 1884, so that Fanny would be nearer to the Divinity School library. *Called Back* (1883), by the British novelist Frederick John Fargus ("Hugh Conway"), was widely popular in its day (see letter no. 1046). Holmes's *Ralph Waldo Emerson* was published in 1885.

To Charles H. Clark   *January 1885*

Dear friend –

Though no New Year be old – to wish yourself and your honored
Father a new and happy one is involuntary and I am sure we are both
reminded of that sacred Past which has forever hallowed us.

I trust the Years which they behold are also new and happy, or
is it a joyous expanse of Year, without bisecting Months, untiring
Anno Domini? Had we but one assenting word, but a Letter is a joy
of Earth – it is denied the Gods.

Vivid in our immortal Group we still behold your Brother, and
never hear Northampton Bells without saluting him.

Should you have any Picture of any Child of my friend, while we
are both below, I hope you may lend it to me for his great sake, as any
circumstance of him is forever precious.

Have you Blossoms and Books, those solaces of sorrow? That, I
would also love to know, and receive for yourself and your Father, the
forgetless sympathy of

Your Friend
E. Dickinson.

MANUSCRIPT: AC. Pencil. Envelope addressed by ED in ink: C. H.
Clark./361. Degraw St./Brooklyn./Long Island. Postmarked: Jan 19. Clark
endorsed the letter: Jan 18/85.

PUBLICATION: L (1894) 364–365; L (1931) 356.

The conclusion of the second paragraph, arranged as verse, is in a
letter to the Loomises (no. 960). ED requests a photograph of Wadsworth's
children.

964

To recipient unknown   *early 1885*

Dear friend –

But of what shall I first speak – the beautiful Child, or it's deep
Possessor, or the little "Book" it is famine to read till I have obtained
it –

[857]

Thank you for the Grave – empty and full – too –

As if I asked a common Alms and in my wondering Hand
A Stranger pressed a Kingdom, and I bewildered stand.
As if I asked the Orient had it for me a Morn,
And it should lift it's Purple Dikes, and shatter me with Dawn –

Your Letter much impressed me – Your every suggestion is Dimension Thought is the Knock which

MANUSCRIPT: AC. Pencil.
PUBLICATION: *NEQ* XXVIII (1955) 299.
This draft remained among ED's papers. It is, however, a fair copy and perhaps was finished on a sheet now missing. The poem is one which she incorporated in a letter to Higginson, written in 1862 (no. 265). There survives another draft (AC – pencil) of the opening of the same letter, likewise a fair copy:
Dear friend,
        But of which shall I first speak – the beautiful Child,
    or its deep Possessor, or the little Book it is Famine to read
    till I have possessed –
A copy in all likelihood was sent, since the letter acknowledges receipt of a photograph of mother and child. A book has been promised.

965

To recipient unknown   *early 1885*

Dear friend –

I thank you with wonder – Should you ask me my comprehension of a starlight Night, Awe were my only reply, and so of the mighty Book – It stills, incites, infatuates – blesses and blames in one. Like Human Affection, we dare not touch it, yet flee, what else remains?

But excuse me – I know but little – Please tell me how it might seem to *you* –

How vast is the chastisement of Beauty, given us by our Maker! A Word is inundation, when it comes from the Sea –

Peter took the Marine Walk at the great risk.

                                                E. Dickinson.

MANUSCRIPT: AC. Pencil.

PUBLICATION: *L* (1894) 423; *Bachelor of Arts*, May 1895; *L* (1931) 411–412.

The provenance of this letter is uncertain. Mrs. Todd had access to it in 1894. Perhaps it was among ED's papers, for though Mrs. Todd published it with other letters in 1894, she named no recipient. It is a complete fair copy, the paper and the writing identical with those of the preceding letter. It seems to have been intended for the same person, since the preceding anticipates the promise of a book, and this thanks the donor. A small prose fragment (AC – pencil) is a variant of the last sentence:

Peter took the Marine walk at a great risk – I think
I am correct but the Apostles misgive me –

The fragment is published in *NEQ* XXVIII (1955) 310–311.

966

To Mrs. J. G. Holland   *February 1885*

Dear Sister,

Horace, the wise, but acrid Man who so long lived with us, was pleased to say of what displeased him, "I hate it, I despise it," and I feel an animadversion similar to the Rheumatism – To wring your shoulder, how brutal, how malign!

Were Revenge accessible, I would surely wreak it, but that, like all the rest of us, is an Apparition –

I trust he will discontinue you for something more befitting – I shall then seek the "Letter" which the "Weird Woman promised" me –

The Winter which you feared has shrunk to Febuary, which limited Expanse has the enchantment of the last, and is therefore beloved. "But the last Leaf fear to touch," says the consummate Browning –

Tell Katrina about the Buttercups that Emily tills, and the Butterflies Emily chases, not catches, alas, because her Hat is torn – but not half so ragged as her Heart, which is barefoot always –

Vinnie wrote you a few Days since, and is sure if you value her as much as you did in Northampton, you will soon reply!

Love for all but the Rheumatism –

Always,

Emily –

[859]

MANUSCRIPT: HCL (H 92). Pencil.
PUBLICATION: *LH* 195–196.
The Browning quotation is from *By the Fireside*, stanza 42: "But a last leaf – fear to touch!" On Horace Church, see Appendix 2.

967

To Benjamin Kimball   *February 1885*

Dear friend –

To take the hand of my friend's friend, even apparitionally, is a hallowed pleasure.

I think you told me you were his kinsman.

I was only his friend – and cannot yet believe that

> "his part in all the pomp that fills
> The circuit of the Southern Hills,
> Is that his Grave is green."

His last words in his last Note were "A Caller comes." I infer it to be Eternity, as he never returned.

Your task must be a fervent one – often one of pain.

To fulfill the will of a powerless friend supersedes the Grave.

Oh, Death, where is thy Chancellor? On my way to my sleep, last night, I paused at the Portrait. Had I not loved it, I had feared it, the Face had such ascension.

> Go thy great way!
> The Stars thou meetst
> Are even as Thyself –
> For what are Stars but Asterisks
> To point a human Life?

Thank you for the nobleness, and for the earnest Note – but *all* are friends, upon a Spar.

> Gratefully,
> E. Dickinson –

MANUSCRIPT: NYPL (Berg collection). Pencil.
PUBLICATION: *Revelation* 68.

Kimball was executor of Judge Lord's estate. Perhaps Lord bequeathed something to ED. (He did not return the letters she had written to him.) This and the letter which follows are in the same collection. With them is an envelope addressed in ink by ED: Benjamin Kimball./8. Congress St./ Boston./Mass. Postmarked: Palmer Mass Feb 20 85. The quoted lines are from Bryant's *June*:

> Whose part, in all the pomp that fills
> The circuit of the summer hills,
> Is that his grave is green.

968

To Benjamin Kimball   *1885*

Dear friend –

Had I known I asked the impossible, should I perhaps have asked it, but Abyss is it's own Apology.

I once asked him what I should do for him when he was not here, referring half unconsciously to the great Expanse – In a tone italic of both Worlds "Remember Me," he said. I have kept his Commandment. But you are a Psychologist, I, only a Scholar who has lost her Preceptor.

For the great kindness of your opinion, I am far indebted.

Perhaps to solidify his faith was for him impossible, and if for him, how more, for us! Your noble and tender words of him were exceedingly precious – I shall cherish them.

He did not tell me he "sang" to you, though to sing in his presence was involuntary, thronged only with Music, like the Decks of Birds.

Abstinence from Melody was what made him die. Calvary and May wrestled in his Nature.

Neither fearing Extinction, nor prizing Redemption, he believed alone. Victory was his Rendezvous –

I hope it took him home.

But I fear I detain you.

I try to thank you and fail.

Perhaps the confiding effort you would not disdain?

Sacredly,
E. Dickinson.

MANUSCRIPT: NYPL (Berg collection). Pencil.
PUBLICATION: *Revelation* 69.
This letter responds to one Kimball had written at ED's request, telling her what he could about Lord as he had known him.

969

To Maria Whitney   *early 1885?*

Dear Friend,

I cannot depict a friend to my mind till I know what he is doing, and three of us want to depict you. I inquire your avocation of Austin, and he says you are "engaged in a great work"! That is momentous but not defining. The thought of you in the great city has a halo of wilderness.

Console us by dispelling it. . . .

Vinnie is happy with her duties, her pussies, and her posies, for the little garden within, though tiny, is triumphant.

There are scarlet carnations, with a witching suggestion, and hyacinths covered with promises which I know they will keep.

How precious to hear you ring at the door, and Vinnie ushering you to those melodious moments of which friends are composed.

This also is fiction.

I fear we shall care very little for the technical resurrection, when to behold the one face that to us comprised it is too much for us, and I dare not think of the voraciousness of that only gaze and its only return.

Remembrance is the great tempter.

Emily.

MANUSCRIPT: missing.
PUBLICATION: *L* (1894) 346–347; *LL* 364; *L* (1931) 335.
Maria Whitney taught in the Brearley School in New York City, 1884–1885, and the first half of 1885–1886.

To Mrs. James S. Cooper   *early 1885*

Dear friend –

Nothing inclusive of a human Heart could be "trivial." That appalling Boon makes all things paltry but itself –

To thank you would profane you – There are moments when even
Gratitude is a desecration –

> Go thy great way!
> The Stars thou meetst
> Are even as Thyself –
> For what are Stars but Asterisks
> To point a human Life?

E – Dickinson,
with love –

MANUSCRIPT: YUL. Pencil.
PUBLICATION: *L* (1894) 395–396; *LL* 335, in part; *L* (1931) 384–385.
The same poem is in letter no. 967.

To Mrs. James S. Cooper   *February 1885*

Trusting an April flower may not curtail your Febuary, that Month
of fleetest sweetness.

E. Dickinson.

MANUSCRIPT: Blaine. Pencil.
PUBLICATION: *L* (1894) 394; *LL* 323; *L* (1931) 383.

To T. W. Higginson   *February 1885*

Dear friend –

It is long since I asked and received your consent to accept the

Book, should it be, and the ratification at last comes, a pleasure I feared to hope –

Biography first convinces us of the fleeing of the Biographied –

> Pass to thy Rendezvous of Light,
> Pangless except for us –
> Who slowly ford the Mystery
> Which thou hast leaped across!

Your Scholar –

MANUSCRIPT: BPL (Higg 115). Pencil.
PUBLICATION: L (1931) 319–320.
In HCL is J. W. Cross, *The Life of George Eliot*, inscribed by Higginson: "T. W. Higginson from Emily Dickinson, 1885." The first volume was published in February 1885; the third, in 1887. The poem is also in letter no. 868.

973

To Mrs. James C. Greenough   *about 1885*

The Flower keeps it's appointment – should the Heart be tardy?
When Memory rings her Bell, let all the Thoughts run in —

Emily —

MANUSCRIPT: AC. Pencil.
PUBLICATION: L (1894) 428; LL 375; L (1931) 416.
The date is conjectured from the handwriting. The note may have been sent on an anniversary.

974

To Maria Whitney   *spring 1885*

Dear friend

I was much quickened toward you and all Celestial things to read (see) that the Life of our loved Mr Bowles would be with us in Autumn, and how fitting (sweet) that his and George Eliots should

be given so near – (should be chosen so near And how strong that his
and George Eliots are in the same year)

On his last arriving from California he told us the Highwayman
did not say your money or your life, but have you read Daniel Deronda
– That wise and tender Book I hope you have seen – It is full of sad
(high) nourishment –

MANUSCRIPT: AC. Pencil. It is an unfinished rough draft, jotted on a
discarded concert program which can be dated 23 March 1885. The fair
copy of the draft presumably was sent to Maria Whitney.

PUBLICATION: *NEQ* XXVIII (1955) 305.

The *Springfield Republican* on 7 March 1885 carried the following
announcement:

> The Century company of New York will publish next
> autumn a biography of the late editor of The Republican,
> under the title, "The Life and Times of Samuel Bowles."

The first volume of Cross's *Life* [of George Eliot] appeared in Feb-
ruary 1885 (see letter no. 972); Merriam's biography of Bowles was pub-
lished late in the year (see letter no. 908). ED had been enthusiastic about
Daniel Deronda when she followed its serial publication in *Scribner's
Monthly* in 1876 (see letter no. 457), but she may have been wrong about
Bowles's last trip to California, which seems to have occurred in 1873. After
the publication of *Daniel Deronda* his only known trip was to Virginia,
Kentucky, and Chicago, in the spring of 1877.

975

To Mary Warner Crowell   early March 1885

Is it too late to touch you, Dear?

> We this moment knew –
> Love Marine and Love terrene –
> Love celestial too –

I give his Angels charge –

                                                            Emily –

MANUSCRIPT: HCL (L 33). Pencil.
PUBLICATION: *L* (1894) 427; *LL* 374; *L* (1931) 415; *Mount Holyoke
Alumnae Quarterly* XXIX (1946) 130.

Endorsed (by Mrs. Crowell?) "Emily Dickinson March 2, 1885." The note was written at the time of Mrs. Crowell's departure for Europe.

976

To Helen Hunt Jackson   *March 1885*

draft no. 1

Dear friend –

To reproach my own Foot in behalf of your's, is involuntary, and finding myself, no solace in "whom he loveth he chasteneth" your Valor astounds me. It was only a small Wasp, said the French Physician, repairing the sting, but the strength to perish is sometimes withheld, though who but you could tell a Foot.

> Take all away from me, but leave me Ecstasy
> And I am richer then, than all my Fellow Men.
> Is it becoming me to dwell so wealthily
> When at my very Door are those possessing more,
> In abject poverty?

That you compass "Japan" before you you [sic] breakfast, not in the least surprises me, clogged only with the Music, like the Wheels of Birds.

Thank you for hoping I am well. Who could be ill in March, that Month of proclamation? Sleigh Bells and Jays contend in my Matinee, and the North surrenders, instead of the South, a reverse of Bugles.

Pity me, however, I have finished Ramona.

Would that like Shakespere, it were just published! Knew I how to pray, to intercede for your Foot were intuitive – but I am but a Pagan.

> Of God we ask one favor,
> That we may be forgiven –

draft no. 2

Dear friend –

To reproach my own foot in behalf of your's is involuntary, and finding meager solace in "whom he chasteneth," your prowess astounds

[866]

me. It was only a small Wasp, said the french physician repairing the sting, but the [   ] tell a foot.

> Take all away from me, but leave me Ecstasy
> And I am richer then I am [   ]

strength to perish is sometimes withheld, yet who but you can [   ] tell a Foot.

> Take all away from me, but leave me Ecstasy,
> And I am richer then, than all my Fellowmen.
> Is it becoming me to dwell so wealthily,
> When at my very Door are those possessing more,
> in abject poverty.

But the strength to perish is sometimes withheld.

That you glance at Japan as you breakfast, not in the least surprises me, thronged only with Music, like the Decks of Birds. Thank you for hoping I am well. Who could be ill in March, that Month of proclamation? Sleigh Bells and Jays contend in my Matinee, and the North surrenders instead of the South, a reverse of Bugles. Pity me, however, I have finished Ramona.

Would that like Shakespeare, it were just published! Knew I how to pray, to intercede for your Foot were intuitive, but I am but a Pagan.

> Of God we ask one favor,
> That we may be forgiven –
> For what, he is presumed to know –
> The Crime, from us, is hidden –
> Immured the whole of Life
> Within a magic Prison
> We reprimand the Happiness
> That too competes with Heaven.

May I once more know, and that you are saved?

Your Dickinson.

MANUSCRIPTS: AC. Pencil.
PUBLICATION: L (1894) 424–425; LL 372–373; L (1931) 413–414. It is a composite of the two drafts.
The actual letter ED wrote is missing, but its contents are clear from

the two drafts left among her papers. Both are fair copies, but show different wording. The first draft is incomplete. The second, which repeats some sentences, has had portions cut out. The repetitions are in fact part of a third draft.

The first poem ED had also incorporated in a letter (no. 960) to the Loomises, written early in January. (See also letter no. 1014.)

There are three fragment drafts (AC – pencil) that incorporate expressions similar to ones in the letter drafts:

> Strength to perish is sometimes withheld
> Afternoon and the West and the gorgeous nothings
> which compose the sunset keep their high Appointment
> Clogged only with Music like the Wheels of Birds
>
> It is very still in the world now – Thronged only
> with Music like the Decks of Birds and the Seasons
> take their hushed places like figures in a Dream –

All are published in *NEQ* XXVIII (1955) 304. (See also letter no. 968.)

The letter is a reply to one (HCL unpublished) written by Helen Jackson, dated: Santa Monica/Cal./By the Sea./Feb. 3. 1885.

976a

My dear Miss Dickinson,

Thank you heartily for the fan. It is pathetic, in its small-ness — poor souls — how did they come to think of making such tiny ones. – I shall wear it sometimes, like a leaf on my breast. –

Your letter found me in Los Angeles, where I have been for two months & a little more. – Sunning myself, and trying to get on my feet. – I had hoped by this time to be able to go without crutches, and venture to New York, for the remainder of the winter — but I am disappointed. So far as the broken leg is concerned, I could walk with a cane now: but the whole leg having been badly strained by doing double duty so long, is obstinate about getting to work again, is very lame and sore, & I am afraid badly given out — so that it will take months for it to recover. – I dislike this exceedingly; – but dare not grumble, lest a worse thing befall me: & if I did grumble, I should deserve it, — for I am absolutely well — drive the whole of every afternoon in an open carriage on roads where larks sing & flowers are in bloom: I can do everything I ever could — except walk! — and if I never walk again it will still remain true that I have had more than a half centurys excellent trotting out of my legs — so even then, I suppose I ought not to be rebellious. – Few people get as much out of one pair of legs as I have! –

This Santa Monica is a lovely little Seaside hamlet, — only eighteen miles from Los Angeles, — one of the most beautiful Seaside places I ever saw: green to the *tip* edge of the cliffs, flowers blooming and choruses of birds, all winter. – There can be nothing in this world nearer perfection than this South California climate for winter. – Cool enough to make a fire necessary, night & morning: but warm enough to keep flowers going, all the time, in the open air, — grass & barley are many inches high – some of the "volunteer" crops already in head. – As I write — (in bed, before breakfast,) I am looking straight off towards Japan — over a silver sea — my foreground is a strip of high grass, and mallows, with a row of Eucalyptus trees sixty or seventy feet high: — and there is a positive cackle of linnets.

Searching here, for Indian relics, especially the mortars or bowls hollowed out of stone, with the solid stone pestles they used to pound their acorns in, I have found two Mexican women called *Ramona*, from whom I have bought the Indian mortars. –

I hope you are well — and at work — I wish I knew what your portfolios, by this time, hold.

Yours ever truly
Helen Jackson.

977

To Mrs. J. G. Holland   *early March 1885*

So Madonna and Daughter were incomplete, and Madonna and Son, must supersede!

Perhaps the Picture is right – But is'nt it rather cool Weather for the Wise Men of the East?

Perhaps their Shining Overcoats obviate the Climate –

The young Man is doubtless an acquisition, but I uphold Katrina, and any encroachment upon her, shall resent to the last –

Congratulate the New Moon on her second Star, and with love for each, and a "Dont wake the Baby," we are heartfeltly

Emily.

Rejoice that you are better.

One more word for Baby –

I send him *Daniel Webster's Hat* for his Golden Wedding. It can be found in the "Century" –

March Number, I think.

Be sure and try it on –

MANUSCRIPT: HCL (H 93). Pencil.

PUBLICATION: LH 197.

A second grandchild, Garrat Bleecker Van Wagenen, was born, 9 February. The March issue of *The Century* contained as frontispiece an illustration of Daniel Webster wearing an enormous beaver hat.

978

To Mabel Loomis Todd   *March 1885*

Dear friend –

Nature forgot – The Circus reminded her –

Thanks for the Ethiopian Face.

The Orient is in the West.

"You knew, Oh Egypt" said the entangled Antony –

MANUSCRIPT: AC. Pencil.

PUBLICATION: L (1894) 432; L (1931) 422.

Mrs. Todd dated the letter, 21 March 1885. Her penciled notation on the letter reads: "On receiving from me a jug of shaded yellow painted with red trumpet-vine blossoms. M. L. T."

979

To Mrs. J. G. Holland   *spring 1885*

Dear Sister,

To "gain the whole World" in the Evening Mail, without the baleful forfeit hinted in the Scripture, was indeed achievement – and I was led resisting to Bed, but Vinnie was firm as the Soudan –

Thank you tenderly – I was breathlessly interested.

Contention "loves a shining Mark." Only *fight* about me, said the dying King, and my Crown is sure –

It is only the Moss upon my Throne that impairs my Dying.

None of us know her enough to judge her, so her Maker must be her "Crowner's Quest" – Saul criticized his Savior till he became enamored of him – then he was less loquacious –

It was lovely to see your Hand again in the old attitude – a literary one, and the Present flew like a Butterfly, and the Past *was*, but there we must not linger – too many linger with us –

Love for the "Holy Family," and say to the Son that the Little Boy in the Trinity had no Grandmama, only a Holy Ghost –

But you must go to Sleep. I, who sleep always, need no Bed.

Foxes have Tenements, and remember, the Speaker was a Carpenter –

Emily –

MANUSCRIPT: HCL (H 94). Pencil.

PUBLICATION: *LH* 198–199.

Mrs. Ward's conjecture in *LH* that the woman here discussed was George Eliot seems probable. Reviews of Cross's biography were coming out and Mrs. Holland evidently sent clippings to ED. Most were laudatory, but some contended that George Eliot had been guilty of moral turpitude. The phrase "loves a shining mark" is from Young's *Night Thoughts* (Night Fifth, line 1013). The opening quotation is from Mark 8.36. "The foxes have holes" are the words of Jesus as given in Matthew 8.20. The expression "Crowner's Quest" is that of the gravedigger (*Hamlet*, V, i), who wonders whether the coroner's inquest will result in a Christian burial for Ophelia.

980

To Mrs. Thomas P. Field   *spring 1885?*

Should you not have this flower, the first of spring with me, I should regret not sending it. Your azaleas are still vivid, though the frailer flowers are flitted away.

E. Dickinson.

[871]

MANUSCRIPT: missing.
PUBLICATION: L (1894) 421; L (1931) 410.
Mrs. Todd dated the letter 1885. Mrs. Field had evidently sent a spray of azaleas to ED, who returned the kindness by sending Mrs. Field a daphne, the flower which ED elsewhere speaks of as being her earliest.

981

To Mrs. Edward Tuckerman   *April 1885*

Dear friend –

We want you to wake – Easter has come and gone –

Morning without you is a dwindled Dawn – quickend [*sic*] toward all celestial things by Crows I heard this Morning.

Accept a loving Caw from a nameless friend,

"Selah."

MANUSCRIPT: AC. Pencil.
PUBLICATION: L (1894) 390; LL 370; L (1931) 379.
The date is conjectured from the handwriting. Easter in 1885 fell on 5 April. Perhaps Mrs. Tuckerman was convalescing from illness. *Selah* is a biblical term, indicating a musical interlude or pause. Here it seems to be connected with the caw.

982

To Mrs. James S. Cooper   *April 1885*

Little Margaret, and April, and the Dog!
"What a Triumvirate"!

MANUSCRIPT: YUL. Pencil. Unpublished. Addressed: Mrs Cooper.
This might refer to a photograph which had been shown her, or to a view of the child seen from her window.

983

To Charles H. Clark   *April 1885*

Dear friend.

The flower for which your Brother cared, resumes it's Siren Cir-

cuit, and choosing a few for his Name's sake, I enclose them to you –
perhaps from some far site he overlooks their transit, and smiles at the
beatitudes so recently his own – Ephemeral – Eternal Heart!

I hope you are in health, and that the fragile Father has every
peace that years possess.

My Sister's tender interest.

We think of your small Mansion with unabated warmth, though
is not any Mansion vast, that contains a *Father?*

That this beloved Spring inspirit both yourself and him, is our
exceeding wish.

E. Dickinson.

MANUSCRIPT: AC. Pencil. Envelope addressed by ED in ink: C. H.
Clark. / 361 Degraw St. / Brooklyn – / Long Island – Postmark illegible.
Clark endorsed the letter: Apl 21/85.

PUBLICATION: *L* (1894) 365; *L* (1931) 356–357.

984

To Mrs. Edward Tuckerman   *1 May 1885*

We trust the repairs of the little friend are progressing swiftly,
though shall we love her as well revamped?

Anatomical dishabille is sweet to those who prize us – A chastened
Grace is twice a Grace. Nay, 'tis a Holiness. With a sweet May Day,

Emily.

MANUSCRIPT: AC. Pencil.

PUBLICATION: *L* (1894) 390; *LL* 371; *L* (1931) 379–380.

Early in March 1885, Mrs. Tuckerman's niece Alice Cooper Tuckerman sprained an ankle and was obliged to use crutches for four or five
months.

985

To Mabel Loomis Todd   *May 1885*

To the Bugle every color is Red –

MANUSCRIPT: AC. Pencil.

PUBLICATION: *L* (1931) 421.

Mrs. Todd's diary for 6 May 1885 says that she painted a scarlet lily which Lavinia had asked her to come to see. This note, in the handwriting of that time, may have been written to Mrs. Todd after ED had seen the painting.

986

To Thomas D. Gilbert   *late May 1885*

There is little to say, dear Mr Gilbert, when the Heart is bruised.
How hallowedly Macbeth said "that sort must heal itself," yet a grieved whisper from a friend might instruct it how –
Though we go by detachments to the strange Home, have no

MANUSCRIPT: AC. Penciled draft. On the verso is the poem "Some one prepared this mighty show." Though a fair copy, this incomplete draft never left ED's desk.
PUBLICATION: *NEQ* XXVIII (1955) 305.
The final draft may have been sent to Susan's brother, as a letter of condolence after the death of Frank Gilbert, 25 May 1885. Susan and her son Ned attended the funeral in Grand Rapids. The quotation attempts to recall the lines of the physician in *Macbeth* (V, iii, 45–46): "Therein the patient/Must minister to himself" (see also letters no. 332 and 669).

987

To Abbie C. Farley   *June 1885*

Dear friends –

When I opened the little Box and the vestal flower sprang out, an instant conviction of it's source overpowered me, and I did not attempt to dispute the Tears which were bolder than I.
Thank the sweet Mother who plotted, and the loved Daughter that executed the spotless commission. Again the vanished lived.
Can the Jasmine outlast the Hand that bore it so joyously away? Then the Mutable is the elder – It lies beside the Portrait.
"Lovely in their Lives, and in their Death, not divided."
How entirely lovely in your Mother to remember one whom she has never seen! I trust she is still well, and may long be a Keepsake to us all.

One of Sue's noble Brothers has died, and Sue and Ned are expected tonight from an absence of two weeks, on that sad account—Mattie comes home occasionally for a Moment's Recess, and fast becomes an imperial Girl.

I hope you may have a charming Trip, and return refreshed.

You have indeed endured.

Can one scant year contain so much?

With Affection,

Emily.

MANUSCRIPT: HCL. Pencil.

PUBLICATION: *Revelation* 66.

Susan and Ned returned on 8 June. The quotation recalls 2 Samuel 1, 23: "Saul and Jonathan were lovely and pleasant in their lives, and in their death they were not divided."

988

To Edward (Ned) Dickinson   *June 1885*

Ned will plead his Cousin's acceptance of the blushing Trifle? To be a Bell and Flower too, is more than Summer's share, but Nature is a Partisan –

MANUSCRIPT: HCL (B 100). Pencil.

PUBLICATION: FF 250–251.

Isabel Cutler, a daughter of Susan Dickinson's sister Harriet, visited early in the summer (see letter no. 961).

A rough draft (AC – pencil) reads:

> Ned will ask his Cousin's perusal of this "Scarlet
> Letter," whose postage is a Solstice –

On the same draft is Prose Fragment 33. It is published in *NEQ* XXVIII (1955) 302.

989

To Joseph K. Chickering   *July 1885*

Dear friend –

The Amherst Heart is plain and whole and permanent and warm.

In childhood I never sowed a seed unless it was perennial – and that is why my Garden lasts.

We dare not trust ourselves to *know* that you indeed have left us.

The Fiction is sufficient pain. To know you better as you flee, may be our recompense. I hope that you are well, and nothing mars your peace but its divinity – for Ecstasy is peril.

With earnest recollection,

E. Dickinson.

MANUSCRIPT: A.C. Pencil.
PUBLICATION: *L* (1894) 415; *LL* 376; *L* (1931) 404–405.
The *Amherst Record* announced on 8 July that Professor Chickering was retiring because of his health.

990

To Joseph K. Chickering   *about 1885*

How charming the magnanimity which conferring a favor on others, by some mirage of valor considers itself receiving one!

Of such is the Kingdom of Knights!

E. Dickinson.

MANUSCRIPT: AC. Envelope addressed: Prof. Chickering. This is rare among letters of the later years in that both envelope and letter are written in ink.
PUBLICATION: *L* (1894) 415; *LL* 341; *L* (1931) 405.
The handwriting is so nearly identical with that of the letter preceding that one conjectures it was written at the same time. Perhaps it acknowledges some token of thanks sent by Chickering upon receiving the preceding letter.

991

To Mrs. Joseph A. Sweetser   *1885?*

Aunt Katie never forgets to be lovely, and the sweet clusters of yesterday only perpetuate a heart warm so many years.

Tropic, indeed, a memory that adheres so long. They were still vivid and fragrant when they reached my fingers, and were the wrist that bears them bolder, it would give reply. As it is, only a kiss and a gratitude, and every grace of being, from your loving niece. "I give his angels charge!"

Should I say his flowers, for qualified as saints they are.

Vinnie's and my transport.

MANUSCRIPT: missing.
PUBLICATION: L (1894) 413; L (1931) 402–403.

ED used the same expression "I give his angels charge" in writing Mrs. Crowell in March 1885 (no. 975). She was ill at the time she wrote this letter.

992

To Mrs. Richard H. Mather   *about 1885*

Is it too late for a Stranger's remembrance —
Is it perhaps too early?

E. Dickinson —

MANUSCRIPT: AC. Pencil. Unpublished.
The date is conjectured from the handwriting. ED never met Mrs. Mather (see letter no. 697).

993

To recipient unknown   *about 1885*

Betrothed to Righteousness might be
An Ecstasy discreet
But Nature relishes the Pinks
Which she was taught to eat —

MANUSCRIPT: AC. Pencil.
PUBLICATION: BM (1945) 327; Poems (1955) 1124.
The date is conjectured from the handwriting. This letter-poem, neatly written on a small sheet of stationery, has been folded as if enclosed in an envelope.

994

To Mrs. William C. Esty   *about 1885*

I bring my Mrs Estey not Treasures, not Temptation, but just this little Vat of Numidian Wine.

Emily

MANUSCRIPT: AC. Discarded penciled draft.
PUBLICATION: facsimile only, in *BM* 311, to illustrate the worksheet of a poem; *NEQ* XXVIII (1955) 306.
The same sheet ED used later to jot down the unfinished poems "Why should we hurry – why indeed," and "Extol thee – could I."

995

To recipients unknown   *about 1885*

Sweet friends.

I send a message by a Mouth that cannot speak –

> The Ecstasy to guess,
> Were a receipted Bliss
> If Grace could talk.
> With love –

MANUSCRIPT: AC. Pencil.
PUBLICATION: *L* (1894) 426; *LL* 373; *L* (1931) 414.
The date is conjectured from the handwriting. See letter no. 1002.

996

To Mrs. Thomas P. Field   *1885?*

I was much chagrined by the delayed flower – please accept its apology.

E. Dickinson.

MANUSCRIPT: missing.
PUBLICATION: *L* (1894) 421; *L* (1931) 410.
Mrs. Todd dated the note 1885.

To Austin Dickinson and family   *about 1885*

Brother, Sister, Ned.

Enclosed please find the Birds which do not go South.

Emily —

MANUSCRIPT: HCL (B 46). Pencil.
PUBLICATION: *FF* 232.
The date is conjectured from the handwriting. A note in *FF* says that
this message accompanied roasting chickens.

To Susan Gilbert Dickinson   *about 1885*

Accept the Firstling of my Flock, to whom also it's Lastling is due.
To broil our Benefits, perhaps, is not the highest way.

Emily.

MANUSCRIPT: HCL (B 115). Pencil.
PUBLICATION: *AM* CXV (1915) 39; *FF* 229.
The date is conjectured from the handwriting. This message accom-
panied broilers.

To Susan Gilbert Dickinson   *summer 1885*

Dear Sue.

I could send you no Note so sweet as the last words of your Boy —
"You will look after Mother"?

Emily.

MANUSCRIPT: HCL (B 41). Pencil.
PUBLICATION: *FF* 262.
During the summer of 1885 Ned vacationed in the Adirondacks, at
Lake Placid. This was probably written on the eve of his departure.

To Edward (Ned) Dickinson   *August 1885*

Dear Boy.

I dared not trust my own Voice among your speechless Mountains, and so I took your Mother's, which mars no Majesty – So you find no treason in Earth or Heaven.

You never will, My Ned –

That is a personal refraction – shall I question you, or let your Story tell itself? "Day unto Day uttereth Speech" if you do not teaze him –

I was stricken with laughter by your Dr Irish – The search for the Syphon is unremitting.

How favorable that something is missing besides Sir John Franklin! Interrogation must be fed –

Your intimacy with the Mountains I heartily endorse – Ties more Eleusinian I must leave to you – Deity will guide you – I do not mean Jehovah – The little God with Epaulettes I spell it in French to conceal it's temerity

What made you quote that sweetest Verse I never heard from Lips but scarcely wake or sleep without re-loving it?

Love for Maria Pearl – and a ruddy remembrance to my Neighbors. Vinnie is still subsoiling, but lays down her Spade to caress you. And ever be sure of me, Lad –

> Fondly,
> Aunt Emily.

Latest from the Dam –

Telegraphed Torricelli to bring a Vacuum, but his Father wrote that he was'nt at Home.

MANUSCRIPT: HCL (B 183). Pencil.

PUBLICATION: *FF* 261–262.

"Maria Pearl" was a nickname for Maria Whitney, who had her own cottage at Lake Placid. The reference to the siphon and the dam has to do with some accident in the town waterworks, of which Ned's father was president. The allusion to Evangelista Torricelli (1608–1647), celebrated physicist and mathematician, was probably clear to Ned, who may have mentioned to his aunt that he had become acquainted with the "Torricellian vacuum," or barometer, in a college science course.

To Eugenia Hall   *about 1885*

I heard a very sweet voice, during the presentation of the Cake, more charming if possible, than the Cake itself, for both of which, my thanks.

May I know how to make it, the Music, and the Cake beside?

Smilingly,
Cousin Emily.

MANUSCRIPT: Mabbott. Pencil. Envelope addressed: Miss E. Hall –
PUBLICATION: *The Collector*, May 1950, in part.
Eugenia was now about twenty or twenty-one years old.

To Eugenia Hall   *about 1885*

Let me thank the little Cousin in flowers, which without lips, have language –

Somewhat Cousin

Emily –

MANUSCRIPT: Barrett. Pencil.
PUBLICATION: L (1894) 427; LL 374; L (1931) 415.
The phrase "Somewhat Cousin" might suggest that ED was ill, or that the cousinship was in fact remote. She is probably thanking Eugenia for the cake by sending flowers. See letter no. 995.

To Benjamin Kimball   *summer 1885*

Dear friend.

Your Note was unspeakable strength.

May I keep it's promise in solemn reserve? To know that there is shelter, sometimes dissuades it's necessity – In this instance defers it.

Even to ask a legal question might so startle me that my Voice would pass to another World before it could be uttered.

In tribute to your fidelity I send you the face of my Father.
Thank you for the *Seal* – it covers the whole area of sanctity.

Confidingly,
E. Dickinson.

MANUSCRIPT: AC. Pencil.
PUBLICATION: *Revelation* 68–69.
Though this letter had been placed by ED in the envelope with letters
and fragments to Lord, Mrs. Bingham's conjecture that it was intended
for Kimball seems probable.

1004

To Mabel Loomis Todd *summer 1885*

Brother and Sister's Friend –

"Sweet Land of Liberty" is a superfluous Carol till it concern ourselves – then it outrealms the Birds.

I saw the American Flag last Night in the shutting West, and I
felt for every Exile.

I trust you are homesick. That is the sweetest courtesy we pay an
absent friend. The Honey you went so far to seek, I trust too you
obtain.

Though was there not an "Humbler" Bee?

"I will sail by thee alone, thou animated Torrid Zone."

Your Hollyhocks endow the House, making Art's inner Summer,
never Treason to Nature's. Nature will be just closing her Picnic,
when you return to America, but you will ride Home by Sunset, which
is far better.

I am glad you cherish the Sea. We correspond, though I never met
him.

I write in the midst of Sweet-Peas and by the side of Orioles, and
could put my Hand on a Butterfly, only he withdraws.

Touch Shakespeare for me.

The Savior's only signature to the Letter he wrote to all mankind,
was, A Stranger and ye took me in.

America.

MANUSCRIPT: AC. Pencil.
PUBLICATION: *L* (1931) 422.

This letter is written in reply to one received from Mrs. Todd, who spent the summer of 1885 in Europe. The quotation in the fifth paragraph attempts to recall lines from Emerson's "The Humble-Bee": "I will follow thee alone,/Thou animated torrid-zone."

1005

To Mrs. James S. Cooper   *about 1885*

With Leopards for Playmates, the beautiful Child defies the Latitudes and I trust that her Session of Domingo has but just begun – With thanks for the little Usher, and the lurking Mama –

E – Dickinson –

MANUSCRIPT: YUL. Pencil. Unpublished.
The date is conjectured from the handwriting. ED has seen a photograph of Mrs. Cooper's grandchild, Margaret Tuckerman, photographed perhaps on a leopard skin.

1006

To Abbie C. Farley   *early August 1885*
Dear friend,

What a reception for you! Did she wait for your approbation?

Her deferring to die until you came seemed to me so confiding – as if nothing should be presumed. It can probably never be real to you.

The Vail that helps us, falls so mercifully over it.

"An envious Sliver broke" was a passage your Uncle peculiarly loved in the drowning Ophelia.

Was it a premonition? To him to whom Events and Omens are at last the same?

I shall certainly think of you in the second departure, so innocent, so cruel.

Isaac pleads again, "but where is the Lamb for the Sacrifice?" The Clock's sweet voice makes no reply.

No faithful pang is silenced, but Anguish sometimes gives a cause which was at first concealed. That you two be not sundered is my holy wish.

Emily, with love.

[883]

MANUSCRIPT: HCL. Pencil.
PUBLICATION: *Revelation* 66.
Abbie's cousin, Mary Farley, was drowned in Walden Pond, 1 August 1885. The two referred to in the last sentence are Abbie and her mother.

1007

To T. W. Higginson   *6 August 1885*

Dear friend.

I was unspeakably shocked to see this in the Morning Paper –
She wrote me in Spring that she could not walk, but not that she would die – I was sure you would know. Please say it is not so.

What a Hazard a Letter is!

When I think of the Hearts it has scuttled and sunk, I almost fear to lift my Hand to so much as a Superscription.

Trusting that all is peace in your loved Abode,

With alarm,
Your Scholar –

MANUSCRIPT: BPL (Higg 116). Pencil. Envelope addressed by ED in ink: Col. T. W. Higginson./Cambridge./Mass. Postmarked: Palmer Aug 6 1885.
PUBLICATION: *L* (1931) 320.
Accompanying the letter is a clipping from the *Springfield Republican* of 6 August, beginning: "Mrs. Helen Hunt Jackson is reported at the point of death in San Francisco, where she has been steadily declining for the past four months." Mrs. Jackson died, 12 August.

A rough draft of two of the sentences (AC – pencil) reads thus:

> What a Hazard a Letter is – When I think of the Hearts
> it has Cleft or healed I almost wince to lift my Hand
> to so much as a superscription but then we always
> except ourselves –

It is published in *NEQ* XXVIII (1955) 305. (See also letter no. 1011.)

1008

To Samuel Bowles the younger   *mid-August 1885*

Dear friend,

May I ask a service so sacred as that you will address and mail a

Note to the friend of my friend Mrs Jackson? I do not know Mr Jackson's address, and desire to write him.

That your loved Confederate and yourself are in ceaseless peace, is my happy faith –

The Sweet Peas you hallowed, stand in Carmine Sheaves. Would that you could plunder them!

Gratefully,

MANUSCRIPT: Bowles. Pencil. The signature is clipped away. Envelope addressed by ED in ink: Samuel Bowles/Springfield/Mass. Postmarked: Palmer Aug 91 1885 [the reversal of the figures in the date make it conjecturally Aug 19, the probable date, since the following letter was mailed the next day].

PUBLICATION: L (1894) 351; L (1931) 339.

ED enclosed the following letter.

1009

To William S. Jackson   *mid-August 1885*

I take the Hand of Mr Bowles to express my sympathy for my grieved Friend, and to ask him when sorrow will allow, if he will tell me a very little of her Life's close? She said in a Note of a few months since, "I am absolutely well."

I next knew of her death. Excuse me for disturbing you in so deep an hour.

Bereavement is my only plea.

Sorrowfully,
E. Dickinson.

MANUSCRIPT: Jackson. Pencil. Envelope addressed by Bowles: Wm S. Jackson Esq./Colorado Springs/Col. Envelope endorsed by Jackson: E Dickenson/Aug 13th 85. Postmarked: Springfield Mass 1885 Aug 20. 1.30 AM. Unpublished. With it ED enclosed a cut envelope showing her name and address.

Immediately after Helen Jackson's death, ED wrote to her publisher Thomas Niles. The letter is missing, but its contents can be inferred by this reply from Niles, dated: Boston, Augt 19 1885. (HCL)

Dear Miss Dickinson

I have yours asking about Mrs Jackson. A year since, she broke her leg & in the autumn she managed to get down to Los Angeles where she passed the winter leaving there in Mch for home but got no farther than San Francisco where she was taken down with what she called Malarial fever. Judging by her continued letters the doctors did not know what her real trouble was. Most likely they did however, but kept it from her. We only know here what has been telegraphed that she died of Cancer in the stomach.

In her last letter to me, recd. since the news of her death, she says she "has but a few days to live and shall be thankful to be released" and she closes thus:

"I shall look in on your new rooms some day, be sure — but you won't see me — Good bye — Affy. forever, H.J."

And by this you will know that *she* thinks it is the "beginning."

I will send you a photograph of her in a day or two

Yrs truly
T. Niles

1010

To Sara Colton (Gillett)   *late summer 1885*

Mattie will hide this little flower in her friend's Hand. Should she ask who sent it, tell her as Desdemona did when they asked who slew her, "Nobody — I myself."

MANUSCRIPT: Holcombe. Pencil.

PUBLICATION: *Amherst Monthly,* May 1910: "The Poetry of Emily Dickinson," by F. J. Pohl, Jr.; LL 61; *Hartford Daily Times* 7 March 1936. See the note to the following letter.

1011

To Sara Colton (Gillett)?   *late summer 1885*

What a hazard an Accent is! When I think of the Hearts it has scuttled or sunk, I hardly dare to raise my voice to so much as a Salutation.

E. Dickinson.

MANUSCRIPT: Holcombe. Pencil.

PUBLICATION: *Hartford Daily Times* 7 March 1936, in part reproduced in facsimile.

The same phraseology ED used in writing Higginson just before Mrs. Jackson's death (no. 1007). Among ED's papers at the time of her death was another draft (AC – pencil):

> What a Hazard an Accent is! When I think of the
> Hearts it has scuttled or sunk, I almost fear to lift my
> Hand to so much as a punctuation.

Sara Colton was a friend of Martha Dickinson, whom she visited in the summer of 1885. She later married the Reverend Arthur L. Gillett, a professor in the Hartford Theological Seminary. The *Hartford Times* article was written from material which Mrs. Gillett supplied, which states "that they [this and the preceding note] were written to Mrs. Gillett when she was a girl. . ."

Sara Colton did not know and never saw ED. The preceding letter (no. 1010) is precisely the kind that ED often wrote and sent across the hedge to friends of her niece and nephews. The tone of this one, the signature, the concern with rhetorical effect, make one seriously doubt that it was in fact sent to Sara Colton. Nor was it sent to Susan Dickinson, for ED never signed notes to Sue thus. Whoever received it perhaps presented it to Sara Colton as a memento, maybe at the same time she received the other note.

1012

To Samuel Bowles the younger   *August 1885*

Dear friend,

I did not know. God bless you indeed!

Extend to that small Hand my own "Right Hand of Fellowship" and guide the Woman of your Heart softly to my own.

I give "his Angels Charge –" Well remembered Angels, whose absence, only, dims our Eyes. The Magnanimity I asked, you how freely gave!

If ever of any act of mine you should be in need, let me reply with the Laureate, "Speak that I live to hear!"

Vitally,
E. Dickinson.

MANUSCRIPT: Bowles. Pencil. Envelope addressed by ED in ink: Mr & Mrs/Samuel Bowles. It was delivered by hand.

PUBLICATION: L (1894) 350; LL 374; L (1931) 339.

Probably Bowles wrote ED that he had forwarded her letter to Jackson, for which act she here commends his "Magnanimity." He also mentioned the birth of their son Samuel, 31 July. She uses the phrase "I give his angels charge" for the third time this year (see letters no. 975 and 991). The final quotation echoes Claudius to Polonius: "Oh, speak of that; that do I long to hear," *Hamlet* II, ii, 50.

1013

To Samuel Bowles the younger   *August 1885*

Dawn and Dew my Bearers be –
Ever,
Butterfly.

MANUSCRIPT: Bowles. Pencil. Addressed by ED in ink: Mr and Mrs/ Samuel Bowles.

PUBLICATION: L (1894) 351; L (1931) 340.

It is said to be a note accompanying sweet peas sent by early train to Springfield. It may well have accompanied the preceding letter.

1014

To Samuel Bowles the younger   *1885*

Dear friends.

Had I not known I was not asleep, I should have feared I dreamed, so blissful was their beauty, but Day and they demurred.

Take all away from me, but leave me Ecstasy, and I am richer then, than all my fellowmen. Is it becoming me, to dwell so wealthily, when at my very door Are those possessing more, in boundless poverty?

With joyous thanks,
E. Dickinson –

MANUSCRIPT: Bowles. Pencil Addressed by ED in ink: Mr and Mrs/ Samuel Bowles. This also was delivered by hand.
PUBLICATION: L (1894) 351; L (1931) 340.
The date is conjectured from the handwriting. The poem, incorporated in a letter for the third time this year (see letters no. 960 and 976), is here arranged as prose.

1015

To William S. Jackson?   *late summer 1885*

Helen of Troy will die, but Helen of Colorado, never. Dear friend, can you walk, were the last words that I wrote her. Dear friend, I can fly – her immortal (soaring) reply. I never saw Mrs Jackson but twice, but those twice are indelible, and one Day more I am deified, was the only impression she ever left on any Heart (House) she entered –

MANUSCRIPT: AC. Rough penciled draft.
PUBLICATION: The first two sentences are in L (1894) 426; LL 373; L (1931) 414. The remainder is in a footnote in AB 84.
This rough draft, from which the published texts derive, is written on two sheets of paper. One conjectures that Mr. Jackson replied to the letter ED wrote him in August (no. 1009), and that this is the draft of her projected answer. The phrase "one Day more I am deified" recalls a line from Browning's "The Last Ride Together."

1016

To Mabel Loomis Todd   *late 1885*

Why should we censure Othello, when the Criterion Lover says, "Thou shalt have no other Gods before Me"?

MANUSCRIPT: AC. Pencil.
PUBLICATION: L (1894) 433; L (1931) 423.
Mrs. Todd dated it September 1885.

To Samuel Bowles the younger   *late September 1885*

Dear friend,

I am sure you will guide the Note to your Brother's Hand. I am unaware of his Residence, and Eden has no number nor street. As I thank you and glance at your own Possessions, may I not touch the words,

"What a Triumvirate"!

Faithfully,
E. Dickinson.

MANUSCRIPT: Bowles. Pencil. Envelope addressed by ED in ink: Samuel Bowles./Springfield./Mass. Postmarked: September 28.

PUBLICATION: L (1931) 340.

It is said to have enclosed a note to Samuel's brother Charles, who had recently become engaged.

To Forrest F. Emerson   *late September 1885*

Dear Clergyman

In a note which you sent my brother soon after the dying of our child, was a passage, our only spar at the time, and solemnly remembered.

We would gladly possess it more accurately, if convenient to you. "And I can but believe that in such a mysterious providence as the dying of little Gilbert, there is a purpose of benevolence which does not include our present happiness." Vinnie hoped, too, to speak with you of Helen of Colorado, whom she understood you to have a friend, a friend also of hers.

Should she know any circumstances of her life's close, would she perhaps lend it to you, that you might lend it to me? Oh had that Keats a Severn!

But I trespass upon your thronged time.

With affection for Mrs Emerson, and my sister's love.

Earnestly,
E. Dickinson.

MANUSCRIPT: missing. The text derives from a transcript (AC) made by Mrs. Todd.

PUBLICATION: L (1931) 394.

The Emersons were in Amherst during the week of 20 September 1885, as guests of President and Mrs. Seelye. Mr. Emerson preached at the First Church on Sunday the twentieth. The Emersons were now living in Newport, Rhode Island, where Mr. Emerson occupied a pulpit.

In referring to Helen Jackson, ED alludes to the deathbed moment of Keats, whose friend Joseph Severn was with him and reported Keats's last words: "Severn, lift me up, for I am dying. I shall die easy. Don't be frightened. Thank God it has come."

1019

To Mrs. Frederick Tuckerman   **autumn 1885**

But if "Little Margaret's love" is so vivid, is it quite safe to ignite it?

I never have taken a Peach in my Hand, so late in the Year. My Lips, also, are guiltless of that pink experience —

Believing Mama to be her Envoy, may I entrust my smiles to her?

E. Dickinson —

MANUSCRIPT: YUL. Pencil. Unpublished.

1020

To Mrs. Edward Tuckerman   *October 1885*

Dear friend.

I thought of you on your lonely journey, certain the hallowed Heroine was gratified, though mute – I trust you return in safety and with closer clutch for that which remains, for Dying whets the grasp.

October is a mighty Month, for in it Little Gilbert died. "Open the Door" was his last Cry – "the Boys are waiting for me!"

Quite used to his Commandment, his little Aunt obeyed, and still two years and many Days, and he does not return.

Where makes my Lark his Nest?

But Corinthians' Bugle obliterates the Birds, so covering your loved Heart to keep it from another shot,

Tenderly,
Emily.

[891]

MANUSCRIPT: AC. Pencil.
PUBLICATION: L (1894) 390–391; LL 376; L (1931) 380.
Except for her sister, Mrs. William Esty, living in Amherst, Mrs. Tuckerman at this time had no surviving close relatives. The journey must have been to the funeral of a more distant relative or a friend. For Gilbert's last words, see letter no. 873. "Corinthians' Bugle" may allude to 1 Corinthians 15.52: ". . . for the trumpet shall sound, and the dead shall be raised incorruptible, and we shall all be changed."

1021

To Eugenia Hall   *mid-October 1885*

Will the sweet Cousin who is about to make the Etruscan Experiment, accept a smile which will last a Life, if ripened in the Sun?

Cousin Emily –

MANUSCRIPT: Barrett. Pencil. Envelope addressed by ED: Eugenia.
PUBLICATION: L (1894) 428; LL 375; L (1931) 416.
Eugenia Hall married Franklin L. Hunt, 20 October 1885.

1022

To Mrs. James C. Greenough   *late October 1885*

Dear friend,

I had the luxury of a Mother a month longer than you, for my own Mother died in November, but the anguish also was granted me to see the first snow upon her Grave, the following Day – which, dear friend, you were spared – but Remembrance engulfs me, and I must cease –

I wish I could speak a word of courage, tho' that Love has already done. Who could be motherless who has a Mother's Grave within confiding reach? Let me enclose the tenderness which is born of bereavement. To have *had* a Mother – how mighty!

Emily.

MANUSCRIPT: AC. Pencil.
PUBLICATION: L (1894) 428–429; LL 375; L (1931) 416–417.
Mrs. Greenough's mother died, 21 October 1885.

[892]

To Edward (Ned) Dickinson   *early November 1885*

Dear Ned –

Burglaries have become so frequent, is it quite safe to leave the Golden Rule out over night?

With sorrow for his illness,

Aunt Emily –

MANUSCRIPT: HCL (B 58). Pencil. Addressed: Ned –
PUBLICATION: *FF* 248.
On 5 November 1885 the Austin Dickinson house was robbed while the family were eating supper.

1024

To Susan Gilbert Dickinson   *late 1885*

The World hath not known her, but *I* have known her, was the sweet Boast of Jesus –

The small Heart cannot break – The Ecstasy of it's penalty solaces the large –

Emerging from an Abyss, and reentering it – that is Life, is it not, Dear?

The tie between us is very fine, but a Hair never dissolves.

Lovingly –
Emily –

MANUSCRIPT: HCL (B 148). Pencil.
PUBLICATION: *LL* 63, in part; *FF* 270, in part.
This and the following note, written to Sue, can be dated by handwriting only. But they sound as if they had been written during a period of illness. ED was so seriously ill after mid-November that for a time during November her brother Austin did not dare leave town.

To Susan Gilbert Dickinson   *late 1885*

Dear Sue –

The Supper was delicate and strange. I ate it with compunction as I would eat a Vision. The Blossoms only were too hearty – those I saved for the Birds – How tenderly I thank you. I often hope you are better – Beneath the Alps the Danube runs –

> MANUSCRIPT: HCL (B 66). Pencil. The signature has been cut out.
> PUBLICATION: *FF* 269.

1026

To Edward (Ned) Dickinson   *late 1885*

What an Embassy –
What an Ambassador!
"And pays his Heart for what his Eyes eat only!"
Excuse the bearded Pronoun –

                                        Ever,

                                              Aunt Emily –

> MANUSCRIPT: HCL (B 118). Pencil.
> PUBLICATION: *AM* CXV (1915) 38; in *FF* 243 the final sentence is attached to letter no. 854, to which the same quotation is attached. This letter is in the same handwriting as the two letters preceding, and was probably written during the same period of illness.

1027

To Kendall Emerson   *Christmas 1885*

Dear Kendall.

I send you a Blossom with my love – Spend it as you will –
The Woods are too deep for your little Feet to grope for Evergreen –

                                        Your friend
                                              Emily –

MANUSCRIPT: AC. Pencil.
PUBLICATION: *Amherst Alumni News* IV (July 1951) 14.
This is the third and last of the Christmas notes ED sent to Gilbert's friend (see letters no. 876 and 956).

1028

To Susan Gilbert Dickinson   *early 1886*

I was just writing these very words to you, "Susan fronts on the Gulf Stream," when Vinnie entered with the Sea. Dare I touch the Coincidence? Do you remember what whispered to "Horatio"?

Emily.

MANUSCRIPT: HCL (B 65). Pencil.
PUBLICATION: FF 242.
This and the two following notes, written to Sue, are in the handwriting of the very latest period. They are thank-you notes, sent to acknowledge small thoughtfulnesses during the period when ED's illness was severe.

1029

To Susan Gilbert Dickinson   *early 1886*

How lovely every solace! This long, short, penance "Even I regain my freedom with a Sigh"

Emily.

MANUSCRIPT: HCL (B 128). Pencil.
PUBLICATION: FF 269.

1030

To Susan Gilbert Dickinson   *early 1886*

Thank you, dear Sue – for every solace –

MANUSCRIPT: HCL (B 101). Pencil.
PUBLICATION: FF 247.

Another manuscript (HCL L 24), unfolded and apparently never sent, was probably a trial start for this letter.

Dear Sue,
Thank y

1031

To Mrs. William Henry Prince   *early 1886*

Dear friend,

Thank you for the tenderness of a Stranger. Life is deep and swift – Spars without the Routes but the Billows designate.

What a Comrade is Human Thought!

The Circumstance you so sweetly recall, steals from my remembrance. Thank you for an Act fragrant so far past.

In behalf of your liquid Note and your delicate Niece, shall I not think of you as the Bird and the Aid de camp?

E. Dickinson.

MANUSCRIPT: AC. Pencil. Envelope addressed: Mrs Prince. Unpublished.

Probably Mrs. Prince called with a niece, one of the Seelye girls, and left a message.

1032

To Alice Skeel Mather   *early 1886*

May it have occurred to my sweet neighbor that the words "found peace in believing" had other than a theological import?

With happy congratulations.

E. Dickinson

MANUSCRIPT: Cushing. Pencil. Unpublished.

This note is said to have been written at the time of the engagement of Alice Mather, daughter of Professor Richard Mather, to the Reverend Williston Walker, of the Hartford Theological Seminary. They were married, 1 June 1886. The quotation echoes Romans 15.13: "Now the God of hope fill you with all joy and peace in believing. . ."

[896]

To Mabel Loomis Todd   28 February 1886

"Or Figs of Thistles?"

MANUSCRIPT: AC. Pencil. The quotation is not closed.
PUBLICATION: L (1931) 421.
Mrs. Todd's diary for 11 February says that she painted a bronze plaque
with thistles for ED. On the fifteenth she sent it, receiving a hyacinth from
ED on the eighteenth, and this note on the twenty-eighth. The message
intends to convey ED's delight by alluding to Matthew 7.16: "Do men
gather grapes of thorns, or figs of thistles?" (See letter no. 883.)

1034

To Louise and Frances Norcross   about March 1886

I scarcely know where to begin, but love is always a safe place. I
have twice been very sick, dears, with a little recess of convalescence,
then to be more sick, and have lain in my bed since November, many
years, for me, stirring as the arbutus does, a pink and russet hope; but
that we will leave with our pillow. When your dear hearts are quite
convenient, tell us of their contents, the fabric cared for most, not a
fondness wanting.

Do you keep musk, as you used to, like Mrs. Morene of Mexico?
Or cassia carnations so big they split their fringes of berry? Was your
winter a tender shelter — perhaps like Keats's bird, "and hops and hops
in little journeys"?

Are you reading and well, and the W[hitney]s near and warm?
When you see Mrs. French and Dan give them a tear from us.

Vinnie would have written, but could not leave my side. Maggie
gives her love. Mine more sweetly still.

Emily.

MANUSCRIPT: destroyed.
PUBLICATION: L (1894) 435; LL 378; L (1931) 427–428.
The quotation is from Keats's Endymion, and used by Higginson in his
essay "The Life of Birds." The Norcrosses were good friends of Daniel
Chester French and his mother, as they were of Maria Whitney, who
lived with her brother in Cambridge.

To Mrs. Edward Tuckerman   mid-March 1886

Dear One,

"Eye hath not seen nor ear heard." What a recompense! The enthusiasm of God at the reception of His sons! How ecstatic! How infinite! Says the blissful voice, not yet a voice, but a vision, "I will not let thee go, except I bless thee."

Emily.

MANUSCRIPT: missing.
PUBLICATION: L (1894) 434; LL 378; L (1931) 427.
Professor Edward Tuckerman died, 15 March 1886. This is the last letter to Mrs. Tuckerman, and seems to be in the nature of a farewell. The opening quotation, from 1 Corinthians 2.9, refers to the nature of things God has prepared for mankind. It was Jacob, wrestling with the angel, who said (Genesis 32.26): "I will not let thee go, except thou bless me." ED again used the expression, with the same inversion, in her next letter to Higginson (no. 1042).

1036

To Mrs. James S. Cooper   spring 1886

Is it too late to express my sorrow for my grieved friend?
Though the first moment of loss is eternity, other eternities remain.

Though the great Waters sleep,
That they are still the Deep,
We cannot doubt.

No vacillating God
Ignited this Abode
To put it out.

MANUSCRIPT: missing.
PUBLICATION: L (1894) 392; LL 296; L (1931) 381.
The Cooper and Tuckerman families were close friends. Professor Tuckerman's nephew married Mrs. Cooper's daughter Alice. Several copies of the poem are extant (see, for instance, letter no. 908). It had been composed about 1884.

1037

To Mrs. George S. Dickerman   *early spring 1886?*

Dear friend,

Daphne always seems to me a more civic Arbutus, though the sweet Barbarian will forgive me if the suggestion is invidious, for are not both as beautiful as Delight can make them?

If we love Flowers, are we not "born again" every Day, without the distractions of Nicodemus? Not to outgrow Genesis, is a sweet monition —

With Affection,
E. Dickinson –

MANUSCRIPT: YUL. Pencil.
PUBLICATION: *Smith Alumnae Quarterly*, February (1954) 79.

Dickerman became pastor of the First Church, 13 June 1883. ED never saw Mrs. Dickerman. Her daughter Miss Elizabeth Dickerman, who possessed the letter, tells in the *Quarterly* how her mother received three items from ED: a poem "There are two Mays" (*Poems* 1955, page 1110), this letter, and a note which from recollection she constructs as "The love of the grape – [signed] Catawba," sent with a glass of jelly. It may very possibly be that ED sent this letter in 1885, though probably not earlier, since an earlier acquaintance would have been too slight to warrant the "With Affection." It is placed here, in spite of ED's severe illness, because the tone fits this final spring, during which on occasion she could communicate with eloquence.

Nicodemus's questions about the meaning of rebirth are answered by Jesus in the opening verses of the third chapter of John.

1038

To Mrs. J. G. Holland   *early spring 1886*

Concerning the little sister, not to assault, not to adjure, but to obtain those constancies which exalt friends, we followed her to St. Augustine, since which the trail was lost, or says George Stearns of his alligator, "there was no such aspect."

The beautiful blossoms waned at last, the charm of all who knew them, resisting the effort of earth or air to persuade them to root, as the great florist says, "The flower that never will in other climate grow."

To thank you for its fragrance would be impossible, but then its other blissful traits are more than can be numbered. And the beloved Christmas, too, for which I never thanked you. I hope the little heart is well, – *big* would have been the width, – and the health solaced; any news of her as sweet as the first arbutus.

Emily and Vinnie give the love greater every hour.

MANUSCRIPT: missing.
PUBLICATION: *L* (1894) 187–188; *L* (1931) 179–180; *LH* 200.

Mrs. Holland first went to Florida to escape attacks of rheumatism during the winter of 1885–1886. She may have known more about ED's illness than this letter of thanks would imply. It is the last letter that ED is known to have written her, and probably the final one. George Stearns of Chicopee, a well-known lawyer and humorist, was a contributor to the *Springfield Republican*. The quotation has not been identified, but may be part of a story told to the Hollands and Dickinsons after Stearns (who described it in the *Republican*) had returned from an alligator hunt. The second quotation is from *Paradise Lost*, II, 272–273: "O flowers/That never will in other climate grow . . ."

1039

To Charles H. Clark   *early April 1886*

Dear friend,

Are you living and well, and your Father in peace, and the Home in Degraw St without effacing chang[e]?

I received your very kind Message, I think in November, since which I have been very ill, and begin to roam in my room a little, an hour at a time.

Do you as time steals on, know anything of the "Willie" whom Mr Wadsworth so loved – and of whom he said with a smile "should he find a gold Watch in the street he would not pick it up, so unsullied was he," and did his Daughter regret her flight from her loved Father, or the son who left the Religion so precious to him? My Sister gives her faithful remembrance to yourself, and your Father, the Brother so cherished, never once forgot. You will recall the flower sacred to your Brother. No Sloth has Memory.

E. Dickinson.

MANUSCRIPT: AC. Pencil. Envelope addressed by Lavinia: C. H. Clark/361 Degraw St/Brooklyn/L.I. Postmarked: Apr 5. Letter endorsed by Clark: Amherst Apl 5/86.

PUBLICATION: *L* (1894) 435–436, in part; *L* (1931) 428, in part.

1040

To Charles H. Clark   *mid-April 1886*

Thank you, Dear friend – I am better. The velocity of the ill, however, is like that of the snail.

I am glad of your Father's tranquility, and of your own courage. Fear makes us all martial.

I could hardly have thought it possible that the scholarly Stranger to whom my Father introduced me, could have mentioned my Friend, almost itself a Vision, or have still left a Legend to relate his name

With the exception of my Sister who never saw Mr Wadsworth, your Name alone remains.

"Going Home," was he not an Aborigine of the sky? The last time he came in Life, I was with my Lilies and Heliotropes, said my sister to me, "the Gentleman with the deep voice wants to see you, Emily," hearing him ask of the servant. "Where did you come from," I said, for he spoke like an Apparition.

"I stepped from my Pulpit [from] to the Train" was my [sic] simple reply, and when I asked "how long," "Twenty Years" said he with inscrutable roguery – but the loved Voice has ceased, and to some one who heard him "Going Home," it was sweet to speak. I am glad his Willie is faithful, of whom he said "the Frogs were his little friends" and I told him they were my Dogs, the last smile that he gave me. Thank you for each circumstance, and tell me all you love to say of what said your lost Brother "The Doctor opened his Heart to Charlie." Excuse me for the Voice, this moment immortal. With my Sister's remembrance,

E. Dickinson.

MANUSCRIPT: AC. Pencil. Envelope addressed by Lavinia: C. H. Clark/361 Degraw St./Brooklyn/L.I. Postmarked: Apr 15 1886. Endorsed by Clark: Amherst April 15. 1886.

PUBLICATION: *L* (1894) 437–438; *L* (1931) 429–430.

To Elizabeth Dickinson Currier   *17 April 1886*

Mr Hunt was tinning a Post this Morning, and told us Libbie did'nt feel quite as well as usual and I hav'nt felt quite as well as usual since the Chestnuts were ripe, though it was'nt the Chestnuts' fault, but the Crocuses are so martial and the Daffodils to the second Joint, let us join Hands and recover.

"I do remember an Apothecary," said that sweeter Robin than Shakespeare, was a loved paragraph which has lain on my Pillow all Winter, but perhaps Shakespeare has been "up street" oftener than I have, this Winter. Would Father's youngest Sister believe that in the "Shire Town," where he and Blackstone went to school, a man was hung in Northampton yesterday for the murder of a man by the name of Dickinson, and that Miss Harriet Merrill was poisoned by a strolling Juggler, and to be tried in the Supreme Court next week?

Dont you think Fumigation ceased when Father died? Poor, romantic Miss Merrill! But perhaps a Police Gazette was better for you than an Essay –

I hope you are both stronger, and ask a word of gain with these ecstatic Days. I give my anxious love, and Vinnie's faithfulness with mine.

Your Emily –

MANUSCRIPT: YUL. Pencil.
PUBLICATION: L (1894) 436–437; LL 379–380; L (1931) 428–429.

ED's aunt Elizabeth (Libbie), to whom this is addressed, died of cancer six months later, 10 October 1886. On 16 April Allen J. Adams was executed at Northampton for the murder of Moses Billings Dickinson of Amherst. The family of Miss Merrill, an aunt of ED's classmate of the same name, were suing her heir, a Dr. De Vore, a man living in her house to whom she left her estate. He was accused by neighbors of having poisoned her. The quotation is from *Romeo and Juliet*, V, i, 37.

To T. W. Higginson   *spring 1886*

"Mars the sacred Loneliness"! What an Elegy! "From Mount Zion below to Mount Zion above"! said President Humphrey of her Father – Gabriel's Oration would adorn his Child –

When she came the last time she had in her Hand as I entered, the "Choir invisible."

"Superb," she said as she shut the Book, stooping to receive me, but fervor suffocates me. Thank you for "the Sonnet" – I have lain it at her loved feet.

> Not knowing when Herself may come
> I open every Door,
> Or has she Feathers, like a Bird,
> Or Billows, like a Shore –

I think she would rather have stayed with us, but perhaps she will learn the Customs of Heaven, as the Prisoner of Chillon of Captivity.

You asked had I read "the Notices."

I have been very ill, Dear friend, since November, bereft of Book and Thought, by the Doctor's reproof, but begin to roam in my Room now –

I think of you with absent Affection, and the Wife and Child I never have seen, Legend and Love in one –

Audacity of Bliss, said Jacob to the Angel "I will not let thee go except I bless thee" – Pugilist and Poet, Jacob was correct –

Your Scholar –

MANUSCRIPT: BPL (Higg 101). Pencil.
PUBLICATION: L (1931) 320–321.

Sometime during the winter Higginson had written, inquiring whether ED had read the notices about the death of Helen Jackson. ED replied as soon as she felt able to do so. The opening of the letter attempts to quote from Higginson's "Decoration" (1874): "And no stone, with feign'd distress,/Mocks the sacred loneliness." Helen Jackson's father, Professor Nathan Fiske, had died while on a trip to the Holy Land. On 30 March 1848, the Reverend Heman Humphrey published *A Tribute to the Memory of Rev. Nathan W. Fiske . . .* : "In Jerusalem he died; on Mount Zion, and near the tomb of David was he buried . . . Who at death would not love to go up from Jerusalem below, to Jerusalem above . . . ?" (For an earlier reference to George Eliot's "The Choir Invisible," see letter no. 951.) Higginson's sonnet "To the Memory of H. H." was published in the May issue of the *Century Magazine*. For the final quotation, see letter no. 1035. This letter to Higginson suggests that she had received from him a transcript of his sonnet in advance of publication. The scripture allusion at the end of the first paragraph is to Luke 1.28.

1043

To T. W. Higginson   *late April 1886*

Dear friend.

The beautiful Sonnet confirms me – Thank you for confiding it –
    The immortality she gave
    We borrowed at her Grave –
    For just one Plaudit famishing,
    The Might of Human Love –
The sweet Acclamation of Death divulges it – There is no Trumpet like the Tomb –
    Of Glory not a Beam is left
    But her Eternal House –
    The Asterisk is for the Dead,
    The Living, for the Stars –
Did you not give her to me?

Your Scholar.

MANUSCRIPT: BPL (Higg 102). Pencil.
PUBLICATION: L (1931) 321.
Since ED had already thanked Higginson, in the preceding letter, for the sonnet, she here probably means that she has now seen it in the *Century* and thanks him for having written it. The last sentence means that Mrs. Jackson and she had been brought together by him. Another variant of the beginning of this letter (AC – pencil) was left among ED's papers. Though it is a fair copy, it probably was an earlier draft, discarded. It was published in L (1894) 402, and L (1931) 391, as a letter to a recipient unknown:

Dear friend –

No "Sonnet" had George Eliot. The sweet Acclamation of Death is forever bounded.

There is no Trumpet like the Tomb.
The Immortality she gave,
We borrowed at her Grave –
For just one Plaudit famishing,
The might of Human Love –
Beautiful as it is it's criminal shortness maims it.

1044

To Mrs. John Jameson   *24 April 1886*

How dare a Tear intrude on so sweet a Cheek?
Gentlest of Neighbors, recall the "Sparrows" and the great Logician –

Tenderly,
E. Dickinson –

MANUSCRIPT: Walcott. Pencil.
PUBLICATION: *L* (1894) 402; *L* (1931) 390.
This note, together with a basket of geraniums, was delivered by Lavinia
on the evening of 24 April (Jameson papers, Library of Congress). A short
time before, Mrs. Jameson had brought over to the Dickinson house a new
photograph of herself. ED alludes to the photograph, for she had never met
Mrs. Jameson. The scripture allusion is to Matthew 10.29.

1045

To T. W. Higginson   *early May 1886*

Deity – does He live now?
My friend – does he breathe?

MANUSCRIPT: BPL (Higg 48). Pencil. The handwriting shows an extreme slant and wide spacing of letters.
PUBLICATION: *L* (1931) 321.
On 30 April the Boston correspondent for the *Springfield Republican*
reported that Higginson was to have read at a Browning Society meeting,
but was prevented by illness from doing so. The report evidently elicited
this message.

To Louise and Frances Norcross   *May 1886*

Little Cousins,
Called back.
Emily.

MANUSCRIPT: destroyed.
PUBLICATION: *L* (1894) 438; *LL* 381; *L* (1931) 430.

It was in a letter written to the Norcrosses in January 1885 (no. 962) that ED spoke of having read Hugh Conway's *Called Back*. During the second week in May she probably came to know that she had but a short time to live. This letter was evidently her last. On the thirteenth she went into a coma. Vinnie sent for Austin and for Dr. Bigelow, who remained with her much of the day. She never regained consciousness, and died about six in the evening, Saturday, 15 May 1886.

ADDITIONAL LETTERS

The letters which follow are placed here because they became known to the editor shortly before publication of this text.

1047

To Lucretia Bullard   *Cambridge, about 1864*

> The lovely flowers embarrass me,
>   They make me regret I am not a Bee –
> Was it my blame or Nature's?
> Thank you, dear Aunt, for the thoughtfulness, I shall slowly forget –
> The beautiful Plant would entice me, did I obey myself, but the Doctor is rigid.
> Will you believe me grateful, who have no Argument?
>
> > Truly,
> >
> > > Emily.

MANUSCRIPT: Currier. Pencil. Unpublished, except the first two lines, which appear in the *Boston Cooking-School Magazine* XI (June–July) No. 1, 1906.

This, and the two notes which follow, ED wrote probably in 1864, when she was in Cambridge undergoing treatment for her eyes. The first two acknowledge thoughtful attentions from her Aunt Lucretia. The above was written after receiving flowers, said to be wistaria; it was therefore presumably written in May. Evidently an invitation to call was declined. Mrs. Asa Bullard was Edward Dickinson's eldest sister, and the Bullards resided in Cambridge, at 24 Center Street.

To Lucretia Bullard   *Cambridge, about 1864*

Dear Aunt,

> The Robin for the Crumb
> Returns no syllable,
> But long records the Lady's name
> In Silver Chronicle.

Affy,

Emily.

MANUSCRIPT: Currier. Pencil.
PUBLICATION: *Boston Cooking-School Magazine* XI (June–July) No.
1, 1906; *Mount Holyoke News*, 9 November 1929; *Boston Transcript*,
9 November 1929.

ED entered this quatrain in one of her packets (see *Poems 1955*, no.
864, where it is dated 1864). This and the packet copy are identical, except
that no punctuation concludes line 2 in the packet copy. The poem was
probably created for this occasion.

To Lucretia Bullard   *Cambridge, about 1864*

The Aunt that has shared her Blossoms with me, must have a cluster of mine. The Golden Sweets are from Grandfather's Tree –

Aff,

Emily.

MANUSCRIPT: Currier. Pencil. Unpublished.
The note, evidently written in the late summer or autumn, seems to
have accompanied apples which ED had received from home.

PROSE FRAGMENTS

PROSE FRAGMENTS

All items that follow are fragmentary in the sense that they are either (1) rough drafts of letters or parts of letters or phrases that were considered for poems or letters, or (2) aphorisms which briefly reflect on aspects of living. In instances where the draft of a letter appears to be complete, where the recipient is known and the letter can be dated, it has been incorporated in the main text (see letter no. 353). So likewise have been placed completed fair copies sent to or intended for unidentified recipients (see letters no. 965 and 995). Several of the fragment scraps are drafts of parts of letters which were in fact sent to identifiable correspondents. Such scraps are placed in the notes to the letters.

Where ED has jotted unrelated thoughts on a single sheet and separated them by a line, they are here likewise separated. Parentheses are used to indicate her alternative suggestions; brackets, to indicate words which she crossed out.

The items are arranged alphabetically in three groups. The first group (PF 1–18) consists of notes or excerpts of notes allegedly sent to Susan Dickinson. No autograph copy of any item in this group is known to survive. The first four are from transcripts (HCL – unpublished) made by Susan Dickinson. None can be dated.

I

To Susan Gilbert Dickinson

PF 1

As one noble Act makes a whole neighborhood tender with the new or forgotten Grace possible to each –

PF 2

No dreaming can compare with reality, for Reality itself is a dream from which but a portion of Mankind have yet waked and part of us is a not familiar Peninsula –

PF 3

That was a beautiful passage – "the Empire on which the Sun never sets" – but it was misapplied – it's meaning is Immortality –

PF 4

The import of that Paragraph "The Word made Flesh"
Had he the faintest intimation Who broached it Yesterday!
"Made Flesh and dwelt among us."

Since no autograph or transcript survives for the remaining fourteen notes to Susan Dickinson, all are here reproduced from *The Life and Letters of Emily Dickinson*. Several are quite evidently excerpts from the letters here identified, or expressions similar to those used in writing to others.

PF 5

Could pathos compete with that simple statement, – "Not that we first loved Him, but that He first loved us"? [*LL* 95. See letter no. 393.]

PF 6

Dear Sue – I should think she would rather be the Bride of the Lamb than that old pill box! Emily. [*LL* 61. The conclusion of this note does not ring true; it sounds as if it had been editorially constructed.]

PF 7

Dreamed of your meeting Tennyson at Ticknor and Fields last night. Where the treasure is the heart is also. [*LL* 82. See letter no. 320.]

PF 8

Gethsemane and Cana are a travelled route – [*LL* 93. See letter no. 598.]

PF 9

"I have finished the faith," he said; we rejoice he did not say *discarded* it. [*LL* 92. See letter no. 727.]

PF 10

It must have been as if he had come from where dreams are born!
[*LL* 82. This is said to have been written after Emerson's visit to Amherst in 1857. On the occasion of his lecture, 16 December 1857, Emerson was a guest in the home of Austin Dickinson.]

PF 11

No message is the utmost message, for what we tell is done.
[*LL* 62]

PF 12

So loved her that he died for her, says the explaining Jesus. [*LL* 93. See letter no. 892.]

PF 13

Tasting the honey and the sting should have ceased with Eden. Pang is the past of peace. [*LL* 62. See letter no. 911.]

PF 14

The beginning of always is more dreadful than the close – for that is sustained by flickering identity. [*LL* 84. See letter no. 534.]

PF 15

The simplest solace with a loved aim has a heavenly quality. [*LL* 95. See letter no. 783.]

PF 16

To die before one fears to die may be a boon. [*LL* 98. See letter no. 596.]

PF 17

To do a magnanimous thing and take oneself by surprise, if one is not in the habit of it, is precisely the finest of joys. Not to do a magnanimous thing, notwithstanding it never be known, notwithstanding it cost us existence, is rapture herself spurned. [*LL* 93]

PF 18

Vinnie is picking a few seeds, for if a pod die, shall it not live again? [*LL* 92. See letter no. 727.]

II

To Unidentified Recipients

Autographs of all this group survive (AC). They were among ED's papers at the time of her death, and came into Mrs. Todd's possession shortly thereafter. All are penciled drafts of letters or parts of letters presumably intended for persons at present not identifiable. Some (for example, nos. 36 and 53) are included in this rather than the third group because they are jotted on the same scrap as items known to be parts of letters. In such instances the distinction is so narrow that any decision about grouping is purely arbitrary.

It is impossible to assign a given year to ED's unformed, worksheet jottings, but the character of the handwriting clearly places all the items in this group in the final decade. Except for PF 29 and PF 45, all are published either in *New England Quarterly* XXVIII (1955) or in *Emily Dickinson: A Revelation*. It is possible that the fragments from *Revelation* were drafts of letters intended for Judge Lord. Following each item are specified the publication and the page number.

PF 19

[A group of students passed the House – one of them said Oh no, like you – the same vagabond Sweetness. I followed the voice –] You know I have a vice for voices – That way lies – (pleading lies) yearning – pathos – [*Rev* 91]

PF 20

Acquainted with Grief through Father's dying it grieves me (us) that neighbors so thoughtful of us must make it's acquaintance – To be willing the Kingdom of Heaven should invade our own requires years of sorrow –

I hope you are resting from the shock and that every Balm which is possible you may have received – [*NEQ* 306. See letter no. 932.]

PF 21

As there are Apartments in our own Minds that – (which) we never enter without Apology – we should respect the seals of others. [Written on a fragment of envelope addressed by ED: Otis P. Lord/ Salem/Mass. It has been published in *L* (1931) xxiv; and *Rev* 20.]

PF 22

But are not all Facts Dreams as soon as we put them behind us?
[*Rev* 91]

PF 23

But ought not the Amanuensis [also] to receive a Commission
also – [*NEQ* 306]

PF 24

But that defeated accent is louder now than him
Eternity may imitate
The Affluence (Ecstasy) of time
But that arrested (suspended) syllable
Is wealthier than him
But Loves dispelled Emolument
Finds (Has) no Abode in him –
Has no retrieve in him
[*NEQ* 295. The lines are jotted down on the verso of PF 41.]

PF 25

Dear Friend,
    Accept this spotless Supper though Midsummer [*NEQ* 306.
See letter no. 928.]

PF 26

Dear friend.
    "*May*" I, or is it still April,
    Reprieve the Mistake [*NEQ* 310]

PF 27

[Dear friends,
    I bring you the first Arbutus, and will add the Robins as fast
as they come –
                Emily] [*NEQ* 307]

PF 28

Dear friends
    I cannot tint in Carbon nor embroider Brass, but send you a home-

spun rustic picture I certainly saw in (at) the [hight of the storm]
terrific storm (awful storm). Please excuse my needlework –

_____

If you have any doubt as to its Authenticity, I sent Oats to the same
Guests by the man at the Barn and received their Acknowledgements –

[This discarded sheet bears in ink in ED's hand the name: Thomas
Niles. The line represents space intended for a poem, perhaps "It
sifts from Leaden Sieves," a copy of which she sent Niles in March
1883. On the verso is the draft of letter no. 809.]

PF 29

Dear Marcia –
I waited to try the Cake, but [unpublished]

PF 30

Did you ever read one of her Poems backward, because the plunge
from the front overturned you? I sometimes (often have, many times)
have – A something overtakes the Mind – [*NEQ* 307. See PF 119.]

PF 31

[Dont you think you could understand if you perhaps tried
The Rafters of the Apocalypse must not be too bare
Of the sweet Adjacency that Exalts by humbling I never knew
When Questions are not needed for answers] [*NEQ* 307]

PF 32

Emerging from an Abyss and entering it again – that is Life, is it
not? [*Rev* 94. See letter no. 1024.]

PF 33

Gilbert's I wont – I wont surpasses Citizen's I wills and when 'tis
interspersed with [little] pretty Execrations tis lovely as a stubborn
Bird – [*NEQ* 300]

PF 34

God cannot discontinue [annul] himself.
This appalling trust is at times all that remains – [*Rev* 95. See also
letter no. 553.]

her eyes were (are) very shrill –

I remember nothing so dear as to see you – [*NEQ* 298. See also letter no. 519.]

PF 36

How invaluable to be ignorant, for by that means one has all in reserve and it is such an Economical Ecstasy [*NEQ* 312. See PF 85.]

PF 37

I hope you have the power of hope – [*NEQ* 309. On verso is PF 67. This fragment is part of the last sentence in letter no. 537.]

PF 38

I send you natures Mittens – they need a little mending

I could not match the Color here but you have wiser shelves – [*NEQ* 309]

PF 39

I send you the last of the Sapphire Flowers so linked with you it's little flight (lapse) feels (seems) like her wan loveliness – A (her) Sabbath on your Breast will cost her no compunction but she will lie as quiet there as on her stem at Home, mysterious human heart – whose accident (one mistake) in Eden has cost it all it's Calm to come (mortal calm, earthly calm) (and therefore all it's calm) [*NEQ* 309]

PF 40

[It is joy to be with (near) you because I love you – if nature makes a distinction as late as tonight I do not know – The happy troupe toward you like a sigh I have] [*NEQ* 304. On verso of PF 46.]

PF 41

[Possibly I did Be sure to bring your text Book – (bring your text book – bring down) though that I add to all other myriad themes (subjects) (to the agile topics) on which to consult you (on which to consult you) for Light would certainly find it (perchance I did –)] [*NEQ* 295. On the back is PF 24. On the same sheet ED wrote:

      Love first and last of all things made
      Of which this (our) living world is but the shade

The lines recall the Prelude to Swinburne's "Tristram of Lyonesse," which open: "Love, that is first and last of all things made,/The light that has the living world for shade."]

PF 42

remained what the Carpenter called the Door he was asked to correct. "Plumb." I asked him what made the Door erroneous, and he said "it was not Plumb" – some rigor of rectitude, I inferred, in which the Door was wanting. [*NEQ* 304]

PF 43

Sunday –

Second of March and the Crow and Snow high as the Spire, and scarlet expectations of things that never come, because forever here.

"The Twilight says to the Turret if you want an Existence. . ." [*Rev* 91–94. The handwriting of this fair copy draft, together with the date, suggest that it was written on 2 March 1884. Mrs. Bingham includes it among those intended as letters to Judge Lord, who died on 13 March 1884. Around the margin in rough draft ED has written: "Of injury too innocent to know it when it passed." She used the verso for worksheet drafts of the poems "Circumference thou Bride of Awe," and "Arrows enamored of his Heart."]

PF 44

Spirit cannot be moved by Flesh – It must be moved by spirit –

It is strange that the most intangible is the heaviest – but Joy and Gravitation have their own ways. My ways are not your ways – [*Rev* 89]

PF 45

Thank my Cousin – [unpublished. Verso of PF 88.]

PF 46

Thank you for knowing I did not spurn it because it was true – I did not – I denied (refused) what Mr Erskine said not from detected feeling but of myself it was not true – I supposed not [care not] of other [*NEQ* 304. On the verso is PF 40.]

PF 47

[Thank you for the Delight.
The Book is fair and lonely, like a Memoir of Evening.

> Of his peculiar light
> We keep one ray –
> To clarify the sight
> To seek him by.

Gratefully,
Emily –]

[*NEQ* 311. ED used the other side for drafts of the poems "A Field of Stubble – lying sere" and "How much the present moment means." See poem no. 1362.]

PF 48

[Throngs who would not prize them, know those holy circumstances which your dear Eyes have sought for mine. I hope it may sometime be that you will chance] [*NEQ* 303. Verso of PF 53.]

PF 49

Tis a dangerous moment for any one when the meaning goes out of things and Life stands straight – and punctual – and yet no content(s) (signal) come(s). Yet such moments are. If we survive them they expand us, if we do not, but that is Death, whose if is everlasting. When I was a little girl I called the Cemetery Tarrytown but now I call it Trans – a wherefore but no more and the if of Deity – (Avalanche or Avenue –) every Heart asks which [*Rev* 95, in part; *NEQ* 301, entire. It is written on the verso of letter no. 938. The final ten words are probably suggested changes for the section following the word "Death." The sentence which comments on the cemetery is in letter no. 892.]

PF 50

We do not think enough of the Dead as exhilirants – they are not dissuaders but Lures – Keepers of that great Romance still to us foreclosed – while coveting (we envy) their wisdom we lament their silence. Grace is still a secret. That they have existed none can take away. That they still exist is a trust so daring we thank thee that thou hast hid these things from us and hast revealed them to them. The power and the glory are the post mortuary gifts. [*Rev* 95]

PF 51

We said she said Lord Jesus – receive my Spirit – We were put in separate rooms to expiate our temerity and thought how hateful Jesus must be to get us into trouble when we had done nothing but Crucify him and that before we were born – [*NEQ* 312]

PF 52

Were Departure Separation, there would be neither Nature nor Art, for there would be no World – Emily [*Rev* 94]

PF 53

When it becomes necessary for us to stake our all upon the belief of another in as for instance Eternity, we find it [is] (discover that it is) impossible to make the transfer – Belief is unconsciously to most of us Ourselves – an Untried Experience [*NEQ* 303–304. PF 48 is on verso.]

PF 54

Why offer Hue – to you – Damsel of Artery? [*NEQ* 312]

PF 55

With love, for Supper – if deferred it will fade like Ice Cream. [*NEQ* 312. On verso is a draft of the poem "Mine Enemy is growing old."]

PF 56

With thanks for my health I send you Antony's Orchard, who paid his Heart for what his eyes ate, only – [*NEQ* 310. See letter no. 854. See PF 104.]

PF 57

With the trust that the little Citizen is already a patriot I send him the national Colors, or such of them as I can find, for hues just now are few – so minute a Veteran will possibly excuse then – [*NEQ* 312. It is on the verso of PF 36.]

III

Aphorisms

Autographs of all this group survive (AC), and have the same provenance as the items in group II. With the exception of PF 124, all are in pencil, and were written in the last decade of ED's life. Fragment 84 is unpublished. The rest are individually identified.

PF 58

. . . a climate of Escape is natural to Fondness . . . [*NEQ* 315. On verso of PF 83.]

PF 59

A cold yet parched alarm that chills and sears [sickens and stings] in one [*NEQ* 315]

PF 60

A little late for spring but early yet for summer – Indian – [*NEQ* 316]

PF 61

A Message from the Meadows – [*NEQ* 306]

PF 62

A prey to Expectation [*NEQ* 312. See PF 85.]

PF 63

a similar mirage of thought [*NEQ* 314. Beneath the phrase, but not connected with what precedes or follows, are the words:
Bottle
Slip –
On the same sheet is PF 95.]

PF 64

A sufficing enchanting wardrobe – [*NEQ* 317. On verso of PF 73.]

PF 65

A woe of Ecstasy [*NEQ* 318. See poem no. 1622.]

As it takes but a moment of imagination to place us anywhere, it would not seem worth while to stay where it was stale –

Sere must be the inertia that could resist this [sunny] Journey – To many (numbers) it is their only Trip, nor would they (one) exchange it –

Other Sails must slack – other steeds (retire) *expire* – but this is it's own divine Relay –

We thank thee Oh Father for this gay (strange) guide (gait) (pace) to Days unbound, and whose Search but surpasses the occupying (– ascertaining – certifying – ratifying –) estimation

Let me not thirst with this Hock at my Lip, nor beg, with Domains in my Pocket – Has any not where to lay his (Heart) *Head*, here is he befriends (provides) him.

A Stranger and ye took me in –

We have (There are) (Men have) two Saviors – an Earthly and a Heavenly – This one is the Heavenly, for the other [one] says of himself he was seen of the Twelve, and (but) this one had no Hours of Flesh. It is his things that the Angels desire to look into and are not permitted – [*NEQ* 294. See poem no. 1772.]

close – Anguish has but (just) so many throes – then Unconsciousness claims it (seals it) [*NEQ* 309. Verso of PF 37.]

Common Sense is almost as omniscient as God [*Rev* 45. It is a fair copy clipped from what may have been a finished letter.]

Consummation is the hurry of fools (exhiliration of fools), but Expectation the Elixir of the Gods – [*NEQ* 312. See PF 85.]

Death being the first form of Life which we have had the power to Contemplate, our entrance here being [before our own comprehension] (preliminary to our own) an Exclusion from comprehension, it is [strange] amazing that the fascination of our predicament does not entice us more. With such sentences as these directly over our Heads we are as exempt from Exultation as the Stones – [*NEQ* 306–307. This thought is expressed in a poem written in 1879: "We knew not that we were to live."]

PF 71

Did we not find (gain) as we lost we should make but a threadbare exhibition after a few years [*NEQ* 313. On verso of PF 117.]

PF 72

Dim is the Heavenly prospective that enlivens some which weary – [*NEQ* 295. See PF 111.]

PF 73

Eve gave (left) her pretty Gowns to the Trees – but they dont (wont) always wear them [*NEQ* 317. On verso is PF 64.]

PF 74

Flowers are so enticing I fear that they are sins – like gambling or apostasy. [*Home* 43]

PF 75

Fly – fly – but as you fly – Remember – the second pass you by – The Second is pursuing the Century – The Century is chasing Eternity – (Ah the) *What a* Responsibility – [Such a – What a – Responsibility] No wonder that the little second flee – Out of it's frightened way – [*NEQ* 313. This raw material for a poem is on the same sheet as PF 99.]

PF 76

Grasped by God – [*NEQ* 318. See poem no. 1718.]

PF 77

Has Human Nature gone –
Unknowing to his dread abode – [*NEQ* 318.
See poem no. 1733. On verso is PF 101.]

[923]

PF 78

Honey grows everywhere but iron (valor) on a Seldom Bush –
[*NEQ* 316]

PF 79

I do not care – why should I care and yet I fear I'm caring
To rock a fretting (crying) (wailing) Truth to sleep –
Is short (no) (frail) (poor) security.
The terror it will wake persistent as perdition
Is harder than to face the frank adversity –
There is an awful yes in every constitution [*NEQ* 314. It is on the
verso of poem no. 1504.]

PF 80

I dont keep the Moth part of the House – I keep the Butterfly part
– [*NEQ* 295; *Rev* 6. See PF 111.]

PF 81

I held it so tight that I lost it said the Child of the Butterfly
Of many a vaster Capture that is the Elegy – [*NEQ* 316]

PF 82

I saw two Bushes fight just now – The wind was to blame – but
to see them differ was pretty as a Lawsuit
    nature is so sudden she makes us all antique – [*NEQ* 318]

PF 83

I should think a faded spirit must be the most dreadful treasure
that one could possess, as a spirit always in bud must be the sweetest –
[*NEQ* 315. On verso is PF 58.]

PF 84

Incredible the Lodging
But limited the Guest [unpublished]

PF 85

Is not the Election of a Daphne much more signal than that of a
President – for Beauty needs no Magistrate and Ecstasy is it's only mob

(is a hushed mob) – [*NEQ* 312. On the same sheet are PF 36, 62, and 69. On the verso is PF 57.]

PF 86

It has a Roof at the Bottom but not any Roof at the top – like a Bird's nest [*NEQ* 316]

PF 87

It is essential to the sanity of mankind that each one should think the other crazy – a condition [which] with which the Cynicism [of Human nature] so cordially (readily) complies, one could wish it were [upon] a [subject] [theme] concurrence more noble [*NEQ* 314]

PF 88

lonesome as entertainments (occupations) of ended minds – [*NEQ* 315. PF 45 is on the verso.]

PF 89

Mansions of Mirage – [*NEQ* 295. See PF 111.]

PF 90

[most enchanting fortune bestowed upon us by a delightful God for he knew what was in men – I remember last May with distinctness and sorrow Today has gratitude of . . .] [*NEQ* 314. On verso of PF 114.]

PF 91

Nature, that Sweet Parishioner, trust *her* – [*NEQ* 310. It is on the verso of poem no. 1443.]

PF 92

necessitates celerity/were better/nay were immemorial/may/to duller/by duller/things [*NEQ* 292n]

PF 93

Not to send errands by John Alden is one of the instructions of History – [*NEQ* 318]

PF 94

Nothing is so old as a dilapidated charm – [*NEQ* 315]

PF 95

Nothing is so resonant with mystery as the [friend] one that forgets us – and the boundlessness (wonder) of her – [him so far transcends Heaven and Hell that it makes them tepid] so dwarfs Heaven and Hell that we think – (recall) of them if at all, as tepid and ignoble trifles (or if we recall them it is as tepid) (or we recall) (and trifles ignoble) (It's intricacy is so boundless that it dispels Heaven and Hell) [*NEQ* 314. On the same sheet as PF 63.]

PF 96

Of our deepest delights there is a solemn shyness [*NEQ* 316. It is on the same sheet as PF 106.]

PF 97

One note from one Bird/Is better than a million words/A scabbard holds (has – needs) but one sword [*NEQ* 316]

PF 98

Or Fame erect her siteless Citadel – [*BM* 319. See poem no. 1183.]

PF 99

Paradise in no Journey because it (he) is within – but for that very cause though – it is the most Arduous of Journeys – because as the Servant Conscientiously says at the Door We are (always – invariably –) out – [*NEQ* 313. On the same sheet is PF 75.]

PF 100

Pompeii – All it's (the) occupations crystallized – Everybody gone away [*NEQ* 318]

PF 101

Revised to Retrospect – [*NEQ* 318. See poem no. 1353. On verso of PF 77.]

PF 102

Science is very near us – I found a megatherium on my strawberry – [NEQ 317. A megatherium is a huge extinct sloth.]

PF 103

Sir Christopher Wren is here prospecting for his nest – I suppose it will have a Dome and Aisles – [NEQ 316]

PF 104

Solomon says that no matter how often we dine we are just as hungry because the meat was killed always – served – but Solomon is a Gourmand and not to be believed – [NEQ 310. On this scrap is poem no. 1768, and the first two lines of poem no. 1594; also PF 56 and 118.]

PF 105

Stolidity is more dreadful (terrible) than sorrow, for it is the stubble of the soil where sorrow grew [NEQ 315]

PF 106

The appetite for silence is seldom an acquired taste [Rev 6; NEQ 316. It is on the same sheet as PF 96.]

PF 107

The Blood is more showy (gaudy) than the Breath.
But cannot dance as well – [BM 319]

PF 108

The consciousness of subsiding power is too startling to be admitted by men – but [best] comprehended by the meadow over which the Flood has quivered (comprehended perhaps by the Meadow, over which Floods have [quivered] – rumbled –), when the waters return to their kindred, and the tillage (acre –) is left alone – [NEQ 314–315]

PF 109

The Fatherless Serpent – [NEQ 318]

[927]

The Grass is the Ground's Hair, and it is singed with heat – Mrs Gamp would say (and it curls like a Girl's, in the damp wind –) [*NEQ* 295. See PF 111.]

The Leaves are very gay – but we know they are elderly – 'Tis pathos to dissimulate, in their departing case – [*NEQ* 295. On the same sheet are PF 72, 80, 89, and 110.]

[The mower is tuning his scythe] [*NEQ* 317. It is jotted on the same slip as poem no. 1625.]

There are those who are shallow intentionally and only profound by accident [*NEQ* 315. On verso is PF 122.]

to know whether we are in Heaven or on Earth is one of the most impossible of the minds decisions, [and] but I think the balance always leans in favor of the negative – if Heaven is negative [*NEQ* 313–314. On the verso is PF 90.]

Train up a Heart in the way it should go and as quick as it can twill depart from it [*Rev* 58]

"Tumultuous privacy of storm" [*NEQ* 317. This phrase from Emerson's poem "The Snow Storm" ED liked so well, as Mrs. Bingham points out, that she copied it onto a sheet of stationery, put it in quotes, and enclosed it in a letter which Lavinia wrote to Mrs. Todd, 5 February 1884.

Two things I have lost with Childhood – the rapture of losing my shoe in the Mud and going Home barefoot, wading for Cardinal flowers and the mothers reproof which was [for] more for my sake than her weary own for she frowned with a smile [now Mother and Cardinal flower are parts of a closed world –] But is that all I have lost – memory drapes her Lips [*NEQ* 313. PF 71 is on the verso.]

PF 118

Undertow of the Organ [*NEQ* 310. See PF 104.]

PF 119

We must travel abreast with Nature if we want to know her, but where shall be obtained the Horse –
A something overtakes the mind – we do not hear it coming [*NEQ* 316]

PF 120

What Lethargies of Loneliness [*NEQ* 310]

PF 121

when most beloved sagacious go (prudential go) [*NEQ* 316. This is verso of PF 123.]

PF 122

[Which has the wisest men undone – (Doubt has the wisest)] [*NEQ* 315. This is verso of PF 113.]

PF 123

Whoever heard of the Blest June delaying or of a tedious visit from the Snow – (Or a protracted session with the Snow –) [*NEQ* 316. PF 121 is on the verso.]

PF 124

With the sincere spite of a *Woman*. [*NEQ* 293n. It is written on a scrap of stationery and is unique among the fragments in that it is in ink and in the handwriting of about 1850.]

APPENDIXES

APPENDIX 1

Persons mentioned casually, who were never significant to ED herself, are briefly identified in the notes to the letters. The names of recipients are starred (*). Localities referred to in the sketches are in Massachusetts unless specified as being elsewhere. For identification of domestic help at the Dickinson house, see Appendix 2.

ADAMS, Elizabeth C. (1810–1873), "our dear teacher," taught at Amherst Academy in the early 1840's. After an absence, she returned in 1846, for another term as preceptress, until her marriage to Albert Clark of Conway, 7 April 1847.

ADAMS, John Sydney, a school friend of ED and of Jane Humphrey, was later proprietor of the local bookstore and drugstore.

*ANTHON, Catherine (Scott) Turner (1831–1917) was the daughter of Henry Scott of Cooperstown, New York. Her acquaintance with Susan Dickinson began in 1848, when they both attended Utica Female Seminary. In 1855 Kate Scott married Campbell Ladd Turner, who died two years later. She visited Sue in 1859, at which time ED met her, and the acquaintance was continued when Kate Turner made subsequent visits to Amherst during the sixties. She married John Anthon in 1866. There is no record that her friendship with ED was pursued after that date. ED is known to have written five letters to her between 1859 and 1866, and to have sent her a few poems.

BARTLETT, Samuel Colcord (1817–1898), a graduate of Dartmouth College (1836), was ordained minister at Monson in 1843. In 1846 he married Mary Learned. Sue was especially fond of the Bartletts, and on occasion visited them after he became pastor of the Franklin Street Church in Manchester, New Hampshire (1851–1857). ED addressed letters to Sue during such visits. Bartlett removed to Chicago, Illinois, in 1857, and was elected president of Dartmouth in 1877. ED probably did not know them.

BELDEN, Pomeroy (1811–1849), a graduate of Amherst College (1833), was pastor of the Second Congregational Church ("East Parish") in Amherst from 1842 until his death.

BLISS, Daniel (1823–1916), a graduate of Amherst College (1852), was ordained in the College Church, Amherst, 17 October 1855, upon graduation from Andover Theological Seminary. In the month following, on 23 November, he married Abby Maria Wood (*q.v.*), one of ED's close childhood friends. He was a leading figure in the founding and development of American Foreign Missions.

*BOLTWOOD, Lucius (1792–1872), a graduate of Williams College (1814), studied law with Samuel Fowler Dickinson and became his law partner in 1817. He married Fanny H. Shepard (1824), a first cousin of R. W. Emerson. From 1828 to 1864 he was Secretary of the Board of Trustees of Amherst College. The Boltwood sons, George and Henry, graduated from Amherst Academy in ED's class of 1847. Though the family was of importance, and the community and college ties of the Boltwoods and Dickinsons were close, one gathers that there was no personal tie between ED and any member of the Boltwood family.

*BOWDOIN, Elbridge Gridley (1820–1893), after graduation from Amherst College (1840), was admitted to the bar in 1847, and practiced law for eight years with ED's father (1847–1855). He then removed to Rockford, Iowa, and set himself up in business. He never married. During the years 1849–1852 ED is known to have sent him two brief notes and a valentine in verse.

*BOWLES, Samuel (1826–1878), was the son of the founder of the *Springfield Daily Republican*, and succeeded his father as editor in 1851. During his lifetime this family paper became one of the most influential in the country, and an organ of liberal Republicanism. A man of wide interests and exhaustless energy, Bowles traveled extensively. His letters were published in the *Republican*, and many of his observations were later collected in books. Greatly admired by all the Dickinsons, with whom he and his family were on intimate terms, he was especially esteemed by Emily. Throughout her lifetime, after 1858, she was steadily in correspondence with him and his wife Mary. She often sent them copies of her poems, and there still survive some fifty letters which she wrote them.

*BOWLES, Samuel the younger (b. 1851), succeeded his father as editor of the *Republican*. After his father's death, ED kept the family tie by communicating with him on special occasions. In May 1884 ED sent regrets to an invitation to his wedding; his marriage to Elizabeth Hoar took place on 12 June.

BREWSTER, Dr. John Milton, Jr., a graduate of Williams College (1839), practiced medicine at Amherst 1843–1853. His wife died 24 December 1851.

*BULLARD, Asa (1804–1888), a graduate of Amherst College (1828), was ordained in 1832, and in the same year, on 16 May, married ED's aunt Lucretia Gunn Dickinson (1806–1885), her father's eldest sister. They lived at 24 Center Street, Cambridge. For forty years (1834–1874) he was general agent for the Congregational Sunday School and Publishing Society. He was author and editor of various religious publications, such as *Sabbath School Chestnuts*.

BURGESS, Ebenezer G. (1826–1877), a graduate of Amherst College in 1852, became a well known physician. He resided at Springfield, 1853–1855.

CARLETON, Anna Newman. *See* Anna Dodge Newman.

*CARMICHAEL, Mrs. Elizabeth, was the mother of the first Mrs. Richard H. Mather (*q.v.*), with whom she made her home until her daughter's death and Professor Mather's remarriage (31 March 1881).

CHAPIN, Lucius D. (1821–1892), a graduate of Amherst College (1851), was ordained for the ministry but later went into business. He lived in the Middle West.

*CHICKERING, Joseph Knowlton (1846–1899), was a graduate of Amherst College (1869), where he taught English from 1873 until 1885, in which latter year he accepted a call to the University of Vermont. At the time of the death of ED's mother (14 November 1882) he was especially thoughtful of the bereaved sisters.

CLARK, Mrs. Albert. *See* Elizabeth C. Adams.

*CLARK, Charles H., was the younger brother of James D. Clark (*q.v.*). He did not, like his brother, attend college. At his death he was the second oldest member of the New York Stock Exchange. ED's correspondence with Charles Clark she initiated during James Clark's fatal illness. All the correspondence with the brothers (a total of some twenty letters) focused upon the memory of Charles Wadsworth.

*CLARK, James D. (1828–1883) was the eldest son of Charles and Temperance Clark of Northampton. After graduation from Williams College (1848), he practiced law, taught school, engaged in business, and retired from active affairs in 1875. ED was introduced to him by her father sometime during the decade of the sixties. He was a lifelong friend of Charles Wadsworth (*q.v.*), and he initiated correspondence with ED after Wadsworth's death.

CLARK, William Smith (1826–1886), a graduate of Amherst College (1848), was a professor of chemistry, botany, and zoology at Amherst, 1852–1867. He served as president of Massachusetts Agricultural College from 1867 until 1878. He married the adopted daughter of Samuel Willis-ton (*q.v.*) on 25 May 1853. They had eleven children.

COLEMAN, Lyman (1796–1882), a graduate of Yale College (1817), was principal of Amherst Academy (1844–1846) during the years that ED and her sister attended it. He taught at the Presbyterian Academy in Phila-delphia from 1849 to 1858, and at Lafayette College from 1861 until his death. He married Maria Flynt (1801–1871) of Monson, a first cousin of ED's mother. Their children Olivia (1827–1847) and Eliza (1832–1871) were friends of the Dickinson girls. Eliza married John Dudley (*q.v.*).

COLTON, Aaron Merrick (1809–1895), a graduate of Yale College (1835), was pastor of the First Church in Amherst from 10 June 1840 until 4 January 1853, when he went to Easthampton.

*COLTON, Sara Philips, of Brooklyn, N. Y., was a lifelong friend of Martha Dickinson Bianchi. In 1911 she married Arthur L. Gillett (AC 1880), throughout his life a professor in the Hartford Theological Sem-inary. See letter no. 1011.

CONKEY, Ithamar (1788–1862), practiced law at Amherst from 1817 until his death. He was a keen political rival of Edward Dickinson.

CONKEY, Ithamar Francis (1823–1875), son of Ithamar Conkey, suc-ceeded his father in law and likewise in politics. He married Luthera Cut-ler, 15 June 1847.

*COOPER, James S. (1802–1870), and his wife Abigail (Girdler) Cooper (1817–1895), removed from Calais, Maine, to Amherst in 1866, where he briefly established a law practice. It had been his intent to edu-cate his sons in Amherst College, and for that reason his widow main-tained her residence and both boys were graduated in the class of 1873. The elder, James I. Cooper, became a law partner of ED's brother. The younger, Dr. Charles W. Cooper, practiced medicine and was for a time the Dickinson family physician. There was a neighborly attachment and ED, until a month or so before her death, sent frequent notes to Mrs. Cooper, often accompanied with small gifts. There were three daughters. Alice married Frederick Tuckerman (*q.v.*).

*COWAN, Perez Dickinson (1843–1923), ED's favorite "Cousin Peter," was graduated from Amherst College (1866) and Union Theo-logical Seminary. Ordained in 1869, he married Margaret Elizabeth Rhea in the following year. He occupied pulpits in his native Tennessee until 1877, and later in New York and New Jersey. ED had known him as an undergraduate and regarded him with especial warmth. His mother was daughter of a brother of Samuel Fowler Dickinson.

*CROWELL, Mary (Warner) (1830–1903), was the daughter of Aaron Warner, professor of Rhetoric and Oratory, and English Literature in Amherst College (1844–1853), and a girlhood friend of ED. In 1861 she married Edward Payson Crowell (Amherst 1853), professor of Latin at Amherst from 1864 until 1908.

*CURRIER, Elizabeth Dickinson (1823–1886), ED's aunt, was the youngest sister of Edward Dickinson. At forty-three she married Augustus Nelson Currier (1820–1896), a widower, on 10 October 1866. They resided in Worcester, where Currier was engaged in the insurance business.

*CUTLER, George, was a brother of William Cutler, the husband of Harriet Cutler (q.v.). The brothers, leading merchants in Amherst, were proprietors of a general store. ED is known to have written one letter to Mrs. Cutler.

CUTLER, Harriet Gilbert (1820–1865), was an older sister of Susan Gilbert Dickinson (q.v.). She married William Cutler (1811–1870) of Amherst, 22 June 1842. He and his brother George (q.v.) were partners in merchandising business with Luke Sweetser (q.v.) until 1854, when they bought Sweetser out. Harriet Cutler died, 18 March 1865.

*DAVIS, Aurelia B. Hinsdale (Mrs. Armon W.), was a sister of Susan Dickinson's friend Harriet Hinsdale. ED is known to have written Mrs. Davis one brief note.

*DICKERMAN, George S. (1843–1937), was a graduate of Yale College (1865) and Yale Divinity School. He married Elizabeth M. Street in 1870, and succeeded the Reverend Mr. F. F. Emerson as pastor of the First Congregational Church in Amherst in June 1883, where he remained until 1891. Together with the Reverend Mr. J. L. Jenkins of Pittsfield, formerly pastor of the same church, he officiated at Emily Dickinson's funeral.

DICKINSON, Austin. *See* William Austin Dickinson.

DICKINSON, Catharine. *See* Catharine Dickinson Sweetser.

DICKINSON, Edward (1803–1874), ED's father, was the eldest child of Samuel Fowler Dickinson and Lucretia Gunn Dickinson. He prepared for college at Amherst Academy, attended Amherst College for one year — the year of its founding — then transferred to Yale College where he was graduated in 1823 at the head of his class. After reading law in his father's office, and further study in the Northampton Law School, he was admitted to the Hampshire County Bar in 1826. He was a lifelong resident of Amherst, where he engaged in the practice of law for forty-eight years. He became treasurer of Amherst College in 1835, and served in that capacity until his resignation in 1872. On 6 May 1828 he married Emily Norcross, daughter of Joel Norcross of Monson. They had three children: William Austin Dickinson, Emily Elizabeth Dickinson, and Lavinia Norcross Dickinson.

Edward Dickinson was a representative in the General Court of Massachusetts in 1838 and 1839, and a delegate to the National Whig Convention in Baltimore, 16 June 1852. He was elected as a representative to the Thirty-third Congress, 1853–1855. In 1874 he again represented his district in the General Court of Massachusetts, and died of apoplexy 16 June 1874 in Boston while attending the legislative session.

*DICKINSON, Edward ("Ned") (1861–1898), ED's nephew, was eldest of the three children of Austin and Susan Dickinson. He was prevented by illness from graduating with his Amherst College class (1884). ED was warmly attached to him. At the time of his death he was assistant librarian of the college library.

*DICKINSON, Elizabeth. See Elizabeth Dickinson Currier.

DICKINSON, Emily Norcross (1804–1882), ED's mother, was a daughter of Joel and Betsy Fay Norcross of Monson. She attended a boarding school in New Haven, Connecticut, 1822–1823, and married Edward Dickinson, 6 May 1828. Domestic by nature, she seldom left home except for brief visits to relatives in Monson or Boston. On 15 June 1875 she suffered a paralytic stroke, and until her death, 14 November 1882, the care of the helpless invalid was largely assumed by Emily.

*DICKINSON, Gilbert (1875–1883), ED's nephew, was the youngest of the three children of Austin and Susan Dickinson. Though named Thomas Gilbert, he was always called Gilbert or "Gib." His sudden and unexpected death from typhoid fever, 5 October 1883, was a blow from which neither his father nor his Aunt Emily fully recovered.

*DICKINSON, Harriet Austin, was a sister of William Cowper Dickinson (q.v.). She and her sisters Martha and Mary attended Amherst Academy, where they became friends of ED's sister Lavinia.

*DICKINSON, Lavinia Norcross (1833–1899), ED's sister, attended Amherst Academy, and Wheaton Female Seminary in Ipswich. Though she visited friends and relatives more frequently than her mother or sister, she remained for the most part at home. After their mother's paralytic stroke, the sisters assumed the burden of caring for the invalid. With the aid of a family retainer, the sisters continued to live at the homestead after their mother's death. The last twelve years of her life she lived alone. It was through her insistent endeavor that the first volume (1890) of ED's poems was published.

DICKINSON, Lucretia Gunn. *See* Asa Bullard.

*DICKINSON, Martha (1866–1943), ED's niece, was the only daughter of Austin and Susan Dickinson. In 1903 she married Alexander E. Bianchi. Her editing of ED's poems began in 1914, with publication of *The Single Hound.*

DICKINSON, Mary. *See* Mark Haskell Newman.

DICKINSON, Samuel Fowler (1775–1838), ED's grandfather, was born in Amherst. Upon graduation from Dartmouth College (1795) he studied law and practiced for many years in Amherst. In 1802 he married Lucretia Gunn (1775–1840) of Montague. Edward Dickinson was the eldest of their nine children. The Squire was instrumental in the founding of Amherst Academy (1814) and Amherst College (1821). He frequently served as representative of the General Court of Massachusetts from 1803 to 1827, and was a member of the state senate in 1828. His support of Amherst College and the cause of education generally brought him acute financial trouble. The homestead he had built in 1813 he was forced to sell twenty years later. He then moved to Cincinnati, and later to Hudson, Ohio, where he continued to further educational causes, and where he died, 22 April 1838.

*DICKINSON, Susan Gilbert (1830–1913), was the youngest daughter of Thomas and Harriet Arms Gilbert. He was a tavern proprietor severally in Amherst, Deerfield (where Susan was born), and Greenfield. Her mother died in 1837, and she was orphaned by the death of her father in 1841. Reared by an aunt in Geneva, New York, she attended Utica Female Academy. Her older sister Harriet had married William Cutler of Amherst and with them (*q.v.*) she came to live about 1850. ED thus came to know her, and during the decade no other friendship came to mean so much to ED. Susan taught school in Baltimore in 1851–1852. She became engaged to ED's brother Austin in November 1853. They were married 1 July 1856, and moved into a house which his father built for them next to the homestead. Emily and Susan thus remained permanently associated.

DICKINSON, (Thomas) Gilbert. *See* Gilbert Dickinson.

DICKINSON, William (1804–1887), ED's uncle, was the second child of S. F. Dickinson, and therefore nearest Edward Dickinson in age. Born in Amherst, he attended Amherst Academy but did not go to college. Instead, he served a ten-year apprenticeship in paper factories, then settled in 1829 in Worcester where he remained, becoming one of the most prominent and successful businessmen in the city. He married Eliza Hawley of

Andover in 1831. She died 31 July 1851, and on 23 October 1852 he married again: Mary Whittier, also of Andover. By his first marriage he was father of William Hawley Dickinson (*q.v.*); by his second, of two sons and one daughter. The brothers Edward and William, though temperamentally different, shared a mutual respect. There was no close bond between ED and her Worcester uncle.

*DICKINSON, William Austin (1829–1895), ED's brother, was in her early years especially close to her. After graduation from Amherst College (1850), he prepared for his profession in the Harvard Law School and his father's office, and was admitted to the bar in 1854. He married Susan Huntington Gilbert (Dickinson) (*q.v.*), 1 July 1856. He practiced law in Amherst throughout his life, succeeding his father as Treasurer of Amherst College in 1873. He was a prominent citizen of the town, especially active in church affairs and village improvements.

*DICKINSON, William Cowper (1827–1899), valedictorian of his Amherst College class (1848), was a tutor at Amherst (1851–1852) before his ordination in 1854. He was a brother of Harriet Austin Dickinson (*q.v.*), and son of the Reverend Baxter Dickinson (1795–1875), a clergyman who taught in several theological schools. The family was distantly related to Edward Dickinson, having a common ancestor four generations back.

*DICKINSON, William Hawley (1832–1883), ED's favorite "cousin Willie," was graduated from Brown University in 1852, and for many years practiced law in New York City. He died, 15 May 1883. No letters which ED wrote to him survive, though at the time of his death there must have been many. A letter from his widow in 1894, in response to a query from Mrs. Todd, revises her original estimate of "a hundred," but states that it was "a considerable number, all of which after my Husband's death I destroyed" (Millicent Todd Bingham, *Ancestors' Brocades*, New York, 1945, 263).

*DOLE, John (1838–1872), after graduation from Amherst College (1861) and Harvard Medical School (1864) practiced medicine in Amherst until his death. In 1867 he married Adelaide Stanton of New Orleans. Dr. Dole died on his way to Europe in 1872, and Mrs. Dole continued to live in Amherst. Mrs. Bianchi says of her (*FF* 35): ". . . Mrs. Dole, well remembered still as an accomplished pianist of wide study . . . always enjoyed playing for Aunt Emily when the coast was clear of callers and the freedom of the house their own."

DUDLEY, John L. (1812–1894), a graduate of Amherst College (1844), married 16 June 1861, one of ED's close friends, Eliza M. Coleman, daughter of Lyman Coleman (*q.v.*). They settled in Middletown, Connecticut, where Dudley had been pastor of the Congregational Church since 1849. They remained there until 1868, when Dudley accepted a call to the Plymouth Congregational Church in Milwaukee, Wisconsin, where he served until 1875. Eliza died 3 June 1871. Dudley married, second, Marion Churchill of Lake Mills, Wisconsin, 23 October 1872.

Eliza's mother, Maria (Flynt) Coleman, was a first cousin of ED's mother. Her youngest brother William Flynt married Eudocia Carter Converse, whose diaries are a repository of much family data.

*DWIGHT, Edward Strong (1820–1890), a graduate of Yale College (1838), was installed as pastor of the First Church in Amherst, 19 June 1854, where he served until 28 August 1860, the illness of his wife Lucy Waterman Dwight compelling his departure from Amherst. She died 11 September 1861. They had two children: Annie Waterman Dwight (b. 4 April 1851) and Edward Huntington Dwight (b. 13 July 1856). Dwight served as a trustee of Amherst College from 1855 until his death.

EASTMAN, Charlotte Sewall, was the wife of Benjamin C. Eastman, a Congressman from Wisconsin during the term of office of Edward Dickinson, in 1853–1855. Mrs. Eastman must have met the Dickinson girls at the time, or soon after, for the friendship with the Dickinson family was shortly well established. After the death of her husband in 1856 she lived in Boston. She visited the Dickinsons, and her name together with theirs is on the register at Mount Holyoke, 20 August 1859. A presentation copy of *Jane Eyre* survives, inscribed: "Emily with the love of Mrs. Eastman. Sept. 20th 1865." In 1872 she wrote from Venice urging the girls to join her in Europe. No letters from ED to Mrs. Eastman are known to exist.

EDWARDS, Henry Luther (1822–1903), was graduated from Amherst College in 1847. He served as tutor in the college, 1849–1852, and after theological studies was ordained in 1857.

*EMERSON, Forrest F., served briefly as pastor of the First Church at Amherst from 12 June 1879 until 21 February 1883. Some eight notes which ED wrote him and his wife are known, but they are brief and suggest that the acquaintance was slight.

EMERSON, John Milton (1826–1869) was graduated from Amherst College as valedictorian in the class of 1849, and later served as tutor (1851–1853). He studied law in the office of Edward Dickinson and practiced briefly at Amherst (1854–1856). From 1856 until his death he practiced law in New York City.

*EMERSON, (Benjamin) Kendall, born in Amherst, was graduated from Amherst College (1897), studied medicine and became an orthopedic surgeon, in active practice until 1928, and as consultant subsequently. ED knew him as a youthful friend of her nephew Gilbert Dickinson, and wrote him Christmas notes thrice annually after Gilbert's death in 1883.

*EMMONS, Henry Vaughan (1832–1912), a graduate of Amherst College (1854) and of Bangor Theological Seminary (1859), was ordained as an evangelist in 1860, and occupied pulpits in various New England churches from 1865 until 1902. His friendship with ED's cousin, John Graves (q.v.), during their undergraduate days at Amherst, brought him often to the Dickinson home, and extended to a like friendship with ED, cordial during his undergraduate years, though it lapsed after his departure from Amherst.

*ESTY, William Cole (1838–1916), a graduate of Amherst College (1860), was a professor of mathematics and astronomy there from 1865 until 1905. In 1867 he married Martha A. Cushing, a sister of Mrs. Edward Tuckerman (q.v.).

*FARLEY, Abbie C. (1846–1932), was a niece of Judge Otis P. Lord (q.v.). The daughter of Mrs. Lord's sister, after the death of Mrs. Lord in 1877 she and her mother kept home for the Judge until his death in 1884. She later married William C. West. She was a close friend of Susan Dickinson, and strongly opposed the attachment of Judge Lord and Emily Dickinson. She was the chief beneficiary of the Judge's will.

*FEARING, Mrs. Henry D., was the wife of an Amherst manufacturer whose hat factory was destroyed by fire, 23 April 1880.

*FIELD, Thomas P. (1814–1894), a graduate of Amherst College (1834), was ordained in 1840, and for ten years occupied various pulpits. For three years (1853–1856) he taught English literature at Amherst, and for the next twenty returned to the ministry. He came back to Amherst (1877) and became professor of Biblical history in 1878, a position he occupied until 1886. Dr. and Mrs. Field were neighbors of the Dickinsons, but only casual acquaintances.

*FISKE, Rebecca W., was a daughter of Deacon David Fiske of Shelburne. She was graduated from Mount Holyoke in 1846, and taught there for three years, until her marriage (1849) to the Reverend Burdett Hart. Samuel Fiske (AC 1848) was her brother.

FISKE, Samuel (1827–1864), was graduated from Amherst College (1848) and taught there for three years (1852–1855). He then studied for the ministry and was later ordained.

*FLYNT, Eudocia Converse, of Monson, was the second wife of William

Norcross Flynt (b. 1818), who was a brother of Mrs. Lyman Coleman. She was ED's first cousin once removed on her mother's side.

*FORD, Emily Ellsworth Fowler (1826–1893), was the daughter of William Chauncey Fowler, professor of Rhetoric and Oratory, and English Literature at Amherst College (1838–1843), and a granddaughter of Noah Webster. She attended Amherst Academy with ED in the early forties. She left Amherst, 16 December 1853, when she married Gordon Lester Ford, a promising lawyer and (later) successful business executive. They made their home in Brooklyn, New York. Herself an author of poems, stories, and essays, she was the mother of two well-known writers, Paul Leicester and Worthington Chauncey Ford.

*FRENCH, Daniel Chester (1850–1931), American sculptor, was the son of Henry Flagg French, who served briefly as first president (1864–1866) of Massachusetts Agricultural College. ED had known him briefly as a boy during the few years his family lived in Amherst.

GILBERT, Harriet Murray. *See* Harriet Gilbert Cutler.

GILBERT, Martha Isabella. *See* Martha Gilbert Smith.

GILBERT, Mary Arms. *See* Mary Gilbert Learned.

GILBERT, Susan Huntington. *See* Susan Gilbert Dickinson.

*GILBERT, Thomas Dwight (1815–1894), eldest of the Gilbert children (see above), was a prosperous lumber dealer in Grand Rapids, Michigan. Before Susan's marriage he contributed liberally to her support, as well as to that of his other sisters, orphaned by the death of their father in 1841 (*see* Susan Gilbert Dickinson). Next to him in age was a brother, Francis Backus Gilbert (1818–1885). The association of the brothers and sisters was close, and remained so throughout their lives.

*GLADDEN, Washington (1836–1918), a graduate of Williams College (1859), was a Congregational clergyman widely known for his lectures and articles popularizing the results of biblical criticism and modern theological views. He was editor of *The Independent* from 1871 to 1875, in which year he resigned his editorship to become pastor of a church in Springfield, where he was residing when ED wrote him in 1882. Shortly thereafter he removed to Columbus, Ohio.

*GOULD, George Henry (1827–1899), who graduated from Amherst College (1850), was a classmate and close friend of Austin Dickinson. After occupying various pulpits, he settled at Worcester in 1872. A "cherished batch" of letters he received from ED was never found (*AB* 254).

*GRAVES, John Long (1831–1915), of Sunderland, was graduated from Amherst College (1855), and ordained in the Congregational ministry in

1860. A few years later he resigned from his calling to go into business, residing in Boston. A cousin of ED, he was always welcome in the Dickinson home during his undergraduate years, as a family member, and this cordiality never abated, although no exchange of letters is known after 1856.

*GREENOUGH, James C., was an assistant principal of the state normal school at Westfield at the time of his marriage in 1860 to Jeanie Ashley Bates, daughter of the Honorable William G. Bates, a widely known Westfield lawyer and politician. It was in Washington in 1855 that ED first met Jeanie Bates. After serving as principal of the Rhode Island Normal School during the seventies, Greenough came to Amherst as president of the Massachusetts Agricultural College, from 1883 until 1886. The only known letters to Mrs. Greenough were written after the Greenoughs came to Amherst.

GRIDLEY, Jane L. (b. 1829), was the daughter of Dr. Timothy Gridley. On 17 September 1849 she married Dr. George S. Woodman.

*HALE, Edward Everett (1822–1909), well-known Unitarian clergyman and writer, was pastor of the Church of the Unity in Worcester when ED wrote to him in January 1854 (see letter no. 153).

*HALL, Eugenia (b. 1864), was the daughter of George and Mary E. Montague Hall of Athens, Georgia. In 1868 she came to Amherst to live with her grandfather George Montague (q.v.). In 1885 she married Franklin L. Hunt of Boston.

HARRINGTON, Brainerd T. (1826–1901), a friend of Austin's, attended Amherst Academy and Amherst College. After graduation (1852) he became a teacher.

HASKELL, Abby Ann (1833–1851), was a schoolmate and friend of ED and Jane Humphrey (q.v.). She died 19 April 1851, at the age of nineteen.

HAVEN, Joseph (1816–1874), a graduate of Amherst College (1835), became professor of philosophy at Amherst (1851–1858), and of systematic theology at the Chicago Theological Seminary (1858–1870). ED is known to have written his wife, *Mary Emerson Haven, three letters (see the note for letter no. 191).

*HIGGINSON, Thomas Wentworth (1823–1911), youngest of the ten children of Stephen and Louisa Storrow Higginson, was graduated from Harvard College in 1841. After taking his degree from Harvard Divinity School (1847), he married his cousin, Mary Elizabeth Channing. He became pastor of the First Religious Society (Unitarian) at Newburyport

(1847–1852) and of the Free Church at Worcester (1852–1861). Resigning from the ministry, he served in the Union Army (1862–1864) as colonel of the First South Carolina Volunteers. He lived at Newport, Rhode Island (1864–1877), until the death of his wife. In February 1879 he married, second, Mary Potter Thacher. Throughout his life he was a crusader for liberal causes and a prolific writer. The correspondence that ED initiated with him in April 1862 is of first importance in the history of American literature.

*HILLS, Henry F. (1833–1896), entered his father's business in Amherst in 1852, as a manufacturer of straw hats: L. M. Hills & Sons. Leonard Hills, father of Henry, died 8 February 1872. Mr. and Mrs. Henry Hills were neighbors of the Dickinsons.

HITCHCOCK, Catharine (1826–1895), was the eldest daughter of President Edward Hitchcock. Kate Hitchcock married Henry M. Storrs (q.v.). Her younger sister Jane married Granville B. Putnam (AC 1861) on 31 August 1864.

HITCHCOCK, Edward (1793–1864), after graduation from Yale College (1818), became the first professor of chemistry at Amherst College in 1825. He served as president of the college from 14 April 1845 until 22 November 1854. In 1821 he married Orra White of Amherst, who died on 26 May 1863. As administrator he served the college ably during its most crucial years. As a geologist he won an international reputation.

*HOAR, Ebenezer Rockwood (1816–1895), a lifelong resident of Concord, was a judge of the Massachusetts Supreme Court 1859–1869, United States attorney-general 1869–1870, and member of Congress from Massachusetts 1873–1875. His daughter Elizabeth married Samuel Bowles the younger (q.v.).

*HOLLAND, Josiah Gilbert (1819–1881), married Elizabeth Luna Chapin (1823–1896) in 1845. In 1849 he began his long association with Samuel Bowles on the *Springfield Daily Republican*. In 1870 he founded *Scribner's Monthly*, and remained its editor until his death. His many books enjoyed considerable popularity in their day. He was known by the title "Doctor" throughout his life, for as a young man he had qualified as a physician, though he soon abandoned the practice of medicine. Dr. and Mrs. Holland were among ED's closest friends, and Mrs. Holland, with whom she exchanged frequent letters all her life, she often designated "Sister." For ED no other friendship was more enduring. Both were vivacious, candid, and perceptive.

HOLLAND, Sophia (1829–1844), was the daughter of Seneca Holland, a leading Amherst businessman. She died on 29 April 1844, aged fifteen.

HOLT, Jacob, of Amherst, attended Amherst Academy and studied dentistry in Boston. He returned to Amherst in 1845, and died of consumption 12 May 1848. While a student at the Academy, he published some verses in the *Northampton Courier*: the issues of 29 August 1843, and 25 June 1844. There seems to have been some kinship between ED and him, presumably engendered by their commonly shared interest in poetry.

HOWE, Sabra, a classmate of ED's at Amherst Academy, was the daughter of A. P. Howe, landlord of the Amherst House.

HOWLAND, George (1824–1892), was graduated from Amherst College (1850) second in his class. From 1852 until 1857 he was a tutor and instructor in Amherst. Most of his life he spent as an educator, in later years as superintendent of schools in Chicago. He served as trustee of Amherst College, 1879–1888. He was a brother of William Howland (*q.v.*).

HOWLAND, William (1822–1880) was graduated from Amherst College (1846), where he served briefly as a tutor (1849–1851). He attended Yale Law School and studied law in the office of Edward Dickinson. From 1852 until his death he practiced law in Lynn. He married in 1860.

HUMPHREY, Helen (1822–1866), a sister of Jane Humphrey (*q.v.*), was one of ED's teachers at Amherst Academy (1841–1842). She married Albert H. Palmer, a lawyer in Racine, Wisconsin, on 27 August 1845. He died 12 September 1846. She married (second) William H. Stoddard of Northampton, 1 January 1852.

HUMPHREY, Heman, a graduate of Yale College (1805), was president of Amherst College from 1823 until 1845.

*HUMPHREY, Jane T. (1829–1908), was the daughter of Dr. Levi W. Humphrey of Southwick. After graduation from Mount Holyoke Female Seminary (1848) she became preceptress of Amherst Academy (1848–1849). She gave up teaching in 1858, and on 26 August of that year married William H. Wilkinson. They resided in Southwick. ED's correspondence with her during the early 1850's was singularly warmhearted, but it was abruptly terminated by Jane's marriage.

HUMPHREY, Leonard (1824–1850), was graduated as valedictorian of his class at Amherst College (1846). He was principal of Amherst Academy (1846–1847) at the time ED attended it. He had served one year as tutor in Amherst College when he was fatally stricken with brain fever.

HUMPHREY, Sarah, a sister of Jane Humphrey (*q.v.*), died on 18 November 1854, of consumption, aged eighteen.

HUNT, Caroline Dutch (1800–1861), was the widow of the Reverend William W. Hunt, pastor of the North Amherst Church. She was preceptress of Amherst Academy from 1840 until 1843.

*JACKSON, Helen Fiske Hunt (1830–1885), was the daughter of Nathan Welby Fiske, professor of moral philosophy and metaphysics in Amherst College, and Deborah Vinal Fiske. Her mother died in 1844, and she was orphaned by the death of her father three years later. She married Edward Bissell Hunt, an army engineer, in 1852. Their first son lived eleven months. In 1863 Major Hunt was accidentally killed in line of duty. Another son Warren ("Rennie") died, aged nine, in 1865. Mrs. Hunt turned to writing and lived for a time in Newport, Rhode Island, where she became acquainted with T. W. Higginson. Though she had attended school briefly with ED in their childhood, she came to know her only in the seventies, by which time "H. H." was acclaimed a leading poet and story writer. In 1875 she married William S. Jackson, and made her home at Colorado Springs. She had seen a few of ED's poems, and was the only contemporary who believed that ED was an authentic poet. Shortly before Helen Jackson's death the acquaintanceship ripened into a friendship of special importance to ED, who probably was deeply touched that Mrs. Jackson had asked to be her literary executor.

*JAMESON, John, was the postmaster at Amherst from 20 December 1876 to 30 March 1885. The Jamesons were neighbors of the Dickinsons, and ED knew and wrote occasional notes to two of their children, Annie and Arthur. The eldest son, John Franklin Jameson (AC 1879), became a well-known historian.

*JENKINS, Jonathan Leavitt (1830–1913), was graduated from Yale College (1851) and Yale Divinity School. In 1862 he married Sarah Maria Eaton. Installed as pastor of the First Church at Amherst in December 1866, he remained until 1877, when he accepted a call to Pittsfield. The Jenkinses were especially admired and loved by all members of the Dickinson family, and their removal to Pittsfield did not break the ties. Together with the incumbent pastor of the Amherst church in 1886, the Reverend Mr. George S. Dickerman, Mr. Jenkins officiated at the funeral of Emily Dickinson.

JEWETT, George Baker (1818–1886), a graduate of Amherst College (1840), was a professor of Latin and modern languages there from 1850 until 1854. He was ordained in 1855.

JONES, Thomas (1787–1853), was a manufacturer of cotton and woolen goods in Amherst.

KARR, William S. (1829–1888), was the commencement orator for his Amherst College class of 1851.

KELLOGG, Emeline (1828–1900), was the daughter of James Kellogg, a prominent Amherst manufacturer. Until 1855 the Kelloggs were next door neighbors of the Dickinsons. On 9 October 1855 Emeline married Henry C. Nash (*q.v.*).

*KIMBALL, Benjamin, was the son of Otis Kimball, of Ipswich, and Lucy Sarah Farley Kimball. At the age of thirty, in 1880, he married Helen Manning Simmons. Throughout his life he practiced law in Boston. He was known to ED because he was a cousin of Judge Otis P. Lord (*q.v.*), and, after Lord's death, Kimball was entrusted with settling the Judge's estate.

KIMBALL, James Parker (1828–1882), a graduate of Amherst College (1849) and Andover Theological Seminary, after ordination became pastor of churches in Falmouth and Haydenville. He served later as secretary for New England of the American Tract Society, and returned to Amherst, where he lived until his death.

KINGMAN, Martha (1832–1851) and Ellen Mary (1838–1851), school friends of ED, were daughters of Cyrus Kingman (1794–1854), who moved from Pelham to Amherst in April 1850. He was paralyzed 9 November 1852. His eldest and only surviving daughter, Jane Juliette, died 26 May 1854. Martha and Ellen died within the space of two weeks. The father died 29 December 1854.

LEARNED, Samuel Julius, a graduate of Amherst College (1845), married Mary Arms Gilbert (1822–1850), a sister of Susan Gilbert Dickinson (*q.v.*), on 19 September 1849, and settled in Sunbury, North Carolina. He was a brother of Mary Learned Bartlett (Mrs. Samuel C. Bartlett, *q.v.*).

LINNELL, Tempe S. (1831–1881), a school friend of ED and Jane Humphrey (*q.v.*), came to Amherst in 1839 with her two brothers and widowed mother, who wished to provide an education for her sons. Tempe never married, and spent her life caring for her mother who died, aged 85, on 11 February 1879. She ran a popular boarding house for students, and died, aged 50, on 6 November 1881.

*LOOMIS, Eben Jenks (1828–1912), and his wife Mary Wilder Loomis were the parents of Mabel Loomis Todd. He was an astronomer, for fifty years assistant in Nautical Almanac (senior assistant 1859–1900) in the

Naval Observatory in Washington. The Loomises visited their daughter in Amherst in the autumn of 1884.

*LORD, Otis Phillips (1812–1884), the son of the Hon. Nathaniel and Eunice Kimball Lord, was born at Ipswich. Graduated from Amherst College in 1832, he studied law and was admitted to the bar in 1835, first in Ipswich, then in 1844 in Salem, where thereafter he resided. In 1843 he married Elizabeth Wise, daughter of Captain Joseph Farley of Ipswich. She died 10 December 1877. During the forties and fifties, Lord served in the Massachusetts legislature and State Senate. With the establishment of the Superior Court in 1859 he was appointed an associate justice, in which capacity he served until his elevation to the state Supreme Court in 1875. Ill health compelled his resignation from the bench in 1882. He died on 13 March 1884. Judge Lord was one of Edward Dickinson's closest friends, and the Lords were frequent guests in the Dickinson home. He continued to visit, for a week or so at a time, during the early eighties, staying with his nieces at the Amherst House. The surviving letters and drafts of letters which ED wrote him about this time indicate that she was very much in love with the Judge. The attachment seems to have been mutual.

*MACK, David, Jr. (1778–1854), the son of Colonel David Mack of Middlefield, served as a major in the War of 1812, and was promoted to brigadier general of militia in 1821. Known generally as Deacon Mack, he was a successful Amherst businessman, and a trustee of Amherst College (1836–1854). He purchased the Dickinson homestead on 22 May 1833, and lived there until his death on 6 September 1854. His first wife, Independence Pease Mack, died in 1809. They had a son, David (1804–1878), who was graduated from Yale College in Edward Dickinson's class of 1823, and a daughter Julia (born in 1806). He married, second, Mary Ely (1787–1842) in 1812. They had one surviving son when they moved to Amherst, Samuel Ely Mack, born in 1815. Mary Ely Mack died 15 December 1842, and Deacon Mack married, third, on 16 May 1844, Harriet Parsons Washburn (1793–1874), daughter of the Reverend Dr. David Parsons of the First Church in Amherst, and widow of Royal W. Washburn, who had been pastor of the same church (1826–1833).

Edward Dickinson and his family occupied the east part of the homestead until April 1840, when they moved to a frame house on North Pleasant Street. This was ED's home until 1855, at which time Edward Dickinson purchased the homestead on Main Street from Samuel E. Mack and his wife Rebecca Robins Mack, of Cincinnati, and moved his family back to it.

MARCH, Francis A. (1825–1911), a graduate of Amherst College (1845), was a tutor at the college, 1847–1849. He became a distinguished Shakespearean scholar.

*MATHER, Richard Henry (1835–1890), a graduate of Amherst College (1857), was a professor of classics there throughout his life. His first wife, Elizabeth Carmichael Mather, died 28 October 1877. On 31 March 1881 he married Ellen A. Mather.

MERRILL, Calvin, married on 9 September 1851 Fanny D. Benjamin. It was the third marriage for both. He was fifty-four years old, and she forty-six.

MERRILL, Harriet, a daughter of Calvin Merrill, was a classmate of ED at Amherst Academy. She taught school first at Amherst Academy and later at Pittsfield. Her aunt of the same name, recalled as an aristocratic spinster who received student lodgers, died under mysterious circumstances, 6 October 1885. (See letter no. 1041.)

*MONTAGUE, George (1804–1893), an older brother of Harriet and Zebina Montague (q.v.), was a first cousin of ED's grandfather Samuel Fowler Dickinson, and a son of Luke and Irene Dickinson Montague. Educated at Amherst Academy, he was in business for thirty years in various cities in the South and West. He returned to Amherst in 1866, and served as treasurer of Massachusetts Agricultural College until his retirement in 1884. He married, first, in Columbus, Georgia, Mary A. Parsons; they had two sons and a daughter, the latter being the mother of Eugenia Hall (q.v.). Three years after the death of his wife Mary, in 1853, he married Sarah M. Seelye of New York. She was still living at the time of ED's death.

MONTAGUE, Zebina (1810–1881), born in Amherst, was the brother of George Montague (q.v.). He resided after 1839, an invalid, at Amherst with his sister Harriet.

NASH, Henry Clark (1829–1900), a graduate of Amherst College (1851), succeeded his father as principal of Mount Pleasant Institute (1854–1877) in Amherst. On 9 October 1855 he married Emeline Kellogg (q.v.).

NASH, John Adams (1798–1877), the father of Henry Nash (q.v.), a graduate of Amherst College (1824), was principal of Mount Pleasant Institute, 1846–1854.

*NEWMAN, Anna Dodge (1846–1887), the youngest daughter of Mark Haskell Newman (q.v.), lived with her sister Clara (q.v.) from 1869 until shortly before her marriage on 3 June 1874 to George H. Carleton of Haverhill. Her daughter Clara Newman Carleton (Mrs. George E. Pearl) was born 21 March 1876.

*NEWMAN, Clarissa (Clara) Badger (1844–1920), sister of Anna (*q.v.*), married, 14 October 1869, Sidney Turner of Norwich, Connecticut. Both Anna and Clara, together with their older sisters Catherine and Sara became wards of their uncle Edward Dickinson, in the charge of their aunt Hannah Haskell Newman (Mrs. Samuel A. Fay) when they were orphaned by the death of their parents in 1852. In October 1858 Clara and Anna (aged respectively 14 and 12) lived with Austin and Susan Dickinson until Clara's marriage in 1869.

NEWMAN, Mark Haskell (1806–1852), a graduate of Bowdoin College (1825), became a publisher of school books in New York City. He married, on 2 October 1828, Mary Dickinson (1809–1852), a daughter of Samuel Fowler Dickinson, and aunt of ED. Of their five children who lived to maturity, the two that ED knew best are described above.

NEWTON, Benjamin Franklin (1821–1853), who did not attend college, studied law in the office of ED's father (1847–1849) and was admitted to the bar in 1850, at Worcester. He was appointed state's attorney for Worcester County in 1852. He married Sarah Warner Rugg on 4 June 1851. He died of consumption on 24 March 1853. His widow survived until 1899. There is every reason to believe that ED corresponded with him after he left Amherst; he had guided her early interest in literature, and his death was for her poignantly distressing. But none of the letters survive, nor could Mrs. Todd trace any even before Mrs. Newton's death.

*NILES, Thomas (1825–1894), was a Boston publisher. Starting his career with the firm of Ticknor, he later became editor of Roberts Brothers. The correspondence between Niles and ED began soon after the publication of *A Masque of Poets*, in 1878, in which her poem "Success" first appeared.

NIMS, Seth (1798–1877), was the postmaster at Amherst from 1845 until 1849, and again from 1853 until 1861.

*NORCROSS, Alfred (1815–1888), ED's uncle, was a younger brother of ED's mother. In 1841 he married Olivia Chapin. Of his five children, the youngest (1860–1862) was named Edward Dickinson Norcross.

NORCROSS, Emily Lavinia (1828–1852) was the daughter of Hiram Norcross (1800–1829), the eldest brother of ED's mother. After the early death of Hiram Norcross, his widow married Charles Stearns of Springfield, but died a few years later. Brought up in Monson, Emily Norcross attended Mount Holyoke Seminary where ED was her roommate during the one year that ED attended. She died, 2 July 1852, and an only brother, William Henry Norcross, died two years later.

*NORCROSS, Joel Warren (1821–1900), was the youngest brother of ED's mother. He married Lamira H. Jones of Chicago, 17 January 1854, after having established himself as a Boston importer, residing at 31 Milk Street. During the year that Austin Dickinson taught school in Boston (1851–1852) his family addressed all letters to him in care of Joel Norcross. Lamira Norcross died, 3 May 1862, and Joel married, second, Maggie P. Gunnison of Roxbury, 24 April 1866. There were two children by the first marriage, and one by the second.

NORCROSS, Loring (1808–1863), a dry goods commission merchant of Boston, married his cousin Lavinia Norcross (1812–1860), a favorite sister of ED's mother. He served as secretary of the Massachusetts Temperance Union and as member of the Boston School Board. She died 17 April 1860, aged 47. He died 17 January 1863, aged 55. Their eldest daughter, Lavinia, died 19 May 1842, aged four. For their other daughters, Louise and Frances, see below.

*NORCROSS, Louise (1842–1919) and Frances Lavinia (1847–1896), daughters of Loring and Lavinia Norcross (q.v.), were ED's "Little Cousins." The girls were orphaned when Louise was twenty-one. As children, Loo and Fanny had always been welcome at the Dickinson home, and it was with them that ED stayed when her eye trouble compelled her to sojourn in Cambridge for several months in 1864 and 1865 to be under the care of a Boston physician. The sisters lived together until Fanny's death, occupied with what genteel employment occasion offered. ED constantly exchanged letters with them, and on a domestic level had an especial affection for them. All the letters, destroyed after Fanny's death, derive from transcripts supplied to Mrs. Todd before 1894.

The spelling of Louise's name is given as *Louisa* in the manuscript Norcross genealogy (New England Historical and Genealogical Society Library) compiled by Joel Warren Norcross of Lynn. But in the Concord death records and in the records of the Old Ladies' Home at Concord, where she died, it is given as *Louise*. A letter from her, among family papers in Monson, is signed *Louise*.

NORCROSS, Sarah Vaill (1788–1854), was the second wife of Joel Norcross of Monson, ED's grandfather. They were married in 1831. He died 5 May 1846; she died 25 April 1854.

PALMER, Helen. *See* Helen Humphrey (Mrs. Albert Palmer).

PARK, Edwards Amasa (1808–1900), a graduate of Brown College

(1826), was professor of Moral Philosophy and Metaphysics briefly at Amherst College (1835–1836). He taught from 1836 until 1881 at Andover Theological Seminary. In January 1844 he declined the presidency of Amherst College.

*PHELPS, Susan Davis, was engaged to Henry Vaughan Emmons. The engagement was broken in May 1860. She died, 2 December 1865.

*PRINCE, Katherine Barber James (1834–1890) was a daughter of the Reverend William James of Albany, and a cousin of William and Henry James. (She was the "Kitty Prince" of William James's *Letters.*) In 1861 she married Dr. William Henry Prince (1817–1883), a psychiatrist, who practiced at Northampton (where he was superintendent of a mental hospital), Newton, and Clifton Springs, New York. Katherine's sister Elizabeth Tillman (1833–1881) married Julius Hawley Seelye (*q.v.*).

*READ, Eliza M. Kellogg, married Hanson L. Read on 25 November 1851. ED attended the wedding. He was engaged in business in Amherst and served there as superintendent of schools, 1868–1871 and 1885–1887. On 26 December 1873 the two Read sons, both in their teens, were drowned while skating on Adams Pond.

*ROOT, Abiah Palmer (b. 1830), was the daughter of Deacon Harvey Root of West Springfield (Feeding Hills). She attended Amherst Academy for one year (1843–1844), and then transferred to Miss Margaret Campbell's school in Springfield. The early friendship with ED was warmhearted, but it seems to have been dropped after Abiah's marriage to the Reverend Samuel W. Strong of Westfield in 1854.

ROOT, Henry Dwight (1832–1855), of Greenfield, was graduated from Amherst College (1852) and attended Harvard Law School. He was a friend of Austin's. He died, 3 September 1855.

*SANBORN, Franklin Benjamin (1831–1917), a graduate of Harvard College (1855), lived in Concord where, after a vigorous participation in the abolition movement, he became editor (1863–1867) of the *Boston Commonwealth*. He served as resident editor (1868–1872) of the *Springfield Republican*, of which he had been corresponding editor since 1856. In 1873 he returned to Concord, acting as special correspondent. He was intimately acquainted with the Concord writers, and in later years devoted his time to editing their literary remains.

SANFORD, Baalis (1825–1875), a graduate of Amherst College (1845), was the older brother of John Sanford (*q.v.*). He studied law with Edward Dickinson in 1850. He was married, 1 June 1853.

SANFORD, John Elliot (1830–1907), was graduated as valedictorian of his Amherst College class (1851), and served as tutor for one year (1853–1854). After studying law in the office of Edward Dickinson he settled in the practice of his profession at Taunton. He was a trustee of Amherst College from 1874 until his death, in later years as president of the board. During his senior year in college he was a frequent caller in the Dickinson home.

*SEELYE, Julius Hawley (1824–1895), a graduate of Amherst College (1849), was ordained in 1853. A professor in the college (1858–1890), he served as President from 1876 until 1890. He was pastor of the College Church, 1877–1892.

SEELYE, L. Clark (1837–1924), a brother of Julius Seelye (q.v.), was graduated from Union College (1857). He was a professor of rhetoric, oratory, and English literature at Amherst College (1865–1873), and the first president of Smith College (1874–1910).

*SLOAN, Timothy W., was a boot and shoemaker in Amherst, living for many years on Spring Street, one block away from the Dickinson home. His daughter, Mary Emma Sloan, died 16 August 1883, aged seventeen.

SMITH, Henry Boynton (1815–1877), was professor of moral philosophy and metaphysics from 1847 until 1850, when he joined the faculty of Union Theological Seminary, where he remained until his death.

*SMITH, Martha Gilbert (1829–1895), was an older sister of Susan Gilbert Dickinson (q.v.). On 20 October 1857 she married John Williams Smith (1822–1878), a dry goods merchant of Geneva, New York. An infant son, Frank, died, 14 June 1861, and a daughter, Susan, died, 3 November 1865, aged two. Their daughter Elizabeth Throop Smith was born, 30 June 1868.

*SNELL, Ebenezer Strong (1801–1876), a graduate of Amherst College (1822), was instructor and professor of mathematics and allied sciences there from 1825 until his death, 18 September 1876. In 1828 he married Sabra Clark. Their daughter Mary was about ED's age.

SPENCER, John Laurens (1818–1851), a graduate of Amherst College (1848), was principal of Amherst Academy from 1848 until 1850. He had undertaken the study of theology at the time of his death, 12 October 1851.

*STEARNS, William Augustus (1805–1876), was a graduate of Harvard College (1827) and Andover Theological Seminary (1831). He was pastor of a church in Cambridgeport, Vermont, when he accepted the presidency of Amherst College in 1854, in which position he served until his death.

*STEARNS, William F., the son of William A. Stearns (*q.v.*), entered business in India, where he died. His widow returned to Amherst where she kept a girls' school. A daughter Ethel died at Amherst, 15 October 1882.

STEBBINS, Milan C. (1828–1889), was salutatorian of the Amherst College class of 1851. On 24 November 1853 he married Sophia Pitts. He was successively a minister, teacher, and merchant.

STODDARD, Mrs. William H. *See* Helen Humphrey.

STORRS, Henry Martyn (1827–1894), was graduated from Amherst College (1846) and Andover Theological Seminary (1851). He married Catharine Hitchcock, 9 March 1852. He became secretary of the American Home Missionary Society. Henry Ward Beecher spoke of him as one of the foremost men in the American pulpit.

STRONG, Mrs. Samuel W. *See* Abiah Root.

*SWEETSER, Catharine Dickinson (1814–1895), ED's favorite aunt Katie, was a sister of Edward Dickinson. She married Joseph A. Sweetser of New York in 1835. He was a brother of Luke Sweetser (*q.v.*). On 21 January 1874 he left their apartment at the Fifth Avenue Hotel to attend a committee meeting at the Madison Square Presbyterian Church, across the street. He was never subsequently heard from or traced.

SWEETSER, Charles Humphreys (1841–1871), was an orphaned nephew of Luke Sweetser. He came to live with the Luke Sweetsers in 1847, and was graduated from Amherst College in 1862. After an apprenticeship on the *Springfield Daily Republican* in 1863, he established with his cousin Henry E. Sweetser a weekly paper, *The Round Table*, in New York. He married his cousin Mary Newman Sweetser, daughter of Catharine and Joseph Sweetser (*qq.v.*), and died of consumption, 1 January 1871.

*SWEETSER, John Howard (1835–1904), was the only child of Luke Sweetser (*q.v.*). He left Amherst College in his junior year to go into business with his uncle Joseph in New York. He received his Bachelor of Arts degree in 1871. On 2 February 1860 he married Cornelia Peck, the "Mrs Nellie" to whom ED often wrote in her later years. Their three children were Alice Munsell Sweetser (Mrs. Henry C. Hall), Howard Sweetser, and "Nettie."

SWEETSER, Luke (1800–1882), born in Athol, came to Amherst in 1824 and became a leading merchant of the town. In 1833 he married Abby Tyler Munsell. In 1834 Abby Wood (*q.v.*), his three-year-old niece, came to live with them. The Sweetsers had one son, John Howard Sweetser (*q.v.*). He died on 27 July 1882, and his wife on 19 October of the same year. The Sweetsers were lifelong neighbors of the Dickinsons.

TAYLOR, Jeremiah (1817–1898), a graduate of Amherst College (1843), was principal of Amherst Academy, 1843–1844. He was subsequently ordained and occupied various New England pulpits.

THOMPSON, John H. (1827–1891), a classmate of Austin Dickinson (AC 1850) and an especially close undergraduate friend, settled as a lawyer in Chicago.

THURSTON, Benjamin Easton (1827–1870), after graduation from Amherst College (1852) went into business.

*TODD, Mabel Loomis (1856–1932), daughter of Eben Jenks Loomis (q.v.), married David Peck Todd (1855–1939), in 1879. A graduate of Amherst College (1875), he returned there as Director of the Observatory (1881–1920) and as professor of Astronomy and Navigation (1892–1920). The account of Mrs. Todd's part in editing the poems and letters of ED is set forth at length in Millicent Todd Bingham's *Ancestors' Brocades* (1945).

TOLMAN, Albert, after graduation from Amherst College (1845) was a tutor there, 1848–1851.

TRACY, Sarah, was one of the "circle of five" who made up ED's intimate Amherst Academy friends. Very little is known about her. She was a boarder, and the last reference to her is of a visit she made in Amherst in August 1851. In the Academy group, ED was "Socrates," Abiah Root was "Plato," and Sarah was "Virgil."

*TUCKERMAN, Edward (1817–1886), was professor of Botany in Amherst College from 1858 until his death, and an international authority on lichens. It was for him that Tuckerman's Ravine in the White Mountains was named. In 1854 he married Sarah Eliza Sigourney Cushing, who survived him by twenty-nine years. They had no children, but Mrs. Tuckerman was always held in loving memory by four orphaned nephews whom she reared, children of her sister, Mrs. William Cole Esty. The warm attachment ED felt for her is attested by the quality of the many notes she wrote her.

*TUCKERMAN, Frederick, a nephew of Professor Edward Tuckerman, married Alice Girdler Cooper on 6 September 1881. *See* James S. Cooper.

*TURNER, Mrs. Sidney. *See* Clara Newman.

TYLER, William Seymour (1810–1897), a graduate of Amherst College (1830), was a professor of Latin and Greek there throughout his life.

VAILL, Joseph (1790–1869), after his graduation from Yale College (1811) was ordained and continued in the ministry all his life. He was a trustee of Amherst College from the date of its founding until his death. After 1854 he lived at Palmer.

VANDERBILT, Gertrude Lefferts (*ca.* 1824–1896), was the wife of Judge John Vanderbilt of King's County, New York. She was a close friend of Catherine Anthon (*q.v.*). It was through Kate Anthon that Mrs. Vanderbilt knew the Dickinsons.

WADSWORTH, Charles (1814–1882), after graduation from Union College (1837), was ordained and became one of the leading pulpit orators of his day. He was pastor of the Arch Street Presbyterian Church in Philadelphia from 1850 until April 1862, when he went to Calvary Church in San Francisco. He returned to Philadelphia in 1870, where he remained until his death. ED probably met him in Philadelphia in 1855. She corresponded with him, and he is known to have called upon her twice, once in 1860, and again in the summer of 1880. She seems to have turned to him for spiritual consolation, but none of her letters to him survive.

*WARD, Horace, a resident of Amherst during the 1860's, was a vestryman of Grace Episcopal Church, a trustee of the Amherst Savings Bank, foreman of the Fire Engine Company, and in 1868 a representative to the General Court of Massachusetts.

WARNER, Aaron (1796–1876), a graduate of Williams College (1815), was a professor of rhetoric and English at Amherst College from the years 1844 until 1853. He was the father of Mary Warner Crowell (*q.v.*).

WASHBURN, William P. (1830–1904), was the son of Royal W. Washburn, whose widow married David Mack (*q.v.*). A graduate of Amherst College (1851), he settled as a lawyer in Knoxville, Kentucky. He attended Williston Seminary with Austin Dickinson.

WHITMAN, Mary C., was graduated from Mount Holyoke in 1839. She served as assistant principal in 1842, and after Miss Lyon's death acted for one year as principal of the institution. In 1851 she married Morton Eddy.

*WHITNEY, Maria (1830–1910), was the daughter of Josiah Dwight Whitney, a Northampton banker. Through the Dwights she was related to Mrs. Samuel Bowles. She spent much time with members of the Bowles family in their home and on their travels, especially during the sixties and seventies. Like the Bowleses she saw a good deal of Austin and Susan Dickinson, and thus knew ED. From 1875 until 1880 she was Teacher of French and German in Smith College. She was a sister of the Yale philologist William Dwight Whitney; of the Harvard geologist Josiah Dwight

Whitney; and of James Lyman Whitney, director of the Boston Public Library.

WILKINSON, Mrs. W. H. *See* Jane Humphrey.

WILLISTON, Lyman Richards (1830–1897), the adopted son of Samuel Williston (*q.v.*), was graduated from Amherst College (1850) and served there for a year as professor of Latin and modern languages (1856–1857).

WILLISTON, Samuel (1795–1874), of Easthampton, founded Williston Seminary in 1841. A well-to-do manufacturer, he was a trustee of Amherst College, 1841–1874, and one of its benefactors.

WOOD, Abby Maria (1830–1915), was a daughter of Joel and Abby Moore Sweetser Wood of Westminster. After her father's death in 1833 and the marriage of her uncle Luke Sweetser (*q.v.*) in December 1833, Abby lived with the Sweetsers. On 23 November 1855 she married the Reverend Daniel Bliss (*q.v.*). She was a girlhood friend of ED.

WOODMAN, George S. (1823–1906), a graduate of Amherst College (1846), married Jane Gridley (*q.v.*) on 17 September 1849. He practiced medicine in Amherst from 1851 until 1858.

APPENDIX 2

A NOTE ON THE DOMESTIC HELP

Through the years the names of persons employed by the Dickinsons to help care for the house, stable, and grounds appear with great frequency in Emily Dickinson's letters. Some persons are easily confused because they bore identical first names. Two of the earliest alluded to are Mrs. Mack, an Irish washerwoman who was working for the Dickinsons in 1851 (see letter no. 60), and Margaret O'Brien. Mrs. Mack was sometimes referred to as "Emerald" Mack (see letter no. 85), to distinguish her from members of the family of Deacon David Mack. Margaret O'Brien, whom ED called Margaret, not Maggie, probably came to the Dickinsons after their return to the old family home in 1855, and remained with them until her marriage to Stephen Lawler in 1865 (see letters no. 285 and 311). In the Pleasant Street house they seem to have had no resident domestic help, but to have called in various women for occasional work by the day. Margaret O'Brien was succeeded, after an interval of four years during which time no housemaid remained for long, by Margaret Maher. Maggie Maher came to the Dickinsons in March 1869, and remained with them until the time of Lavinia's death in 1899. She is first mentioned in a letter to the Norcross cousins in the autumn of 1869 (letter no. 337), and thereafter ED often speaks of her, for Maggie became a part of the Dickinson family life (see especially letter no. 651). Maggie came from Ireland, and before she began working for the Dickinsons had returned to her homeland to bring her parents to Amherst. Her brothers and an older sister Mary also came. The sister married an earlier Irish arrival, Thomas Kelley, and the Kelleys lived nearby (see letter no. 752). After the departure of her brothers to seek work elsewhere, and the death of her parents, the Kelley house was Maggie's home. (See letters no. 375, 389, 670, and 771.) She is described in some detail by Jay Leyda, "Miss Emily's Maggie," *New World Writing* (Third Mentor Selection), May 1953, 255–267.

Another family on whom the Dickinsons depended over the years was one which emigrated from England. Richard (Dick) Matthews and his wife Ann lived in a small house in back of the Dickinson place on North Pleasant Street. Of their sixteen children, nine died young. Allusions to the family are made in a number of letters, notably those to the Norcross cousins, who knew them. (See letter no. 206.) Dick had become the Dickinson stableman by 1858, for ED so speaks of him in a letter to

Mrs. Holland, telling of the death of a daughter Harriet (letter no. 195).

The numerous Scannell family, whose names are variously spelled in newspapers and town records as Scanlan, Scanlin, Scanelly, etc., also played a part in the domestic life of the Dickinsons. Timothy and Catherine Scannell emigrated from Ireland and settled in Amherst in the 1840's. Timothy made his living as a farmer and day laborer. His son Dennis worked for the Dickinsons in the 1870's, and is the subject of letters no. 605 and 616. Dennis's son, Jerry, a boy of fourteen, is mentioned in letter no. 685. The Tim mentioned in letters no. 333, 337, and 343 as a coachman was perhaps also a member of the family.

The man responsible for keeping the garden and grounds in order was Horace Church, a farmer, and the sexton of the First Church. He is referred to as early as 1854 (letter no. 165), and he remained in the Dickinson employ until his death in 1881 (see letters 337, 692, and 966).

In later years another Stephen — Stephen Sullivan — became one of the Dickinson workmen. He is the "gracious boy at the barn" (letter no. 907), first mentioned early in 1884 (no. 888). He was married in 1887, aged twenty-three.

Jeremiah Holden, who took care of the Dickinsons' horse during Austin's absence at the Harvard Law School (see letter no. 80), seems to have been succeeded in the spring of 1854 by "little Pat," who is mentioned in letters no. 165 and 172. His family name has not been identified with certainty, but later allusions to Pat indicate that his connection with the Dickinsons continued through the years. (See letters no. 412 and 414.) It seems probable, therefore, that he can be identified with the Pat Ward who was one of ED's pallbearers.

There seem also to have been a succession of youthful handymen and errand boys, such as the young Scannells, Austin Grout (letter no. 45), and Johnnie Beston, first alluded to in letter no. 110. Other helpers are named, but probably were transient (see letter no. 49). Some of the seamstresses who annually came to the Dickinson house to outfit Mrs. Dickinson and the girls are identified in brief notes: such were Miss Baker, Miss Bartlett, and Miss Leonard, Mrs. Aiken, Mrs. Godfrey, Mrs. Kimberly, and Mrs. Noyes.

Mrs. Bianchi (FF 62 note) quotes Ellery Strickland, an Amherst funeral director called in after Emily Dickinson's death, thus: "Then the cortège across the lawn, through the hedge, across the fields, a special bier borne by faithful workmen of her father's grounds, Dennis Scanlon, Owen Courtney, Pat Ward, Steven Sullivan, Dennis Cashman, and Dan Moynihan."

APPENDIX 3

Bowles, Samuel, the younger
  (1879) 590
  (1880) 651
  (1882) 761
  (1883) 864, 865
  (1884) 902, 935
  (1885) 1008, 1012, 1013, 1014, 1017
Bullard, Lucretia
  (ca 1864) 1047, 1048, 1049
Carleton, Anna Newman
  (1884) 925
Carmichael, Elizabeth
  (1880) 665
  (1883) 875
  (1884) 879
Chickering, Joseph K.
  (1882) 784, 786
  (1883) 798
  (1885) 989, 990
Clark, Charles H.
  (1883) 817, 818, 821, 825, 826, 827, 859, 872
  (1884) 880, 884, 896
  (1885) 963, 983
  (1886) 1039, 1040
Clark, James D.
  (1882) 766, 773, 776, 788
  (1883) 804, 807
Cooper, Mrs. James S.
  (1874) 416, 419
  (1875) 445
  (1876) 462, 468, 469
  (1877) 504, 509, 510, 529
  (1878) 543, 569
  (1879) 606, 607, 608
  (1880) 647, 648, 672
  (1881) 706
  (1884) 905, 931, 947
  (1885) 970, 971, 982, 1005
  (1886) 1036

(1877) 487, 490, 491, 492, 502, 521, 525
(1878) 542, 544, 547, 551, 555
(1879) 589, 619
(1880) 650, 667, 678, 683
(1881) 685, 687, 689, 692, 715, 721, 723, 729, 730, 731, 732, 733, 738,
    740, 742, 743
(1882) 747, 775, 779, 792, 794
(1883) 801, 802, 805, 806, 808, 820, 822, 833, 866, 873
(1884) 882, 888, 890, 901, 936, 950
(1885) 966, 977, 979
(1886) 1038
Holland, Theodore
(1884) 921
Humphrey, Jane
(1842) 3
(1850) 30, 35
(1852) 81, 86
(1855) 180
Jackson, Helen Hunt
(1875) 444, 444a (HHJ to ED)
(1876) 476a (HHJ to ED), 476c (HHJ to ED)
(1878) 573a (HHJ to ED), 573b (HHJ to ED), 573c (HHJ to ED)
(1879) 601, 601a (HHJ to ED), 602
(1883) 816
(1884) 937, 937a (HHJ to ED)
(1885) 976, 976a (HHJ to ED)
Jackson, William S.
(1885) 1009, 1015
Jameson, Mrs. John, and family
(1883) 863, 878
(1884) 924, 933, 957
(1886) 1044
Jenkins, Jonathan L., and family
(1874) 411, 422, 423
(1876) 464, 482, 483
(1877) 485, 495, 496, 497, 499, 501, 506, 520
(1878) 564
(1879) 592
(1880) 646, 682

(1881) 717, 718, 719
(1883) 810, 811, 812, 844
Kimball, Benjamin
(1885) 967, 968, 1003
Loomis, Mr. and Mrs. Eben J.
(1884) 944, 945, 946, 953, 955
(1885) 960
Lord, Otis Phillips
(1878) 559, 560, 561, 562, 563
(1879) 600
(1880) 645
(1881) 695
(1882) 750, 752, 780, 790, 791
(1883) 842, 843
Mack, Mrs. Samuel E.
(1884) 939, 940
Maher, Margaret
(1882) 771
"Marcia"
PF 29
Mather, Alice Skeel
(1886) 1032
Mather, Mr. and Mrs. Richard H.
(1877) 523
(1881) 697
(1882) 764
(1883) 841
(1884) 927, 928, 929, 930
(1885) 992
Montague, Mr. and Mrs. George
(1881) 700, 701, 702, 703, 704, 705, 713, 716
Niles, Thomas
(1878) 573d (TN to ED)
(1882) 749, 749a (TN to ED), 749b (TN to ED)
(1883) 813, 813a (TN to ED) 813b (TN to ED), 814, 814a (TN to ED)
(1885) 1009a (TN to ED)
Norcross, Alfred
(1883) 800

(1882) 746
(1883) 828
(1884) 892, 897, 952
(1885) 991
Sweetser, Mrs. Luke
  (1868) 326
Todd, Mabel Loomis
  (1881) 736
  (1882) 748, 769, 770
  (1883) 831
  (1884) 906
  (1885) 978, 985, 1004, 1016
  (1886) 1033
Tuckerman, Mrs. Edward
  (1874) 406
  (1875) 433, 437
  (1877) 528
  (1878) 545, 556, 558, 565
  (1879) 588, 611
  (1880) 627, 628, 637, 673, 677
  (1881) 684, 725, 739, 741
  (1882) 745
  (1883) 795, 832
  (1884) 883, 895
  (1885) 981, 984, 1020
  (1886) 1035
Tuckerman, Mrs. Frederick
  (1884) 903, 904
  (1885) 959, 1019
Turner, Clara Newman
  (1874) 425
  (1884) 926
Wadsworth, Charles
  (1862?) 248a (CW to ED)
Ward, Mrs. Horace
  (1860) 218
Whitney, Maria
  (1877) 524
  (1878) 537, 538, 539, 540, 573

(1879) 591
(1880) 643
(1882) 777
(1883) 815, 824, 830, 860
(1884) 889, 948
(1885) 969, 974
Recipients Unknown
(1858) 187
(1861) 233
(1862) 248
(1875) 446
(1878) 568
(1881) 720.
(1883) 809
(1884) 923
(1885) 964, 965, 993, 995

INDEX

INDEX OF POEMS

INDEX

Asterisks indicate a book that ED is reading, or one from which she quotes. The poems which she incorporates in her letters, indexed by first lines, are grouped, and follow in a separate *Index of Poems*.

INDEX OF POEMS

This part of the index shows those poems by ED, either used or adapted for her correspondence, or referred to in the editorial notes. The number in parentheses following the first line of the poem is that assigned in the 1955 edition of the *Poems*.